SIXTH EDITION

TEN STEPS
TO
IMPROVING
COLLEGE
READING SKILLS

SIXTH EDITION

TEN STEPS
TO
IMPROVING
COLLEGE
READING SKILLS

JOHN LANGAN

ATLANTIC CAPE COMMUNITY COLLEGE

Books in the Townsend Press Reading Series

Groundwork for College Reading with Phonics
Groundwork for College Reading
Ten Steps to Building College Reading Skills
Ten Steps to Improving College Reading Skills
Ten Steps to Advancing College Reading Skills
Ten Steps to Advanced Reading

Books in the Townsend Press Vocabulary Series

Vocabulary Basics
Groundwork for a Better Vocabulary
Building Vocabulary Skills
Building Vocabulary Skills, Short Version
Improving Vocabulary Skills
Improving Vocabulary Skills, Short Version
Advancing Vocabulary Skills
Advancing Vocabulary Skills, Short Version
Advanced Word Power

Supplements Available for Most Books

Instructor's Edition
Instructor's Manual and Test Bank
Online Exercises
PowerPoint Slides

Copyright © 2014 by Townsend Press, Inc.
Printed in the United States of America
9 8 7 6 5 4 3 2 1

Cover design: Akisia Grigsby

ISBN (Student Edition): 978-1-59194-423-2
ISBN (Instructor's Edition): 978-1-59194-424-9

Send book orders and requests for desk copies or supplements to:
Townsend Press Book Center
439 Kelley Drive
West Berlin, New Jersey 08091

For even faster service, contact us in any of the following ways:
By telephone: 1-800-772-6410
By fax: 1-800-225-8894
By e-mail: cs@townsendpress.com
Through our website: www.townsendpress.com

Contents

Preface: To the Instructor   vii

Introduction

1 How to Become a Better Reader and Thinker   **3**

2 Reading for Pleasure and Power   **10**

3 Some Quick Study Tips   **17**

Part One   Ten Steps to Improving College Reading Skills

1 **Vocabulary in Context**   **21**
Reading: Night Watch   *Roy Popkin*   41
Mastery Tests   45

2 **Main Ideas**   **57**
Reading: Here's to Your Health   *Joan Dunayer*   85
Mastery Tests   91

3 **Supporting Details**   **103**
Reading: Child-Rearing Styles
    Diane E. Papalia and Sally Wendkos Olds   125
Mastery Tests   129

4 **Implied Main Ideas**   **141**
Reading: Rowing the Bus   *Paul Logan*   161
Mastery Tests   169

5 **Relationships I**   **181**
Reading: Wonder in the Air   *Jeff Gammage*   203
Mastery Tests   209

6 **Relationships II**   **221**
Reading: Students in Shock   *John Kellmayer and Alina Wyden*   247
Mastery Tests   253

7 **Inferences**   **273**
Reading: Relationships in the 21st Century   *James M. Henslin*   299
Mastery Tests   307

8 **Purpose and Tone**   **319**
Reading: The Scholarship Jacket   *Marta Salinas*   343
Mastery Tests   351

9   **Argument**   **363**
    Reading: In Praise of the F Word   *Mary Sherry*   381
    Mastery Tests   387

10 **Critical Reading**   **399**
    Reading: The 2,000-Year-Old Wonder Drug   *David B. Agus*   423
    Mastery Tests   429

Part Two   Ten Reading Selections

1   **The Yellow Ribbon**   *Pete Hamill*   **443**
2   **College Athletes Should Be Paid**   *Ann Kaufmann*   **451**
3   **Shame**   *Dick Gregory*   **463**
4   **The Bystander Effect**   *Dorothy Barkin*   **472**
5   **Growing Less Dumb**   *Eileen Brenoff*   **483**
6   **Coping with Nervousness**   *Rudolph F. Verderber*   **495**
7   **Compliance Techniques: Getting People to Say Yes**
    Shelley E. Taylor, Letitia Anne Peplau, and David O. Sears   **505**
8   **Lizzie Borden**   *James Kirby Martin and others*   **516**
9   **Nonverbal Communication**   *Anthony F. Grasha*   **526**
10 **The Power Within**   *John Langan*   **534**

Part Three   Relationships and Combined-Skills Tests

1   **Relationships Tests**   **551**
2   **Combined-Skills Tests**   **563**

Appendixes

Pronunciation Guide   **617**
Writing Assignments   **619**
Limited Answer Key   **637**

Acknowledgments   645
Index   649
Reading Performance Chart   Inside back cover

Preface: To the Instructor

We all know that many students entering college today do not have the reading skills needed to do effective work in their courses. A related problem, apparent even in class discussions, is that students often lack the skills required to think in a clear and logical way.

The purpose of *Ten Steps to Improving College Reading Skills, Sixth Edition,* is to develop effective reading and clear thinking. To do so, **Part One** presents a sequence of ten reading skills that are widely recognized as essential for basic and advanced comprehension. The first six skills concern the more literal levels of comprehension:

- Understanding vocabulary in context
- Recognizing main ideas
- Identifying supporting details
- Recognizing implied main ideas
- Understanding relationships that involve addition and time
- Understanding relationships that involve examples, comparison and/or contrast, and cause and effect

The remaining skills cover the more advanced, critical levels of comprehension:

- Making inferences
- Identifying an author's purpose and tone
- Evaluating arguments
- Separating fact from opinion, detecting propaganda, and recognizing errors in reasoning

In every chapter in Part One, the key aspects of a skill are explained and illustrated clearly and simply. Explanations are accompanied by a series of practices, and each chapter ends with four review tests. The last review test consists of a reading selection so that students can apply the skill just learned to real-world reading materials, including newspaper and magazine articles and textbook selections. Together, the ten chapters provide students with the skills needed for both basic and more advanced reading comprehension.

Following each chapter in Part One are **at least six mastery tests for the skill in question.** The tests progress in difficulty, giving students the additional practice and challenge they may need for the solid learning of each skill. While designed for quick grading, the tests also require students to think carefully before answering each question.

Part Two is made up of ten additional readings that will improve both reading and thinking skills. Each reading is followed by *Basic Skill Questions* and *Advanced Skill Questions* so that students can practice all ten skills presented in Part One. In addition, an *Outlining, Mapping,* or *Summarizing* activity after each reading helps students think carefully about the basic content and organization of a selection. *Discussion Questions* then afford instructors a final opportunity to engage students in a variety of reading and thinking skills and thus deepen their understanding of a selection.

Part Three consists of a set of two relationships tests and a series of twenty-five combined-skills tests that review the skills in Part One and help students prepare for the standardized reading test that is often a requirement at the end of a semester.

The **appendixes** that follow include a pronunciation guide and a limited answer key as well as writing assignments for the twenty readings in Parts One and Two of the text. When time permits, asking students to write about a selection will help reinforce the reading and thinking skills they have practiced in the book.

Important Features of the Book

- **Focus on the basics.** The book is designed to explain, in a clear, step-by-step way, the essential elements of each skill. Many examples are provided to ensure that students understand each point. In general, the focus is on teaching the skills—not just on explaining or testing them.

- **Frequent practice and feedback.** Because abundant practice and careful feedback are essential to learning, this book includes numerous activities. Students can get immediate feedback on the practice exercises in Part One by turning to the limited answer key at the back of the book. The answers to the review and mastery tests in Part One, the reading questions in Part Two, and the relationships and combined-skills tests in Part Three are in the *Instructor's Manual.*

The limited answer key increases the active role that students take in their own learning. They are likely to use the answer key in an honest and positive way if they know they will be tested on the many activities and selections for which answers are not provided. (Answers not in the book can be easily copied from the *Instructor's Edition* or the *Instructor's Manual* and passed out at the teacher's discretion.)

● **High interest level.** Dull and unvaried readings and exercises work against learning. Students need to experience genuine interest and enjoyment in what they read. Teachers as well should be able to take pleasure in the selections, for their own good feeling can carry over favorably into class work. The readings in the book, then, have been chosen not only for the appropriateness of their reading level but also for their compelling content. They should engage teachers and students alike.

● **Ease of use.** The logical sequence in each chapter—from explanation to example to practice to review test to mastery test—helps make the skills easy to teach. The book's organization into distinct parts also makes for ease of use. Within a single class, for instance, teachers can work on a new skill in Part One, review other skills with one or more mastery tests, and provide variety by having students read one of the selections in Part Two. The limited answer key at the back of the text also makes for versatility: the teacher can assign some chapters for self-teaching. Finally, the mastery tests—each on its own tear-out page—and the combined-skills tests make it a simple matter for teachers to test and evaluate student progress.

● **Integration of skills.** Students do more than learn the skills individually in Part One. They also learn to apply the skills together through the reading selections in Parts One and Two as well as the combined-skills tests in Part Three. They become effective readers and thinkers through repeated practice in applying a combination of skills.

● **Integrated online resources.** Through the use of TP's acclaimed Learning Center, *Ten Steps to Improving College Reading Skills,* 6/e, features powerful online components to enhance learning, including:

    1 **Online practice exercises and mastery tests.** Each chapter of the book is supported by additional practice exercises *and* online versions of the book's mastery tests. These materials can be used to reinforce skills taught in the chapter *or* to assess students' learning.

    2 **Helpful PowerPoint files.** A comprehensive collection of PowerPoint files covering the book's ten key chapters is available for immediate downloading.

3   **Downloadable supplements.** Electronic (PDF) versions of the instructor's manual and test bank can be downloaded directly from the Learning Center. These files give you the resources you need whenever and wherever you are—24 hours a day.

4   **Class management controls.** The Learning Center allows you to control which assignments and tests your students can access. It also allows you to create unique assignments for each class you teach, track students' progress, and simplify grading. To learn more, e-mail **cs@townsendpress.com** or visit the Learning Center at **www.townsendpress.net**.

● **Thinking activities.** Thinking activities—in the form of outlining, mapping, and summarizing—are a distinctive feature of the book. While educators agree that such organizational abilities are important, these skills are all too seldom taught. From a practical standpoint, it is almost impossible for a teacher to respond in detail to entire collections of class outlines or summaries. This book, then, presents activities that truly involve students in outlining, mapping, and summarizing—in other words, that truly make students *think*— and yet enable a teacher to give immediate feedback. Again, it is through continued practice *and* feedback on challenging material that a student becomes a more effective reader and thinker.

● **Supplementary materials.**

Print Supplements

The two helpful supplements listed below are available at no charge to instructors who have adopted the text. They can be obtained quickly by writing or calling Townsend Press (439 Kelley Drive, West Berlin, New Jersey 08091; 1-800-772-6410), by sending a fax to 1-800-225-8894, or by e-mailing Customer Service at **cs@townsendpress.com**.

1   An *Instructor's Edition*—chances are that you are holding it in your hand—is identical to the student book except that it also provides hints for teachers (see the front of the book), answers to all the practices and tests, and comments on selected items. *No other book on the market has such detailed and helpful annotations.*

2   A combined *Instructor's Manual and Test Bank* includes suggestions for teaching the course, a model syllabus, and readability levels for the text and the reading selections. The test bank contains four additional mastery tests for each of the ten skills and four additional combined-skills tests—all on letter-sized sheets so they can be copied easily for use with students.

Online Supplements

As indicated above, online supplements are available through the TP website by going to the "Supplements" area for instructors at **www.townsendpress.net**.

1 PowerPoint presentations.

2 Online exercises.

● **One of a sequence of books.** This text is the fourth in a series of six books.

Groundwork for College Reading with Phonics and *Groundwork for College Reading* are the basic texts in the series. They are suitable for ESL students and basic adult learners.

Ten Steps to Building College Reading Skills is often the choice for a first college reading course.

Ten Steps to Improving College Reading Skills is an intermediate text appropriate for the core developmental reading course offered at most colleges.

Ten Steps to Advancing College Reading Skills is a higher-level developmental text than the *Improving* book. It can be used as the core book for a more advanced class, as a sequel to *Ten Steps to Improving,* or as a second-semester alternative to it.

Finally, *Ten Steps to Advanced Reading* is the most advanced text in the series. It can also be used as a sequel (or a second-semester alternative) to either the *Improving* or the *Advancing* text.

A companion set of vocabulary books, listed on the copyright page, has been designed to go with the *Ten Steps* books. Recommended to accompany this book is *Improving Vocabulary Skills* (300 words and word parts) or *Improving Vocabulary Skills, Short Version* (200 words).

Together, the books and all their supplements form a sequence that should be ideal for any college reading program.

To summarize, *Ten Steps to Improving College Reading Skills, Sixth Edition,* teaches and reinforces ten essential reading skills. Through an appealing collection of readings and a carefully designed series of activities and tests, students receive extensive guided practice in the skills. The result is an integrated approach to learning that will, by the end of the course, produce better readers and stronger thinkers.

Changes in the Sixth Edition

Changes in this edition include four new readings, a set of relationships tests, five added combined-skills tests, and a freshening of illustrations and practice materials throughout. In addition, the book will be available in electronic as well as print format, and online support for the book has been expanded.

Acknowledgments

I am grateful for the many helpful suggestions provided by the following reviewers: Glenda Bell, University of Arkansas Community College at Batesville; Carol Brenner, Pellissippi State Technical Community College; Gwendolyne Bunch, Midlands Technical College; Donna Clack, Schoolcraft College; Rochelle Favale, College of DuPage; Kay Fell, Tarrant County College; Linda Gilmore, Carroll Community College; Marianne Friedell, College of the Mainland; Belinda C. Hauenstein, Burlington County College; Iris Hill, Wake Technical Community College; Mary Huffer, Lake Sumter Community College; Nancy Joseph, Southeast Community College; Ellen Kaiden, Ramapo College; Miriam Kinard, Trident Technical College; Evelyn Koperwas, Broward Community College; Jackie Lumsden, Greenville Technical College; Denise May, Bucks County Community College; Vashti Muse, Hinds Community College; Joanne Nelson, Hillsborough Community College; Helen Sabin, El Camino College; Annis Shields, Catawba Valley Community College; Tonya Strickland, Bainbridge College; Eileen Suruda, Essex Community College; Mary Temerson, Richmond Community College; Posy Thurow, Fox Valley Technical College; José Rafael Trevino, Laredo Community College; B. Jean Van Meter, Montgomery College; Paula Wimbish, Hinds Community College; and Leta Wium, Florida Community College at Jacksonville.

At Townsend Press, I thank Kathryn Bernstein, Bill Blauvelt, Denton Cairnes, Beth Johnson, Paul Langan, Ruth A. Rouff, and Tanya Savory for the help they provided along the way. I also want to acknowledge the remarkable talent of Akisia Grigsby, who is responsible for the new and dynamic cover design of the book. And I owe special thanks to two TP editors who brought their exceptional talents to this revision. Barbara Solot is responsible for a layout and full-color text design that are as clear as they are inviting. The result of her artistry is a strikingly attractive book that both students and teachers will appreciate. Janet Goldstein has provided design input along with her usual superb editorial skills. Her insights, coupled with her many years of classroom teaching, have strengthened the clarity and pedagogy of the book.

It is always a special pleasure to work with people who aspire toward excellence. With help from my colleagues in the teaching profession and at Townsend Press, I have been able to create a much better book than I could have managed on my own.

John Langan

Introduction

1 How to Become a Better Reader and Thinker

The chances are that you are not as good a reader as you should be to do well in college. If so, it's not surprising. You live in a culture where people watch an average of *five hours of video every day!!!* All that passive viewing does not allow much time for reading. Reading is a skill that must be actively practiced. The simple fact is that people who do not read very often are not likely to be strong readers.

● How much TV do you guess you watch on an average day? _____

Another reason besides TV for not reading much is that you may have a lot of responsibilities. You may be going to school and working at the same time, and you may have a lot of family duties as well. Given your hectic schedule, you're not going to have much time to read. When you have free time, you're exhausted, and it's easier to turn on the TV than to open up a book.

● Do you do any regular reading (for example, a daily newspaper, weekly

magazines, occasional novels)? _____

● When are you most likely to do your reading? _____

A third reason for not reading is that school may have caused you to associate reading with worksheets and drills and book reports and test scores. Experts agree that many schools have not done a good job of helping students discover the pleasures and rewards of reading. If reading was an unpleasant experience in school, you may have concluded that reading in general is not for you.

● Do you think that school made you dislike reading, rather than enjoy it?

_____

Here are three final questions to ask yourself:

● Do you feel that perhaps you don't need a reading course, since you "already know how to read"? _____

● If you had a choice, would you be taking a reading course? (It's okay to be honest.) _____

● Do you think that a bit of speed reading may be all you need? _____

Chances are that you don't need to read *faster* as much as you need to read *smarter*. And it's a safe bet that if you don't read much, you can benefit enormously from the reading course in which you are using this book.

One goal of the book is to help you become a better reader. You will learn and practice ten key reading comprehension skills. As a result, you'll be better able to read and understand the many materials in your other college courses. The skills in this book have direct and practical value: they can help you perform better and more quickly—giving you an edge for success—in all of your college work.

The book is also concerned with helping you become a stronger thinker, a person able not just to *understand* what you read but to *analyze* and *evaluate* it as well. In fact, reading and thinking are closely related skills, and practice in thoughtful reading will also strengthen your ability to think clearly and logically. To find out just how the book will help you achieve these goals, read the next several pages and do the brief activities as well. The activities are easily completed and will give you a quick, helpful overview of the book.

How the Book Is Organized

The book is organized into four main parts:

Introduction (pages 1–18)

In addition to this chapter, which will give you a good sense of the book, there are two other parts to the introduction. "Reading for Pleasure and Power" is a personal essay that describes my own experience in becoming a reader and suggests ways for you to develop the reading habit. Turn to page 13 and write, on the line below, the first of the suggestions:

_____

"Some Quick Study Tips" presents four hints that can make you a better student. If I had time to say just four things to incoming college students based on my thirty years of teaching experience, these are the things I would say. Turn to page 17 and write, in the space below, the first of these tips:

_____

_____

Part One: Ten Steps to Improving College Reading Skills (pages 19–440)

To help you become a more effective reader and thinker, this book presents a series of ten key reading skills. They are listed in the table of contents on pages v and vi. Turn to those pages to fill in the skills missing below:

1 Vocabulary in Context

2 _____

3 _____

4 Implied Main Ideas

5 Relationships I

6 Relationships II

7 _____

8 Purpose and Tone

9 _____

10 Critical Reading

Each chapter is developed in the same way.

   First of all, clear explanations and examples help you *understand* each skill. Practices then give you the "hands-on" experience needed to *learn* the skill.

   ● How many practices are there for the second chapter, "Main Ideas" (pages 57–90)? _____

   Closing each chapter are four review tests. The first review test provides a check of the information presented in the chapter.

   ● On which page is the first review test for "Main Ideas"? _____

The second and third review tests consist of activities that help you practice the skill learned in the chapter.

   ● On which pages are Review Tests 2 and 3 for "Main Ideas"? _____

The fourth review test consists of a story, essay, or textbook selection that both gets you reading and gives you practice in the skill learned in the chapter as well as skills learned in previous chapters.

   ● What is the title of the reading selection in the "Main Ideas" chapter?

_____

Following each chapter are at least six mastery tests which gradually increase in difficulty.

● On what pages are the mastery tests for the "Main Ideas" chapter? _____

The tests are on tear-out pages and so can be easily removed and handed in to your instructor. So that you can track your progress, there is a score box at the top of each test. Your score can also be entered into the "Reading Performance Chart" on the inside back cover of the book.

Part Two: Ten Reading Selections (pages 441–548)

The ten reading selections that make up Part Two are followed by activities that give you practice in all of the skills studied in Part One. Each reading begins in the same way. Look, for example, at "The Yellow Ribbon," which starts on page 443. What are the headings of the two sections that come before the reading itself?

● _____

● _____

Note that the vocabulary words in "Words to Watch" are followed by the numbers of the paragraphs in which the words appear. Look at the first page of "The Yellow Ribbon" and explain how each vocabulary word is marked in the reading itself.

● _____

Activities Following Each Reading Selection

After each selection, there are four kinds of activities that will help you to improve the reading and thinking skills you learned in Part One of the book.

1 The first activity consists of **basic skill questions**—questions involving vocabulary in context, main ideas (including implied main ideas and central points), supporting details, and relationships.

● Look at the basic skill questions for "The Yellow Ribbon" on pages 445–447. Note that the questions are labeled so you know what skill you are practicing in each case. How many questions deal with understanding vocabulary in context? _____

2 The second activity is made up of **advanced skill questions**—those involving inferences, purpose and tone, argument, and critical reading.

● Look at the advanced skill questions on pages 447–449. How many questions deal with making inferences? _____

3 The third activity involves **outlining, mapping,** or **summarizing**. Each of these activities will sharpen your ability to get to the heart of a selection and to think logically and clearly about what you read.

- What kind of activity is provided for "The Yellow Ribbon" on page 449?

  _____

- What kind of activity is provided for the reading titled "College Athletes Should Be Paid" on page 460? _____

Note that a map, or diagram, is a highly visual way of organizing material. Like an outline, it shows at a glance the main parts of a selection.

4 The fourth activity consists of **discussion questions**. These questions provide a chance for you to deepen your understanding of each selection.

- How many discussion questions are there for "College Athletes Should Be Paid" (page 461)—and indeed for nearly every other reading?

  _____

Part Three: Relationships and Combined-Skills Tests (pages 549–614)

The first chapter in Part Three contains three tests that provide additional practice with the relationships you studied in Chapters 5 and 6.

- How many items are in each test? _____

The second chapter in Part Three consists of short passages that give you practice in all the reading skills taught in the book.

- How many such tests are there in all? _____

Appendixes (pages 615–644)

Following Part Three are appendixes that include a pronunciation guide, a limited answer key, and writing assignments for all twenty of the reading selections in the book. Reading and writing are closely connected skills, and writing practice will improve your ability to read closely and to think carefully.

Helpful Features of the Book

1 The book centers on *what you really need to know* to become a better reader and thinker. It presents ten key comprehension skills and explains the most important points about each one.

2 The book gives you *lots of practice.* We seldom learn a skill only by hearing or reading about it; we make it part of us by repeated practice. There are, then, numerous activities in the text. They are not "busywork," but carefully designed materials that should help you truly learn each skill.

   Notice that after you learn each skill in Part One, you progress to review tests and mastery tests that enable you to apply the skill. And as you move from one skill to the next, the reading selections help you practice and reinforce the skills already learned.

3 The selections throughout the book are *lively and appealing.* Dull and unvaried readings work against learning, so subjects have been carefully chosen for their high interest level. Almost all of the selections here are good examples of how what we read can capture our attention. For instance, begin "The Yellow Ribbon," which is about a repentant man just released from prison who is wondering if his wife will allow him to return home—and try to *stop* reading. Or read the textbook selection "Relationships in the 21st Century," which offers some surprising facts about the changing patterns of marriage and childbirth in the United States. Or look at the textbook selection on pages 516–525, which considers the question of whether Lizzie Borden really was an ax-murderer.

4 The readings include *six selections from college textbooks.* Therefore, you will be practicing on some materials very much like the ones in your other courses. Doing so will increase your chances of transferring what you learn in your reading class to your other college courses.

How to Use the Book

1 A good way to proceed is to read and review the explanations and examples in a given chapter in Part One until you feel you understand the ideas presented. Then carefully work through the practices. As you finish each one, check your answers with the "Limited Answer Key" that starts on page 637.

For your own sake, *don't just copy in the answers without trying to do the practices!* The only way to learn a skill is to practice it first and then use the answer key to give yourself feedback. Also, take whatever time is needed to figure out just why you got some answers wrong. By using the answer key to help teach yourself the skills, you will prepare yourself for the review and mastery tests at the end of each chapter as well as the other reading tests in the book. Your instructor can supply you with answers to those tests.

If you have trouble catching on to a particular skill, stick with it. In time, you will learn each of the ten skills.

2 Read the selections first with the intent of simply enjoying them. There will be time afterward for rereading each selection and using it to develop your comprehension skills.

3 Keep track of your progress. Fill in the charts at the end of each chapter in Part One and each reading in Part Two. And in the "Reading Performance Chart" on the inside back cover, enter your scores for all of the review and mastery tests as well as the reading selections and combined-skills tests. These scores can give you a good view of your overall performance as you work through the book.

In summary, *Ten Steps to Improving College Reading Skills* has been designed to interest and benefit you as much as possible. Its format is straightforward, its explanations are clear, its readings are appealing, and its many practices will help you learn through doing. *It is a book that has been created to reward effort,* and if you provide that effort, you will make yourself a better reader and a stronger thinker. I wish you success.

John Langan

2 Reading for Pleasure and Power

Why Read?

Recently I was at a conference where a panel of first-year college students were asked, "If you could give just one bit of advice to high-school kids, what would it be?" One student answered, "I can answer that in one word: **Read.** Read everything you can. The more you read, the better off you're going to be." Up and down the panel, heads nodded. No one disagreed with this advice.

All these students agreed because they had learned the truth about reading—that it is the very heart of education. They had been in college long enough to realize that the habit of regular reading is the best possible preparation for college and for success in life. Here are four specific reasons why you should become a regular reader:

1 **Real Pleasure.** Chances are that you have done little reading for pleasure in your life. You may be an unpracticed reader who has never gotten into the habit of regular reading.

  Perhaps you grew up in a home like mine where a television set dominated the household. Perhaps you got off to a bad start in reading class and never seemed to catch up. Or maybe you were eager to learn about reading when you began school but then soured on it. If you were given uninteresting and irrelevant material to read in school, you may have decided (mistakenly) that reading cannot be rewarding for you.

  The truth is that reading can open the door to a lifetime of pleasure and adventure. If you take the time to walk through that door, chances are you will learn that one of the great experiences of life is the joy of reading for its own sake.

2 **Language Power.** Research has shown beyond any question that frequent reading improves vocabulary, spelling, and reading speed and comprehension, as well as grammar and writing style. If you become a regular reader, all of these language and thinking abilities develop almost automatically!

3 **Job Power.** Regular reading will increase your chances for job success. In today's world more than ever before, jobs involve the processing of information, with words being the tools of the trade. Studies have found that the better your command of words, the more success you are likely to have. *Nothing will give you a command of words like regular reading.*

4 **Human Power.** Reading enlarges the mind and the heart. It frees us from the narrow confines of our own experience. Knowing how other people view important matters helps us decide what we ourselves think and feel. Reading also helps us connect with others and realize our shared humanity. Someone once wrote, "We read in order to know that we are not alone." We become less isolated as we share the common experiences, emotions, and thoughts that make us human. We grow more sympathetic and understanding because we realize that others are like us.

A Personal Story about the Value of Reading

I did little reading as a boy, with one notable exception: I loved comic books. In particular, I can remember reading comics at lunchtime. Since I attended a grade school that was only several blocks away, I could walk home at noon. There I would drink chocolate milk and eat my favorite sandwich—baloney, mustard, and potato chips layered between two pieces of white bread. I would sit at the kitchen table with my two sisters, home from the same school, as well as my father, home for lunch from his job with a local insurance company. The four of us sat silently because we were all reading. My sisters and I read mostly Donald Duck, Scrooge McDuck, and Mickey Mouse comic books, while my father read *Reader's Digest, Life* magazine, or the morning newspaper. Coffee cup in hand, my mother hovered nearby, always a bit frustrated, I suspect. She was in the mood for conversation, but her family was too busy reading.

Even when I went on to high school, I was more likely to read a comic book than anything else. Each year my English teachers typically assigned two books for students to read and report on—books such as Sir Walter Scott's *Ivanhoe* and Charles Dickens's *A Tale of Two Cities.* I had no interest in reading such books, especially ones that seemed to be about, as I remember saying at the time, "old dead stuff." How, then, did I deal with these assignments? I was rescued by a series of classic comic books, which were illustrated stories of famous novels. Classic comics helped me pass tests and do book reports. They also kept me from actually having to sit down and read a book—an activity that I never imagined could be a source of enjoyment.

What did give me pleasure was watching television. I developed a routine after school: get my homework done, do any household chores, eat dinner, and then spend the whole evening watching the tube.

Fortunately, something happened in the summer before my junior year that changed my life. The country was in the middle of a recession, so I was not able to get a job. I felt too old to spend the summer playing back-alley baseball with neighborhood buddies, and there was not enough on daytime TV (this was before cable) to hold my interest. Except for a once-a-week job of cutting my aunt's grass, I had nothing to do and felt restless and empty.

Then, sitting on my front porch one day in early June, I saw a public service message on the side of a bus that was rumbling noisily down the street. I remember the exact words: "Open your mind—read a book." Such messages had always annoyed me. On general principle I never liked being told what I should do. I also resented the implication that my mind was closed just because I didn't read books. I thought to myself, "For the heck of it, I'm going to read a book just so I know for sure there's nothing there."

That afternoon I walked to the one bookstore in town, browsed around, and picked out a paperback book—*The Swiss Family Robinson*—about a family that had been shipwrecked on an island and had to find a way to survive until rescue came. I spent a couple of days reading the story. When I was done, I had to admit that I had enjoyed it and that I was proud of myself for actually having read an entire book.

But in the perverse frame of mind that was typical of me at age 15, I thought to myself, "I just happened to pick out the one story in the world that is actually interesting. Chances are there aren't any more." But the more reasonable part of me wondered, "What if there are other books that wouldn't waste my time?"

I remembered that upstairs in my closet were some books that my aunt had once given me but I had never read. I selected one that I had heard of and that seemed to have some promise. It was *The Adventures of Tom Sawyer*, by Mark Twain, and it was a hardbound book now so old that its binding cracked when I opened it. I began reading, and while the activities of Tom were interesting enough, it was his girlfriend Becky Thatcher who soon captured my complete attention. My adolescent heart raced when I thought of her, and for a while I thought about her night and day. For the first time in my life, I had fallen in love— incredibly enough, with a character in a book! The character of Becky helped show me what power a book can have.

Tom had a friend named Huck Finn, about whom Mark Twain had written another book. So when I finished Tom's story, I went to the library, got a library card, and checked out *The Adventures of Huckleberry Finn*. I figured this book might tell me more about Becky. As it turned out, it didn't, but by pure chance I wound up reading one of the great works of American literature.

If Becky had made my blood race, the story of Huck Finn and the trip that he and his friend Jim took on a raft down the Mississippi River caught me up in a different but equally compelling way. While I could not express what happened at the time, the book made me look at people in a new light. I saw a whole stage of characters who felt very human and whose stories seemed very real. Some of these characters were mean and stupid and cowardly and hateful, others were loyal and courageous and dignified and loving, and a few were a blend of good and evil. By the time I finished Huck's story, I knew that books could be a source of pleasure, and I sensed also that they could be a source of power—that they could help me learn important things about the world and the people around me. I was now hooked on books. By the end of the summer, I had read over twenty novels, and I have been reading ever since.

How to Become a Regular Reader

How, you might be wondering, does one become a regular reader? The key, as simple as it might sound, is to do a great deal of reading. The truth of the matter is that reading is like any other skill. The more you practice, the better you get. In his book *The Power of Reading: Insights from the Research*, the reading scholar Stephen Krashen surveys an extensive number of studies and concludes that reading itself is the "way that we become good readers." The value of regular reading is a point about which common sense and research are in complete agreement.

The following suggestions will help you make reading a part of your life. Remember, though: These suggestions are only words on a page. You must decide to become a regular reader, and you must follow through on that decision. Only then will reading become a source of pleasure and power.

- Create a half hour or an hour of reading in your daily schedule. That time might be during your lunch hour, or late afternoon before dinner, or the half hour or so before you turn off your light at night. Find a time that is possible for you, and make reading then a habit. The result will be both recreation time and personal growth.

- Subscribe to a daily newspaper and read the sections that interest you. Keep in mind that it is not *what* you read that matters—for example, you should not feel obliged to read the editorial section if opinion columns are not your interest. What does matter is *the very fact that you read*. Feel perfectly free to read whatever you like: the sports page, the fashion section, movie reviews, front-page stories—even the comics.

- Subscribe to one or more magazines. Browse in the magazine section of your library, a local bookstore, or online; chances are you'll find some magazines that interest you. You may want to consider a weekly news magazine, such as *Time*; a weekly general-interest magazine, such as *People*; or any number of special-interest monthly magazines, such as *Glamour, Sports Illustrated, Essence,* or *Health and Fitness*.

    You'll find subscription cards within most magazines; and on many college bulletin boards, you'll see display cards offering magazines at discount rates for students. In addition, you can now access a wide variety of magazines in digital format and read them on your computer, smartphone, or tablet.

● Read aloud to children in your family, whether younger brothers or sisters or sons or daughters or nephews or nieces. Alternatively, have a family reading time when you and the children take turns reading.

● Read books on your own. This is the most important step on the road to becoming a regular reader. Reading is most enjoyable when you get drawn into the special world created by a book. You can travel in that world for hours, unmindful for a while of everyday concerns. In that timeless zone, you will come to experience the joy of reading. Too many people are addicted to smoking or drugs or television; you should try, instead, to get hooked on books.

What should you read? Select anything that interests you. That might be comic books, fantasies or science fiction, horror and mystery stories, romances, adventure and sports stories, biographies and autobiographies, or how-to books. To select a book, browse in a bookstore, library, or reading center. Find something you like and begin reading. If you stick to it and become a regular reader, you may find that you have done nothing less than change your life.

Questions

1. Was reading a priority in the home where you grew up? If so, tell how reading was emphasized. If not, describe what seemed to be the attitude towards reading in your home. How did your family's attitude (positive or negative) about reading affect your development as a reader?

2. When you were growing up, what role did school play in encouraging or discouraging you to read? Describe experiences in school that made you feel positive or negative about reading.

3. What do you think that parents and schools could do to make reading a source of pleasure for children? Suggest some specific ideas that would have worked for you as a child.

4. Of the five suggestions that appear in the section in this chapter titled "How to Become a Regular Reader," which one or two seem the most appealing and realistic to you?

5. Read one of the books recommended on the Townsend Press website. Go to **www.townsendpress.com** and click on "TP Library and Bluford Series." More than one hundred books are available, each at only $1 apiece plus shipping and handling.

A Special Offer

To promote your reading growth, Townsend Press will send you five books at no charge except for postage and handling. Here are the five books:

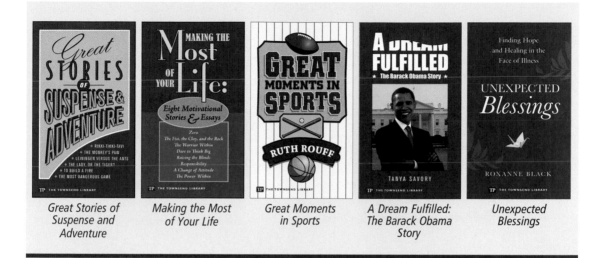

Great Stories of Suspense and Adventure

Making the Most of Your Life

Great Moments in Sports

A Dream Fulfilled: The Barack Obama Story

Unexpected Blessings

Cut out the actual order form below (not a copy), enclosing five dollars to cover the cost of shipping and handling. You'll then be sent these five very readable books.

ORDER FORM

YES! Please send me copies of *Great Stories, Making the Most of Your Life, Great Moments in Sports, A Dream Fulfilled,* and *Unexpected Blessings.* Enclosed is five dollars to cover the shipping and handling of the books.

Please PRINT the following very clearly. It will be your shipping label.

Name _____

Address _____

City _____ *State* _____ *Zip* _____

MAIL TO: TP Book Center, 439 Kelley Drive, West Berlin, NJ 08091.

3 Some Quick Study Tips

While it's not my purpose in this book to teach study skills, I do want to give you four quick hints that can make you a better student. The hints are based on my thirty years of experience working with first-year college students and teaching reading and study skills.

 TIP 1 The most important steps you can take to succeed in school are to go to every class and take a lot of notes. If you don't go to class, or you go but just sit there without taking notes, chances are you're heading for a heap of trouble.

 TIP 2 Let me ask you a question: Which is more important—learning how to read a textbook or learning how to read your professor?

Write your answer here: _____

You may be surprised at the answer: What is far more important is learning how to read your professor—to understand what he or she expects you to learn in the course and to know for tests.

I remember becoming a good student in college only after I learned the truth of this statement. And I have interviewed hundreds of today's students who have said the same thing. Let me quote just one of them:

> *You absolutely have to be in class. Then you learn how to read the teacher and to know what he or she is going to want on tests. You could read an entire textbook, but that wouldn't be as good as being in class and writing down a teacher's understanding of ideas.*

 TIP 3 Many teachers base their tests mainly on the ideas they present in class. But when you have to learn a textbook chapter, do the following.

First, read the first and last few paragraphs of the chapter; they may give you a good overview of what the chapter is about.

Second, as you read the chapter, look for and mark off definitions of key terms and examples of those definitions.

Third, as you read the chapter, number any lists of items; if there is a series of items and you number the items *1, 2, 3,* and so on, it will be easier to understand and remember them.

Fourth, after you've read the chapter, take notes on the most important material and test yourself on those notes until you can say them to yourself without looking at them.

TIP **TIP 4** Here's another question: Are you an organized person? Do you get out of bed on time, do you get to places on time, do you keep up with school work, do you allow time to study for tests and write papers?

If you are *not* an organized person, you're going to have trouble in school. Here are three steps to take to control your time:

First, pay close attention to the course outline, or *syllabus,* your instructors will probably pass out at the start of a semester. Chances are that the syllabus will give you the dates of exams and tell you when papers or reports are due.

Second, move all those dates onto a *large monthly calendar*—a calendar that has a good-sized block of white space for each date. Hang the calendar in a place where you'll be sure to see it every day—perhaps above your desk or on a bedroom wall.

Third, buy a small notebook and write down every day a *"to do" list* of things that need to get done that day. Decide which items are most important, and focus on them first. (If you have classes that day, going to those classes will be "A" priority items.) Carry your list with you during the day, referring to it every so often and checking off items as you complete them.

Questions

1. Of the four hints listed above, which is the most important one for you? Why?

2. Which hint is the second most important for you, and why?

3. A graph later in this book makes clear just how quickly we forget new material. For example, how much class material do you think most people forget in just two weeks? Check (✓) the answer you think is correct.

   _____ 20 percent is forgotten within two weeks

   _____ 40 percent is forgotten within two weeks

   _____ 60 percent is forgotten within two weeks

   _____ 80 percent is forgotten within two weeks

   The truth is that within two weeks most people forget almost 80% of what they have heard! Given that fact, what should you be sure to do in all your

   classes? _____

Part One

**Ten Steps to
Improving
College Reading
Skills**

1 Vocabulary in Context

If you were asked to define the words *ambivalent*, *adverse*, and *incessant*, you might have some difficulty. On the other hand, if you saw these words in sentences, chances are you could come up with fairly accurate definitions. For example, see if you can define the words in *italics* in the three sentences below. Then, using a capital letter, write the letter of your choice on the answer line.

Do not use a dictionary for this work. Instead, in each sentence, try the word you think is the answer. For example, put *mixed* or *critical* or *approving* into the sentence in place of *ambivalent* to see which one makes the best sense.

____ Many of us have *ambivalent* (ăm-bĭv′ə-lənt) feelings about our politicians, admiring them but also distrusting them.

Ambivalent means

A. mixed.　　　　B. critical.　　　　C. approving.

____ The *adverse* (ăd-vûrs′) effects of this drug, including dizziness, nausea, and headaches, have caused it to be withdrawn from the market.

Adverse means

A. artificial.　　　　B. energetic.　　　　C. harmful.

____ I prefer the occasional disturbance of ear-splitting thunder to the *incessant* (ĭn-sĕs′ənt) dripping of our kitchen sink.

Incessant means

A. harmless.　　　　B. exciting.　　　　C. nonstop.

In each sentence above, the **context**—the words surrounding the unfamiliar word—provides clues to the word's meaning. You may have guessed from the context that *ambivalent* means "mixed," that *adverse* means "harmful," and that *incessant* is "nonstop."

Using context clues to understand the meaning of unfamiliar words will help you in several ways:

● It will save you time when reading. You will not have to stop to look up words in the dictionary. (Of course, you won't always be able to understand a word from its context, so you should always have a dictionary nearby as you read.)

● After you figure out the meaning of the same word more than once through its context, it may become a part of your working vocabulary. You will therefore add to your vocabulary simply by reading thoughtfully.

● You will get a good sense of how a word is actually used, including any shades of meaning it might have.

Types of Context Clues

There are four common types of context clues:

1 Examples
2 Synonyms
3 Antonyms
4 General Sense of the Sentence or Passage

In the following sections, you will read about and practice using each type. The practices will sharpen your skills in recognizing and using context clues. They will also help you add new words to your vocabulary.

Remember *not* to use a dictionary for these practices. Their purpose is to help you develop the skill of figuring out what words mean without using a dictionary. Pronunciations are provided in parentheses for the words, and a brief guide to pronunciation is on pages 617–618.

1   Examples

Examples may suggest the meaning of an unknown word. To understand how this type of clue works, look again at the sentence on page 21: "The *adverse* effects of this drug, including dizziness, nausea, and headaches, have caused it to be withdrawn from the market." The examples—dizziness, nausea, and headaches—helped you figure out that the word *adverse* means "harmful."

Look also at the cartoon on the next page. What do you think the word *initiative* (ĭ-nĭsh′ə-tĭv′) means?

A. anger   B. willpower   C. ability to take charge

"If we had any initiative, we'd be chasing mice right now instead of letting them run wild in the kitchen."

Note that the example of the cats' having initiative—chasing mice—helps you understand that *initiative* means "ability to take charge."

 ## Check Your Understanding

Now read the items that follow. An *italicized* word in each sentence is followed by examples that serve as context clues for that word. These examples, which are **boldfaced,** will help you figure out the meaning of each word. On each line, write the letter of the answer you think is correct. Then read the explanation that follows.

Note that examples are often introduced with signal words and phrases like *for example*, *for instance*, *including*, and *such as*.

_____ 1. *Nocturnal* creatures, such as **bats and owls**, have highly developed senses that enable them to function in the dark.

        Nocturnal (nŏk-tûr′nəl) means
        A. feathery.   B. living.   C. active at night.

_____ 2. *Mundane* activities such as **doing the laundry or dishes** or **going food shopping** or **reading the newspaper** all help me relax.

        Mundane (mŭn-dān′) means
        A. exciting.   B. painful.   C. ordinary.

_____ 3. Instances of common *euphemisms* include **"final resting place"** (for *grave*), **"intoxicated"** (for *drunk*), and **"restroom"** (for *toilet*).

Euphemisms (yoō′fə-mĭz′əmz) means
A. unpleasant reactions.
B. answers.
C. substitutes for offensive terms.

Explanation

In each sentence, the examples probably helped you to figure out the meanings of the words in italics:

● In sentence 1, the examples given of nocturnal creatures—bats and owls—may have helped you to guess that nocturnal creatures are those that are "active at night," since bats and owls do come out at night.

● In sentence 2, the activities referred to are clues to the meaning of *mundane,* which is "ordinary."

● In sentence 3, as the examples indicate, *euphemisms* means "substitutes for offensive terms."

PRACTICE 1: Examples

For each item below, underline the examples that suggest the meaning of the italicized term. Then write the letter of the meaning of that term on the answer line. Note that the last five sentences have been taken from college textbooks.

_____ 1. Today I had to deal with one *mishap* after another. I couldn't find my car keys, I dropped a bowl of soup at lunchtime, and my computer crashed twice.

Mishap (mĭs′hăp′) means
A. unlucky accident.
B. event.
C. unexpected question.

Hint: For this and all the exercises in this chapter, actually insert into the sentence the word you think is the answer. For example, substitute *unlucky accident* or *event* or *unexpected question* in the sentence in place of *mishap* to see which one fits.

_____ 2. Some mentally ill people have *bizarre* ideas. For instance, they may think the TV is talking to them or that others can steal their thoughts.

Bizarre (bĭ-zär′) means
A. limited.
B. ordinary.
C. odd.

_____ 3. Some animals have remarkable *longevity*. For example, the giant land tortoise can live several hundred years.

Longevity (lŏn-jĕv′ĭ-tē) means
A. appearances.   B. length of life.   C. habits.

_____ 4. Before the invention of television, people spent more time on *diversions* such as going to town concerts and ball games, visiting neighborhood friends, and playing board games.

Diversions (dĭ-vûr′zhənz) means
A. amusements.   B. differences.   C. chores.

_____ 5. Since my grandfather retired, he has developed several new *avocations*. For instance, he now enjoys gardening and chat groups on the Internet.

Avocations (ăv′ō-kā′shənz) means
A. hobbies.   B. vacations.   C. jobs.

_____ 6. Children who move to a foreign country *adapt* much more easily than their parents, soon picking up the language and customs of their new home.

Adapt (ə-dăpt′) means
A. adjust.   B. struggle.   C. become bored.

_____ 7. The Chinese government provides *incentives* for married couples to have only one child. For example, couples with one child get financial help and free medical care.

Incentives (ĭn-sĕn′tĭvz) means
A. warnings.   B. penalties.   C. encouragements.

_____ 8. Changes in such abilities as learning, reasoning, thinking, and language are aspects of *cognitive* development.

Cognitive (kŏg′nĭ-tĭv) means
A. physical.   B. mental.   C. spiritual.

_____ 9. Today was a day of *turmoil* at work. The phones were constantly ringing, people were running back and forth, and several offices were being painted.

Turmoil (tûr′moil′) means
A. discussion.   B. confusion.   C. harmony.

_____ 10. *White-collar crime*—for example, accepting a bribe from a customer or stealing from an employer—is more costly than "common" crime.

White-collar crime (hwīt-kŏl′ər krīm) means crime committed by
A. gang members.   B. strangers.   C. people in the workplace.

2 Synonyms

A context clue is often available in the form of a **synonym**: a word that means the same or almost the same as the unknown word. A synonym may appear anywhere in a passage to provide the same meaning as the unknown word.

Look at the cartoon below.

"My doctor said smoking could terminate my life. But I told him, 'Everybody's life has to end some time.'"

© Randy Glasbergen. www.glasbergen.com

Notice that the synonym that helps you understand the meaning of *terminate* is *end*.

✓ *Check Your Understanding*

In each of the following items, the word to be defined is italicized. Underline the synonym for the italicized word in each sentence.

1. Fresh garlic may not *enhance* (ĕn-hăns′) the breath, but it certainly does improve spaghetti sauce.

2. As soon as I made a *flippant* (flĭp′ənt) remark to my boss, I regretted sounding so disrespectful.

3. Although the salesperson tried to *assuage* (ə-swāj′) the angry customer, there was no way to soothe her.

Explanation

In each sentence, the synonym given should have helped you understand the meaning of the word in italics:

● *Enhance* means "improve."
● *Flippant* means "disrespectful."
● *Assuage* means "soothe."

PRACTICE 2: Synonyms

Each item below includes a word that is a synonym of the italicized word. Write the synonym of the italicized word in the space provided. Note that the last five sentences have been taken from college textbooks.

_____ 1. Speaking in front of a group *disconcerts* (dĭs′kən-sûrtz′) Alan. Even answering a question in class embarrasses him.

Hint: How does speaking in public affect Alan?

_____ 2. Because my friends had advised me to *scrutinize* (skrōōt′n-īz′) the lease, I took time to examine all the fine print.

_____ 3. The presidential candidate vowed to discuss *pragmatic* (prăg-măt′ĭk) solutions. He said the American people want practical answers, not empty theory.

_____ 4. I asked the instructor to explain a confusing passage in the textbook. She said, "I wish I could, but it's *obscure* (ŏb-skyŏŏr′) to me, too."

_____ 5. Teachers may overlook it when a student is two minutes late. But they are not going to *condone* (kən-dōn′) someone's walking into class a half hour late.

_____ 6. When people are broke, they find that many things which seem *indispensable* (ĭn′dĭ-spĕn′sə-bəl) are not so necessary after all.

_____ 7. Managers should beware of having *adversaries* (ăd′vər-sĕr′ēz) work together; opponents often do not cooperate well.

_____ 8. In the same way that the arrival of mechanical equipment meant fewer farm jobs, the *advent* (ăd′vĕnt′) of the computer has led to fewer manufacturing jobs.

_____ 9. Many corporations like to be seen as *benevolent* (bə-nĕv′ə-lənt) and will actively seek publicity for their charitable donations.

_____ 10. Throughout history, the *prevalent* (prĕv′ə-lənt) authority pattern in families has been patriarchy, in which males are in control. In only a few societies has matriarchy been the customary authority pattern.

3 Antonyms

An **antonym**—a word that means the opposite of another word—is also a useful context clue. Antonyms are often signaled by words and phrases such as *however, but, yet, on the other hand*, and *in contrast.*

Look again at the sentence on page 21: "I prefer the occasional disturbance of ear-splitting thunder to the *incessant* dripping of our kitchen sink." Here the word *occasional* is an antonym that helps us realize that the word *incessant* means "nonstop."

Look also at the cartoon below.

Note that the antonym *lowers* help you figure out that *amplifies* must mean "increases."

✓ *Check Your Understanding*

In each sentence below, underline the word that means the opposite of the italicized word. Then, on the answer line, write the letter of the meaning of the italicized word.

_____ 1. Many people have pointed out the harmful effects that a working mother may have on the family, yet there are many *salutary* effects as well.

Salutary (săl′yə-tĕr′ē) means
A. well-known.   B. beneficial.   C. hurtful.

_____ 2. Trying to control everything your teens do can *impede* their growth. To advance their development, allow them to make some decisions on their own.

Impede (ĭm-pēd′) means
A. block.   B. predict.   C. improve.

_____ 3. During their training, police officers must respond to *simulated* emergencies in preparation for dealing with real ones.

Simulated (sĭm′yə-lā′tĭd) means
A. made-up.   B. mild.   C. actual.

Explanation

In the first sentence, salutary effects are the opposite of harmful effects, so *salutary* means "beneficial." In the second sentence, *impede* is the opposite of *advance*, so *impede* means "block." Last, the opposite of *real* is *simulated*; *simulated* means "made-up."

PRACTICE 3: Antonyms

Each item below includes a word that is an antonym of the italicized word. Underline the antonym of each italicized word. Then, on the answer line, write the letter of the meaning of the italicized word. Note that the last five sentences have been taken from college textbooks.

_____ 1. Many politicians do not give *succinct* answers. They prefer long ones that help them avoid the point.

Hint: If politicians prefer to give long answers, what kind of answer do they usually *not* give?

Succinct (sək-sĭngkt′) means
A. brief.   B. accurate.   C. complete.

_____ 2. Although investments in the stock market can be *lucrative,* they can also result in great financial loss.

Lucrative (loo′krə-tĭv) means
A. required.   B. financially rewarding.   C. risky.

_____ 3. "I've seen students *surreptitiously* check answer sheets during exams," said the professor. "However, until today I never saw one openly lay out a cheat sheet on his desk."

Surreptitiously (sûr′əp-tĭsh′əs-lē) means
A. legally.   B. secretly.   C. loudly.

_____ 4. While Melba's apartment is decorated plainly, her clothing is very *flamboyant*.

Flamboyant (flăm-boi′ənt) means
A. inexpensive.   B. flashy.   C. washable.

_____ 5. To keep healthy, older people need to stay active. Remaining *stagnant* results in loss of strength and health.

Stagnant (stăg′nənt) means
A. inactive.   B. lively.   C. unhealthy.

_____ 6. In formal communication, be sure to avoid *ambiguous* language. Clear language prevents confusion.

Ambiguous (ăm-bĭg′yoo-əs) means
A. wordy.   B. ineffective.   C. unclear.

_____ 7. Being raised with conflicting values can be a *detriment* to boys' and girls' relationships with each other. In contrast, shared values can be a benefit.

Detriment (dĕt′rə-mənt) means
A. improvement.   B. drawback.   C. relationship.

_____ 8. While houses and antiques often increase in value, most things, such as cars and TVs, *depreciate*.

Depreciate (dĭ-prē′shē-āt′) means
A. remain useful.   B. lose value.   C. break.

_____ 9. Reliable scientific theories are based not upon careless work, but rather upon *meticulous* research and experimentation.

Meticulous (mĭ-tĭk′yə-ləs) means
A. hasty.   B. expensive.   C. careful.

_____ 10. In the early days of automobile manufacturing, *stringent* laws controlled motorists' speed. In contrast, the laws designed to protect consumers from faulty products were extremely weak.

Stringent (strĭn′jənt) means
A. informal.   B. not effective.   C. strict.

4   General Sense of the Sentence or Passage

Sometimes it takes a bit more detective work to puzzle out the meaning of an unfamiliar word. In such cases, you must draw conclusions based on the information given with the word. Asking yourself questions about the passage may help you make a fairly accurate guess about the meaning of the unfamiliar word.

Look at the cartoon below.

Copyright 2006 by Randy Glasbergen.
www.glasbergen.com

GLASBERGEN

"I'd like a prescription that will alleviate my aches and pains and also make me younger and thinner."

To figure out the meaning of *alleviate*, try asking this question: What would the patient want the prescription to do to his aches and pains? The patient's words to his doctor strongly suggest that *alleviate* means "lessen."

✔ *Check Your Understanding*

Each of the sentences below is followed by a question. Think about each question; then, on the answer line, write the letter of the answer you think is the correct meaning of the italicized word.

_____ 1. A hilarious video of a little dog playing the piano and "singing" went *viral* almost immediately, with millions of people viewing it on the Internet.

(What must have happened if millions viewed the video?)

Viral (vī′rəl) means
A. unpopular.   B. spreading quickly.   C. making money.

_____ 2. Despite the *proximity* of Ron's house to his sister's, he rarely sees her.

(What about Ron's house would make it surprising that he didn't see his sister more often?)

Proximity (prŏk-sĭm′ĭ-tē) means

A. similarity.   B. nearness.   C. superiority.

_____ 3. The car wash we organized to raise funds was a *fiasco*—it rained all day.

(How successful would a car wash be on a rainy day?)

Fiasco (fē-ăs′kō) means

A. great financial   B. welcome surprise.   C. complete disaster.
success.

Explanation

The first sentence provides enough evidence for you to guess that *viral* means "spread quickly." *Proximity* in the second sentence means "nearness." And a *fiasco* is a "complete disaster." (You may not hit on the exact dictionary definition of a word by using context clues, but you will often be accurate enough to make good sense of what you are reading.)

 PRACTICE 4: General Sense of the Sentence or Passage

Try to answer the question that follows each item below. Then use the logic of each answer to help you write the letter of the meaning you think is correct. Note that the last five sentences have been taken from college textbooks.

_____ 1. The lizard was so *lethargic* that I wasn't sure if it was alive or dead. It didn't even blink.

(Would an animal that seemed dead be green, inactive, or big?)

Lethargic (lə-thär′jĭk) means

A. green.   B. inactive.   C. big.

_____ 2. Jamal didn't want to tell Tina the entire plot of the movie, so he just gave her the *gist* of the story.

(What kind of information would Jamal have given Tina?)

Gist (jĭst) means

A. ending.   B. title.   C. main idea.

_____   3. After the accident, I was angered when the other driver told the police officer a complete *fabrication* about what happened. He claimed that I was the person at fault.

(How truthful was the other driver's information?)

Fabrication (făb′rĭ-kā′shən) means
A. lie.   B. description.   C. confession.

_____   4. The public knows very little about the *covert* activities of CIA spies.

(What kind of activities would the CIA spies be involved in that the public wouldn't know much about?)

Covert (kŭv′ərt *or* kōv′ərt *or* kō-vûrt′) means
A. public.   B. secret.   C. family.

_____   5. Whether or not there is life in outer space is an *enigma*. We may never know for sure until we are capable of space travel or aliens actually land on our planet.

(What would we call something to which we have no answer?)

Enigma (ĭ-nĭg′mə) means
A. reason.   B. certainty.   C. mystery.

_____   6. Suicide rates tend to *fluctuate* with the seasons, with much higher rates in the winter than in the summer.

(What happens to the suicide rate from season to season?)

Fluctuate (flŭk′chōō-āt′) means
A. go up and down.   B. disappear.   C. stay the same.

_____   7. Human beings are *resilient* creatures—they can often bounce back from negative experiences and adjust well to life.

(What point is the author making about the nature of human beings?)

Resilient (rĭ-zĭl′yənt) means
A. not flexible.   B. living.   C. able to recover.

_____   8. A major accomplishment of sociology is *dispelling* the myths and prejudices that groups of people have about each other.

(What would a profession do to "myths and prejudices" that could be considered a "major accomplishment"?)

Dispelling (dĭ-spĕl′ĭng) means
A. ignoring.   B. making vanish.   C. creating again.

_____ 9. Ten years of research *culminated* in a report explaining the mysterious behavior of the praying mantis, a large green or brownish insect.

(What would be the relationship of the report to the research?)

Culminated (kŭl'mə-nā'tĭd) means

A. failed.   B. began.   C. concluded.

_____ 10. Despite complaints from parents, educators, and government officials, violence and sex on television seem to go on *unabated*.

(In spite of the complaints, does anything happen?)

Unabated (ŭn'ə-bā'tĭd) means

A. more slowly.   B. unstopped.   C. at great expense.

An Important Point about Textbook Definitions

You don't always have to use context clues or the dictionary to find definitions. Very often, textbook authors define important terms. Also, after giving a definition, authors usually follow it with one or more examples to ensure that you understand the new term. For instance, here is a short textbook passage that includes a definition and an example:

> [1]People do not always satisfy their needs directly; sometimes they use a substitute object. [2]Use of a substitute is known as **displacement**. [3]This is the process that takes place, for instance, when you control your impulse to yell at your boss and then go home and yell at the first member of your family who is unlucky enough to cross your path.

Textbook authors, then, often do more than provide context clues: they define a word, set it off in *italic* or **boldface** type, and provide examples as well. When they take the time to define and illustrate a word, you should assume that the term is important enough to learn.

More about textbook definitions and examples appears on pages 224–225 in the "Relationships II" chapter.

CHAPTER REVIEW

In this chapter, you learned the following:

- To save time when reading, you should try to figure out the meanings of unfamiliar words. You can do so by looking at their **context**—the words surrounding them.

- There are four kinds of context clues: **examples** (marked by words like *for example, for instance, including,* and *such as*); **synonyms** (words that mean the same as unknown words); **antonyms** (words that mean the opposite of unknown words); and **general sense of the sentence or passage** (clues in the sentence or surrounding sentences about what words might mean).

- Textbook authors typically set off important words in *italic* or **boldface** and define those words for you, often providing examples as well.

The next chapter—Chapter 2—will introduce you to the most important of all comprehension skills: finding the main idea.

 On the Web: If you are using this book in class, you can visit our website for additional practice in understanding vocabulary in context. Go to **www.townsendpress.com** and click on "Learning Center."

REVIEW TEST 1

To review what you've learned in this chapter, answer the following questions by filling in the blank or writing the letter of the correct answer.

1. Often, a reader can figure out the meaning of a new word without using the dictionary—by paying attention to the word's _____.

_____ 2. In the sentence below, which type of context clue is used for the italicized word?

    A. example   B. synonym   C. antonym

    You can't take certain courses unless you've taken a *prerequisite* (prĕ-rĕk′wĭ-zĭt); for instance, you can't take Spanish Literature I unless you've taken Spanish III.

_____ 3. In the sentence below, which type of context clue is used for the italicized word?

    A. example   B. synonym   C. antonym

    There are thick pine forests at the foot of the mountain, but higher up, the trees become *sparse* (spärs).

_____ 4. In the sentences below, which type of context clue is used for the italicized word?

    A. example   B. synonym   C. antonym

    Talent may take years to surface. When Beethoven was a young child, his great *aptitude* (ăp′tĭ-to͞od′) in music was not at all apparent to his teachers.

5. Often when textbook authors introduce a new word, they provide you with a _____ and follow it with _____ that help make the meaning of the word clear.

REVIEW TEST 2

A. Look at the cartoon below, and then answer the questions that follow.

Copyright 2002 © Randy Glasbergen.
www.glasbergen.com

GLASBERGEN

"I'm trying to curtail my coffee drinking by
cutting down to just one cup a day."

_____ 1. Using the context clues in the cartoon, write the letter of the best
meaning of *curtail* (kər-tāl′) in the space provided.
A. improve   B. reduce   C. supplement

_____ 2. What kind of context clue helps you understand the meaning of the
cartoon?
A. Examples clue   B. Synonym clue   C. Antonym clue

B. Using context clues for help, write the letter of the best meaning for each italicized
word. Use the space provided.

_____ 3. *Nepotism* (nĕp′ə-tĭz′əm) is commonplace where I work: the boss's
daughter is vice-president of the company, her husband runs the order
department, and their son has just started working in the warehouse.
A. good managerial practice   C. arguments among employees
B. favoritism to relatives   D. confusion among management

_____ 4. Because the professor's explanation was *nebulous* (nĕb′yə-ləs), several
of the students asked him to make himself clear.
A. vague   C. fascinating
B. boring   D. brief

_____ 5. The bank robber was apparently *nondescript* (nŏn′dĭ-skrĭpt′)—none of the witnesses could think of any special characteristics that might identify him.

A. poorly disguised   C. memorable
B. lacking distinctive qualities   D. cruel

C. Using context clues for help, write the definition for each italicized word. Then write the letter of the definition in the space provided. Choose from the definitions in the box below. Each definition will be used once.

A. discouraged	B. doubtful	C. nag
D. overjoyed	E. provided	

_____ 6. I would not just be glad if I won the lottery; I'd be *ecstatic*.

Ecstatic (ĕk-stăt′ĭk) means _____.

_____ 7. Nature has *endowed* hummingbirds with the ability to fly backward.

Endowed (ĕn-doud′) means _____.

_____ 8. Opponents of the death penalty say it has never actually *deterred* anyone from committing murder.

Deterred (dĭ-tûrd′) means _____.

_____ 9. Around the age of two or three, small children like to *badger* their parents with endless questions beginning with the word "why."

Badger (băj′ər) means _____.

_____ 10. While four-year-old Mattie claimed she was going to stay up until midnight on New Year's Eve, her parents were *dubious* of her ability to remain awake that late.

Dubious (dōō′bē-əs) means _____.

REVIEW TEST 3

A. Use context clues to figure out the meaning of the italicized word in each of the following sentences, and write your definition in the space provided.

1. While it's often not *feasible* to work full-time while going to school, it may be practical to hold down a part-time job.

   Feasible (fē′zə-bəl) means _____.

2. It's amazing that my neighbors always appear *immaculate*, yet their apartment is often quite dirty.

   Immaculate (ĭ-măk′yə-lĭt) means _____ .

3. It's against the law to ask people to *divulge* their ages at job interviews.

   Divulge (dĭ-vŭlj′) means _____.

4. Doctors should *alleviate* the pain of terminally ill patients so that their final days are as comfortable as possible.

   Alleviate (ə-lē′vē-āt′) means _____ .

5. When rain and sunshine are *simultaneous*, the rain is often described as a sun shower.

   Simultaneous (sī′məl-tā′nē-əs) means _____ .

B. Use context clues to figure out the meanings of the italicized words in the following textbook passages. Write your definitions in the spaces provided.

[1]Although mysteries and science fiction may seem like very different kinds of writing, the two forms share some basic similarities. [2]First of all, both are action-directed, emphasizing plot at the expense of character development. [3]Possibly for this reason, both types of literature have been *scorned* by critics as being merely "entertainment" rather than "literature." [4]But this attack is unjustified, for both mysteries and science fiction share a concern with moral issues. [5]Science fiction often raises the question of whether or not scientific advances are of benefit to humanity. [6]And a mystery story rarely ends without the *culpable* person being brought to justice.

6. *Scorned* (skôrnd) means _____.

7. *Culpable* (kŭl′pə-bəl) means _____ .

¹Why did people begin to live in cities? ²To answer this question, we must start by looking back some ten thousand years ago. ³In certain parts of the world (probably those where the natural food supply was fairly unreliable), people *endeavored* to tame nature for their own purposes. ⁴They began weeding and watering groups of edible plants, adding organic matter to help fertilize the soil, and saving the seeds from the strongest, most desirable plants to sow the next spring. ⁵At the same time, they began protecting herds of small wild animals that were often hunted by larger animals. ⁶They would move them to more plentiful pastures during the dry months of summer. ⁷During the harshest periods of winter, they would *supplement* whatever fresh food was available with stored food. ⁸These changes, *coupled* with a few simple techniques for storing grain and meat, enabled people to abandon a wandering lifestyle in favor of settlement in small villages. ⁹These villages were the basic form of human social organization for the next several thousand years.

8. *Endeavored* (ĕn-dĕv′ərd) means _____ .

9. *Supplement* (sŭp′lə-mənt) means _____ .

10. *Coupled* (kŭp′əld) means _____ .

 REVIEW TEST 4

Here is a chance to apply the skill of understanding vocabulary in context to a full-length selection. Read the story below, a version of which appeared in *Reader's Digest*, and then answer the questions that follow.

Words to Watch

Below are some words in the reading that do not have strong context support. Each word is followed by the number of the paragraph in which it appears and its meaning there. These words are indicated in the article by a small circle (°).

smudged (2): dirty with streaks or stains
boondocks (3): a rural region
maneuvers (3): military exercises

NIGHT WATCH

Roy Popkin

1   The story began on a downtown Brooklyn street corner. An elderly man had collapsed while crossing the street, and an ambulance rushed him to Kings County Hospital. There, during his few returns to consciousness, the man repeatedly called for his son.

2   From a smudged°, often-read letter, an emergency-room nurse learned that the son was a Marine stationed in North Carolina. Apparently, there were no other relatives.

3   Someone at the hospital called the Red Cross office in Brooklyn, and a request for the boy to rush to Brooklyn was relayed to the Red Cross director of the North Carolina Marine Corps camp. Because time was short—the patient was dying—the Red Cross man and an officer set out in a jeep. They located the sought-after young man wading through marshy boondocks° on maneuvers°. He was rushed to the airport in time to catch the one plane that might enable him to reach his dying father.

4   It was mid-evening when the young Marine walked into the entrance lobby of Kings County Hospital. A nurse took the tired, anxious serviceman to the bedside.

5   "Your son is here," she said to the old man. She had to repeat the words several times before the patient's eyes opened. Heavily sedated because of the pain of his heart attack, he dimly saw the

young man in the Marine Corps uniform standing outside the oxygen tent. He reached out his hand. The Marine wrapped his toughened fingers around the old man's limp ones, squeezing a message of love and encouragement. The nurse brought a chair, so the Marine could sit alongside the bed.

6   Nights are long in hospitals, but all through the night the young Marine sat there in the poorly lighted ward, holding the old man's hand and offering words of hope and strength. Occasionally, the nurse suggested that the Marine move away and rest a while. He refused.

7   Whenever the nurse came into the ward, the Marine was there. His full attention was on the dying man, and he was oblivious of her and of the night noises of the hospital—the clanking of an oxygen tank, the laughter of night-staff members exchanging greetings, the cries and moans and snores of other patients. Now and then she heard him say a few gentle words. The dying man

said nothing, only held tightly to his son through most of the night.

8   Along toward dawn, the patient died. The Marine placed on the bed the lifeless hand he had been holding, and went to tell the nurse. While she did what she had to do, he relaxed—for the first time since he got to the hospital.

9   Finally, she returned to the nurse's station, where he was waiting. She started to offer words of condolence for his loss, but the Marine interrupted her. "Who was that man?" he asked.

10   "He was your father," she answered, startled.

11   "No, he wasn't," the Marine replied. "I never saw him before in my life."

12   "Why didn't you say something when I took you to him?" the nurse asked.

13   "I knew right off there'd been a mistake, but I also knew he needed his son, and his son just wasn't here. When I realized he was too sick to tell whether or not I was his son, I figured he really needed me. So I stayed."

14   With that, the Marine turned and left the hospital. Two days later a routine message came in from the North Carolina Marine Corps base informing the Brooklyn Red Cross that the real son was on his way to Brooklyn for his father's funeral. It turned out there had been two Marines with the same name and similar serial numbers in the camp. Someone in the personnel office had pulled out the wrong record.

15   But the wrong Marine had become the right son at the right time. And he proved, in a uniquely human way, that there are people who care what happens to their fellow human beings.

Vocabulary Questions

Use context clues to help you decide on the best definition for each italicized word. Then, on the answer line, write the letter of each choice.

_____ 1. In the sentence below, the word *relayed* (rē′lād) means
        A. hidden.
        B. passed along.
        C. made a gift.
        D. ignored.

"Someone at the hospital called the Red Cross office in Brooklyn, and a request for the boy to rush to Brooklyn was relayed to the Red Cross director of the North Carolina Marine Corps camp." (Paragraph 3)

_____ 2. In the sentence below, the words *enable him* (ĕ-nā′bəl hǐm) mean
        A. stop him.
        B. encourage him.
        C. know him.
        D. make him able.

"He was rushed to the airport in time to catch the one plane that might enable him to reach his dying father." (Paragraph 3)

_____ 3. In the excerpt below, the word *sedated* (sĭ-dāt′ĭd) means
    A. spoken loudly.   C. armed.
    B. wide awake.   D. drugged with a pain reliever.

    "'Your son is here,' she said to the old man. She had to repeat the words several times before the patient's eyes opened. Heavily sedated because of the pain of his heart attack, he dimly saw the young man …" (Paragraph 5)

_____ 4. In the excerpt below, the word *dimly* (dĭm′lē) means
    A. clearly.   C. rarely.
    B. unclearly.   D. often.

    "She had to repeat the words several times before the patient's eyes opened. Heavily sedated because of the pain of his heart attack, he dimly saw the young man …" (Paragraph 5)

_____ 5. In the sentence below, the word *limp* (lĭmp) means
    A. lacking firmness and strength.   C. long.
    B. equally tough.   D. bleeding.

    "The Marine wrapped his toughened fingers around the old man's limp ones, squeezing a message of love and encouragement." (Paragraph 5)

_____ 6. A clue to the meaning of *limp* in the sentence above is the antonym
    A. *toughened.*   C. *message.*
    B. *old.*   D. *love.*

_____ 7. In the excerpt below, the word *oblivious* (ə-blĭv′ē-əs) means
    A. mindful.   C. unaware.
    B. bothered.   D. informed.

    "Whenever the nurse came into the ward, the Marine was there. His full attention was on the dying man, and he was oblivious of her and of the night noises of the hospital …" (Paragraph 7)

_____ 8. In the excerpt below, the word *condolence* (kən-dŏ′ləns) means
    A. excuse.   C. surprise.
    B. bitterness.   D. sympathy.

    "She started to offer words of condolence for his loss …" (Paragraph 9)

_____ 9. In the excerpt below, the word *startled* (stär′tld) means
    A. very pleased.   C. angry.
    B. with admiration.   D. surprised.

    "'Who was that man?' he asked. 'He was your father,' she answered, startled." (Paragraphs 9–10)

_____ 10. In the sentence below, the words *uniquely human* (yōō-nēk′lē hyōō′mən) mean

A. impossible for humans.
B. scary to humans.
C. done only by humans.
D. sudden by human standards.

> "And he proved, in a uniquely human way, that there are people who care what happens to their fellow human beings." (Paragraph 15)

Discussion Questions

1. When do you think the Marine realized that calling him to the hospital was a mistake? Was it when he first saw the old man or before? What parts of the reading support your conclusion?

2. How do you think the dead man's real son felt about the other Marine being with his dying father? How would you feel?

3. The incident in the reading took place because of some surprising coincidences. What were they? Has a surprising or interesting coincidence ever taken place in your life? If so, what was it, and how did it affect you?

4. By going out of his way for a stranger, the Marine showed "in a uniquely human way that there are people who care what happens to others." Have you ever gone out of your way to help a stranger? Or have you seen someone else do so? Tell what the situation was and what happened.

Note: Writing assignments for this selection appear on page 621.

Check Your Performance   VOCABULARY IN CONTEXT

Activity		Number Right	Points		Score
Review Test 1	(5 items)	_____	× 2	=	_____
Review Test 2	(10 items)	_____	× 3	=	_____
Review Test 3	(10 items)	_____	× 3	=	_____
Review Test 4	(10 items)	_____	× 3	=	_____
			TOTAL SCORE	=	_____ %

Enter your total score into the **Reading Performance Chart: Review Tests** on the inside back cover.

VOCABULARY IN CONTEXT: Mastery Test 1

A. Look at the cartoon below, and then answer the question that follows.

_____ 1. Using the context clues in the cartoon, write the letter of the meaning of *gullibility* (gŭl′lə-bəl′ĭ-tē) in the space provided.
   A. state of being easily fooled
   B. assertiveness
   C. irritability

B. For each item below, underline the **examples** that suggest the meaning of the italicized word. Then, on the answer line, write the letter of the meaning of that word.

_____ 2. When I finally get around to cleaning out my refrigerator, I always find something *vile* (vīl) at the back of a shelf, such as moldy fruit or old smelly beans.
   A. tempting   C. false
   B. recent   D. disgusting

_____ 3. The Easter egg hunt featured *cryptic* (krĭp′tĭk) clues such as, "You'll find a prize somewhere narrow" and "Look for the pink."
   A. rhyming   C. clear
   B. puzzling   D. overused

(Continues on next page)

45

_____ 4. *Verbose* (vər-bōs′) writing can be hard to follow. For instance, "At this point in time, we have an urgently felt need for more and greater financial resources" is less clear than "We need money now."
    A. realistic   C. wordy
    B. informal   D. ungrammatical

C. Each item below includes a word or words that are a **synonym** of the italicized word. Write the synonym of the italicized word in the space provided.

_____ 5. Americans spend millions each year on a *quest* (kwĕst) for the perfect weight-loss plan. Their search is for a pill or diet that will allow them to eat much and exercise little.

_____ 6. Samuel Langhorne Clemens wasn't the first author to use the *pseudonym* (sōōd′n-ĭm′) Mark Twain. A newspaper writer of the time used the same false name.

D. Each item below includes a word or words that are an **antonym** of the italicized word. Underline the antonym of each italicized word. Then, on the answer line, write the letter of the meaning of the italicized word.

_____ 7. Computer manuals are often very hard to understand, so I was surprised to discover how *lucid* (lōō′sĭd) this one is.
    A. long   C. clear
    B. expensive   D. new

_____ 8. When my sister first got her job at the recording studio, she was excited to go to work each day. Now, after ten years, she's *blasé* (blä-zā′) about her work and wants to change jobs.
    A. tardy   C. thrilled
    B. bored   D. curious

E. Use the **general sense of each sentence** to figure out the meaning of each italicized word. Then, on the answer line, write the letter of the meaning of the italicized word.

_____ 9. A person can be very intelligent and yet be *deficient* (dĭ-fĭsh′ənt) in common sense.
    A. lacking   C. overqualified
    B. well supplied   D. lucky

_____10. The store detective faced the *dilemma* (dĭ-lĕm′ə) of either having an elderly, needy man arrested or ignoring store rules about shoplifters.
    A. memory   C. proof
    B. difficult choice   D. reason

VOCABULARY IN CONTEXT: Mastery Test 2

A. Look at the cartoon below, and then answer the question that follows.

_____ 1. Using the context clues in the cartoon, write the letter of the meaning of *degraded* (dĭ-grād′ĭd) in the space provided.
   A. treated with disrespect
   B. treated with care
   C. treated with fear

B. For each item below, underline the **examples** that suggest the meaning of the italicized word. Then, on the answer line, write the letter of the meaning of that word.

_____ 2. Every *habitat* (hăb′ĭ-tăt′) in the world, from volcano tops to icebergs, can support some sort of life.
   A. country   C. food source
   B. environment   D. practice

_____ 3. Common *redundant* (rĭ-dŭn′dənt) phrases include "cooperate together" (instead of simply "cooperate") and "postponed until later" (instead of "postponed").
   A. repetitious   C. difficult
   B. descriptive   D. useful

C. Each textbook item below includes a word that is a **synonym** of the italicized word. Write the synonym of the italicized word in the space provided.

_____ 4. The Amish people prefer *austere* (ô-stîr′) styles—their clothing and homes are plain.

_____ 5. Airport security guards must observe people's *demeanor* (dĭ-mē′nər) in order to notice any suspicious conduct.

(Continues on next page)

_____ 6. In business, it can be harmful to be too *unassuming* (ŭn′ə-sōo′mĭng). If you're overly modest about your achievements, for example, you may be passed up for a promotion.

D. Each textbook item below includes a word that is an **antonym** of the italicized word. Underline the antonym of each italicized word. Then, on the answer line, write the letter of the meaning of the italicized word.

_____ 7. Even when textbooks are *standardized* (stăn′dər-dīzd′) throughout a school system, methods of teaching with them may be greatly varied.
   A. different   C. made the same
   B. expensive   D. lacking

_____ 8. During the Middle Ages, everyone—from the rich landowner down to the most *impoverished* (ĭm-pŏv′ər-ĭsht) peasant—had a clear place in society.
   A. weak   C. poor
   B. common   D. decent

E. Use the **general sense of each sentence** to figure out the meaning of each italicized word. Then, on the answer line, write the letter of the meaning of the italicized word.

_____ 9. It is odd how often public figures who loudly *espouse* (ĭ-spouz′) "traditional family values" are later caught in some scandal concerning their own private lives.
   A. recognize   C. reject
   B. remember   D. argue for

_____10. It is widely believed that Columbus sailed westward to *validate* (văl′ĭ-dāt′) the theory that the world is round. In fact, it was already well known at that time that the world is round.
   A. think up   C. contradict
   B. prove   D. foresee

VOCABULARY IN CONTEXT: Mastery Test 3

Using context clues for help, write, in the space provided, the letter of the best meaning for each italicized word.

_____ 1. It's a good idea for married couples to discuss their plans in case of each other's *demise* (dĭ-mīz′). For example, do they wish to be buried or cremated?
   A. death   C. desire to divorce
   B. success   D. concern

_____ 2. The press *assailed* (ə-sāld′) the mayor for giving large city construction jobs to his brother-in-law's firm.
   A. searched for   C. attacked
   B. paid   D. fined

_____ 3. One *tenet* (tĕn′ĭt) of Islam is that its followers should not drink alcohol.
   A. answer   C. teaching
   B. prediction   D. guarantee

_____ 4. Toddlers are naturally *inquisitive* (ĭn-kwĭz′ĭ-tĭv). Because they are so interested in their surroundings, they are eager to explore everything.
   A. unreliable   C. curious
   B. clumsy   D. tired

_____ 5. After x-rays were discovered in 1895, there were some *preposterous* (prĭ-pŏs′tər-əs) reactions. For example, London merchants sold x-ray-proof underwear.
   A. logical   C. dangerous
   B. ridiculous   D. delayed

_____ 6. The foolish defendant *waived* (wāvd) his right to an attorney and instead spoke for himself in court.
   A. depended upon   C. wrote
   B. greeted   D. gave up

(Continues on next page)

_____ 7. Sexual standards in England during the 1800s were so strict that it was considered *sordid* (sôr'dĭd) for women to reveal their legs in public.
    A. proper   C. popular
    B. impossible   D. indecent

_____ 8. Young children believe their parents are perfect—until the children become teenagers, when their parents suddenly become quite *fallible* (făl'ə-bəl).
    A. unhealthy   C. imperfect
    B. dangerous   D. skilled

_____ 9. America has often been called a "melting pot" into which people of many different cultures *assimilate* (ə-sĭm'ə-lāt').
    A. learn   C. avoid each other
    B. leave   D. blend

_____10. The Englishman John Merrick's illness gave him such a *grotesque* (grō-tĕsk') appearance that he was called "the Elephant Man." Despite people's reactions to his abnormally large head and twisted body, Merrick remained affectionate and gentle.
    A. strong   C. gray
    B. deformed   D. childlike

VOCABULARY IN CONTEXT: Mastery Test 4

Using context clues for help, write, in the space provided, the letter of the best meaning for each italicized word or words. Note that all of the sentences have been taken from college textbooks.

_____ 1. After the Civil War, trolleys and streetcars greatly expanded workers' *mobility* (mō-bĭl'ĭ-tē), permitting them to move beyond walking distance from factories.
 A. pay   C. ability to move
 B. skills   D. interests

_____ 2. What people say may not reflect accurately what they are actually feeling. It is sometimes necessary to *resort to* (rĭ-zôrt' tōō) clues other than their spoken words to understand them fully.
 A. remove from   C. make use of
 B. make light of   D. ignore

_____ 3. Individual political organizations often join together to form *coalitions* (kō'ə-lĭsh'ənz) to increase the support for their issues.
 A. partnerships   C. contests
 B. lines   D. questions

_____ 4. Surveys about people's sexual habits are often inaccurate because people may lie, and there is no way to *corroborate* (kə-rŏbə-rāt') what they say.
 A. forget   C. change
 B. prove the truth of   D. recall

_____ 5. Everyone at the party was shocked by how *blatantly* (blāt'nt-lē) the woman insulted her former boss. She refused to shake his hand, saying, "I don't want to get my hand dirty."
 A. secretly   C. barely
 B. accidentally   D. obviously

_____ 6. Following the English principle that voters had to have a *stake* (stāk) in the community, the colonies generally required citizens to own a certain minimum amount of land in order to vote.
 A. job   C. investment
 B. relative   D. employee

(Continues on next page)

51

_____ 7. William Henry Harrison's 1840 campaign brought many *innovations* (ĭn′ə-vā′shənz) to the art of electioneering. For example, for the first time, a presidential candidate spoke out on his own behalf.
   A. new things   C. crimes
   B. people   D. financial skills

_____ 8. To fully *assess* (ə-sĕs′) patients in order to place them in appropriate programs, mental health professionals need information on emotional adjustment and physical health.
   A. find   C. hide
   B. recognize   D. evaluate

_____ 9. In the eating disorder known as bulimia nervosa, a person will go on huge eating binges and then will try to *nullify* (nŭl′ə-fī′) the outrageous food intake by purposely vomiting or strictly dieting.
   A. increase   C. forget
   B. undo   D. delay

_____10. Adults who have both children of their own and elderly parents need to balance their commitments. They must look after their children and also *allocate* (ăl′ə-kāt′) time and energy to care for their parents.
   A. recall   C. set aside
   B. pay for   D. view

VOCABULARY IN CONTEXT: Mastery Test 5

A. Using context clues for help, write, in the space provided, the letter of the best meaning for each italicized word. Note that all of the sentences have been taken from college textbooks.

_____ 1. The possibility of developing a top seller is so *alluring* (ə-loor′ĭng) that American companies spend billions of dollars a year trying to create new products or improve old ones.
   A. dangerous   C. attractive
   B. final   D. unreasonable

_____ 2. Using sign language, chimpanzees can *convey* (kən-vā′) such ideas as "Candy sweet" and "Give me hug."
   A. reject   C. think of
   B. accept   D. communicate

_____ 3. Smoking or chewing tobacco, wrote King James I, was "*loathsome* (lōth′səm) to the eye, hateful to the nose, harmful to the brain, and dangerous to the lungs."
   A. appealing   C. disgusting
   B. hidden   D. healthy

_____ 4. The death of a spouse can cause *profound* (prə-found′) depression that, in some cases, can even lead to the death of the partner.
   A. deep   C. occasional
   B. accidental   D. mild

_____ 5. The healthiest type of parents are those who guide and instruct their children, but also grant them a degree of *autonomy* (ô-tŏn′ə-mē), encouraging the children to make their own decisions and form their own opinions.
   A. financing   C. independence
   B. knowledge   D. guidance

(Continues on next page)

B. Use context clues to figure out the meaning of the italicized word in each of the following items. Then write your definition in the space provided.

6. A person giving first aid needs to make sure a body part that has been completely *severed* is sent to the hospital with the victim. Surgeons can often reattach the body part with microsurgery.

   Severed (sĕv′ərd) means _____

7. Tabloid newspapers often *distort* the news by reporting rumors as if they were true.

   Distort (dĭ-stôrt′) means _____

8. It's not always necessary for adults to *intervene* in children's fights; sometimes it's best to let children handle quarrels themselves.

   Intervene (ĭn′tər-vēn′) means _____

9. Many companies once had retirement policies that made it *mandatory* for people to quit working as soon as they turned a certain age.

   Mandatory (măn′də-tôr′ē) means _____

10. After a heavy public relations campaign against the union, the hospital finally *relented* and allowed its workers to join.

   Relented (rĭ-lĕnt′ĭd) means _____

VOCABULARY IN CONTEXT: Mastery Test 6

A. Five words are italicized in the textbook passage below. Write the definition for each italicized word, choosing from the definitions in the box. Also, write the letter of the definition in the space provided.

Be sure to read the entire passage before making your choices. Note that five definitions will be left over.

A. causing	**B.** deadly	**C.** delay	**D.** die
E. enjoyable	**F.** forced to experience	**G.** give credit for	**H.** helpful
I. pay for	**J.** reducing		

¹In the early days of medicine, there were few drugs or treatments that gave any real physical benefit. ²As a result, patients were treated in a variety of strange, largely ineffective ways. ³For instance, Egyptian patients were medicated with "lizard's blood, crocodile dung, the teeth of swine, the hoof of an ass, rotten meat, and fly specks." ⁴If the disease itself didn't cause the patient to *succumb*, he or she had a good chance of dying instead from the treatment. ⁵Medical treatments of the Middle Ages were somewhat less *lethal*, but not much more effective. ⁶And as late as the eighteenth century, patients were *subjected to* bloodletting, freezing, and repeatedly induced vomiting to bring about a cure.

⁷Amazingly, people often seemed to get relief from such treatments. ⁸Physicians have, for centuries, been objects of great respect, and this was no less true when few remedies were actually effective. ⁹To what can one *attribute* the fair level of success that these treatments provided and the widespread faith in the effectiveness of physicians? ¹⁰The most likely answer is that these are examples of the tremendous power of the placebo effect—"any medical procedure that produces an effect in a patient because of its therapeutic intent and not its specific nature, whether chemical or physical." ¹¹Even today, the role of placebos in *curtailing* pain and discomfort is substantial. ¹²Many patients who swallow useless substances or who undergo useless procedures find that, as a result, their symptoms disappear and their health improves.

_____ 1. In sentence 4, *succumb* (sə-kŭm′) means _____ .

_____ 2. In sentence 5, *lethal* (lē′thəl) means _____ .

_____ 3. In sentence 6, *subjected to* (səb-jĕk′tĭd tōō) means _____ .

_____ 4. In sentence 9, *attribute* (ə-trĭb′yōōt) means _____ .

_____ 5. In sentence 11, *curtailing* (kər-tāl′ĭng) means _____ .

(Continues on next page)

55

B. Five words are italicized in the textbook passage below. Write the definition for each italicized word, choosing from the definitions in the box. Then write the letter of the definition in the space provided.

Be sure to read the entire passage before making your choices. Note that five definitions will be left over.

A. colorful	B. delayed	C. disappeared	D. increased
E. most common	F. passed	G. pray	H. punished
I. stir up interest	J. uncontrolled		

¹A century ago, the *prevailing* view among industrialists was that business had only one responsibility: to make a profit. ²By and large those were not good times to be a low-level worker or an incautious consumer. ³People worked sixty-hour weeks under harsh conditions for a dollar or two a day. ⁴The few people who tried to fight the system faced violence and unemployment. ⁵Consumers were not much better off. ⁶If you bought a product, you paid the price and took the consequences. ⁷There were no consumer groups or government agencies to come to your defense if the product was defective or caused harm. ⁸If you tried to sue the company, chances were you would lose.

⁹These conditions caught the attention of a few crusading journalists and novelists known as muckrakers. ¹⁰They used the power of the pen to create public anger and *agitate* for reform. ¹¹Largely through their efforts, a number of laws were passed to limit the power of monopolies and to establish safety standards for food and drugs.

¹²Despite these reforms, business continued to pursue profits above all else until the Great Depression. ¹³When the economic system collapsed in 1929 and 25 percent of the work force was unemployed, people lost their faith in *unbridled* capitalism. ¹⁴Pressure *mounted* for government to fix the system.

¹⁵At the urging of President Franklin Roosevelt, Congress voted in laws to protect workers, consumers, and investors. ¹⁶The Social Security system was set up, employees were given the right to join unions and bargain collectively, the minimum wage was established, and the length of the workweek was limited. ¹⁷Legislation was also *enacted* to prevent unfair competition and false advertising.

_____ 6. In sentence 1, *prevailing* (prĭ-vā′lĭng) means _____ .

_____ 7. In sentence 10, *agitate* (ăj′ĭ-tāt′) means _____ .

_____ 8. In sentence 13, *unbridled* (ŭn-brīd′ld) means _____ .

_____ 9. In sentence 14, *mounted* (moun′tĭd) means _____ .

_____ 10. In sentence 17, *enacted* (ĕn-ăk′tĭd) means _____ .

2 Main Ideas

What Is the Main Idea?

"You are just not a dateworthy guy. You need to wear different clothes, put some meat on those bones, and get rid of that scythe."

"**W**hat's the point?" You've probably heard these words before. It's a question people ask when they want to know the main idea that someone is trying to express. The same question can guide you as you read. Recognizing the **main idea**, or point, is the most important key to good comprehension. Sometimes a main idea is immediately clear, as in the above cartoon. The humorous point—that the figure of death is not a desirable date—is supported by the woman's three reasons.

To find the main idea of a reading selection, ask yourself, "What's the point the author is trying to make?" For instance, read the paragraph on the following page, asking yourself as you do, "What is the author's point?"

¹School bullies have been around as long as there have been schools. ²Studies reveal several reasons why some children become bullies. ³Research shows that a certain combination of size and personality may be one factor. ⁴Bigger, more aggressive children are more likely to try to dominate their smaller, quieter peers. ⁵Another factor linked to bullying is overexposure to violent TV programs. ⁶By the time the average American child is ten years old, he or she has watched thousands of acts of violence, including assault and murder. ⁷Such exposure can lead to aggression and violence. ⁸Finally, exposure to *real* violence is a factor in bullying. ⁹Studies indicate that victims of bullies often turn into bullies themselves. ¹⁰Whether abused by family members or tormented by other kids, bullies typically learn their behavior from others. ¹¹Look closely into the eyes of a bully, and you may be looking into the eyes of a former victim.

A good way to find an author's point, or main idea, is to look for a general statement. Then decide if that statement is supported by most of the other material in the paragraph. If it is, you have found the main idea.

✓ Check Your Understanding

Following are four statements from the passage. Pick out the one that is both a general statement *and* that is supported by the other material in the passage. Write the letter of that statement in the space provided. Then read the explanation that follows.

Four statements from the passage

A. School bullies have been around as long as there have been schools.

B. Studies reveal several reasons why some children become bullies.

C. Research shows that a certain combination of size and personality may be one factor.

D. Studies indicate that victims of bullies often turn into bullies themselves.

The general statement that expresses the main idea of the passage is _____.

Explanation

Sentence A: While this *is* a general statement, the paragraph does not go on to show how bullying has been a problem from when schools first began to the present day. Sentence A, then, is not the main idea.

Sentence B: The phrase "several reasons" is a general one. And in fact the rest of the passage goes on to describe a series of three supporting reasons why some children become bullies. Sentence B, then, is the sentence that expresses the main idea of the passage.

Sentence C: This sentence is about only one reason. It is not general enough to include the other reasons for bullying.

Sentence D: This sentence provides detailed support for the third reason for bullying—"exposure to *real* violence." It does not cover the other material in the paragraph.

The Main Idea as an "Umbrella" Idea

Think of the main idea as an "umbrella" idea. The main idea is the author's general point; all the other material of the paragraph fits under it. That other material is made up of **supporting details**—specific evidence such as examples, causes, reasons, or facts. The diagram below shows the relationship.

STUDIES REVEAL
REASONS SOME CHILDREN
BECOME BULLIES

Combination of size and personality
Overexposure to violent TV programs
Exposure to *real* violence

The explanations and activities on the following pages will deepen your understanding of the main idea.

Recognizing a Main Idea

As you read through a passage, you must **think as you read**. If you merely take in words, you will come to the end of the passage without understanding much of what you have read. Reading is an active process, as opposed to watching television, which is passive. You must actively engage your mind, and, as you read, keep asking yourself, "What's the point?" Here are three strategies that will help you find the main idea.

1 Look for general versus specific ideas.
2 Use the topic to lead you to the main idea.
3 Use key words to lead you to the main idea.

Each strategy is explained on the following pages.

1 Look for General versus Specific Ideas

You saw with the bullying paragraph that the main idea is a *general* idea supported by *specific* ideas. The following practices will improve your skill at separating general from specific ideas. Learning how to tell the difference between general and specific ideas will help you locate the main idea.

PRACTICE 1

Each group of words below has one general idea and three specific ideas. The general idea includes all the specific ideas. Identify each general idea with a **G** and the specific ideas with an **S**. Look first at the example.

Example

S   dogs
S   goldfish
S   hamsters
G   pets

(*Pets* is the general idea which includes three specific types of pets: dogs, goldfish, and hamsters.)

1. ___ home cooking
   ___ take-out
   ___ ways to eat dinner
   ___ frozen foods

2. ___ hot and humid
   ___ cold and rainy
   ___ cloudy with scattered showers
   ___ weather forecasts

3. ___ oversleeping
   ___ bad habits
   ___ overeating
   ___ smoking

4. ___ traffic delays
   ___ head cold
   ___ bad coffee
   ___ minor problems

5. ___ deadbolt locks
   ___ alarm system
   ___ barking dog
   ___ kinds of security

6. ___ divorce
   ___ failing grades
   ___ major problems
   ___ eviction

7. ___ not taking notes in class
   ___ poor study habits
   ___ missing classes
   ___ cramming for exams

8. ___ surprised
   ___ tone of voice
   ___ enthusiastic
   ___ bored

9. ___ communicating
   ___ writing
   ___ reading
   ___ speaking

10. ___ hurry up
    ___ get to bed
    ___ commands
    ___ clean up this mess

PRACTICE 2

Write the answers to each question in the spaces provided. For each question, the answers will be specific details that illustrate the general idea.

1. Let's say you are describing a good friend. That he or she is a good friend is a general idea. List three *specific* reasons why he or she is a good friend.

   _____   _____   _____

2. All of us have certain valued material possessions in our lives. What are three *specific* objects that are very important to you?

   _____   _____   _____

3. Everyone has goals. What are three of the *specific* goals in your life?

   _____

   _____

   _____

4. Most students have had teachers whom they admire. Name one such teacher and three *specific* qualities or behaviors that made you like or respect that teacher.

   Name of teacher: _____

   Specific qualities or behaviors: _____

   _____

   _____

   _____

5. At one time or another, you've probably had to do a really unpleasant chore or job. Write three *specific* reasons why that chore or job was so unpleasant.

   _____

   _____

   _____

PRACTICE 3

In the following groups, one statement is the general point, and the other statements are specific support for the point. Identify each point with a **P** and each statement of support with an **S**.

1. ___ My family has real problems.
   ___ My mother has cancer.
   ___ My sister is pregnant.
   ___ I lost my job.

2. ___ Iris has a great smile.
   ___ Iris asks you questions about yourself.
   ___ Iris is a pleasure to be around.
   ___ Iris really listens when you talk.

3. ___ I feel short of breath.
   ___ I'm getting dizzy and sweating.
   ___ There is a pain in my chest.
   ___ I may be having a heart attack.

4. ___ My boss is hard to work for.
   ___ He lacks a sense of humor.
   ___ He never gives praise.
   ___ He times all our breaks to the second.

5. ___ We had different political beliefs.
   ___ The date was a nightmare.
   ___ We were dressed completely differently.
   ___ Both of us were too nervous to say much.

PRACTICE 4

In each of the following groups, one statement is the general point, and the other statements are specific support for the point. Identify each point with a **P** and each statement of support with an **S**.

1. ___ A. Last night we could hear and smell a large animal prowling outside our tent.

   ___ B. Green flies with stinging bites are in abundance around our campsite.

   ___ C. The time has come to find a new campsite.

   ___ D. This morning we discovered a nest of baby rattlesnakes nearby.

2. ___ A. Children are at risk at the school.

   ___ B. There are two active gangs in the school.

   ___ C. Knives and guns have been found in lockers.

   ___ D. Drug busts have been made at the school.

3. ___ A. Cats are clean and do not require much attention.

   ___ B. There are definite advantages to having a cat as a pet.

   ___ C. Cats like living indoors and are safe to have around children.

   ___ D. Cats are inexpensive to feed and easy to keep healthy.

4. ___ A. Communicating with family and friends using computer e-mail takes very little effort or time.

   ___ B. Finding information is as easy as typing several key words.

   ___ C. Shopping can be quickly handled online with a few clicks of the mouse and the use of a credit card.

   ___ D. Computers make everyday matters much easier.

5. ___ A. Instead of working full-time, many of today's employees work part-time with little job security and few benefits.

   ___ B. Job security and our ideas about work have changed dramatically in recent years.

   ___ C. Unlike in years past, most people entering the work force today will change jobs several times during their careers.

   ___ D. Rather than work for someone else, many of today's workers hope to start their own businesses.

2   Use the Topic to Lead You to the Main Idea

You already know that to find the main idea of a selection, you look first for a general statement, which is often at the beginning of a selection. You then check to see if that statement is supported by most of the other material in the paragraph. If it is, you've found the main idea. Another approach that can help you find the main idea is to decide on the topic of a given selection.

The **topic** is the general subject of a selection. It can often be expressed in one or more words. Knowing the topic can help you find a writer's main point about that topic. Paying close attention to the topic of a selection can lead you to the main idea.

Textbook authors use the title of each chapter to state the overall topic of that chapter. They also provide many topics and subtopics in boldface headings within the chapter. For example, here is the title of a chapter in a sociology textbook:

Aggression: Hurting Others (a 38-page chapter)

And here are the subtopics:

Theories of Aggression (a 12-page section)

Influences on Aggression (a 20-page section)

Reducing Aggression (a 6-page section)

If you were studying the above chapter, you could use the topics to help find the main ideas. (Pages 17–18 explain just how to do so, as well as other textbook study tips.)

But there are many times when you are not given topics—with standardized reading tests, for example, or with individual paragraphs in articles or textbooks. To find the topic of a selection when the topic is not given, ask this simple question:

Who or what is the selection about?

For example, look again at the beginning of the paragraph that started this chapter:

School bullies have been around as long as there have been schools. Studies reveal several reasons why some children become bullies.

What, in a single word, is the above paragraph about? On the line below, write what you think is the topic.

Topic: _____

You probably answered that the topic is "Bullies." As you read the paragraph again, you saw that, in fact, every sentence in it is about bullying.

The next step after finding the topic is to decide what main point the author is making about the topic. Authors often present their main idea in a single sentence. (This sentence is also known as the **main idea sentence** or the **topic sentence**.) As we have already seen, the main point that is made about bullying is that "Studies reveal several reasons why some children become bullies."

✓ *Check Your Understanding*

Let's look now at another paragraph. Read it and then see if you can answer the questions that follow.

> ¹Though fun to watch, chimpanzees should not be kept as pets. ²They are dangerously stronger than any NFL lineman. ³Adult chimps weigh only 100 to 160 pounds, but have been measured pulling six to nine times their own weight—*with one hand*. ⁴Thus, to match the strength of an average chimp, a human being would have to be able to register a two-handed pull of about a ton; it takes a very strong man to pull a quarter of that. ⁵Combined with this strength is the fact that a chimp is capable of losing its temper—for reasons known only to the chimp. ⁶Chimps signal their feelings with subtle cues of behavior that aren't apparent to most humans. ⁷It's quite possible for a chimp to be on the verge of violence while its owner sits unaware or even unknowingly continues to provoke it. ⁸Furthermore, it's not wise to keep a cute young chimp and release it into the wild when it becomes dangerous. ⁹Wild-raised chimps will routinely gang up on and kill those raised in captivity.

1. What is the *topic* of the paragraph? In other words, what is the paragraph about? _____

   Hint: It often helps to look for (and even circle) a word or idea that is repeated in the paragraph.

2. What is the *main idea* of the paragraph? In other words, what point is the author making about the topic? (Remember that the main idea will be supported by the other material in the paragraph.)

   _____

Explanation

As the first sentence of the paragraph suggests, the topic is "chimpanzees." Reading the paragraph, you see that, in fact, everything in it is about chimpanzees. And the main idea is clearly that "chimpanzees should not be kept as pets." This idea is a general one that sums up what the entire paragraph is about. It is an "umbrella" statement under which all the other material in the paragraph fits. The parts of the paragraph could be shown as follows:

Topic: Chimpanzees

Main idea: Chimpanzees should not be kept as pets.

Supporting details:
1. Dangerously strong
2. Capable of losing temper
3. Liable to be attacked if released in the wild

The following practices will sharpen your sense of the difference between a topic, the point about the topic (the main idea), and supporting details.

PRACTICE 5

Below are groups of four items. In each case, one item is the topic, one is the main idea, and two are details that support and develop the main idea. Label each item with one of the following:

T — for the **topic** of the paragraph
MI — for the **main idea**
SD — for the **supporting details**

Note that an explanation is provided for the first group; reading it will help you do this practice.

Group 1

_____ A. The creakings of a house settling may sound like a monster coming out of a grave.

_____ B. Gusts of wind rattling a bedroom window can sound like invaders about to break in.

_____ C. Nighttime noises can be frightening to children.

_____ D. Noises at night.

Explanation

All of the statements in Group 1 are about noises at night, so item D must be the topic. Statements A and B each describe specific nighttime noises. Statement C, however, presents the general idea that nighttime noises can be frightening to children. It is the main idea about the topic "noises at night," and statements A and B are supporting details that illustrate that main idea.

Group 2

_____ A. People vary in the amount of daydreaming they do.

_____ B. Around 2 to 4 percent of the population spend at least half their free time fantasizing.

_____ C. Almost everyone daydreams about 10 percent of the time.

_____ D. Daydreaming.

Group 3

_____ A. Global warming.

_____ B. Melting ice caps will raise ocean water levels and flood coastal areas.

_____ C. A warmer atmosphere may cause droughts that will turn farmlands to deserts.

_____ D. Global warming may cause destructive changes to life on Earth.

Group 4

_____ A. There are ways to remain healthy in old age.

_____ B. One way for people to remain healthy as they age is to continue to find mental challenges.

_____ C. Sticking to a balanced, low-cholesterol diet and a reasonable exercise program helps keep people in good shape throughout their lives.

_____ D. Health in old age.

Group 5

_____ A. Love at first sight is a poor basis for a happy marriage, according to a study of one thousand married and divorced couples.

_____ B. Couples who knew each other only slightly but fell instantly in love found that their feelings for each other grew weaker instead of stronger.

_____ C. Love at first sight.

_____ D. The couples who considered themselves happily married reported that they were not powerfully attracted to their partners when they first met, but that they gradually found each other more attractive as they grew to know and understand each other.

PRACTICE 6

Following are five paragraphs. Read each paragraph and do the following:

1   Ask yourself, "What seems to be the topic of the paragraph?" (It often helps to look for and even circle a word or idea that is repeated in the paragraph.)

2   Next, ask yourself, "What is the writer's main point about this topic?" This will be the main idea. It is stated in one of the sentences in the paragraph.

3   Then test what you think is the main idea sentence by asking, "Is this statement supported by all or most of the other material in the paragraph?"

> *Hint:* When looking for the topic, make sure you do not pick one that is either **too broad** (covering a great deal more than is in the selection) or **too narrow** (covering only part of the selection). The topic and the main idea of a selection must include everything in that selection—no more and no less.
>
> For example, in Group 1 on page 66, the topic is "noises at night." "Noises" would be too broad, since there are many other types of noises that are not mentioned. "The creakings of a house" would be too narrow, since this is only one type of nighttime noise mentioned.

Paragraph 1

¹Stories have the magic to focus our attention and maintain our interest. ²The politician or preacher who says, "That reminds me of a story . . . " has an audience's attention immediately. ³Consider the success of television's *60 Minutes*, the longest-running and most profitable prime-time show in the history of television. ⁴The person behind its success, producer Don Hewitt, says, "The secret of our show is so simple I can't believe the formula hasn't been followed by others. ⁵It's four words that every kid knows: 'Tell me a story.' ⁶I look at things in screening rooms and I say, 'That's an interesting guy and those are some great scenes you've got, but what's the story?'" ⁷Without the "story," Hewitt knows the audience is leaving.

1.   What is the *topic* of the paragraph? In other words, what (in one or more words) is the paragraph about? _____

_____ 2.   What point is the writer making about this topic? In other words, what is the *main idea* of the paragraph? In the space provided, write the number of the sentence containing the main idea. (Remember that the main idea will be supported by the other material in the paragraph.)

Paragraph 2

¹Extrasensory perception, or ESP, is an area that fascinates people. ²However, ESP is not documented by any convincing evidence. ³For instance, it would seem that ESP would be an excellent way of winning at games of chance, such as those played at gambling casinos. ⁴But casino owners in Las Vegas and Atlantic City report no problem with "psychics" winning great sums of money. ⁵Also, although great publicity is generated when a psychic seems to help police solve a crime, the value of such help has never been scientifically proven. ⁶Tips from psychics are usually worthless, and almost all cases are solved through traditional police work. ⁷And while audiences may be amazed at the feats of "mind readers," the fact is that mind readers use simple psychological tricks to exploit their audiences' willingness to believe.

1. What is the *topic* of the paragraph? _____

_____ 2. What point is the writer making about this topic? In other words, what is the *main idea* of the paragraph? In the space provided, write the number of the sentence containing the main idea.

Paragraph 3

¹Though some people still stubbornly resist the winds of change, Americans are becoming increasingly supportive of the idea of gay marriage. ²The numbers alone are astounding. ³In 1996, only 27 percent of Americans thought that gay people should be allowed to marry. ⁴Not even twenty years later, the majority of people in this country, 53 percent, feel that allowing gay people to marry is the right thing to do. ⁵Why the change? ⁶Some people say that they're better informed than they used to be. ⁷Others just shrug and say it's not as big a deal as it used to be. ⁸But the vast majority of people say it's because they know and care about someone who is gay. ⁹Nearly 80 percent of Americans have a gay friend, family member, or coworker. ¹⁰"Their love is no different from mine," said an 80-year-old woman who once opposed gay marriage. ¹¹"Their rights should be no different." ¹²Perhaps most important, however, is the overwhelming support of young people. ¹³Three out of four people aged 18–29 are pushing for equal rights for gay people. ¹⁴That's a sure indicator that the winds of change are blowing ever more strongly.

1. What is the *topic* of the paragraph? _____

_____ 2. What point is the writer making about this topic? In other words, what is the *main idea* of the paragraph? In the space provided, write the number of the sentence containing the main idea.

Paragraph 4

¹Some people persist in believing that they can drink and be alert drivers. ²Yet alcohol is estimated to be a factor in at least half of all fatal highway accidents. ³Another poor attitude about driving is the refusal to wear seat belts. ⁴Statistics show that the chances of being seriously hurt or dying in a car accident are greater when a seat belt is not worn. ⁵Also potentially deadly is the view that the best driving is fast driving. ⁶Again, statistics contradict this attitude—fast driving is more likely to be deadly driving. ⁷After speed limits are lowered, traffic fatalities fall significantly. ⁸A final mistaken attitude is that speaking on a cell phone will not detract from a driver's attention and response time to unexpected traffic conditions. ⁹Studies prove otherwise, with the result that many have called for a ban on cell phones while driving. ¹⁰There is simply no question that poor attitudes about driving contribute to the high rate of traffic accidents and their brutal effects.

    1. What is the *topic* of the paragraph? _____

           _____

_____ 2. What point is the writer making about this topic? In other words, what is the *main idea* of the paragraph? In the space provided, write the number of the sentence containing the main idea.

Paragraph 5

¹In some ways, dark chocolate is a health food. ²Rich in iron, magnesium, and fiber, it's also loaded with flavonoids, compounds known to reduce cell damage. ³Medical journals report that regularly eating a moderate amount of dark chocolate (about 3 ounces a day) reduces blood pressure both in healthy people and in patients with high blood pressure. ⁴Lower blood pressure means less risk of irregular heartbeat, heart attack, and heart failure. ⁵Continuous moderate consumption of dark chocolate also lowers bad cholesterol (the type that clogs arteries) and raises good cholesterol (the type that counters clogging). ⁶In addition, dark chocolate helps prevent blood clots and arterial plaque, and so protects against stroke. ⁷Dark chocolate even boosts the body's ability to metabolize sugar, thereby reducing the risk of diabetes.

    1. What is the *topic* of the paragraph? _____

           _____

_____ 2. What point is the writer making about this topic? In other words, what is the *main idea* of the paragraph? In the space provided, write the number of the sentence containing the main idea.

3   Find and Use Key Words to Lead You to the Main Idea

Sometimes authors make it fairly easy to find their main idea. They announce it by using **key words**—verbal clues that are easy to recognize. First to note are **list words**, which tell you a list of items is to follow. For example, the main idea in the paragraph about bullies was stated like this: "Studies reveal several reasons why some children become bullies." The expression *several reasons* helps you zero in on your target: the main idea. You realize that the paragraph is going to be about specific reasons why some children become bullies.

Here are some common word groups that often announce a main idea. Note that each of them contains a word that ends in *s*—a plural that suggests the supporting details will be a list of items.

List Words

several kinds (or ways) of	several causes of	some factors in
three advantages of	five steps	among the results
various reasons for	a number of effects	a series of

When expressions like these appear in a sentence, look carefully to see if that sentence might be the main idea. Chances are a sentence containing list words will be followed by a list of major supporting details.

Note Many other list-word expressions are possible. For example, a writer could begin a paragraph with a sentence containing "four kinds of" or "some advantages of" or "three reasons for." So if you see a sentence with a word group like the ones above, you've probably found the main idea.

✔ *Check Your Understanding*

Underline the list words in the following sentences.

Hint: Remember that list words usually end in **s**.

Example Certain kinds of behavior can quickly get you fired from a job.

1. American workers can be said to earn several types of income.

2. Water pollution takes two forms.

3. The purchase price of a house is only one of various costs that buyers must consider.

4. Problem solving usually involves a series of four steps.

5. The increasing flow of women into the labor force was caused by a number of economic factors.

Explanation

You should have underlined the following groups of words: *several types of, two forms, various costs, a series of four steps,* and *a number of economic factors.* Each of these phrases tells you that a list of details will follow.

Besides list words, addition words can alert you to the main idea. **Addition words** are generally used right before a supporting detail. When you see this type of clue, you can assume that the detail it introduces fits under the umbrella of a main idea.

Here are some of the addition words that often introduce supporting details and help you discover the main idea.

Addition Words

one	to begin with	also	further
first (of all)	for one thing	in addition	furthermore
second(ly)	other	next	last (of all)
third(ly)	another	moreover	final(ly)

✓ Check Your Understanding

Reread the paragraph about bullies, underlining the addition words that alert you to supporting details.

[1]School bullies have been around as long as there have been schools. [2]Studies reveal several reasons why some children become bullies. [3]Research shows that a certain combination of size and personality may be one factor. [4]Bigger, more aggressive children are more likely to try to dominate their smaller, quieter peers. [5]Another factor linked to bullying is overexposure to violent TV programs. [6]By the time the average American child is ten years old, he or she has watched thousands of acts of violence, including assault and murder. [7]Such exposure can lead to aggression and violence. [8]Finally, exposure to real violence is a factor in bullying. [9]Studies indicate that victims of bullies often turn into bullies themselves. [10]Whether abused by family members or tormented by other kids, bullies typically learn their behavior from others. [11]Look closely into the eyes of a bully, and you may be looking into the eyes of a former victim.

Explanation

The words that introduce each new supporting detail for the main idea are *one,* *Another*, and *Finally*. These addition words introduce each of the three reasons for bullying.

Note also that the main idea includes the list words *several reasons*, which signal that the supporting details will be a list of the reasons for bullying. In this and many paragraphs, list words and addition words often work hand in hand.

The following chapter, "Supporting Details," includes further information about words that alert you to the main idea and the details that support it. But what you have already learned here will help you find main ideas.

Locations of the Main Idea

Now you know how to recognize a main idea by 1) distinguishing between the general and the specific, 2) identifying the topic of a passage, and 3) using key words. You are ready to find the main idea no matter where it is located in a paragraph.

A main idea may appear at any point within a paragraph. Very commonly, it shows up at the beginning, as either the first or the second sentence. However, main ideas may also appear further within a paragraph or even at the very end.

Main Idea at the Beginning

In textbooks, it is very common for the main idea to be either the first or the second sentence. See if you can underline the main idea in the paragraph on the following page.

¹Spanking is a poor way to shape a child's behavior. ²For one thing, spanking will result in feelings of anger and frustration. ³The child, then, will not learn anything positive from the punishment. ⁴In addition, spanking may actually lead to more bad behavior. ⁵Having learned that hitting is okay, the child may attack smaller children. ⁶Finally, spanking teaches children to hide certain actions from their parents. ⁷Once out of their parents' sight, however, children may feel they can get away with the bad behavior.

In this paragraph, the main idea is in the *first* sentence. All the following sentences in the paragraph provide details about the negative effects of spanking.

✓ ## Check Your Understanding

Now read the following paragraph and see if you can underline its main idea:

¹Tailgating—following too closely behind another vehicle—is a common cause of accidents. ²Yet tailgating accidents could be avoided if drivers followed some clear-cut guidelines. ³Any car that is less than two seconds behind the one ahead is definitely too close. ⁴Two car lengths is a safe following distance to maintain in local driving. ⁵Two-car accidents often become chain-reaction pileups when a number of drivers are all tailgating in a line. ⁶At freeway speeds, or in snowy, icy or foggy conditions, people should increase following distance well beyond what is normally safe. ⁷Finally, drivers who are impatient or aggressive need to develop the self-control not to express those feelings through dangerous behaviors like tailgating.

Explanation

In the preceding paragraph, the main idea is stated in the *second* sentence. The first sentence introduces the topic, but it is the idea in the second sentence—tailgating can be avoided by following clear-cut guidelines—that is supported in the rest of the paragraph. So keep in mind that the first sentence may simply introduce or lead into the main idea of a paragraph. Very often, a contrast word like *yet, but,* or *however* signals the main idea, as in the paragraph you have just read:

Tailgating—following too closely behind another vehicle—is a common cause of accidents. **Yet** tailgating accidents could be avoided if drivers followed some clear-cut guidelines.

Main Idea in the Middle

The main idea at times appears in the middle of a paragraph. Here is an example of a paragraph in which the main idea is somewhere in the middle. Try to find it and underline it. Then read the explanation that follows.

> [1]Many of us are annoyed by telemarketers who call us day and night, trying to sell us everything from magazine subscriptions to vacation homes. [2]These electronic intruders don't seem to care how much they are inconveniencing us and refuse to take "no" for an answer. [3]However, nuisance callers can be stopped if we take charge of the conversation. [4]As soon as one of them asks if we are Mr. or Ms. X, we should respond, "Yes, and are you a telephone solicitor?" [5]This technique puts them on the defensive. [6]We then have an opening to say that we don't accept solicitations over the phone, only through the mail. [7]This puts a quick end to the conversation.

If you thought the third sentence states the main idea, you were correct. The two sentences before the main idea introduce the topic: the problem of annoying telemarketers. Then the writer presents the main idea, which is that we can stop telemarketers from going on by taking charge of the conversation. The rest of the paragraph develops that idea by telling us how we can take charge of the conversation.

Main Idea at the End

Sometimes all the sentences in a paragraph will lead up to the main idea, which is presented at the end. On the next page is an example of such a paragraph.

¹A study at one prison showed that owning a pet can change a hardened prison inmate into a more caring person. ²Another study discovered that senior citizens, both those living alone and those in nursing homes, became more interested in life when they were given pets to care for. ³Even emotionally disturbed children have been observed to smile and react with interest if there is a cuddly kitten or puppy to hold. ⁴Animals, then, can be a means of therapy for many kinds of individuals.

Main Idea at the Beginning and the End

Main Idea
Supporting Detail
Supporting Detail
Supporting Detail
Main Idea

At times an author may choose to state the main idea near the beginning of the paragraph and then emphasize it by restating it later in the paragraph. In such cases, the main idea is at both the beginning and the end. Such is the case in the following paragraph.

¹People react strongly to red. ²The next time you go into a bookstore, notice which books catch your eye. ³Those with red covers are likely to stand out. ⁴The color of blood, red puts us on the alert. ⁵Often it signals danger. ⁶Red traffic lights and stop signs tell us to halt. ⁷Red also flags problems. ⁸Errors commonly are marked in red. ⁹Debts place us "in the red." ¹⁰Red is the color of negative emotion. ¹¹We redden with overexertion or embarrassment. ¹²When we're angry, we "see red." ¹³But red also is associated with strong positive feelings. ¹⁴The red hearts and roses of Valentine's Day speak of romance. ¹⁵Red cheeks convey health; red lips and nails, sexuality. ¹⁶Red can even confer a competitive advantage. ¹⁷When the colors worn by Olympic athletes in sports such as boxing were analyzed, researchers found that athletes who wore red tended to outperform opponents in blue. ¹⁸Apparently, red suggests power. ¹⁹Physiologically, our eyes are more sensitive to red than to blue or green. ²⁰Asked to name any color, most adults respond, "Red." ²¹Red is the one color that humans simply cannot ignore.

PRACTICE 7

The main ideas of the following paragraphs appear at different locations—in the beginning, somewhere in the middle, or at the end. Identify each main idea by filling in its sentence number in the space provided.

_____ 1. ¹Nearly every day, we all use expressions that have unusual and not commonly-known origins. ²For example, if you've ever said or heard that someone is the "spitting image" of someone else, here's some news: it has nothing to do with spit! ³The original phrase, "spirit and image," was used by slaves hundreds of years ago to describe a child who was so similar to another family member that it was believed that the same spirit occupied both people. ⁴Over the years, the words have run together to give us "spitting image." ⁵And everyone knows that to "live high on the hog" implies living well, but where did such a phrase come from? ⁶This expression originally referred to those who could afford the more expensive cuts of meat higher up on a hog, such as the shoulder roasts and the ribs, as opposed to the cheap "lower" parts, the pig's feet and the bacon from the belly. ⁷Finally, when we say that someone "takes the cake," we don't really mean that that person is going to receive a cake. ⁸However, originally, that's exactly what it meant! ⁹In the 1800s, a dance that made fun of stuffy ballroom dancing became so popular that eventually contests were held to see who could look the most ridiculous. ¹⁰Over time, this dance became known as the "Cakewalk" because winners were awarded cakes. ¹¹So those who really stood out in a comical and memorable way did, in fact, "take the cake."

_____ 2. ¹Recently while I was sitting in a small auditorium waiting for a play to begin, I saw three audience members chatting on cell phones. ²In fact, people converse on their cell phones while they drive, shop, walk down the street, use public transportation, eat in restaurants, or go to the bathroom. ³Let's face it: in the 21st century, cell phones are everywhere. ⁴In addition to using cell phones to talk, people use them to e-mail, text-message, surf the Web, organize their day, take photos, listen to music, watch videos, play games, and, by means of the phone's light, find something in the dark, such as a keyhole. ⁵More than 200 million Americans, including about half of those aged thirteen to sixteen, carry a cell phone. ⁶In a 2005 survey of U.S. cell-phone users, 26 percent said they would rather leave home without their wallet than without their cell phone. ⁷Almost three-fourths of U.S. households have at least one cell phone; many have three or more. ⁸In the United States, cell phones now far outnumber wired phones. ⁹Americans clearly love cell phones, right? ¹⁰Wrong. ¹¹A survey asked U.S. adults which invention they most hate. ¹²The most frequent reply? ¹³The cell phone.

_____ 3. [1]Caffeine is a natural ingredient in coffee, tea, colas, cocoa, and chocolate, and is added to some prescription and non-prescription drugs. [2]Despite being "natural," caffeine is also a powerful drug which greatly affects the body. [3]In healthy, rested people, a dose of 100 milligrams (about one cup of coffee) increases alertness, banishes drowsiness, quickens reaction time, enhances intellectual and muscular effort, and increases heart and respiratory rates. [4]Drinking one to two cups of coffee an hour before exercise encourages the body to preserve glycogen and burn fat—something that results in greater endurance. [5]In addition, caffeine masks fatigue. [6]In doses above 300 milligrams, caffeine can produce sleeplessness, nervousness, irritability, headaches, heart palpitations, and muscle twitches. [7]Caffeine is also habit-forming, and those who try to suddenly stop after heavy use may experience such withdrawal symptoms as headaches, lethargy, irritability, and difficulty in concentrating.

_____ 4. [1]Queen Isabella of Spain, who died in 1504, boasted that she'd had only two baths in her life—at birth and before her marriage. [2]In colonial America, leaders frowned on bathing, because it involved nudity, which, they feared, could lead to loose morals. [3]Indeed, laws in Virginia and Pennsylvania either limited or outright banned bathing—and for a time in Philadelphia, anyone who bathed more than once a month faced jail. [4]Furthermore, some of the early Christian churches discouraged sudsing up because of its association with the immorality common in the Roman baths. [5]Clearly, the notion that cleanliness is next to godliness has not always been a popular one.

_____ 5. [1]Research has demonstrated our self-centered tendency to rate ourselves more favorably than others rate us. [2]In one study, members of a random sample of men were asked to rank themselves on their ability to get along with others. [3]Defying mathematical laws, all subjects—every last one—put themselves in the top half of the population. [4]Sixty percent rated themselves in the top 10 percent of the population, and an amazing 25 percent rated themselves in the top 1 percent. [5]In the same study, 70 percent of the men ranked their leadership in the top quarter of the population, whereas only 2 percent ranked their leadership as below average. [6]Sixty percent said they were in the top quarter in athletic abilities, whereas only 6 percent said they were below average.

A Note on the Central Point

Just as a paragraph may have a main idea, a longer selection may have a **central point**, also known as a **central idea** or **thesis**. The longer selection might be an essay, an article, or a section of a textbook chapter. You can find a central point in the same way that you find a main idea—by identifying the topic (which is often suggested by the title of the selection) and then looking at the supporting material. The paragraphs within the longer reading will provide supporting details for the central point. You will see, for example, that the essay that ends this chapter has a central point.

A Final Thought

Whether we are readers, writers, listeners, or speakers, the "heart" of clear communication is the main idea, or point, and the support for the main idea. Look at the following diagram:

The diagram underscores the importance of the most important of all reading skills: the ability to identify main ideas. The diagram also shows that the ability to identify supporting details for the main idea is an almost equally important skill.

CHAPTER REVIEW

In this chapter, you learned the following:

- Recognizing the main idea is the most important key to good comprehension. The main idea is a general "umbrella" idea; all the specific supporting material of the passage fits under it.

- Three strategies that will help you find the main idea are to 1) look for general versus specific ideas; 2) use the topic (the general subject of a selection) to lead you to the main idea; 3) use key words—verbal clues that lead you to the main idea.

- The main idea often appears at the beginning of a paragraph, though it may appear elsewhere in a paragraph.

The next chapter—Chapter 3—will sharpen your understanding of the specific details that authors use to support and develop their main ideas.

 On the Web: If you are using this book in class, you can visit our website for additional practice in recognizing main ideas. Go to **www.townsendpress.com** and click on "Learning Center."

REVIEW TEST 1

To review what you've learned in this chapter, answer the following questions by filling in the blank or writing the letter of the correct answer.

_____ 1. The umbrella statement that covers all of the material in a paragraph is called the

A. topic.   B. main idea.   C. supporting details.

2. Supporting details are always more (*general or specific?*) _____ than the main idea.

_____ 3. To locate the main idea of a selection, you may find it helpful to first decide on its

A. topic.   B. structure.   C. length.

_____ 4. While a main idea may appear anywhere within a paragraph, in textbooks it very commonly appears

A. at the beginning.   B. in the middle.   C. at the end.

5. To help you decide if a certain sentence is the main idea, ask yourself, "Is this statement supported by all or most of the _____

_____?"

REVIEW TEST 2

A. In each of the following groups, one statement is the general point, and the other statements are specific support for the point. Identify each point with a **P** and each statement of support with an **S**.

1. ___ A. Executives kept fake accounting records to hide the fact that the company was losing money.

___ B. Employees were strongly encouraged to buy company stock, which is now worthless.

___ C. Top company executives made millions of dollars while the company was failing.

___ D. Officers of that failed energy company should be put in jail for a long time.

2. ___ A. Traditional Japanese culture emphasizes self-discipline and respect for authority.

   ___ B. No one in Japan, including police officers, may keep a handgun at home.

   ___ C. The crime rate in Tokyo is the lowest of any major city in the world for a number of reasons.

   ___ D. At least once a year, police officers visit every home in Japan to discuss neighborhood conditions.

B. Each group of statements below includes one topic, one main idea, and two supporting details. In the space provided, label each item with one of the following:

   T — for the **topic** of the paragraph
   MI — for the **main idea**
   SD — for the **supporting details**

Group 1

   _____ A. Staying in the sun too long can cause sunstroke.

   _____ B. People develop skin cancer after years of "working in the sun" or after years of exposure to direct sunlight.

   _____ C. Time in the sun.

   _____ D. Spending time in the sun can be dangerous.

Group 2

   _____ A. Rubbing one's nose and eyes transfers viruses to the hands, which then contaminate whatever they touch, such as a doorknob, serving spoon, or telephone.

   _____ B. Because the dried cold virus can live as long as three hours, you can pick it up from an object after the person with a cold is gone.

   _____ C. Catching a cold.

   _____ D. The most likely way to catch a cold is by touching an object that someone suffering from a cold has handled.

REVIEW TEST 3

The main idea appears at various places in the following paragraphs. Write the number of each main idea in the space provided.

_____ 1. ¹Two unlikely heroes, the goose and the canary, have earned their places in history as protectors of humans. ²In 390 B.C., the Romans placed geese (and dogs) in lookout positions on castle towers to warn of approaching enemies. ³A goose, the Romans knew, has remarkable powers of perceiving motion and sound, even in the middle of the night. ⁴As a result, while the dogs slept right through the approach of the fierce Gaul army, the guard geese sensed the Gallic invasion and warned the Romans well in advance with their thunderous honking and frantic wing flapping. ⁵Fifteen hundred years later, the use of canaries in coal mines saved more than a few coal miners from suffocation. ⁶Miners, who were always threatened by pockets of poisonous gases in the mines, used to carry canaries in small cages, holding them in front of them as they descended deeper and deeper into new mines. ⁷Because a canary's lungs are significantly more sensitive than a human's, the canary would show the effects of bad air long before the miners could sense it. ⁸Therefore, when the canary either appeared to be sick or (unfortunately) suddenly died, the miners were warned of the deadly air ahead, and they retreated quickly to safety.

_____ 2. ¹Criticism is a valuable means of helping ourselves and others achieve personal growth. ²However, because it is often done carelessly or cruelly, criticism has a bad reputation. ³Here are some guidelines for offering criticism constructively. ⁴First, wait until the person asks for feedback on his or her performance or actions. ⁵Unasked-for criticism is not usually valuable. ⁶Second, describe the person's behavior as specifically as possible before you criticize it. ⁷Instead of just saying, "You were awful," tell the person exactly what you observed. ⁸And finally, try to balance your criticism with positive statements. ⁹Look for significant points in the other person's performance that you can honestly praise.

_____ 3. ¹In Bulgaria, one nods one's head for "no" and shakes it back and forth for "yes." ²If you make the "A-OK" sign in Brazil, with the index finger and thumb making a circle, it's not only not okay, it's very impolite. ³To show the bottom of one's feet to a Turk is a serious insult, implying that "you are lower than the ground I walk on." ⁴Throughout the Middle East, to offer the left hand in a handshake— or to wave it at someone—will give deep offense. ⁵The Japanese consider it polite to bow to varying levels, depending on the message one is trying to convey. [6]When a Frenchman wants to make a strong point, he waves his upraised index finger from side to side. [7]In many Mediterranean cultures, men who are nonromantic friends walk hand in hand. [8]And in America—especially out West—a firm handshake and a direct look in the eye are expected when men meet one another; in many cultures, this would be considered very rude. [9]Clearly, body language that is perfectly normal or meaningless in one culture may mean something quite different in another.

_____ 4. [1]Some Americans believe that colonials cleverly won the Revolutionary War by hiding behind rocks and trees and sniping at the British, who marched and fought in bright red rows and didn't even aim their muskets. [2]In fact, the British were worn down in the American colonies by a combination of factors. [3]While the colonies never had a powerful army, they had a steady source of plentiful manpower and could easily replace their losses. [4]The British regular soldiers (or German soldiers for hire), by contrast, took more time to train and generally had to be shipped across the Atlantic Ocean. [5]Also, the colonies were not Britain's only worry; a much greater concern was France, with which the British were consistently at odds. [6]If too much energy had been spent holding the colonies, France might well have invaded and conquered Britain. [7]France was well aware of this, so it began sending supplies to the colonials early in the war and soon sent a fleet and an army. [8]The French contributions proved decisive at Yorktown in 1781, where the French and American armies held Lord Cornwallis's army at bay in Virginia while the French fleet turned back the Royal Navy's rescue effort.

_____ 5. [1]People often think of shame as a strong form of embarrassment. [2]A psychological study of 104 persons, however, suggests that shame and embarrassment are quite different experiences. [3]In general, embarrassment results from a relatively minor event that occurs while others are around. [4]It is more likely to cause a person to blush. [5]Also, an embarrassing event is likely to include an element of surprise and to be remembered with smiles or jokes. [6]Embarrassment generally does not lead to a feeling that one must correct a situation. [7]Shame is felt when people reveal a personal flaw to themselves and perhaps to others. [8]Unlike embarrassment, it is likely to make one feel that a situation needs repairing. [9]In addition, while embarrassment is strongly related to how we believe others view us, shame is often felt when one is alone. [10]And it is not generally looked upon later as humorous.

Here is a chance to apply your understanding of main ideas to a full-length selection. Read the article below about the popularity of alcohol in our culture, and then answer the questions on main ideas that follow. There are also questions to help you continue practicing the skill of understanding vocabulary in context.

Words to Watch

Below are some words in the reading that do not have strong context support. Each word is followed by the number of the paragraph in which it appears and its meaning there. These words are indicated in the reading by a small circle (°).

> *myth* (3): a false belief
> *irony* (11): a meaning that is the opposite of what is actually said

HERE'S TO YOUR HEALTH

Joan Dunayer

1   As the only freshman on his high school's varsity wrestling team, Tod was anxious to fit in with his older teammates. One night after a match, a teammate offered him a ride home. Several other teammates also were passengers. One of them took out a bottle of tequila and started passing it around. When the bottle reached Tod, he felt he had to drink, or he would seem like a "sissy." He took a swallow. Each time a teammate passed the bottle back to him, Tod took another swallow. After seven swallows he passed out. Terrified, his teammates carried him into his house. Tod's mother rushed him to the hospital, where his stomach was pumped. Tod recovered, but his blood alcohol level had been so high that he was lucky not to be in a coma or dead.

Although alcohol can cause rapid   2 poisoning, frequently leads to long-term addiction, and always threatens self-control, U.S. society encourages drinking. By their example, many parents give children like Tod the impression that alcohol is an essential ingredient of social gatherings. Peer pressure turns bachelor parties, fraternity initiations, and spring-semester beach vacations into competitions in "getting trashed." In soap operas, glamorous characters pour

Scotch whisky from crystal decanters as readily as most people turn on the faucet for tap water. In movies and music videos, trendsetters party by drinking in nightclubs and bars. The worst culprit of all is advertising. Alcohol ads appear with pounding frequency in magazines, on billboards, in newspapers, and on television. Who can recall a televised baseball or basketball game without a beer commercial? In 2005 more than 300,000 alcohol commercials appeared on U.S. television. It is no surprise that 70 percent of 21- to 25-year-olds report using alcohol in the last month, and nearly 48 percent of 21-year-olds are binge drinkers, downing five or more drinks in one session.

3   This nonstop promotion of alcohol in the mass media has resulted in several harmful beliefs about drinking that have spread throughout U.S. society. One alcohol myth° is that liquor signals professional success. In a slick men's magazine, one full-page ad for Scotch whiskey shows two men seated in an elegant restaurant. Both are in their thirties, perfectly groomed, and wearing expensive-looking gray suits. The windows are draped with velvet, the table with spotless white linen. Each place setting consists of a long-stemmed water goblet, silver utensils, and thick silver plates. On each plate is a half-empty cocktail glass. The two men are grinning and shaking hands, as if they've just concluded a business deal. The caption reads, "The taste of success."

4   Contrary to what the liquor company would have us believe, drinking is more closely related to failure than to achievement. Among students, the heaviest drinkers generally have the lowest grades. In the work force, alcoholics are frequently late or absent, tend to perform poorly, and often get fired. Although alcohol abuse occurs in all economic classes, it remains most prevalent among the poor.

5   Another alcohol myth that non-stop advertising supports is that drinking makes a person more sexually attractive. "Hot, hot, hot," one commercial's sound–track begins, as the camera scans a crowd of college-age beachgoers. The camera then zooms in on one woman sitting amid the crowd. She is beautiful, wearing a bikini. The camera follows the shape of her leg up to her bare hip and lingers there. Carrying an ice chest, a man

positions himself near the woman. He is handsome, tan, muscular. The woman doesn't show much interest—until the man opens the chest and takes out a beer. Now she smiles at him. He raises his eyebrows and invitingly holds up another can. The woman joins him. The advertised beer "attracts like no other," the commercial's song concludes.

6   The truth, however, is that beer doesn't make anyone sexier. Like all alcohol, it lowers the levels of male hormones in men and of female hormones in women—even when drunk in small amounts. In substantial amounts, alcohol can cause infertility in women and impotence in men. Some alcoholic men even develop enlarged breasts.

7   Yet another myth is that alcohol and athletics are a good combination. One billboard features three high-action images: a sprinter running at top speed, a surfer riding a wave, and a basketball player leaping to make a dunk shot. A particular light beer, the billboard declares, "won't slow you down."

8   But "slow you down" is exactly what alcohol does. Even in small amounts, alcohol dulls the brain, reducing muscle coordination and slowing reaction time. It also interferes with the ability to focus the eyes and adjust to a sudden change in brightness, such as the flash of a car's headlights. The leading cause of death among U.S. teenagers, drinking and driving is responsible for about 40 percent of all U.S. traffic fatalities. Drinking also results in many home and workplace accidents, such as falls, that cause injury or death. Continued alcohol abuse can physically change the brain,

permanently impairing learning and memory. Long-term drinking is related to malnutrition, weakening of the bones, and ulcers. It increases the risk of liver failure, heart disease, and stomach cancer. Drinking during pregnancy can lead to miscarriage and is a major cause of birth defects such as limb deformities and brain damage.

9   Finally, advertising creates the myth that alcohol fosters happy relationships. In one TV commercial, an overweight man sits alone in his drab living room. He reaches into a cooler, takes out a bottle of beer, and twists off the cap. Instantly, dance music plays, and dozens of attractive young adults appear in a shower of party streamers and confetti. "Where the party begins," a voice announces. The previously lonely man now is surrounded by male and female friends. The message: drinking solves social problems.

10   In reality, relationships in which alcohol plays a major role are unlikely to be happy. Heavy drinking destroys relationships and contributes to antisocial feelings and behavior. Alcoholics are about twenty-one times more likely than nonalcoholics to have antisocial personality disorder. In the United States, an estimated 30 percent of violent crimes are committed by people who had been drinking, and three-fourths of reported cases of spouse abuse involve alcohol. Parents with a drinking problem are more likely to neglect or abuse their children. Approximately 30 percent of Americans who commit suicide are alcoholics; the suicide rate among alcoholics is fifty

times the rate among nonalcoholics.

11   Alcohol, many would have us believe, is part of being successful, sexy, healthy, and happy. Those who have suffered from alcohol's destructive effects know otherwise. For alcohol's victims, "Here's to your health" rings with a terrible irony° when it is accompanied by the clink of liquor glasses.

Reading Comprehension Questions

Vocabulary in Context

_____ 1. In the excerpt below, the word *caption* (kăp′shən) means
   A. man.
   B. menu.
   C. contract that seals the business deal.
   D. words accompanying the picture.

   "In a slick men's magazine, one full-page ad for Scotch whiskey shows two men seated in an elegant restaurant. . . . The caption reads, 'The taste of success.'" (Paragraph 3)

_____ 2. In the sentence below, the word *prevalent* (prĕv′ə-lənt) means
   A. weak.
   B. colorful.
   C. widespread.
   D. inexpensive.

   "Although alcohol abuse occurs in all economic classes, it remains most prevalent among the poor." (Paragraph 4)

_____ 3. In the excerpt below, the word *substantial* (səb-stăn′shəl) means
   A. large.
   B. reasonable.
   C. weak.
   D. pleasing.

   ". . . beer . . . lowers the levels of male hormones in men and of female hormones in women—even when drunk in small amounts. In substantial amounts, alcohol can cause infertility in women and impotence in men." (Paragraph 6)

_____ 4. In the sentence below, the word *impairing* (ĭm-pâr′ĭng) means
   A. damaging.
   B. doubling.
   C. postponing.
   D. teaching.

   "Continued alcohol abuse can physically change the brain, permanently impairing learning and memory." (Paragraph 8)

_____ 5. In the sentence below, the word *fosters* (fŏs′tərz) means
   A. removes.
   B. hides.
   C. produces.
   D. follows.

   "Finally, advertising creates the myth that alcohol fosters happy relationships." (Paragraph 9)

Central Point and Main Ideas

_____ 6. The main idea of paragraph 2 is its
   A. first sentence.
   B. second sentence.
   C. third sentence.
   D. last sentence.

_____ 7. The main idea of paragraph 3 is its
   A. first sentence.
   B. second sentence.
   C. third sentence.
   D. seventh sentence.

_____ 8. The topic of paragraph 4 is drinking and
   A. grades.
   B. work.
   C. the poor.
   D. lack of success.

_____ 9. The main idea of paragraph 10 is its
   A. first sentence.
   B. second sentence.
   C. third sentence.
   D. fourth sentence.

_____ 10. Which sentence best expresses the central point of this selection?
   A. Although U.S. society encourages drinking, alcohol consumption is harmful in a number of ways.
   B. Alcohol ads appear very often in magazines, on billboards, in newspapers, and on television.
   C. Contrary to what the liquor industry wants us to believe, drinking is more closely related to failure than to achievement.
   D. Alcohol's victims know that alcohol is not part of being successful, sexy, healthy, and happy.

Discussion Questions

1. Unfortunately, Tod's experience with alcohol is not so rare. Do you know anyone who has had a negative experience because of drinking or because of drinking and driving? Where was that person drinking, and how much did he or she have? Explain what eventually happened.

2. If it's true that "beer doesn't make anyone sexier," why do you think so many young people drink so much beer in social situations?

3. Think about a wine, beer, or liquor ad you have seen in a magazine, in a newspaper, or on television. Which alcohol myth described in "Here's to Your Health" does that ad promote? What details of the ad contribute to that myth?

4. Cigarette advertising is no longer allowed on television. Do you think beer ads should also be outlawed on TV? In college newspapers? Explain your answers.

Note: Writing assignments for this selection appear on page 622.

Check Your Performance   MAIN IDEAS

Activity		Number Right	Points	Score
Review Test 1	(5 items)	_____	× 2 =	_____
Review Test 2	(16 items)	_____	× 2.5 =	_____
Review Test 3	(5 items)	_____	× 4 =	_____
Review Test 4	(10 items)	_____	× 3 =	_____
			TOTAL SCORE =	_____ %

Enter your total score into the **Reading Performance Chart: Review Tests** on the inside back cover.

MAIN IDEAS: Mastery Test 1

A. In each of the following groups, one statement is the general point, and the other statements are specific support for the point. Identify each point with a **P** and each statement of support with an **S**.

1. ___A. I'm a good example of someone who has "math anxiety."

   ___B. I feel dread every time I sit down to take our Friday math quiz.

   ___C. During the math midterm, I "froze" and didn't even try to answer most of the questions.

   ___D. I turned down a job as a salesclerk because I would have had to figure out how much change customers should get back.

2. ___A. Hungry bears searching for food often threaten hikers.

   ___B. Hiking on that mountain trail can be very dangerous.

   ___C. Severe weather develops quickly, leaving hikers exposed to storms and cold.

   ___D. When it rains, the trail—which is very steep at some points—becomes slippery.

3. ___A. A student at Virginia Tech shot and killed 32 people and wounded 17 others before committing suicide.

   ___B. During a midnight movie showing in Aurora, Colorado, a gunman walked into the theater and began shooting, killing 12 people and injuring 58 more.

   ___C. After shooting his mother, a young man drove to Sandy Hook Elementary School in Connecticut and shot 20 children and 6 adults to death.

   ___D. When disturbed people have access to guns, terrible tragedies can result.

(Continues on next page)

B. Each group of statements below includes one topic, one main idea, and two supporting details. In the space provided, label each item with one of the following:

T — for the **topic** of the paragraph
MI — for the **main idea**
SD — for the **supporting details**

Group 1

_____ A. Some people knock on wood when talking about good luck.

_____ B. Everyday superstitions.

_____ C. Some people believe they should leave a house through the same door they entered.

_____ D. There are many superstitions that are practiced in everyday life.

Group 2

_____ A. Vegetarian diets.

_____ B. The incidence of heart disease is much lower for vegetarians than for non-vegetarians.

_____ C. People who eat vegetarian diets are generally healthier than non-vegetarians.

_____ D. Vegetarians have a lower rate of cancer than non-vegetarians.

MAIN IDEAS: Mastery Test 2

A. In each of the following groups, one statement is the general point, and the other statements are specific support for the point. Identify each point with a **P** and each statement of support with an **S**.

1. ___A. Elected officials could spend more time on their jobs and less on raising money.

   ___B. There should be a limit on how much can be spent for political campaigns.

   ___C. Candidates with less money would have a fairer chance of competing.

   ___D. Elected officials would be less likely to be influenced by rich contributors to their campaigns.

2. ___A. Often you'll wait half an hour for a Route 27 bus, and then three will show up at once.

   ___B. Sometimes Route 27 buses will roar right past you at a bus stop, even though they aren't full.

   ___C. Route 27 seems to be assigned the oldest buses, ones that rattle and have broken seats.

   ___D. It is wise to avoid the Route 27 bus whenever possible.

3. ___A. Congress should enact a comprehensive highway program.

   ___B. Some of the numerous accidents, injuries, and fatalities on our nation's roads are the result of poor highway design.

   ___C. There is an urgent need for bridge construction and maintenance throughout this country.

   ___D. This nation needs programs to alleviate traffic jams.

(Continues on next page)

B. Each group of statements below includes one topic, one main idea, and two supporting details. In the space provided, label each item with one of the following:

T — for the **topic** of the paragraph
MI — for the **main idea**
SD — for the **supporting details**

Group 1

_____ A. School officials complain that students damage school property, and parents complain their children can't read or do math.

_____ B. Teachers complain about the low salaries they get for their difficult and important jobs.

_____ C. Problems in our schools.

_____ D. The problems within our school systems are varied and affect almost everyone involved.

Group 2

_____ A. Self-help groups based on the Alcoholics Anonymous model exist to serve people with a variety of problems.

_____ B. Self-help groups.

_____ C. Narcotics Anonymous sponsors meetings where drug abusers and their loved ones can get support.

_____ D. Overeaters Anonymous assists people whose eating has gotten out of control.

MAIN IDEAS: Mastery Test 3

The main idea may appear at any place within each of the five paragraphs that follow. Write the number of each main idea sentence in the space provided.

_____ 1. [1]Creatures that are very sensitive to the changes in the air before a storm can "predict" a change in the weather. [2]Birds, for example, sense the pressure change and fly lower. [3]Low-flying birds, then, indicate that rain is coming. [4]Similarly, houseflies detect this change and move indoors to avoid the downpour. [5]And cats are known to groom themselves just before a storm. [6]In doing so, they are reacting to the static electricity that enters the air before a thunderstorm. [7]The electricity separates their fur and makes them feel dirty, so they lick themselves to make the fur smooth and "clean" again.

_____ 2. [1]Men, we are reminded over and over, are the stronger sex. [2]Yet men are more likely than women to have a number of health problems at every age. [3]More males than females are miscarried, are stillborn, or die in their first year of life. [4]In all societies, men die earlier than women do. [5]American men are more likely than women to die from heart disease, lung disease, and cirrhosis of the liver. [6]They are more likely to suffer from stress-related diseases, such as hypertension, ulcers, and asthma. [7]They are hospitalized for mental illness more frequently. [8]Women attempt suicide more often than men, but men succeed in killing themselves three times as often (largely because they use violent means—guns rather than sleeping pills).

_____ 3. [1]The eruption of volcanoes has caused death and misery throughout the centuries. [2]But in parts of Italy, Iceland, Chile, and Bolivia, volcanic steam is used to run heat and power plants. [3]Pumice, which is made from volcanic lava, is used as a grinder and polisher. [4]Sulfur produced by volcanoes is useful to the chemical industry. [5]Hawaiian farmers grow crops on land made rich by decayed volcanic material. [6]Clearly, in spite of all the damage they cause, volcanoes do benefit us in various ways.

(Continues on next page)

_____ 4.   [1]Adult children who move back home can avoid family conflicts by following some helpful tips. [2]First, they should contribute what they can—and it doesn't necessarily have to be in terms of money. [3]Being productive family members will help them earn their keep. [4]This can involve tutoring or coaching younger sisters or brothers, or helping Mom and Dad with household chores and errands. [5]Second, grown children at home should not expect their parents to rescue them from difficulties. [6]As adults, they are responsible for getting out of their own scrapes—and for trying to avoid scrapes in the first place. [7]Last, they must respect their parents' lifestyles and own needs for independence. [8]It is unrealistic to expect parents' lives to revolve around the needs of a grown child, as they may have when the child was younger.

_____ 5.   [1]Police estimate that only 1 to 2 percent of hitchhiking crimes are reported, so there are no accurate statistics on such events. [2]But frequent horror stories indicate that hitchhiking can be dangerous to both hitchhiker and driver. [3]There was the nineteen-year-old woman who accepted a lift from three young men in New Jersey, expecting a ride across the bridge to New York City. [4]Instead they drove to a motel, where they repeatedly raped her. [5]Luckily, she escaped with her life. [6]Less fortunate was the eighteen-year-old woman student who disappeared from campus after accepting a ride with a stranger and whose decomposed body was found in a suburban sewage plant two years later. [7]Male hitchhikers are less open to assault, but a number of incidents show that they are far from immune. [8]Hitchhikers also face the hazards of riding with an intoxicated or stoned driver, not the least of which is an accident. [9]They also risk assault or robbery by other hitchhikers and being stranded in out-of-the-way places. [10]Drivers, too, are subject to assault and robbery. [11]And they risk an accident by stopping on a busy highway, or arrest if their passengers happen to be carrying drugs. [12]Some male drivers have picked up young girls who threatened to call the police and cry rape unless the men handed over all their money.

MAIN IDEAS: Mastery Test 4

The main idea may appear at any place within each of the five paragraphs that follow. Write the number of each main idea sentence in the space provided.

_____ 1. [1]Fire extended humans' geographical boundaries by allowing them to travel into regions that were previously too cold to explore. [2]It also kept predators away, allowing early humans to sleep securely. [3]Fire, in fact, has been a significant factor in human development and progress in many ways. [4]Other obvious benefits of fire are its uses in cooking and in hunting. [5]Probably even more important, however, is that learning to control fire allowed people to change the very rhythm of their lives. [6]Before fire, the human daily cycle coincided with the rising and setting of the sun. [7]With fire, though, humans gained time to think and talk about the day's events and to prepare strategies for coping with tomorrow.

_____ 2. [1]The stages of life, from birth to death, may seem controlled by biology. [2]However, the way we think about life's stages is shaped by society. [3]During the Middle Ages, for example, children dressed—and were expected to act—just like little adults. [4]Adolescence became a distinct stage of life only fairly recently, when a separate teenage subculture began to appear. [5]But in the Middle Ages, young people were "children" until about age 16. [6]Then they went to work, married, and had their own children. [7]Today, "young adulthood" has become a new stage of life, stretching from about age 20 to 30. [8]As life expectancy becomes longer and people spend years in active retirement, older adulthood has also become a distinct life stage.

_____ 3. [1]New technology often creates unanticipated problems. [2]Automobiles, for example, provide numerous benefits, but they also pollute the air and kill more than thirty thousand Americans each year. [3]It is difficult to imagine life without electricity and heat, but power plants pollute the air, cause the thermal pollution of rivers, and contribute to global warming. [4]Insecticides and chemical fertilizers have performed miracles in agriculture but have polluted food and streams (and even "killed" some lakes). [5]Jet planes, while helping us in many ways, cause air pollution (one jet taking off emits the same amount of hydrocarbon as the exhausts from ten thousand automobiles) and noise pollution near busy airports.

(Continues on next page)

_____ 4.   ¹By the end of the first series of Sherlock Holmes stories, the author, Sir Arthur Conan Doyle, had become tired of writing detective stories. ²So at the end of his second book of Holmes stories, he decided to have the detective die. ³The book ends with Holmes and his archenemy, Moriarty, plunging to their deaths from a high cliff overlooking a waterfall. ⁴After that, hundreds of letters poured in to Conan Doyle, begging him to bring Holmes back. ⁵Also, magazines offered him huge sums of money for additional Sherlock Holmes adventures. ⁶Finally, after nine years, Conan Doyle wrote a new story in which Holmes reappears and tells Dr. Watson that he did not die after all. ⁷Sometimes it is the reader, not the author, who determines how long fictional heroes will live.

_____ 5.   ¹With so many young, single people having babies, the question arises as to how happy they are being young parents. ²A national survey of young, single mothers and fathers reveals that most were happier before they became parents. ³Sixty-seven percent of the nine thousand new parents who responded to the survey said having a baby presented more problems than they envisioned. ⁴Fifty-six percent of the respondents said they had to drop out of school, despite their hopes that they could manage schoolwork plus rearing a baby. ⁵A majority (73 percent) said they were forced to seek financial help from family, friends, and/or government agencies, and 37 percent said they accepted low-paying, unsatisfying jobs out of necessity. ⁶Also, 70 percent said they missed the "good times" with friends that they enjoyed before their babies were born.

MAIN IDEAS: Mastery Test 5

The five paragraphs that follow are all taken from college textbooks. The main idea may appear at any place within each paragraph. Write the number of each main idea sentence in the space provided.

_____ 1. [1]An author doing research for a book asked thousands of Americans what made them happy. [2]Among the popular responses she received were eating ice-cream sandwiches and candy, being offered a football ticket, and visiting city parks. [3]Other specific responses included eating ravioli, feeling the cool underside of a pillow, and rereading old love letters. [4]The most frequently cited response was simply spending time with family. [5]Almost no one gave the answer of owning flashy jewelry, showy cars, or other fancy things. [6]The author concluded that most of the things that put a smile on our face are simple and free or inexpensive.

_____ 2. [1]To erase or not to erase? [2]That is the question in many students' minds after they've penciled in one of those small circles in multiple-choice tests. [3]Folk wisdom has long held that when answering questions on such tests—or on any test—you should trust your first instincts. [4]However, a research instructor has found that students who change answers they're unsure of usually improve their scores. [5]The instructor spent three years compiling and analyzing college students' tests, watching for telltale erasure marks that would indicate that the student had, indeed, revised his or her answer. [6]What the instructor found was that revised answers were two and a half times as likely to go from wrong to right as vice-versa. [7]This statistic held up even across such variables as sex, age, and race; the subject matter of the tests studied also proved not to be a factor.

_____ 3. [1]Finding a good way to get rid of garbage is a problem that faces many municipalities today. [2]It may be of some consolation for them to know that getting rid of garbage has almost always involved problems. [3]When settlements were very small, garbage was simply thrown outdoors, where it eventually decomposed. [4]But as communities grew, pigs and other animals helped clear away garbage by eating it; of course, the animals, in turn, recycled that garbage and thus created an even less appealing waste problem. [5]The first municipal effort to deal with garbage was begun in Philadelphia by Benjamin Franklin, whose solution was to have it dumped into the Delaware River. [6]A century later, municipal incinerators, generally located in the most crowded part of town, burned garbage and produced the worst of odors as a by-product.

(Continues on next page)

_____ 4.   ¹In both Canada and the United States, many people arrested for a crime never receive appropriate punishment. ²Prosecutors often drop charges because of flaws in the arrest procedures—officers didn't follow the rules with sufficient care or file their paperwork properly. ³In many other cases, the charges are dismissed at preliminary hearings because of problems of evidence, such as key witnesses failing to appear. ⁴Of cases surviving these barriers, many are resolved by a plea bargain. ⁵That is, the charges are reduced in exchange for a plea of guilty. ⁶This spares the government the expense of a trial, but it also makes punishment less severe. ⁷And of those who do go to prison, very few will serve their full sentence. ⁸Time off for good behavior often equals 25 percent of one's sentence, so most will be out on parole well before their time is up.

_____ 5.   ¹If we compressed the entire history of life on the planet into a single year, the first modern human would not appear until December 31 at about 11:53 p.m., and the first civilizations would emerge only about a minute before the end of the year. ²Yet humanity's achievements in its brief history on Earth have been remarkable. ³Some 15,000 years ago, our ancestors practiced religious rituals and painted superb pictures on the walls of their caves. ⁴Around 11,000 years ago, some human groups began to domesticate animals and plants, thereby freeing themselves from total dependence on hunting and gathering food. ⁵About 6,000 years ago, people began to live in cities, to specialize in different forms of labor, to divide into social classes, and to create distinct political and economic institutions. ⁶Within a few thousand years, empires were created, linking isolated groups and bringing millions under centralized rule. ⁷Advanced agricultural practices improved farming, resulting in growing populations and the emergence of large nation-states. ⁸A mere 250 years ago, the Industrial Revolution began, thrusting us into the modern world of factories and computers, jets and nuclear reactors, instantaneous global communications, and terrifying military technologies.

MAIN IDEAS: Mastery Test 6

The five paragraphs that follow are all taken from college textbooks. The main idea may appear at any place within each paragraph. Write the number of each main idea sentence in the space provided.

_____ 1. [1]People may think that love and romantic feelings are enough of a basis for choosing a spouse. [2]The chances of a marriage surviving, however, would improve if prospective marriage partners considered a few unromantic questions before deciding on matrimony. [3]For example, do the two individuals involved share a common socioeconomic background? [4]The more similar they are in their social, economic, religious, and cultural backgrounds, the more similar their expectations about married life will be. [5]In addition, what are their goals? [6]It's a big advantage to the marriage if they know and share one another's goals concerning career, lifestyle, and family. [7]Finally, and maybe most important, how does the prospective spouse treat others in his or her life? [8]During the courtship, the boyfriend or girlfriend may get special consideration, but in the long run, spouses will probably treat each other about the same way they treat their own family members.

_____ 2. [1]There is a tendency in our society to turn important decisions over to groups. [2]In the business world, most important decisions are made around a conference table rather than behind one person's desk. [3]In politics, major policy decisions are seldom made by just one person. [4]Groups of advisers, cabinet officers, committee members, or aides meet to deliberate and decide. [5]In the courts, a defendant may request a trial by jury, and for some serious crimes, a jury trial is required by law. [6]And of course, the U.S. Supreme Court renders group decisions on issues of major importance.

_____ 3. [1]The American ideal of a lush green lawn is borrowed from England, where the cool, misty climate makes it easy to grow grass. [2]In America, however, lawns are an energy-intensive, wasteful, and nonproductive form of landscaping. [3]To begin with, achieving a picture-perfect lawn requires gallons of expensive fertilizer and hazardous pesticides that pollute groundwater and run off into lakes and rivers. [4]In addition, lawn owners often exterminate the insects, moles, and gophers that play a part in the balance of nature. [5]Equally destructive is the constant watering lawns require, often where water is a limited resource. [6]Finally, the lawn must be mowed on a regular basis to give it that green carpet effect, requiring endless output of human and mechanical energy. [7]After all the labor and expense, the final result is a flat covering that lacks interesting features, wildlife, or edible produce.

(Continues on next page)

_____ 4. [1]Propaganda is information that is methodically spread in order to persuade audiences to adopt a certain opinion. [2]Advertising is an ever-present form of propaganda in our lives. [3]Four common propaganda techniques are present in the advertising we see and hear every day. [4]One technique, the testimonial, involves having a well-known person appear on behalf of the product being sold. [5]Advertisers assume, for example, that if we admire a sports star, we'll want to eat the cereal he or she endorses. [6]Another common propaganda technique, the bandwagon, makes us want to be "one of the gang." [7]"Everybody's switching to . . . " "Don't be left out . . . " and "All across America, people are discovering . . . " are phrases that signal a bandwagon approach. [8]The plain-folks propaganda technique is especially popular on TV. [9]In plain-folks commercials, we see and hear "regular" consumers talk about their experience using a certain phone company, headache remedy, or brand of coffee. [10]The fourth common propaganda technique, the transfer, encourages us to link two unrelated objects in our mind. [11]When a powerful cougar prowls around a shiny new car, for example, advertisers hope we will transfer our sense of the wild cat's speed, strength, and beauty to our vision of their product.

_____ 5. [1]Stories of the mythical Camelot, the location in England of King Arthur's court, depict a world of dashing knights in shining armor and beautiful damsels in distress. [2]In actuality, the real world of that time probably consisted of smelly men in rusty tin suits and damsels in a certain kind of distress—the distress of being constantly pregnant and of having no rights in a male-dominated society. [3]Those same stories often glorified the brave men who fought to the death for king and country. [4]However, most battle fatalities of the time resulted from medieval medicine. [5]Letting the "bad blood" out of a sick person was a common medical practice, and cleanliness was not. [6]Other stories of the fabled Camelot housed royalty in glittering palaces, clothed them in silks, and covered them in mystery and awe. [7]But what is awesome about living in a cold, stone, rat-infested fortress with poor ventilation? [8]As for silks, war-indebted kings could rarely afford such foreign commodities. [9]Wool from home usually did the trick. [10]And there's certainly nothing silky about the discomfort caused by coarse woolen undergarments. [11]It is obvious that the Camelot myth ignores the harsh realities of life in the Middle Ages in favor of a fantastic, unrealistic view of history.

3 Supporting Details

In Chapter 2 you worked on the most important reading skill—finding the main idea. A closely related reading skill is locating *supporting details*—the added information that is needed for you to make sense of a main idea.

This chapter describes supporting details and presents three techniques to help you take study notes on main ideas and their supporting details: outlining, mapping, and summarizing.

What Are Supporting Details?

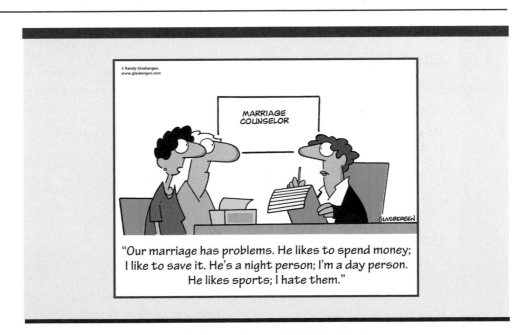

"Our marriage has problems. He likes to spend money; I like to save it. He's a night person; I'm a day person. He likes sports; I hate them."

Supporting details are reasons, examples, facts, steps, or other kinds of evidence that explain a main idea. In the cartoon above, the main idea—that the marriage has problems—is well supported by the three differences stated by the wife.

On the next page is a paragraph with strong support for its point.

A Paragraph with Strong Support

In the paragraph below, three major details support the main idea that many people are strangely passive when they visit a doctor. As you read the paragraph, try to identify and check (✓) the three major details.

[1]Many people are strangely passive when they visit a doctor. [2]First of all, they often fail to provide the doctor with complete information about their medical problem. [3]They may barely describe their symptoms, believing that a skilled doctor—like a master car mechanic—will somehow easily be able to diagnose what is wrong with them. [4]Secondly, many people fail to ask their doctors for a full and clear explanation of their condition. [5]They don't want to appear ignorant in front of their "all-knowing" doctor, and they don't want to take up too much of this Important Person's time, so they say little and ask almost nothing. [6]Last of all, they often fail to understand a doctor's orders. [7]Studies show that many patients don't understand why they should take a certain medication or for how long they should take it. [8]Incredibly enough, some patients are not even sure, as they are about to be rolled into an operating room, why they are having surgery!

✓
Check Your Understanding

See if you can complete the basic outline below that shows the three major details supporting the main idea.

Main idea: Many people are strangely passive when they visit a doctor.

Supporting detail 1: _____

Supporting detail 2: _____

Supporting detail 3: _____

Explanation

You should have added that patients fail to 1) provide enough information about their problem, 2) get a full explanation of their problem, and 3) understand a doctor's orders. These major supporting details help you fully understand the main idea. To read effectively, you must often learn to recognize main ideas *and* the details that support those ideas.

Understanding Major and Minor Details

There are often two levels of supporting details—major and minor. The **major details** explain and develop the main idea. In turn, the **minor details** help fill out and make clear the major details.

In the paragraph below, the main idea is stated in the first sentence. Read the paragraph and put a check (✓) by the two major details that support the main idea. The major details are in turn supported by minor details, which are examples in this case. The first major detail is followed by three examples, and the second major detail is followed by one long example.

> ¹There are two ways to relate to people in our lives. ²One way is to see them as *objects*: we get something from them, but we are not concerned with how they feel. ³They are there only for our use. ⁴For example, we might treat as an object the person who sells us items in a convenience store or waits on us in a restaurant or even teaches a class we are taking. ⁵The second way we can see people is as *subjects*, letting ourselves be aware that they have feelings just as we do. ⁶There is a story about a British woman who was expecting important guests for tea one afternoon. ⁷She looked out from her front porch after lunch and was horrified to see that her gardener had not shown up for work. ⁸When he finally arrived, she tore into him. ⁹"Do you know who is coming here in an hour? ¹⁰I ought to fire you!" ¹¹Without looking up, the man quietly said, "I'm sorry. ¹²My little girl died during the night, and we had to bury her today." ¹³For the first time, the woman saw the man as a human being, not simply as a device for keeping her lawn attractive. ¹⁴He stopped being an object and became a subject, a possessor of feelings, needs, pains, and relationships to which she had never given a thought.

Explanation

The major details are the "two ways to relate to people in our lives" mentioned in the main idea. The first major detail is to see people as objects, and the second detail is to see them as subjects. The minor details are the examples the author has used to make those two major details clear. The relationships between the main idea and its major and minor details can be seen at a glance in this brief, informal outline:

Main idea: Two ways to relate to people in our lives

1. See them as objects
   Examples: convenience-store salesperson, waiter, teacher

2. See them as subjects
   Example: British woman and her gardener

Notice that just as the main idea is more general than its supporting details, the major details are more general than the minor ones. For example, to see people as subjects is more general than the specific example of the British woman and her gardener.

The purpose of the rest of this chapter is to sharpen your sense of the relationships between main ideas and their major and minor supporting details. You will practice three note-taking techniques that will make you a better reader: outlining, mapping, and summarizing.

Outlining

Preparing an outline of a passage will help you understand and see clearly the relationship between a main idea and its supporting details. Outlines start with a main idea (or a heading that summarizes the main idea), followed by major supporting details. Sometimes there will be a level of minor details as well.

Suppose you wanted to outline the paragraph on bullying that appeared in Chapter 2. Reread the paragraph, trying to identify and check (✓) the three major supporting details.

[1]School bullies have been around as long as there have been schools. [2]Studies reveal several reasons why some children become bullies. [3]Research shows that a certain combination of size and personality may be one factor. [4]Bigger, more aggressive children are more likely to try to dominate their smaller, quieter peers. [5]Another factor linked to bullying is overexposure to violent TV programs. [6]By the time the average American child is ten years old, he or she has watched thousands of acts of violence, including assault and murder. [7]Such exposure can lead to aggression and violence. [8]Finally, exposure to *real* violence is a factor in bullying. [9]Studies indicate that victims of bullies often turn into bullies themselves. [10]Whether abused by family members or tormented by other kids, bullies typically learn their behavior from others. [11]Look closely into the eyes of a bully, and you may be looking into the eyes of a former victim.

✔ *Check Your Understanding*

Now see if you can fill in the missing items in the following outline of the paragraph, which shows both major and minor details.

Main idea: Studies reveal several reasons why some children become bullies.

    Major detail: **1.** A certain combination of size and personality

        Minor details: Bigger, more aggressive children may dominate their smaller, quieter peers.

Major detail: 2.   _____

_____

Minor details: _____

_____

Major detail: 3.   _____

Minor details: Kids abused by family members or bullied by other kids often become bullies.

Explanation

You should have added two major supporting details: (2) overexposure to violent TV programs; (3) exposure to *real* violence. And to the second major supporting detail, you should have added the minor detail that the average American ten-year-old has watched thousands of acts of violence on television.

Notice that just as the main idea is more general than its supporting details, so major details are more general than minor ones. For instance, the major detail that "overexposure to violent TV programs" is a factor in bullying is more general than the minor detail that the average American child of ten "has watched thousands of acts of violence."

Outlining Tips

The following tips will help you prepare outlines:

 TIP 1   Look for words that tell you a list of details is coming. Here are some common list words:

List Words

several kinds of	various causes	a few reasons
a number of	a series of	three factors
four steps	among the results	several advantages

For example, look again at the main ideas in two paragraphs already discussed and underline the list words:

- Studies reveal several reasons why some children become bullies.
- There are two ways to relate to people in our lives.

Here the words *several reasons* and *two ways* tell us that a list of major details is coming. You will not always be given such helpful signals that a list of details will follow. For example, there are no list words in the paragraph with this main idea, "Though fun to watch, chimpanzees should not be kept as pets." However, you will want to note such words when they are present. *Such list words help you to understand quickly the basic organization of a passage.*

 TIP 2   Look for words that signal major details. Such words are called **addition words**, and they will be explained further on page 182. Here are some common addition words:

Addition Words

one	to begin with	also	further
first (of all)	for one thing	in addition	furthermore
second(ly)	other	next	last (of all)
third(ly)	another	moreover	final(ly)

✔ Check Your Understanding

Now look again at the paragraph on bullying on page 106:

1. The word *one* (in *one factor*) signals the first major supporting detail.

2. Which addition word introduces the second major supporting detail?

   _____

3. Which addition word introduces the third major supporting detail?

   _____

And look again at the selection on two ways of relating to people on page 105:

1. Which word introduces the first major detail? _____

2. Which word introduces the second major detail? _____

Explanation

In the paragraph on bullying, the second major detail is introduced by the word *Another (factor)* and the third by the word *Finally*. In the selection on relating to people, the first major detail is introduced by the word *One* and the second by the word *second*.

TIP 3 When making an outline, put all supporting details of equal importance at the same distance from the left margin. In the outline of the paragraph on bullying on pages 106–107, the three major supporting details all begin at the same point on the margin. Likewise, the minor supporting details are indented at the same distance from the margin. You can therefore see at a glance the main idea, the major details, and the minor details.

✓ Check Your Understanding

Put appropriate numbers *(1, 2, 3)* and letters *(a, b)* in front of the items in the following outline.

Main idea
　_____ **Major detail**
　　_____ Minor detail
　　_____ Minor detail
　_____ **Major detail**
　　_____ Minor detail
　　_____ Minor detail
　_____ **Major detail**

Explanation

You should have put a *1, 2,* and *3* in front of the major details and an *a* and *b* in front of the minor details. Note that an outline proceeds from the most general to the most specific, from main idea to major details to minor details.

The practice on the following pages will give you experience in finding major details, in separating major details from minor details, and in preparing outlines.

PRACTICE 1

Read and then outline each passage. Begin by writing in the main idea, and then fill in the supporting details. The first outline requires only major details; the second calls for you to add minor details as well.

A. [1]Parents can take several steps to discourage TV watching and encourage reading. [2]For one thing, have only one television set, and place it in the family room. [3]Then if your child wants privacy, he or she will have to go elsewhere, away from the TV. [4]Secondly, connect reading with eating. [5]Put a bookcase rather than a television in the kitchen, and make sure it is filled with comics, magazines, local newspapers, and so on. [6]Explain that all snacks have to be eaten in the kitchen. [7]Given the fact that most kids can go only a short time without putting food in their mouths, your kids should get a lot of reading done while they're snacking. [8]Last of all, don't even dream of putting a television set in a child's bedroom. [9]You want your kids to fall asleep over books, not glued to a flickering screen.

Main idea: _____

_____

    Major detail: 1. _____

_____

    Major detail: 2. _____

_____

    Major detail: 3. _____

_____

B. [1]Colleges of the early nineteenth century had distinct differences from today's schools. [2]First, the student body during this time was almost entirely white males. [3]Higher education was considered a final polishing for upper-class gentlemen—a privilege unnecessary for those who had lower social status. [4]In addition, no matter what their interests were, all students had to take the same courses. [5]They were required to study the ancient languages (Latin, Greek, sometimes Hebrew), literature, natural science, mathematics, and political and moral philosophy. [6]A third feature of nineteenth-century colleges was their small size. [7]Except for a few of the very oldest institutions, most colleges had a student body of only a few dozen students. [8]The typical faculty consisted of just three or four professors and an equal number of tutors. [9]A final difference was that student life in the early 1800s was much more regulated than today. [10]Strict curfews determined what times students had to turn the lamps out in their rooms, and most schools required students to attend religious services on campus.

Note: Don't write in *all* the minor details, but try to summarize them in a few words.

Main idea: _____

_____

Major detail: 1. _____

    Minor details: _____

_____

Major detail: 2. _____

    Minor details: _____

_____

Major detail: 3. _____

    Minor details: _____

_____

Major detail: 4. _____

    Minor details: _____

_____

Study Hint: At times you will want to include minor details in your study notes; at other times, it may not be necessary to do so. If you are taking notes on one or more textbook chapters, use your judgment. It is often best to be aware of minor details but to concentrate on writing down the main ideas and major details.

Mapping

Students sometimes find it helpful to use maps rather than outlines. **Maps,** or diagrams, are highly visual outlines in which circles, boxes, or other shapes show the relationships between main ideas and supporting details. Each major detail is connected to the main idea. If minor details are included, each is connected to the major detail it explains.

✓

Check Your Understanding

Read the following passage, and then see if you can complete the map and the questions that follow.

> [1]Several factors can interfere with having a good memory. [2]One such factor is a lack of motivation. [3]Without a real desire to learn or remember something, you probably won't. [4]Another cause is a lack of practice. [5]To stay sharp, memory skills, like any other skill, must be used on a regular basis. [6]A third factor that can hurt memory is self-doubt. [7]If you're convinced you won't remember something, you probably won't. [8]A person with a positive attitude will do much better on a test than someone who is sure he or she won't remember the material. [9]Last, distraction can interfere with memory. [10]If you are being distracted by the sound of a television or a conversation nearby, try to find a quiet environment before you attempt to commit something to memory.

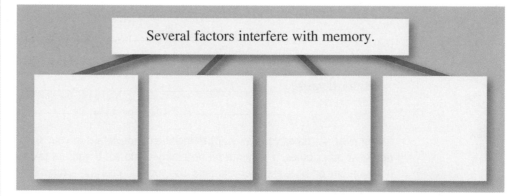

Several factors interfere with memory.

Which words introduce:

1. The first major detail? _____

2. The second major detail? _____

3. The third major detail _____

4. The last major detail? _____

Explanation

The map sets off the major details in a very visual way. You see at a glance the four factors that can interfere with memory: lack of motivation, lack of practice, self-doubt, and distraction. The words that introduce the major details are *One, Another, A third,* and *Last.*

PRACTICE 2

Read each passage, and then complete the maps that follow. The main ideas are given so that you can focus on finding the supporting details. The first passage requires only major details. The second passage calls for you to add both major and minor details.

A. ¹Many people become nearly tongue-tied when they want to meet other people. ²For those of us who find starting conversations with strangers difficult, the following four strategies may be useful. ³Notice that each is developed in question form, inviting the other person to respond. ⁴One approach is to introduce yourself, giving your name and asking the name of the other person. ⁵"Hi, I'm Shelby. ⁶And who are you?" ⁷A second approach is to refer to the physical setting in a question. ⁸You might, for example, make such a comment as, "This is awful weather for a game, isn't it?" ⁹Another approach is to give the other person a compliment and ask a question related to it. ¹⁰You might say, for instance, "Your braid looks great. ¹¹Did it take long to do?" ¹²Finally, you can seek direct information from the other person. ¹³At a work gathering, you can ask such a question as, "Which department do you work in?" ¹⁴At a party, you might say, "Walt and Jan give a really nice party. ¹⁵How do you happen to know them?"

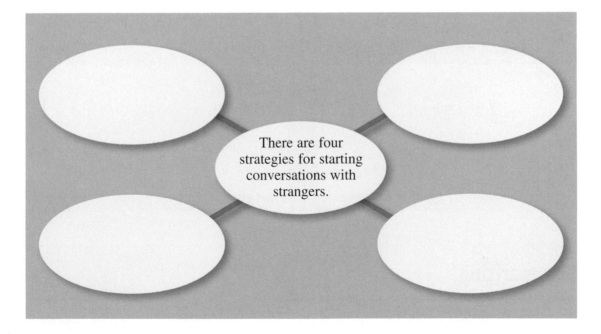

There are four strategies for starting conversations with strangers.

B. ¹Industrialized dairy farming differs from old-fashioned dairy farming in two basic respects. ²First of all, there is an immense saving of labor in industrial farming. ³Industrial farms have milking machines installed on a huge carousel, and each revolution allows sufficient time for a cow to be milked. ⁴Consequently, it takes only one operator to place and release cows as each milking station comes by the gateway. ⁵In contrast, in many nations milking is still done by hand and takes about 10 minutes per cow. ⁶The second major difference is the higher milk output per cow on industrial farms. ⁷The average American cow gives 7.5 times more milk than does the average cow in Brazil, where farms are old-fashioned. ⁸The productivity differences are so great that milk is far cheaper in the United States than in Brazil.

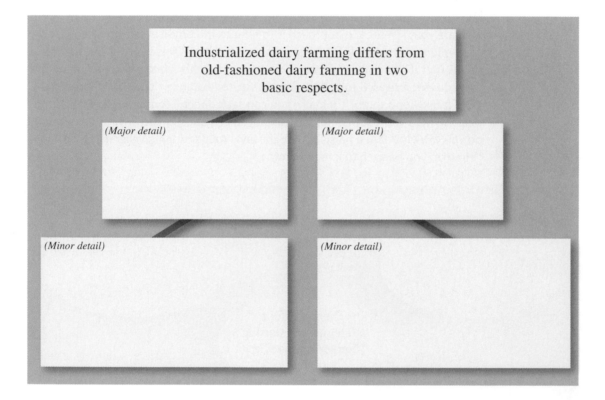

Industrialized dairy farming differs from old-fashioned dairy farming in two basic respects.

(Major detail)

(Major detail)

(Minor detail)

(Minor detail)

Summarizing

A **summary** is the reduction of a large amount of information to its most important points. The length and kind of summary will depend upon one's purpose as well as on the material in question. Often, a summary will consist of a main idea and its major supporting details. As a general guideline, a paragraph might be reduced to a sentence or two, an article might be reduced to a paragraph, and a textbook chapter might be reduced to about three pages of notes.

One of the most common types of summarizing occurs when you are taking study notes on textbook material. Very often you will find it helpful to summarize examples of key terms. For instance, look at the textbook passage below and the summary that follows.

> [1]In some circumstances, the most effective way of coping with stress is **withdrawal**—avoiding the situation. [2]A person at an amusement park who is overcome by anxiety when just looking at a roller coaster can walk on to a less threatening ride or even leave the park entirely. [3]A woman whose promotion depends on temporarily relocating might simply quit her job and join another company. [4]Or she might withdraw emotionally from the stressful situation by deciding that promotion no longer matters to her and that she has already advanced in her career as far as she wants to go.

Summary

Withdrawal—coping with stress by avoiding the situation. For example, a person made anxious by being near a roller coaster can walk elsewhere.

Note that a textbook definition of a key term (such as *withdrawal*) should generally not be summarized, but should be worded in the language chosen by the author. On the other hand, it usually makes sense to summarize the supporting information. Summarizing often involves two steps:

1 *Select* one example from several that might be given. Which example you select is up to you, as long as it makes the term clear for you. In the summary above, the example about the roller coaster has been chosen to illustrate withdrawal.

2 *Condense* the example if it's not already very brief. Notice that the example about the roller coaster has been condensed from a very long sentence to a short one.

A definition of a key term followed by one condensed example is a very useful way to take notes—especially in introductory college courses, where many terms are defined and illustrated.

> *Study Hint:* If you have a textbook chapter to learn, very often you can get what you need by doing two things: 1) writing down the definitions in the chapter along with summarized examples of the definitions, and 2) writing down lists of major supporting details and any minor details that you think are important.

Summarizing a Passage

Read the selection below, taken from an introductory textbook for a college social science course. As is often the case in such introductory texts, a new term is presented and then followed by an extended example. Complete the study notes by circling the letter of the answer choice that best summarizes that example.

[1]Bureaucracies have become a part of modern life because they are a powerful form of social organization. [2]Once in existence, however, they tend to take on a life of their own. [3]In a process called **goal displacement**, an organization continues even after it achieves its goal and no longer has a reason to go on. [4]A classic example is the National Foundation for the March of Dimes, organized in the 1930s to fight polio. [5]At that time, the origin of polio was a mystery. [6]Parents lived in fear because no one knew whose child might be stricken next with this crippling disease. [7]To raise money to discover the cause and a cure, the March of Dimes placed posters of children on crutches near cash registers in almost every store in the United States. [8]The U.S. public took the campaign to heart and contributed heavily. [9]The organization raised money beyond its wildest dreams. [10]During the 1950s, Dr. Jonas Salk developed a vaccine for polio, and this threat was wiped out almost overnight.

[11]What then? [12]Did the organization fold? [13]After all, its purpose had been fulfilled. [14]But, of course, the March of Dimes is still around. [15]Faced with the loss of their jobs, the professional staff that ran the organization quickly found a way to keep its bureaucracy intact by pursuing a new enemy—birth defects. [16]Their choice of enemy is striking, for it is doubtful that we will ever run out of birth defects—and thus unlikely that these people will ever run out of jobs.

Study notes

Goal displacement—An organization finds a way to continue even after it achieves its goal and no longer has a reason to go on.

Example—

A. A classic example is the National Foundation for the March of Dimes, organized in the 1930s to fight polio.
B. After the March of Dimes achieved its goal of wiping out polio, it found a way to continue by taking on a new enemy, birth defects.
C. The March of Dimes successfully raised money to discover a cause and cure for polio, and when Dr. Jonas Salk developed a vaccine for polio, the threat was wiped out almost overnight.

Explanation

Useful study notes should clearly show how an example illustrates a new term. In the case of the paragraph above, the notes should include the key point that an organization finds a way to continue even after reaching its goal. Neither answer A nor answer C explains how the organization in question, the March of Dimes, found a way to continue. Answer B does, so it is the correct answer. Remember, the purpose of an example is to make a definition clear.

PRACTICE 3

Read each textbook selection below. Then complete the study notes by circling the letter of the answer that best summarizes an example of the term being defined.

A. ¹People deceive themselves in various ways to cope better with problems. ²One such way is **denial**, the unconscious refusal to recognize a painful or threatening reality. ³One researcher cites the example of a woman who was near death from severe burns. ⁴At first, she was depressed and frightened, but after a few days she began to feel sure that she would soon be able to return home and care for her children, although all her medical indications were to the contrary. ⁵By denying the extent of her injuries, this woman was able to stay calm and cheerful. ⁶She was not merely putting on an act for her relatives and friends; she actually believed she would recover. ⁷In another situation, researchers interviewed the parents of children who were dying of leukemia. ⁸Some parents denied their children's condition; others accepted it. ⁹Physical examinations revealed that those who denied the illness did not have the physiological symptoms of stress, such as excessive stomach acid, found in those who accepted their children's illness.

Study notes

Denial—the unconscious refusal to recognize a painful or threatening reality.

Example—

A. Being near death from extreme burns depressed and frightened a woman.
B. According to all the medical indications, the woman who had suffered severe burns was near death.
C. By refusing to believe her burn injuries were deadly, a woman near death was able to stay calm and cheerful.

B. ¹Imagine a ball lying on a level table. ²Left alone, the ball stays where it is. ³Given a gentle push, the ball rolls a short way and then comes to a stop. ⁴The smoother the ball and the tabletop, the farther the ball rolls before stopping. ⁵Suppose that we have a perfectly round ball and a perfectly smooth and level tabletop, and that no air is present to slow down the ball. ⁶If the table is infinitely long and we give the ball a push, will it ever stop rolling? ⁷In fact, we can reasonably expect that under ideal conditions the ball would keep rolling forever. ⁸This conclusion was first reached by Galileo and later stated by Newton as the first law of motion: An object will continue in its state of rest or of motion in a straight line at constant speed if the object does not interact with anything else.

Study notes

Newton's first law of motion—an object will continue in its state of rest or of motion in a straight line at constant speed if the object does not interact with anything else.

Example—

A. If a ball lying on a level table is given a gentle push, it won't roll too far.
B. A perfectly round ball on an endless table won't move if left alone, but can roll forever if pushed.
C. Galileo first came to a conclusion which Newton later stated as his first law of motion.

PRACTICE 4

Read each textbook selection below. Then take study notes by 1) writing down the key term and its definition, 2) selecting an example that makes the definition clear, and 3) writing that example in your notes, condensing it if possible.

A. [1]**Passive listening** occurs when a listener tries to make sense out of a speaker's remarks without being able to interact with the speaker. [2]Probably the most familiar example of passive listening would be students hearing an instructor's lecture without having the opportunity to ask questions or otherwise interact with the speaker. [3]Passive listening also takes place in interpersonal settings, as when one person dominates a conversation while the others fall into the role of audience members, or when some parents lecture their children without allowing them to respond.

Study notes

_____ _ _____

_____

Example—_____

_____

B. [1]In an attempt to convince ourselves and others that the positive face we show to the world is true, we tend to judge ourselves in the most generous terms possible. [2]Social scientists have labeled this tendency the **self-serving bias**. [3]On one hand, when others suffer, we often blame the problem on their personal qualities. [4]On the other hand, when we suffer, we blame the problem on forces outside ourselves. [5]Consider a few examples. [6]When *they* botch a job, we might think they were not listening well or trying hard enough; when *we* botch a job, the problem was unclear directions or not enough time. [7]When *he* lashes out angrily, we say he's being moody; when *we* lash out angrily, it's because of the pressure we've been under. [8]When *she* gets caught speeding, we say she should have been more careful; when *we* get caught speeding, we deny that we were driving too fast, or we say, "Everybody does it."

Study notes

_____ — _____

_____

Example—_____

_____

A Final Note

This chapter has centered on supporting details as they appear in well-organized paragraphs. But keep in mind that supporting details are part of readings of any length, including selections that may not have an easy-to-follow list of one major detail after another. Starting with the reading at the end of this chapter (page 125), you will be given practice in answering all kinds of questions about key supporting details. These questions will develop your ability to pay close attention to what you are reading.

CHAPTER REVIEW

In this chapter, you learned the following:

- Major and minor details provide the added information you need to make sense of a main idea.

- List words and addition words can help you to find major and minor supporting details.

- Outlining, mapping, and summarizing are useful note-taking strategies.

- Outlines show the relationship between the main idea, major details, and minor details of a passage.

- Maps are very visual outlines.

- Writing a definition and summarizing an example is a good way to take notes on a new term.

The next chapter—Chapter 4—will show you how to find implied main ideas and central points.

On the Web: If you are using this book in class, you can visit our website for additional practice in identifying supporting details. Go to **www.townsendpress.com** and click on "Learning Center."

REVIEW TEST 1

To review what you've learned in this chapter, answer each of these questions about supporting details.

1. *Fill in the blanks:* Major supporting details are more *(general, specific)* _____ than main ideas. Minor supporting details are more *(general, specific)* _____ than major details.

2. _____ TRUE OR FALSE? Supporting details can be reasons, examples, facts, or other specific information.

3. Outlining is a way to show at a glance the relationship between a main idea and its _____.

4. In _____, you create a visual outline using circles, boxes, and other shapes to set off main ideas and supporting details.

5. When taking notes on textbook material, you will often find it useful to write out each definition in full and then select and _____ one example of that definition.

REVIEW TEST 2

A. (1–7.) Complete the outline of the following paragraph by adding words to the main idea and filling in the missing major and minor details. Note that addition words introduce the major details and some of the minor details as well.

> [1]Several factors influence the justice system's treatment of criminals. [2]For one thing, the sex of offenders affects the severity of sentences. [3]A woman is less likely to receive the death penalty than a man. [4]Also, the court is more reluctant to send a mother to prison than a father. [5]Another factor in the treatment of offenders is their race. [6]Nonwhites are awarded parole and probation less often. [7]In addition, blacks are executed more often for capital crimes. [8]Finally, the age of offenders is considered in sentencing. [9]Young offenders are given special treatment. [10]And the elderly are given more lenient sentences.

Main idea: _____ influence the justice system's treatment of criminals.

Major detail: **1.** _____

   Minor details: a. Woman less likely to receive death penalty than a man

   b. _____

Major detail: **2.** _____

   Minor details: a. _____

   b. _____

Major detail: **3.** Age of offenders considered in sentencing

   Minor details: a. _____

   b. More lenient sentences for the elderly

B. (8–10.) Answer the questions about supporting details that follow the passage. Note that the main idea is boldfaced.

> [1]More than one anthropologist has taken the time to explore old cemeteries in New England and look at the gravestones there. [2]**The anthropologists discovered that over different time periods, there were three different types of images carved on the gravestones.** [3]The first, which appears on the oldest stones (from the 1600s into the mid-1700s), is the death's head: a grinning skull. [4]The death's head corresponds with the pessimistic view of life and death held by the Puritans that populated New England at that time. [5]But as more liberal thought took hold in New England in the mid-1700s, another image began to be seen on headstones. [6]This was a cherub—a smiling, baby-faced angel. [7]The cherub seemed to represent

a more hopeful view of death and a happy afterlife in heaven. [8]In the late 1700s, there was a preference for the classic-looking urn and willow. [9]This image indicates a turn to a more intellectual and less emotional attitude toward death.

_____ 8. The addition word that signals the second major detail is
  A. *one*.
  B. *first*.
  C. *another*.
  D. *This*.

_____ 9. The list words that tell what types of details will follow are
  A. "more than one anthropologist."
  B. "old cemeteries."
  C. "three different types of images."

_____ 10. How many major supporting details are in the paragraph?
  A. Two   B. Three   C. Four

REVIEW TEST 3

A. (1–5.) Outline the following passage by completing the main idea and filling in the major supporting details.

[1]Serious depression, as opposed to the fleeting kind we all feel at times, has definite warning signs. [2]Some or all of these signs may be present within the affected individual. [3]One symptom of depression is a change in sleep patterns— either sleeplessness or sleeping too much. [4]Another sign is abnormal eating patterns, either eating too much or loss of appetite. [5]A third sign is trouble in thinking or concentrating—even to the point of finding it difficult to read a magazine or newspaper. [6]Finally, a general feeling of hopelessness may signal depression. [7]People feel indifferent to their families and jobs and may begin to think that life is not worth living.

Main idea: Serious depression has _____

  1. _____
  2. _____
  3. _____
  4. _____

B. (6–9.) Map the following paragraph by filling in the main idea and the major supporting details.

> ¹There are three common ways that people deal with their feelings. ²One way is to withhold them—to keep them inside without giving any verbal or nonverbal clues to their existence. ³Such people use "poker faces" in relationships, so that others have to guess about whether they are happy or sad inside. ⁴A second and often more appropriate way to deal with feelings is to display them—expressing them verbally or through facial or body language. ⁵For example, a person who displays feelings would cheer at a sporting event, laugh or cry at a moving scene in a movie, or openly admire an unexpected act of kindness. ⁶Displays must always be handled carefully if the feelings are negative. ⁷Often the best method of dealing with feelings is to describe them—put them into words in a calm, nonjudgmental way. ⁸If someone borrows one of your books without asking or otherwise takes advantage of you, tell him or her that makes you feel angry. ⁹If someone does you a favor, let him or her know how much you appreciate it. ¹⁰Describing feelings helps you keep open the clear lines of communication with other people.

C. (10.) Read the textbook selection below. Then complete the study notes by circling the letter of the answer choice that best summarizes the example of the term being defined.

> [1]**Cultural lag** refers to a practice or belief that once made sense and still persists even though it is no longer useful. [2]You can see an example of cultural lag every time that you eat. [3]Americans, after they cut their meat, put down the knife and switch the fork from the left hand to the right. [4]Only then do they put the food in their mouths. [5]This differs from the European practice of simply raising the food to the mouth with the fork in the left hand after cutting the meat. [6]Why did Americans develop this habit? [7]Some experts guess that in the old days of the American frontier, Americans needed to keep a hand free in case they had to grab a weapon to fight an intruder. [8]Today the frontier is gone, and putting down the knife and switching the fork to the other hand is no longer of practical use. [9]Americans continue to do it anyway, and to eat in the European style is considered to be "bad manners."

Study notes

Cultural lag—a practice or belief that once made sense and still persists even though it is no longer useful.

Example—

A. Europeans eat with a fork in the left hand, but Americans put the knife down after cutting and switch the fork to the right hand.

B. Americans consider the European style of eating with a fork in the left hand to be bad manners even though that method is more practical than switching the fork to the right hand.

C. Americans consider it correct to switch the fork to the right hand after cutting even though the supposed purpose—keeping the left hand free for a weapon—no longer exists.

REVIEW TEST 4

Here is a chance to apply your understanding of supporting details to a passage from a college textbook: *Psychology*, Second Edition, by Diane E. Papalia and Sally Wendkos Olds. Read the passage, and then answer the questions that follow.

To help you continue to strengthen your work on the skills taught in previous chapters, there are also questions on vocabulary in context and main ideas.

Words to Watch

Below are some words in the reading that do not have strong context support. Each word is followed by the number of the paragraph in which it appears and its meaning there. These words are indicated in the article by a small circle (°).

provocation (1): annoyance
loath (1): reluctant
temperament (1): emotional makeup
competence (2): skill
thrive (3): grow well
self-reliant (3): independent
assertive (3): positive and confident
detached (4): emotionally apart from others
withdrawn (4): shy

CHILD-REARING STYLES

Diane E. Papalia and Sally Wendkos Olds

1   What makes Mary burst into tears of frustration when she can't finish a jigsaw puzzle, while Gary will shrug and walk away from it, and Cary will sit with it for hours until he finishes? What makes Polly independent and Molly a clinger? What makes Tim ready to hit out at the slightest provocation° and Jim loath° to fight? One answer lies in the basic temperament° children are born with. A second very important influence on behavioral styles is the early emotional environment—how children are treated by their parents.

2   The psychologist Diana Baumrind set out to discover relationships between different styles of child rearing and the social competence° of children. She reviewed the research literature and conducted her own studies with ninety-five families of children in nursery school. Using a combination of long interviews, standardized testing, and observations at school and home, she identified three categories of parenting styles and linked them to children's behavior.

3   *Authoritative* parents exert firm control when necessary, but they explain why they take a stand and encourage children to express their opinions. They feel confident in their ability to guide their children, while respecting the children's interests, opinions, and unique personalities. They combine firm control with encouragement and love. Their children know that they are expected to perform well, fulfill commitments, and carry out duties in

the family. They know when they are meeting expectations and when it is worth risking their parents' displeasure to pursue some other goal. They seem to thrive° on their parents' reasonable expectations and realistic standards, and they are most self-reliant°, self-controlled, assertive°, exploratory, and content.

4   *Authoritarian* parents value unquestioning obedience and punish their children forcibly for not conforming to set and quite absolute standards. They are somewhat detached°, controlling, and distant. Their children tend to be discontented, withdrawn°, and distrustful of others.

5   *Permissive* parents make few demands on their children, set few rules, and hardly ever punish. As preschoolers, their children are immature—the least self-reliant, the least self-controlled, the least exploratory.

On the basis of her research, 6 Baumrind has recommended that parents who want to raise competent, socially responsible, independent children should do several things:

- Teach by example; that is, behave the way you want your children to behave.

- Reward behaviors you want to encourage and punish behaviors you want to discourage, giving explanations in both cases.

- Show interest in children.

- Bestow approval only when the child has earned it.

- Demand achievement and the meeting of standards, while being open to hearing the child's point of view.

- Encourage original thinking.

Baumrind's work raises important issues about child-rearing practices, but before we conclude that parenting is all that matters, we have to remember what children bring to the family. Through their own inborn temperaments, children influence their parents. It is possible, for example, that "easy" children will elicit an authoritative attitude from their parents, while "difficult" children may make tyrants out of theirs.

Reading Comprehension Questions

Vocabulary in Context

_____ 1. In the sentence below, the word *bestow* (bǐ-stō′) means
   A. deny.   C. accept.
   B. give.   D. risk.

> "Bestow approval only when the child has earned it." (Paragraph 6)

_____ 2. In the excerpt below, the word *elicit* (ǐ-lǐs′ǐt) means
   A. draw out.   C. imitate.
   B. dislike.   D. abuse.

> "Through their own inborn temperaments, children influence their parents. It is possible, for example, that 'easy' children will elicit an authoritative attitude from their parents, while 'difficult' children may make tyrants out of theirs." (Paragraph 7)

Main Ideas

_____ 3. The topic of paragraph 6 is
   A. Diana Baumrind.
   B. teaching by example.
   C. giving approval.
   D. raising children.

_____ 4. Which sentence best expresses the main idea of paragraph 6?
   A. "On the basis of her research, Baumrind has recommended that parents who want to raise competent, socially responsible, independent children should do several things:"
   B. "Teach by example, that is, behave the way you want your children to behave."
   C. "Reward behaviors you want to encourage and punish behaviors you want to discourage, giving explanations in both cases."
   D. "Demand achievement and the meeting of standards, while being open to hearing the child's point of view."

Supporting Details

5. Complete the sentence: To study the ninety-five families of children in nursery school, Baumrind used standardized tests, observations at school and at home, and _____.

6–10.   Complete the following outline of parts of the reading by filling in the blanks.

A.   Two influences on how a child behaves

1. _____

2. _____

B.   Three parenting styles

1. _____

2. _____

3. _____

Discussion Questions

1.   What type of parenting style did you grow up with? Would you say this style was effective? Why or why not?

2.   Why do you think Diana Baumrind feels that teaching by example is useful?

3.   Baumrind encourages parents to show interest in children. What are some ways in which parents can show interest in children?

4.   The authors feel that children are born with "their own inborn temperaments." Has your experience with children confirmed or contradicted their idea that children have different temperaments, starting from the time they are born? Give some examples.

Note: Writing assignments for this selection appear on pages 622–623.

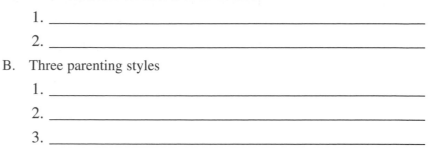

Check Your Performance   SUPPORTING DETAILS

Activity		Number Right	Points	Score
Review Test 1	(5 items)	_____	× 2 =	_____
Review Test 2	(10 items)	_____	× 3 =	_____
Review Test 3	(10 items)	_____	× 3 =	_____
Review Test 4	(10 items)	_____	× 3 =	_____
		TOTAL SCORE	=	_____ %

Enter your total score into the **Reading Performance Chart: Review Tests** on the inside back cover.

SUPPORTING DETAILS: Mastery Test 1

A. (1–6.) Complete the outline of the following textbook passage by adding the main idea and the missing major or minor details.

> [1]Divorce has serious negative consequences. [2]First, social adjustment after the divorce is a troublesome time. [3]The former couple often finds that starting to date again can be nerve-racking. [4]Also, married friends may exclude singles from social plans. [5]Secondly, emotional difficulties among the original family members are common. [6]Feelings of guilt and resentment may persist between the former husband and wife. [7]At the same time, children may be confused and hurt; many also feel guilty, imagining that they were somehow to blame for the divorce. [8]A third consequence is that financial adjustments are necessary. [9]Alimony, child support, and property dispersal must be dealt with. [10]Also, the high fees that lawyers charge can be a burden.

Main idea: _____.

   Major detail: **1.** Social adjustment is troublesome.

     Minor details: a. _____

                     _____

                     b. Married friends may exclude singles from social plans.

   Major detail: **2.** _____

                     _____

     Minor details: a. _____

                     _____

                     b. Children may be confused and hurt and feel guilty.

   Major detail: **3.** _____

     Minor details: a. _____

                     _____

                     _____

                     b. High fees charged by lawyers can be a burden.

(Continues on next page)

B. (7–10.) Answer the questions about supporting details that follow the passage.

[1]When we call someone "pig" or "swine," we do not mean it as a compliment. [2]But pigs do not deserve to be used as a symbol for an insult. [3]They are probably not as dirty as they are made out to be. [4]According to one pig keeper, swine are very clean when allowed to live in a clean environment. [5]He feels that pigs are usually dirty simply because their keepers don't clean their pens. [6]In any case, no one has proven that the pig that wallows in mud prefers that to a cool bath. [7]Furthermore, pigs are smarter than most people think. [8]Many farmers, for example, have observed that pigs frequently undo complicated bolts on gates in search of adventure or romance. [9]So the next time you call someone a pig, perhaps he or she ought to be someone you wish to praise.

_____ 7. In general, the major details of this passage are
   A. reasons why pigs are dirty.
   B. reasons why pigs should not be used as symbols for insults.
   C. ways to insult or compliment people.

_____ 8. Specifically, the major details are
   A. Pigs are probably not as dirty as people think; pigs are smarter than most people think.
   B. Pigs may be dirty because their pens are dirty; it hasn't been proved that pigs prefer mud to a cool bath; pigs have been seen undoing complicated bolts.
   C. People use "pig" and "swine" as insults; "pig" and "swine" should be considered praise.

_____ 9. One pig keeper feels that pigs will stay clean if they are
   A. given baths.
   B. praised.
   C. kept in a clean environment.

10. What example is used to show that pigs are smarter than they are often thought to be? _____

_____

SUPPORTING DETAILS: Mastery Test 2

A. Answer the questions about supporting details that follow the textbook passage.

[1]A **social dilemma** is a situation in which the most rewarding short-term choice for an individual will ultimately lead to negative outcomes for all concerned. [2]For example, as you hike along a beautiful mountain trail, you stop for a snack. [3]You are tempted to throw away your empty water containers and granola bar wrappers, knowing that your backpack will be lighter if you don't have to carry your trash to the top of the mountain and back. [4]But you hesitate, knowing that if all hikers litter the trail, it will soon be unpleasant for all who use it. [5]Or consider the situation of many communities in the Southwest that have suffered severe drought for years, so that water conservation is essential. [6]Individuals living in such drought-stricken areas face personal decisions. [7]For instance, should I forgo the pleasure of a long shower today so that there will be more water for all in the future?

_____ 1. The main idea is expressed in sentence
    A. 1.
    B. 2.
    C. 7.

_____ 2. In general, the major supporting details of this paragraph are
    A. rewarding short-term choices.
    B. examples of social dilemmas.
    C. examples of negative outcomes.

_____ 3. How many major details are in this paragraph?
    A. Two
    B. Three
    C. Four

_____ 4. The second major detail of the paragraph begins in sentence
    A. 1.
    B. 2.
    C. 5.

_____ 5. In the Southwest, the desire to take a long shower presents a social dilemma because
    A. a pleasant long shower could mean less water for others.
    B. the water is polluted.
    C. water costs more there, so long showers are expensive.

(Continues on next page)

_____ 6. Which summary best completes the study notes of the paragraph?

> Social dilemma—a situation in which the most rewarding short-term choice for an individual will ultimately lead to negative outcomes for all concerned.
>
> **Example—**
> A. Littering a beautiful trail is tempting, but would soon make for an unpleasant trail for all.
> B. Littering a beautiful trail is convenient because then you wouldn't have to carry trash to the top of the mountain and back.
> C. To avoid littering when hiking in public places, carry empty containers and wrappers until you get to a trash can.

B. (7–10.) Complete the outline of the textbook passage by filling in the missing main idea and major details, including a brief explanation of each. One explanation has been done for you.

> [1]The three types of human memory allow a person to remove or retain information, as needed. [2]Everything that we notice—see, smell, hear, or touch—forms a brief mental impression called a sensory memory. [3]Information is stored in this sensory memory for only a few tenths of a second before it disappears forever. [4]Information that is retained for slightly longer enters what's called short-term memory. [5]This form of memory can store about seven items for about thirty seconds—about enough information to dial a telephone number. [6]In order to be remembered for a long period, information must pass into long-term memory. [7]No one knows just how much information can be stored in a person's long-term memory, but the capacity seems enormous.

Main idea: _____

_____.

   1. _____—stores memory for a few tenths of a second.

   2. _____

       _____

   3. _____

SUPPORTING DETAILS: Mastery Test 3

A. Answer the questions about supporting details that follow the textbook passage.

¹Contemporary American society has a variety of markers of entrance into adulthood. ²There are legal definitions: at 17, young people may enlist in the armed forces; at age 18, in most states, they may marry without their parents' permission; at 18 to 21 (depending on the state), they may enter into binding contracts. ³Using sociological definitions, people may call themselves adults when they are self-supporting or have chosen a career, have married or formed a significant relationship, or have founded a family. ⁴There are also psychological definitions. ⁵Cognitive maturity is often considered to correspond with the capacity for abstract thought. ⁶Emotional maturity may depend on such achievements as discovering one's identity, becoming independent of parents, developing a system of values, and forming relationships. ⁷Some people never leave adolescence, no matter what their chronological age.

_____ 1. The main idea is expressed in sentence
    A. 1.
    B. 2.
    C. 3.

_____ 2. The paragraph is made up of a series of
    A. types of adults.
    B. definitions of adulthood.
    C. stages of adulthood.

_____ 3. The second major detail of the paragraph is introduced in sentence
    A. 3.
    B. 4.
    C. 5.

_____ 4. Sentence 4 contains
    A. the main idea.
    B. a major supporting detail.
    C. a minor supporting detail.

_____ 5. Sentences 5–7 contain
    A. major supporting details.
    B. minor supporting details.

_____ 6. Which is the best outline of the paragraph?

    A. Markers for adulthood
      1. Legal definitions
      2. Sociological definitions
      3. Psychological definitions
      4. Cognitive maturity
      5. Emotional maturity

    B. Markers for adulthood
      1. Age when entering the armed forces or marrying without parents' permission
      2. Age when self-supporting or when starting a family
      3. Age of discovering one's identity or learning to think abstractly

    C. Markers for adulthood
      1. Legal definitions
      2. Sociological definitions
      3. Psychological definitions

B. (7–10.) Outline the following textbook passage by filling in the main idea and the major supporting details. Condense the major details.

[1]Chimpanzees, skillful tool-users, use several objects found in their environment as tools. [2]First of all, they use sticks. [3]They have been seen inserting carefully trimmed sticks into termite mounds and then withdrawing the sticks and eating the termites that cling to them; they also are known to use sticks to steal honey from beehives. [4]In addition, chimps use leaves in a variety of ingenious ways. [5]For example, they have been seen rolling leaves into cones to use as drinking cups, dampening them and using them to clean their bodies, and chewing them until they can serve as sponges. [6]Finally, chimpanzees have been observed using stones to crack open nuts.

Main idea: _____

_____.

    1. _____

       _____

    2. _____

    3. _____

SUPPORTING DETAILS: Mastery Test 4

A. (1–5.) Outline the following textbook passage by filling in the main idea and a brief statement of each major supporting detail.

[1]After studying all night for an important exam, most college students find themselves wishing for one thing after their big test: sleep. [2]Although the exact reasons why people sleep are still being debated, researchers have come up with a number of theories to explain the functions of sleep. [3]First of all, sleep is believed to give the body time to repair burned-out brain cells and make more of the special chemical that makes it possible for the brain to think. [4]Another theory holds that sleep enables the body to save energy because when we sleep, the body temperature is lower, so less energy is needed to create heat. [5]This method of energy conservation may have helped people survive thousands of years ago when food was hard to find. [6]Sleep may also have helped humanity survive by keeping people out of trouble. [7]In prehistoric times, when many large predators like the saber-toothed tiger hunted in darkness, the habit of sleeping at night helped prevent people from being an animal's dinner. [8]Scientists also believe that sleep, in addition to being a survival tactic, is used to reduce memory. [9]It allows the brain to forget or unlearn things that are not necessary. [10]Otherwise, the mind would become cluttered and overwhelmed with unneeded information.

Main idea: _____

_____.

1. _____

   _____

2. _____

3. _____

4. _____

B. (6.) Read the textbook excerpt below. Then complete the study notes on the next page by circling the letter of the best summary of the supporting details.

[1]The **multiplier effect** refers to any change in one part of our economic system that creates changes elsewhere. [2]For example, if a university decides to build a new dormitory, some construction workers will have more income. [3]If some of these workers decide to spend the extra income on new boats, boat-builders will have more income. [4]The boat-builders, in turn, might spend this income in neighborhood restaurants, and the restaurant owners might spend it on cars. [5]Money never stays in one place, and every market decision has an impact on other markets.

(Continues on next page)

Study notes

Multiplier effect—Any change in one part of our economic system that creates changes elsewhere.

Example—

A. The decision to build a new university dormitory will lead to work for some construction workers.

B. Our economic system is very complicated.

C. Building a dorm allows construction workers to buy boats, giving boat-builders money for restaurants, and so on.

C. Answer the questions about supporting details that follow the textbook passage.

¹Studies done in the 1930s in New Guinea by the social scientist Margaret Mead show that not all cultures share our views of the differences between the sexes. ²The mountain people called the Arapesh, for example, do not think men and women are different in temperament. ³They expect both sexes to be equally gentle, home-loving, and what we would call "maternal" in their relations with others. ⁴The neighboring Mundugumor people, by contrast, are as fierce as the Arapesh are gentle. ⁵Men and women are equally "macho," paying less attention to their children than to plotting for power and position. ⁶A third tribe, the Tchambuli, do believe the sexes are different in temperament, but their sex roles are the reverse of ours. ⁷Tchambuli women are the practical, hard-headed providers, while the men of the tribe spend their days beautifying themselves and looking for approval from the women.

_____ 7. Sentence 1 provides

A. the main idea.

B. a major supporting detail.

C. a minor supporting detail.

_____ 8. In general, the major supporting details of this paragraph are

A. differences between the sexes.

B. examples of differing cultural views of the sexes.

C. a series of stereotypes about Western culture.

_____ 9. How many major details are in this paragraph?

A. Two

B. Three

C. Four

_____ 10. The Arapesh do not think that men and women are

A. equally gentle.

B. "maternal."

C. different in temperament.

SUPPORTING DETAILS: Mastery Test 5

A. Answer the questions that follow the textbook passage.

[1]Suburbs arose out of a complex set of social factors. [2]One factor was the economic and technological developments that made it possible for people to live far from where they worked. [3]Early in this century, most people were limited in where they could live by the need to find transportation to work. [4]This meant that most had to live in the cities near where the jobs were. [5]Because there were relatively few automobiles and highways, people walked or used public transportation to get to work and go shopping. [6]This encouraged the concentration of population, and central cities served as the commercial and cultural core of urban areas. [7]By the 1940s and 1950s, the increasing prosperity of many Americans, along with the automobile, made it possible for them to live farther from work and opened up suburban life to middle-class Americans.

[8]In addition, government policy was also a factor contributing to suburbanization. [9]First of all, the government paid 80 percent of the cost of developing the interstate highway system. [10]With cars and high-speed highways, people can now live far from where they work and shop. [11]In sprawling cities such as Los Angeles, for example, it is common to live fifty or more miles from where you work. [12]Also, government agencies made available federally guaranteed mortgage loans for the purchase of new homes. [13]Because land outside of the cities was both inexpensive and available, this is where much of the construction took place.

_____ 1. In general, the major details of this passage are
   A. economic developments that led to the growth of suburbs.
   B. factors that contributed to suburbanization.
   C. ways the government helped suburbs to develop.

_____ 2. Specifically, the major details of the passage are
   A. suburbs; cities.
   B. central cities; federally guaranteed mortgage loans for new homes.
   C. economic and technological developments; government policy.

_____ 3. Sentence 1 provides
   A. the main idea of the passage.
   B. a major detail of the passage.
   C. a minor detail of the passage.

(Continues on next page)

_____ 4. Sentence 8 provides
    A. the main idea of the passage.
    B. a major detail of the passage.
    C. a minor detail of the passage.

_____ 5. Sentence 12 provides
    A. the main idea of the passage.
    B. a major detail of the passage.
    C. a minor detail of the passage.

B. (6–10.) Complete the map of the following textbook passage by filling in the main idea and the four major supporting details.

> ¹Through the years, experts in our country have suggested various purposes of imprisonment. ²Prior to 1800 it was widely assumed that the punishment of those who did not follow society's rules was necessary if the community was to feel morally satisfied. ³In recent years there has been a renewed interest in punishment—not for the sake of vengeance, but to restore a sense of moral order. ⁴During the last century and a half, a second purpose of imprisonment has been rehabilitation. ⁵In this view, crime resembles "disease," something foreign and abnormal to most people. ⁶It is presumed that individuals are not to blame for the disease, and that we should focus on curing them. ⁷Another purpose of imprisonment has been to deter crime. ⁸Some studies suggest that the certainty of arrest and punishment does tend to lower crime rates. ⁹Last, some argue that neither rehabilitation nor deterrence really works, so that it is useless to send people to prison with these goals in mind. ¹⁰Instead, imprisonment should be used as selective confinement, reducing crime rates by keeping "hard-core" criminals off the streets. ¹¹One study of young men in Philadelphia showed that 6 percent of the men were responsible for over half the crimes committed by the entire group.

SUPPORTING DETAILS: Mastery Test 6

A. (1–6.) Outline the following textbook passage by filling in the missing major and minor details.

> [1]Certain significant differences exist between the House and the Senate. [2]The most obvious difference, of course, is size—the House has 435 members and the Senate 100. [3]This factor leads to differences in style. [4]Perhaps, as one author has stated, "the most striking difference noticed by most visitors to the Capitol is the apparent formality and impersonality in the House chamber as contrasted to the relatively informal and friendly atmosphere in the Senate." [5]Size also influences the procedures followed by the House and the Senate. [6]House rules are many and complex; Senate rules are short and relatively simple. [7]House rules, for example, sharply limit the time in which a member may speak during a debate, whereas senators are subject to few limits.
>
> [8]Another difference between the two houses of Congress is the political outlook of their members. [9]Most representatives have smaller constituencies; each speaks for the residents of a particular district. [10]The representative's concerns, therefore, are often limited to local issues that are of interest to fewer groups. [11]Senators have statewide constituencies. [12]As a result, they must keep in mind the interests of a variety of groups.
>
> [13]A further major difference between the two houses of Congress derives from the different terms of office of their members (two years in the House, six years in the Senate). [14]This means that most representatives are campaigning almost all the time, whereas senators have more time before they must seek reelection. [15]As a result, senators can pay more attention to aspects of legislation that do not directly affect their chances of winning or losing voters' support.

Main idea: Significant differences exist between the House and the Senate.

A. Differences in size: 435 in House vs. 100 in Senate
  1. Style differences
     a. Formal style in the House
     b. _____
  2. _____
     a. _____
     b. _____
B. _____
  1. _____
  2. Statewide outlook of senators
C. Differences in terms of office: 2 years in House vs. 6 years in Senate
  1. Constant campaigning of representatives
  2. More time for senators to spend on legislation not affecting their campaigns

(Continues on next page)

B. (7–10.) Complete the map of the following textbook passage by filling in the main idea and the missing major supporting details.

¹To a greater or lesser extent, all of us have learned aggressive responses. ²We are each a potential aggressor. ³A number of conditions have been found to stimulate aggression. ⁴For one thing, pain—both mental and physical— heightens aggressiveness. ⁵Any decidedly hurtful event, whether a big disappointment, a personal insult, or a physical pain, can incite an emotional outburst. ⁶Environmental irritants can also stimulate aggression. ⁷The most studied environmental irritant is heat. ⁸Studies have found that, compared with students who answered questionnaires in a room with a normal temperature, those who did so in an uncomfortably hot room (over 90° F) reported feeling more tired and aggressive and expressed more hostility toward a stranger they were asked to rate. ⁹A third condition, one that especially provokes aggression, is attacks by another. ¹⁰Experiments confirm that attacks bring counterattacks, especially when the victim perceives the attack as intentional. ¹¹Finally, crowding—the feeling of not having enough space—can be stressful. ¹²The stress experienced by animals allowed to overpopulate a confined environment produces heightened aggressiveness. ¹³And it is undeniably true that dense urban areas suffer higher rates of crime and emotional distress.

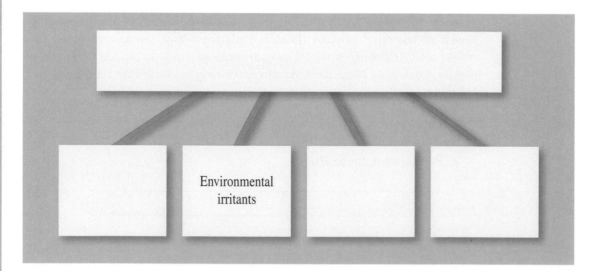

4 Implied Main Ideas

"The others are complaining that you don't leave any coffee for anyone else."

In Chapters 2 and 3, you learned the two basic parts of anything you read: a *main idea* and the *supporting details* that explain and develop that idea. As you have seen, the main idea may be clearly stated in one sentence of a selection.

However, sometimes the main idea is **implied**—only suggested by the supporting details and not clearly stated in one sentence. The reader must figure out such an implied main idea by considering the supporting details. In the above cartoon, you can figure out the implied main idea by noting the details: the man's coworkers are complaining that he doesn't leave coffee for anyone else; also, he has such a caffeine high that he is flying! The clearly implied idea is that he is drinking too much coffee.

This chapter offers practice in finding implied main ideas, whether in paragraphs or in longer selections.

Implied Main Ideas in Paragraphs

Sometimes a selection lacks a sentence that directly states the main idea. In such cases, the author has simply decided to let the details of the selection suggest the main idea. You must figure out what that implied idea is by deciding upon the point all the details support. For example, read the following paragraph.

> [1]All people are concerned about a few great questions: the existence of God, the purpose of life, the existence of an afterlife, and morality. [2]About the first, science has nothing to say: no test tube has either proved or disproved God's existence. [3]As to the purpose of life, although science can provide a definition of life and describe the characteristics of living organisms, it has nothing to say about ultimate purpose. [4]Regarding an afterlife, science can offer no information, for it has no tests that it can use to detect a "hereafter." [5]As for the question of morality, science can demonstrate the consequences of behavior but not the *moral* superiority of one action compared with another. [6]Science cannot even prove that loving your family and neighbor is superior to hurting and killing them.

The above paragraph has no good "umbrella" statement that covers all of the other sentences. To decide on the main idea, we must ask the same three questions we've already used to find main ideas:

- ● "Who or what is this paragraph about?"
- ● "What is the main point the author is trying to make about that topic?"
- ● And when we think we know the main point, we can test it by asking, "Does *all or most* of the material in the paragraph support this idea?"

In the paragraph above, all of the details are about science and great human concerns, so that must be the topic. Which of the following statements expresses the general point that the author is trying to make about the topic? Check (✔) the answer you think is correct.

_____   A.   Science alone cannot tell us about the four main concerns that all people have.

_____   B.   Science alone has not contributed any answer to the question of whether God exists.

_____   C.   There is no scientific data on whether there is life after death.

_____   D.   Science alone cannot provide us with any guidance on whether we should love our neighbor as ourselves.

The details reveal the author's general point to be answer A: science alone cannot tell us about the four main concerns that all people have. All the other statements on the previous page are supporting details for this main idea. Although the main idea is not directly stated, it is clearly implied by all the material in the paragraph.

Figuring Out Implied Main Ideas in Paragraphs

To find implied main ideas, it often helps to decide on the topic first. Do so by asking yourself, "Who or what is the selection about?" After you find the topic, then ask yourself, "What is the author's main point about the topic?"

✔ *Check Your Understanding*

Read the following selection, and then try to answer the questions that follow.

[1]The original intention of a school worksheet was intelligent: to discover which students didn't understand the reading lesson, so the teacher could work with them individually. [2]Unfortunately, the teacher had to keep the rest of the class busy while doing that, so more worksheets were passed out. [3]The assessment tool soon turned into a crowd control device. [4]To make matters worse, the worksheets multiplied faster than the loaves and fishes, often reaching 1,000 per child per school year. [5]But research shows no connection between the number of worksheets a student does and how good a reader the child eventually becomes. [6]If you're fed reading as six worksheets a day, 1,000 sheets a year, under the pronouncement, "Boys and girls, it's time for reading," by the time you reach fourth grade you think worksheets *are* reading, and you mistakenly think you hate reading.

_____ 1. What is the topic of the above paragraph?
   A. School worksheets
   B. Books
   C. Teaching tools
   D. Crowd control devices

_____ 2. Which statement best expresses the unstated main idea of this paragraph?
   A. School worksheets may do more harm than good.
   B. Reading is one of the most difficult skills for teachers to teach and students to learn.
   C. Over the years, school worksheets have served as both an assessment tool and a crowd control device.
   D. Teachers have a variety of teaching tools to choose from.

Explanation

The topic, referred to in a number of sentences in the paragraph, is school worksheets. The implied main idea about worksheets is that they may do more harm than good.

When you think you have determined an implied main idea, test yourself by asking, "Does all or most of the material in the paragraph support this idea?" In this paragraph, the author (Jim Trelease, in his book *The Read-Aloud Handbook*) describes how worksheets turned into a student control device and multiplied out of control. He also notes that research has showed no benefit from worksheets and that students given too many worksheets may wind up thinking they "hate reading." So the paragraph clearly supports the idea that worksheets may do more harm than good.

PRACTICE 1

Read each paragraph, and then answer the questions that follow. Remember to find a topic by asking "Who or what is the selection about?" and to find an implied main idea by asking "What is the author's point about the topic?"

> *Hint:* Noticing addition words (such as *first, another, also, moreover,* and *finally*) will help you identify the major supporting details that can suggest the main idea.

Paragraph 1

¹Are you one of the millions of people who are terrified of going to the dentist? ²You should know that some dentists actually specialize in treating people who are very fearful of dental work. ³These dentists encourage patients to discuss their fears and will answer questions in an honest, understanding manner. ⁴Even if your dentist does not have such a specialty, you can arrange with him or her to use a signal, such as raising your right hand, if you experience too much pain. ⁵This will give you a feeling of control and the assurance that the pain—if any—will not go beyond what you can tolerate. ⁶You can also try the relaxation technique of breathing deeply, before and during appointments. ⁷A last good idea is to bring headphones and listen to your favorite music in the dental chair. ⁸It's hard for the brain to register pain when your favorite rap group or classical musician is filling your head.

_____ 1. What is the topic of the above paragraph?
A. Dentists
B. Ways to relax
C. Better communication with your dentist
D. Less scary dental visits

_____ 2. Which statement best expresses the unstated main idea?
   A. Millions of people are frightened of visits to the dentist.
   B. There are ways to make visits to the dentist less painful and frightening.
   C. There are dentists who specialize in treating patients who are very fearful of dental work.
   D. If you are frightened of going to the dentist, try the relaxation technique of breathing deeply before and during appointments.

Paragraph 2

¹Mining coal is dangerous to the miner and usually leaves large areas of land unfit for further use. ²Acid rain from the burning of coal harms plant and animal life on a large scale. ³Also, the air pollution from the same source damages the health of millions of people. ⁴Moreover, coal-burning power plants expose the people living around them to more radioactivity, from traces of uranium, thorium, and radon in their smoke, than nuclear plants do. ⁵Most estimates put the number of deaths in the United States from cancer and respiratory diseases caused by burning coal at over ten thousand per year.

_____ 3. What is the topic of the above paragraph?
   A. Air pollution
   B. Mining
   C. Effects of acid rain
   D. Drawbacks of coal

_____ 4. Which statement best expresses the unstated main idea?
   A. Coal is far from being a desirable fuel.
   B. Acid rain is a major environmental problem.
   C. More people are dying from cancer and respiratory diseases than at any time in the past.
   D. Air pollution has become our largest single environmental problem today.

Paragraph 3

¹Scientists count such animals as elephants, timber wolves, ducks, and whistling swans by flying over them and counting them. ²Small animals such as field mice are counted by trapping every single one in a given area and then counting them. ³Microscopic creatures are gathered in a sample and counted little by little under a microscope. ⁴Songbirds are counted by people walking through every part of a certain area at the same time, with each person counting every single songbird seen in his or her assigned space.

_____ 5. What is the topic of the above paragraph?
   A. Counting microscopic creatures
   B. Counting
   C. Methods of counting animals
   D. Scientists who count animals

_____ 6. Which statement best expresses the unstated main idea?
   A. There are various reasons for counting the population of certain types of animals.
   B. The methods scientists use to count animals vary according to the species.
   C. The microscope is one of the tools used by biologists in counting the populations of species.
   D. Biologists face many difficult tasks in studying the large variety of animal life on Earth.

PRACTICE 2

The main idea of each of the following paragraphs is unstated, and each paragraph is followed by four sentences. In the space provided, write the letter of the sentence that best expresses each unstated main idea.

Remember to consider carefully all of the information given and to ask yourself the following two questions:

● Who or what is the selection about? (In other words, what is the topic?)

● What is the author's main point about that topic? (In other words, what is the implied main idea?)

Then test your answer by asking:

● Does *all or most* of the material in the paragraph support this idea?

Paragraph 1

[1]The work homemakers do is essential to the economy. [2]The estimated value of the cleaning, cooking, nursing, shopping, child care, home maintenance, money management, errands, entertaining, and other services homemakers perform has been estimated at equal to roughly one-fourth of the gross national product. [3]In fact, the Commerce Department's Bureau of Economic Analysis has proposed a revision of the gross national product that would take into account the value of the homemaker's services. [4]But homemaking is not formal employment that brings money or prestige. [5]No financial compensation is associated with this position, and the *Dictionary of Occupational Titles* places mothering and homemaking skills in the lowest category of skills, lower than the occupation of "dog trainer."

_____ Which statement best expresses the unstated main idea of the paragraph?
   A. We no longer value the work done by homemakers.
   B. Homemakers should receive salaries for their work.
   C. Although homemaking is essential to the economy, it brings no money or prestige.
   D. It's better to be a dog trainer than a homemaker.

Paragraph 2

[1]Albanian legend adheres to the traditional method for killing a vampire—a stake through the heart as the proper method. [2]According to legend, the Hungarian method of killing a vampire advised a stake through the heart, but insisted that a nail be driven through the temples as well. [3]The Irish way is less colorful; one simply piled rocks on the vampire's grave. [4]Macedonians were supposed to pour boiling oil on the vampire and then hammer a nail through its navel. [5]Their neighbors, the Serbs, held to a variant of that method: they proposed cutting off the undead creature's toes and pounding a nail through its neck. [6]Saxon legend says that a lemon in the mouth will do the trick, but in Prussian legend, you should instead put poppy seeds in the grave. [7]In Poland, it was believed that just burying the vampire face downward would kill it. [8]And from Romania itself—the home of the original Dracula—comes one of the most complicated methods: cut out the heart and slice it in two, put garlic in the monster's mouth, and pound a nail into its head.

_____ Which statement best expresses the unstated main idea of the paragraph?
   A. Nails play an important role in many European legends about killing vampires.
   B. Macedonia and Serbia, two neighboring nations, share similar legends about how to kill vampires.
   C. Vampires are popular legendary creatures in many European countries.
   D. Although many European countries have legends about vampires, those countries vary wildly on the best way to kill a vampire.

Paragraph 3

[1]During the Civil War, soldiers first gathered into companies of a hundred men and then formed into regiments (ten companies). [2]When two or three regiments were assembled—2,000 to 3,000 men—they were called a brigade and then sent off to battle. [3]Under the command of a brigadier general, the soldiers formed double lines that advanced over a front of a thousand yards. [4]From there, junior officers led the army's charge through clouds of grapeshot, bullets, and thick gunpowder smoke. [5]Men who panicked or broke from ranks were often shot by their own officers, who remained behind the advancing line. [6]Once the advancing army neared the enemy, they had to scramble through fortifications of earth and timber. [7]Finally, if they made it this far, the soldiers had to engage in hand-to-hand combat. [8]The attackers and defenders fought until everyone was killed or wounded or until one side gave up and ran away.

_____ Which statement best expresses the unstated main idea of the paragraph?
A. Hand-to-hand combat played an important role in most Civil War battles.
B. A battle during the Civil War followed a clear plan.
C. Officers in the Civil War had no sympathy for frightened soldiers.
D. Earth and timber fortifications were easy to defend and difficult to attack.

Putting Implied Main Ideas into Your Own Words

When you read, you often have to **infer**—figure out on your own—an author's unstated main idea. The implied main idea that you come up with should cover all or most of the details in the paragraph.

See if you can find and write the topic of the paragraph below. Then write the implied main idea in your own words. Finally, read the explanation that follows.

Hints: Remember that you can help yourself identify the topic and main idea if you 1) look for repeated words as you read and 2) try to mark major supporting details. Major details are often signaled by such common addition words as the following:

Addition Words

one	to begin with	also	further
first (of all)	for one thing	in addition	furthermore
second(ly)	other	next	last (of all)
third(ly)	another	moreover	final(ly)

¹A mistaken belief about sleepwalking is that sleepwalkers drift about in a ghost-like way, with arms extended. ²The fact is most sleepwalkers walk around quite normally, though their eyes are usually closed or glazed. ³It is also commonly believed that one should never wake a sleepwalker. ⁴But it is advisable to do so if the walker seems in immediate danger—for example, if he or she is going toward an open window or handling a sharp object. ⁵Another popular misconception is that sleepwalkers are not "really" sleeping or are only half-asleep. ⁶In fact, they are in a very deep state of sleep. ⁷A last commonly held belief is that sleepwalkers are easy to spot because they're in nighties or pajamas. ⁸Often this isn't true because sleepwalkers can do routine tasks, including getting completely dressed.

What is the topic of this paragraph?_____

What is the implied main idea of this paragraph? _____

_____

Explanation

One key to the topic here is the word *sleepwalkers*, which is repeated throughout the paragraph. The other key to the topic is major details in the paragraph. Three of the details are signaled by addition words (*also* in "It is also commonly believed," *Another* in "Another popular misconception," and *last* in "A last commonly held belief"). Here are the four major details in the paragraph:

- Sleepwalkers drift in a ghost-like way.
- One should never wake a sleepwalker.
- Sleepwalkers are not really sleeping.
- Sleepwalkers are easy to spot.

What do those four major details have in common? They're all *beliefs about sleepwalkers*, so that phrase can be considered the topic. And the author's main point about the topic could be stated like this: *There are several mistaken beliefs about sleepwalkers.*

PRACTICE 3

In the spaces provided, fill in the topic of each paragraph. Then write the implied main ideas of the paragraphs in your own words.

Hints:

1. Remember that to find the topic, it often helps to look for repeated words in a paragraph.
2. Remember that you can help yourself identify the topic and main idea if you mark major supporting details as you read. These major details are often signaled by such common addition words as the ones shown in the box on the previous page.

1. ¹One of the reasons for lying is to save face. ²For example, you might pretend to remember someone at a party in order to save that person from the embarrassment of being forgotten. ³A second reason for lying is to avoid tension or conflict. ⁴You might, for instance, say you really like a friend's new hairstyle or a new outfit in order to prevent the hassle that would result if you expressed your real feelings. ⁵Lies are also told in order to make everyday relationships run smoothly. ⁶You might pretend to be glad to see someone you dislike, or you might fake interest in a person's boring stories just to make a social event pass quickly. ⁷An additional reason for lying is to expand or reduce relationships. ⁸In one study, a majority of college students willingly lied to improve their chances of getting a date with an attractive partner. ⁹Sometimes people lie to reduce interaction with others: "I really have to go. ¹⁰I should be studying for a test tomorrow." ¹¹A final reason for lying is to gain power. ¹²A person might turn down a last-minute request for a date by claiming to be busy, saying in effect, "Don't expect me to sit around waiting for you to call."

   Topic: _____

   Implied main idea: _____

   _____

2.   ¹Many people think that children without brothers or sisters are lucky because of the material goods and attention they receive. ²But consider that an only child has no privacy—parents always feel entitled to know everything that's going on in his or her life. ³A second drawback of being an only child is the lack of certain advantages that children with brothers and sisters have. ⁴An only child can never blame a sibling for something that goes wrong or ask for a privilege that an older brother or sister was given earlier. ⁵In addition, only children miss the companionship of siblings. ⁶The result can be loneliness as well as trouble making friends later in life because they never learned to get along with a brother or sister.

Topic: _____

Implied main idea: _____

_____

3.   ¹Some people have opposed the death penalty for religious reasons. ²The Quakers, for instance, were the first to institute prison sentences in an effort to eliminate torture and execution. ³Others have opposed capital punishment on grounds of racism because African Americans were executed more often than whites. ⁴Some have even argued that executions actually increase murders by brutalizing the public sense of the value of life. ⁵Still others point to social-science research that seems to show capital punishment does not deter murder. ⁶If that's true, they say, there is no good reason for risking the execution of an innocent person.

Topic: _____

Implied main idea: _____

_____

Figuring Out Implied Central Ideas in Longer Passages

When you read a longer passage, you may have to infer an author's unstated central idea (also called a **central point** or **thesis**). As you learned in Chapter 2, you can find a central point in the same way that you find a main idea—by looking for a topic and considering the supporting material. The implied central idea that you come up with should cover all or most of the details in the passage. For example, read the following passage:

¹Ben Franklin said that the only sure things in life are death and taxes. ²He left something out, however: disappointment. ³No one gets through life without experiencing many disappointments.

⁴Depression is a common negative response to disappointment. ⁵Yvonne, for example, works hard for over a year in her department, trying to win a promotion. ⁶She is so sure she will get it, in fact, that she has already picked out the car she will buy when her salary increase comes through. ⁷However, the boss names one of her coworkers to the spot. ⁸The fact that all the other department employees tell Yvonne she really deserved the promotion doesn't help her deal with the crushing disappointment. ⁹Deeply depressed, Yvonne decides that all her goals are doomed to defeat. ¹⁰She loses her enthusiasm for her job and can barely force herself to show up every day. ¹¹She tells herself that she is a failure and that doing a good job just isn't worth the work.

¹²Another negative reaction to disappointment is escape. ¹³Kevin fails to get into the college his brother is attending, the college that was the focus of all his dreams, and reacts to his disappointment by escaping his circumstances. ¹⁴Why worry about college at all? ¹⁵Instead, he covers up his real feelings by giving up on his schoolwork and getting completely involved with friends, parties, and "good times." ¹⁶Or Linda doesn't make the varsity basketball team—something she wanted very badly—and so refuses to play sports at all. ¹⁷She decides to hang around with a new set of friends who get high every day; then she won't have to confront her disappointment and learn to live with it.

¹⁸The positive way to react to disappointment is to use it as a chance for growth. ¹⁹This isn't easy, but it's the only useful way to deal with an inevitable part of life. ²⁰Yvonne, the woman who wasn't promoted, could have handled her disappointment by looking at other options. ²¹If her boss doesn't recognize talent and hard work, perhaps she could transfer to another department. ²²Or she could ask the boss how she could improve her performance so that she would be a shoo-in for the next promotion. ²³Kevin, the young man who didn't get into the college of his choice, should look into other schools. ²⁴Going to another college may encourage him to be his own person, step out of his brother's shadow, and realize that being turned down by one college isn't a final judgment on his abilities or potential. ²⁵Rather than escape into drugs, Linda could improve her basketball skills for a year or pick up another sport, like swimming or tennis, that might turn out to be more useful to her as an adult.

²⁶Disappointments are unwelcome but regular visitors to everyone's life. ²⁷The best response is to step over the unwelcome visitor on the doorstep and get on with life.

You can see that no sentence in the passage is a good "umbrella" statement that covers all of the other sentences. To decide on the implied central point, we must ask the same three questions we've already used to find main ideas:

- "Who or what is this passage about?" That will be the topic.

- "What is the point the author is trying to make about that topic?"

- And when we think we know the central point, we can test it by asking, "Does all or most of the material in the passage support this idea?"

✓ Check Your Understanding

In the passage on the previous page, all of the details concern disappointment, so that must be the topic. Which of the following statements expresses the central point that the author is trying to make about the topic? Check (✓) the answer you think is correct.

_____ A. Death, taxes, and disappointment are three inevitable parts of daily living.

_____ B. Many people react to disappointment in a negative way.

_____ C. One of the challenges of life is to react to disappointment in a positive way.

_____ D. Many people react to disappointment with depression or escape, rather than using it as an opportunity for growth.

Explanation

The details reveal the author's central point to be answer D: Many people react to disappointment with depression or escape, rather than using it as an opportunity for growth. Answer A implies that the passage will deal equally with death and taxes, rather than simply disappointment. Answers B and C are both supporting details for the implied main idea, but neither in itself is the "umbrella" idea that covers all of the material in the passage.

PRACTICE 4

The central point of each of the following two passages is unstated, and each passage is followed by four sentences. In the space provided, write the letter of the sentence that best expresses each unstated central idea.

Remember to first ask yourself, "What is the implied central point?" Then test your answer by asking, "Does all or most of the material in the passage support this idea?"

Passage 1

¹For many people, the image of the woman in movies about the old West is a gentle one of a mother quietly tending to her kitchen, shopping at the general store, and raising her children.

²But preparing even a simple meal was a time- and energy-consuming chore. ³Prior to the twentieth century, cooking was performed on a coal- or wood-burning stove. ⁴Unlike an electric or a gas range, which can be turned on with the flick of a single switch, cast-iron and steel stoves were especially difficult to use. ⁵Housewives would first have to clean out the ashes left from previous fires. ⁶Then, paper and kindling had to be set inside the stove, dampers and flues had to be carefully adjusted, and a fire had to be lit. ⁷Since there were no thermostats to regulate the stove's temperature, a woman had to keep an eye on the contraption all day long. ⁸Any time the fire slackened, she had to adjust a flue or add more fuel. ⁹All day long, the stove had to be fed with new supplies of coal or wood—an average of fifty pounds or more. ¹⁰At least twice a day, the ash box under the fire had to be emptied. ¹¹All together, a housewife spent four hours every day rubbing the stove with thick black wax to keep it from rusting, lighting the fire, adjusting dampers, sifting ashes, and carrying wood or coal.

¹²It was not enough for a housewife to know how to use a cast-iron stove. ¹³She also had to know how to prepare unprocessed foods for consumption. ¹⁴Prior to the 1890s, there were few factory-prepared foods. ¹⁵Shoppers bought poultry that was still alive and then had to kill and pluck the birds. ¹⁶Fish had to have scales removed. ¹⁷Green coffee had to be roasted and ground. ¹⁸Loaves of sugar had to be pounded, flour sifted, nuts shelled, and raisins seeded.

¹⁹Cleaning was an even more arduous task than cooking. ²⁰The soot and smoke from coal- and wood-burning stoves blackened walls and dirtied drapes and carpets. ²¹Gas and kerosene lamps left smelly deposits of black soot on furniture and curtains. ²²Each day, the lamps' glass chimneys had to be wiped and the wicks trimmed or replaced. ²³And periodically floors had to be scrubbed, rugs beaten, and windows washed.

²⁴Since indoor plumbing was available only to the wealthy, chores that involved the use of water were especially demanding. ²⁵The mere job of bringing water into the house was a challenge. ²⁶According to calculations made in 1886, a typical North Carolina housewife had to carry water from a pump or well or a

spring eight to ten times each day. [27]Washing, boiling, and rinsing a single load of laundry used about fifty gallons of water. [28]Over the course of a year, she walked 148 miles toting over 36 tons of water! [29]Homes without running water also lacked the simplest way to dispose of dirty water: sinks with drains. [30]That meant that women had to remove dirty dishwater, kitchen slops, and, worst of all, the contents of chamber pots from their house by hand.

_____ Which sentence best expresses the implied central point of the entire selection?

    A. For nineteenth-century housewives, preparing even a simple meal was a time- and energy-consuming chore.

    B. During the nineteenth century, indoor plumbing was available only to the wealthy, so a typical housewife walked 148 miles, carrying over 36 tons of water, during the course of a year.

    C. In nineteenth-century America, a housewife's days were spent in harsh physical labor.

    D. Because coal-and wood-burning stoves were especially difficult to use and because most foods required intensive preparation, most nineteenth-century housewives were tied to their kitchens.

Passage 2

[1]Moderate drinking can bring social benefits, such as relaxation and recreation with others. [2]However, excessive use of alcohol is a factor in the relatively high rate of _automobile accidents_, the leading cause of death among young people in the United States. [3]Over half of each year's automobile deaths and injuries can be traced to excessive drinking. [4]As the National Institute on Alcohol Abuse and Alcoholism has found, "Most people killed in traffic accidents after drinking . . . have very high blood-alcohol concentration, averaging twice the level of alcohol considered legally impairing." [5]Those young people most likely to have auto accidents, including deadly ones, are more likely to drink excessively, use illicit drugs, violate various traffic laws, enjoy taking risks, and exhibit aggressiveness or hostility toward others.

[6]Excessive drinking also leads to a high rate of _other criminal offenses_. [7]The offenses include public drunkenness, disorderly conduct, and vagrancy. [8]Such crimes result in so many arrests that they put a severe strain on the operation of the criminal justice system. [9]Since 1970 many treatment programs for problem drinkers have helped reduce the number of arrests for alcohol-related offenses, but they still constitute the largest arrest category today. [10]The majority (over 90 percent) of the crimes committed by students on college campuses are also alcohol-related. [11]The perpetrators usually commit multiple crimes, including vandalism, fighting, theft, and alcohol violations.

[12]Heavy drinking further plays a significant part, albeit indirectly, in the commission of more serious _violent crimes_, such as homicide, aggravated assault,

and forcible rape. [13]In fact, alcohol is implicated in 42 percent of all violent crimes in the United States. [14]Those who commit these crimes seem to use alcohol as an excuse for expressing their aggression. [15]Alcohol can thus become dynamite in the hands of an aggressive person. [16]According to one study, subjects with a history of arguments and other aggressive acts were more likely to get involved in interpersonal aggression after they had done some heavy drinking.

_____   Which sentence best expresses the implied central point of the entire selection?

A. If many people didn't abuse alcohol, the United States would have far fewer deadly automobile accidents.

B. Excessive use of alcohol contributes to a number of negative social consequences.

C. While moderate drinking can bring social benefits, excessive use of alcohol plays a significant part in the commission of violent crimes.

D. Alcohol can become dynamite in the hands of an aggressive person, or a person who drinks and drives.

CHAPTER REVIEW

In this chapter, you learned the following:

- At times authors imply, or suggest, a main idea without stating it clearly in one sentence. In such cases, you must figure out that main idea by considering the supporting details. When you think you know the main idea, test it by asking, "Does *all or most* of the material support this idea?"

- To find implied central ideas in longer reading selections, you must again look closely at the supporting material.

The next two chapters—Chapters 5 and 6—will explain common ways that authors organize their material.

On the Web: If you are using this book in class, you can visit our website for additional practice in recognizing implied main and central ideas. Go to **www.townsendpress.com** and click on "Learning Center."

REVIEW TEST 1

To review what you've learned in this chapter, complete each of the following sentences.

1. When a paragraph has no sentence that states the main idea, we say the main idea is *(central, general, implied)* _____.

2. If you have trouble finding an implied main idea, it may help to first determine the *(topic, central point)* _____ of the paragraph.

3. After you figure out what you think is the implied main idea of a paragraph, test yourself by asking, "Does all or most of the material in the paragraph _____ this idea?"

4. The "main idea" of a selection that is longer than several paragraphs is called the *(topic, central point)* _____.

5. The central point is *(never, sometimes, always)* _____ implied.

REVIEW TEST 2

A. In the space provided, write the letter of the sentence that best expresses the implied main idea of each of the following paragraphs.

_____ 1. ¹Lean against a tree almost anywhere, and the first creature that crawls on you will probably be an ant. ²Stroll down a suburban sidewalk—or anywhere else—with your eyes fixed on the ground, counting the different kinds of animals you see. ³The ants will win hands down. ⁴The British entomologist C.B. Williams once calculated that the number of insects alive on Earth at a given moment is one million trillion. ⁵If, to take a conservative figure, 1 percent of those insects are ants, their total population is ten thousand trillion. ⁶Individual workers weigh on average between one and five milligrams, according to the species. ⁷When combined, all ants in the world taken together weigh about as much as all human beings.

A. Ants are commonplace in the suburbs.
B. There are huge numbers of ants on Earth.
C. There are too many ants in the world.
D. C.B. Williams, the British entomologist, calculated the number of insects alive on Earth at any one time.

_____ 2. ¹Some actors and rock stars are paid more than a hundred times as much per year as schoolteachers are. ²We enjoy such performers, but certainly they do not do work that is many times more important than those who teach and guide our nation's students. ³Indeed, the reverse is true. ⁴Also, professional athletes earn vastly more than firefighters. ⁵The first group may bring enjoyable diversion to our lives, but the latter literally save lives. ⁶Again, there can be little doubt that the lower-paid group, firefighters, makes the more important, indeed essential, contribution to society. ⁷Similarly, most high-fashion designers, who can make up to $50,000 for a single gown, far outearn police officers. ⁸Now, we can easily live without sophisticated clothes (and probably about 99.9 percent of us do), but a society without law-enforcement officers would be unlivable for all of us.

    A. Workers in our society are not necessarily paid according to how important their work is.

    B. Teachers deserve to be paid as much as actors and rock stars.

    C. High-fashion designers should be paid less money for their work.

    D. Entertainment is a valuable and needed diversion in our society—one which commands a high salary.

B. Write out the implied main idea of the following paragraphs.

3. ¹TV is our favorite way of relaxing. ²After a stressful day it's restful to just put our feet up and enjoy a favorite program. ³And, of course, TV is entertaining for all ages. ⁴Movies, video games, and special cable offerings, as well as regular network programming, provide a choice of amusements for the whole family. ⁵TV is also deservedly popular for being informative. ⁶When history is being made—for example, during the terrorist attacks on September 11, 2001—we are often there, thanks to TV. ⁷Perhaps the most important benefit of television is that it is a real educational tool. ⁸From *Sesame Street* to public television's nature programs, it teaches in a colorful and interesting fashion.

Implied main idea: _____

_____

4. ¹Lower-class criminals are more likely to be caught than wealthy criminals. ²And once caught, they are less likely to be able to afford highly skilled legal representation. ³When they appear in court, their life history—which often includes quitting school, unemployment, divorce, and an apparent lack of responsibility when judged by middle-class standards—may work against them. ⁴As a result, lower-income criminals are likely to receive heavier penalties than higher-income criminals for the same crime. ⁵And because they often cannot afford bail, lower-income criminals often have to wait for trial in jail cells rather than in the comfort of their own homes.

Implied main idea: _____

_____

REVIEW TEST 3

A. In the space provided, write the letter of the sentence that best expresses the implied main idea of each of the following paragraphs.

_____ 1. ¹After anti-smoking campaigns made teens aware of the risk of smoking, the percentage of teens smoking dropped from 28 to 20 percent in 10 years. ²Additionally, in schools where students have access to health clinics which provide birth control information and devices, pregnancy rates have declined by 30 percent. ³Furthermore, another study demonstrated that students in schools with comprehensive health education were less likely to use alcohol, to try drugs, or to attempt suicide.

A. If more schools would conduct anti-smoking campaigns, the number of teens who smoke would greatly decline.

B. Evidence suggests that health education programs have a favorable effect on teenagers' behavior.

C. Health education clinics are a positive influence on how people of all ages take care of themselves.

D. One study found that students in schools with comprehensive health education were less likely to use drugs or to attempt suicide.

_____ 2. ¹President John Adams's wife, Abigail, helped him with speeches, public relations, and policy decisions. ²Abraham Lincoln's wife, Mary, and Ulysses S. Grant's wife, Julia, both advised their husbands on political appointments. ³When Woodrow Wilson suffered a paralyzing stroke, his wife, Edith, became his intermediary; she determined what papers he saw and when, kept high officials out of his bedroom, and relayed his instructions. ⁴Eleanor Roosevelt actively advised her husband, Franklin, on the New Deal and championed the cause of black people at a time when it was politically inconvenient for him to do so. ⁵With her husband confined to a wheelchair, she traveled widely to observe and report back to him on social and economic conditions and New Deal projects. ⁶Nancy Reagan protected her husband, Ronald, from those advisors she judged unfit, pushed him hard toward arms-control talks, and rewrote his speeches. ⁷More recently, Hillary Clinton acted as one of her husband Bill's chief advisors. ⁸Her strong behind-the-scenes role led to her own successful campaign for political office.

A. Presidents' wives have played a major role in shaping U.S. political appointments.

B. Many presidential wives have served as champions for important social causes.

C. Certain presidential wives have had great political power—especially when their husbands were ill.

D. Many presidential wives have been quite influential in government during their husbands' administrations.

B. Write out the implied main idea of the following paragraph.

3. ¹If you have trouble getting a good night's sleep, don't have an alcoholic drink before bedtime. ²While alcohol can certainly knock you out, it also damages the quality of sleep you'll get. ³That's because it chemically interferes with dreaming, an important part of restful sleep. ⁴Also, avoid beverages and foods that contain caffeine, such as coffee, most teas, colas, and chocolate. ⁵Caffeine can stimulate you, making sleep difficult or impossible. ⁶A better before-bed choice is milk, which contains a mild, sleep-inducing type of protein. ⁷Another piece of good advice is to exercise during the day; this can leave you tuckered out enough at night to fall promptly and soundly asleep. ⁸But do avoid exercise right before bedtime, as its immediate effects are more stimulating than relaxing. ⁹Last, try to get up at about the same time every day; this practice will help your body establish a solid sleep and wake cycle. ¹⁰Varying your hours too much can confuse your body's "inner clock."

Implied main idea: _____

_____

C. In the space provided, write the letter of the sentence that best expresses the implied central point of the following selection from a sociology textbook.

4. ¹Compared to middle-income people, the poor are ill more often, receive poorer and more limited medical care, and live shorter lives. ²The poor have a higher rate of mental illness, particularly for the more serious illnesses such as depression, schizophrenia, and personality disorders. ³They also report lower levels of personal happiness than the nonpoor.

⁴The children of the poor are at greater risk of dying in infancy, and if they survive, they have a greater risk than nonpoor children of getting into trouble with the law or becoming pregnant as teenagers. ⁵Their education is inferior to that of nonpoor children, and they are far less likely to complete high school. ⁶One study showed that in Chicago's public schools, where a large proportion of the students are from poverty-stricken families, fewer than half graduated on time, and of those who did graduate, only one out of three could read at a twelfth-grade level.

⁷Poor people spend more of their income on food and housing than the nonpoor, but they are still worse fed and worse housed. ⁸A study of housing in southern Illinois revealed that poor people were several times as likely as the general public to live in overcrowded housing, yet 80 to 90 percent of these poor people were paying more than the government standard of 25 percent of their incomes for rent.

[9]Poor people are more likely to commit street crimes and to be the victims of such crimes. [10]Crime rates are highest in poor neighborhoods, for criminals tend to victimize those who are close by and available. [11]As a result, a highly disproportionate number of victims of robbery, assault, and homicide are poor. [12]So high is the incidence of crimes in some poor neighborhoods that poor people are afraid to venture outside their homes. [13]Summer after summer in major cities, elderly poor people have died from heat-related illnesses because they could not afford air conditioning and were afraid to open their windows because of crime.

_____ Which sentence best expresses the implied central point of the entire selection?

A. Children of the poor are at a greater risk of dying in infancy, of teenage pregnancies, and of not completing high school.

B. The victims of crime are more likely to be the poor than the nonpoor.

C. In virtually every way imaginable, life is more difficult for people living in poverty.

D. Poor people pay more of their income for food and housing than the nonpoor and at the same time are worse fed and worse housed.

REVIEW TEST 4

Here is a chance to apply your understanding of implied and central ideas to a reading about childhood cruelty.

To help you continue to strengthen your skills, the reading is followed by questions not only on what you've learned in this chapter but also on what you've learned in previous chapters.

Words to Watch

Below are some words in the reading that do not have strong context support. Each word is followed by the number of the paragraph in which it appears and its meaning there. These words are indicated in the article by a small circle (°).

simulate (1): imitate
musty (3): stale or moldy in odor
trudge (5): walk in a heavy, tired way
brunt (6): greatest part
taunted (6): mocked and insulted
gait (7): manner of moving
sinister (7): evil
distracted (9): interested in something else
stoic (13): emotionless
vulnerable (25): defenseless

ROWING THE BUS

Paul Logan

1   When I was in elementary school, some older kids made me row the bus. Rowing meant that on the way to school I had to sit in the dirty bus aisle littered with paper, gum wads, and spitballs. Then I had to simulate° the motion of rowing while the kids around me laughed and chanted, "Row, row, row the bus." I was forced to do this by a group of bullies who spent most of their time picking on me.

2   I was the perfect target for them. I was small. I had no father. And my mother, though she worked hard to support me, was unable to afford clothes and sneakers that were "cool." Instead she dressed me in outfits that we got from "the bags"—hand-me-downs given as donations to a local church.

3   Each Wednesday, she'd bring several bags of clothes to the house and pull out musty°, wrinkled shirts and worn

bell-bottom pants that other families no longer wanted. I knew that people were kind to give things to us, but I hated wearing clothes that might have been donated by my classmates. Each time I wore something from the bags, I feared that the other kids might recognize something that was once theirs.

4   Besides my outdated clothes, I wore thick glasses, had crossed eyes, and spoke with a persistent lisp. For whatever reason, I had never learned to say the "s" sound properly, and I pronounced words that began with "th" as if they began with a "d." In addition, because of my severely crossed eyes, I lacked the hand and eye coordination necessary to hit or catch flying objects.

5   As a result, footballs, baseballs, soccer balls and basketballs became my enemies. I knew, before I stepped on the field or court, that I would do something clumsy or foolish and that everyone would laugh at me. I feared humiliation so much that I became skillful at feigning illnesses to get out of gym class. Eventually I learned how to give myself low-grade fevers so the nurse would write me an excuse. It worked for a while, until the gym teachers caught on. When I did have to play, I was always the last one chosen to be on any team. In fact, team captains did everything in their power to make their opponents get stuck with me. When the unlucky team captain was forced to call my name, I would trudge° over to the team, knowing that no one there liked or wanted me. For four years, from second through fifth grade, I prayed nightly for God to give me school days in which I

would not be insulted, embarrassed, or made to feel ashamed.

6   I thought my prayers were answered when my mother decided to move during the summer before sixth grade. The move meant that I got to start sixth grade in a different school, a place where I had no reputation. Although the older kids laughed and snorted at me as soon as I got on my new bus— they couldn't miss my thick glasses and strange clothes—I soon discovered that there was another kid who received the brunt° of their insults. His name was George, and everyone made fun of him. The kids taunted° him because he was skinny; they belittled him because he had acne that pocked and blotched his face, and they teased him because his voice was squeaky. During my first gym class at my new school, I wasn't the last one chosen for kickball; George was.

7   George tried hard to be friends with me, coming up to me in the cafeteria on the first day of school. "Hi. My name's George. Can I sit with you?" he asked with a peculiar squeakiness that made each word high-pitched and raspy. As I nodded for him to sit down, I noticed an uncomfortable silence in the cafeteria as

many of the students who had mocked George's clumsy gait° during gym class began watching the two of us and whispering among themselves. By letting him sit with me, I had violated an unspoken law of school, a sinister° code of childhood that demands there must always be someone to pick on. I began to realize two things. If I befriended George, I would soon receive the same treatment that I had gotten at my old school. If I stayed away from him, I might actually have a chance to escape being at the bottom.

8   Within days, the kids started taunting us whenever we were together. "Who's your new little buddy, Georgie?" In the hallways, groups of students began mumbling about me just loud enough for me to hear, "Look, it's George's ugly boyfriend." On the bus rides to and from school, wads of paper and wet chewing gum were tossed at me by the bigger, older kids in the back of the bus.

9   It became clear that my friendship with George was going to cause me several more years of misery at my new school. I decided to stop being friends with George. In class and at lunch, I spent less and less time with him. Sometimes I told him I was too busy to talk; other times I acted distracted° and gave one-word responses to whatever he said. Our classmates, sensing that they had created a rift between George and me, intensified their attacks on him. Each day, George grew more desperate as he realized that the one person who could prevent him from being completely isolated was closing him off. I knew that I shouldn't avoid him, that he was feeling the same way I felt for so long, but I was so afraid that my life would become the hell it had been in my old school that I continued to ignore him.

10   Then, at recess one day, the meanest kid in the school, Chris, decided he had had enough of George. He vowed that he was going to beat up George and anyone else who claimed to be his friend. A mob of kids formed and came after me. Chris led the way and cornered me near our school's swing sets. He grabbed me by my shirt and raised his fist over my head. A huge gathering of kids surrounded us, urging him to beat me up, chanting "Go, Chris, go!"

11   "You're Georgie's new little boy-friend, aren't you?" he yelled. The hot blast of his breath carried droplets of his spit into my face. In a complete betrayal of the only kid who was nice to me, I denied George's friendship.

12   "No, I'm not George's friend. I don't like him. He's stupid," I blurted out. Several kids snickered and mumbled under their breath. Chris stared at me for a few seconds and then threw me to the ground.

13   "Wimp. Where's George?" he demanded, standing over me. Someone pointed to George sitting alone on top of the monkey bars about thirty yards from where we were. He was watching me. Chris and his followers sprinted over to George and yanked him off the bars to the ground. Although the mob quickly encircled them, I could still see the two of them at the center of the crowd, looking at each other. George seemed stoic°, staring straight through

Chris. I heard the familiar chant of "Go, Chris, go!" and watched as his fists began slamming into George's head and body. His face bloodied and his nose broken, George crumpled to the ground and sobbed without even throwing a punch. The mob cheered with pleasure and darted off into the playground to avoid an approaching teacher.

14   Chris was suspended, and after a few days, George came back to school. I wanted to talk to him, to ask him how he was, to apologize for leaving him alone and for not trying to stop him from getting hurt. But I couldn't go near him. Filled with shame for denying George and angered by my own cowardice, I never spoke to him again.

15   Several months later, without telling any students, George transferred to another school. Once in a while, in those last weeks before he left, I caught him watching me as I sat with the rest of the kids in the cafeteria. He never yelled at me or expressed anger, disappointment, or even sadness. Instead he just looked at me.

16   In the years that followed, George's silent stare remained with me. It was there in eighth grade when I saw a gang of popular kids beat up a sixth-grader because, they said, he was "ugly and stupid." It was there my first year in high school, when I saw a group of older kids steal another freshman's clothes and throw them into the showers. It was there a year later, when I watched several seniors press a wad of chewing gum into the hair of a new girl on the bus. Each time that I witnessed another awkward, uncomfortable, scared kid being tormented, I thought of George, and gradually his haunting stare began to

speak to me. No longer silent, it told me that every child who is picked on and taunted deserves better, that no one—no matter how big, strong, attractive or popular— has the right to abuse another person.

17   Finally, in my junior year when a loudmouthed, pink-skinned bully named Donald began picking on two freshmen on the bus, I could no longer deny George. Donald was crumpling a large wad of paper and preparing to bounce it off the back of the head of one of the young students when I interrupted him.

18   "Leave them alone, Don," I said. By then I was six inches taller and, after two years of high-school wrestling, thirty pounds heavier than I had been in my freshman year. Though Donald was still two years older than me, he wasn't much bigger. He stopped what he was doing, squinted, and stared at me.

19   "What's your problem, Paul?"

20   I felt the way I had many years earlier on the playground when I watched the mob of kids begin to surround George.

21   "Just leave them alone. They aren't bothering you," I responded quietly.

22   "What's it to you?" he challenged. A glimpse of my own past, of rowing the bus, of being mocked for my clothes, my lisp, my glasses, and my absent father flashed in my mind.

23   "Just don't mess with them. That's all I am saying, Don." My fingertips were tingling. The bus was silent. He got up from his seat and leaned over me, and I rose from my seat to face him. For a minute, both of us just stood there, without a word, staring.

24   "I'm just playing with them, Paul," he said, chuckling. "You don't have to

go psycho on me or anything." Then he shook his head, slapped me firmly on the chest with the back of his hand, and sat down. But he never threw that wad of paper. For the rest of the year, whenever I was on the bus, Don and the other troublemakers were noticeably quiet.

25 Although it has been years since my days on the playground and the school bus, George's look still haunts me. Today, I see it on the faces of a few scared kids at my sister's school—she is in fifth grade. Or once in a while I'll catch a glimpse of someone like George on the evening news, in a story about a child who brought a gun to school to stop the kids from picking on him, or in a feature about a teenager who killed herself because everyone teased her. In each school, in almost every classroom, there is a George with a stricken face, hoping that someone nearby will be strong enough to be kind—despite what the crowd says—and brave enough to stand up against people who attack, tease or hurt those who are vulnerable°.

26 If asked about their behavior, I'm sure the bullies would say, "What's it to you? It's just a joke. It's nothing." But to George and me, and everyone else who has been humiliated or laughed at or spat on, it is everything. No one should have to row the bus.

Reading Comprehension Questions

Vocabulary in Context

_____ 1. In the sentence below, the word *feigning* (fān′ĭng) means
   A. escaping.
   B. faking.
   C. recognizing.
   D. curing.

"I feared humiliation so much that I became skillful at feigning illnesses to get out of gym class." (Paragraph 5)

_____ 2. In the excerpt below, the word *rift* (rĭft) means
   A. friendship.
   B. agreement.
   C. break.
   D. joke.

> "I decided to stop being friends with George. . . . Our classmates, sensing that they had created a rift between George and me, intensified their attacks on him." (Paragraph 9)

Central Point and Main Ideas

_____ 3. Which sentence best expresses the central point of the selection?
   A. Although Paul Logan was a target of other students' abuse when he was a young boy, their attacks stopped as he grew taller and stronger.
   B. When Logan moved to a different school, he discovered that another student, George, was the target of more bullying than he was.
   C. Logan's experience of being bullied and his shame at how he treated George eventually made him speak up for someone else who was teased.
   D. Logan is ashamed that he did not stand up for George when George was being attacked by a bully on the playground.

_____ 4. At times, a main idea may cover more than one paragraph. Which sentence best expresses the main idea of paragraphs 2–4?
   A. The first sentence of paragraph 2
   B. The first sentence of paragraph 3
   C. The first sentence of paragraph 4
   D. The first sentence of paragraph 5

_____ 5. The topic sentence of paragraph 8 is its
   A. first sentence.
   B. second sentence.
   C. third sentence.
   D. final sentence.

Supporting Details

_____ 6. When Chris attacked George, George reacted by
      A. fighting back hard.
      B. shouting for Logan to help him.
      C. running away.
      D. accepting the beating.

_____ 7. Logan finally found the courage to stand up for abused students when he saw
      A. Donald throwing paper at a younger student.
      B. older kids throwing a freshman's clothes into the showers.
      C. seniors putting bubble gum in a new student's hair.
      D. a gang beating up a sixth-grader whom they disliked.

Implied Main Ideas

_____ 8. Which sentence best expresses the implied main idea of paragraph 5?
      A. Because of Logan's clumsiness, gym was a miserable experience for him in elementary school.
      B. Because Logan hated gym so much, he made up excuses to avoid it.
      C. The gym teacher caught on to Logan's excuses.
      D. Logan knew that other students did not want him to be a member of their team when games were played.

_____ 9. Which sentence best expresses the implied main idea of paragraph 6?
      A. Logan's mother moved so that Logan could get a fresh start in a new school.
      B. Even at the new school, students laughed at Logan's appearance.
      C. Riding on the bus was the worst part of Logan's school experience.
      D. When Logan started at his new school, he realized that a student named George was more unpopular than he was.

_____ 10. Which sentence best expresses the implied main idea of paragraph 16?
      A. Older kids were often cruel to younger students at Logan's schools.
      B. Because of what happened to George, Logan became increasingly bothered by students' picking on other students.
      C. In Logan's first year in high school, some students threw a freshman's clothes into the showers.
      D. In school, Logan learned a great deal about how people behave in various situations throughout life.

Discussion Questions

1. Paul Logan titled his selection "Rowing the Bus." Yet very little of the reading actually deals with the incident the title describes—only the first and last paragraphs. Why do you think Logan chose that title?

2. Logan wanted to be kind to George, but he wanted even more to be accepted by the other students. Have you ever found yourself in a similar situation—where you wanted to do the right thing but felt that it had too high a price? Explain what happened.

3. Logan refers to "a sinister code of childhood that demands there must always be someone to pick on." Why do children need someone to pick on?

4. The novelist Henry James once said, "Three things in human life are important. The first is to be kind. The second is to be kind. And the third is to be kind." What do you think schools or concerned adults could do to encourage young people to treat one another with kindness, rather than with cruelty?

Note: Writing assignments for this selection appear on pages 623–624.

Check Your Performance   **IMPLIED MAIN IDEAS**

Activity		Number Right	Points	Score
Review Test 1	(5 items)	_____	× 2 =	_____
Review Test 2	(4 items)	_____	× 7.5 =	_____
Review Test 3	(4 items)	_____	× 7.5 =	_____
Review Test 4	(10 items)	_____	× 3 =	_____
			TOTAL SCORE =	_____%

Enter your total score into the **Reading Performance Chart: Review Tests** on the inside back cover.

IMPLIED MAIN IDEAS: Mastery Test 1

In the space provided, write the letter of the sentence that best expresses the implied main idea of each of the following paragraphs.

_____ 1. [1]Children in Finland are the highest-scoring young readers in the world, but they also spend more time watching TV than reading. [2]A Finnish national research coordinator has pointed out a key relationship between reading and Finnish TV: "Many programs have captions, and watching these programs seems to motivate and enhance reading among young students." [3]In fact, almost 50 percent of Finnish television consists of foreign TV programs and movies whose subtitles must be read—and read quickly—for the shows to be understood. [4]Finnish nine-year-olds want to learn to read in order to understand TV and therefore watch a moderately heavy amount.

A. Children in Finland are the best young readers in the world.
B. Finnish television is very different from television in the United States.
C. Finnish teenagers watch less TV than younger children do.
D. Captioned television appears to help children learn to read.

_____ 2. [1]Intellectual curiosity is a desire for knowledge simply for its own sake—not to get a good grade, pass a test, get a diploma, or get a job. [2]Intellectual curiosity prevents boredom and apathy—and bored, apathetic people are dreary people, to themselves and to others. [3]Such curiosity also broadens our horizons. [4]If we pursue only the knowledge that we think we need for "success," our possibilities will be limited. [5]Moreover, curiosity of the mind makes us versatile. [6]People with broad knowledge and wide interests can change the course of their work and activities if they need to—as they well might, given the rapid pace of change in our world—or simply if they want to. [7]Last, although practicality is not its aim, intellectual curiosity can have practical advantages; at any time, any kind of knowledge may turn out to be useful to our happiness and growth in life.

A. Intellectual curiosity has many benefits.
B. Intellectual curiosity prevents boredom and apathy.
C. People with intellectual curiosity can change their jobs if they want or need to.
D. Intellectual curiosity has practical advantages.

(Continues on next page)

_____ 3. [1]Many people think there is no difference between an alligator and a crocodile. [2]However, the alligator's snout is shorter and broader than that of a crocodile. [3]A more dramatic difference between the two creatures lies in how dangerous they are to humans. [4]There are very few documented instances in which alligators have killed a person. [5]On the other hand, crocodiles, particularly those along the Nile River, are quite dangerous to humans. [6]It is said, in fact, that as far as killing people is concerned, crocodiles are second only to poisonous snakes.

A. Poisonous snakes are more dangerous to humans than crocodiles.
B. Many people believe that alligators and crocodiles are the same.
C. There are clear differences between alligators and crocodiles.
D. Alligators aren't particularly dangerous to humans.

_____ 4. [1]Adolescents and old people are both often segregated from the rest of society: young people are isolated in schools, and many old people live in retirement communities, assisted-living facilities, and nursing homes. [2]Also, both groups tend to be poorer than young adults or middle-aged people: adolescents because they do not yet have the education or experience to command high salaries, and old people because they are retired and living on their savings and social security. [3]Third, independence is important for both groups—they are conscious of wanting it, whereas young adults and middle-aged people take it for granted. [4]Adolescents want to become independent of their parents; old people want to keep their independence and not have to rely on their children or on social institutions. [5]Fourth, they both tend to have a relatively large amount of leisure time or, at least, time that they can choose or not choose to fill with study or work. [6]By contrast, young and middle-aged adults typically spend most of their time at their jobs or taking care of home duties such as child-rearing.

A. Adolescents and old people, more than other social groups, strongly value their independence.
B. Both adolescents and old people have different economic conditions from young and middle-aged adults.
C. Young and middle-aged adults spend much of their time taking care of home duties such as child-rearing.
D. Adolescents and old people, as groups in our culture, are very similar in certain ways.

IMPLIED MAIN IDEAS: Mastery Test 2

In the space provided, write the letter of the sentence that best expresses the implied main idea of each of the following paragraphs.

_____ 1. ¹Many people dream of being celebrities, but do they consider what celebrities' lives are really like? ²For one thing, celebrities have to look perfect all the time. ³There's always a photographer ready to take an unflattering picture of a famous person looking dumpy in old clothes. ⁴Celebrities also sacrifice their private lives. ⁵Their personal struggles, divorces, or family tragedies all end up as front-page news. ⁶Most frighteningly, celebrities are in constant danger of the wrong kind of attention. ⁷Threatening letters and even physical attacks from crazy fans are things the celebrity must contend with.

    A. Many people dream of being celebrities.
    B. Being a celebrity is often difficult.
    C. Being a celebrity means having to look good all the time.
    D. Celebrities face dangers.

_____ 2. ¹As you speak with someone, you can easily gather clues about how much he or she understands or agrees with you and adjust your conversation accordingly. ²But when you write, you must try to anticipate the reader's reactions without such clues. ³You also have to provide stronger evidence in writing than in conversation. ⁴A friend may accept an unsupported statement such as "He's a lousy boss." ⁵But in writing, the reader expects you to back up such a statement with proof.

    A. There are special techniques for communicating verbally with others.
    B. Speaking and writing are both challenging ways of communicating.
    C. Communicating effectively in writing is more demanding than communicating verbally.
    D. When speaking, you get feedback about a person's reaction that helps you to make your conversation more effective.

(Continues on next page)

_____ 3. ¹In murders investigated by the FBI, more than one-third have been committed by one family member against another. ²Three percent of them involve the murder of a child by a parent. ³Aggression by parents toward children also takes a less drastic form. ⁴Each year two million children are kicked, beaten, or punched by their parents. ⁵Aggression is evident in marriages as well. ⁶Each year, four million husbands and wives violently attack each other. ⁷These attacks result in severe injuries in a quarter of a million cases.

A. Abuse of children by parents is widespread in the United States.
B. Aggression is part of many marriages in this country.
C. In the United States, family violence is increasing steadily.
D. In the United States, aggression is often directed toward members of one's own family.

_____ 4. ¹A baby's most basic cry consists of a rhythmic pattern which begins with a cry followed by a brief silence and then a shorter higher-pitched whistling sound. ²Experts believe the basic cry is triggered by hunger, tiredness, or mild discomfort. ³Researchers have also identified an anger cry. ⁴A bit more forceful than the basic cry, the anger cry involves larger volumes of air passing over the baby's vocal chords. ⁵Such a sound might be made when a baby wants to be picked up and is not, or when a baby is put in a crib when it wants to be held. ⁶A third type of cry that babies use is the pain cry. ⁷A sudden loud wail followed by an extended period of breath-holding, the pain cry is the loudest sound a baby can make.

A. Babies have three distinct cries to communicate what they are feeling.
B. The pain cry is the loudest sound a baby can make.
C. Babies communicate differently at different ages.
D. Experts believe that hunger, tiredness, or mild discomfort may cause the basic cry.

IMPLIED MAIN IDEAS: Mastery Test 3

A. In the space provided, write the letter of the sentence that best expresses the implied main idea of each of the following paragraphs.

_____ 1. ¹The earliest humans probably used the lengthening and shortening of shadows on the ground to measure the passage of time. ²Later, the sundial was invented to tell time more precisely, but still by using the shadow principle. ³The hourglass, a slightly more recent invention, measured time by allowing grains of sand to fall from one container to another. ⁴In about the year 1300, a primitive clock was invented. ⁵It had only an hour hand, but it became the most exact way yet to tell the time. ⁶Since then, clocks have been so improved technically that today's clocks and watches can be depended upon to be quite precise.

   A. Throughout history, people have found better and better ways to measure the passing of time.
   B. The hourglass is a slightly more recent invention than the sundial.
   C. The first methods of measuring the passing of time took advantage of the changing shadows cast by the sun throughout a day.
   D. A primitive clock invented in about 1300 was the most exact way to tell time up to that point.

_____ 2. ¹Earth is surrounded by a thick gaseous envelope called the atmosphere. ²The atmosphere provides the air that we breathe and protects us from the sun's intense heat and dangerous radiation. ³The energy exchanges that continually occur between the atmosphere and space produce the effects we call weather. ⁴If, like the moon, Earth had no atmosphere, our planet would be lifeless, and many of the processes and interactions that make the surface such an energetic place could not operate. ⁵Without weathering and friction, the face of our planet might more closely resemble the lunar surface, which has not changed much in nearly three billion years.

   A. The atmosphere is a thick gaseous layer covering the entire Earth.
   B. The moon, unlike Earth, has no atmosphere and has therefore not changed much in almost three billion years.
   C. There are many influences on Earth's development.
   D. The atmosphere is a key part of our environment and of Earth's processes.

(Continues on next page)

B. Write out the implied main idea of the following paragraph:

3. ¹You don't have to scare your family with statistics about heart attacks. ²To get them to exercise more often, emphasize instead how good they'll feel and how much better they'll look if they work out daily. ³Another method you can use is to set an example. ⁴If they see you walking to the convenience store instead of driving, they might be encouraged to do likewise the next time they have errands in the neighborhood. ⁵Finally, make exercise a family activity. ⁶Suggest that the whole family go swimming together, take up early morning jogging, or join the Y at the group rate.

Implied main idea: _____

_____

_____

C. In the space provided, write the letter of the item below that best expresses the implied central idea of the following textbook passage.

_____ 4. ¹A researcher at Johns Hopkins University has repeatedly done a simple experiment with two rats. ²He holds one rat firmly in hand so that, no matter how much the rat struggles, he cannot escape. ³The rat will finally give up. ⁴The researcher then throws that unmoving rat into a tank of warm water, and the rat sinks, not swims. ⁵He has "learned" that there is nothing he can do, that there is no point in struggling. ⁶The researcher then throws another rat into the water—one that doesn't "know" that his situation is hopeless and that he is therefore helpless. ⁷This rat will swim to safety.

⁸A comparable experiment involving people has been conducted by Martin E.P. Seligman of the University of Pennsylvania. ⁹Two groups of college students are put in rooms where they are blasted with noise turned up to almost intolerable levels. ¹⁰In one room there is a button that turns off the noise. ¹¹The students quickly notice it, push it, and are rewarded with blissful silence. ¹²In the other room, however, there is no turn-off button. ¹³The students look for one, find nothing, and finally give up. ¹⁴There is no way to escape the noise (except to leave the room before a previously agreed-upon time period has elapsed), so they simply endure the noise.

¹⁵Later, the same two groups are put in two other rooms. ¹⁶This time, both rooms contain a switch-off mechanism—though not a simple button this time and not as easy to find. ¹⁷Nevertheless, the group that found the button the first time succeeds in finding the "off" switch the second time, too. ¹⁸But the second group, already schooled in the hopelessness of their circumstances, doesn't even search; its members just sit it out again.

A. Experiments suggest that humans and rats have similar reactions to unpleasant situations.

B. Experimenters at two leading universities have subjected both humans and rats to frustrating situations.

C. As strange as it may seem, both rats and humans give up trying in certain situations.

D. Experiments have revealed that past failures can teach both rats and humans to feel helpless and, as a result, to give up trying.

IMPLIED MAIN IDEAS: Mastery Test 4

A. In the space provided, write the letter of the sentence that best expresses the implied main idea of each of the following paragraphs.

_____ 1. ¹There is no doubt that businesses can improve their productivity. ²If every person and machine did things right the first time, the same number of people could handle much larger volumes of work. ³High costs of inspection could be channeled into productive activities, and managers could take all the time they spend checking and devote it to productive tasks. ⁴Wasted materials would become a thing of the past. ⁵In fact, it's been estimated that attention to quality can reduce the total cost of operations anywhere from 10 to 50 percent. ⁶As Philip Crosby said: "Quality is free. ⁷What costs money are the unquality things—all the actions that involve not doing jobs right the first time."

    A. Philip Crosby is an expert in quality in business.
    B. It is wasteful to spend so much money on plant inspections.
    C. Businesses can improve their sales in several ways.
    D. If quality is improved, productivity improves.

_____ 2. ¹In nineteenth-century America, people shared beds, both at homes with relatives and in hotels with strangers, without inquiring about their bed partner's health. ²They exchanged combs, hairbrushes, and even toothbrushes; and they fed babies from their mouths and spoons, with no sense of danger. ³They coughed, sneezed, and spat without concern for their own health or the health of those around them. ⁴They cooked and stored their meals with little worry about food-borne illness. ⁵They drank unfiltered water from wells and streams, often using a common dipper or drinking cup. ⁶Last but not least, they used chamber pots and outhouses with little regard for where the contents ended up in relation to the community water supply.

    A. Nineteenth-century Americans were friendlier than modern Americans.
    B. There was less water pollution in nineteenth-century America than there is today.
    C. In nineteenth-century America, people were probably as concerned about health as they were about survival.
    D. Nineteenth-century Americans engaged in behaviors that could easily spread disease.

(Continues on next page)

B. In the space provided, write the letter of the sentence that best expresses the implied main idea of each of the following paragraphs.

_____ 3.   ¹Some baby animals are born nearly helpless. ²They cannot survive if they are not cared for, usually by older members of their species. ³Food and shelter are the most obvious needs of a baby animal. ⁴But scientists have also observed another, less obvious need. ⁵Monkeys who are raised alone, with no physical contact with other animals, develop strange habits such as constantly rocking or moving in circles. ⁶In addition, they cannot relate normally to other monkeys. ⁷The males can rarely breed with females. ⁸The females who do bear young ignore or abuse their babies. ⁹When monkeys who were raised alone are put in contact with friendly, "motherly" monkeys who touch and cuddle them, they eventually develop normal monkey behaviors.

   A. Baby animals need to be given food and shelter.
   B. Studies suggest that for certain animals, touching, like food and shelter, is essential for normal development.
   C. All animals that are raised without physical contact with other animals develop strange habits.
   D. Scientists have done studies of monkeys raised without physical contact with other animals.

_____ 4.   ¹As an alternative to marriage, a marriage contract would be valid for three years, at which time the partners would decide whether or not to renew the agreement. ²If they did not choose to stay together, no divorce would be necessary. ³They would simply file a paper stating that they would not be renewing their contract. ⁴One advantage of the marriage contract system is that it would force couples to think in practical terms about their marriages. ⁵They would have to talk ahead of time about such questions as the handling of money, the dividing of household chores, and the matter of children. ⁶In addition, a contract would encourage couples to work harder at their marriages. ⁷If they knew their contract was coming up for renewal at a certain point, they would closely consider the reasons why it should or should not be extended. ⁸Finally, a renewable marriage contract would make ending a marriage far easier than it is today. ⁹A couple would not have to hire expensive lawyers and endure long waits in divorce courts. ¹⁰The simple filing of a paper in the courthouse would close out the contract and end a marriage. ¹¹The couple would then go their separate ways.

   A. People who want to marry would be better off if, instead, they signed a renewable marriage contract.
   B. A marriage contract is an alternative to marriage.
   C. A marriage contract would be a far easier and less costly way than divorce of ending a marriage.
   D. A marriage contract would encourage a couple to think carefully in advance about what it would mean to live together.

IMPLIED MAIN IDEAS: Mastery Test 5

A. In the space provided, write the letter of the sentence that best expresses the implied main idea of each of the following paragraphs.

_____ 1. [1]In one Ohio prison each maximum-security inmate is confined, alone, for up to 23 hours a day, in a cell that has a solid metal door and is 7 by 14 feet. [2]Some cells in other U.S. prisons are even smaller. [3]Alfred McCoy, the author of *A Question of Torture*, says that solitary confinement can cause rage, stupor, and insanity. [4]Psychiatrist Stuart Grassian agrees that solitary confinement can drive prisoners "crazy." [5]After only a few days in solitary confinement, prisoners show altered brain waves typical of stupor and delirium. [6]Most U.S. prisoners placed in solitary confinement stay there for more than five years; many stay there for more than twenty. [7]In California and Texas prisons, most suicides occur among inmates in solitary confinement.

    A. Solitary confinement is necessary for certain prisoners.
    B. Solitary confinement is cruel.
    C. Solitary confinement is widespread in American prisons.
    D. Solitary confinement is no longer a preferred treatment.

_____ 2. [1]A Senate committee estimates the loss of earnings of men ages 25 to 34 who have less than high school-level skills at $236 billion. [2]Half of the heads of households classified below the federal poverty line cannot read an eighth-grade book. [3]More than a third of mothers on welfare are also functionally illiterate. [4](Functional illiteracy is the inability to read and write well enough for everyday practical needs.) [5]So are 60 percent of the adult prison population and 84 percent of juveniles who come before the courts. [6]Businesses have difficulty filling such entry-level jobs as clerk, bank teller, and paralegal assistant. [7]A major insurance firm reports that 70 percent of dictated letters must be retyped "at least once" because secretaries cannot spell and punctuate correctly. [8]The military, too, pays a price for functional illiteracy. [9]The navy has stated that 30 percent of new recruits are "a danger to themselves and costly to naval equipment" because they cannot read very well or understand simple instructions.

    A. Americans are among the most poorly educated people in the world.
    B. Functional illiteracy, widespread among Americans, is costly for individuals and society.
    C. Businesses must face the problem of poorly prepared workers.
    D. Our prisons and courts are filled with adults and juveniles who are functionally illiterate.

B. Write out the implied main idea of the following paragraph:

3. [1]According to study experts, one tip for exam success is regular daily and weekly study. [2]Another tip is to focus on, in your study sessions, ideas that the instructor has emphasized in class. [3]In addition, use the night before an exam for a careful review rather than a stressful cramming. [4]Then get up a bit early the next morning and review your notes one more time. [5]Arriving early for an exam is another helpful tip that experts suggest. [6]Sit in a quiet spot and go through a final reading of notes. [7]Last, once the test begins, the advice of experts is to answer

(Continues on next page)

the easier questions first; then go back and tackle the hard ones. [8]And on essay questions, it's most productive to think a few minutes and make a brief outline before beginning to write.

Implied main idea: _____

_____

_____

C. Read the following textbook passage and in the space provided, write the letter of the sentence that best expresses the implied main idea.

_____ 4. [1]In the 1800s, reformers wanted to persuade Americans to adopt more godly personal habits. [2]They set up associations to battle profanity and Sabbath-breaking, to place a Bible in every American home, and to provide religious education for the children of the poor.

[3]At the start of the century, heavy drinking was an integral part of American life. [4]Many people believed that downing a glass of whiskey before breakfast was healthful. [5]Instead of taking coffee breaks, people took a dram of liquor at eleven and again at four o'clock as well as drinks after meals "to aid digestion" and a nightcap before going to sleep. [6]Campaigning politicians offered voters generous amounts of liquor during campaigns and as rewards for "voting right" on Election Day.

[7]By 1820 the typical adult American consumed more than 7 gallons of absolute alcohol a year (compared with 2.6 gallons today). [8]Consumption had risen markedly in two decades, fueled by the growing amounts of corn distilled by farmers into cheap whiskey, which could be transported more easily than bulk corn. [9]In the 1820s, a gallon of whiskey cost just a quarter.

[10]In their campaign, reformers identified liquor as the cause of a wide range of social, family, and personal problems. [11]Alcohol was blamed for the abuse of wives and children and the squandering of family resources. [12]Many businesspeople linked drinking with crime, poverty, and inefficient and unproductive employees.

[13]The stage was clearly set for the appearance of an organized movement against liquor. [14]In 1826 the nation's first formal national temperance organization was born: the American Society for the Promotion of Temperance. [15]Led by socially prominent clergy and laypeople, the new organization called for total abstinence from distilled liquor. [16]Within three years, 222 state and local anti-liquor groups were laboring to spread this message.

A. At the start of the 1800s, many Americans were heavy drinkers, but as the century wore on, the consumption of alcohol became less socially acceptable.

B. The American Society for the Promotion of Temperance helped reduce per capita consumption of alcohol and forced thousands of distillers to close.

C. In the early 1800s, an organized movement against liquor began as part of a larger moral reform campaign.

D. Although alcohol abuse is still a problem, it appears that Americans in the early 1800s drank much more than they do today.

IMPLIED MAIN IDEAS: Mastery Test 6

A. Read the following textbook passage, and then follow the instructions to select the implied main idea.

[1]Today's world puts a lot of pressure on teenagers to work. [2]By working, they gain more independence from their families, and they also get the spending money needed to keep up with their peers. [3]Many people argue that working can be a valuable experience for the young.

[4]However, schoolwork and the benefits of extracurricular activities tend to go by the wayside when adolescents work more than fifteen hours a week. [5]Teachers are then faced with the problems of keeping the attention of tired pupils and of giving homework to students who simply don't have the time to do it. [6]In addition, educators have noticed less involvement in the extracurricular events many consider healthy influences on young people. [7]School bands and athletic teams are losing players to work, and sports events are poorly attended by working students. [8]Those teenagers who try to do it all—homework, extracurricular activities, and work—may find themselves exhausted and prone to illness.

[9]Another drawback of too much work is that it may promote materialism and an unrealistic lifestyle. [10]Some parents say that work teaches adolescents the value of a dollar. [11]Undoubtedly, it can, and it's true that some teenagers work to help out with the family budget or save for college. [12]But surveys have shown that the majority of working teens use their earnings to buy luxuries—iPads, smartphones, clothing, even cars. [13]These young people, some of whom earn $300 and more a month, don't worry about spending wisely—they can just about have it all. [14]In many cases, experts point out, they are becoming accustomed to a lifestyle they won't be able to afford several years down the road, when they'll no longer have parents to pay for car insurance, food and lodging, and so on. [15]At that point, they'll be hard pressed to pay for necessities as well as luxuries.

_____ 1. Write the letter of the sentence that best expresses the implied main idea.
   A. Teenagers who work more than fifteen hours a week find that they have little or no time for homework and extracurricular activities.
   B. Some people believe that work teaches teenagers the value of a dollar, but others believe that it leads to materialism.
   C. These days, students who work often use their earnings to buy luxuries that they will no longer be able to afford when they're no longer living at home.
   D. By limiting their working hours, teenagers can benefit from both work *and* school—and also avoid an unrealistic lifestyle.

(Continues on next page)

B. Read the following textbook passage, and then follow the instructions to select the implied main idea.

¹Many of the world's girls and women are missing from schools. ²In sub-Saharan Africa, for every ten boys, only six girls are enrolled in secondary school, and in southern Asia, only four. ³In these regions, three-quarters of women aged 25 and over are still illiterate. ⁴A major reason why girls leave school is that they are married off, often to older men, and begin bearing children in their teens. ⁵Some are sold by their parents to prostitution rings, where young girls are in demand because they are considered less likely to carry the AIDS virus.

⁶Women are missing from the paid labor force. ⁷Women work as hard as or harder than men (on average, thirteen more hours a week worldwide). ⁸But the work women do—caring for children; providing food and health care to their families; tending gardens and livestock; processing crops; gathering firewood and hauling water; weaving cloth, carpets, and baskets; and selling home-grown food and home-made crafts at local markets—is not considered "real" work. ⁹When women do work for wages, they are usually employed in clerical, sales, and service occupations, and they are excluded from higher-paying jobs in manufacturing, transportation, and management. ¹⁰Even when women do the same work as men, they earn—on average worldwide—30 to 40 percent less.

¹¹Women are missing in the halls of power, policy, and decision making. ¹²Although women make up more than half the world's population, less than 5 percent of heads of state, heads of corporations, and directors of international organizations are female.

¹³Until recently, women were missing from the battlefield; however, they have never been missing from the ranks of the dead and wounded. ¹⁴In the many ethnic and civil wars in the world today, hostile groups are fighting for towns and cities, and civilians are caught in the crossfire. ¹⁵Hundreds of thousands of women and children have become widows, orphans, and refugees.

¹⁶War or not, women the world over are regularly abused sexually, physically injured, and even killed simply because they are women. ¹⁷In 1987 in India, 1,786 "dowry deaths"—in which the husband and/or his family kill a woman because her dowry was insufficient—were recorded. ¹⁸In Thailand, more than 50 percent of married women living in Bangkok's largest squatter settlement said they were regularly beaten by their husbands. ¹⁹Not until 1991 did the Brazilian Supreme Court outlaw the "honor" defense, which excused a man who murdered an adulterous wife on the grounds that he was defending his honor.

_____ 2. Write the letter of the sentence that best expresses the implied main idea.

A. Throughout the world, women's work is usually undervalued, even though women work as hard or harder than men.

B. All over the world, women and girls are sexually exploited and murdered by men simply because they are female.

C. Because girls and women receive far fewer educational opportunities than men throughout the world, they have far fewer opportunities to become decision-makers.

D. Throughout the world, females are clearly second-class citizens or worse.

5 Relationships I

Authors use two common methods to show relationships and make their ideas clear. The two methods—**transitions** and **patterns of organization**—are explained in turn in this chapter. The chapter also explains two common types of relationships:

- Relationships that involve **addition**
- Relationships that involve **time**

Transitions

Look at the following items and put a check (✓) by the one that is easier to read and understand:

____ One way to lose friends is to talk but not listen. A way to end friendships is to borrow money and not pay it back.

____ One way to lose friends is to talk but not listen. Another way to end friendships is to borrow money and not pay it back.

You probably found the second item easier to understand. The word *another* makes it clear that the writer is adding a second way to lose friends. **Transitions** are words or phrases (like *another*) that show relationships between ideas. They are like signs on the road that guide travelers. Or they can be seen as "bridge" words, carrying the reader across from one idea to the next:

One way to lose friends **ANOTHER** way to end friendships is to is to talk but not listen. borrow money and not pay it back.

Two major types of transitions are words that show addition and words that show time.

Words That Show Addition

Once again, put a check (✓) beside the item that is easier to read and understand.

___ Many people rent DVDs because rental is cheaper than tickets to a movie theater. DVDs are now available online as well as in stores.

___ Many people rent DVDs because rental is cheaper than tickets to a movie theater. Also, DVDs are now available online as well as in stores.

The word *also* in the second item makes the relationship between the sentences clearer. The author is providing reasons why renting movies is popular. The first reason is that renting DVDs is cheaper than buying tickets to the movies. A *second* reason is that the movies are so readily available. The word *also* makes it clear that another reason is being given. *Also* is an addition word.

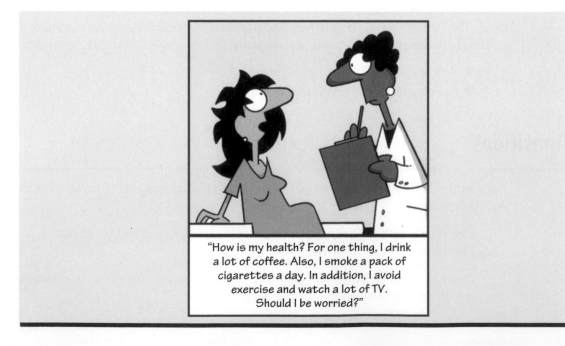

"How is my health? For one thing, I drink a lot of coffee. Also, I smoke a pack of cigarettes a day. In addition, I avoid exercise and watch a lot of TV. Should I be worried?"

Addition words signal added ideas. These words tell you a writer is presenting one or more ideas that continue along the same line of thought as a previous idea. Like all transitions, addition words help writers organize their information and present it clearly to readers. In the cartoon on the previous page, the speaker is presenting three pieces of information about her health. The joke is that if she smokes and drinks a lot and doesn't exercise, she *should* be worried.

Here are some common words that show addition:

Addition Words

one	to begin with	also	further
first (of all)	for one thing	in addition	furthermore
second(ly)	other	next	last (of all)
third(ly)	another	moreover	final(ly)

Examples

The following examples contain addition words. Notice how these words introduce ideas that *add to* what has already been said.

- Garlic improves the flavor of many dishes. *In addition*, it lowers cholesterol, fights heart disease, and kills certain viruses.

- Rivers serve as highways for migrating birds. *Also*, the nearby wetlands provide the birds with places in which to rest and feed.

- My neighbors are so safety-conscious that they had the wooden front door of their apartment replaced with a steel one. *Moreover*, they had iron bars installed on all their apartment windows.

PRACTICE 1

Complete each sentence with a suitable addition word from the box above. Try to use a variety of transitions.

> *Hint:* Make sure that each addition word or phrase that you choose fits smoothly into the flow of the sentence. Test each choice by reading the sentence aloud.

1. To avoid car thieves, lock valuables in the trunk or glove compartment. You should _____ try to park in the middle of a block on a busy, well-lit street.

2. There are several ways to use old jeans. _____, you can use them for patching other jeans.

3. One million stray dogs live in the New York City metropolitan area. _____, there are more than 500,000 stray cats in the same area.

4. "_____, and most important," said my adviser, "you've got to complete that term paper or you won't graduate on time."

5. Part-time workers have second-class status. For one thing, they are easily laid off. Second, they get no fringe benefits. _____, they are often paid less than half the hourly rate of a full-timer.

Words That Show Time

Put a check (✓) beside the item that is easier to read and understand:

____ The two neighboring families used to get along well. They are not on speaking terms.

____ Previously, the two neighboring families got along well. Now they are not on speaking terms.

The words *previously* and *now* in the second item clarify the relationship between the sentences: *Before*, the families got along well; and *now* they don't speak to each other. *Previously* and *now* and words like them are time words.

GLASBERGEN

"I started in the mail room. Next, I was in sales.
Then I became a district manager. Now I'm at the
top and worried about you replacing me!"

These transitions indicate a time relationship. **Time words** tell us *when* something happened in relation to when something else happened. In the above cartoon, the words, *Next, Then,* and *Now* indicate when each of the events happened in the speaker's career.

Below are some common words that show time:

Time Words

before	immediately	when	until
previously	next	whenever	often
first (of all)	then	while	frequently
second (ly)	following	during	eventually
third (ly)	later	as (soon as)	final(ly)
now	after	by	last (of all)

Note: Some additional ways of showing time are dates ("In 1890 . . . ," "Throughout the 20th century . . . ," "By 2018 . . .") and other time references ("Within a week . . . ," "by the end of the month . . . ," "in two years . . .").

Examples

The following examples contain time words. Notice how these words show us *when* something takes place.

- *While* the nurse prepared the needle, I rolled up my sleeve. *Then* I looked away.

- Many people get sleepy *after* eating a heavy meal.

- *During* my last semester in college, I spent more time job hunting than I did studying.

Helpful Tips about Transitions

Here are two points to keep in mind about transitions.

 TIP 1 Some transition words have the same meaning. For example, *also, moreover,* and *furthermore* all mean "in addition." Authors typically use a variety of transitions to avoid repetition.

 TIP 2 In some cases the same word can serve as two different types of transitions, depending on how it is used. For example, the word *first* may be used as an addition word to show that the author is presenting a series of points, as in the following sentences:

> For many athletes, life after a sports career is a letdown. *First,* they are often not prepared for nonathletic careers. In addition, they . . .

First may also may be used to signal a time sequence, as in these sentences:

> A trip to a giant supermarket can be quite frustrating. *First,* you have trouble finding a parking space close to the store. Then, . . .

PRACTICE 2

Complete each sentence with a suitable time word from the box on the previous page. Try to use a variety of transitions.

> *Hint:* Make sure that each time word or phrase that you choose fits smoothly into the flow of the sentence. Test each choice by reading the sentence aloud.

1. _____ my cousin took a long shower, there was no hot water left for anyone else in the house.

2. To make chicken stock, begin by putting a pot of water on the stove to boil. _____ drop in a chicken and some diced celery and onions.

3. Gerald waited impatiently all day for the Monday night football game to begin on TV, but _____ the first half, he fell asleep.

4. Recent advances in medicine make it possible to treat babies even _____ they are born.

5. Some students listen to their iPods, eat snacks, and talk on their cell phones _____ doing their homework.

Patterns of Organization

You have learned that transitions show the relationships between ideas in sentences. In the same way, **patterns of organization** show the relationships between supporting details in paragraphs, essays, and chapters. It helps to recognize the common patterns in which authors arrange information. You will then be better able to understand and remember what you read.

The rest of this chapter discusses two major patterns of organization:

- The **list of items pattern**
  (Addition words are often used in this pattern of organization.)

- The **time order pattern**
  (Time words are often used in this pattern of organization.)

Noticing the transitions in a passage can often help you become aware of its pattern of organization. Transitions can also help you locate the major supporting details.

1   The List of Items Pattern

```
┌──────────────────────────┐
│      List of Items       │
├──────────────────────────┤
│           Item 1         │
│           Item 2         │
│           Item 3         │
└──────────────────────────┘
```

To get a sense of the list of items pattern, try to arrange the following sentences in a logical order. Put a *1* in front of the sentence that should come first, a *2* in front of the sentence that comes next, a *3* in front of the third sentence, and a *4* in front of the sentence that should come last. The result will be a short paragraph. Use the addition words as a guide.

____   One common strategy is to consume massive quantities of junk food, which is easily done thanks to all the ever-present convenience stores and fast-food restaurants.

____   There are some widely popular, inappropriate methods that people use to combat stress.

____   Finally, watching hours of nonstop TV can put people in a stupor that helps them forget the problems of everyday life.

____   Another way to deal with stress is to doze or sleep for hours and hours, even during the day.

This paragraph begins with the main idea: "There are some widely popular, inappropriate methods that people use to combat stress." The next three sentences go on to list three of those methods, resulting in the pattern of organization known as a list of items. The transitions *One, Another,* and *Finally* introduce the points being listed and indicate their order:

> [1]There are some widely popular, inappropriate methods that people use to combat stress. [2]One common strategy is to consume massive quantities of junk food, which is easily done thanks to all the ever-present convenience stores and fast-food restaurants. [3]Another way to deal with stress is to doze or sleep for hours and hours, even during the day. [4]Finally, watching hours of nonstop TV can put people in a stupor that helps them forget the problems of everyday life.

A **list of items** refers to a series of reasons, examples, or other points that support an idea. The items have no time order, but are listed in whatever order the author prefers. Addition words, such as those in the box on the following page, are often used in a list of items to tell us that other supporting points are being added to a point already mentioned. Textbook authors frequently organize material into lists of items, such as a list of types of economic systems, symptoms of heart disease, or reasons for teenage drinking.

Addition Words Used in the List of Items Pattern

one	to begin with	also	further
first (of all)	for one thing	in addition	furthermore
second(ly)	other	next	last (of all)
third(ly)	another	moreover	final(ly)

✔ ## Check Your Understanding

The paragraph below is organized as a list of items. Complete the outline of the paragraph by first filling in the missing part of the main idea. Then add to the outline the three major details listed in the paragraph.

To help you find the major details, do two things to the paragraph:

● Underline the addition words that introduce the major details in the list;

● Number (*1, 2, . . .*) each item in the list.

> ¹Like all social institutions, sports serve various purposes. ²First, they provide the leisure-time exercise so necessary in a society in which most jobs provide little or no physical activity. ³Second, sports supply an outlet for energies that might otherwise strain the social order. ⁴Emotions such as anger and frustration can be expressed in ways that are acceptable to society—through both watching and participating in sports. ⁵Finally, sports give society role models. ⁶At their best, athletes, especially famous ones, are examples of dedication, hard work, and conduct for others to imitate.

Main idea: Sports serve _____

1. _____

2. _____

3. _____

Explanation

The main idea is that sports serve several purposes. (You may also express main ideas at times in a short heading; the heading here could be "Purposes of sports.") Following are the three purposes you should have added to the outline:

1. They provide leisure-time exercise. (This point is signaled with the addition transition *First*.)

2. They supply an outlet for energies that might otherwise strain the social order. (This point is signaled with the addition transition *Second*.)

3. They give society role models. (This point is signaled with the addition transition *Finally*.)

PRACTICE 3

A. The following passage uses a listing pattern. Outline the passage by filling in the main idea and the major details.

> *Hint:* Underline the addition words that introduce the items in the list, and number the items.

> [1]Today, beef is America's favorite meat. [2]But, for several reasons, America's most popular meat a hundred years ago was pork. [3]First of all, pigs grew quickly. [4]They could multiply their weight 150 times in just 8 months by eating nuts, roots, fallen orchard fruit, spoiled food, and garbage. [5]Another reason for the popularity of pork was that pigs required almost no attention. [6]In a nation with lots of land and not enough workers, pigs were perfect because they could take care of themselves. [7]Indeed, wild pigs, such as the American razorback, were so fierce that they didn't need a farmer's protection. [8]A third reason for the preference for pigs was that they could be cheaply preserved. [9]A butchered pig could be packed into barrels filled with heavily salted water and saved for up to a year. [10]Indeed, it was salted pork—not hamburger—that fed most people in the first century and a half of the growing United States.

Main idea: _____

_____

1. _____

2. _____

3. _____

B. The following passage uses a listing pattern. Complete the map of the passage by completing the main idea and filling in the missing major details.

> [1]Various theories explain the aging process. [2]The most obvious is that our bodies simply wear out. [3]Yet since many bodily systems are able to replace or repair their worn components (wounds heal, for example, and skin cells are constantly being generated), this version cannot be the whole story. [4]A related theory is that as cells repeatedly divide, more and more contain genetic errors and stop working properly. [5]A third theory holds that our body chemistry loses its delicate balance over the years. [6]For example, our excretory system, after years of filtering pollutants from our bloodstream, becomes less efficient. [7]The resulting change in our blood chemistry can produce a variety of other malfunctions. [8]Finally, according to another theory, our bodies tend with age to reject some of their own tissues.

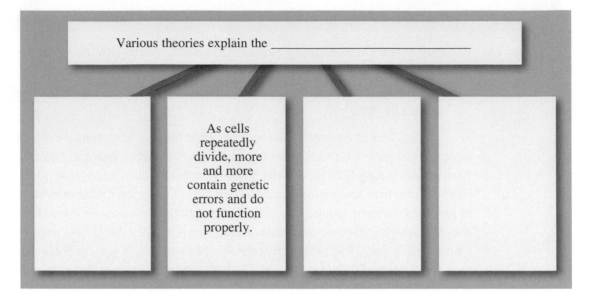

Various theories explain the _____

As cells repeatedly divide, more and more contain genetic errors and do not function properly.

2   The Time Order Pattern

To get a sense of the time order pattern, try to arrange the following sentences in a logical order. Put a *1* in front of the sentence that should come first, a *2* in front of the sentence that comes next, a *3* in front of the third sentence, and a *4* in front of the sentence that should come last. The result will be a short paragraph. Use the time words as a guide.

____ Next, the two people declare themselves a couple, telling friends and relatives about the new person in their lives.

____ The two people then make a commitment to have an exclusive relationship with each other.

____ A relationship begins when two people show interest in each other and choose to spend time together.

____ Last, the two people formalize the relationship by cohabitation or marriage.

Authors usually present events in the order in which they happen, resulting in the **time order** pattern of organization. Clues to the order of the above sentences are time transitions (*Next, then, when,* and *Last*). The paragraph should read as follows:

[1]A relationship begins when two people show interest in each other and choose to spend time together. [2]The two people then make a commitment to have an exclusive relationship with each other. [3]Next, the two people declare themselves a couple, telling friends and relatives about the new person in their lives. [4]Last, the two people formalize the relationship by cohabitation or marriage.

As a student, you will see time order used frequently. Textbooks in all fields describe events and processes, such as the events leading to the Boston Tea Party, the important incidents in Abraham Lincoln's life, the steps involved for a bill to travel through Congress, the process involved in writing a paper, or the stages in the development of a cell.

In addition to the time transitions listed on page 185, as well as dates and other time references, signals for the time order pattern include such words as *stages, series, steps,* and *process.*

The two most common kinds of time order are 1) a series of events or stages and 2) a series of steps (directions for how to do something). Each is discussed on the following pages.

Series of Events or Stages

Time Order: Events

Event 1
Event 2
Event 3

Time Order: Stages

Stage 1
Stage 2
Stage 3

Check Your Understanding

Following is a paragraph that is organized according to time order. Complete the outline of the paragraph by listing the missing stages in the order in which they happen.

To help you find the stages, do two things to the paragraph:

● Underline the words that introduce each stage;
● Number (*1, 2, . . .*) each stage.

¹Children master language in predictable stages. ²First, at about six months, babies start to repeat simple sounds, such as "ma-ma-me-me." ³About three or four months later, they can repeat sounds that others make and carry on little conversations. ⁴These interchanges are rich in emotional meaning, although the sounds themselves are meaningless. ⁵At the next stage, toddlers learn the meanings of many words, but they cannot yet talk. ⁶A toddler might understand a sentence such as "Bring me your sock" but be unable to say any of the words. ⁷Finally, the child begins to talk in single words and in two-word sentences.

Main idea: Children master language in predictable stages.

1. _____

   _____

2. Three or four months later, babies can repeat sounds and carry on little "conversations."

3. _____

   _____

4. _____

   _____

Explanation

You should have added these points to the outline:

1. At about six months, babies begin to repeat simple sounds. (The author signals this stage with the time transition *First* and the mention of age: "at about six months.")

3. Toddlers understand many words but cannot talk. (The author signals this stage with the time word *next:* "At the next stage, . . .")

4. Finally, the child talks in single words and two-word sentences. (The author signals this stage with the time word *Finally.*)

As emphasized by the transitions used, the relationship between the points is one of time: The second stage happens *after* the first, and so on.

PRACTICE 4

The following passage describes a sequence of events. Outline the paragraph by filling in the main idea and major details. Note that the major details are signaled by time words and dates.

> *Hint:* Underline the time word or words that introduce each major detail, and number each major detail.

¹The 1960s were a time of profound events in America. ²The first thunderclap occurred in 1963, with the bullets that assassinated President John Kennedy, depressing the spirit of the country. ³Then in 1965, urban riots moved the long-simmering issue of racial equality onto center stage. ⁴A minor summer incident involving police in Watts, a black section of Los Angeles, set off five days of looting and rioting that left thirty-four people dead. ⁵Over a hundred major urban riots, all centered in black ghettos in cities like Newark and Detroit, were to follow. ⁶The next profound explosion was a series of protests against the increasing American

presence in Vietnam. **⁷**The protests began in 1968 and spread across the country, centering on college campuses. **⁸**Soon almost every major campus in the United States was torn by rallies, teach-ins, and riots.

Main idea: _____.

1. _____

2. _____

3. _____

PRACTICE 5

The following passage describes a series of stages. Complete the map by writing the main idea in the top box and filling in the three major details (the stages).

¹Many people pass through three stages in reacting to their unemployment. **²**At first they experience shock, followed by relief. **³**In many cases they had anticipated that they were about to lose their jobs, so when the dismissal comes, they may feel a sense of relief that at last the suspense is over. **⁴**On the whole, they remain confident and hopeful that they will find a new job when they are ready. **⁵**During this time, they maintain normal relationships with their family and friends. **⁶**The first stage lasts for about a month or two. **⁷**The second stage centers on a strong effort to find a new job. **⁸**If workers have been upset or angry about losing their jobs, the feeling tends to evaporate as they marshal their resources and concentrate on finding a new job. **⁹**This stage may last for up to four months. **¹⁰**But if another job is not found during this time, people move into a third stage, one of self-doubt and anxiety, which lasts about six weeks. **¹¹**They must struggle to maintain their self-esteem as they question their own personal power and worth.

Series of Steps (Directions)

When authors give directions, they use time order. They explain step 1, then step 2, and so on through the entire sequence of steps that must be taken toward a specific goal.

✓ Check Your Understanding

Below is a paragraph that gives directions. Complete the outline of the paragraph by listing the missing steps in the correct sequence. To help yourself identify each step, do two things:

● Underline the time words that introduce each item in the sequence;

● Number (1, 2, . . .) each step in the sequence.

> ¹Here is a six-step technique that will help you relax quickly. ²First, lie down with your arms at your sides and your fingers open. ³When you are comfortable, close your eyes and put all distracting thoughts out of your mind. ⁴Next, tighten all the muscles of your body at once. ⁵Do this by pushing your toes together, tightening your buttocks and abdomen, clenching your fists, and squeezing your eyes shut. ⁶Then, let everything relax, and feel the tension flow out of your body. ⁷After that, take a deep breath through your mouth, hold it for twenty seconds, and then let it out slowly, breathing slowly and easily, as you do when you are sleeping. ⁸Finally, think of a pleasant scene as you feel your whole body becoming calm and relaxed.

Main idea: Here is a six-step technique that will help you relax quickly.

1. _____

2. _____

3. Tighten all muscles at once.

4. _____

5. _____

6. _____

Explanation

You should have added these steps to the outline:

1. Lie down, arms at your sides and fingers open. (The author signals this stage with the time word *First.*)

2. When you are comfortable, close your eyes and clear your mind. (The author signals this stage with the time word *When*.)

4. Let everything relax, and feel the tension flow out of your body. (The author signals this stage with the time word *Then*.)

5. Take a deep breath, hold it, let it out, and breathe slowly and easily. (The author's signal is the time word *After*.)

6. Think of a pleasant scene as you feel yourself relax. (The author signals this last step with the time word *Finally*.)

As indicated by the transitions used, the relationship between the steps is one of time: The second step happens *after* the first, and so on.

PRACTICE 6

The following passage gives directions involving several steps that must be done in order. Complete the map below by writing the main idea in the top box and filling in the three missing steps.

Hint: Underline the time words that introduce each step in the sequence, and number each step.

[1]There are several steps to remembering your dreams. [2]To begin with, you must make up your mind to do so, for consciously deciding that you want to remember increases the likelihood that it will happen. [3]Then put a pen and a notebook near your bed, so that you can write down what you remember as soon as you wake up. [4]When possible, turn off your alarm before you go to sleep so that you can wake up gradually; this will increase the likelihood of remembering your dreams. [5]Finally, when you wake up in the morning and remember a dream, write it down immediately, even before getting out of bed.

Make up your mind to remember your dreams.

A Note on Main Ideas and Patterns of Organization

A paragraph's main idea often indicates its pattern of organization. For example, here's the main idea of the paragraph you just read: "There are several steps to remembering your dreams." The words *several steps* suggest that this paragraph will be organized according to time order. Another good example is the main idea of the earlier paragraph on aging: "Various theories explain the aging process." The words *various theories* suggest that this paragraph will be a list of items.

Paying close attention to the main idea, then, can give you a quick sense of a paragraph's pattern of organization. Try, for instance, to guess the pattern of the paragraph with this main idea:

> While there are thousands of self-help groups, they all fall into three basic categories.

The phrase "three basic categories" is a strong indication that the paragraph will list those categories. The main idea helps us guess that the paragraph will be a list of three items.

PRACTICE 7

Most of the main ideas below have been taken from college textbooks. In the space provided, write the letter of the pattern of organization that each main idea suggests.

_____ 1. The process of digestion can be divided into four stages.
      A. List of items   B. Time order

_____ 2. A federal form of government has advantages and disadvantages.
      A. List of items   B. Time order

_____ 3. The stock market crash resulted from a number of basic weaknesses in the economy.
      A. List of items   B. Time order

_____ 4. Serious relationships in our lives often evolve gradually, going through several phases.
      A. List of items   B. Time order

_____ 5. Law enforcement officers are taught a series of steps to follow upon arriving at the scene of a violent crime.
      A. List of items   B. Time order

_____ 6. There are several search aids that can be of great help when you are looking for information online.
   A. List of items   B. Time order

_____ 7. Educational opportunities vary greatly in different regions of the United States.
   A. List of items   B. Time order

_____ 8. Treating the allergic patient often involves a three-stage process.
   A. List of items   B. Time order

_____ 9. Convenience products can be subdivided into four groups on the basis of how people buy them.
   A. List of items   B. Time order

_____10. The worldwide fall of communism was marked by a series of dramatic events.
   A. List of items   B. Time order

Three Final Points

1 While many passages have just one pattern of organization, often the patterns are mixed. For example, you may find that part of a passage uses a list of items pattern, and another part of the same passage uses a time pattern.

2 You may have noted that when an author presents a series of events or stages or steps, that series is itself a list of items. For example, here's a time order passage:

> [1]To read and study a textbook more effectively, follow a few helpful steps. [2]**First**, preview the reading, taking a couple of minutes to get a quick sense of what the selection is about. [3]**Next**, read and mark the selection, using a highlighter pen to set off important points. [4]**Then** write up a set of study notes that summarize the most important ideas in the selection. [5]**Last**, go over and over the ideas in your notes until you know the material.

The above passage is indeed made up of a list of items. But what makes it a time order passage is that the list of items appears not at random but in a *time sequence*. Realizing that there is a time sequence will help you achieve your study purpose, which is probably to take effective notes on the material.

3 Remember that not all relationships between ideas are signaled by transitions. An author may present a list of items, for example, without using addition words. So as you read, watch for the relationships themselves, not just the transitions.

CHAPTER REVIEW

In this chapter, you learned how authors use transitions and patterns of organization to make their ideas clear. Just as transitions show relationships between ideas in sentences, patterns of organization show relationships between supporting details in paragraphs and longer pieces of writing.

You also learned two common kinds of relationships that authors use to make their ideas clear:

- **Addition relationships**

    — Authors often present a list or series of reasons, examples, or other details that support an idea. The items have no time order, but are listed in whatever order the author prefers.
    — Transition words and phrases that signal such addition relationships include *for one thing, second, also, in addition,* and *finally.*

- **Time relationships**

    — Authors usually discuss a series of events or steps in the order in which they happen, resulting in a time order.
    — Transition words that signal such time relationships include *first, next, then, after,* and *last.*

The next chapter—Chapter 6—will help you learn three other important kinds of relationships: definition-example, comparison and/or contrast, and cause-effect.

 On the Web: If you are using this book in class, you can visit our website for additional practice in understanding relationships that involve addition and time. Go to **www.townsendpress.com** and click on "Learning Center."

REVIEW TEST 1

To review what you've learned in this chapter, fill in the blanks in the following items.

1. Transitions are words that signal *(parts of, the relationships between, the importance of)* _____ ideas.

2. A(n) *(addition, time)* _____ transition signals that the writer is adding to an idea or ideas already mentioned.

3. When a passage provides a series of directions or steps, or a sequence of events, it is likely to use *(addition, time)* _____ transitions.

4. _____ TRUE OR FALSE? A main idea often suggests a paragraph's pattern of organization.

5. A passage's pattern of organization is the pattern in which its *(supporting details, main ideas, causes and effects)* _____ are organized.

REVIEW TEST 2

A. Fill in each blank with one of the words in the box. Use each transition once. Then write the letter of the transition in the space provided.

A. also	B. before	C. final
D. one	E. second	F. then

_____ 1. Rubber tires were invented in 1845, _____ cars existed. At that time, the tires were meant for bicycles.

_____ 2. The average square inch of human skin includes 19 million cells. It _____ includes 625 sweat glands and 60 hairs.

_____ 3. There are two main kinds of fats: _____ is saturated fats; the other is unsaturated fats.

_____ 4. Read the paragraph carefully and _____ answer the questions that follow.

_____ 5. First dig a hole and work peat moss into the soil. Then put the plant in and pile in enough dirt to refill the hole. The _____ step is to water the plant liberally.

_____ 6. The first type of small business is often called the "mom-and-pop operation." The majority of small businesses fall into this category. The _____ type is the high-growth enterprise. This type of business aims to outgrow its small-business status as quickly as possible.

B. Read the textbook paragraph below, and then answer the questions that follow.

[1]The first professional baseball team, the Cincinnati Red Stockings, was founded in 1869. [2]After only a short time, there were teams in all the major Eastern and Midwestern cities. [3]The ballpark brought together crowds of strangers who could experience a sense of community within the big city as they watched a baseball game. [4]Immigrants were able to shake loose their ethnic ties and become absorbed in the new national game. [5]The green fields and fresh air of the ballpark were a welcome change from the sea of bricks and stone that dominated the city scene. [6]Workers could temporarily escape the routine of their daily lives. [7]They loved indirectly participating in the competition and accomplishment that baseball games symbolized. [8]The ballpark also provided a means for spectators to release their frustrations against authority figures. [9]The umpire became a symbol of scorn, and frequent cries of "kill the umpire" were heard.

_____ 7. The relationship of sentence 2 to the sentence before it is one of
A. addition.   B. time.

8. The key transition word in sentence 2 is _____.

_____ 9. Sentences 3–9 present a
A. list of benefits people found in attending baseball games.
B. series of events in baseball's history.
C. series of stages in the history of baseball.

10. The relationship of sentence 8 to the sentences before it is signaled by the transition _____.

REVIEW TEST 3

A. (1–5.) Fill in each blank with the appropriate transition from the box. Use each transition once.

A. after	B. as	C. first
D. later	E. then	

¹In one of the most terrifying scenes in all of literature, George Orwell in his classic novel *1984* describes how a government known as Big Brother destroys a couple's love. ²The couple, Winston and Julia, fall in love and meet secretly, knowing the government would not approve. ³(1) _____ informers turn them in, a government agent named O'Brien takes steps to end their love. ⁴(2) _____ he straps Winston down and explains that he has discovered Winston's worst fear. ⁵(3) _____ he sets a cage with two giant, starving sewer rats on the table next to Winston. ⁶He says that when he presses a lever, the door of the cage will slide up, and the rats will shoot out like bullets and bore straight into Winston's face. ⁷(4) _____ Winston's eyes dart back and forth, revealing his terror, O'Brien places his hand on the lever. ⁸Winston realizes that the only way out is for Julia to take his place. ⁹Suddenly, he hears his own voice screaming, "Do it to Julia! Not me! Julia!" ¹⁰Orwell does not describe Julia's interrogation, but (5) _____, when Julia and Winston see each other, they realize that each has betrayed the other. ¹¹Their love is gone. ¹²Big Brother has won.

_____ 6. The pattern of organization for the above selection is
A. list of items.   B. time order.

B. Below are the beginnings of four passages. Label each one with the letter of its pattern of organization. (You may find it helpful to underline the transition or transitions in each item.)

   A   List of items
   B   Time order

_____ 7.   ¹The process of labor during childbirth takes place in three overlapping phases. ²The first stage is the longest, lasting an average twelve to twenty-four hours for a woman having her first child. ³The second stage typically lasts about one and a half hours. . . .

_____ 8.   ¹There are various ways to combat fatigue. ²One excellent way is exercise—walking, running, or lifting weights several times a week. ³Another useful strategy is to take a daily nap of twenty minutes or less, preferably in mid-afternoon, a low-energy period for many people. . . .

_____ 9.   ¹Even before he meets the three witches, Macbeth dreams of becoming king of Scotland. ²Then the witches predict he will be king, intensifying his ambition. ³Finally, his wife persuades him to murder King Duncan and take over the country. . . .

_____10.   ¹Today's smartphones offer many convenient features. ²Voice mail allows you to leave and receive messages. ³Another helpful feature is texting, which allows you to send a quick message without even making a call. ⁴Also, a camera is built in so you can take photos on the spur of the moment. ⁵And finally, more than 100,000 apps offer everything from maps and restaurant reviews to e-readers, music, and popular games like Words with Friends.

REVIEW TEST 4

Here is a chance to apply your understanding of addition and time relationships to a full-length reading. The following story tells about a loving father who decides never to lie to his child—and then has to deal with Santa Claus. Read it, and then answer the relationships questions that follow. There are also questions on understanding vocabulary in context, finding main ideas, and identifying supporting details.

Words to Watch

Below are some words in the reading that do not have strong context support. Each word is followed by the number of the paragraph in which it appears and its meaning there. These words are indicated in the reading by a small circle (°).

> *innumerable* (3): too many to count
> *leprechauns* (5): Irish elves
> *by osmosis* (7): like a sponge
> *allegedly* and *purportedly* (7): supposedly
> *deceived* (8): misled
> *literal* (9): factual
> *weasel words* (9): deliberately misleading language
> *prevalent* (14): widely held
> *stark* (17): plain
> *ponder* (23): think over
> *subtleties* (24): details

WONDER IN THE AIR

Jeff Gammage

1 When my wife and I had our first child, we established one firm parental rule:

2   No lies.

3   Our daughter, Jin Yu, spent her first two years in an orphanage in China, and we knew that as she grew, she would ask innumerable° questions about her life there. We wanted to be able to answer from an established position of truth-telling.

4   For me, the "All the truth, all the time" policy extended onto the symbols and myths of the holidays.

5   Every April, I gladly helped fill a basket with candy rabbits and colored eggs for our daughter, and then for her new sister, but skipped the story of the Easter bunny. I avoided any mention of leprechauns°, tried to ignore the tooth fairy.

6   Most of all, I was adamant about not telling Jin Yu tales about a certain red-suited fat man who spends every

December 24 breaking into people's homes.

7   Of course, like the Grinch, I couldn't stop Christmas—or Santa Claus—from coming. Jin Yu absorbed a belief in Santa as if by osmosis°. By age 4 she knew who he (allegedly°) was, how he (purportedly°) looked, and what he (supposedly) did.

8   I didn't want to ruin her fun, but also didn't want her to feel deceived° later on.

9   So, I responded to her questions about the big man with what I liked to think of as precise and technically accurate versions of the literal° truth—and what she would no doubt characterize as weasel words°.

10   At the mall, we'd walk past a jolly Santa sitting upon a velvet throne.

11   "Is that really Santa?" my daughter would ask.

12   I'd reply with a lawyerly, "The people in line must think so."

13   The worst was when she wondered if Santa truly kept lists of children who behaved and misbehaved.

14   "That's the prevalent° belief," I said.

15   By last Christmas Eve, I had done such an expert job of parenting, made such a successful effort to be truthful, that as I tucked my daughter into bed, she was confused and near tears.

16   "Daddy, will Santa"—here her voice almost broke—"bring me any presents?"

17   This was it, the question squarely placed, a moment that offered a stark° choice between fable and fact, that demanded a reasoned response from a father grounded in principle. I looked at my adored child, her dark brown eyes threatening to overflow, knowing there was but one choice, and I made it:

I lied.   18

On Christmas Eve, the holy of holy   19 nights, I lied to my 5-year-old daughter so fully, so deliberately and in such compelling detail that I nearly believed it myself.

"Darling, of course Santa is going   20 to bring you presents. He would never overlook you. You're such a good girl [that part was true] that I know Santa will stop here. Listen, do you hear that sound outside? I think it's jingle bells! It must be his sleigh!"

Jin Yu turned to the window,   21 hoping to glimpse a team of reindeer in flight, then lay back and drifted off, content, or at least relieved.

22   The next morning, she awoke to find that, sure enough, Santa had visited her home, proving his existence by magically delivering a wardrobe of princess gowns and dress-up shoes in exactly her size.

23   I think he left something for me as well: The power of a child's belief. A reminder that the best things in life cannot be seen with the naked eye. And that while there will be plenty of time for my daughter to ponder° cold and painful truths, her time of wonder should be savored.

24   This year, fully 6, Jin Yu is happily preparing for Santa by drawing crayon snowscapes and discussing his impending arrival with friends. She counsels her 3-year-old sister, Zhao Gu, on the subtleties° of naughty and nice.

25   Last week Jin Yu came to me with a very specific Christmas question, the sort that once again required a father's sure guidance: What kind of cookies should she leave for Santa on Christmas Eve?

26   I was firm in my response: Chocolate chip. Definitely, I told her, Santa likes chocolate chip.

Reading Comprehension Questions

Vocabulary in Context

_____ 1. In the sentence below, the word *adamant* (ăd′ə-mənt) means
    A. undecided.
    B. determined.
    C. flexible.
    D. angry.

    "Most of all, I was adamant about not telling Jin Yu tales about a certain red-suited fat man who spends every December 24 breaking into people's homes." (Paragraph 6)

_____ 2. In the sentence below, the word *savored* (sā′vərd) means
  A. unnoticed.
  B. discouraged.
  C. fully enjoyed.
  D. explained.

> "And that while there will be plenty of time for my daughter to ponder cold and painful truths, her time of wonder should be savored." (Paragraph 23)

_____ 3. In the sentence below, the word *impending* (ĭm-pĕnd′ĭng) means
  A. late.
  B. soon to take place.
  C. surprising.
  D. possible.

> "This year, fully 6, Jin Yu is happily preparing for Santa by drawing crayon snowscapes and discussing his impending arrival with friends." (Paragraph 24)

Central Point and Main Ideas

_____ 4. Which sentence best expresses the central point of the selection?
  A. Holiday myths are so common in our culture that it is impossible to always tell the truth to children.
  B. If a child wants to believe in Santa Claus, there is little a parent can do to stop her.
  C. The author reluctantly goes along with his daughter's belief in Santa Claus.
  D. When he sees how important a belief in Santa Claus is to his daughter, the author comes to understand that all children should be permitted their time of wonder.

_____ 5. The main idea of paragraphs 1–5 is that
  A. the author's daughter was adopted from an orphanage in China as a two-year-old.
  B. the author knew that his adopted daughter would ask questions about her first two years in China.
  C. the author and his wife vowed never to lie to their adopted daughter, even about holiday symbols and myths.
  D. the author allowed his daughter to celebrate holidays, but skipped telling her holiday myths.

Supporting Details

_____ 6. The author breaks his vow never to lie to his daughter
  A. when they see a Santa at the shopping mall.
  B. a few days before Easter.
  C. on Christmas Eve.
  D. when she asks him what kind of cookies she should leave for Santa on Christmas Eve.

_____ 7. For Jin Yu, Santa's existence is proven when
  A. she sees him at the shopping mall.
  B. she finds that he has eaten all the chocolate chip cookies she left him on Christmas Eve.
  C. she finds that he has magically delivered princess gowns and dress-up shoes in exactly her size.
  D. all her friends tell her that he exists.

Transitions

_____ 8. Read the two sentences below and then answer the question that follows.

"Jin Yu turned to the window, hoping to glimpse a team of reindeer in flight, then lay back and drifted off, content, or at least relieved.

"The next morning, she awoke to find that, sure enough, Santa had visited her home, . . ." (Paragraphs 21–22)

What does the second sentence do?
  A. It adds more detail to the first sentence.
  B. It shows a time order relationship.

Patterns of Organization

_____ 9. Paragraph 23 mainly
  A. lists ways that the author benefited from his daughter's belief in Santa Claus.
  B. presents a series of events in time order.

_____ 10. The main pattern of organization of this selection is
  A. a list of items.
  B. time order.

Discussion Questions

1. Was the author right to lie to his daughter? Why or why not?

2. When you were a child, did you believe in Santa Claus? How did you find out that he doesn't really exist?

3. When or if you have children, will you encourage them to believe in Santa, the Easter Bunny, and the tooth fairy? Why or why not?

4. The author and his wife decided that "no lies" would be their "one firm parental rule." What do you think are some other good parental rules?

Note: Writing assignments for this selection appear on page 624.

Check Your Performance   **RELATIONSHIPS I**

Activity		Number Right	Points	Score
Review Test 1	(5 items)	_____	× 2 =	_____
Review Test 2	(10 items)	_____	× 3 =	_____
Review Test 3	(10 items)	_____	× 3 =	_____
Review Test 4	(10 items)	_____	× 3 =	_____
			TOTAL SCORE =	_____ %

Enter your total score into the **Reading Performance Chart: Review Tests** on the inside back cover.

RELATIONSHIPS I: Mastery Test 1

A. Fill in each blank with an appropriate transition from the box. Use each transition once. Then, in the spaces provided, write the letter of the transition you have chosen.

A. after	B. also	C. another
D. moreover	E. then	

Hint: Make sure that each word or phrase that you choose fits smoothly into the flow of the sentence. Test your choices by reading each sentence to yourself.

_____ 1. ¹If you're used to e-mail, sending an actual letter can seem like a long, drawn-out process. ²First you have to get a pen and paper, an envelope, and stamps. ³_____ you write the letter, you have to fold it, place it in the envelope, and attach a stamp. ⁴Finally you need to find a place to mail the letter. ⁵No wonder people mail so few real letters these days!

_____ 2. ¹I have a limited interest in people whose main topic of conversation is themselves and who never show any interest in what is happening to me. ²_____ group I avoid is people who never allow facts to interfere with their opinions.

_____ 3. ¹The world of business is one area in which technology has isolated us. ²Many people now work alone at a display terminal that connects to a large central computer. ³Personal banking has _____ become a detached process. ⁴To deposit or withdraw money from their accounts, customers often interact with machines rather than people.

_____ 4. ¹By today's standards, early automobiles were difficult to operate and uncomfortable to drive. ²A driver had to start the car's engine by cranking it by hand, and the crank sometimes sprang back and broke the driver's thumb. ³_____, early cars were open on top, so driving on unpaved roads left riders choking on dust and dirt.

_____ 5. ¹Many television ads proceed in three stages: the problem, the advice, and the resolution. ²For example, a mouthwash commercial will first establish the problem—that someone has bad breath. ³_____ it will suggest that the person try the advertised mouthwash. ⁴This is followed by an obvious resolution of the problem: the person's being chased by attractive members of the opposite sex.

(Continues on next page)

B. (6–9.) Fill in each blank with an appropriate transition word from the box. Use each transition once.

A. after	B. last	C. next
D. then		

¹Two Minnesota brothers, Ed and Norman, are engaged in a war. ²It all started (6)_____ Ed's wife gave him a pair of pants that didn't fit. ³Ed wrapped up the pants and put them under Norman's Christmas tree. ⁴As soon as Norman opened the box, he recognized the unwanted pants.

⁵The (7)_____ year, he gave them back to Ed, sealed in a heavy carton tied with knotted ropes. ⁶The War of the Pants was on. ⁷Each year, on one of the brothers' birthdays, or on Christmas, the dreaded pants reappear. ⁸Two years ago, Norman bought an old safe, put the pants in it, welded it shut, and delivered it to Ed's house. ⁹Somehow, Ed retrieved the pants. ¹⁰(One of the rules of the war is that the pants must not be damaged.)

¹¹(8)_____ year Ed took the pants to an auto junkyard. ¹²The pants were placed in an ancient Ford's backseat, and the car (9)_____ went through the auto crusher. ¹³On his birthday, Norman found a four-foot square of smashed metal on his doorstep. ¹⁴He knew it could only be Ed's doing, and the pants must be inside. ¹⁵Norman is still trying to get at the pants and prepare next year's "topper."

_____10. The pattern of organization of the above selection is
     A. list of items.
     B. time order.

RELATIONSHIPS I: Mastery Test 2

A. Fill in each blank with an appropriate transition from the box. Use each transition once. Then, in the spaces provided, write the letter of the transition you have chosen.

A. also	**B. before**	**C. first**
D. then	**E. when**	

_____ 1. ¹Big snapping turtles don't get to weigh so much without eating a lot of food. ²Here's how they do it: ³Most snapping turtles float, or lie motionless on the bottom of a pond or river. ⁴_____ a fish, frog, or other prey swims close enough, the turtle snaps very fast with powerful jaws.

_____ 2. ¹Experts cite several reasons for Japan's low crime rate. ²_____, Japan has had strict gun control for four hundred years. ³In addition, the country relies on some fifteen thousand small neighborhood police stations known as *koban*. ⁴Police officers and their families actually live as part of the neighborhood, helping prevent the growth of conditions that might lead to crime.

_____ 3. ¹For much of my life, I have been haunted by dreams of falling. ²In a typical dream, I have fallen off a tall building or over the edge of a cliff or out of a plane, and I am plunging at a breathtaking speed toward the ground. ³_____, just as I am about to crash into the ground, I wake up in a cold sweat, my heart racing.

_____ 4. ¹According to legend, tea was discovered quite by accident. ²One day about 4,000 years ago, a Chinese emperor was boiling water outside when leaves from a bush fell into the open pot. ³_____ the emperor could remove the leaves, they began to brew. ⁴He smelled the sweet aroma of the mixture, and once he tasted it, tea was born.

_____ 5. ¹Whoever you are, whatever you look like, chances are you're not happy with your appearance. ²Our culture constantly sends out the message that you're not attractive enough. ³Television is one of the most powerful message-carriers, showing you an endless parade of impossibly thin, beautiful people. ⁴Magazines are _____ designed to make you feel ugly, with glossy airbrushed models on every page providing an impossible ideal of thin, ageless beauty.

(Continues on next page)

B. Read the passage and answer the question that follows.

¹Probably every child remembers digging a hole in his or her backyard and being told, "If you dig deep enough, you'll go to China." ²What would really happen if a man dug a hole through the center of the Earth and then jumped into it? ³The traveler entering the tunnel would first fall rapidly under the force of gravity. ⁴Eventually, as he approached the Earth's center, the jumper's weight would decrease. ⁵By the time he reached the center of the Earth, he would be weightless. ⁶An equal amount of the Earth's mass on all sides of him would cancel out the forces of gravity. ⁷Still, the traveler's original momentum would carry him past the center toward the opening on the far side of the world. ⁸After almost reaching that point, he would fall back up the hole toward his starting point. ⁹Back and forth he would then go, like a yo-yo, gradually slowing down until coming to a stop at the very center of the Earth.

_____ 6. The main pattern of organization of the passage is
     A. list of items.
     B. time order.

C. (7–9.) Fill in each blank with an appropriate transition word from the box. Use each transition once. Then answer the question that follows.

A. also	B. finally	C. first

¹The microbes that cause infection are transmitted to people in several ways.

²(7)_____, there is direct transmission, which involves bodily contact with an infected person. ³Examples are passing along a cold through handshaking or herpes through sexual relations. ⁴There is (8)_____ indirect transmission, which occurs when microbes are passed from an infected person to an individual via airborne particles, water, food, or anything else the infected person touches. ⁵For example, someone might catch the flu by drinking from a glass that has been used by a person with the flu. ⁶(9)_____, animals and insects can transmit microbes. ⁷Flies, for instance, carry harmful microbes on their feet, and can transmit them to people by landing on their food.

_____10. The pattern of organization of the above selection is
     A. list of items.
     B. time order.

RELATIONSHIPS I: Mastery Test 3

A. (1–4.) Arrange the scrambled sentences below into a logical paragraph by numbering them *1, 2, 3,* and *4* in an order that makes sense. Then, in the space provided, write the letter of the pattern of organization used.

Note that transitions will help you by clarifying the relationships between sentences.

___ In addition, check the puppy's personality by watching how it plays with other puppies.

___ There are some important points to keep in mind when choosing a puppy.

___ Last, since curiosity is a sign of intelligence, clap your hands to see if the puppy is curious and interested.

___ For one thing, look for signs of good health, including clear, bright eyes and firm, pink gums.

_____ 5. The pattern of organization of the above selection is
   A. list of items.
   B. time order.

B. Read the passage and answer the question that follows. You may find it helpful to underline transitions as you read.

¹In January of 1954, Ernest and Mary Hemingway left Nairobi on a vacation trip on which they flew over grazing elephants, hippos bathing in the lakes, and huge flocks of feeding flamingos. ²As they were circling a spectacular waterfall, a flock of ibises flew in front of the plane. ³When the pilot dived to avoid the birds, he struck an abandoned telegraph wire that crossed the gorge. ⁴In the crash that followed, Ernest sprained his shoulder; Mary was only slightly injured. ⁵Luckily, a boat came down the river the next morning, and its crew rescued them. ⁶By that evening, they were on board a small plane bound for Entebbe. ⁷The plane lifted from the plowed field that served as a runway, then crashed and burst into flames. ⁸Ernest escaped by breaking through a window with his head and injured shoulder, and Mary got out through another window. ⁹Twice in two days they had crashed and come out alive, but Ernest had injured his head, his backbone, and a kidney. ¹⁰After this, even writing a letter was difficult for him.

_____ 6. The pattern of organization of the above selection is
   A. list of items.
   B. time order.

(Continues on next page)

C. Read the textbook passage below, and then answer the question and complete the outline.

> [1]Prevention against injury involves a combination of two types of preventive measures. [2]First is active prevention, which refers to methods that require people to do something to reduce the risk of being injured. [3]Examples include the use of nonautomatic seat belts, the use of bicycle and motorcycle helmets, following drunk driving laws, and obeying traffic regulations. [4]The second type of preventive measure is passive prevention. [5]Passive prevention refers to methods requiring little or no action on the part of those being protected. [6]These measures include seat belts that automatically engage when a person enters a car, automobile air bags, better street lighting, and built-in safety switches on power tools and electrical equipment.

_____ 7. The pattern of organization of the above selection is
     A. list of items.
     B. time order.

8–10. Complete the outline of the passage.

Main idea: _____

_____

    Major supporting details:

    1. _____

       _____

       Examples—use of nonautomatic seat belts; bike helmets

    2. _____

       _____

       Examples—automatic seat belts; air bags

RELATIONSHIPS I: Mastery Test 4

A. (1–5.) Arrange the scrambled sentences below into a logical paragraph by numbering them *1, 2, 3,* and *4* in an order that makes sense. Then, in the space provided, write the letter of the pattern of organization used.

Note that transitions will help you by clarifying the relationships between sentences.

____ When you have chosen your apartment, have a lawyer or another person knowledgeable about leases examine your lease before you sign it.

____ If you're looking for an apartment, begin by making a list of promising openings. Check the classified ads and two or three real estate offices for apartments within your price range and desired locale.

____ As you inspect each apartment, make sure that faucets, toilets, stoves, and electrical wiring and outlets are functioning efficiently and safely.

____ After you have made a solid list, visit at least five of the most promising available apartments.

_____ 5. The pattern of organization of the above selection is
   A. list of items.
   B. time order.

B. Read the textbook passage below and answer the question that follows.

¹Did you ever wonder how trainers get porpoises to do all those tricks, like leaping over a high bar or jumping through a hoop? ²Wild porpoises are first taught to eat fish from their trainer's hand. ³When the animal accepts a fish, the trainer blows a whistle. ⁴The porpoise associates the whistle with "correct" behavior. ⁵Once the porpoise touches a human hand to get a fish, it will touch other things, like a red target ball. ⁶For example, the trainer will hold the ball high above the water while leaning over a kind of pulpit. ⁷Seeing the ball, the porpoise leaps out of the water; it knows it will be rewarded with a fish. ⁸A hoop can then be substituted for a ball, and the porpoise's behavior can be "shaped" so it will jump through the hoop. ⁹If the porpoise misses by jumping too low, the fish reward is withheld. ¹⁰The intelligent animal will associate "no fish" with "wrong" behavior; very quickly, the porpoise will be leaping gracefully through the center of the hoop.

_____ 6. The pattern of organization of the above selection is
   A. list of items.
   B. time order.

(Continues on next page)

C. (7–10.) Complete the map of the following textbook passage.

¹Work shapes human lives in fundamental ways. ²First, work consumes enormous amounts of people's time. ³Most people spend about one-third of their adult lives working. ⁴According to a recent survey, almost half of all employed people spend 40 hours or more per week at work; only 10 percent work less than 30 hours a week. ⁵Work also gives life a structure and rhythm. ⁶The traditional eight-hour "shift" allows people to balance their days with productive time and recreational time. ⁷This daily pattern promotes mental health. ⁸In fact, many studies show that when people are unable to work, they experience emotional distress and low self-esteem. ⁹A third way work shapes life is that it causes stress. ¹⁰For some this stress can be positive—resulting in increased performance and professional success. ¹¹For others, however, the stress can be extreme and lead to health problems and illness.

RELATIONSHIPS I: Mastery Test 5

Read each textbook passage, and then answer the questions or follow the directions provided.

A. ¹Scoundrels have cheated their victims throughout history, but the term "confidence man" was apparently coined only in 1849, and it immediately achieved widespread currency. ²It originated in the story of a swindler of gentlemanly appearance and remarkable boldness named Samuel Thompson. ³He would approach a well-dressed stranger on the streets of a city and greet him as if he were an old acquaintance. ⁴After a brief conversation, Thompson would ask, "Have you confidence in me to trust me with your watch until tomorrow?" ⁵The victim, embarrassed to have forgotten this courteous and friendly gentleman and reluctant to deny such a direct request, would lend his watch. ⁶Then the "confidence man" would walk off laughing, never to return. ⁷He was finally caught by the police only after he was spotted by a previous victim.

_____ 1. The pattern of organization of the above selection is
   A. list of items.
   B. time order.

2. One of the transitions that signals the pattern of organization is

   _____.

B. ¹Many food products are stamped with dates that tell consumers when the product is still fresh. ²Products are dated in one of three ways. ³Some food products contain the words "sell by" followed by the date. ⁴These foods remain fresh for about one week after the date on the label. ⁵Other foods list the date after the words "best if used by." ⁶Products with this label can still be used for a few weeks after the date on the label, but they might not have the same quality.

⁷_____, certain products, such as baby formulas, have an expiration date. ⁸These products should not be used after the date on the label.

_____ 3. The paragraph
   A. lists ways in which food products are dated.
   B. describes stages in dating food products.

_____ 4. The transition that would best fit the blank space in sentence 7 is
   A. *After.*
   B. *Eventually.*
   C. *Third.*

(Continues on next page)

C.   ¹Dr. Elisabeth Kübler-Ross has identified five stages in the reactions of dying patients. ²The first stage, she says, is denial. ³Patients will at first deny the seriousness of their illness, claiming that some error has been made. ⁴Then patients become angry. ⁵They ask, "Why me?" ⁶Their anger may be directed against God, fate, or even their doctors. ⁷Next comes depression. ⁸During this stage, patients feel hopeless and lose interest in life. ⁹After depression comes bargaining—patients try to bargain for their lives. ¹⁰They may promise God or their doctors that they'll be good, stop smoking, give up alcohol, or do whatever is necessary if only they can survive. ¹¹The fifth stage is that of acceptance. ¹²Patients finally resign themselves to the inevitable. ¹³They are not joyful, but they gain a sense of inner peace. ¹⁴While there has been some criticism of Kübler-Ross's stages, her work has contributed much to making death a more comfortable and better-understood subject.

_____   5.   The pattern of organization of the above selection is
            A. list of items.
            B. time order.

6–10.   Complete the map of the paragraph.

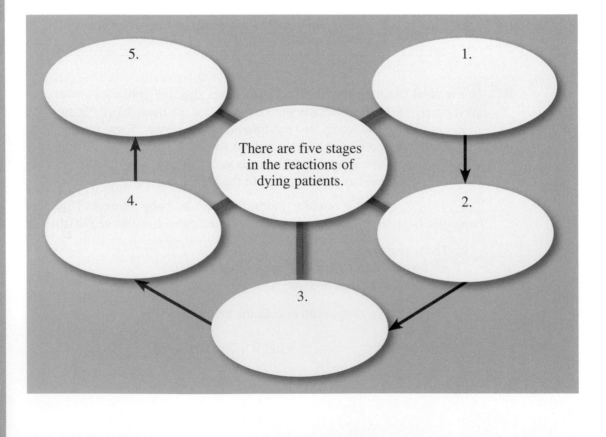

RELATIONSHIPS I: Mastery Test 6

Read each textbook passage, and then answer the questions or follow the directions provided.

A. [1]According to the National Institute on Drug Abuse, thirty million Americans—one out of eight people—suffer from a drug or alcohol dependency. [2]The development of an addiction typically unfolds in four stages. [3]First, some stimulus—drugs, alcohol, sex, chocolate—holds out the promise of short-lived pleasure or excitement. [4]Next, a person discovers that indulging in one of these activities temporarily satisfies some psychological need, making him or her feel good, if only for a short time. [5]Third, certain recurring situations start to trigger the addictive behavior, and the pattern repeats itself. [6]Finally, the habit takes control, and the individual loses self-control. [7]Often, by this stage, a physical dependency will have been added to a psychological one, thereby making the addictive behavior pattern even more difficult to break.

_____ 1. The pattern of organization of the above selection is
   A. list of items.
   B. time order.

2–3. Two of the transitions that introduce the major details of the paragraph are

   _____   _____

B. [1]After World War II began, women's roles changed. [2]The most visible change was the sudden appearance of large numbers of women in uniform. [3]The military organized them into auxiliary units with special uniforms, their own officers, and, amazingly, equal pay. [4]Most either filled traditional women's roles, such as nursing, or replaced men in noncombat situations.

[5]Women also substituted for men on the home front. [6]During the war, three million women entered the labor force, and for the first time in history, married working women outnumbered single working women. [7]The war challenged the public's image of proper female behavior, as "Rosie the Riveter" became the popular symbol of women who abandoned traditional jobs as domestic servants and store clerks to work in construction and heavy industry.

_____ 4. The pattern of organization of the above selection is
   A. list of items.
   B. time order.

5. The second major detail is signaled with the transition _____.

_____ 6. The total number of major details is
   A. two.
   B. three.
   C. four.

(Continues on next page)

C.   ¹There are three main ways that children learn their gender roles. ²One is conditioning through rewards and punishments. ³For example, boys who play with model airplanes and girls who play with dolls will usually be encouraged by their parents. ⁴On the other hand, boys who prefer dolls and girls who prefer airplanes will often be criticized or even punished. ⁵Another element is imitation. ⁶Young children will usually imitate adults who they think are like themselves. ⁷This means that boys will usually imitate their fathers and girls their mothers. ⁸The third and perhaps most important element is self-definition. ⁹Children quickly learn that all people are either male or female and define themselves as belonging to one sex rather than the other. ¹⁰They then use this self-definition to choose their future interests and to develop their personalities and social roles.

_____ 7.   The pattern of organization of the above selection is
   A. list of items.
   B. time order.

8–10. Complete the outline of the paragraph.

Main idea: _____

   Major supporting details:

   1.   Conditioning through rewards and punishments

   2.   _____

   3.   _____

6 Relationships II

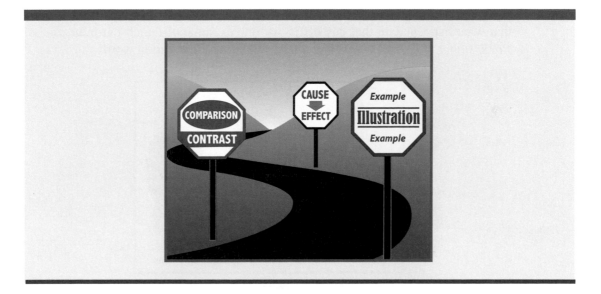

In the previous chapter, you learned how authors use transitions and patterns of organization to show relationships and make their ideas clear. You also learned about two common types of relationships:

- Relationships that involve **addition**
- Relationships that involve **time**

In this chapter, you will learn about three other types of relationships:

- Relationships that involve **illustration**
- Relationships that involve **comparison and contrast**
- Relationships that involve **cause and effect**

1 Illustration

Words That Show Illustration

Put a check (✓) beside the item that is easier to understand:

___ I've become very absent-minded. Last week I went to work on my day off.

___ I've become very absent-minded. Last week, for instance, I went to work on my day off.

The second item is easier to understand. The words *for instance* make it clear that what happened on that day off is just one example of the absent-mindedness. *For instance* and other words and phrases like it are illustration words.

Illustration words indicate that an author will provide one or more *examples* to develop and clarify a given idea. In the cartoon above, the husband gives examples of what, to him, are deep emotions.

Here are some common words that introduce examples:

Illustration Words

(for) example	including	(as an) illustration	one
(for) instance	specifically	to illustrate	once
such as	to be specific		

Examples

The following items contain illustration words. Notice how these words signal that one or more *examples* are coming.

● Certain colors are associated with particular emotions. *For instance*, green represents jealousy, red stands for anger, and blue means "gloomy."

- My grandmother doesn't hear well anymore. *For example,* whenever I say, "Hi, Granny," she answers, "Fine, just fine."
- A cat's curiosity can get it into ridiculous situations. *Once,* a neighbor's cat got its head stuck in the garbage disposal.

PRACTICE 1

Complete each item with a suitable illustration word or phrase from the box on the previous page. Try to use a variety of transitions.

> *Hint:* Make sure that each word or phrase that you choose fits smoothly into the flow of the sentence. Test each choice by reading the sentence aloud.

1. Animals were once tried for crimes. _____, in 1740 a cow convicted of witchcraft was hanged by the neck until dead.

2. Some soap opera fans take the shows too seriously. There are viewers, _____, who actually send threats to soap opera "villains."

3. My mother believes in various superstitions, _____ the idea that if you drop a fork, it means company's coming.

4. When a couple divorces, the partners often experience a wide range of emotions, _____ anger, regret, depression, and relief.

5. People have chosen to end their lives in a variety of unusual ways. As an _____, in ancient China, people committed suicide by eating a pound of salt.

Illustration words are common in all types of writing. One way they are used in textbooks is in the pattern of organization known as the definition and example pattern.

The Definition and Example Pattern

Definition and Example

Definition

Example   Example

To get a sense of the definition and example pattern, try to arrange the following sentences in an order that makes sense. Put a *1* in front of the sentence that should come first, a *2* in front of the sentence that comes next, and a *3* in front of the sentence that should be last. The result will be a short paragraph.

___ Someone might, for instance, sit calmly through a friend's criticism and act as if it didn't bother him or her.

___ Apathy is an avoidance response in which a person acknowledges unpleasant information but pretends he or she does not care about it.

___ Another example is responding to the loss of a job by acting indifferent: "Who cares? It was a dumb job anyhow."

This paragraph begins with a definition: "Apathy is an avoidance response in which a person acknowledges unpleasant information but pretends he or she does not care about it." The second sentence makes clear this meaning of *apathy* with an example: "Someone might, for instance, sit calmly through a friend's criticism and act as if it didn't bother him or her." The third sentence then provides an added example: "Another example is responding to the loss of a job by acting indifferent: 'Who cares? It was a dumb job anyhow.'" The second and third sentences include the illustration words *for instance* and *example*. As you can see, the **definition and example** pattern of organization includes just what its name suggests: a definition and one or more examples.

> *An Important Study Hint:* Good textbook authors want to help readers understand the important ideas and terms in a subject—whether it is psychology, sociology, business, biology, or any other field. Such authors often take time, then, to include key definitions. The ideas and terms being defined are usually set off in *italic* or **boldface** type, and the definitions are signaled by such words as *is, are, is called, termed,* and *refers to.* Here are some definitions from a variety of textbooks:
>
> ● An **instinct** is a form of behavior that occurs in all normal members of a species without having been learned.
>
> ● **Phobias** are fears that are out of proportion to the actual danger involved in a situation.
>
> ● **Divergent thinking** refers to the ability to generate unusual, yet nonetheless appropriate, responses to problems or questions.
>
> ● Once a tumor has been detected, cells can be removed from it in a procedure called a **biopsy**; the cells are then examined under the microscope by a pathologist.
>
> ● Party funding, along with the money a candidate receives from individual contributors and interest groups, is termed **hard money** since it goes directly to the candidate and can be spent as he or she chooses.
>
> ● Both rapidly growing countries and slowly growing countries can have a problem with their **dependency ratio**—the number of nonworking compared to working individuals in a population.

If an author defines a term, you can assume that it is important enough to learn. So when reading and taking notes on a textbook, always do two things:

1)   Write down key definitions.

2)   Put an "Ex" in the margin next to a helpful example for each definition. When a definition is general and abstract, examples are often essential to make its meaning clear.

✓ Check Your Understanding

The following paragraph defines a word, explains it a bit, and then gives an example of it. After reading the paragraph, see if you can answer the questions that follow.

¹Acrophobia is an intense, unreasonable fear of high places. ²People with acrophobia exhibit emotional and physical symptoms in response to being at great heights. ³For instance, one sufferer of extreme acrophobia, Sally Maxwell, is unable to go above the third floor of any building without feeling enormous anxiety. ⁴Her acrophobia began one evening when she was working alone in her office on the eighth floor of a large building. ⁵Suddenly she was struck with terror by the idea that she might jump or fall out the open window. ⁶She crouched behind a steel filing cabinet, trembling, unable to move. ⁷When she finally gathered her belongings and left the building, she was sweating, her breathing was rapid, and her heart was pounding. ⁸Yet she had no rational explanation for her fears.

What word is being defined? _____

What is the definition?   _____

_____

Which sentence explains more about the word? _____

In which sentence does the example begin? _____

Explanation

The word *acrophobia* is defined in the first sentence—"an intense, unreasonable fear of high places." The second sentence explains a bit more about acrophobia. The story about Sally Maxwell, which begins in the third sentence, provides an example of how acrophobia affects one sufferer. The example helps make the new term clear to the reader. The author introduces that illustration with the transition *For instance*.

PRACTICE 2

A. The following passage includes a definition and two examples. Underline the term being defined. Then, in the spaces provided, write the number of the definition sentence and the number of the sentence where each example begins.

> [1]Shaping is a way to teach a new behavior by encouraging a series of small bits of the whole behavior. [2]This approach, for instance, was used to teach a disturbed little boy named Dickey to wear eyeglasses after cataract surgery. [3]His physician feared that without glasses, his vision would deteriorate permanently. [4]At the mere mention of eyeglasses, however, Dickey threw terrible temper tantrums. [5]So researchers used shaping to ease him into the idea of wearing his glasses. [6]Dickey was deprived of his breakfast so that food could be used as a reward. [7]He received a bit of food each time he picked up some glasses frames. [8]Later in the procedure, he had to put glasses on in order to receive a reward. [9]Within eighteen days, Dickey had learned through gradual steps to wear his glasses for twelve hours a day.
>
> [10]Another example is teaching a circus tiger to jump through a flaming hoop. [11]The tiger might first be rewarded for jumping up on a pedestal and then for leaping from that pedestal to another. [12]Eventually, the hoop would be set on fire, and the tiger would have to leap through the burning hoop to be rewarded.

Definition _____ *Example 1* _____ *Example 2* _____

B. The following passage includes a definition and one example. Underline the term being defined. Then outline the selection by doing two things: 1) filling in the word being defined and its definition; 2) in a few words, summarizing the example.

> [1]Jonathan Swift (1667–1745), author of *Gulliver's Travels,* often used irony— saying one thing but meaning another—in his writing. [2]For example, in his famous essay "A Modest Proposal," he makes this suggestion for ending the famine in Ireland: the Irish should raise babies to be eaten. [3]Swift did not mean his suggestion to be taken seriously. [4]His actual goal was to shock his British audience into facing the mass starvation and misery in Ireland that British policies had produced at that time.

_____ — _____

_____

Example— _____

_____

2 Comparison and Contrast

Words That Show Comparison

Put a check (✓) beside the item that is easier to understand:

____ Driving a car is a skill that we learn through practice. Writing a paper is a skill that we learn through hands-on experience.

____ Driving a car is a skill that we learn through practice. Similarly, writing a paper is a skill that we learn through hands-on experience.

The first item makes us wonder, "What has learning to drive a car got to do with writing a paper?" The word *similarly* makes it clear that the author intends to compare learning to write a paper with learning to drive a car. *Similarly* and words like it are comparison words.

DRABBLE © 2000 Kevin Fagin. Reprinted with permission of UNIVERSAL UCLICK for UFS. All rights reserved.

Comparison words signal similarities. Authors use a comparison transition to show that a second idea is *like* the first one in some way. In the cartoon above, the word *resemble* helps show a comparison is being made.

Here are some common words that show comparison:

Comparison Words

(just) as	both	in like fashion	in a similar fashion
(just) like	equal(ly)	in like manner	in a similar manner
alike	resemble	similar(ly)	(in) the same way
same	likewise	similarity	(in) common

Examples

The sentences below contain comparison words. Notice how these words show that things are *alike* in some way.

- When buying milk, my mother always takes a bottle from the back of the shelf. *Similarly,* when my father buys a newspaper, he usually grabs one from the middle of the pile.

- Moviemakers with a big hit tend to repeat the winning idea in their next film, *just like* authors who use a successful plot over and over.

- The printing press greatly changed the way people learned news and ideas. *In a similar manner,* the Internet has revolutionized the way in which people obtain information.

PRACTICE 3

Complete each sentence with a suitable comparison word or phrase from the box on the previous page. Try to use a variety of transitions.

1. Using a smartphone in a darkened theater will not win you any friends. _____, talking out loud with your movie partner will soon make people scowl in your direction.

2. _____ an athlete in training, the mind of a reader grows stronger with practice.

3. Spicy foods make me very thirsty. Believe it or not, ice cream affects me _____.

4. The Amish people farm their land _____ their 18th-century relatives did, without benefit of gasoline-powered tractors or other modern equipment.

5. _____ rats become hostile when they live in a crowded cage, humans become aggressive in crowded conditions.

Words That Show Contrast

Put a check (✓) beside the item that is easier to understand:

____ A roller coaster scares many people. They love riding on it.

____ Even though a roller coaster scares many people, they love riding on it.

In the first item, the two sentences seem to contradict each other. We want to ask, "Do people like a roller coaster, or don't they?" In the second item, the phrase *even though* makes clear the relationship between the two ideas: In spite of the fact that a roller coaster is scary, people still love riding on it. *Even though* and other words and phrases like it are contrast words.

"Smoking may kill me. On the other hand, the non-smokers are inside working themselves to death."

Contrast words show that things *differ* in one or more ways. In the above cartoon, the speaker is contrasting two possible ways to die.

Here are some common words that show contrast:

Contrast Words

but	instead (of)	even though	difference
yet	in contrast	as opposed to	different(ly)
however	on the other hand	in spite of	differ (from)
although	(on the) contrary	despite	unlike
nevertheless	converse(ly)	rather than	while
still	opposite		

Examples

The above cartoon and the sentences that follow contain contrast words. Notice how these words signal that one idea is *different from* another idea.

● People used to think that getting chilled would lead to catching a cold. *However,* getting chilled has nothing to do with getting sick.

- Skunks are unpopular creatures, *yet* they eat lots of mice and bugs and don't spray unless they feel threatened.

- Some people look upon eating as something to be done quickly so they can get on to better things. *In contrast,* others think eating *is* one of the better things.

PRACTICE 4

Complete each sentence with a suitable contrast word or phrase from the box on the previous page. Try to use a variety of transitions.

1. Most of us could live without food for a month; _____, we need two quarts of water a day to survive.

2. _____ going up a ladder is easy, looking down from the top can be difficult.

3. At first we were planning on spending our vacation at a campground,

   _____ now we've decided to save money by relaxing at home.

4. Paula was not satisfied with her paper _____ the fact that she had already written five drafts.

5. We use seventeen muscles to smile. _____, we have to use forty-three muscles to frown.

Comparison and contrast transitions are often used in paragraphs organized in the comparison and/or contrast pattern.

The Comparison and/or Contrast Pattern

To get a sense of the comparison and/or contrast pattern, try to arrange the following sentences in an order that makes sense. Put a *1* in front of the sentence that should come first, a *2* in front of the sentence that comes next, and a *3* in front of the sentence that should be last. The result will be a short paragraph.

____ Yet the large, hairy tarantula is relatively harmless, while the small brown recluse is dangerously poisonous.

____ The tarantula and the brown recluse are more different than they are similar.

____ It's true that both spiders are alike in inspiring a great deal of fear.

The first sentence of this paragraph is the general one, the one with the main idea: "The tarantula and the brown recluse are more different than they are similar." The words *similar* and *different* suggest a comparison and/or contrast pattern of organization. The comparison word *alike* and the contrast words *yet* and *while* in the other two sentences show that the spiders are indeed being compared *and* contrasted: "It's true that both spiders are alike in inspiring a great deal of fear. Yet the large, hairy tarantula is relatively harmless, while the small brown recluse is dangerously poisonous."

The **comparison-contrast** pattern shows how two things are alike or how they are different, or both. When things are compared, their similarities are pointed out; when they are contrasted, their differences are discussed. (The tarantula and the brown recluse spider are alike in the fear they inspire; they are different in the effects of their bites, as well as in their appearance.)

You will find authors using a **comparison** pattern to show how two things are alike and a **contrast** pattern to show how they are different. Sometimes an author will compare and contrast in the same paragraph, pointing out both similarities and differences between two things. Comparison or contrast transitions will signal what an author is doing.

✔ *Check Your Understanding*

In the following paragraph, the main idea is stated in the first sentence. As is often the case, the main idea suggests a paragraph's pattern of organization. Here the transition *differently* is a hint that the paragraph may be organized in a comparison and/or contrast pattern. Read the paragraph and answer the questions below. Then read the explanation that follows.

[1]In middle age, men and women often view life very differently, especially if they are couples who have led traditional lives. [2]By middle age, the husband is often comfortable in his position at work and has given up any dreams of advancing further. [3]He may then become more family-oriented. [4]In contrast, once the children are grown, the wife may find herself free to explore interests and develop abilities she has had no time for in the previous fifteen or twenty years. [5]Unlike her husband, she may be more interested in non-family activities than she was before.

1. Is this paragraph comparing, contrasting, or both? _____

2. What two things are being compared and/or contrasted? _____

   _____

3. What three comparison or contrast transition words or phrases are used in

   the paragraph? _____

Explanation

This paragraph is only contrasting, not comparing—it discusses only differences, not similarities. The two things being contrasted are the views of traditional middle-aged men and women. The transition words or phrases that show contrast are *differently, In contrast,* and *Unlike.*

PRACTICE 5

A. The following passage uses the pattern of either comparison or contrast. Read the passage and answer the questions that follow.

> [1]Employment policies are quite different in Japan and the United States. [2]In Japan, teamwork is an essential part of hiring and promotion. [3]College graduates who join a corporation are all paid about the same starting salary. [4]To learn about the company's various departments, they are rotated as a team through the organization. [5]They are also promoted as a team. [6]Only in later years are individuals singled out for recognition. [7]When there is an opening in the firm, outsiders are not even considered.
>
> [8]In the United States, on the other hand, an employee is hired on the basis of what the firm thinks that individual can contribute. [9]Employees try to outperform others, and they strive for raises and promotions as signs of personal success. [10]The individual's loyalty is to himself or herself, not to the company. [11]Outsiders are considered for openings in U.S. firms.

Check (✓) the pattern which is used in this passage:

____ Comparison

____ Contrast

What two things are being compared or contrasted?

1. _____   2. _____

B. The following paragraph uses the pattern of either comparison or contrast. Read the passage and then answer the questions and complete the map that follows.

> [1]Among the school experiences new to young children is the regimented environment. [2]At home, children may have been able to do what they wanted when they wanted to do it. [3]But in school, they are given a set time for talking, working, playing, eating, and even going to the toilet. [4]Another source of anxiety may be the public method of discipline that some teachers use. [5]Whereas at home children are scolded in private, in school they may be held up to embarrassment in front of their peers. [6]"Mandy," the teacher may say, "why are you the only one in

the class who didn't do your homework?" [7]Or, "Scott, why are you the only one who can't work quietly at your seat?" [8]Last, a child may be scared by the competitive atmosphere of the school. [9]At home, one hopes, such competition for attention is minimal. [10]In school, however, children may vie for the teacher's approving glance or tone of voice, or for stars on a paper, or for favored seats in the front row.

Check (✓) the pattern which is used in this passage:

____   Comparison

____   Contrast

Complete the following map of the paragraph:

There are three differences between _____ and _____.	
1. Regimentation in school	Free movement at home
2.	
3.	

3 Cause and Effect

Words That Show Cause and Effect

Put a check (✓) beside the item that is easier to understand:

____   The paint has worn off the wooden siding. Fungus has begun to grow on it.

____   Because the paint has worn off the wooden siding, fungus has begun to grow on it.

In the first item, it seems the author is simply listing two things that have happened to the wooden siding. The word *because* in the second item makes clear the relationship between the two ideas—the protective paint wore off, and for this reason, the fungus was able to grow. *Because* and words like it are cause and effect words.

Cause and effect words signal that the author is explaining *the reason why* something happened or *the result* of something happening. In the cartoon above, the applicant is told that the result of interest rates going up or down will, unfortunately for him, be the same: Either way, his mortgage payment will go up!

Here are some common words that show cause and effect:

Cause and Effect Words

therefore	so	owing to	because (of)
thus	(as a) result	effect	reason
(as a) consequence	results in	cause	explanation
consequently	leads (led) to	if . . . then	accordingly
due to	since	affect	depend(s) on

Examples

The above cartoon and the sentences that follow contain cause and effect words. Notice how these words introduce a *reason* for something or the *result* of something.

- My sister became a vegetarian *because* she doesn't want to eat anything that had a mother.

- *If* the weather gets too humid, *then* the wooden doors in our house swell up and begin to stick.

- At one time in history, birth records were not kept for ordinary people. *As a result,* the only birthday parties given were for kings, queens, and other royalty.

PRACTICE 6

Complete each sentence with a suitable cause and effect word or phrase from the box on the previous page. Try to use a variety of transitions.

1. _____ property taxes in the city have gone sky-high, many corporations are moving to the suburbs.

2. Maria's resumé is impressive; _____, she has already had several job interviews.

3. My family is full of great Italian cooks, _____ canned ravioli tastes like cardboard to me.

4. _____ car dealers have a monthly quota of cars to sell, they are more likely to offer good deals near the end of a month.

5. Some zoo animals have not learned how to be good parents. _____, baby animals are sometimes brought up in zoo nurseries and even in private homes.

Cause and effect transitions often signal the cause and effect pattern of organization.

The Cause and Effect Pattern

To get a sense of the cause and effect pattern, try to arrange the following sentences in an order that makes sense. Put a *1* in front of the sentence that should come first, a *2* in front of the sentence that comes next, and a *3* in front of the sentence that should be last. The result will be a short paragraph.

____ Growing up without parents around resulted in the monkeys drinking enormous amounts of alcohol.

____ A study of monkeys suggests two factors may lead to alcoholism.

____ Low levels of serotonin in the brain also caused the monkeys to drink more.

As the words *resulted in, lead to,* and *caused* suggest, this paragraph is organized in a cause and effect pattern. The paragraph begins with the general idea: "A study of monkeys suggests two factors may lead to alcoholism." Next come two causes: "Growing up without parents around resulted in the monkeys drinking enormous amounts of alcohol. Low levels of serotonin in the brain also caused the monkeys to drink more."

Note that even in the cause and effect pattern—or any other pattern—addition words may be used to introduce points and show their order. The last sentence of the above paragraph, for example, includes the word *also,* showing that a second point is being added to the first: "Low levels of serotonin in the brain also caused the monkeys to drink more."

Information in a **cause and effect** pattern addresses the questions "Why does a behavior or event happen?" and/or "What are the results of a behavior or event?" An author may then discuss causes, or effects, or both causes and effects.

Authors usually don't just tell what happened; they try to explain both what happened and why. A textbook section on the sinking of the ship *Titanic*, for example, would be incomplete if it did not include the cause of the disaster—going at a high speed, the ship collided with an iceberg. Or if the number of homeless families in the country increases, journalists will not simply report the increase. They would also explore the reasons for and effects of that increase.

✔ Check Your Understanding

Read the paragraph below and see if you can answer the questions about cause and effect that follow. Then read the explanation to see how you did.

¹Even the best listeners are unable to listen carefully to everything they hear. ²One reason is the overload of messages we encounter each day. ³Besides the numerous hours we spend hearing others speak, we may spend several more hours listening to the radio or television. ⁴It just isn't possible to avoid having our attention wander at least part of this time. ⁵Another cause of poor listening is a preoccupation with personal concerns. ⁶A romance gone sour or a good grade on a test may take prominence in our mind even as someone is speaking to us. ⁷In addition, being surrounded by noise may result in poor listening. ⁸For example, many voices at a noisy party or the sound of traffic may make it difficult for us to hear everything that is being said.

1. What are the three causes described in this paragraph?

    A. _____

    B. _____

    C. _____

2. The three causes lead to what result or effect? _____

_____

3. What three cause and effect signal words or phrases are used?

_____

Explanation

The paragraph begins with the main idea: "The best listeners are unable to listen carefully to everything they hear." That point is then supported by three reasons, or causes. The first is the overload of messages we hear each day. The second reason is our preoccupation with personal concerns. The third cause given is that we are at times surrounded by interfering noise. The effect is stated in the main idea—our inability to listen carefully to everything we hear. The cause and effect signals used are *reason, cause,* and *result in.*

PRACTICE 7

A. Read the paragraph below, looking for one cause and three main effects (the three major details). Then complete the map that follows.

> ¹Chronic stress can lead to many serious health problems. ²One effect of stress is painful muscle tension. ³Headaches, backaches and sore shoulders are direct consequences of this tension. ⁴Another result of long-term exposure to stress is a weakening of the body's immune system. ⁵The body is then more vulnerable to infection and diseases, and normal colds or minor infections are more likely to develop into serious illnesses. ⁶Third, stress can result in psychological disorders, including depression, anxiety, phobias, and addictions. ⁷In one way or another, our bodies will eventually protest a prolonged exposure to stressful situations.

(Cause)

(Effect)

(Effect)

(Effect)

B. Read the paragraph below, looking for the one effect and the four causes. Then complete the outline that follows.

> ¹Why do people daydream? ²One reason is boring jobs that are tolerable only when workers imagine themselves doing something else. ³Deprivation also leads to daydreaming. ⁴During World War II, conscientious objectors who volunteered to go on semistarvation diets for six months fantasized about food. ⁵Some even hung enticing pictures of foods on their walls to give themselves something to dream about. ⁶Another reason people daydream is to discharge hostile feelings. ⁷For example, an angry student may imagine getting his instructor fired, helping him to laugh at and dismiss his annoyance with her. ⁸Last, some people fantasize as a way to plan for the future so that by the time they face future situations, they will know what to say and how to act.

Main idea *(the effect):* _____

    Major supporting details *(the causes):*

      1. _____

      2. _____

      3. _____

      4. _____

A Note on Main Ideas and Patterns of Organization

Remember that a paragraph's main idea often indicates its pattern of organization. For example, here is the main idea of a paragraph you worked on earlier:

> In middle age, men and women often view life very differently, especially if they are couples who have led traditional lives.

This sentence may have made you expect that the paragraph would go on to contrast the views of middle-aged men and women. If so, the paragraph would be organized according to the comparison and/or contrast pattern.

✓ ### *Check Your Understanding*

Finding the main idea of a paragraph may help you decide on its pattern of organization. Try, for instance, to guess the pattern of paragraphs with these main ideas:

> The development of the automobile in the early twentieth century resulted in a number of changes in U.S. society.

Pattern: _____

A franchise is a business arrangement in which an individual obtains rights from a larger company to sell a well-known product or service.

Pattern: _____

Explanation

In the first sentence, the words *resulted in* suggest that the paragraph will have a cause and effect pattern, discussing the social effects of the introduction of the automobile. In the second sentence, the word *franchise* is defined, suggesting that the paragraph will follow a definition and example pattern, with examples of various franchises to follow.

PRACTICE 8

Most of the main ideas below come from college textbooks. In the space provided, write the letter of the pattern of organization that each suggests.

_____ 1. A communicable disease is one in which an infectious organism is usually passed from person to person.
   A. Definition and   B. Comparison and/or   C. Cause and effect
      example   contrast

_____ 2. Following are three reasons for the existence of stereotypes.
   A. Definition and   B. Comparison and/or   C. Cause and effect
      example   contrast

_____ 3. College students in their thirties and forties face many of the same pressures as younger students, but they are often better equipped to withstand these pressures.
   A. Definition and   B. Comparison and/or   C. Cause and effect
      example   contrast

_____ 4. A growing concern with health has affected the way that many Americans eat.
   A. Definition and   B. Comparison and/or   C. Cause and effect
      example   contrast

_____ 5. A mission statement is an organization's declaration of how it will achieve its purpose.
   A. Definition and   B. Comparison and/or   C. Cause and effect
      example   contrast

_____ 6. Americans typically think of men as naturally better suited to perform the most strenuous physical labor, but not all peoples of the world hold the same view.
A. Definition and example
B. Comparison and/or contrast
C. Cause and effect

_____ 7. Because of economic pressures, increasing numbers of people are seeking housing assistance.
A. Definition and example
B. Comparison and/or contrast
C. Cause and effect

_____ 8. Nonverbal communication behaviors are those bodily actions and vocal qualities that accompany a verbal message and have agreed-upon interpretations within a culture.
A. Definition and example
B. Comparison and/or contrast
C. Cause and effect

_____ 9. There are several possible explanations for why retail prices often end on certain numbers.
A. Definition and example
B. Comparison and/or contrast
C. Cause and effect

_____10. First-year college students who expect to do well in school need to learn quickly the right and wrong ways of preparing for exams.
A. Definition and example
B. Comparison and/or contrast
C. Cause and effect

A Final Point

Keep in mind that a passage may often be made up of more than one pattern of organization. For instance, the paragraph in this chapter about acrophobia (the unreasonable fear of high places) uses the definition and example pattern. But the example itself—a series of events on one evening in Sally Maxwell's life—uses a time order pattern.

Or consider the following passage:

[1]Have you ever had the experience of recognizing someone's face but not being able to recall his or her name? [2]The reason is that the information about that person is split up and stored in the two different sides of your brain, and each side has its own way of thinking and remembering. [3]Recalling someone's face is the task of the right side of your brain, which understands whole things at once and is responsible for visualizing, recognizing similarities, and supplying intuitions. [4]This side of your brain provides insights that are hard to put into words. [5]The left side of your brain deals with language and stores words themselves, including the person's name that you have temporarily forgotten. [6]This is the side responsible for speaking, reading, writing, and listening.

The paragraph uses, in part, a cause and effect pattern, explaining the reason why we may recognize a face but not recall a name. It also uses a contrast pattern, explaining the different functions of the two sides of the brain. Pages 265–272 offer practice on passages with more than one pattern of organization.

CHAPTER REVIEW

In this chapter, you learned about three kinds of relationships that authors use to make their ideas clear:

- ● **Definitions and examples**
  - — To help readers understand the important ideas and terms in a subject, textbook authors often take time to include key definitions (often setting them off in *italic* or **boldface**) and examples of those definitions. When reading a textbook, it is usually a good idea to mark off both definitions and examples. (Underline each definition, and put *Ex* in the margin next to each example.)
  - — Transition words that signal the definition and example pattern include *for example, for instance, to illustrate,* and *such as*.

- ● **Comparison and/or contrast**
  - — Authors often discuss how two things are alike or how they are different, or both.
  - — Transition words that signal comparisons include *alike* and *similar*.
  - — Transition words that signal contrasts include *but, however,* and *in contrast*.

- ● **Cause and effect**
  - — Authors often discuss the reasons why something happens or the effects of something that has happened.
  - — Transition words that signal causes include *reason* and *because*.
  - — Transition words that signal effects include *therefore, consequently,* and *as a result*.

Note that pages 265–272 list and offer practice in all the transitions and patterns of organization you have studied in "Relationships I" and "Relationships II."

The next chapter—Chapter 7—will sharpen your ability to make inferences in reading.

On the Web: If you are using this book in class, you can visit our website for additional practice in in understanding relationships that involve examples, comparison or contrast, and cause and effect. Go to **www.townsendpress.com** and click on "Learning Center."

REVIEW TEST 1

To review what you've learned in this chapter, fill in the blanks or choose the best answer for the following items.

1. When textbook authors provide a definition of a term, they are also likely to provide one or more _____ to help make that definition clear.

2. A(n) _____ transition signals that two things are alike in some way.

3. A(n) _____ transition signals that two things are different in some way.

_____ 4. A cause and effect paragraph might be about
   A. reasons.
   B. results.
   C. reasons and/or results.

_____ 5. The pattern of organization of a paragraph may be suggested by
   A. the transitions it contains.
   B. its topic sentence.
   C. both A and B.

REVIEW TEST 2

A. Fill in each blank with one of the words or phrases in the box. Use each transition once. Then write the letter of the transition in the space provided.

A. because	B. effects	C. however
D. just like	E. such as	

_____ 1. Strong emotions can have negative _____ on digestion.

_____ 2. Mariah claims her teenage brother is _____ a cockroach—he enjoys going out at night and eating junk food.

_____ 3. An adult elephant weighs about 12,000 pounds. _____,
          its eyes are almost exactly the size of a human's.

_____ 4. _____ Ray's father and grandfather have both become
          bald, Ray expects to lose his hair, too.

_____ 5. For people who wish to work with children, there are many career
          choices, _____ teaching, school counseling, and working
          at a day-care center.

B. Below are the beginnings of five passages. Label each one with the letter of its
   pattern of organization. (You may find it helpful to underline the transition or
   transitions in each item.)

   A Definition and example
   B Comparison and/or contrast
   C Cause and effect

_____ 6. [1]Television news stories resemble newspaper articles in being timely
          and appealing to a wide audience. [2]However, TV coverage tends to be
          more superficial, emphasizing the visual aspects of a story rather than
          important background issues. . . .

_____ 7. [1]Many drivers take to the roads in July and August, when families
          traditionally go on vacation. [2]As a result, oil companies often raise the
          price of gasoline during the summer months. . . .

_____ 8. [1]In a mystery story, the term _red herring_ refers to a false or misleading
          clue meant to deceive the reader. [2]One famous red herring is Sherlock
          Holmes's farewell note to Dr. Watson in "The Final Problem," which
          leads the reader to believe Holmes has fallen to his death. . . .

_____ 9. [1]One type of hearing loss is caused by damage to the nerve cells in
          the inner ear. [2]The damage may be the result of loud noises, allergic
          reactions to medicines, or a hard blow to the ear or skull. [3]Certain
          diseases can also cause damage to the nerve cells of the inner ear. . . .

_____10. [1]A complementary relationship is one in which the distribution of power
          is unequal. [2]One partner says, "Let's go to a movie tonight," and the
          other says, "Sure." [3]The boss asks several employees to work overtime,
          and they all agree. . . .

REVIEW TEST 3

Read each paragraph and answer the questions that follow.

A. ¹Pessimists have long had a poor image as sourpusses and doomsayers, but a concept called "defensive pessimism" is beginning to be recognized as a useful, helpful attitude. ²Defensive pessimism means acting positively—taking specific steps—to reduce the anxiety and stress of expecting the worst. ³For instance, taking the time to back up important files eliminates worries about computer crashes, viruses, and mistakes that can wipe out days or months of work. ⁴Diversifying one's savings and investments eliminates the fear of being financially ruined if a company in which one holds too much stock goes bankrupt. ⁵And rather than worry about being arrested for speeding or jailed for tax evasion, for example, the defensive pessimist drives within the speed limit and pays taxes honestly.

_____ 1. The main pattern of organization of the paragraph is
         A. definition and example.
         B. cause and effect.
         C. comparison and/or contrast.

        2. One transition that signals the pattern of organization of this paragraph

            is _____.

B. ¹The three most common non-prescription pain relievers are aspirin, acetaminophen, and ibuprofen. ²They are alike in inhibiting the production of prostaglandins in the body, which are hormone-like substances that trigger pain, inflammation, and fever. ³But while aspirin and ibuprofen can reduce all three symptoms, acetaminophen does not reduce inflammation. ⁴Aspirin is considered to have the greatest number of uses but also has the greatest number of side effects, including allergic reactions, stomach upset, and bleeding. ⁵In contrast, ibuprofen generally has fewer side effects than aspirin. ⁶Acetaminophen has the fewest side effects; its only drawback is that it is probably the least effective of the three pain killers.

_____ 3. The main pattern of organization of the paragraph is
         A. definition and example.
         B. cause and effect.
         C. comparison and/or contrast.

        4. One transition that signals the pattern of organization of this paragraph

            is _____.

C.   ¹Alternate freezing and thawing is one of the most important processes of mechanical weathering. ²Water has the unique property of expanding about 9 percent as it freezes. ³This increase in volume occurs because as water solidifies, the water molecules arrange themselves into a very open crystalline structure. ⁴As a result, when water freezes, it exerts a tremendous outward force. ⁵In nature, water works its way into cracks or voids in rock. ⁶When the water then freezes and expands, the effect is to break the rock into angular fragments.

_____ 5. The main pattern of organization of the paragraph is
     A. definition and example.
     B. cause and effect.
     C. comparison and/or contrast.

6. One transition that signals the pattern of organization of this paragraph

    is _____.

D.   ¹Corporate welfare refers to financial aid given by the government to corporations, especially when the handout is considered unjust. ²The government aid to Borden Chemicals in Louisiana is a good example. ³The company buried hazardous wastes without a permit and released hazardous chemicals so thick that to protect drivers, the police sometimes shut down the highway that runs near the plant. ⁴Borden even contaminated the groundwater beneath its plant, threatening the aquifer that provides drinking water for residents of Louisiana and Texas. ⁵Borden's pollution has cost the company a hefty $7 million, but thanks to corporate welfare, the company didn't make out so badly. ⁶With $15 million in reduced and canceled property taxes, Borden has enjoyed a net gain of $8 million.

_____ 7. The main pattern of organization of the paragraph is
     A. definition and example.
     B. cause and effect.
     C. comparison and/or contrast.

8. The transition that signals the pattern of organization of this paragraph

    is _____.

E.   ¹The use of fire by prehistoric people probably affected wildlife both intentionally and unintentionally. ²In all likelihood, early people used fire to drive game toward waiting hunters. ³Later, new plant growth in the burned areas would attract more wild animals. ⁴In addition, accidental fires must have occurred frequently. ⁵Because prehistoric people had trouble starting fires, they would have kept burning embers on hand. ⁶The result must have been widespread accidental fires, especially in dry areas. ⁷Certainly, these fires also would have greatly altered the habitat for wildlife.

_____ 9. The main pattern of organization of the paragraph is
            A. definition and example.
            B. cause and effect.
            C. comparison and/or contrast.

       10. One transition that signals the pattern of organization of this paragraph

            is _____.

REVIEW TEST 4

Here is a chance to apply your understanding of relationships to a full-length reading—an article about stress in college.

To help you continue to strengthen your skills, the reading is followed by questions not only on what you've learned in this chapter but also on what you've learned in previous chapters.

Words to Watch

Below are some words in the reading that do not have strong context support. Each word is followed by the number of the paragraph in which it appears and its meaning there. These words are indicated in the article by a small circle (°).

aptitude (5): natural ability
anorexia (8): an abnormal lack of appetite which can result in serious illness or death
bulimia (8):   an abnormal craving for food that leads to heavy eating and then intentional vomiting
stability (12): steadiness
bombarded (12): attacked
devastating (12): very destructive
magnitude (13): great importance

STUDENTS IN SHOCK

John Kellmayer and Alina Wyden

1   For several generations, young people have heard the same promise: If they worked hard and went to college, the American dream would be theirs. A college degree would be the ticket to a satisfying career, an income that would allow them to buy a home and raise a family, and eventually, a comfortable retirement. And for previous generations, that promise has generally been true.

2   But for today's young people, the rosy promise of college is too often replaced by anxiety, disappointment, and crushing debt. The result is that many of today's college students are suffering from a form of shock. Going to college has always had its ups and downs, but today the "downs" of the college experience are more numerous and difficult than ever before.

3   Lisa is a good example of a student in shock. She is an attractive, intelligent twenty-year-old junior at a state university. Having been a straight-A student in high school and a member of the basketball and softball teams there, she remembers her high-school days with fondness. Lisa was popular then and had a steady boyfriend for the last two years of school.

4   Now, only three years later, Lisa is miserable. She has changed her major four times already and is forced to hold down two part-time jobs in order to pay her tuition. She suffers from sleeping and eating disorders and believes she has no close friends. Sometimes she bursts out crying for no apparent reason. On more than one occasion, she has considered taking her own life.

5   Dan, too, suffers from student shock. He is nineteen and a freshman at a local community college. He began college as an accounting major, but hated that field. So he switched to computer programming, because he heard job prospects were good in that area. Unfortunately, he discovered that he had little aptitude° for programming and changed majors again, this time to psychology. He likes psychology but has heard horror stories about the difficulty of finding a job in that field without a graduate degree. Now he is considering switching majors again, but is panicking at the idea that he has already invested money in courses that won't count toward his eventual degree. To help pay for school, Dan works nights and weekends as a sales clerk at Walmart. He doesn't get along with his boss, but as so many of his friends can't find any job at all, he doesn't dare quit to look for another one. A few months ago, his longtime girlfriend broke up with him.

6   Not surprisingly, Dan has started to suffer from depression and migraine headaches. He believes that in spite of all his hard work, he just isn't getting anywhere. He can't remember ever being this unhappy. He has considered talking to somebody in the college counseling center. He rejected that

idea, though, because he doesn't want people to think there's something wrong with him.

7   What is happening to Lisa and Dan is happening to more college students every year. Increasing numbers of young people are suffering from "student shock." The evidence is disturbing. A national annual survey of college freshmen reports that by 2012 the emotional health of incoming students was at its lowest point since the survey began in 1985. "The American Freshman: National Norms" reported that the percentage of students who rated their emotional health as "above average" had fallen to 52 percent.

8   This kind of emotional distress means that large numbers of students will experience depression intense enough to warrant professional help. At schools across the country, psychological counselors are booked months in advance. Stress-related problems such as anxiety, migraine headaches, insomnia, anorexia°, and bulimia° are epidemic on college campuses.

9   Suicide rates and self-inflicted injuries such as deliberate cutting among college students are higher now than at any other time in history. There are approximately 1,100 college suicides per year, making suicide the second most common cause of death among college students.

10   College health officials believe that these reported problems represent only the tip of the iceberg. They fear that most students, like Lisa and Dan, suffer in silence, convinced that "everyone else" is doing just fine.

But many college students *aren't* 11 doing just fine, and there are three significant reasons why—reasons that, in many cases, are intertwined.

The first reason that today's 12 college students are suffering more than students of earlier generations is a weakening family support structure. The transition from high school to college has always been difficult. But in the past, students typically had firm family support to help them get through it. Today, with divorce rates at a historical high and many parents experiencing their own psychological and financial difficulties, that solid familial support and guidance may not be available. And when students who do not find stability° at home are bombarded° with numerous new and stressful experiences, the results can be devastating°.

Another problem college students 13 face is the large and bewildering selection of majors available. Because of the magnitude° and difficulty of choosing a major, and thereby preparing for a career, many students are wracked by indecision. Students often switch majors, many more than once. As a result, it is becoming commonplace to take five or six years to earn a bachelor's degree. Students who have changed majors are often depressed to realize the courses they have completed will not count towards the new major. They feel they have wasted not only time, but precious tuition dollars. Rather than accumulate more debt, many students drop out. Forty-three percent of all four-year college students start college but never complete it.

14   The related, and final, major cause of "student shock" is the ugly reality of today's economy. At the same time that a college degree is considered the minimum qualification for most American jobs, today's college graduates are facing a job market that is the worst since World War II. The current U.S. unemployment rate is about 7.9 percent, but for 20- to 24-year-olds, it is closer to 14 percent. Just as alarming, only half of recent college graduates who *are* working are in jobs that require a college degree. Most are waiting tables, foaming lattes, and doing other low-wage work. There are 80,000 bartenders in America with bachelor's degrees.

15   Even while college degrees are worth less in the job market, their price is skyrocketing. In the last thirty years, the cost of tuition and fees has tripled for all colleges—public, private, and community. At the same time, student financial aid has been slashed to the bone. Students are graduating with more debt than ever before—an average of $25,000. Without a well-paying job to move into, and in many cases without health insurance, many new graduates will carry that ever-increasing debt with

them for decades, making it difficult for them to move ahead with plans to marry, buy a house or a car, or make other traditional inroads into adult life.

It's not a pretty picture. And while   16 there is no magic cure-all, students can—and should—take steps to insure against falling into student shock. If you are a college student, or soon to be one, here is some serious advice:

First, you should never hesitate to   17 make use of any helpful services offered by your college. You are paying for those services, and you deserve them. Just a few sessions of psychological counseling can be tremendously helpful when you're feeling depressed, panicky, or paralyzed with indecision. Campus stress-management workshops may be available; and these, too, can be helpful and also make it clear that you're not the only one to experience college stress.

But more importantly, students   18 today, more than at any time previously, must take a coldly realistic look at their plans for college and a career. When you are considering a college and a major, you must realize that you are making what amounts to a business decision that will significantly affect your life for years to come. It is therefore essential to shop around for the school that will offer the best possible combination of affordability and the courses that you want. It is imperative that as you choose a major, you research the job possibilities in that field and how you can best position yourself to land one of those jobs. You can achieve this result by going to your school's vocational counseling office to ask what fields are expected to be hiring in the near future; by interviewing people in the line of work you are considering; and by looking at the "Fastest Growing" occupations in the online *Occupational Outlook Handbook*, a publication of the Bureau of Labor Statistics that provides information about hiring trends for hundreds of careers (**http://www.bls.gov/ooh/**).

It's a tough time to be a college 19 student or new graduate. But "student shock" does not have to defeat you. If you go into college with a realistic perspective about why you are there and what you want to get out of your degree, you will lessen any "shocks" that might lie ahead.

Reading Comprehension Questions

Vocabulary in Context

_____ 1. In the sentence below, the word *prospects* (prŏs′pĕkts′) means
    A. failures.
    B. possibilities.
    C. candidates.
    D. limitations.

"So he switched to computer programming because he heard the job prospects were excellent in that area." (Paragraph 5)

_____ 2. In the excerpt below, the word *warrant* (wôr′ənt) means
    A. fight.
    B. have no need for.
    C. get degrees in.
    D. justify.

"This kind of emotional distress means that large numbers of students will experience depression intense enough to warrant professional help. At schools across the country, psychological counselors are booked months in advance." (Paragraph 8)

Central Point and Main Ideas

_____ 3. Which sentence best expresses the central point of the selection?
    A. Going to college is a depressing experience for many students.
    B. To lessen student shock, students need to be realistic about why they are in college and what they can get out of their degree.
    C. Lisa and Dan have experienced too much stress at school to enjoy college life.
    D. Unlike previous generations, today's college graduates are not assured an income that will allow them to live the American Dream.

.

_____ 4. At times, a main idea may cover more than one paragraph. The main idea of paragraphs 3 and 4 is stated in the
   A. first sentence of paragraph 3.
   B. second sentence of paragraph 3.
   C. first sentence of paragraph 4.
   D. last sentence of paragraph 4.

_____ 5. The main idea of paragraph 14 is stated in the
   A. first sentence.
   B. second sentence.
   C. third sentence.
   D. last sentence.

Supporting Details

_____ 6. According to the authors, students are graduating with more debt than ever before because
   A. lenders have made it too easy for students to obtain credit cards.
   B. college costs have risen steeply while financial aid has been slashed.
   C. most students no longer work while they attend college.
   D. parents can no longer afford to contribute to the cost of their children's education.

Transitions

_____ 7. The sentence below expresses a relationship of
   A. contrast.   C. illustration.
   B. cause and effect.   D. addition.

   "Stress-related problems such as anxiety, migraine headaches, insomnia, anorexia, and bulimia are epidemic on college campuses." (Paragraph 8)

_____ 8. Read the two sentences below, and then answer the question that follows.

   "Students often switch majors, many more than once. As a result, it is becoming commonplace to take five or six years to earn a bachelor's degree." (Paragraph 13)

   What does the second sentence do?
   A. It adds more detail to the first sentence.
   B. It establishes a time order relationship.
   C. It establishes a cause and effect relationship with the first sentence.
   D. It contrasts how easy it is to switch majors with how hard it is to earn a college degree.

Patterns of Organization

_____ 9. Paragraphs 11–15
   A. compare college life as it used to be to college life today.
   B. list reasons that students today are suffering more than those in earlier generations.
   C. contrast college life today with what it used to be like.
   D. provide examples of students who are in shock.

_____ 10. The main pattern of organization of paragraph 18 is
   A. list of items.   C. definition and example.
   B. comparison and/or contrast. D. cause and effect.

Discussion Questions

1. If you were a peer counselor for Lisa or Dan, what advice might you give her or him?

2. Do you think most people enter college with a realistic idea of what they want to accomplish there? Explain your answer.

3. What were—or are—the most stressful parts of college life for you? Explain why. What ways have you found for dealing with that stress?

4. The authors state, "First, you should never hesitate to make use of any helpful services offered by your college." What services does your college offer? Have you tried any of them? How do you think your school could improve the services it offers to help students deal with "student shock"?

Note: Writing assignments for this selection appear on page 625.

Check Your Performance   RELATIONSHIPS II

Activity	Number Right	Points	Score
Review Test 1 (5 items)	_____	× 2 =	_____
Review Test 2 (10 items)	_____	× 3 =	_____
Review Test 3 (10 items)	_____	× 3 =	_____
Review Test 4 (10 items)	_____	× 3 =	_____
		TOTAL SCORE =	_____ %

Enter your total score into the **Reading Performance Chart: Review Tests** on the inside back cover.

RELATIONSHIPS II: Mastery Test 1

A. Fill in each blank with an appropriate transition from the box. Use each transition once. Then, in the spaces provided, write the letter of the transition you have chosen.

A. because	**B.** for example	**C.** in contrast
D. just as	**E.** therefore	

Hint: Make sure that each word or phrase that you choose fits smoothly into the flow of the sentence. Test your choices by reading each sentence to yourself.

_____ 1. [1]Some thieves read the newspapers to find out good times to rob houses.
[2]_____, after reading the obituaries, such thieves may "clean out" a home while the family is at a loved one's funeral.

_____ 2. [1]Whenever something bad happens to me, my grandmother tries to help me through it. [2]When I was depressed after breaking up with my boyfriend, she told me, "_____ we must go through the storm before seeing the rainbow, we often must experience sorrow before joy."

_____ 3. [1]Honeybees attack just to protect their hives. [2]_____, if you run away from the hive when attacked, the bees will eventually lose interest in you.

_____ 4. [1]_____ there are no clocks in gambling casinos, gamblers can easily lose all sense of time. [2]That is clearly what the casino management wants to happen. [3]The longer people stay at the tables or in front of the slot machines, the better.

_____ 5. [1]Most birds are born in either of two very different states. [2]Some are born weak, blind, and usually naked. [3]About all they can do for themselves is open their mouths for food. [4]_____, other newborn baby birds are bright-eyed and covered with down. [5]As soon as their down is dry, they are able to peck at things and run after their parents.

(Continues on next page)

B. Label each item with the letter of its main pattern of organization.

    A Definition and example
    B Comparison and/or contrast
    C Cause and effect

_____ 6. ¹Phobias are intense, irrational fears that are out of proportion to the actual danger in a situation. ²For example, people with the fear of open places (agoraphobia) are often reluctant to leave their homes.

_____ 7. ¹Bread made with whole-wheat flour is brown, but not all brown bread is whole-wheat bread. ²Some manufacturers add molasses or honey to white-flour dough to give it a brown color, and they are allowed to label the product "wheat bread." ³For this reason, it is important to read the package label before buying.

_____ 8. ¹Prison overcrowding is dangerous because it increases unrest among inmates and produces a climate in which violence is more likely. ²Riots, escapes, and hostage taking become more of a problem. ³Prison overcrowding also makes it more difficult for correctional officers and prison administrators to manage the prison. ⁴The result is that prisons are more costly to run.

_____ 9. ¹In the 1890s, most Americans were struggling to reach a middle-class lifestyle. ²By the 1990s, in contrast, an overwhelming majority had achieved the middle class but were either losing it or struggling to hold on to it. ³In the 1890s, government responded to the prodding of reform-minded citizens and began to create a framework of rules to control the excesses of giant businesses and to protect the interests of the average citizen. ⁴But in the 1990s, that framework of controls on large corporations was steadily dismantled.

_____10. ¹What sociologist George Ritzer has termed the "McDonaldization of society"—the standardization of everyday life—does not refer just to the robotlike assembly of food. ²As Ritzer points out, this process is occurring throughout our society—and it is transforming our lives. ³For instance, shopping malls offer one-stop shopping in controlled environments. ⁴Travel agencies offer "package" tours. ⁵They will transport middle-class Americans to ten European capitals in fourteen days. ⁶All visitors experience the same hotels, restaurants, and other scheduled sites—and no one need fear meeting a "real" native. ⁷The newspaper *USA Today* spews out McNews—short, blank, unanalytical pieces that can be digested between gulps of the McShake or the McBurger.

RELATIONSHIPS II: Mastery Test 2

Read each textbook passage and answer the questions or follow the directions provided.

A. [1]The incomes of middle- and working-class Americans were dealt a severe blow during the 1980s. [2]A major reason was a decline in industrial jobs. [3]The economy became less devoted to manufacturing goods and more focused on providing services. [4]Many manufacturing jobs, especially in the steel and auto industries, were transferred from the United States to Third World countries. [5]As a result, millions of blue-collar workers in the Midwest and Northeast were stranded. [6]They were forced into much lower-paying jobs with fewer benefits and opportunities for advancement.

_____ 1. The main pattern of organization of the paragraph is
    A. definition and example.
    B. cause and effect.
    C. comparison and/or contrast.

    2. One transition that signals the pattern of organization of this paragraph is _____.

B. [1]Boys who mature early physically have a decided advantage over their more slowly maturing peers. [2]Early maturers become heroes in sports and leaders in both formal and informal activities. [3]Other boys look up to them; girls have crushes on them. [4]Even adults tend to trust them. [5]They are more self-confident and independent than other boys. [6]In contrast, their less mature male peers, with their high-pitched voices and underdeveloped physiques, feel inadequate. [7]They are weaker at sports and more awkward with girls.

_____ 3. The main pattern of organization of the paragraph is
    A. definition and example.
    B. cause and effect.
    C. comparison and/or contrast.

    4. The transition that signals the pattern of organization of this paragraph is _____.

C. [1]There are often more than two sides to a question, and offering only two choices when more actually exist is called an either-or fallacy. [2]For example, the statement "You are either with us or against us" assumes that there is no middle ground. [3]Or consider the following conclusion: People opposed to total freedom of speech are really in favor of censorship. [4]This argument ignores the fact that a person could believe in free speech as well as in laws that prohibit slander or that punish someone for falsely yelling "Fire!" in a crowded theater.

(Continues on next page)

_____ 5. The main pattern of organization of the paragraph is
   A. definition and example.
   B. cause and effect.
   C. comparison and/or contrast.

6. The transition that signals the pattern of organization of this paragraph

   is _____.

D.   ¹Why does lightning make such a loud sound? ²The answer has to do with the electrical energy it gives off. ³A single bolt may produce as much as 3,750 million kilowatts of electrical energy. ⁴Most of this energy—75 percent—turns into heat, causing the temperature of the surrounding air to rise greatly. ⁵Since heated air expands, the sudden increase in temperature leads to a rapid expansion of the air around the lightning. ⁶And that air expansion causes sound waves—thunder—which can be heard up to eighteen miles away.

_____ 7. The main pattern of organization of the paragraph is
   A. definition and example.
   B. cause and effect.
   C. comparison and/or contrast.

8. One transition that signals the pattern of organization of this paragraph

   is _____.

E.   ¹People are different from other primates, but not as different as they might like to think. ²It's true that that there are significant contrasts in size and proportion between humans and other primates. ³And, of course, humans are by far the more intelligent. ⁴Nevertheless, to use chimpanzees as an example, both they and humans have the same muscles and bones, located in almost the same places and working in nearly the same ways. ⁵The internal organs of both animals are also very much alike, as are their blood and other body fluids. ⁶Seen under a microscope, even their genes are strikingly similar.

_____ 9. The main pattern of organization of the paragraph is
   A. definition and example.
   B. cause and effect.
   C. comparison and/or contrast.

10. One transition that signals the pattern of organization of this paragraph

   is _____.

RELATIONSHIPS II: Mastery Test 3

A. (1–4.) Arrange the scrambled sentences below into a logical paragraph by numbering them *1, 2, 3,* and *4* in an order that makes sense. Then, in the space provided, write the letter of the pattern of organization used.

   Note that transitions will help you by clarifying the relationships between sentences.

____ Also, high tuitions affect the amount of time available for studying; because loans and scholarships are hard to get, many students have to put in numerous hours at work in order to afford school.

____ For one thing, it undoubtedly prevents some students from attending college in the first place.

____ Finally, those who do manage to get loans know that they must begin their careers with large debts.

____ The high cost of college today causes problems for many students in more ways than one.

_____ 5. The main pattern of organization is
   A. contrast.
   B. comparison.
   C. cause and effect.
   D. definition and example.

B. Read the passages and answer the questions that follow. You may find it helpful to underline transitions as you read.

> ¹Men and women may interpret women's actions on a date very differently. ²One study found that acts such as speaking in a low voice or smiling were interpreted by men as indicating that the woman was interested in sex. ³Women, in contrast, tended to see the same behaviors as simply friendly. ⁴Drinking with a man, going to the man's apartment, or wearing sexy clothes were all seen by men as indicating a desire for sex, while women regarded these behaviors as appropriate or fashionable.

_____ 6. The main pattern of organization of the paragraph is
   A. definition and example.
   B. cause and effect.
   C. comparison and/or contrast.

7. One transition that signals the main pattern of organization of this

   paragraph is _____.

(Continues on next page)

¹Mass hysteria is a type of group behavior that involves a widely held and contagious anxiety, usually as a result of a false belief. ²The reaction in part of the country to the 1938 radio broadcast of *The War of the Worlds* is one example. ³This dramatization of Martians landing on Earth was so realistic that people began to panic and flee before the realization set in that they were reacting to a radio play. ⁴The medieval witch-hunts are another good example of mass hysteria. ⁵They were based on the belief that witches were the cause of many problems in late medieval society, including natural disasters and illness. ⁶Those accused of being witches (mainly old women) were tortured until they confessed or they died. ⁷As many as 500,000 people were burned to death by the clergy between the fifteenth and seventeenth centuries.

_____ 8. The major supporting details of the selection are
     A. definitions.
     B. causes.
     C. comparisons.
     D. examples.

_____ 9. The main pattern of organization of the paragraph is
     A. definition and example.
     B. cause and effect.
     C. comparison and/or contrast.

    10. The transition that signals the main pattern of organization of this paragraph is _____.

RELATIONSHIPS II: Mastery Test 4

A. (1–4.) Arrange the scrambled sentences below into a logical paragraph by numbering them *1, 2, 3,* and *4* in an order that makes sense. Then, in the space provided, write the letter of the main pattern of organization used.

Note that transitions will help you by clarifying the relationships between sentences.

___ In contrast, the original Italian story is the gruesome tale of the Princess Talia, who falls into a deep magical sleep in the woods, where she is raped by a nobleman and, later on, gives birth to twins, whom the nobleman's wife tries to have killed and cooked for dinner.

___ It is often said that fairy tales, with their heavy doses of terror and violence, are too scary for young children.

___ Consider the story of Sleeping Beauty that today's children know, which involves a princess who is put to sleep by a wicked witch and then awakened by the kiss of her true love.

___ But today's versions of fairy tales are actually less frightening than the original stories.

_____ 5. The main pattern of organization is
    A. contrast.
    B. comparison.
    C. cause and effect.
    D. definition and example.

B. Read each paragraph and answer the questions that follow.

¹A small sausage in a bun received the name "hot dog" in 1906 as the result of a cartoonist's poor spelling ability. ²A sausage vendor, Harry Stevens, sold what he called "dachshund sausages" (named after the short-legged dog) at New York City baseball games. ³During one of those games, newspaper cartoonist Tad Dorgan was in the audience. ⁴He sketched a cartoon of a live dachshund, smeared with mustard and folded into a bun. ⁵Not knowing how to spell "dachshund," however, he settled on "dog," giving the cartoon the caption "Get your hot dogs!" ⁶Once the cartoon was published in newspapers, readers began demanding their own "hot dogs."

_____ 6. The main idea is expressed in the
    A. first sentence.
    B. second sentence.
    C. last sentence.

(Continues on next page)

_____ 7. The selection mainly
  A. defines and illustrates the term "hot dog."
  B. gives the reason small sausages are now called hot dogs.
  C. contrasts "dachshund sausage" with "hot dog."

8. The transition that signals the main pattern of organization of this paragraph is _____.

¹When a crowd is watching as someone threatens to jump from a building, its behavior seems affected by the time of day. ²In daylight, the crowd is usually quite quiet, but under the cover of darkness, many individual members will shout encouragement to the person to kill himself or herself. ³A similar reaction was seen when women college students took part in an experiment where they were asked to press a button to shock other volunteers. ⁴When the women pushing the buttons were visible to the victims, they administered only brief shocks. ⁵However, when they were allowed to wear gowns and masks that hid their identity, they shocked the volunteers twice as much. ⁶Clearly the feeling of being anonymous causes people to engage in antisocial behavior.

_____ 9. One pattern of organization of the selection is
  A. definition and example.
  B. cause and effect.
  C. comparison and/or contrast.

_____10. Another pattern of organization of the selection is
  A. definition and example.
  B. cause and effect.
  C. comparison and/or contrast.

RELATIONSHIPS II: Mastery Test 5

A. Read the textbook paragraph below. Then answer the question and complete the outline that follows.

> ¹There are several reasons why middle-aged adults are returning to school. ²Some want to learn to do their jobs better. ³College courses can help them improve their job skills and keep up in their fields. ⁴Others return to school because more credits may mean a raise or promotion. ⁵Teachers, for instance, get raises for reaching certain levels of education. ⁶Also, some adults return to the classroom because of interest in a new field, such as telecommunications or computer programming. ⁷Finally, others want to study subjects such as foreign languages, history, or literature for the sake of learning. ⁸Such classes help adults spend their time in more productive and interesting ways and deepen their understanding of themselves and their world.

_____ 1. The organizational patterns of the paragraph are list of items and
   A. definition and example.
   B. cause and effect.
   C. comparison and/or contrast.

2–5. Complete the outline of the paragraph by writing in the four major supporting details.

Main idea: There are several reasons why middle-aged adults are returning to school.

Major supporting details:

1. _____

2. _____

3. _____

4. _____

(Continues on next page)

B. Read the textbook paragraph below. Then answer the question and complete the map that follows.

> ¹While management styles vary, there are certain factors that separate the good administrator from the poor one. ²A good manager anticipates problems and prepares for them, but a poor manager is often taken by surprise. ³The effective administrator makes changes to eliminate repeated problems; the less effective boss deals with one crisis at a time, never seeing patterns of problems. ⁴In addition, a good boss delegates work to others, while the poor one prefers to take on one extra task after another rather than train employees to do the work right. ⁵The effective administrator is also flexible enough to adapt to changing situations. ⁶In contrast, the poor one often clings to the old rules, whether or not they apply.

_____ 6. The organizational patterns of the paragraph are list of items and
   A. definition and example.
   B. comparison and/or contrast.
   C. cause and effect.

7–10. Complete the map of the paragraph by writing in the missing supporting details.

Certain factors separate the good administrator from the poor one.

Good manager

1. Anticipates problems
2. Eliminates repeat problems
3. Delegates work

4. _____

   _____

Poor manager

1. _____

   _____

2. Deals with one problem at a time, not noticing repetition

3. _____

   _____

4. _____

   _____

RELATIONSHIPS II: Mastery Test 6

A. Read the textbook paragraph below. Then answer the question and complete the outline that follows.

> ¹One researcher has identified five basic causes of frustration above and beyond daily hassles. ²To begin with, delays are hard for us to accept because our culture stresses the value of time. ³Anyone who has been caught in a traffic jam is familiar with the frustration of delay. ⁴Lack of resources is another cause of frustration, especially to low-income Americans, who cannot afford the new cars or vacations that TV programs and magazine articles would have us believe everyone must have. ⁵Losses, such as the end of a love affair or a cherished friendship, are frustrating because they often make us feel helpless, unimportant, and worthless. ⁶Failure is a frequent source of frustration in our competitive society. ⁷The aspect of failure that is hardest to cope with is guilt. ⁸We imagine that if we had done certain things differently, we might have succeeded, and so we feel responsible for our own or someone else's pain and disappointment. ⁹Discrimination can also be a source of frustration. ¹⁰Being denied opportunities or recognition simply because of one's sex, age, religion, or skin color, regardless of one's personal qualifications or accomplishments, is immensely frustrating.

_____ 1. The organizational patterns of the paragraph are list of items and
  A. definition and example.
  B. comparison and/or contrast.
  C. cause and effect.

2–6. Complete the outline of the paragraph by writing in the five major supporting details.

Main idea: There are five causes of frustration above and beyond daily hassles.

Major supporting details:

1. _____

2. _____

3. _____

4. _____

5. _____

B. Read the textbook paragraph below. Then answer the question and complete the map that follows.

> ¹Role conflict is a situation in which the different roles an individual is expected to play make incompatible demands. ²A working mother provides one example. ³In meeting the requirements of a full-time job, she automatically violates the expectation that a mother will put her children's needs before everything else. ⁴In meeting the cultural demands of motherhood (staying home if the child is sick, attending school plays), she automatically violates the requirements of a nine-to-five job. ⁵A priest provides another example. ⁶He is expected to treat confessions as strictly confidential. ⁷But a priest, like any other citizen, has responsibilities toward the community. ⁸What should he do if a parishioner confesses that he has committed several rapes and cannot control his behavior? ⁹In living up to one role expectation (confidentiality), the priest violates another (community responsibility). ¹⁰The key point here is that the difficulties the individuals in these positions experience—the feelings of conflict, inadequacy, and anguish—are not of their own making. ¹¹They are built into their roles.

_____ 7. The main pattern of organization of the passage is
  A. cause and effect.
  B. definition and example.
  C. comparison.
  D. contrast.

8–10. Complete the map of the passage. In doing so, you will need to summarize the main idea and the two supporting details.

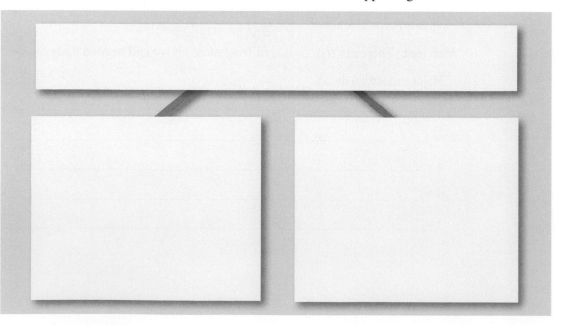

TO THE STUDENT

The pages that follow contain three mastery tests that offer additional practice in the skills covered in Chapters 5 and 6:

- Relationships that involve **addition**

- Relationships that involve **time**

- Relationships that involve **illustration**

- Relationships that involve **comparison and/or contrast**

- Relationships that involve **cause and effect**

For ease in reference, the lists of words that show these relationships have been reprinted on the next page.

Addition Words

one	to begin with	also	further
first (of all)	for one thing	in addition	furthermore
second(ly)	other	next	last (of all)
third(ly)	another	moreover	final(ly)

Time Words

before	immediately	when	until
previously	next	whenever	often
first (of all)	then	while	frequently
second(ly)	following	during	eventually
third(ly)	later	as (soon as)	final(ly)
now	after (ward)	by	last (of all)

Illustration Words

(for) example	including	(as an) illustration	one
(for) instance	specifically	to illustrate	once
such as	to be specific		

Comparison Words

(just) as	both	in like fashion	in a similar fashion
(just) like	equal(ly)	in like manner	in a similar manner
alike	resemble	similar(ly)	(in) the same way
same	likewise	similarity	(in) common

Contrast Words

but	instead (of)	even though	difference
yet	in contrast	as opposed to	different(ly)
however	on the other hand	in spite of	differ (from)
although	on the contrary	despite	unlike
nevertheless	converse(ly)	rather than	while
still	opposite		

Cause and Effect Words

therefore	so	owing to	because (of)
thus	(as a) result	effect	reason
(as a) consequence	results in	cause	explanation
consequently	leads (led) to	if . . . then	accordingly
due to	since	affect	depend(s) on

RELATIONSHIPS I & II: Mastery Test 1

A. Fill in each blank with an appropriate transition from the box. Use each transition once. Then, in the spaces provided, write the letter of the transition you have chosen.

A. cause	B. first	C. for example
D. then	E. unlike	

_____ 1. [1]If you are approached by a vicious neighborhood or stray dog, you have a good chance of avoiding being attacked or bitten if you do the following. [2]First of all, stand still. [3]Secondly, do not look the dog directly in the eyes; instead, look just over the top of its head. [4]Next, talk in as soft and unconcerned a way as you can to the dog, saying, "Hey, what's up, pal?" [5]_____ slowly back away while facing the dog.

_____ 2. [1]Public opinion can be defined as those opinions held by ordinary citizens that they are willing to express openly. [2]This expression need not be verbal. [3]It could also take the form, _____, of a protest demonstration or a vote for one candidate rather than another.

_____ 3. [1]The opossum reacts to danger in one of several ways. [2]_____, some varieties of opossum can spray an unpleasant odor. [3]A second reaction to danger used by opossums is to bluff their way out of a tight spot by hissing and baring their teeth. [4]Finally, the best-known of opossum defenses is to "play dead" by entering into a coma-like state brought on by fear.

_____ 4. [1]Swollen glands can be uncomfortable, but they are a welcome sign that your body is working to defend itself. [2]They are often associated with an illness such as mumps, German measles, a cold, or flu; but an insect bite or infected cut can also result in swelling. [3]A blocked duct in a salivary gland is another possible _____ of a swollen gland. [4]Still, if swollen glands last more than a few days, they can be a sign of a serious illness, such as Hodgkin's disease.

_____ 5. [1]The feeling of awe is similar to fear in some ways. [2]With both, we have a sense of being overwhelmed, of confronting someone or something much more powerful than we are. [3]But _____ fear, awe is a positive feeling, an expansive feeling. [4]While fear makes us want to run away, awe makes us want to draw closer even as we hesitate to get too close.

(Continues on next page)

B. Fill in each blank with an appropriate transition from the box. Use each transition once. Then, in the spaces provided, write the letter of the transition you have chosen.

A. after	B. as a result	C. for instance
D. however	E. next	

_____ 6. [1]There are more than a few similarities between the ancient Egyptian religion and our modern religions of today. [2]_____, a belief that you "could take it with you" is a prime difference. [3]In fact, the Egyptians thought the dead could take a considerable number of items with them. [4]In many cases, Egyptian royalty and high officials began stocking their tombs with goods long before their death.

_____ 7. [1]Scotch tape is not wound up in the factory in the little rolls found in stores. [2]During the manufacturing process, sheets of cellophane several feet wide are first run through a machine that coats them with adhesive. [3]_____ that, a machine winds the sticky film around tubes that are also several feet wide. [4]Next, this wide roll of Scotch tape is fed through a slicing machine, which produces the thin rolls of tape sold to consumers.

_____ 8. [1]For two decades, the Chinese government tried to control population by limiting most rural families to one child. [2]Because boys are prized in rural areas—they can work the land and give more support to their families— many couples aborted female fetuses, killed newborn daughters, or neglected them to death. [3]_____, China in 2002 was short 50 million females. [4]With so few brides to go around, desperate bachelors have taken to marrying relatives.

_____ 9. [1]Communicators who want to set themselves apart from others adopt the strategy of divergence, speaking in a way that emphasizes their differences from others. [2]_____, an attorney who wants to impress a client might speak formally and use professional jargon to create a sense of distance. [3]The implicit message here is, "I'm different (and more knowledgeable) than you."

_____10. [1]Almost all good writing begins with terrible first efforts. [2]You need to start somewhere. [3]Start by getting something—anything—down on paper. [4]A friend of mine says that the first draft is the down draft—you just get it down. [5]The _____ draft is the up draft—you fix it up. [6]You try to say what you have to say more accurately. [7]And the third draft is the dental draft, where you check every tooth, to see if it's loose or cramped or decayed, or even, God help us, healthy.

RELATIONSHIPS I & II: Mastery Test 2

A. ¹Americans have mixed feelings about government. ²We complain about highway and bridge tolls, but we insist that every road be in good repair and wide enough to get us quickly to wherever we are going. ³Our consumption of tobacco and alcohol is among the highest in the world, yet we insist on strict regulations on who can buy them and where they can be sold and consumed. ⁴We complain without fail about our taxes; at the same time, however, we demand that government spend more on everything from cleaner air and higher-quality schools to safer streets and more jobs. ⁵We dislike "welfare" programs and those who use them. ⁶Still, we want government to provide all Americans with an economic "safety net" to protect them during hard times.

_____ 1. The main pattern of organization of the selection is
   A. time order.   B. list of items.   C. comparison and/or contrast.

2. One transition that signals the pattern of organization of this paragraph is _____.

B. ¹Pictures of starving Africans leave the impression that Africa is overpopulated. ²Why else would all those people be starving? ³But the truth is far different. ⁴Africa has 22 percent of the earth's land, but only 10.5 percent of the earth's population. ⁵The reason for famines in Africa, then, cannot be too many people living on too little land. ⁶In fact, Africa contains some of the world's largest untapped lands suitable for agriculture. ⁷The reality is that famines are due to three primary causes: drought, inefficient farming techniques, and wars that disrupt harvests and food distribution.

_____ 3. The main pattern of organization of the selection is
   A. time order.   B. definition and example.   C. cause and effect.

4. One transition that signals the pattern of organization of this paragraph is _____.

C. ¹Sawing a woman in half is an easy illusion for magicians. ²The trick begins when a table holding a coffin-like box is rolled onstage. ³A female assistant is hiding inside that table. ⁴When the magician displays the box to the audience, it is, of course, empty. ⁵Then the magician asks a female assistant on stage to climb into the box. ⁶As she does this, the hidden woman enters the box through a trapdoor in the table, sticks her feet out one end, and curls up with her head between her knees. ⁷The other woman, drawing her knees up to her chin, puts her head out the other end of the box. ⁸Now the box appears to be holding one woman, and the magician can saw

(Continues on next page)

right through. ⁹After he does so, the woman at the foot end slides back into the table as the magician reopens the box.

_____ 5. The main pattern of organization of the selection is
   A. time order.   B. definition-example.   C. comparison and/or contrast.

6. One transition that signals the pattern of organization of this paragraph

is _____.

D. ¹A conflict of interest exists when a businessperson is faced with a situation in which an action benefiting one person or group has the potential to harm another. ²For instance, lawyers, business consultants, or advertising agencies would face a conflict of interest if they represented two competing companies; a strategy that would most benefit one of the client companies might harm the other client. ³Another example would be a real estate agent who faces an ethical conflict if he or she represents both the buyer and seller in a transaction. ⁴In general, the buyer benefits from a low price, and the seller benefits from a high price. ⁵Handling the situation responsibly may be possible, but it would also be difficult.

_____ 7. The main pattern of organization of the selection is
   A. time order.   B. definition and example.   C. list of items.

8. One transition that signals the pattern of organization of this paragraph

is _____.

E. ¹Three musical instruments played an important role in eighteenth-century warfare. ²One of the most important was the snare drum. ³Often played by boys between 12 and 16 years old, snare drums were used to set the marching rhythm for soldiers. ⁴With a skilled drummer playing 96 beats per minute, a commander could march his troops three miles in fifty minutes, allowing ten minutes each hour for a breather and a drink. ⁵Another important instrument was a small flute called a fife. ⁶The fife's role in an army was to entertain soldiers and communicate orders. ⁷For example, the song "Pioneer's March" was the signal for road-clearing crews to get started ahead of the infantry. ⁸Fifes were also used to give orders to soldiers during battle since they could be heard above the roar of firearms. ⁹A third instrument used in warfare was the trumpet. ¹⁰Requiring just one hand to play, it was used by soldiers on horseback to send messages to soldiers in battle and on the march.

_____ 9. The main pattern of organization of the selection is
   A. time order.   B. list of items.   C. comparison and/or contrast.

10. One transition that signals the pattern of organization of this paragraph

is _____.

RELATIONSHIPS I & II: Mastery Test 3

Each of the following selections uses **two** patterns of organization. Read each selection and then, in the spaces provided, write the letter of the two patterns of organization.

A. ¹A boycott is an expression of protest consisting of an organized refusal by a group of people to deal with another person or group. ²An illustration is the famous boycott that began in 1955 when Mrs. Rosa Parks of Montgomery, Alabama, refused to obey a local ordinance requiring black people to sit at the back of city buses. ³Mrs. Parks was arrested, which resulted in a boycott of the Montgomery bus system by blacks. ⁴The boycott was organized and led by Dr. Martin Luther King, Jr. ⁵Rather than continue to lose revenue needed to run the bus system, the city repealed the ordinance.

_____ 1. The main patterns of organization of the selection are
   A. definition-example and list of items.
   B. cause-effect and contrast.
   C. definition-example and cause-effect.

B. ¹On May 18, 1980, Mt. St. Helens in the state of Washington erupted violently, killing nearly one hundred people and leveling thousands of acres of timber. ²By contrast, many volcanoes in Hawaii never explode, but simply have lava flowing out of them. ³The difference between volcanic eruptions and simple lava flows is the result of the differing composition of the molten rock that comes to the surface as lava. ⁴The lava from Mt. St. Helens is a type that cools more quickly, which causes it to build a lava dome that plugs up the flow. ⁵Eventually the pressure becomes so intense that a tremendous explosion blows the lava dome off and sends a massive cloud of ash into the air. ⁶By contrast, the lava from Hawaiian volcanoes contains enough iron to keep it from hardening to rock when it reaches the air; it flows down the side of the cone until it hits an obstacle or eventually cools and becomes solid. ⁷It never plugs the volcano; therefore, there is no explosion.

_____ 2. The main patterns of organization of the selection are
   A. definition-example and time order.
   B. contrast and cause-effect.
   C. list of items and comparison.

C. ¹The United States ranks near the bottom among the world's democracies in the percentage of eligible citizens who participate in national elections. ²One reason for the low voter turnout is that individual Americans are responsible for registering to vote, whereas in most other democracies, voters are automatically registered by government officials. ³In addition, unlike some other democracies, the United States does not

(Continues on next page)

encourage voting by holding elections on the weekend or by imposing penalties, such as fines, on those who do not participate.

_____ 3. The main patterns of organization of the selection are
    A. cause-effect and contrast.
    B. time order and comparison.
    C. definition-example and time order.

D. [1]What caused our distant ancestors to move from walking on all fours to standing upright? [2]First, and probably most important, standing upright freed the forelimbs to carry things. [3]With dangerous animals around more than willing to make a meal out of a small primate, the ability to search for food while possibly carrying one's offspring and to carry the food back to a safe location would certainly be a benefit. [4]Second, by elevating the head, walking upright provided better views of food and danger. [5]In addition, the vertical orientation helped cool the body by presenting a smaller target for the intense equatorial rays of the sun and by placing more of the body above the ground to catch cooling air currents. [6]Finally, standing upright, while using a great deal of energy for running, was very efficient for walking. [7]Long periods of steady walking in search of food required less energy if done in an upright position.

_____ 4. The main patterns of organization of the selection are
    A. cause-effect and list of items.
    B. definition-example and time order.
    C. list of items and time order.

E. [1]When a honeybee finds a new source of food—flower pollen and nectar—she flies back to the hive. [2]Within minutes, more bees emerge and, amazingly, fly straight to the food. [3]Their ability to do this is a result of what goes on in the hive after that first bee flies in. [4]Inside the hive, that bee does a dance, called a waggling dance, to communicate to the other bees the direction, distance, and identity of the food. [5]First, because it's usually dark in the hive, she emits sound signals that help the other bees determine where she is and how she's moving. [6]She then dances in a figure-eight pattern, waggling only when she is facing the direction of the food source in relation to the sun. [7]The pace of her dancing tells how far away the food is; the faster she dances, the closer the food. [8]At some point, the bees observing the dance emit sounds that vibrate the honeycomb. [9]This causes the dancer to stop, and she gives the watchers small samples of the food so they know its taste, smell, and quality. [10]After receiving the necessary information, the other bees then fly out to find the food.

_____ 5. The main patterns of organization of the selection are
    A. definition-example and list of items.
    B. cause-effect and time order.
    C. comparison and time order.

7 Inferences

You have probably heard the expression "to read between the lines." When you "read between the lines," you pick up ideas that are not directly stated in what you are reading. These implied ideas are often important for a full understanding of what an author means. Discovering the ideas that are not stated directly in writing is called **making inferences**, or **drawing conclusions**.

Look at the cartoon below. What inferences can you make about it? Check (✓) the **two** inferences that are most logically based on the information suggested by the cartoon.

_____ A. The couple is not likely to have a good dining experience at the restaurant.

_____ B. The couple will never eat at the restaurant.

_____ C. The restaurant was recently closed for health violations.

_____ D. Whoever is running the restaurant is not doing a good job.

Explanation

A. *The couple is not likely to have a good dining experience at the restaurant.*

The "help wanted" sign indicates that the restaurant is seriously understaffed. It would be logical, then, to infer that the restaurant cannot provide patrons with a good dining experience. You should have checked this item.

B. *The couple will never eat at the restaurant.*

The man's comment that "this isn't the best time" suggests that he may be willing to try the restaurant once it has solved its staffing problems. Also, experience suggests that it is common for restaurants to change ownership and/or management. You should not have checked this item.

C. *The restaurant was recently closed for health violations.*

Nothing in the cartoon suggests that the restaurant was recently closed for health violations. Perhaps if it continues to operate without sufficient staff, it *may* be closed, but we have no way of knowing that. You should not have checked this item.

D. *Whoever is running the restaurant is not doing a good job.*

Experience tells us that good managers are able to hire and retain qualified employees. The "help wanted" sign suggests quite the opposite—that a number of employees have recently quit or been fired. The lack of staff, in turn, has caused the couple to decide against dining there. Clearly, this is no way to run a business! You should have checked this item.

Inferences in Reading

In reading, we make logical leaps from information stated directly to ideas that are not stated directly. As one scholar has said, inferences are "statements about the unknown made on the basis of the known." To draw inferences, we use all the clues provided by the writer, our own experience, and logic.

You have already practiced making inferences in this book. Do you remember the following sentence from "Vocabulary in Context" on page 21?

Many of us have *ambivalent* feelings about our politicians, admiring them but also distrusting them.

That sentence does not tell us the meaning of *ambivalent*, but it does suggest that *ambivalent* involves both positive and negative feelings. Thus you can infer from this sentence that *ambivalent feelings* probably means "mixed feelings," and you'd be correct.

✓ *Check Your Understanding 1*

Read the following passage and check (✔) the **two** inferences that are most firmly based on the information given. Then read the explanation that follows.

> [1]A sociology professor wrote on the board, "A woman without her man is nothing" and, with a smile, asked students to punctuate the sentence correctly. [2]The men all wrote, "A woman, without her man, is nothing." [3]However, the women wrote, "A woman: Without her, man is nothing."

____ A. The professor was definitely a man.

____ B. The professor did not believe students could punctuate the words correctly.

____ C. The professor knew there was more than one way to punctuate the words correctly.

____ D. The professor is not a good teacher.

____ E. Gender differences caused students to read and punctuate the professor's words differently.

Explanation

A. There is no indication of the professor's gender in the passage. You should not have checked this item.

B. Nothing in the passage implies that the professor doubted students' ability to punctuate the words correctly. You should not have checked this item.

C. Since the professor chose the particular sentence and smiled while writing the words, we can conclude that the professor was aware of more than one punctuation possibility. Therefore, you should have checked this item.

D. There is no suggestion in the passage that the professor is a poor teacher. In fact, the professor has chosen a dramatic way to suggest that each sex sees the world from its own point of view. You should not have checked this item.

E. Male and female students had very different responses to the sentence. Gender was the only apparent difference among the students, so we can conclude that it caused the different responses. You should have checked this item.

✔ *Check Your Understanding 2*

Read the following passage, and then check (✓) the **three** inferences that can most logically be drawn from it. Then read the explanation that follows.

> [1]A famous psychology experiment conducted by Dr. John B. Watson demonstrates that people, like animals, can be conditioned—trained to respond in a particular way to certain stimulations. [2]Watson gave an eleven-month-old baby named Albert a soft, furry white rat. [3]Each time Albert tried to stroke the rat, Dr. Watson hit a metal bar with a hammer. [4]Before long, Albert was afraid not only of white rats but also of white rabbits, white dogs, and white fur coats. [5]He even screamed at the sight of a Santa Claus mask.

____ A. Dr. Watson did not like small children.

____ B. Before the experiment, Albert was not afraid of white rats.

____ C. Albert had been familiar with rats before the experiment.

____ D. If he had seen a black fur coat, Albert would have screamed.

____ E. Albert connected the loud noise of the hammer striking the metal bar with the white rat.

____ F. Albert was afraid of unexpected loud noises.

Explanation

A. This is not a logical inference. We might certainly question the way the baby was used, but the passage doesn't give enough information for us to infer logically that Watson did not like small children.

B. This is a logical inference. Because Albert tried to pet the rat, it is fair to assume that he wasn't frightened of the animal.

C. This is not a logical inference. The passage gives no clues about Albert's having previous experience with rats.

D. This is not a logical inference. The passage makes no mention of Albert's response to any color but white.

E. This is a logical inference. Because the noise appears to have changed Albert's attitude toward the rat, we can assume he associated the noise with the rat.

F. This is a logical inference. Since the noise is what made Albert afraid of the rat, we have to infer that he was afraid of the noise. In addition, experience tells us that babies are likely to be frightened of unexpected loud noises.

Guidelines for Making Inferences in Reading

The exercises in this chapter provide practice in making careful inferences when you read. Here are three guidelines for that process:

1   **Never lose sight of the available information.** As much as possible, base your inferences on the facts. For instance, in the paragraph about Watson's experiment, we are told, "Albert tried to stroke the rat." On the basis of that fact, we can readily conclude that the baby had no fear of rats.

   It's also important to note when a conclusion lacks support. For instance, the idea that Albert would have screamed at the sight of a black fur coat has no support in the paragraph. We are told only that Albert was frightened by white furry things.

2   **Use your background information and experience to help you in making inferences.** Our understanding and experience with babies, for example, help us realize that Albert was frightened of unexpected loud noises.

   The more you know about a subject, the better your inferences are likely to be. So keep in mind that if your background in an area is weak, your inferences may be shaky. For example, if you develop a rash and fever that will not go away, a doctor's inferences about the cause are likely to be more helpful than your inferences.

3   **Consider the alternatives.** Don't simply accept the first inference that comes to mind. Instead, consider all the facts of a case and all the possible explanations. For example, the doctor analyzing your rash and fever may first think of and then eliminate several possibilities before coming to the right conclusion.

PRACTICE 1

Read the following passages. Then, in the space provided, write the letter of the most logical answer to each question, based on the information given in the passage.

A.   [1]A corporate president recently made a visit to a nearby Native American reservation as part of his firm's public-relations program. [2]"We realize that we have not hired any Indians in the five years our company has been located in this area," he told the assembled tribespeople, "but we are looking into the matter very carefully." [3]"*Hora, hora,*" said some of the audience. [4]"We would like to eventually hire 5 percent of our total work force from this reservation," he said. [5]"*Hora, hora,*" shouted more of the audience. [6]Encouraged by their enthusiasm, the president closed his short address by telling them that he hoped his firm would be able to take some hiring action within the next couple of years. [7]"*Hora, hora, hora,*" cried the total group. [8]With a feeling of satisfaction, the president left the hall and was taken on a tour of the reservation. [9]Stopping in a field to admire some of the horses grazing there, the president asked if he could walk up closer to the animals. [10]"Certainly," said his guide, "but be careful not to step in the *hora*."

_____ 1. To get the main point of this passage, the reader must infer
A. the location of the reservation.
B. what kind of company the president headed.
C. the meaning of the word *hora*.

_____ 2. From the passage, we can infer that the audience
A. believed the president's speech.
B. did not believe the president's speech.
C. was confused by the president's speech.

_____ 3. From the passage, we can infer that the president
A. thought the Native Americans deserved to be hired.
B. thought his company should not hire the Native Americans.
C. misinterpreted the Native Americans' reaction to his speech.

_____ 4. From the passage, we can infer that the main reason the president spoke to the Native Americans about jobs was that
A. they needed the jobs.
B. he thought promising jobs to Native Americans would make his company look good.
C. he thought hiring Native Americans would be good for his company.

B.   [1]Parents bewildered by their teen alien can take comfort from one sign that Junior may be from the same species as they are: High-school status ladders look just as they did when Corvettes were the hot cars of choice.

[2]A new study of social systems at eighteen high schools in various states reveals some familiar patterns, reports sociologist Murray Milner, Jr. [3]Still tops in popularity: male athletes and attractive girls. [4]Just beneath them stand well-dressed "preppies" who try to act indifferent to school and snag the "right" party invitations.

[5]"Nerds" cluster near the bottom. [6]Their sin? [7]Open preoccupation with academic success. [8]But they're not lowest. [9]The "dorks," Milner says, "were hopelessly inept" about clothes and social events. [10]They often had low grades and poor athletic ability, too.

[11]Kids typically date only within their status level, which is set in stone by the first year and seldom can be upgraded. [12]Downgrading is a danger, though. [13]A girl dating a star athlete who later got injured and couldn't play found his status—and hers—suddenly declining. [14]And being seen talking to classmates "beneath" one's status can pull students down very fast.

[15]"High school is a very scary place," Milner says.

[16]It often is, agrees San Diego psychiatrist Martin Greenberg. [17]To take the

pressure off at home, consider cutting teens some slack on minor disputes, he advises. [18]"Try to be flexible because a lot of them are having a hard time. [19]No matter how it looks," he says, "they're desperate for love."

_____ 5. From the beginning of the passage, we can conclude that a generation ago
A. teens became popular for very different reasons than they do today.
B. social status was not very important in high schools.
C. good-looking girls and athletic boys were the most popular kids.
D. only "dorks" drove Corvettes.

_____ 6. We can infer from the passage that
A. teenagers generally don't care about their social status.
B. the high-school years are stressful ones for many teens.
C. most teens admire students who openly care about school.
D. teens typically behave lovingly when they are home.

_____ 7. The passage suggests that in high school,
A. boys are most valued for their athletic ability and girls for their appearance.
B. female athletes are generally as popular as male athletes.
C. a nonathletic boy can be very popular as long as he is a good student.
D. athletes don't care about getting invited to parties.

_____ 8. The passage suggests that
A. teenagers are independent thinkers who aren't bothered by other people's opinions.
B. popular teens often make friends with less popular kids.
C. outward appearance is an important factor in determining high-schoolers' status.
D. a teenager's social status often changes from year to year.

C.   [1]During World War II, the troop ship *SS Dorchester* steamed out of New York harbor with 904 men headed for Greenland. [2]Among those leaving anxious families behind were four chaplains: Methodist preacher George Fox, Rabbi Alexander Goode, Catholic priest John Washington, and Reformed Church minister Clark Poling. [3]Some 150 miles from their destination, a Nazi submarine sighted the *Dorchester* in its cross hairs. [4]Within moments of a torpedo's impact, reports a survivor, stunned men were pouring out from their bunks as the ship began tilting. [5]With power cut off, the escort vessels, unaware of the unfolding tragedy, pushed on in the darkness. [6]Onboard, chaos ruled as panicky men came up from the hold without life jackets and leaped into overcrowded lifeboats.

[7]When the four chaplains made it up to the steeply sloping deck, they began guiding the men to their boat stations. [8]They opened a storage locker, distributed life jackets, and coaxed the men over the side. [9]In the icy, oil-smeared water, Private William Bednar heard the chaplains preaching courage and found the strength to

swim until he reached a life raft. [10]Still onboard, Grady Clark watched in awe as the chaplains handed out the last life jackets, and then, with ultimate selflessness, gave away their own. [11]As Clark slipped into the water, he saw the chaplains standing—their arms linked—praying, in Latin, Hebrew, and English. [12]Other men, now calm, joined them in a huddle as the *Dorchester* slid beneath the sea.

_____ 9. We can infer from this passage that
  A. the Nazis had been hunting for the *Dorchester* for a long time.
  B. the *Dorchester*'s passengers and their families knew that because the ship carried soldiers, it might be attacked.
  C. the Nazi submarine was eventually found and destroyed.

_____ 10. We can infer that the chaplains and others remaining on the boat didn't jump off because
  A. there was no more room in the lifeboats, and they knew they could not survive in the icy sea without a life jacket.
  B. they couldn't swim.
  C. they assumed a friendly ship would soon pass by and save them.

_____ 11. We can infer from the passage that Grady Clark
  A. was one of the men who died in the *Dorchester* tragedy.
  B. survived the attack and reported what the chaplains had done.
  C. was the sole survivor of the attack on the *Dorchester*.

_____ 12. The passage suggests that
  A. the chaplains had known each other for many years.
  B. religious faith may strengthen courage.
  C. the chaplains had no fear of death.

PRACTICE 2

Read the following textbook passages. Then put a check (✓) by the **three** inferences that are most logically based on the given facts in each passage.

A. [1]George Washington's honesty is a trait that has been well publicized. [2]The famous story of how little George chopped down his father's favorite cherry tree, then bravely admitted to the deed, has an honored place in American presidential history. [3]The cherry tree story was first recorded in 1806 by Parson Mason Weems, a Maryland preacher and storyteller. [4]Unfortunately, Parson Weems was none too honest himself, and it appears that he invented the story of George and the cherry tree. [5]There is no record of the cherry tree incident anywhere until it appears in Weems's book. [6]The parson, it seems, thought it acceptable to teach the virtue of honesty through a made-up story. [7]We can judge Weems's own truthfulness by the fact that he describes himself in the book as "formerly rector of Mount Vernon Parish." [8]Such a parish never existed.

_____ 1. The passage suggests that George Washington was not so honest after all.

_____ 2. We can conclude that Parson Weems knew George Washington well.

_____ 3. Widely accepted stories about history are not necessarily true.

_____ 4. Parson Weems wrote about a virtue he didn't have himself.

_____ 5. The author of this passage doubts that George Washington was a great leader and president.

_____ 6. In his stories and sermons, Weems may well have told other false stories.

B. [1]The *Chicago Tribune* once wrote that Henry Ford, the founder of the Ford Motor Company, was an ignorant man. [2]Ford sued, challenging the paper to "prove it." [3]During the trial, Ford was asked dozens of simple, general information questions: "When was the Civil War?" "Name the presidents of the United States," and so on. [4]Ford, who had little formal education, could answer very few. [5]Finally, exasperated, he said, "I don't know the answers to those questions, but I could find a man in five minutes who does. [6]I use my brain to think, not store up a lot of useless facts."

_____ 1. Henry Ford was probably angered by the article in the *Chicago Tribune*.

_____ 2. Ford frequently sued people.

_____ 3. The *Tribune* won the case in court.

_____ 4. Ford believed that knowing where to find a fact is good enough.

_____ 5. Ford would have been even more successful in his career had he had a formal education.

_____ 6. Ford believed that knowing how to think is more important than knowing facts.

C. [1]Most people would like to think that they choose their friends solely on the basis of personal characteristics. [2]A classic study of a housing complex for married students at the Massachusetts Institute of Technology (MIT) suggests that proximity— nearness and availability—can be an important factor. [3]Researchers asked couples to list their friends in the complex. [4]They found that residents were far more likely to list the couple in the next apartment than one that lived two doors away, and more likely to visit with a couple two doors away than with one three or four doors away. [5]A distance of thirty feet or a short elevator ride made the difference between friends and strangers! [6]More recent studies have confirmed the importance of proximity. [7]One possible explanation is that whenever people encounter strangers, they feel tense. [8]The more they see a person, the more they come to think of that person as predictable and safe, and hence the more likely they are to strike up a conversation that leads to friendship. [9]This would explain why the most popular couples in the MIT housing complex were those who lived at the bottom of the stairs near the garbage cans that everyone used.

____ 1. Most people probably think their personal preferences determine whom they choose for friends.

____ 2. In fact, our personal preferences have no effect on who our friends are.

____ 3. A person who lives in a big country is more likely to have more friends than someone who lives in a small country.

____ 4. Someone living in an apartment house is likely to have more friends than someone who lives on a farm.

____ 5. A garbage collector is likely to have more friends than a letter carrier.

____ 6. Someone who works in a busy office is likely to have more friends than someone who works at home.

Inferences in Literature

Inferences are very important in reading literature. While writers of factual material usually state directly much of what they mean, creative writers often provide verbal pictures that *show* us what they mean. It is up to the reader to infer the point of what the creative writer has said. For instance, a nonfiction author might write the following:

A man got angry at the person using a cell phone in the theater.

But a novelist might write this:

Thomas turned to face the laughing red-haired girl sitting behind him in the theater. A vein on his forehead was throbbing. "Would you mind very much turning off that cell phone?" he hissed. "A few of us are here to actually see the movie."

Rather than merely stating that Thomas was angry, the author shows the anger with vivid details. To get the most out of literature, you must often infer meanings—just as you do in everyday life. Your may have inferred, for example, that the laughing girl is insensitive to the rights of others in the theater. You could also have concluded that Thomas has probably been waiting a while for her to quiet down, but she has not, and his temper is now boiling.

Now look at the following statement that a nonfiction writer might produce:

A farmer is about to kill a small pig, but his daughter objects, so the farmer decides to let his daughter learn for herself that a small pig can be a problem.

Compare the above line with the following scene from *Charlotte's Web*, a literary classic that is beloved by young and old alike:

[1]"Fern," said Mr. Arable, "I know more about raising a litter of pigs than you do. [2]A weakling makes trouble. [3]Now run along!"

[4]"But it's unfair," cried Fern. [5]"The pig couldn't help being born small, could it? [6]If I had been very small at birth, would you have killed me?"

[7]Mr. Arable smiled. [8]"Certainly not," he said, looking down at his daughter with love. [9]"But this is different. [10]A little girl is one thing, a little runty pig is another."

[11]"I see no difference," replied Fern, still hanging on to the ax. [12]"This is the most terrible case of injustice I ever heard of."

[13]A queer look came over John Arable's face. [14]He seemed almost ready to cry himself.

[15]"All right," he said. [16]"You go back to the house and I will bring the runt when I come in. [17]I'll let you start it on a bottle, like a baby. [18]Then you'll see what trouble a pig can be."

✔ ## *Check Your Understanding*

See if you can answer the following inference questions about the excerpt.

_____ 1. Fern and Mr. Arable probably live
   A. in a city.
   B. in a small town.
   C. on a farm.

_____ 2. We can infer from the excerpt that Mr. Arable
   A. has probably raised many pigs in his lifetime.
   B. has had little experience raising pigs.
   C. does not like pigs.

_____ 3. Mr. Arable appears almost ready to cry because he
   A. gets worried about how difficult it would be to raise the pig.
   B. does not like to lose an argument with his daughter.
   C. is touched by his daughter's willingness to stand up for the small pig.

_____ 4. We can conclude that Mr. Arable agrees to spare the pig because
   A. Fern has convinced him that it is unfair to kill pigs, no matter what their size.
   B. he believes that raising a pig will teach Fern some lessons.
   C. he realizes that taking care of a runt pig is not that difficult.

_____ 5. By the end of this passage, we can infer that Mr. Arable is
   A. a cruel man.
   B. a reasonable man.
   C. not a very patient man.

Explanation

1. Fern and Mr. Arable live in a place where pigs are born and raised. That strongly suggests that they live on a farm. The correct answer, then, is C.

2. Mr. Arable mentions that he knows about "raising a litter of pigs." He also tells Fern how to begin feeding the pig. These details suggest that he has raised pigs before. Therefore, the answer is A.

3. Mr. Arable seems near crying after Fern insists there's no difference between killing a runt pig and killing a small daughter. And the passage has already described Mr. Arable looking at his daughter with love. So we can conclude that the plea for justice from the young daughter he adores is what touched him so. Thus the answer is C.

4. When Mr. Arable agrees to let his daughter raise the pig, he says "you'll see what trouble a pig can be." His words suggest that he expects Fern to learn a lesson. Therefore B is the answer.

5. Mr. Arable talks to Fern, listens to her opinions, and agrees to allow her to do something he does not fully support. These actions suggest he is a fair and reasonable man. So answer B is correct.

The excerpt from *Charlotte's Web* is a small example of how inference skills can increase your appreciation of literary forms—fiction, poetry, autobiographies, and other imaginative literature.

Poetry, especially, by its nature implies much of its meaning. Poets often imply their meanings through comparisons. For example, Emily Dickinson begins one of her poems with the following lines:

> Hope is the thing with feathers
> That perches in the soul,
> And sings the tune without the words,
> And never stops at all . . . .

Here, Dickinson uses a figure of speech known as a metaphor, comparing hope to a singing bird. The comparison implies, among other things, that hope is a sweet and welcome thing. (More about metaphors appears on the next page.)

A Note on Figures of Speech

Creative writers often use **figures of speech** to give us a fresh way of looking at something. The two most common figures of speech are similes and metaphors.

Simile—a comparison introduced with *like, as,* or *as if.*

In the cartoon, the boy, Linus, says that getting back his lost security blanket is "like seeing the flood waters recede . . . like a reunion with old friends . . . like a drop of water to a man lost in the desert . . . like coming out of a dark cave into the wonderful sunlight." (The joke, of course, is that he overdoes the similes, which is why Lucy ties the blanket around his mouth.)

Here is another example. Instead of saying, "The window shade snapped up," you could express it more vividly by saying, "The window shade snapped up like a gunshot." The simile shows that the noise of the window shade was loud and startling.

Here are some other similes:

- That Halloween night was *as dark as the inside of a witch's hat.*
- After you've broken up with a boyfriend or girlfriend, every day feels *like a cloudy, cold Monday morning.*
- If he senses you don't know the material, our math teacher attacks *like a shark.*
- That runner moves *as gracefully as a gazelle.*

Metaphor—an implied comparison, with *like, as,* or *as if* omitted.

The thought "No person can be self-sufficient" was expressed vividly in a metaphor by the poet John Donne, who wrote: "No man is an island." His comparison says no one can be completely disconnected from the mainland—the rest of humanity.

Here are some other metaphors:

- The grade on the paper was *a dash of ice water in my face.*
- When Nate got up to speak, he was *a mass of quivering Jell-O.*
- *The warm honey* of her voice melted my anger.
- Watching TV for hours, the children were *glassy-eyed statues.*
- The dancer's head was *a rose* on *the slender stem* of her neck.

PRACTICE 3

Use a check (✔) to identify each figure of speech as a simile or a metaphor. Then, in the space provided, answer each inference question that follows.

_____ 1. His friendship is as genuine as a plastic Christmas tree.

___ simile   ___ metaphor

You can infer that the friendship is
A. easy to maintain.
B. fake and cheap.
C. seasonal and glittery.

_____ 2. A gang of teenaged boys moved through the mall like a pack of wild dogs.

___ simile   ___ metaphor

You can infer that the boys were
A. polite and friendly.
B. sneaky and quiet.
C. loud and disruptive.

_____ 3. The executives did not admit that the company was a sinking ship until after they had taken millions of dollars for themselves.

___ simile   ___ metaphor

You can infer that the company
A. was well-managed.
B. was failing.
C. was going in more than one direction.

_____ 4. Everyone at work thinks that Jasmine is a real gem.

___ simile   ___ metaphor

You can infer that Jasmine is
A. disliked and unfriendly.
B. shy and quiet.
C. admired and valued.

_____ 5. I'm writing a family history so that my grandparents' stories do not go up in smoke and ashes.

___ simile   ___ metaphor

You can infer that the grandparents' stories are
A. full of fire and passion.
B. uneventful and unimportant.
C. in danger of being lost forever.

PRACTICE 4

George Orwell is famous for his novels *Animal Farm* and *1984* as well as his classic literary essays. Following is an excerpt from "A Hanging," an essay Orwell wrote about an execution he witnessed while he was an English police officer stationed in Burma. Read the excerpt, and then answer the inference questions that follow.

Note that the meanings of a few words in the excerpt are given below.

reiterated: repeated
Ram: Hindu god
abominable: hateful
timorously: timidly
oscillated: swung back and forth

¹We stood waiting, five yards away. ²The warders had formed in a rough circle round the gallows. ³And then, when the noose was fixed, the prisoner began crying out to his god. ⁴It was a high, reiterated° cry of "Ram°! Ram! Ram! Ram!" not urgent and fearful like a prayer or a cry for help, but steady, rhythmical, almost like the tolling of a bell. ⁵The dog answered the sound with a whine. ⁶The hangman, still standing on the gallows, produced a small cotton bag like a flour bag and drew it down over the prisoner's face. ⁷But the sound, muffled by the cloth, still persisted, over and over again: "Ram! Ram! Ram! Ram!"

⁸The hangman climbed down and stood ready, holding the lever. ⁹Minutes seemed to pass. ¹⁰The steady, muffled crying from the prisoner went on and on, "Ram! Ram! Ram!" never faltering for an instant. ¹¹The superintendent, his head on his chest, was slowly poking the ground with his stick; perhaps he was counting the cries, allowing the prisoner a fixed number—fifty, perhaps, or a hundred. ¹²Everyone had changed color. ¹³The Indians had gone grey like bad coffee, and one or two of the bayonets were wavering. ¹⁴We looked at the lashed, hooded man on the drop, and listened to his cries—each cry another second of life; the same thought was in all our minds: oh, kill him quickly, get it over, stop that abominable° noise!

¹⁵Suddenly the superintendent made up his mind. ¹⁶Throwing up his head, he made a swift motion with his stick. ¹⁷"Chalo!" he shouted almost fiercely.

¹⁸There was a clanking noise, and then dead silence. ¹⁹The prisoner had vanished, and the rope was twisting on itself. ²⁰I let go of the dog, and it galloped immediately to the back of the gallows; but when it got there, it stopped short, barked, and then retreated into a corner of the yard, where it stood among the weeds, looking timorously° out at us. ²¹We went round the gallows to inspect the prisoner's body. ²²He was dangling with his toes pointed straight downward, very slowly revolving, as dead as a stone.

²³The superintendent reached out with his stick and poked the bare body; it oscillated°, slightly. ²⁴"*He's* all right," said the superintendent. ²⁵He backed out from under the gallows, and blew out a deep breath. ²⁶The moody look had gone out of his face quite suddenly. ²⁷He glanced at his wristwatch. ²⁸"Eight minutes past eight. ²⁹Well, that's all for this morning, thank God."

_____ 1. We can infer from the simile below that the prisoner's cry was like
    A. wedding bells.
    B. a funeral bell.
    C. a doorbell.

      "It was a high . . . cry . . . steady, rhythmical, . . . like the tolling of a bell."

_____ 2. The reaction of the Indian spectators, described in the simile below, suggests they are
    A. sympathetic to the superintendent's duty.
    B. disturbed by the prisoner's hanging.
    C. relieved that the prisoner was about to die.

      "Everyone had changed color. The Indians had gone grey like bad coffee . . ."

_____ 3. In the second paragraph, we can conclude that the superintendent waited for the prisoner to say his prayers because he
    A. had the same religious beliefs as the prisoner.
    B. was distracted by something on the ground.
    C. understood the prisoner's fear and showed him respect.

_____ 4. We can infer from the passage that the word *chalo* was a
    A. word of protest against the hanging.
    B. cheer in support of the hanging.
    C. command used to begin the hanging.

_____ 5. Orwell's description of the prisoner being as "dead as a stone" is a simile that suggests the prisoner was
    A. still and lifeless.
    B. dirty and round.
    C. solid and strong.

_____ 6. The author implies that the dog
    A. belonged to the superintendent.
    B. sensed that something terrible had happened.
    C. had no understanding of what was going on around him.

_____ 7. When the superintendent says, "Well, that's all for this morning," he implies that
    A. there may be more executions in the afternoon.
    B. there has been only one execution that morning.
    C. there will be no other work to do in the morning.

_____ 8. When the superintendent says, "*He's* all right," he means that
    A. while the prisoner is at peace, everyone else is still shaken.
    B. the prisoner got the punishment that he deserved.
    C. the prisoner had wanted to die and got his wish.

_____ 9. We can infer from the superintendent's behavior that he
    A. was a cruel man who enjoyed seeing others executed.
    B. refused to attend any more executions after this one.
    C. considered executions an unpleasant part of his duty.

_____ 10. We can infer from the details in this passage and another excerpt from the essay, shown below, that the author probably was
    A. in favor of capital punishment.
    B. troubled by capital punishment.
    C. not interested in the issue of capital punishment.

> "He [the prisoner] and we were a party of men, walking together, seeing, hearing, feeling, understanding the same world; and in two minutes, with a sudden snap, one of us would be gone—one mind less, one world less."

Inferences in Graphs and Tables

You have already tried your hand at making inferences from a picture, the cartoon about the couple deciding not to eat at the restaurant. Many of the cartoons in newspapers and magazines depend on your inference skills. Other "pictures" that require inferences are graphs and tables, which combine words with visual representations. Authors of textbooks, professional and newspaper articles, and other materials often organize large amounts of material into graphs and tables. Very often, the graphs and tables are used to show comparisons and changes that take place over time.

As with other reading material, to infer the ideas presented in graphs and tables, you must consider all the information presented.

Steps in Reading a Graph or Table

To find and make sense of the information in a graph or table, follow a few steps.

1 Read the title. It will tell you what the table or graph is about in general.

   ● What is the title of the graph on the next page? _____

   _____

2 Check the source. At the bottom of a table or graph, you will usually find the source of the information, an indication of the reliability of its material.

   ● What is the source of the graph on the next page? _____

   _____

3 Read any labels or captions at the top, the side, or underneath that tell exactly what each column, line, bar, number, or other item represents. This information includes such things as quantities, percentages, and years.

   ● What is the span of years covered in the graph? _____

   ● Which types of work does the graph cover? _____

   _____

4 Once you have taken the above steps, you are ready to infer from the graph or table whatever information you seek from it.

Changes in U.S. Work Force, 1900–2010

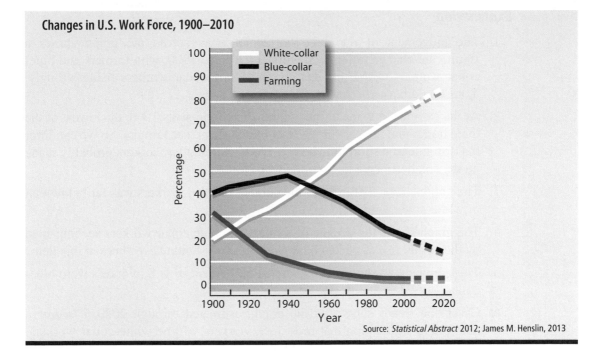

Source: *Statistical Abstract* 2012; James M. Henslin, 2013

✓ *Check Your Understanding*

See if you can put a check (✓) by the **three** inferences that are most logically based on the above graph.

____ 1. The work force of 1900 was very different from the work force of today.

____ 2. Before 1900, farmers made up the smallest percentage of workers.

____ 3. In 1940, the percentages of farm workers and white-collar workers were about equal.

____ 4. In general, as the number of farming and blue-collar workers has decreased, the number of white-collar workers has increased.

____ 5. In 1940, blue-collar workers made up about 25 percent of the U.S. work force.

____ 6. In the future, most U.S. workers are likely to be white-collar workers.

Explanation

1. The movement of the three horizontal lines across the graph shows a significant change in the U.S. work force since 1900, with farmers and blue-collar workers decreasing sharply and white-collar workers rising strongly. You should have checked this item.

2. At the extreme left side of the graph, which represents 1900, the lowest of the three horizontal lines is for white-collar workers, not farmers. So we can infer that for at least a short time before 1900, white-collar workers probably made up the smallest percentage of the work force.

3. The graph shows that in 1940 the number of farm workers was far below that of white-collar workers.

4. The graph shows the decline of farmers and blue-collar workers accompanied by the steady rise of white-collar workers. You should have checked this item.

5. The graph shows that in 1940, almost 50 percent of U.S. workers were blue-collar.

6. Given the trends shown on the graph, estimated through 2020, it seems a reasonable assumption that most U.S. workers will be white-collar workers. You should have checked this item.

PRACTICE 5

Read the table on the next page, following the steps for reading graphs and tables on page 290. Then put a check (✓) by the **three** inferences that are most logically based on the table.

_____ 1. The percentage of Americans who vote has declined steadily since 1992.

_____ 2. Women are more likely to vote than men.

_____ 3. The older a person gets, the more likely he or she is to vote.

_____ 4. The more education and money people have, the more likely they are to vote.

_____ 5. African Americans are far less likely to vote than white Americans.

_____ 6. A person's employment status has little effect on his or her voting record.

TABLE 11.1 Who Votes for President?

	1988	1992	1996	2000	2004	2008
Overall						
Americans Who Voted	57%	61%	54%	55%	58%	58%
Age						
18–20	33%	39%	31%	28%	41%	41%
21–24	46%	46%	33%	35%	43%	47%
25–34	48%	53%	43%	44%	47%	49%
35–44	61%	64%	55%	55%	57%	55%
45–64	68%	70%	64%	64%	67%	65%
65 and older	69%	70%	67%	68%	69%	68%
Sex						
Male	56%	60%	53%	53%	56%	56%
Female	58%	62%	56%	56%	60%	60%
Race–Ethnicity						
Whites	64%	70%	56%	56%	60%	60%
African Americans	55%	59%	51%	54%	56%	61%
Asian Americans	NA	54%	NA	25%	30%	32%
Latinos	48%	52%	27%	28%	28%	32%
Education						
High school dropouts	41%	41%	34%	34%	35%	34%
High school graduates	55%	58%	49%	49%	52%	51%
Some college	65%	69%	61%	60%	66%	65%
College graduates	78%	81%	73%	72%	74%	73%
Marital Status						
Married	NA	NA	66%	67%	71%	70%
Divorced	NA	NA	50%	53%	58%	59%
Labor Force						
Employed	58%	64%	55%	56%	60%	60%
Unemployed	39%	46%	37%	35%	46%	49%
Income						
Under $20,000	NA	NA	NA	NA	48%	52%
$20,000 to $30,000	NA	NA	NA	NA	58%	56%
$30,000 to $40,000	NA	NA	NA	NA	62%	62%
$40,000 to $50,000	NA	NA	NA	NA	69%	65%
$50,000 to $75,000	NA	NA	NA	NA	72%	71%
$75,000 to 100,000	NA	NA	NA	NA	78%	76%
Over $100,000	NA	NA	NA	NA	81%	92%

Sources: James M. Henslin. Based on Casper and Bass 1996; Jamieson et al. 2002; Holder 2006; File and Crissey 2010:Table 1; *Statistical Abstract of the United States* 1991:Table 450; 1997:Table 462; 2012: Table 399.

CHAPTER REVIEW

In this chapter, you learned the following:

- Many important ideas in reading are not stated directly but must be inferred. To make inferences about implied ideas, use the information provided as well as your own experience and logic.

- Inferences are also a key part of reading literature and such visual materials as cartoons, tables, and graphs.

The next chapter—Chapter 8—will help make you aware of an author's purpose and tone.

On the Web: If you are using this book in class, you can visit our website for additional practice in making inferences. Go to **www.townsendpress.com** and click on "Learning Center."

REVIEW TEST 1

To review what you've learned in this chapter, answer each of the following questions about inferences.

1. An inference is an idea that is *(directly stated, suggested)* _____ by the author.

2. When making inferences, it is *(a mistake, useful)* _____ to use our own experience as well as the author's clues.

3. When making inferences, it is *(a mistake, useful)* _____ to use our sense of logic as well as the author's clues.

4. _____ TRUE OR FALSE? A reader must make inferences when finding the meaning of words through context and when finding implied main ideas.

5. Making inferences is a key skill in reading literature because writers of fiction do not so much *(tell, show)* _____ us what they mean as *(tell, show)* _____ us with vivid specific details.

REVIEW TEST 2

A. (1–4.) Put a check (✓) by the **four** inferences that are most logically based on the information given in the cartoon.

___ 1. The man with glasses thinks the boss is unfair to temporary workers.

___ 2. The man with glasses agrees with the boss's behavior.

___ 3. The boss values saving money more than he values caring for workers.

___ 4. The boss feels a bit guilty about his treatment of temporary workers.

___ 5. The boss has probably hired and fired other temporary workers.

___ 6. The worker in the boss's arms is about to be promoted.

___ 7. The cartoonist implies that temporary workers have no power in the workplace.

___ 8. The cartoonist implies that companies should not hire temporary workers.

B. (5–8.) Read the following textbook passage, and then put a check (✓) by the **four** inferences that are most logically supported by the information given.

> ¹Your sister has a new boyfriend. ²The first time you meet him, he corners you and talks to you for an hour about football, a subject in which you have no interest at all. ³You come away with the impression that he is an inconsiderate bore. ⁴The next two times you see him, however, he says not a word about football; instead, he participates in the general conversation and makes some witty and intelligent remarks. ⁵What is your impression of him now? ⁶Do you find him likable and interesting on the basis of the last two encounters? ⁷Do you average out the early minus and the later plus and come out with a neutral zero? ⁸Neither is likely. ⁹What

is likely is that you still think of him as an inconsiderate bore, for research suggests that first impressions, as our mothers and fathers told us, are quite lasting.

____ 1. First impressions are usually negative.

____ 2. It is useful to make good first impressions.

____ 3. It's a bad idea to discuss football when you first meet someone.

____ 4. To make a good impression, it helps to notice what interests the other person.

____ 5. A "neutral zero" impression of someone would be negative.

____ 6. A "neutral zero" impression of someone would be neither positive nor negative.

____ 7. It's not so easy to be objective about others.

____ 8. Second impressions can be even more powerful than first impressions.

C. (9–10.) After reading the following passage, put a check (✓) by the **two** inferences that are most firmly based on the given facts.

> [1]A man is talking to the Lord, trying to understand His eternal nature. [2]"Lord," he asks, "what's a million years to you?" [3]"A million years is but a second to me," the Lord explains. [4]"And a million dollars?" [5]"A penny," the Lord replies. [6]The man feels bold and now proceeds to ask, "Lord, would you give me a million dollars?" [7]"Sure," the Lord replies. [8]"Just a second."

____ 1. In comparison with eternity, a million years is a short time.

____ 2. The man will not live long enough to collect his million dollars.

____ 3. The Lord knows the man would just waste the money.

____ 4. The man is poor.

REVIEW TEST 3

A. (1–4.) Read the graph below. Then put a check (✓) by the **four** statements that are most logically supported by the graph.

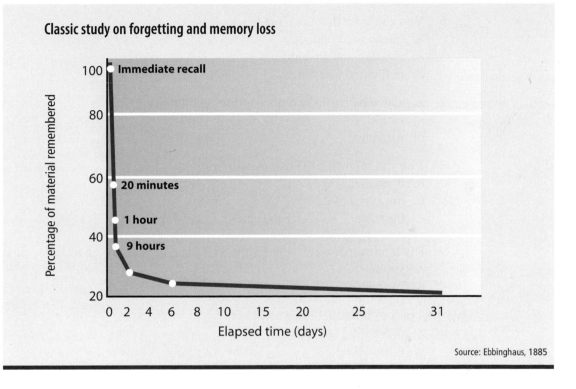

Classic study on forgetting and memory loss

Percentage of material remembered

100 — Immediate recall
80
60 — 20 minutes
— 1 hour
40 — 9 hours
20

0 2 4 6 8 10 15 20 25 31
Elapsed time (days)

Source: Ebbinghaus, 1885

_____ 1. The most rapid memory loss takes place in the first twenty minutes after exposure to new material.

_____ 2. After one month, most people remember only half of the new material they've learned.

_____ 3. In a single day, people are likely to forget over half of the new material they've learned.

_____ 4. By the end of a month, people tend to forget 100 percent of new material learned.

_____ 5. After two days, the rate of forgetting slows down greatly.

_____ 6. Since people rapidly forget new material, taking notes in classes and reviewing them regularly are useful study techniques.

_____ 7. A student who sits in class and listens carefully but does not take notes can often do just as well as a student who takes notes.

B. Identify each figure of speech as a simile or a metaphor. Then answer each inference question that follows.

_____ 5. My mother's angry gaze bored into me like twin laser beams.
   A. simile
   B. metaphor

_____ 6. You can infer that the mother's gaze was
   A. intense and cutting.
   B. exciting and adventurous.
   C. unfocused and bored.

_____ 7. A tidal wave of bad events overtook the family.
   A. simile
   B. metaphor

_____ 8. You can infer that the bad events were
   A. overwhelming.
   B. unexpected.
   C. bearable.

_____ 9. His kind words were as welcome as a flash of sunlight on a cloudy day.
   A. simile
   B. metaphor

_____ 10. You can infer that the words were
   A. depressing and sad.
   B. disorienting.
   C. warm and unexpected.

REVIEW TEST 4

Society is constantly changing, and one of the most significant areas of change is the ways that couples court, marry, and reproduce. In this excerpt from his textbook *Essentials of Sociology: A Down-to-Earth Approach,* sociologist James Henslin demonstrates how sharply that pattern has altered in recent years.

Words to Watch

Below are some words in the reading that do not have strong context support. Each word is followed by the number of the paragraph in which it appears and its meaning there. These words are indicated in the article by a small circle (°).

significant (1): important
norm (2): custom
engrained in (2): deeply a part of
subtle (7): mild
essential (8): important

RELATIONSHIPS IN THE 21ST CENTURY

James M. Henslin

The Changing Timetable of Family Life: Marriage and Childbirth

1 Figure 12.10 illustrates one of the most significant° changes in U. S. marriages. As you can see, the average age of first-time brides and grooms declined from 1890 to about 1950. In 1890, the typical first-time bride was 22, but by 1950, she had just left her teens. For about twenty years, there was little change. Then in 1970, the average age started to increase sharply. Today's average first-time bride and groom are older than at any other time in U.S. history.

2 Since postponing marriage is today's norm°, it may surprise you to learn that most U.S. women used to be married before they turned 24. To see this remarkable change, look at Figure 12.11. This change is so engrained in° our culture that the percentage of women between 20 and 24 who are married is now less than a fourth of what it was in 1970. For men, it is less than a third. Just as couples are postponing marriage, so they are putting off having children. Today's average U.S. woman now has her first child at age 25, the

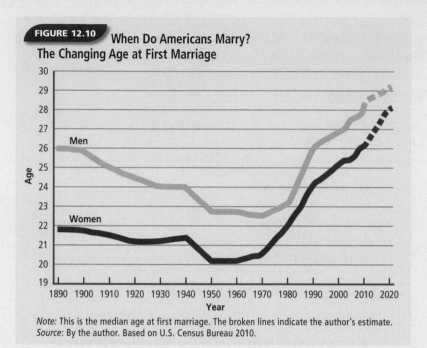

FIGURE 12.10   **When Do Americans Marry? The Changing Age at First Marriage**

Note: This is the median age at first marriage. The broken lines indicate the author's estimate.
Source: By the author. Based on U.S. Census Bureau 2010.

highest age in U.S. history (Matthews and Hamilton 2009).

3   Why have these changes occurred? The primary reason is cohabitation. Although Americans have postponed the age at which they first marry, they have not postponed the age at which they first set up housekeeping with someone of the opposite sex. Let's look at this trend.

Cohabitation

4   Figure 12.12 shows the increase in cohabitation, adults living together in a sexual relationship without being married. This figure is one of the most remarkable in sociology. I know of no other social trend that increases this steeply and consistently. Cohabitation is twelve times more common than it was in the 1970's. From a furtive activity, cohabitation has moved into the mainstream, and today about two-thirds of couples who marry may have cohabited (Huang et al. 2011). Cohabitation has become so common that about 44 percent of U.S. children will spend some time in a cohabiting family (Kennedy and Bumpass 2011).

5   *Commitment* is the essential difference between cohabitation and marriage. In marriage, the assumption is permanence; in cohabitation, couples agree to remain together for "as long as

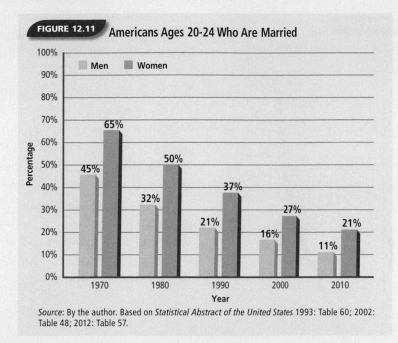

FIGURE 12.11 Americans Ages 20-24 Who Are Married

Source: By the author. Based on *Statistical Abstract of the United States* 1993: Table 60; 2002: Table 48; 2012: Table 57.

it works out." For marriage, individuals make public vows that legally bind them as a couple; for cohabitation, they simply move in together. Marriage requires a judge to authorize its termination, but if a cohabiting relationship sours, the couple separates, telling friends and family that "it didn't work out."

Does Cohabitation Make Marriage Stronger?

6 If couples set up housekeeping before they marry, are they less likely to divorce than couples who did not live together before marriage? It would seem that cohabitation would make marriage stronger. Cohabiting couples have the chance to work out so many real-life problems before marriage—and they marry only after sharing these experiences. To find out, sociologists compared divorce rates. It turns out that couples who cohabit before marriages were more likely to divorce (Osborne et al. 2007; Lichter and Qian 2008).

7 This went directly against what we would expect. Sociologists suggested this reason: People are less picky about choosing someone to live with than choosing someone to marry (Dush et al. 2003). After couples cohabit, however, many experience a "push" toward marriage—from having common possessions, pets, and children to the

FIGURE 12.12

Cohabitation in the United States

Note: Broken line indicates author's estimate.
Source: By the author. Based on US Census Bureau 2007 and *Statistical Abstract of the United States* 1995: Table 60; 2012: Table 63.

subtle and not-so-subtle° hints of family and friends. As a result, many end up marrying someone they would not otherwise have chosen as a spouse.

As cohabitation has developed into a more essential° part of the courtship/mating process, the initial findings of higher divorce are washing out. The latest research shows that of the recently married, the divorce rate of those who did and did not cohabit before marriage is about the same (Manning and Cohen 2011). If this finding holds, we can conclude that cohabitation neither weakens nor strengthens marriage.

8

Reading Comprehension Questions

Vocabulary in Context

_____ 1. In the excerpt below, the word *declined* (dǐ-klīnd′) means
  A. became higher.
  B. became lower.
  C. stayed the same.
  D. was unknown.

> "As you can see, the average age of first-time brides and grooms declined from 1890 to about 1950. In 1890, the typical first-time bride was 22, but by 1950, she had just left her teens." (Paragraph 1)

Central Point and Main Ideas

_____ 2. Which sentence best expresses the central point of the selection?
  A. Since 1970, American couples have been postponing both marriage and having children.
  B. Cohabitation, adults living together in a sexual relationship without being married, has greatly increased in the United States since 1970.
  C. Researchers no longer believe that couples who cohabit before they get married are more likely to divorce.
  D. Although increased cohabitation has led American couples to postpone marriage and having children, it seems to have had no effect on divorce rates.

_____ 3. Which sentence best expresses the main idea of paragraph 2?
  A. Both American women and American men are putting off getting married.
  B. Surprisingly, most American women used to be married before they turned 24.
  C. Just as American couples are postponing marriage, so they are putting off having children.
  D. Today's average U.S. woman is waiting longer to have her first child than at any time in U.S. history.

Supporting Details

_____ 4. According to the selection,
   A. most U.S. women are putting off marrying but not putting off having children.
   B. on average, Americans who marry for the first time are older than at any other time in U.S. history.
   C. about one-third of U.S. couples cohabit before they marry.
   D. early studies indicated that couples who cohabited before marriage were less likely to divorce.

_____ 5. The relationship between the two sentences below is one of
   A. contrast.
   B. addition.
   C. illustration.
   D. cause and effect.

   "After couples cohabit, however, many experience a "push" toward marriage—from having common possessions, pets, and children to the subtle and not-so-subtle hints of family and friends. As a result, many end up marrying someone they would not otherwise have chosen as a spouse." (Paragraph 7)

Patterns of Organization

_____ 6. Paragraph 5 mainly
   A. contrasts cohabitation and marriage.
   B. explains why couples are putting off making a commitment to each other.
   C. presents statistics showing the rising rate of cohabitation.
   D. illustrates typical problems that cohabiting couples face.

Inferences

_____ 7. Paragraph 7 suggests that
   A. marriage is less highly valued than cohabitation.
   B. cohabitation sometimes leads people to get married when they don't really want to.
   C. most people see no reason to get married if they are already living together.
   D. people cohabit only with people they are interested in marrying.

_____ 8. Figure 12.10 suggests that
   A. the average age at which men and women marry will continue to increase.
   B. between 2010 and 2020, the average age at which women marry will rise more quickly than the average age at which men marry.
   C. for over a hundred years, men have tended to be older when they first marry than women.
   D. all of the above.

_____ 9. Figure 12.11 suggests
   A. by 2020, the average marriage age for American women will be about the same as it was in 2010.
   B. by 2020, only about 5% of American men between the ages of 20–24 will be married.
   C. 1970 was the last year in which at least half of American women between the ages of 20–24 were married.
   D. in 2000, American men were half as likely as American women to be married between the ages of 20–24.

_____ 10. We can infer from Figure 12.12 that
   A. if present trends continue, very few American couples will ever marry.
   B. by 2020, over 9 million U.S. couples will be cohabiting.
   C. the rate at which couples cohabit is slowing down.
   D. all of the above.

Discussion Questions

1. Do you know any couples who cohabit? If so, why did they choose to cohabit rather than to marry? Do they eventually plan to marry? Why or why not?

2. According to Figure 12.10, the average marriage age for American men and women dropped sharply beginning in 1940 and stayed low throughout the 1950s. Why do you think early marriage was so much more attractive to couples in the 1940s and 1950s than it is today?

3. As the selection suggests, cohabitation does not involve the same level of commitment as marriage. Why, in your opinion, are couples today so reluctant to make a permanent commitment to each other?

4. Some social critics view the rise in cohabitation as evidence of a decline in American morals. Do you agree with these critics? Why or why not?

Note: Writing assignments for this selection appear on pages 625–626.

Check Your Performance   INFERENCES

Activity	Number Right	Points		Score
Review Test 1 (5 items)	_____	× 2	=	_____
Review Test 2 (10 items)	_____	× 3	=	_____
Review Test 3 (10 items)	_____	× 3	=	_____
Review Test 4 (10 items)	_____	× 3	=	_____
		TOTAL SCORE	=	_____ %

Enter your total score into the **Reading Performance Chart: Review Tests** on the inside back cover.

INFERENCES: Mastery Test 1

A. (1–3.) Put a check (✓) by the **three** inferences that are most logically based on the information suggested by the cartoon.

____ 1. Lucy has just criticized the boy, Linus.

____ 2. Linus feels Lucy's criticism is valid.

____ 3. Lucy feels very guilty that Linus has taken her criticism badly.

____ 4. Lucy doesn't seem to realize that people may accept constructive criticism but not destructive criticism.

____ 5. The cartoonist believes we should never criticize others.

____ 6. The cartoonist believes it's best to criticize others in a constructive way.

B. (4–6.) Read the passage below. Then check (✓) the **three** inferences that are most logically supported by the information given.

[1]Shortly after the young woman sat down in the bus, she lit a cigarette. [2]The man next to her waved some smoke away, nudged her, and pointed to the sign at the front of the bus.

[3]The woman did not turn to look at the man and continued smoking calmly. [4]The man got up and spoke to the bus driver, who continued driving and shook his head. [5]At the next stop, the man, looking disgusted, got off the bus.

____ 1. The man had never smoked.

____ 2. The smoke was bothering the man.

____ 3. The man pointed to a no-smoking sign.

____ 4. The driver refused to get involved.

____ 5. The man got off the bus because it was his stop.

____ 6. The driver was related to the woman.

(Continues on next page)

C. (7–10.) Read each passage below. Then check (✓) the **two** inferences after each passage which are most logically supported by the information given.

1.   ¹My day has not ended. ²When I get home I suddenly realize that I have between thirty and forty pounds of fish to clean—rockfish yet, all full of spines and pricklers and razor-sharp teeth. ³When I'm finished, I have so many holes in me I look like a composite of George Custer, Saint Sebastian, and Bonnie and Clyde, but my family comes out to view the catch and restore my faith in the whole enterprise.
⁴"Yuk," says my daughter.
⁵"That's a lot of rockfish for people who aren't all that into rockfish," says my wife.
⁶"I wouldn't eat that on a bet," says my son.

____ 1. The family is on vacation.

____ 2. Rockfish are difficult to clean.

____ 3. The author's family appreciates his hard work to feed them.

____ 4. The man enjoys the challenge of cleaning rockfish.

____ 5. When he praises his family for restoring his faith, the author is being sarcastic.

2.   ¹I guess I did it because I hadn't studied very much. ²And it seemed so easy—everybody knows that Mr. Wagner keeps his office door unlocked. ³It's just too bad things didn't work out for me. ⁴Now my classmates are mad at me because they must re-study for the new test Mr. Wagner is making up. ⁵My parents have taken away my car keys. ⁶And even worse, I'll have to go to summer school for biology.

____ 1. The speaker stole a test.

____ 2. The speaker had been failing the course.

____ 3. The speaker deeply regrets not studying more.

____ 4. The speaker will never cheat again.

____ 5. The speaker does not seem to have a guilty conscience about what he did.

INFERENCES: Mastery Test 2

A. (1–3.) Put a check (✓) by the **three** inferences that are most logically based on the information suggested by the cartoon.

© 1997 Randy Glasbergen. www.glasbergen.com

GLASBERGEN

"Let's try getting up every night at 2:00 AM to feed the cat. If we enjoy doing that, then we can talk about having a baby."

____ 1. The woman would like to have a baby.

____ 2. The couple often have serious disagreements.

____ 3. The couple will divorce because of the man's unwillingness to have a baby.

____ 4. The man is not enthusiastic about becoming a father.

____ 5. The woman is dismayed by the man's lack of enthusiasm for having a baby.

____ 6. The woman has been trying to get pregnant for a long time.

B. (4–6.) Read the following quotation. Then put a check (✓) by the **three** inferences that are most logically based on the information given.

> [1]"Good character is more to be praised than outstanding talent. [2]Most talents are, to some extent, a gift. [3]Good character, by contrast, is not given to us. [4]We have to build it piece by piece—by thought, choice, courage and determination."
>
> — John Luther

____ 1. You can't earn talent, but you can earn a reputation for being good.

____ 2. People of good character tend to look down on talented people.

____ 3. People who possess outstanding talent don't deserve praise.

____ 4. In some ways, people with talent have it easier than people without talent.

(Continues on next page)

___ 5. People with outstanding talent are often selfish and lazy.

___ 6. Talented people often receive more attention than people of good character.

C. Read the following passage. Then, in the spaces provided, write the letter of the most logical answer to each question, based on the information given in the passage.

¹My friends have no friends. ²They are men. ³They think they have friends, and if you ask them whether they have friends they will say yes, but they don't really. ⁴They think, for instance, that I'm their friend, but I'm not. ⁵It's OK. ⁶They're not my friends either.

⁷The reason for that is that we are all men—and men, I have come to believe, cannot or will not have real friends. ⁸They have something else—companions, buddies, pals, chums, someone to drink with and someone to lunch with, but no one when it comes to saying how they feel—especially how they hurt.

⁹Women know this. ¹⁰They talk about it among themselves. ¹¹To women, this inability of men to say what they feel is a source of amazement and then anguish and then, finally, betrayal. ¹²Women will tell you all the time that they don't know the men they live with. ¹³They talk of long silences and of drifting off and of keeping feelings hidden and never letting on about troubles or bothers or whatever.

_____ 7. We can infer that the author of this passage
   A. has genuine friends himself.
   B. believes men have no need of genuine friends.
   C. feels something prevents men from having genuine friends.

_____ 8. We can infer that the author
   A. is proud he is able to share his feelings better than other men.
   B. believes women want the men in their lives to share their feelings.
   C. believes men have more hurt feelings than women do.

_____ 9. We can infer that the author believes women
   A. have genuine friends.
   B. prefer "strong, silent" men.
   C. understand why men do not talk about their feelings.

_____ 10. We can conclude that the author thinks
   A. men realize they don't have friends.
   B. women should try to be more like men when it comes to friendship.
   C. men's relationships aren't deep enough to be genuine friendships.

INFERENCES: Mastery Test 3

A. (1–3.) Put a check (✓) by the **three** inferences that are most logically based on the information suggested by the cartoon.

____ 1. The two young men have committed a serious crime.

____ 2. The two young men will be invited to wear masks and carry axes, also.

____ 3. The committee members have already made up their minds about the two young men.

____ 4. The two young men in the doorway expect something bad is about to happen to them.

____ 5. The two young men are powerful members of a corporation.

____ 6. The two young men in the doorway work for a corporation.

B. (4–6.) Read the following textbook passage. Then put a check (✓) by the **three** inferences which are most logically supported by the information given.

> [1]The swim team at the University of California at Berkeley was having a practice. [2]After a race, the coach told each swimmer his time—but it wasn't his real time. [3]The coach falsified the time, making it slower than it really was. [4]During the next race, the coach watched what happened. [5]Some of his swimmers swam significantly faster than before, while others swam considerably slower than their usual pace.

(Continues on next page)

____ 1. The swim coach at Berkeley expected his swimmers to react exactly the way they did.

____ 2. Some of the Berkeley swimmers probably knew about their coach's experiment before it took place.

____ 3. Giving disappointing news to athletes is the best way to increase their performance.

____ 4. Disappointing news about performance can make some athletes try harder and perform better.

____ 5. People's ability to perform certain tasks is often related to their thoughts and attitudes.

____ 6. Disappointing news about performance can make some athletes grow discouraged and perform poorly.

C. Read the passage below, taken from the autobiographical book *Move On* by the television journalist Linda Ellerbee. Then, in the spaces provided, write the letter of the most logical answer to each question, based on the information given in the passage.

[1]Television changed my family forever. [2]We stopped eating dinner at the dining-room table after my mother found out about TV trays. [3]We kept the TV trays behind the kitchen door and served ourselves from pots on the stove. [4]Setting and clearing the dining-room table used to be my job; now, setting and clearing meant unfolding and wiping our TV trays, then, when we'd finished, wiping and folding our TV trays. [5]Dinner was served in time for one program and finished in time for another. [6]During dinner we used to talk to one another. [7]Now television talked to us. [8]If you had something you absolutely had to say, you waited until the commercial, which is, I suspect, where I learned to speak in thirty-second bursts. [9]As a future writer, it was good practice in editing my thoughts. [10]As a little girl, it was lonely as hell. [11]Once in a while, I'd pass our dining-room table and stop, thinking I heard our ghosts sitting around talking to one another, saying stuff.

_____ 7. We can infer that as a child, Ellerbee
   A. preferred eating at the dining-room table to eating in front of TV.
   B. was glad that she no longer had to set and clear the dining-room table.
   C. wished that her parents watched TV programs that she enjoyed.

_____ 8. Ellerbee suggests that
   A. TV can help people feel less lonely.
   B. it's possible to feel lonely even when others are around.
   C. talking with others does not help to reduce loneliness.

_____ 9. We can infer that in Ellerbee's home
   A. her mother was aware that Ellerbee was unhappy with TV.
   B. there were no other children for Ellerbee to talk to.
   C. watching TV became more important than talking and listening to family members.

_____ 10. We can infer that when Ellerbee imagined ghosts, she
   A. was remembering better times with her family.
   B. was scared of passing by the dining room.
   C. realized her childhood home was haunted.

INFERENCES: Mastery Test 4

A. After reading the following textbook passage, write the letter of the best answer to each question.

> [1]Suppose a man works six or seven days a week in a factory, trying to support his family, but never seems to be able to make ends meet. [2]If he analyzed his situation rationally, he would probably blame the well-to-do generally, and his employers specifically, for failing to pay him an adequate wage. [3]But these people have the power to cut off his income; to oppose them openly would be self-destructive. [4]He could also blame himself for his financial problems, but this too makes him uncomfortable. [5]Instead, he looks to the immigrants who have begun working in his factory. [6]He doesn't really know them, but he suspects they're willing to work for low wages and that many other immigrants are eager to take his job. [7]By a process of twisted logic, he blames these people for his poverty. [8]Soon he is exchanging rumors about "them" with his cronies and supporting efforts to close the border. [9]Hating immigrants makes the man and his friends feel a little better.

_____ 1. We can infer that the author of the passage thinks
   A. factory workers are not good at managing money.
   B. all factory workers are underpaid.
   C. the man in the example is underpaid.

_____ 2. We can infer that the author
   A. agrees with what the man in the example thinks.
   B. feels that employers and other well-to-do's should hire only immigrants.
   C. is critical of both the man in the example and his well-to-do employers.

_____ 3. We can infer that the man in the example probably
   A. has many friends and neighbors who are immigrants.
   B. understands what immigrants think and is aware of their problems.
   C. has no understanding of or meaningful contact with immigrants.

_____ 4. We can infer from the passage that
   A. immigrants are eager to take other people's jobs.
   B. the man in the example would probably oppose hiring immigrants.
   C. most immigrants don't do their jobs as well as domestic workers.

_____ 5. The passage suggests that
   A. some people make themselves feel better by thinking less of others.
   B. immigration should be limited or reduced to protect workers' jobs.
   C. employers are wrong to hire immigrants when domestic workers are available.

(Continues on next page)

B. Read the following textbook passage. Then, in the space provided, write the letter of the best answer to each question.

> ¹People interrupt for various reasons. ²One is believing that what they have to say is more important than what the other person is saying. ³Another reason people interrupt is that they believe they know what the other person is going to say and want the person to know that they already know. ⁴People may also interrupt when they are not paying close attention. ⁵The interruption communicates a lack of sensitivity, a superior attitude, or both. ⁶People need to be able to verbalize their ideas and feelings fully; inappropriate interruptions are bound to damage their self-concepts or make them hostile—and possibly both. ⁷Simply stated, whatever you have to say is seldom so important that it requires you to interrupt a person. ⁸When you do interrupt, you should realize that you may be perceived as putting a person down. ⁹The more frequent the interruptions, the greater the potential harm.

_____ 6. The author of the above passage suggests that people
   A. feel good if others listen carefully to their ideas.
   B. who interrupt don't mind being interrupted themselves.
   C. should learn not to feel insulted when they are interrupted.

_____ 7. The author suggests that people may interrupt because they
   A. don't realize that the speaker is in the middle of a point.
   B. are nervous and want the speaker to like and respect them.
   C. are angry at the speaker.

_____ 8. The author suggests that
   A. it is okay to interrupt others if you feel you are superior to them.
   B. you will never be interrupted if you don't interrupt others.
   C. interruptions can make people feel that their ideas are not worth listening to.

_____ 9. We can conclude from this paragraph that
   A. it is okay for a parent to interrupt a child.
   B. a boss will gain more cooperation by not interrupting workers.
   C. the author of the passage has never been interrupted in a conversation.

_____ 10. The passage suggests that people who interrupt
   A. usually are able to predict what others will think about their behavior.
   B. don't always realize how the other person will view the interruption.
   C. should not worry about trying to guess what others are thinking about them.

INFERENCES: Mastery Test 5

A. (1–6.) Read the passage below, taken from an essay titled "Darkness at Noon" by Harold Krents, an attorney who was born blind. Then check the **six** statements which are most logically supported by the information given.

Note that the meaning of one word in the passage is given below.

cum laude: with honor

[1]There are those who assume that since I can't see, I obviously also cannot hear. [2]Very often people will converse with me at the top of their lungs, enunciating each word very carefully. [3]Conversely, people will also often whisper, assuming that since my eyes don't work, my ears don't either.

[4]For example, when I go to the airport and ask the ticket agent for assistance to the plane, he or she will invariably pick up the phone, call a ground hostess and whisper: "Hi, Jane, we've got a 76 here." [5]I have concluded that the word "blind" is not used for one of two reasons: Either they fear that if the dread word is spoken, the ticket agent's retina will immediately detach, or they are reluctant to inform me of my condition, of which I may not have been previously aware.

[6]On the other hand, others know that of course I can hear but believe that I can't talk. [7]Often, therefore, when my wife and I go out to dinner, a waiter or waitress will ask Kit if "he would like a drink," to which I respond that "indeed he would.". . .

[8]The toughest misconception of all is the view that because I can't see, I can't work. [9]I was turned down by over forty law firms because of my blindness, even though my qualifications included a cum laude° degree from Harvard College and a good ranking in my Harvard Law School class.

____ 1. It would offend Krents if people were to use the word "blind" in reference to him.

____ 2. The airline's code for a blind passenger was "76."

____ 3. It is better to whisper to blind people than to speak to them loudly.

____ 4. Krents prefers that people speak to him in a normal tone of voice.

____ 5. Sighted persons are sometimes uncomfortable directing conversation toward a blind person.

____ 6. Krents's wife is not blind.

____ 7. Blindness seems to harm a person's intelligence.

____ 8. Some employers are biased against blind workers.

____ 9. Harvard is apparently biased against blind students.

____ 10. Krents speaks frankly about his blindness.

(Continues on next page)

B. (7–10.) Read the paragraph below. Then check the **four** statements which are most logically supported by the information given.

> ¹In 1995, the American Academy of Pediatrics declared that "advertising directed at children is inherently deceptive and exploits children under eight years of age." ²The academy did not recommend a ban on such advertising because it seemed impractical and would infringe upon advertisers' freedom of speech. ³Today the health risks faced by the nation's children far outweigh the needs of its mass marketers. ⁴Congress should immediately ban all advertisements aimed at children that promote foods high in fat and sugar. ⁵Thirty years ago Congress banned cigarette ads from radio and television as a public health measure—and those ads were directed at adults. ⁶Smoking has declined ever since. ⁷A ban on advertising unhealthy foods to children would discourage eating habits that are not only hard to break, but potentially life-threatening. ⁸Moreover, such a ban would encourage the fast-food chains to alter the recipes for their children's meals. ⁹Greatly reducing the fat content of McDonald's Happy Meals, for example, could have an immediate effect on the diet of the nation's kids. ¹⁰Every month more than 90 percent of the children in the United States eat at McDonald's.

____ 1. Cigarette advertisements were effective in encouraging people to continue smoking.

____ 2. The author values advertisers' freedom of speech, especially as it relates to commercials targeting children.

____ 3. The author believes the number of children at risk of health problems due to poor diets has increased since 1995.

____ 4. Banning fast-food ads is unlikely to have any lasting effect on children's diets, according to the author.

____ 5. The author feels that the advertisers' right to free speech is less important than the health of the nation's children.

____ 6. TV commercials and other ads probably have little effect on children's behaviors.

____ 7. The author believes fast-food chains can be convinced to voluntarily refrain from advertising unhealthy foods for young children.

____ 8. The author suggests that children's poor eating habits are as serious a health problem as adults' smoking.

INFERENCES: Mastery Test 6

A. (1–5.) Read the table below. Then put a check by the **five** statements that are most logically based on the table.

Voter Turnout among the World's Democracies

Country	Approximate Voter Turnout	Automatic Registration	Election Day a Holiday or Weekend Day?
Belgium	90%	Yes	Yes
Italy	90%	Yes	Yes
Denmark	85%	Yes	No
Austria	80%	Yes	Yes
France	80%	No	Yes
Germany	80%	Yes	Yes
Great Britain	70%	Yes	No
Canada	65%	Yes	No
Japan	60%	Yes	Yes
United States	50%	No	No

Source: Thomas E. Patterson, *The American Democracy*, 2001.

____ 1. About a third of voters in the United States do not vote.

____ 2. Election Day holidays tend to increase voter turnout rates.

____ 3. Voter turnout might increase if the United States had automatic voter registration and an Election Day holiday.

____ 4. Low voter turnout in the United States probably has little to do with automatic voter registration or Election Day holidays.

____ 5. Factors that have increased voter participation in other countries have not worked as well in Japan.

____ 6. Compared to the United States, other countries make it easier for voters to participate in elections.

____ 7. Voter turnout would be better if elections were held on weekend days rather than on holidays.

____ 8. Voter turnout would be better if elections were held on holidays rather than on weekend days.

____ 9. Voters in Belgium and Italy care more about political issues than U.S. voters do.

(Continues on next page)

B. Following is a passage from *A Hole in the World,* an autobiographical account by the Pulitzer Prize-winning author Richard Rhodes. Read the passage, and then choose the inferences which are most logically supported by the information given.

> [1]We played dodgeball at recess. [2]Dodgeball was my sport. [3]I was light and quick and often managed to escape being picked off until I was the last of my team inside the circle, the winner of the round. [4]My friend was usually my competition. [5]One day I kidded him too sharply when he lost and I won. [6]He gathered a knot of classmates afterward, the girl I dreamed about among them. [7]They strolled over and surrounded me. [8]They were smiling and I thought they were friendly; it didn't occur to me to dodge. [9]The boys grabbed me. [10]My friend led them. [11]"You stink," he told me happily. [12]"We think you're dirty. [13]We want to see." [14]They jerked down the straps on my bib overalls, held my arms high, peeled off my ragged shirt. [15]They exposed my filth, my black armpits, my dirty neck for everyone to see. [16]The faces of those children, the girl well forward among them, filled with horror perverted with glee. [17]I went the only way I could go, down, dropping to the asphalt of the playground. [18]They formed a circle around me, laughing and pointing. [19]I couldn't get away. [20]I covered my head and drew up my knees. [21]I knew how to make myself invisible. [22]I'd learned to make myself invisible when my stepmother attacked. [23]It worked because I couldn't see her even if she could still see me. [24]I made myself invisible. [25]They couldn't hear me crying.

_____ 6. We can infer from the passage that the author's friend
    A. felt sorry for him.
    B. meant to embarrass him.
    C. did not expect the other kids to laugh.

_____ 7. We can infer from the passage that the girl in the crowd
    A. made the author's humiliation greater.
    B. had strong feelings for the author.
    C. was against teasing the author.

_____ 8. The author implies that his stepmother
    A. was very fond of him.
    B. worried about him.
    C. abused him.

_____ 9. We can infer from the passage that the author
    A. probably wasn't very well cared for at home.
    B. was usually clean, but just happened to be dirty that day.
    C. expected kids to tease him about his dirtiness.

_____ 10. We can infer that when the author made himself "invisible,"
    A. he was really putting others out of sight.
    B. he was free from the hurt caused by the other kids.
    C. the other kids stopped teasing him.

8 Purpose and Tone

There is an author—a person with thoughts, feelings, and opinions—behind everything you read. Whether this person is a cartoonist, a sportswriter, a newspaper columnist, a novelist, or a friend sending you a letter or an e-mail, he or she writes from a personal point of view. That point of view is reflected in (1) the *purpose* of a piece of writing—to inform, to persuade, or to entertain—as well as (2) its *tone:* the expression of attitude and feeling.

The *purpose* of the above cartoon, like all cartoons, is to entertain. Can you tell what the *tone* of each speaker is? Which one is sincere in what he says? Which is insincere? After you have decided on your answers, read the explanation that follows.

Explanation

The boss is insincere. If he decided to fire the worker, he most likely is not sorry. He doesn't know if the worker will "land on his feet" and find another job. The worker, on the other hand, is sincere in his anger at being fired and his wish that he could stomp on his ex-boss's chest.

Purpose

Authors write with a reason in mind, and you can better evaluate their ideas by determining what that reason is. The author's reason for writing is also called the **purpose** of a selection. Three common purposes are as follows:

- To **inform**—to give information about a subject. Authors with this purpose wish to provide facts that will explain or teach something to readers.

  For example, the author of an informative paragraph about sandwiches might begin, "Eating food between two slices of bread—a sandwich—is a practice that has its origins in eighteenth-century England."

- To **persuade**—to convince the reader to agree with the author's point of view on a subject. Authors with this purpose may give facts, but their main goal is to argue or prove a point to readers.

  The author of a persuasive paragraph about sandwiches might begin, "There are good reasons why every sandwich should be made with whole-grain bread."

- To **entertain**—to amuse and delight; to appeal to the reader's senses and imagination. Authors with this purpose entertain in various ways, through fiction and nonfiction.

  The author of an entertaining paragraph about sandwiches might begin, "What I wanted was a midnight snack, but what I got was better—the biggest, most magical sandwich in the entire world."

While the cover and title of anything you read—books, articles, and so on—don't necessarily suggest the author's main purpose, often they do. On the next page are the covers of three books. See if you can guess the primary purpose of each of these books.

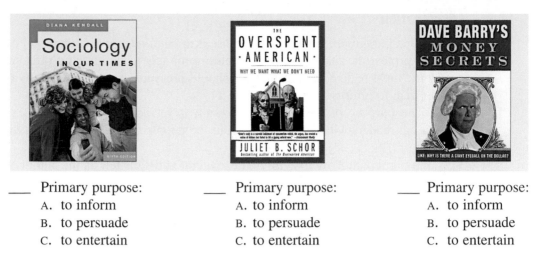

___ Primary purpose:
A. to inform
B. to persuade
C. to entertain

___ Primary purpose:
A. to inform
B. to persuade
C. to entertain

___ Primary purpose:
A. to inform
B. to persuade
C. to entertain

As you probably concluded, the main purpose of the textbook is to inform; the main purpose of *The Overspent American* is to persuade; and the main purpose of *Dave Barry's Money Secrets* is to entertain.

✓ Check Your Understanding

Read each of the three paragraphs below and decide whether the author's purpose is to inform, to persuade, or to entertain. Write in your answers, and then read the explanations that follow.

1. Each Saturday morning, TV commercials advertise fast foods and high-calorie cereals directly to children. These ads teach children unhealthy eating habits and have been linked to childhood obesity. Parents must realize how harmful such commercials are and should pressure companies to stop marketing unhealthy products to children.

   Purpose: _____

2. About 113 billion people have lived and died in the history of our planet, according to scientific estimates. Of all these people, the names of about 7 billion, or approximately 6 percent, are recorded in some way—on monuments or in books, manuscripts, and public records. The other 106 billion people are gone without a trace.

   Purpose: _____

3. Because of the war between his medium-size shirts and pants and his extra-large-size body, my brother has made a commitment to only three meals a day. His definition of a meal, however, is as broad as his belly. If we spot a pretzel salesman or a hot-dog stand on our way to a restaurant, for example, he is not beyond suggesting that we stop. "It'll make a good appetizer," he says.

   Purpose: _____

Explanation

In the first paragraph, the writer's purpose is to *persuade* the audience that parents should protest the marketing of unhealthy products to children. Words such as *must* in "must realize" and *should* in "should pressure" are meant to convince us rather than to inform us.

The purpose of the second paragraph is to *inform*. The author is simply providing readers with information about the people who have lived and died on Earth.

In paragraph 3, the playful and exaggerated details tell us the author's main goal is to *entertain* with humor.

A Note about Writing with More Than One Purpose

At times, writing may combine two or even all three purposes. A persuasive letter to an editor, for example, may contain factual information, or an informative article on losing weight may include comic touches and some implied persuasion.

- What would you say is the main purpose of this book?

    A. To inform   B. To persuade   C. To entertain

If you chose answer A, you're correct—my main purpose is to inform and provide practice. But I also have two other purposes at times. For example, on the first page (page 10) of an earlier section, "Reading for Pleasure and Power," what is my main purpose?

    A. To inform   B. To persuade   C. To entertain

My main purpose on page 10 is to persuade you about the importance of becoming a regular reader.

You'll notice, too, that I have included in this book high-interest readings such as the story of Lizzie Borden (page 516) or amusing passages such as the one about not stepping in the *hora* (page 277). What is my purpose in choosing such content?

    A. To inform   B. To persuade   C. To entertain

While my main purpose is to inform, I do at times have a second and even third purpose—to persuade and to entertain. And that is the case for other authors as well. What you need to remember when trying to determine purpose is to ask yourself, "What is the author's *main* purpose here?"

PRACTICE 1

Label each item according to its main purpose: to inform (**I**), to persuade (**P**), or to entertain (**E**).

_____ 1. Professional athletes do not deserve their inflated salaries, nor does their behavior merit so much media attention.

_____ 2. The career of a professional athlete is usually quite short.

_____ 3. Nurses assigned to intensive-care units should be given shorter shifts and higher pay because the work is unusually demanding and stressful.

_____ 4. On average, women dream more than men, and children dream more than adults.

_____ 5. The best approach to take when you feel the urge to exercise is to lie down quickly in a darkened room until the feeling goes away.

_____ 6. It's easy to quit smoking; I've done it hundreds of times.

_____ 7. More women should get involved in local politics and support the growing number of female candidates for public office.

_____ 8. An artificial odor is added to natural gas so that people can tell whether or not gas is leaking.

_____ 9. Once football season begins, Matt starts jogging every night—to the refrigerator during commercial breaks.

_____10. The first person to die of radiation poisoning was a co-discoverer of radium, Marie Curie.

PRACTICE 2

Following are three passages, one each from a textbook, a humor book, and a collection of essays. In the spaces provided, write the letter of the best description of the purpose of each passage.

_____ 1. ¹We have all heard the story of how the young, impoverished Abraham Lincoln trekked miles to borrow books from a neighbor and then read them by firelight. ²We know that nineteenth-century readers would rush to the wharf to greet the ship carrying the latest chapters of a Dickens novel. ³Today, reading seems less urgent and less exciting to many of us. ⁴Worse, few people impart a passion for books to their children. ⁵Instead, they leave the children in front of the television and hope, weakly, that too much watching won't be bad for them. ⁶But we cannot afford to stop reading. ⁷Books shed a light that illuminates our problems and crises. ⁸They are also mirrors that reflect the truest image of ourselves.

The main purpose of this passage is to
A. explain something about Abraham Lincoln and Dickens to readers.
B. convince readers of the importance of books.
C. delight readers with entertaining material from books.

_____ 2. ¹Most of what I know about carpentry, which is almost nothing, I learned in Shop. ²You should know that I took Shop during the Eisenhower administration, when boys took Shop and girls took Home Economics—a code name for "cooking." ³Schools are not allowed to separate boys and girls like that anymore. ⁴They're also not allowed to put students' heads in vises and tighten them, which is what our Shop teacher, Mr. Schmidt, did to Ronnie Miller in the fifth grade when Ronnie used a chisel when he should have used a screwdriver. ⁵(Mr. Schmidt had strong feelings about how to use tools properly.) ⁶I guess he shouldn't have put Ronnie's head in the vise, but it (Ronnie's head) was no great prize to begin with, and you can bet Ronnie never confused chisels and screwdrivers in later life—assuming he made it to later life.

The main purpose of this passage is to
A. inform readers about the nature of shop classes.
B. argue that shop classes should be eliminated from public schools.
C. amuse readers with humorous details about shop classes.

_____ 3. ¹Studies of job satisfaction indicate that the vast majority of workers are at least somewhat satisfied with their jobs and would continue to work even if they didn't have to. ²The meaning of work varies from person to person. ³To some, it is a source of self-respect and life purpose. ⁴For others, work is a means of passing time. ⁵To still others, it is primarily a source of financial independence. ⁶Among women, available work is often less satisfying than home management. ⁷Yet most women report increases in self-esteem when employed, especially if they experience support from their families.

The main purpose of this passage is to
A. report on what has been learned through studies of job satisfaction.
B. convince readers of the importance of job satisfaction.
C. entertain readers with rich, sensual descriptions of job satisfaction.

Tone

A writer's **tone** reveals the attitude that he or she has toward a subject. Tone is expressed through the words and details the writer selects. Just as a speaker's voice can project a range of feelings, a writer's voice can project one or more tones, or feelings: anger, sympathy, hopefulness, sadness, respect, dislike, and so on. Understanding tone is, then, an important part of understanding what an author has written.

To appreciate the differences in tone that writers can employ, look at the following versions of a murder confession. Then read them aloud—in the tone of voice appropriate in each case.

"I just shot my husband five times in the chest with this .357 Magnum." (*Tone:* matter-of-fact, objective.)

"How could I ever have killed him? I just can't believe I did that!" (*Tone:* shocked, disbelieving.)

"Oh, my God. I've murdered my husband. How can I ever be forgiven for this dreadful deed?" (*Tone:* guilty, regretful.)

"That dirty rat. He's had it coming for years. I'm glad I finally had the nerve to do it." (*Tone:* revengeful, self-satisfied.)

PRACTICE 3

Following are five reactions to a fender-bender accident (in which one car hits and slightly damages the rear fender of another car). Label each statement with the tone of voice that you think is present. Choose each tone from the following box, and use each tone only once.

A. angry	**B.** apologetic	**C.** calm
D. concerned	**E.** defensive	

_____ 1. "Are you hurt? Are you sure you're okay? Don't move too quickly. Take your time getting out of the car."

_____ 2. "I am really sorry. I was daydreaming a bit, which is no excuse. I should have been more careful."

_____ 3. "You idiot! If you hadn't stopped short, I would never have hit you. You should be tossed in jail. You could have gotten us both killed."

_____ 4. "It's no big deal. Neither of us was hurt, which is all that counts. The damage is slight. Don't worry about it."

_____ 5. "Hey, this wasn't my fault. Don't even think about blaming me. You're the one that stopped too quickly, not me. I did nothing wrong here."

Words That Describe Tone

Below and on the next page are two lists of words commonly used to describe tone. With the exception of the words *matter-of-fact* and *objective,* the words reflect a feeling or judgment. The words on this page are more familiar ones. Brief meanings are given in italics for the words on the next page. Refer to these meanings as needed to learn any words you don't know yet.

Some Words That Describe Tone

accepting	cheerful	fearful	self-critical
admiring	conceited	forgiving	self-pitying
affectionate	concerned	frightened	serious
alarmed	critical	grateful	sorrowful
amused	cruel	humorous	sympathetic
angry	curious	insulting	threatening
apologetic	defensive	joyous	tragic
appreciative	determined	loving	warm
approving	disapproving	playful	worried
ashamed	doubtful	praising	
calming	encouraging	regretful	
caring	excited	respectful	

More Words That Describe Tone—with Their Meanings

ambivalent	*uncertain about a choice*
arrogant	*full of self-importance; conceited*
bewildered	*confused; puzzled*
bitter	*angry; full of hate*
compassionate	*deeply sympathetic*
depressed	*very sad or discouraged*
detached	*emotionally uninvolved*
disbelieving	*unbelieving*
distressed	*suffering sorrow, misery, or pain*
hypocritical	*false*
impassioned	*filled with strong feeling*
indignant	*angry about something unfair or mean*
instructive	*teaching*
ironic	*meaning the opposite of what is expressed*
lighthearted	*happy and carefree*
matter-of-fact	*sticking to facts; unemotional*
mocking	*making fun of and/or looking down upon something*
nostalgic	*longing for something or someone in the past*
objective	*not influenced by feelings or personal prejudices*
optimistic	*looking on the bright side of things*
outraged	*fiercely angered and shocked*
pessimistic	*looking on the gloomy, unfavorable side of things*
pleading	*begging*
prideful	*full of pride or exaggerated self-esteem*
remorseful	*guilty over a wrong one has done*
revengeful	*wanting to hurt someone in return for an injury*
sarcastic	*sharp or wounding; ironic*
scheming	*tricky*
scornful	*looking down on someone or something*
self-mocking	*making fun of or looking down on oneself*
sentimental	*showing tender feelings; romantic; overly emotional*
solemn	*involved with serious concerns*
straightforward	*direct and honest*
superior	*looking down on others*
tolerant	*respectful of other views and behavior; patient about problems*
uncertain	*doubting*

✓

Check Your Understanding

Below are five statements expressing different attitudes about a shabby apartment. Five different tones are used:

bitter	humorous	optimistic
sentimental	tolerant	

Label each statement with the tone you think is present. Use each tone once. Then read the explanation that follows. (Feel free to check the list on page 327 for the meanings of any unfamiliar tone words.)

_____ 1. This place may be shabby, but since both of my children were born while we lived here, it has a special place in my heart.

_____ 2. This isn't the greatest apartment in the world, but it's not really that bad.

_____ 3. If only there were some decent jobs out there, I wouldn't be reduced to living in this miserable dump.

_____ 4. This place does need some repairs, but I'm sure the landlord will be making improvements sometime soon.

_____ 5. When we move away, we're planning to release three hundred cockroaches and two mice so we can leave the place exactly as we found it.

Explanation

The tone of item 1 is sentimental. "It has a special place in my heart" expresses tender emotions. In item 2, the words "it's not really that bad" show that the writer is tolerant, accepting the situation while recognizing that it could be better. We could describe the tone of item 3 as bitter. The writer resents a situation that forces him or her to live in a "miserable dump." Item 4 is optimistic since the writer is expecting the apartment to be improved soon. Finally, the tone of item 5 is humorous. Its writer claims to be planning a comic revenge on the landlord by returning the apartment to the terrible condition it was in when the tenants moved in.

A Note on Irony

One commonly used tone is irony. When writing has an **ironic** tone, it says one thing but means the opposite. Irony is found in everyday conversation as well as in writing. Following are a few examples of verbal irony (also known as **sarcasm**); notice that the quotation in each says the opposite of what is meant.

- If at the beginning of a semester you discover that one of your instructors is particularly demanding, you might comment, "This class is sure going to be a piece of cake."

- After seeing a terrible performance in a movie, someone might say about the actor involved, "Now there's a person with a great chance for an Oscar."

- While standing in a long, slow line at a supermarket or bank, you might say to people in line with you, "My, this is exciting."

- If a friend arrives at your place two hours late, you might say, "Well, thanks for showing up on time."

- If you're suffering from the flu and someone asks how you feel, you might say: "I feel terrific today."

Irony also refers to situations in which what happens is the opposite of what we might expect. We would call it ironic, for example, if a young woman who failed English in high school went on to become a well-known writer, or if a young man who was cut from his Little League baseball team went on to star in the major leagues. Here are a few more examples of this type of irony:

- Security cameras installed to stop crime were stolen during a robbery.

- A new computer purchased to help a small business crashes, causing the business to lose many of its customers.

- An instructor at a health club smokes a cigarette during lunch break.

- Albert Einstein, one of the century's most brilliant scientists, did poorly in school.

- Beethoven's music teacher once said of him, "As a composer, he is hopeless."

- A newspaper editor fired Walt Disney because he "lacked imagination and had no good ideas."

As you can see, irony is a useful tone for humor and can be used to imply exactly the opposite of what is said or what is done.

✔ Check Your Understanding

Look now at the cartoon below. See if you can explain the irony.

The irony in the little girl's comment "People are so self-absorbed" is that

_____

_____

Explanation

The irony is that the little girl herself is completely self-absorbed. She shows no interest in the people around her and is concerned only about their paying attention to her new hair style.

PRACTICE 4

A. Below are five statements expressing different attitudes about a boss. Five different tones are used:

admiring	critical	ironic
objective	sympathetic	

For each statement, write the tone that you think is present. Use each tone once.

_____   1. Tony is an excellent manager—the best one I've ever had.

_____ 2. I know Tony's daughter has been sick. Naturally it's hard for him to concentrate on work right now.

_____ 3. Tony's too ambitious for his own good. That ambition may destroy both him and the company.

_____ 4. Since Tony Roberts became manager, sales in the appliance division have increased 30 percent.

_____ 5. Tony's wonderful, all right. He's gotten as far as he has without the slightest idea of how to manage a division.

B. The following conversation between a mother and son involves five of the tones shown in the box below. For each statement, write the tone that you think is present. Five tones will be left over.

disbelieving	joyful	nostalgic	pessimistic
sarcastic	self-pitying	solemn	straightforward
sympathetic	threatening		

_____ 6. "Please take the garbage out on your way to school this morning."

_____ 7. "Sure, Mom. I've been looking forward to that chore all morning."

_____ 8. "Listen, young man, if you don't start fulfilling your responsibilities around this house, your father and I will start asking you to pay rent or find your own place."

_____ 9. "Okay, I'll take the garbage out. But you know it's not easy going to school full-time and working twenty hours a week when I'm just getting over a bad case of the flu."

_____ 10. "I know, honey, this semester has been an especially difficult one for you."

PRACTICE 5

Each passage illustrates one of the tones in the box below. In each space, put the letter of the tone that best applies. Don't use any letter more than once. Five tones will be left over.

Remember that the tone of a selection reflects the author's attitude. To find the tone of a paragraph, ask yourself what attitude is revealed by its words and phrases.

A. accepting	B. affectionate	C. alarmed	D. ambivalent
E. ashamed	F. bitter	G. forgiving	H. grateful
I. playful	J. revengeful		

_____ 1. [1]In my fantasies I have ways of dealing with drivers who irritate the heck out of me. [2]At times I have 50-caliber machine guns instead of headlights on the front of my car. [3]That way, I can send several hundred rounds of burning lead into the slow-moving gas-guzzler car in front of me. [4]I also have a fantasy to deal with another driver I really despise—the truck driver who tailgates just inches from my rear bumper. [5]In his case, I have flame-throwers that rise up out of the trunk of my car and melt down his front tires; that gets him out of my life fast. [6]I also have a way to deal at night with the guy behind me who has his high beams on. [7]It feels like a spotlight is shining into my car. [8]In this case, I'm driving a rented car, so I suddenly slam on my brakes, causing him to plow into me. [9]That puts his lights out in a hurry. [10]Then I drive on, leaving him to find his way home in the dark. [11]My motto is, "Don't just get mad, get even."

_____ 2. [1]The percentage of children who are classified as overweight has more than doubled in the last thirty years. [2]A lack of exercise and increasingly unhealthy, junk-food-filled diets are making kids heavier and heavier. [3]More than 22 percent—that's close to one in four—are classified as dangerously obese. [4]One in four! [5]This is an urgent public health crisis that people need to wake up to and recognize. [6]Most overweight children become overweight adults, and overweight adults are at risk for developing heart disease, cancer, diabetes, and stroke. [7]The costs of dealing with those health problems—from work-hours lost to medical expenses—are going to be immense. [8]If we don't start dealing with this problem immediately, we're going to be in big trouble. [9]Parents, schools, the government, and the media need to join forces to do something about it before it's too late.

_____ 3.   ¹I'm at peace now with my husband's death. ²I had been out shopping when a sudden intuition prompted me to call him. ³My husband had been diagnosed six months before his death with a rare cancer of the body's soft tissues that had since spread to his lungs. ⁴"Are you all right?" I asked him. ⁵"No," he replied. ⁶"I'm having trouble breathing here." ⁷I rushed home and drove him to the ER. ⁸That's where the house of cards came tumbling down. ⁹During the week that followed, my husband developed serious complications. ¹⁰In his final hours, he told me he wanted everything done for him because he wanted to live so much. ¹¹But as I watched his condition deteriorate, I made the most difficult decision of my life. ¹²It had gotten to the point that life support wasn't the right thing to do. ¹³I went in and held him. ¹⁴And I said, "I want you to let go and come into my heart because it's safe there." ¹⁵He stopped breathing. ¹⁶And now he's in my heart. ¹⁷I can feel his arms around me.

_____ 4.   ¹The proposal has been made that students in our schools be required to wear uniforms. ²In some ways, this sounds good. ³It is true that shopping for fashionable clothing and deciding what to wear in the morning take up a lot of money and time. ⁴But kids need to learn to deal with social pressure about things like clothing, and school might be as good a place as any for that lesson. ⁵Also, the way people dress is one way they express themselves, and maybe students should have that avenue of expression open to them too. ⁶However, it is a shame if they constantly worry about their appearance and waste valuable class time by wishing they could have the name-brand shirt across the room. ⁷So uniforms might be helpful in keeping students' minds on their education. ⁸Uniforms could save students and their parents money, too, which is certainly a good thing. ⁹On the other hand, those uniforms are not cheap, and most students will want to have several sets, so the savings might not be all that significant. ¹⁰It's really hard to say whether uniforms are a good idea or not.

_____ 5.   ¹After twenty-two years of business in this community, Acme Supplies closed its doors for the final time today. ²Ninety-seven people lost their jobs. ³Many of them had worked for Acme since it opened. ⁴You might think the management of Acme would feel it owed those loyal workers something, but you would be wrong. ⁵Despite the factory's record of efficiency and high production, Acme executives leaped at the chance to make more money by moving the plant to Mexico, where wages are lower. ⁶In doing so, they turned their backs on the men and women who have made their company so successful over the years. ⁷Some of those employees were only months away from retirement. ⁸Instead of looking forward to some well-deserved rest, those employees are frantically trying to adjust to having had the rug pulled out from under their feet by their greedy employers. ⁹Although Acme always claimed to treat its workers "like family," the reality is that those workers were never more than tools used to fatten the bank accounts of the company's unscrupulous managers.

PRACTICE 6

Read the following letter to the late Ann Landers, along with her response. Then answer the questions about purpose and tone that follow.

[1]**Dear Ann Landers:** [2]When our daughter won a scholarship to a very fine university in the East last year, we were thrilled and proud of her.

[3]"Mary" does not drink or smoke and has high moral standards. [4]We were not the least bit uneasy about her moving so far from home to go to school, and we didn't worry about peer pressure. [5]She has always been a leader, not a follower.

[6]Mary's letters, however, are depressing. [7]She says so many people who live in her dorm (it's mixed, both men and women) get drunk at least four nights a week, and they make so much noise she can't study. [8]She also has spent several nights taking care of sick, hung-over friends. [9]Her roommate, she says, often stays out until 3 or 4 in the morning, comes in dead drunk, and throws up. [10]Mary resents having to clean up after her, but she has no choice.

[11]We did not anticipate this sort of thing when we sent our daughter away to college. [12]We asked Mary if she would consider changing schools next year (we would be willing to forgo the scholarship and pay her tuition). [13]She said, "No, an Ivy League school has always been my dream, and these problems exist all over."

[14]What on Earth is going on? [15]Can you tell us?

[16]**Dear Parents:** [17]You ask, "What's going on?" [18]You just described it, according to the information I receive regularly from the National Clearinghouse for Alcohol and Drug Information. [19]College students spend $5.5 billion a year on alcohol. [20]Harvard School of Public Health researchers have reported that excessive use of alcohol on college campuses may be hazardous not only to the health of drinkers but to nondrinkers as well. [21]Nondrinkers suffer from loss of sleep and study time, vandalism, physical assault, unwanted sexual advances, and rape.

[22]Dr. Henry Wechsler, director of college alcohol studies at the Harvard School of Public Health, was the lead author of a report that studied the drinking habits of 17,592 students from 140 colleges. [23]The study found that alcohol on college campuses poses a serious hazard to the physical health and emotional well-being of students. [24]One student said she was fed up with people urinating in the elevators, vomiting in the halls, wrecking the bathroom, and pounding holes in the walls.

[25]Wechsler's research revealed that nearly half the college students are binge drinkers who cause most of the trouble by depriving others of study time and sleep and by attacking classmates. [26]College security officers and administrators report that alcohol is involved in the majority of rapes and almost all violent incidents on campus.

²⁷Wechsler urges students who do not drink to speak up and demand their rights. ²⁸*Time* magazine quoted Wechsler as saying, "If your roommate gets drunk every night, either insist on a new roommate or demand that you be moved." ²⁹He urges people who are bothered by excessive drinking to complain. ³⁰He said, "I want students to complain. ³¹I want parents to complain. ³²That's the only way we will get change."

³³Although Wechsler does not beat the drum for total abstinence (he says it is not "realistic"), I disagree. ³⁴If you don't drink at all, you will never have to worry about how much is too much.

_____ 1. The first paragraph of the parents' letter has a
     A. tragic tone.
     B. prideful tone.
     C. pleading tone.

_____ 2. In its third paragraph, the parents' letter takes on a
     A. distressed tone.
     B. revengeful tone.
     C. doubtful tone.

_____ 3. The parents' letter ends in a(n)
     A. instructive tone.
     B. bewildered tone.
     C. sentimental tone.

_____ 4. The purpose of much of the parents' letter is to
     A. inform Ann Landers of their daughter's situation.
     B. persuade Ann Landers to convince their daughter to leave her school.
     C. amuse Ann Landers with the ridiculous behavior of today's college students.

_____ 5. On the basis of the facts she has chosen to include and her last paragraph, we can conclude that Landers's main purpose is
     A. simply to inform people about various views of alcohol.
     B. to persuade readers that it is best to drink little or no alcohol.
     C. to entertain readers with colorful views about alcohol.

CHAPTER REVIEW

In this chapter, you learned that part of effective reading is to do the following:

● Be aware of an author's **purpose**: the reason why he or she writes. Three common purposes are to inform, to persuade, and to entertain.

● Be aware of **tone**—the expression of the author's attitude and feeling about a subject. A writer's tone might be objective—the case in most textbook writing—or it might be lighthearted, sympathetic, angry, affectionate, respectful, or any of many other tones shown on pages 326–327.

● One important tone to recognize is **irony**: saying one thing but meaning the opposite.

The next chapter—Chapter 9—will explain another part of effective reading: recognizing the point in an argument and evaluating the support for that point.

On the Web: If you are using this book in class, you can visit our website for additional practice in identifying an author's purpose and tone. Go to **www.townsendpress.com** and click on "Learning Center."

REVIEW TEST 1

To review what you've learned in this chapter, fill in the blank(s) or write, in the space provided, the letter of the correct answer for each question.

1. The author's reason for writing something is called the _____ of a selection.

2–4. What is the purpose of each of the types of writing below? Label each according to its usual main purpose: to inform, to persuade, or to entertain.

   A news report: _____

   A mystery novel: _____

   An editorial: _____

5. The tone of a selection reveals the author's _____ toward his or her subject.

6. An ironic comment is one that means the _____ of what is said.

_____ 7. Imagine a bad morning when everything goes wrong—there is no hot water for the shower, milk for the cereal is sour, a pool of oil is under the car, and so on. Which of the following would be an ironic comment on the situation?
   A. "What a lousy start to the day."
   B. "What a great day this is going to be."
   C. "Good grief. What did I do to deserve this?"

_____ 8. Which of the following tones reveals no personal feeling?
   A. Forgiving
   B. Critical
   C. Matter-of-fact

_____ 9. An arrogant tone suggests that the speaker or writer
   A. is angry.
   B. looks on the unfavorable side of things.
   C. thinks a lot of himself or herself.

_____10. An objective tone indicates that the speaker or writer is telling something
   A. dishonestly.
   B. without personal prejudice.
   C. with a longing for something in the past.

REVIEW TEST 2: PURPOSE

In the space provided, indicate whether the primary purpose of each passage is to inform (**I**), to persuade (**P**), or to entertain (**E**).

_____ 1.   ¹Let's pretend for a moment. ²Suppose that in the hospital room where your mother lies dying with terminal cancer, there is a button. ³You have the power, by pushing that button, to quickly and painlessly end the life of this person you dearly love. ⁴You know your mother will be confined to that hospital room for her remaining days. ⁵Would you push the button for her? ⁶You watch as she is hooked up to a life-support machine, and you also watch and listen as her pain increases and she pleads for you to help. ⁷You watch her worsen day after day until she reaches a point where she can no longer talk or hear, and she is alive only because of that machine. ⁸Now would you push that button? ⁹If you can imagine the horror of what I have described, then you may agree our country should reconsider its laws against mercy killing.

_____ 2.   ¹Traditionally, English grammar called for the use of the masculine pronoun *he* to stand for the entire class of humans regardless of sex. ²Thus in the past, the following sentence would have been considered proper English: "Everyone in class must hand in his paper tomorrow." ³Today, many language experts would consider that sentence sexist because it excludes females. ⁴They say that one way to avoid the problem is to recast a sentence using plurals: "All students in the class must hand in their papers tomorrow." ⁵Alternately, they advise using *both* male and female singular pronouns: "Everyone in class must hand in his or her paper tomorrow."

_____ 3.   ¹An elderly woman in a Cadillac was preparing to back into a parking space. ²Suddenly a small red sports car appeared and pulled into the space. ³"That's what you can do when you're young and fast," the young man in the car yelled to the old woman. ⁴As he strolled away, laughing, he heard a terrible crunching sound. ⁵"What's that noise?" he asked. ⁶Turning around, he saw the old woman backing repeatedly into his small car and crushing it. ⁷"You can't do that, old lady!" he yelled.

⁸"What do you mean, I can't?" she yelled back, as metal grated against metal. ⁹"This is what you can do when you're old and rich."

_____ 4. ¹College students who contract mononucleosis ("mono") can be forced into a long period of bed rest during a semester when they can least afford it. ²Other common diseases can be managed with minimal disruption, but the overall weakness and fatigue seen in many people with mono sometimes requires a month or two of rest and recuperation. ³Mono is a viral infection in which the body produces an excess of one type of white blood cells. ⁴After an uncertain, perhaps long, incubation, the acute symptoms of mono can appear, including weakness, headache, low-grade fever, swollen lymph glands (especially in the neck), and sore throat. ⁵Mental fatigue and depression are sometimes reported as side effects of mono. ⁶After the acute symptoms disappear, the weakness and fatigue usually persist, sometimes for a few months.

_____ 5. ¹Americans love parks and wildlife refuges, but the crowding they find there is a national disgrace. ²Parking lots are packed, and roadways through parks and refuges are often so jammed that they might as well be the parking lots. ³Playing fields and barbecue grills are claimed early in the day, and even on remote trails, voices can be heard from every direction. ⁴Americans badly need more land devoted to open space where nature walks, picnics, and camping can take place in uncrowded tranquillity. ⁵Communities across the nation should establish parks and trails that provide free access to open space for everyone.

REVIEW TEST 3: TONE

The cartoon and the four passages that follow each illustrate one of the tones in the box below. In the space provided, put the letter of the tone that best applies in each case. Don't use any letter more than once. Three tones will be left over.

Remember that tone reflects an author's (or speaker's) attitude. In each case, ask yourself what attitude is revealed by the words used.

A. ashamed	B. forgiving	C. indignant	D. ironic
E. objective	F. pessimistic	G. sentimental	H. tolerant

_____ 1. What is the tone of the man holding the cup of coffee in the cartoon below?

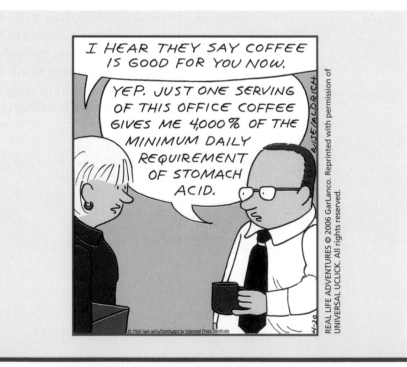

_____ 2. ¹Most animals have a "sweet tooth," and humans are no exception. ²That's why food manufacturers often add sugars and other sweeteners to their products. ³Indeed, many commercial breakfast cereals are 40% sugar by weight. ⁴Because added sugar provides calories but no essential nutrients, sugar is usually described as contributing "empty calories" to the diet. ⁵Excess calories from added sugar are converted to fat, which in some cases may contribute to overweight problems. [6]Populations that consume large amounts of sugar exhibit high rates of heart disease, obesity, diabetes, and tooth decay. [7]Sugar consumption in the United States averages about 133 pounds per person per year.

_____ 3.   [1]Relentless greed and horrifying dishonesty characterized the treatment of Indians in the 1860s and 1870s, when massacres of Native Americans were commonplace. [2]The massacre at Sand Creek in Colorado in 1864 was sadly typical. [3]The territorial governor had persuaded the Indians to gather there and had promised them protection. [4]Despite this pledge, Colonel J. M. Chivington's militia attacked the defenseless Indian camp. [5]They disregarded that sacred symbol, the American flag, and the white flag of truce that the Indians were flying at Sand Creek. [6]Four hundred fifty peaceful Indians—men, women, and children—were slaughtered in what has been called "the foulest and most unjustified crime in the annals of America." [7]This was only one of the heartless massacres of Native Americans recorded by history.

_____ 4.   [1]During my last physical, the doctor found a little lump in my throat. [2]I'm going into the hospital tomorrow so they can check out what it is. [3]The doctor said it was most likely a harmless cyst, but of course he would say that. [4]What's he going to say: "Sorry—looks like cancer to me"? [5]He also said that if it is cancer, it's probably of a kind that is easily treated. [6]Right, I thought. [7]He's trying to be nice, I know, but I also know how these things go. [8]First he'll say it's nothing; then he'll say it's cancer but no big deal; and finally he'll tell me the truth. [9]I'm done for.

_____ 5.   [1]I can't look my best friend in the eye. [2]He doesn't know what happened last weekend, and I hope he never will. [3]We were all at a party at a friend's house. [4]It was pretty loud and wild, and I was having a good time. [5]I found myself in the corner of a crowded room with the girl he's been dating all year. [6]We were joking around, and then we started dancing. [7]I don't even know how it began, but somehow we ended up alone in a bathroom. [8]I started kissing her and she kissed me back. [9]We stayed in there until somebody started pounding on the door. [10]That night it didn't seem like a big deal, but the next day I couldn't believe I had done it. [11]This is a girl he really cares for a lot, and she doesn't mean a thing to me. [12]Now everything is a mess. [13]I'm so uncomfortable around her I don't know what to do. [14]And I know he considers me one of his best friends. [15]I feel like such a jerk for betraying him.

REVIEW TEST 4

Here is a chance to apply your understanding of purpose and tone to a full-length selection. In "The Scholarship Jacket," Marta Salinas writes about a moment of disappointment in her childhood in southern Texas. By focusing on an award that school authorities decided she should not receive, Salinas shows us the pain of discrimination as well as the need for inner strength.

To help you continue to strengthen your skills, the reading is followed by questions not only on what you've learned in this chapter but also on what you've learned in previous chapters.

Words to Watch

Below are some words in the reading that do not have strong context support. Each word is followed by the number of the paragraph in which it appears and its meaning there. These words are indicated in the article by a small circle (°).

agile (2): able to move quickly
P.E. (3): the abbreviation for physical-education class
eavesdrop (4): secretly listen
filtered through (7): passed through
fidgeted (8): fussed
muster (12): call forth
mesquite (15): a sweet-smelling thorny tree
clod (15): lump of earth
gaunt (25): thin and bony
vile (29): very unpleasant
adrenaline (31): a hormone that responds to emotion, raising blood pressure and stimulating the heart

THE SCHOLARSHIP JACKET

Marta Salinas

1   The small Texas school that I attended carried out a tradition every year during the eighth grade graduation: a beautiful gold and green jacket, the school colors, was awarded to the class valedictorian, the student who had maintained the highest grades for eight years. The scholarship jacket had a big gold S on the left front side, and the winner's name was written in gold letters on the pocket.

2   My oldest sister, Rosie, had won the jacket a few years back, and I fully expected to win also. I was fourteen and in the eighth grade. I had been a straight-A student since the first grade, and the last year I had looked forward to owning that jacket. My father was a farm laborer who couldn't earn enough money to feed eight children, so when I

was six I was given to my grandparents to raise. We couldn't participate in sports at school because there were registration fees, uniform costs, and trips out of town; so even though we were quite agile° and athletic, there would never be a sports school jacket for us. This one, the scholarship jacket, was our only chance.

3   In May, close to graduation, spring fever struck, and no one paid any attention to class; instead we stared out the windows and at each other, wanting to speed up the last few weeks of school. I despaired every time I looked in the mirror. Pencil thin, not a curve anywhere, I was called "Beanpole" and "String Bean," and I knew that's what I looked like. A flat chest, no hips, and a brain, that's what I had. That really isn't much for a fourteen-year-old to work with, I thought, as I absentmindedly wandered from my history class to the gym. Another hour of sweating during basketball and displaying my toothpick legs was coming up. Then I remembered my P.E.° shorts were still in a bag under my desk where I'd forgotten them. I had to walk all the way back and get them. Coach Thompson was a real bear if anyone wasn't dressed for P.E. She had said I was a good forward and once she even tried to talk Grandma into letting me join the team. Grandma, of course, said no.

4   I was almost back at my classroom door when I heard angry voices and arguing. I stopped. I didn't mean to eavesdrop°; I just hesitated, not knowing what to do. I needed those shorts and I was going to be late, but I didn't want to interrupt an argument between my teachers. I recognized the voices: Mr. Schmidt, my history teacher, and Mr. Boone, my math teacher. They seemed to be arguing about me. I couldn't believe it. I still remember the shock that rooted me flat against the wall as if I were trying to blend in with the graffiti written there.

5   "I refuse to do it! I don't care who her father is, her grades don't even begin to compare to Martha's. I won't lie or falsify records. Martha has a straight-A-plus average and you know it." That was Mr. Schmidt, and he sounded very angry. Mr. Boone's voice sounded calm and quiet.

6   "Look, Joann's father is not only on the Board, he owns the only store in town; we could say it was a close tie and—"

7   The pounding in my ears drowned out the rest of the words, only a word here and there filtered through°. "Martha is Mexican . . . resign . . . won't do it . . . ." Mr. Schmidt came rushing out, and luckily for me went down the opposite way toward the auditorium, so he didn't see me. Shaking, I waited a few minutes and then went in and grabbed my bag and fled from the room. Mr. Boone looked up when I came in but didn't say anything. To this day I don't remember if I got in trouble in P.E. for being late or how I made it through the rest of the afternoon. I went home very sad and cried into my pillow that night so Grandmother wouldn't hear me. It seemed a cruel coincidence that I had overheard that conversation.

8   The next day when the principal called me into his office, I knew what it would be about. He looked uncomfortable and unhappy. I decided I wasn't going to make it any easier for him, so I looked him straight in the eye. He looked away and fidgeted° with the papers on his desk.

9   "Martha," he said, "there's been a change in policy this year regarding the scholarship jacket. As you know, it has always been free." He cleared his throat and continued. "This year the Board decided to charge fifteen dollars— which still won't cover the complete cost of the jacket."

10   I stared at him in shock, and a small sound of dismay escaped my throat. I hadn't expected this. He still avoided looking in my eyes.

11   "So if you are unable to pay the fifteen dollars for the jacket, it will be given to the next one in line."

12   Standing with all the dignity I could muster°, I said, "I'll speak to my grandfather about it, sir, and let you know tomorrow." I cried on the walk home from the bus stop. The dirt road was a quarter of a mile from the highway, so by the time I got home, my eyes were red and puffy.

13   "Where's Grandpa?" I asked Grandma, looking down at the floor so she wouldn't ask me why I'd been crying. She was sewing on a quilt and didn't look up.

14   "I think he's out back working in the bean field."

15   I went outside and looked out at the fields. There he was. I could see him walking between the rows, his body bent over the little plants, hoe in hand. I walked slowly out to him, trying to think how I could best ask him for the money. There was a cool breeze blowing and a sweet smell of mesquite° in the air, but I didn't appreciate it. I kicked at a dirt clod°. I wanted that jacket so much. It was more than just being a valedictorian and giving a little thank-you speech for the jacket on graduation night. It represented eight years of hard work and expectation. I knew I had to be honest with Grandpa; it was my only chance. He saw me and looked up.

16   He waited for me to speak. I cleared my throat nervously and clasped my hands behind my back so he wouldn't see them shaking. "Grandpa, I have a big favor to ask you," I said in Spanish, the only language he knew. He still waited silently. I tried again. "Grandpa, this year the principal said the scholarship jacket is not going to be free. It's going to cost fifteen dollars and I have to take the money in tomorrow, otherwise it'll be given to someone else." The last words came out in an eager rush. Grandpa straightened up tiredly and leaned his chin on the hoe handle. He looked out over the field that was filled with the tiny green bean plants. I waited, desperately hoping he'd say I could have the money.

17   He turned to me and asked quietly, "What does a scholarship jacket mean?"

18   I answered quickly; maybe there was a chance. "It means you've earned it by having the highest grades for eight years and that's why they're giving it to you." Too late I realized the significance of my words. Grandpa knew that I understood it was not a matter of money. It wasn't that. He went back to hoeing the weeds that sprang up between the delicate little bean plants. It was a time-consuming job; sometimes the small shoots were right next to each other. Finally he spoke again.

19   "Then if you pay for it, Marta, it's not a scholarship jacket, is it? Tell your principal I will not pay the fifteen dollars."

20   I walked back to the house and locked myself in the bathroom for a long time. I was angry with Grandfather even though I knew he was right, and I was angry with the Board, whoever they were. Why did they have to change the rules just when it was my turn to win the jacket?

21   It was a very sad and withdrawn girl who dragged into the principal's office the next day. This time he did look me in the eyes.

22   "What did your grandfather say?"

23   I sat very straight in my chair.

24   "He said to tell you he won't pay the fifteen dollars."

25   The principal muttered something I couldn't understand under his breath, and walked over to the window. He stood looking out at something outside. He looked bigger than usual when he stood up; he was a tall, gaunt° man with gray hair, and I watched the back of his head while I waited for him to speak.

26   "Why?" he finally asked. "Your grandfather has the money. Doesn't he own a small bean farm?"

27   I looked at him, forcing my eyes to stay dry. "He said if I had to pay for it, then it wouldn't be a scholarship jacket," I said and stood up to leave. "I guess you'll just have to give it to Joann." I hadn't meant to say that; it had just slipped out. I was almost to the door when he stopped me.

28   "Martha—wait."

29   I turned and looked at him, waiting. What did he want now? I could feel my heart pounding. Something bitter and vile° tasting was coming up in my mouth; I was afraid I was going to be sick. I didn't need any sympathy speeches. He sighed loudly and went back to his big desk. He looked at me, biting his lip, as if thinking.

30   "Okay, damn it. We'll make an exception in your case. I'll tell the Board, you'll get your jacket."

31   I could hardly believe it. I spoke in a trembling rush. "Oh, thank you, sir!" Suddenly I felt great. I didn't know about adrenaline° in those days, but I knew something was pumping through me, making me feel as tall as the sky. I wanted to yell, jump, run the mile, do something. I ran out so I could cry in the hall where there was no one to see me. At the end of the day, Mr. Schmidt winked at me and said, "I hear you're getting a scholarship jacket this year."

32   His face looked as happy and innocent as a baby's, but I knew better. Without answering I gave him a quick hug and ran to the bus. I cried on the walk home again, but this time because I was so happy. I couldn't wait to tell Grandpa and ran straight to the field. I joined him in the row where he was working and without saying anything I crouched down and started pulling up the weeds with my hands. Grandpa worked alongside me for a few minutes, but he didn't ask what had happened. After I had a little pile of weeds between the rows, I stood up and faced him.

33   "The principal said he's making an exception for me, Grandpa, and I'm getting the jacket after all. That's after I told him what you said."

34   Grandpa didn't say anything; he just gave me a pat on the shoulder and a smile. He pulled out the crumpled red handkerchief that he always carried in his back pocket and wiped the sweat off his forehead.

35   "Better go see if your grandmother needs any help with supper."

36   I gave him a big grin. He didn't fool me. I skipped and ran back to the house, whistling some silly tune.

Reading Comprehension Questions

Vocabulary in Context

_____ 1. In the excerpt below, the word *dismay* (dĭs-mā′) means
    A. joy.
    B. comfort.
    C. surprise and relief.
    D. sudden discouragement.

> "I stared at him in shock, and a small sound of dismay escaped my throat. I hadn't expected this." (Paragraph 10)

Central Point and Main Ideas

_____ 2. Which sentence best expresses the central point of this selection?
    A. When she went to pick up her gym clothes, Marta overheard a conversation between two teachers that shocked and saddened her.
    B. At Marta's school, it was a tradition to award a beautiful gold and green jacket to the eighth-grade valedictorian.
    C. Although fourteen-year-old Marta had earned a school jacket awarded for scholarship, she almost lost this award because of discrimination.
    D. Marta's sister had won the scholarship jacket, and Marta deeply wanted to win it as well.

_____ 3. Which sentence best expresses the main idea of paragraph 7?
    A. Marta was unable to hear every word of Mr. Schmidt's and Mr. Boone's conversation.
    B. Marta was shocked and saddened when she overheard two teachers arguing about her.
    C. Mr. Schmidt didn't see Marta when he rushed out of the room.
    D. Marta didn't want her grandmother to know she was crying.

Supporting Details

_____ 4. Which of the following statements is false?
    A. Marta was being raised by her grandparents because her parents were dead.
    B. Mr. Schmidt was angry at the attempt to give the scholarship jacket to someone less deserving than Marta.
    C. Marta's grandfather refused to give her the money for the scholarship jacket.
    D. Marta was called by a different name at school.

Transitions

_____ 5. The relationship between the two parts of the sentence below is one of
A. time.
B. contrast.
C. comparison.
D. cause and effect.

"I decided I wasn't going to make it any easier for him, so I looked him straight in the eye." (Paragraph 8)

Patterns of Organization

_____ 6. The overall pattern of organization of the selection is
A. cause and effect.
B. time order.
C. comparison.
D. contrast.

Inferences

_____ 7. We can infer from paragraph 8 that the principal was "uncomfortable and unhappy" because
A. the students had not been paying attention in class during the last few weeks before graduation.
B. his office was very hot.
C. he was ashamed to tell Marta that she had to pay fifteen dollars for a jacket that she had earned.
D. Mr. Boone and Mr. Schmidt were fighting in the hallway.

_____ 8. By saying, "If you pay for it, Marta, it's not a scholarship jacket, is it?" Marta's grandfather was implying that
A. the jacket was not worth fifteen dollars.
B. a real award should not have to be bought with money.
C. Marta did not deserve to win the scholarship jacket.
D. he did not understand the purpose of the scholarship jacket.

Purpose and Tone

_____ 9. The author's purpose in this selection is to
   A. inform and engage readers with an interesting and meaningful anecdote.
   B. persuade schools not to charge students for academic awards.
   C. entertain with an amusing, light-hearted story about a young girl in school.

_____10. The tone of paragraph 31 can be described as
   A. contented.
   B. angry.
   C. joyous.
   D. conceited.

Discussion Questions

1. In her first meeting with the principal, Marta could have challenged him by telling what she had overheard the two teachers saying. Why do you think she stayed silent? What do you think the principal would have said or done if she'd told him she knew the real reason she wasn't being given the jacket?

2. Why do you think the principal gave in during his second meeting with Marta? What do you think that shows about Marta's grandfather's decision? What do you think might happen when the principal has to face the Board again? If you were the principal, what would you have said to the Board?

3. Marta implies that she was discriminated against because of her ethnic background (she was Mexican) and her family's economic condition (they were poor). Have you ever experienced discrimination, or do you know of a friend who has experienced it? Explain.

4. Marta stresses again and again how important the scholarship jacket was to her and how hard she worked to win it. Is there something you worked hard to achieve when you were younger? How long did you work toward that goal? How did you feel when you finally succeeded—or did not succeed? What lessons, if any, did you learn from the experience?

Note: Writing assignments for this selection appear on page 626.

Check Your Performance   PURPOSE AND TONE

Activity		Number Right	Points	Score
Review Test 1	(10 items)	_____	× 1 =	_____
Review Test 2	(5 items)	_____	× 6 =	_____
Review Test 3	(5 items)	_____	× 6 =	_____
Review Test 4	(10 items)	_____	× 3 =	_____
		TOTAL SCORE	=	_____ %

Enter your total score into the **Reading Performance Chart: Review Tests** on the inside back cover.

PURPOSE AND TONE: Mastery Test 1

A. In the space provided, indicate whether the primary purpose of each item is to inform (**I**), to persuade (**P**), or to entertain (**E**).

_____ 1. Every month more than 90 percent of the children in the United States eat at McDonald's.

_____ 2. Fast-food chains must be encouraged to offer meals that are healthier for our children.

_____ 3. Fred's idea of healthy eating is to have a double cheeseburger without putting any salt on it.

_____ 4. The federal government needs to hire more inspectors to insure the safety of the meals served to our schoolchildren.

_____ 5. Rachel says she eats a balanced diet by choosing items from the four major food groups: chips, soda, candy, and pastries.

B. Each of the following passages illustrates one of the five tones in the box below. In the space provided, write the letter of the tone that applies to each passage.

A. caring	**B.** critical	**C.** humorous
D. pessimistic	**E.** self-mocking	

_____ 6. ¹Recently, my sister asked me to baby-sit her two sons for the evening. ²I figured I would get them dinner, let them watch a little TV, and then put them to bed early. ³The rest of the night I planned to watch TV and collect an easy twenty dollars. ⁴Well, right before we sat down for a pizza dinner, Rickie let the parakeet out of its cage. ⁵The dog started chasing the bird as it flew around the house, so I decided to catch it before the dog did. ⁶The boys and I had the bird cornered by the fireplace when Rickie jumped for it and knocked over the hamster cage. ⁷The hamsters took off under the sofa while the bird flew away. ⁸Fortunately, the dog had disappeared at this point. ⁹I took care of the hamsters while the boys caught the parakeet and put it back in its cage. ¹⁰When we returned to the kitchen to eat cold pizza, I discovered why the dog had lost interest in the bird chase. ¹¹What was left of the pizza was lying on the floor, and tomato sauce was dripping like blood from the dog's chin. ¹²Later, when my sister returned, I took the twenty dollars and told her to get someone else next time.

(Continues on next page)

_____ 7. ¹Whatever happened to the practice of saving up for what you want? ²It seems nobody has that kind of patience any more. ³Many Americans buy what they want when they want it and worry about paying for it later. ⁴The average American spends significantly more than he or she earns, much to the enjoyment of the credit-card companies. ⁵Apparently people need to reach a financial crisis before they realize that it's downright stupid to neglect balancing their budgets and saving for a rainy day.

_____ 8. ¹Machines are complete mysteries to me, and this has resulted in some embarrassing service calls at my home. ²For example, there was the time I called in a repairman because our refrigerator was too warm. ³Imagine my humiliation when he told me that the cause of the problem was a dirty filter, which I didn't know existed and therefore hadn't cleaned even once in the two years we owned the refrigerator. ⁴The best example of my brilliance with machines, however, has to be the time I called for someone to fix my washing machine. ⁵The repairman's solution was simply to put the plug back in the outlet, from which it had been jarred loose by the constant vibration of the washer.

_____ 9. ¹Research on rats shows that when animals live in crowded conditions, they live disorderly, violent lives. ²Humans are no different. ³Crowded inner cities are models of lawlessness; the crowded highways of Los Angeles encourage aggression by drivers, and even shootings. ⁴As our urban areas continue to grow in population density, these types of problems will surely also grow. ⁵That means more family violence and more fighting over available resources. ⁶The American dream will become just that—only a dream.

_____ 10. ¹Those addicted to drugs and alcohol probably feel terrible about themselves—even if they don't show it—and harsh judgments only worsen their self-image. ²What these people need are programs to help rid themselves of their addictions. ³It is also important that we all open our hearts and minds to these troubled people. ⁴Their addiction does not make them any less "children of God"; nor does it mean that they deserve to be stripped of the dignity that is the birthright of every human being. ⁵We must strive to create an environment of hope and help for those who so desperately need it.

PURPOSE AND TONE: Mastery Test 2

A. In the space provided, indicate whether the primary purpose of each item is to inform (**I**), to persuade (**P**), or to entertain (**E**).

_____ 1. The world's first ads were neither printed nor broadcast electronically; they were vocal, called out by street peddlers promoting their wares.

_____ 2. Billboard advertising is a form of visual pollution and should be banned.

_____ 3. Instead of nagging my father to lose weight, my mother bought him an extra-large T-shirt imprinted with the message "This space for rent."

_____ 4. For television, the top advertising spenders are manufacturers of cars and light trucks; automobile dealers spend the most on newspaper ads.

_____ 5. Advertisers should not be allowed to continue misleading consumers by lying or exaggerating.

_____ 6. On average, each person in the United States and Canada uses more than 300 gigajoules (GJ) (equivalent to about 60 barrels) of oil per year. By contrast, in some of the poorest countries of the world, such as Ethiopia, Nepal, and Bhutan, each person generally consumes less than 1 GJ per year.

_____ 7. The foundation of public education has always been reading, writing, and arithmetic—the "three R's." Yet the schools insist that students who have not mastered these fundamentals continue to take all the other subjects as well. What good does it do for young people to sit in a history or science class if they can't read or calculate well? Schools ought to require students who are very far behind in the fundamentals to devote all their time to the three R's until they are reading at or near grade level.

(Continues on next page)

B. Each of the following passages illustrates one of the tones identified in the box below. In each space provided, put the letter of the tone that applies to the passage. (Three tone choices will be left over.)

A. amused	B. arrogant	C. critical
D. depressed	E. objective	F. optimistic

_____ 8. [1]When I was younger, I thought that by this age, I would be pretty well set for life. [2]I imagined that I would have a nice house, some money in the bank, and a decent job. [3]But things haven't worked out that way at all. [4]I'm living in a one-bedroom apartment with shabby furniture and a view of a parking lot. [5]My office job is dull and unrewarding, and I bring home hardly enough to cover my rent and expenses, much less put anything away. [6]My place is so unattractive that I don't want to invite anyone over, so I'm alone most of the time. [7]Whatever dreams I had in my youth are pretty well gone now. [8]Sometimes I think about going back to school and trying to prepare for a different career, but at my age there doesn't seem to be much point in doing that. [9]I guess this is just what life had in store for me.

_____ 9. [1]Parents who do not read to their children often excuse themselves by claiming a lack of time. [2]But with few exceptions, their failure to read is a matter of priorities. [3]Most parents find the time to put in a full workday, take several coffee breaks, eat lunch and dinner, read the newspaper, watch the nightly newscast or ball game, do the dishes, talk on the phone for thirty minutes (mostly about nothing), run to the store for a pack of cigarettes or a lottery ticket, drive to the mall, and never miss that favorite prime-time show. [4]Somehow they find the time for those things—important or unimportant as they are—but can't find time to read to a child, which is much more important than all the other items on a leisure priority list.

_____ 10. [1]Scientists say grilling meat creates cancer-causing substances that affect the meat in two ways. [2]First, when fat drips onto the source of heat, the substances are formed and then carried up to the food by smoke. [3]They are also formed when flames touch the meat. [4]There are, however, a few ways that experts say will minimize the risk of grilling meat: (1) Use low-fat meats and nonfat sauces. [5](2) Partially cook meat before grilling. [6](3) Cover the grill with foil; punch holes in the foil to let fat drip down. [7](4) Avoid fire flare-ups, which cause harmful smoke. [8](5) Scrape off blackened material on the surface of meat before eating it. [9](6) Don't cook out every day.

PURPOSE AND TONE: Mastery Test 3

A. Seven quotations in the story below are preceded by a blank space. Identify the tone of each italicized quotation by writing in the letter of one of these tones. (Three tone choices will be left over.)

A. angry	**B.** curious	**C.** depressed	**D.** excited
E. frightened	**F.** pleading	**G.** scheming	**H.** straightforward
I. superior	**J.** sympathetic		

The television reporter knocked on the door of the small row home. A woman opened the door.

____ 1. *"My name is Tod Hunter,"* the reporter said. *"I'm with* Action News, *and I'd like to talk to the woman who lost her daughter in the school fire last night."*

"Oh, I'm sorry, but she's not much in the mood for visitors."

"I understand," the reporter said. "Please tell her that we only want a moment of her time."

While the woman was gone, the reporter turned to his crew.

____ 2. *"You could shoot from this angle,"* he whispered, *"but let's try to get inside. If she's at all responsive to my questions, let's gradually move in* through the doorway."

Children in the neighborhood crowded around the TV crew.

____ 3. *"Those are TV cameras!"* some shouted, laughing. *"Wow, real TV cameras!"*

____ 4. Pausing to look at the crew standing outside the house, passersby asked, *"What do you suppose happened there?"*

Then the mother of the fire victim appeared at the door, looking drawn and exhausted. "What do you want?"

"I'm really very sorry for your great loss, Ma'am." Hunter continued, "I'm here for *Action News*. Do you know what caused the terrible fire?"

"Please, no interviews."

"Our viewers want to know about this awful fire."

____ 5. *"I don't care about your viewers!"* she shouted. *"It's none of their business. It's none of your business, either, young man."*

____ 6. *"Run! She's mad!"* shouted the children as they raced away.

____ 7. *"All I want is two minutes,"* the reporter said. *"Please, just two minutes of your time."*

But the door had already slammed in his face.

"Let's get out of here," the frustrated reporter said to his crew. "I'm starved."

(Continues on next page)

B. In the space provided, indicate whether the primary purpose of each passage is to inform (**I**), to persuade (**P**), or to entertain (**E**).

_____ 8. ¹Why do people swear and engage in coarse language? ²One researcher suggests that swearing is a way of asserting independence by breaking adult taboos. ³In a society that prizes adulthood and independence, the increasing use of vulgar and profane language at younger and younger ages is not surprising. ⁴When used infrequently, profanity and vulgar expressions communicate strong emotions for which there may be no other appropriate words. ⁵They are meant to shock and to communicate one's deep disgust or contempt.

_____ 9. ¹Advertising aimed at children is not just annoying—it is destructive and should be controlled. ²Especially around the holiday season, children are hammered with media messages intended to make them want the latest toy, game, computer, sneakers, doll, music, and clothing on the market. ³While manufacturers are busy sucking money from the pockets of children and their families, they are contributing to a growing sense of dissatisfaction and greed. ⁴That serves the manufacturers' purpose—after all, if children were ever satisfied, they would not ask their parents to buy more merchandise. ⁵But the effect is to produce a nation of selfish men and women whose lives are ruled by the need to have more, more, more. ⁶It is frightening to see a generation being trained from childhood to be greedy consumers. ⁷What chance do they have to ever become contented adults whose values extend beyond a price tag?

_____ 10. ¹While I was watching a cartoon with my daughter, she said, "Dad, why does Bugs Bunny wear gloves?" ²The question has bothered me ever since. ³Why do Mickey Mouse, Bugs and Woody Woodpecker all wear gloves? ⁴And who decides which characters get pants? ⁵Mickey always wears them, yet Donald Duck just wears that sailor shirt. ⁶Porky has a jacket and a bow tie, but no shirt or pants, and Daffy just has his feathers. ⁷And, come to think of it, how did Goofy, a dog, make the evolutionary leap to stand up on his hind legs, put on pants, a shirt, and a vest, and talk? ⁸Yet Pluto is content to hang out in the doghouse getting his butt kicked by the chipmunks Chip 'n Dale.

PURPOSE AND TONE: Mastery Test 4

A. Seven quotations in the story below are preceded by a blank space. Identify the tone of each italicized quotation by writing in the letter of one of these tones. (Three tone choices will be left over.)

A. amused	B. ashamed	C. cheerful	D. disgusted
E. joyous	F. outraged	G. sorrowful	H. straightforward
I. understanding	J. vengeful		

The scene is a busy restaurant on a Saturday evening.

_____ 1.   *"Good evening!"* a young waitress chirped to a table of diners. *"It's so nice to see you here tonight! My name is Annette, and I'll be your server this evening."*

_____ 2.   Meanwhile, across the room, a man stared at his food as he pushed it around with his fork. *"Yuk! They call this 'ocean-fresh fish,'"* he said, *"but it sure doesn't smell all that fresh. It's making me gag!"*

But at the next table, a young man said to his friend, "This great spaghetti really hits the spot. I was starved."

_____ 3.   Nearby, in a dimly lit corner of the restaurant, a young man and woman sat close together, smiling at the diamond ring on the woman's finger. *"Oh, darling,"* sighed the woman. *"This is the happiest night of my life. This restaurant will always be my favorite because this is where you asked me to marry you."*

_____ 4.   A conversation of a different sort was taking place at another table: *"I cannot believe you would do this!"* a woman hissed at her husband. *"What kind of man takes his wife into a public place to tell her he's having an affair with her best friend? What am I supposed to do now—order an appetizer?"*

_____ 5.   Back in the kitchen, the restaurant manager was instructing the staff. *"Annette, you cover tables one through four. Ben, you're responsible for five through eight. A party of sixteen people is coming in at eight o'clock; Lisa and Suzette will take care of them."*

"Well, we got passed over again, didn't we?" Ben remarked to Annette after the manager was gone. "Lisa and Suzette always get the big groups and the big tips. It makes me wonder why I try to do a good job here."

_____ 6.   *"Oh, I don't mind,"* Annette said. *"Lisa and Suzette do work a lot more hours than you or I do. I can see why the manager thinks they deserve the best assignments."* Then Annette walked out of the kitchen.

_____ 7.   *"Well, it's not okay with me,"* Ben muttered to himself. *"When I quit this lousy job, they're going to pay for the way they've treated me. I'll get back at them somehow."*

(Continues on next page)

B. (8.) In the space provided, indicate whether the primary purpose of the following passage is to inform (**I**), to persuade (**P**), or to entertain (**E**).

_____   ¹Eye contact, also referred to as gaze, is how and how much we look at people with whom we are communicating. ²By maintaining our eye contact, we can tell when or whether people are paying attention to us, when people are involved in what we are saying, and whether what we are saying is eliciting feelings. ³The amount of eye contact differs from person to person and from situation to situation. ⁴Studies show that talkers hold eye contact about 40 percent of the time and listeners nearly 70 percent of the time. ⁵We generally maintain better eye contact when we are discussing topics with which we are comfortable, when we are genuinely interested in a person's comments or reactions, or when we are trying to influence the other person. ⁶On the other hand, we tend to avoid eye contact when we are discussing topics that make us uncomfortable, when we lack interest in the topic or person, or when we are embarrassed, ashamed, or trying to hide something.

C. Read the paragraph below. Then carefully consider the questions that follow, and write the letters of the best responses.

¹There are certain types of people you should not trust. ²One type is people who tell you that God told them to ask you to send them money. ³You know the guys I mean. ⁴They get on television and say: "God told me He wants you to send me some money, say $100, or even just $10, if that's all you can afford, but in all honesty I must point out that God is less likely to give you some horrible disease if your gift is in the $100 range." ⁵The theory here seems to be that God talks only to the guys on television. ⁶I always thought that if God needed money all that badly, He would get in touch with us directly.

_____ 9. The purpose of this paragraph is
      A. to persuade readers that they should not send money to television evangelists.
      B. to entertain readers by exaggerating points.
      C. both of the above.

_____ 10. The tone of this paragraph can be described as
      A. straightforward and serious.
      B. humorous and mocking.
      C. prayerful and respectful.
      D. sentimental and warm.

PURPOSE AND TONE: Mastery Test 5

Read the paragraphs below. Then carefully consider the questions that follow, and, in the spaces provided, write the letters of the best responses.

A. ¹A successful doctor is scheduled to operate on a patient at 8 a.m., but it has snowed during the night, and driving is difficult. ²Do you think the doctor will stay home in bed? ³Not if he or she is professional. ⁴This attitude of professionalism is the key to being a successful college student, too. ⁵And it is within your reach, no matter how well or how poorly you have done in school up until now. ⁶You cannot undo the past, but you can adopt an attitude of professionalism from now on. ⁷All you have to do is intend to take school seriously, and the rest will follow. ⁸By attending classes, turning in assignments on time, and coming prepared for tests, you will gradually build your skills.

_____ 1. The primary purpose of this paragraph is to
   A. present facts on student behavior.
   B. inspire students to be conscientious.
   C. entertain students with a dramatic story about professionalism.

_____ 2. In general, the tone of this paragraph can be described as
   A. critical.
   B. pessimistic.
   C. encouraging.
   D. praising.

B. ¹According to memory experts, there are ways you can improve your chances of remembering the names of people you meet. ²One way is to make associations between a person's name and looks. ³For example, if you meet a man named Baker, you might picture him wearing a baker's hat. ⁴If the name is a difficult one, ask for the spelling and visualize the letters mentally. ⁵It's also useful to repeat the person's name as you converse, keeping your mental images in mind. ⁶And when your conversation ends, repeat the person's name as you say goodbye.

_____ 3. The primary purpose of this paragraph is to
   A. inform.
   B. persuade.
   C. entertain.

_____ 4. The overall tone of this paragraph can be described as
   A. critical and angry.
   B. obviously humorous.
   C. doubtful.
   D. straightforward and instructive.

(Continues on next page)

C. ¹I was sitting on a beach one summer day, watching two children, a boy and a girl, playing in the sand. ²They were hard at work building an elaborate sandcastle by the water's edge, with gates and towers and moats and internal passages. ³Just when they had nearly finished their project, a big wave came along and knocked it down, reducing it to a heap of wet sand. ⁴I expected the children to burst into tears, devastated by what had happened to all their hard work. ⁵But they surprised me. ⁶Instead, they ran up the shore away from the water, laughing and holding hands, and sat down to build another castle. ⁷I realized that they had taught me an important lesson. ⁸All the things in our lives, all the complicated structures we spend so much time and energy creating, are built on sand. ⁹Only our relationships with other people endure. ¹⁰Sooner or later, a wave will come along and knock down what we have worked so hard to build up. ¹¹When that happens, only the person who has somebody's hand to hold will be able to laugh.

_____ 5. The primary purpose of this paragraph is to
    A. inform readers about how children behave.
    B. persuade readers of the importance of relationships.
    C. delight readers with a story of childhood playfulness.

_____ 6. The tone of this paragraph can be described as
    A. forgiving.
    B. humorous.
    C. self-pitying.
    D. instructive.

D. ¹My best school report was in first grade from Mrs. Varulo. ²First, she told my parents about my amazing physical energy: "Lisa never tires of chasing and punching her classmates." ³Next, she praised my class participation and active, questioning mind: "After every instruction—even one as simple as 'Please take out your pencils'—Lisa asks 'Why?'" ⁴Mrs. Varulo was so impressed with my vocabulary that she commented, "I don't know where Lisa has picked up some of the words she uses—certainly not in my classroom." ⁵Somehow she even knew I would become a famous fiction writer. ⁶"More than any other student I have ever taught," she wrote, "Lisa is a born liar."

_____ 7. The primary purpose of this paragraph is to
    A. inform.
    B. persuade.
    C. entertain.

_____ 8. The tone of this paragraph can best be described as
    A. enthusiastic and cheerful.
    B. annoyed and bitter.
    C. cheerful and nostalgic.
    D. ironic and humorous.

PURPOSE AND TONE: Mastery Test 6

Read the paragraphs below. Then carefully consider the questions that follow, and, in the spaces provided, write the letters of the best responses.

A. ¹Throughout history, people have suffered from ailments that could have been easily avoided if they had only been understood. ²For instance, it used to be common for hat makers to be tortured by uncontrollable trembling, slurred speech, and mental confusion. ³The condition led to Lewis Carroll's creation of the Mad Hatter in his book *Alice's Adventures in Wonderland*. ⁴Sadly, the hatters did not know that the mercury they used in creating felt hats was poisoning them, leading to their strange symptoms. ⁵Similarly, many of the world's greatest artists suffered from terrible depression. ⁶Today we know that the lead in the paint they used probably affected their mental state. ⁷How tragic that so many lives were destroyed for want of a little knowledge.

_____ 1. The primary purpose of the passage is
  A. to tell readers about formerly misunderstood ailments.
  B. to persuade readers to protect themselves against easily avoidable ailments.
  C. both of the above.

_____ 2. The tone of the passage can be described as
  A. regretful.
  B. angry.
  C. alarmed.
  D. pessimistic.

B. ¹Al Smith, the Democratic candidate for President in 1928, was known for his ready wit and quick comebacks. ²Once he was heckled while making a campaign speech. ³"Tell 'em everything you know, Al," yelled the heckler. ⁴"It won't take very long."
  ⁵Al Smith answered with a grin, "I'll tell 'em everything we both know—it won't take any longer."

_____ 3. The primary purpose of this passage is to
  A. inform students about a humorous aspect of a historical figure.
  B. persuade people to support the Democrats.
  C. argue that Al Smith should have won the 1928 presidential campaign.

_____ 4. The tone of the passage can be described as
  A. forgiving.
  B. amused.
  C. bitter.
  D. disbelieving.

(Continues on next page)

C. ¹Three people were killed because a man was angry that his girlfriend wanted to break up with him. ²He shot both her and two people who tried to stop him. ³Now the state is planning to kill him, and that's as it should be. ⁴Some may argue that taking a life is always wrong, that two wrongs don't make a right. ⁵But there is nothing right about making taxpayers give free room and board to a person who killed innocent people. ⁶And there's nothing right about putting such a dangerous person in prison, from which he will probably one day be released to again threaten society.

_____ 5. The primary purpose of this paragraph is to
   A. report on facts about the death penalty.
   B. persuade readers that the death penalty has merit.
   C. entertain readers with a description of an interesting problem.

_____ 6. The overall tone of this paragraph can be described as
   A. forceful.
   B. insulting.
   C. compassionate.
   D. excited.

D. ¹When people are unemployed, two major sources of stress come into play. ²One is the loss of income, with all the financial hardships that this brings. ³Suddenly there are the difficulties of paying the monthly rent or mortgage, of making the car payment and paying credit-card bills, of dealing with utility costs, and the fundamental matter of putting enough food to eat on the table. ⁴The other source of stress is the effect of the loss of income on workers' feelings about themselves. ⁵Workers who derive their identity from their work, men who define manhood as supporting a family, and people who define their worth in terms of their work's dollar value lose more than their paychecks when they lose their jobs. ⁶They lose a piece of themselves; they lose their self-esteem.

_____ 7. The primary purpose of this paragraph is
   A. to inform readers about the major sources of stress for the unemployed.
   B. to persuade readers that unemployment should be eliminated.
   C. to amuse readers with observations about human nature.

_____ 8. The tone of this paragraph can be described as
   A. depressed and sorrowful.
   B. angry and desperate.
   C. surprised but optimistic.
   D. serious and sympathetic.

9 Argument

"I shall now punch a huge hole in your argument."

Many of us enjoy a good argument. A good argument is not an emotional experience in which people's feelings get out of control, leaving them ready to start throwing things. Instead, it is a rational discussion in which each person advances and supports a point of view about some matter. We might argue with a friend, for example, about where to eat or what movie to go to. We might argue about whether a boss or a parent or an instructor is acting in a fair or an unfair manner. We might argue about whether certain performers or sports stars deserve to get paid as much as they do. In a good argument (such as the one that appears to be going on in the above cartoon), the other person listens carefully as we state our case, waiting to see if we really have solid evidence to support our point of view.

Argumentation is, then, a part of our everyday dealings with other people. It is also an important part of much of what we read. Authors often try to convince us of their opinions and interpretations. Very often there are three important things we must do as critical readers:

1 Recognize the **point** the author is making.

2 Decide if the author's support is **relevant**.

3 Decide if the author's support is **adequate**.

This chapter will give you practice in doing the above, first in everyday arguments and then in textbook material.

The Basics of Argument: Point and Support

A good **argument** is one in which you make a point and then provide persuasive and logical evidence to back it up. Here is a point:

Point: The Beef and Burger Shop is a poor fast-food restaurant.

This statement hardly discourages us from visiting the Beef and Burger Shop. "Why do you say that?" we might legitimately say. "Give your reasons." Support is needed so we can decide for ourselves whether a valid point has been made. Suppose the point is followed by these three reasons:

1. The burgers are full of gristle.

2. The roast beef sandwiches have a chemical taste.

3. The fries are lukewarm and soggy.

Clearly, the details provide solid support for the point. They give us a basis for understanding and agreeing with the point. In light of these details, our mouths are not watering for lunch at the Beef and Burger Shop.

We see here, then, a small example of what clear thinking in an argument is about: making a point and providing support that truly backs up that point. A **valid argument** may also be described as a conclusion supported by logical reasons, facts, examples, and other evidence.

Let's look at another example:

Point: There are certain creatures in particular that you would never want to bite you.

Of course, we would not want *any* creature to bite us. But in this statement we're told that certain creatures in particular can be nasty biters. We'd like to get supporting details so we can see and judge for ourselves. Here are details:

1. A bite from the venomous king cobra can cause muscle paralysis and lead to respiratory failure in a matter of minutes.

2. A lion's bite is powerful enough to rip off your arm or take large chunks out of your body.

3. A crocodile's jaws will snap closed like a steel trap, and if the crocodile then decides to roll, you can usually say goodbye to your arm, leg, or whatever is in its mouth.

With such solid support, you're likely to agree that the king cobra, lion, and crocodile are especially scary biters and that a logical point has been made.

The Point and Support of an Argument

In everyday life, of course, people don't simply say, "Here is my point" and "Here is my support." Nor do writers state their ideas so directly. Even so, the basic structure of point and support is still at work beneath the surface, and to evaluate an argument, you need to recognize its point and support.

The following activity will help you distinguish between a point and its support.

PRACTICE 1

In each group of statements, one statement is the point, and the other statement or statements are support for the point. Identify each point with a **P** and each statement of support with an **S**.

> *Hint:* If it sounds right to insert the word *because* in front of a sentence, you probably have a statement of support. For example, we could say, "Because the burgers are full of gristle, because the roast beef sandwiches have a chemical taste, and because the fries are lukewarm and soggy, I've come to the conclusion that the Beef and Burger Shop is a poor fast-food restaurant."

1. _____ A. You have constant headaches and blurred vision.

   _____ B. You should see a doctor.

2. _____ A. A number of accidents have occurred at that intersection.

   _____ B. A traffic light is needed at the intersection.

3. _____ A. A television is always blaring in one corner of the lounge.

   _____ B. The student lounge is not a place for quiet study.

   _____ C. There are always people there talking loudly to each other.

4. _____ A. High schools need to teach personal finance skills.

_____ B. Many young people do not know how to budget their money.

_____ C. More and more people are getting into serious credit-card debt.

5. _____ A. Cats refuse to learn silly tricks just to amuse people.

_____ B. Cats are more sensible than dogs.

_____ C. Dogs will accept cruel mistreatment, but if a cat is mistreated, it will run away.

6. _____ A. Scientists have proved that acid rain harms trees and bodies of water.

_____ B. Laws should be passed to reduce acid rain.

_____ C. The damage done by acid rain is hard or impossible to undo.

7. _____ A. Fewer companies are offering health plans and retirement benefits.

_____ B. Conditions in the workplace are tougher than they used to be.

_____ C. In many industries, workers have had to take wage cuts.

8. _____ A. The people upstairs make a lot of noise.

_____ B. We'd better look for another apartment.

_____ C. Roaches seem to be taking over this apartment.

_____ D. The landlord does nothing but promise to fix the leaky faucets.

9. _____ A. Almost half of the stores in the shopping center are empty.

_____ B. A deathly hush fills the building.

_____ C. That shopping center is a depressing place.

_____ D. Unhappy-looking store owners stare out at the few passing shoppers.

10. _____ A. The stimulant effects of a daily cup of coffee have been proved to reduce suicide rates.

_____ B. Coffee flushes from the bloodstream the excess fat that clogs arteries.

_____ C. Coffee supplies a large dose of antioxidants, chemicals which prevent the formation of tumors.

_____ D. Even though coffee can make you jittery and interfere with sleep, there are real health benefits to drinking coffee.

Relevant Support

Once you identify the point and support of an argument, you need to decide if each piece of evidence is **relevant**—in other words, if it really applies to the point. The critical reader must ask, "Is this reason relevant support for the argument?" In their enthusiasm for making an argument, people often bring up irrelevant support. For example, in trying to persuade you to lend him some money this week, a friend might say, "You didn't lend me money last week when I needed it." But last week is beside the point; the question is whether or not you should lend him money *this* week.

An excellent way to develop your skill in recognizing relevant support is to work on simple point-support outlines of arguments. By isolating the reasons of an argument, such outlines help you think about whether each reason is truly relevant. Paying close attention to the relevance of support will help your writing as well as your reading.

✔ ## Check Your Understanding

Consider the following outline. The point is followed by six "facts," only three of which are relevant support for the point. See if you can check (✔) the **three** relevant statements of support.

> **Point:** My dog Otis is not very bright.
> ____ 1. He's five years old and doesn't respond to his name yet.
> ____ 2. He cries when I leave for work every day.
> ____ 3. He always gets excited when visitors arrive.
> ____ 4. He often attacks the backyard hedge as if it's a hostile animal.
> ____ 5. He gets along very well with my neighbor's cat.
> ____ 6. I often have to put food in front of him because he can't find it by himself.

Now read the following comments on the six items to see which ones you should have checked and why.

Explanation

1. Most dogs know their names, so Otis's unfamiliarity with his own name reveals a weak memory, and memory is one aspect of intelligence. You should have checked this item.

2. Even an intelligent dog might be sad when its companions leave the house.

3. Both bright and not-so-bright dogs are happy to see old and new human friends.

4. The inability to distinguish between a bush and an animal—friendly or hostile—suggests a lack of analytical skills. This is the second item you should have checked.

5. Dogs of all degrees of intelligence have been known to be friendly with cats.

6. Since most dogs recognize food much more often than their owners would like them to, Otis's inability to find food clearly indicates poor problem-solving skills. You should also have checked this item.

PRACTICE 2

Each point is followed by three statements that provide relevant support and three that do not. In the spaces, write the letters of the **three** relevant statements of support.

> *Hint:* To help you decide if a sentence is relevant or not, ask yourself, "Does this provide logical support for the point being argued?"

1. **Point: Wildlife can be found even in the middle of the city.**
   A. Raccoons sometimes raid the garbage containers near urban apartments.
   B. Many animals have been pushed out of their homes by building development.
   C. Squirrels, chipmunks, and rabbits make their home in city parks.
   D. Heavy traffic makes it dangerous for animals in the city.
   E. Many city dwellers own a cat or a dog.
   F. Hawks build their nests on the window ledges of skyscrapers.

   Items that logically support the point: _____   _____   _____

2. **Point: Singapore is a society with strict controls on people's behavior.**
   A. There are four official languages spoken in Singapore.
   B. Singapore declared its independence from Malaysia in 1965.
   C. Chewing gum on the street is prohibited by law.
   D. Most Singaporeans are of Chinese, Malay, or Indian descent.
   E. Persons convicted of vandalism are whipped with a long rattan cane.
   F. There is a $95 fine for failing to flush a public toilet.

   Items that logically support the point: _____   _____   _____

3. **Point:** Alcohol and tobacco are among the most dangerous drugs that Americans use today.

    A. Cancer from cigarette smoking kills numerous Americans every year.

    B. During Prohibition (1920–1933), liquor bootleggers fought one another as drug dealers do today.

    C. About half of all fatal traffic accidents are due to drunk driving.

    D. Nothing is more annoying than trying to enjoy a restaurant meal when the people at nearby tables are smoking and drinking heavily.

    E. We often don't think of alcohol and tobacco as "drugs" because they are legal.

    F. Alcohol abuse causes many people to become more aggressive and violent.

    Items that logically support the point: _____   _____   _____

4. **Point:** Psychologically healthy people have some general characteristics in common.

    A. Depression, stress, or fatigue can interfere with a person's normal functioning.

    B. A person who is psychologically healthy is productive, doing tasks without making a big deal of them.

    C. The culture we live in has a great deal to do with what we consider "normal" behavior.

    D. People who are well-balanced psychologically get along well with most other people.

    E. Psychologically healthy persons can focus their attention on people or things outside of themselves.

    F. Consistently inappropriate behavior can be a symptom of mental illness.

    Items that logically support the point: _____   _____   _____

Relevant Support in Paragraphs

The point, or main idea, of the argument in the paragraph on the next page is stated in the first sentence. One of the other sentences is **not** relevant support for that point.

✓ Check Your Understanding

Read the paragraph below and see if you can find the statement that does **not** support the point of the argument.

> [1]Every high-school student should be required to take a class in parenting skills. [2]The absence of such classes shows how little our schools do for young people. [3]Numerous young people today are bearing children without having the least idea of how to be a good parent. [4]Many of them have grown up in families where poor parenting was the norm, and so they have no good parenting models. [5]Well-planned parenting classes could give future parents at least an idea of what responsible parenting is all about. [6]The classes might then reduce future problems, including child abuse.

The number of the irrelevant sentence: _____

Explanation

The point of this argument is stated in the first sentence: "Every high-school student should be required to take a class in parenting skills." Any statement that doesn't help prove this point is irrelevant. Sentences 3–6 support that argument: Sentences 5–6 tell the benefits of parenting classes. Sentences 3–4 explain why students need those benefits. Sentence 2, however, is about something else altogether—it complains about how little is being done for young people by schools. Whether that is true or not doesn't change the point and support of the argument. Even if the schools did a great deal for young people, parenting classes could still be useful. Thus sentence 2 is irrelevant to the argument.

PRACTICE 3

The point of the argument in each paragraph that follows is stated in the first sentence. One sentence in the paragraph does not support that point. Read each paragraph, and decide which sentence is **not** relevant evidence. Then write its letter in the space provided.

Hint: To decide if a sentence is relevant, ask yourself, "Does this really provide logical support for the point being argued?"

_____ 1. [1]Nobody in this neighborhood will miss the Martins when they move. [2]They keep their poor dog chained to a tree 24 hours a day, and it howls for most of that time. [3]When the neighborhood kids play ball anywhere near their house, Mr. Martin yells at them, "Don't you dare hit that ball into my yard!"

⁴Of course he has had a lot of illness, so you can understand his being short-tempered. ⁵In addition, the Martins refuse to come to neighborhood block parties, and then they complain about the noise. ⁶And they mow their lawn at 6 a.m. on Saturday morning, when other people are trying to get a little extra sleep.

Which of the following statements does **not** support the author's argument that no one will miss the Martins when they move?

A. Sentence 3   C. Sentence 5
B. Sentence 4   D. Sentence 6

_____ 2. ¹National health insurance is entirely possible, as many industrialized countries have proven. ²The National Health Service in Great Britain provides free health care to all citizens. ³The Health Service is almost completely tax-supported. ⁴That doesn't help the immigrants living in Britain, however. ⁵In Sweden, medical care is provided by publicly funded hospitals and clinics. ⁶A national health insurance system reimburses the providers. ⁷Canadians rely on private physicians and hospitals for day-to-day care, but health care is guaranteed as a right for all citizens. ⁸Income taxes are used to finance Canada's public medical insurance.

Which of the following statements does **not** support the author's argument that providing national health insurance is entirely possible?

A. Sentence 3   C. Sentence 5
B. Sentence 4   D. Sentence 6

_____ 3. ¹Short-term goals encourage self-discipline better than distant aims. ²For instance, dieters lose more weight by attempting to shed two pounds a week than by worrying about a total of twenty pounds or more. ³Low-fat diets are another help for dieters. ⁴Also, students who try to increase study time by a half hour each day do better than those who think only about compiling straight A averages. ⁵And alcoholics and drug addicts achieve more lasting recovery when they deal with their problems one day at a time.

Which sentence is **not** relevant support for the argument that short-term goals are better for will power than long-term goals?

A. Sentence 2   C. Sentence 4
B. Sentence 3   D. Sentence 5

_____ 4. ¹The wish for acceptance by the dominant culture sometimes causes people to turn their backs on their own cultural tradition. ²In Australia, Aborigines who have become part of the dominant society may refuse to acknowledge their darker-skinned grandparents on the street. ³In India, the well-off Indians who dominate the culture copy the traditions and prejudices of the

British, leaving many Hindus unhappy about their behavior. ⁴India won its independence from Britain after Mahatma Gandhi led a campaign of peaceful resistance. ⁵And in the United States, many descendants of immigrants have changed their ethnic-sounding family names to names like those of white Protestants. ⁶Also, children of U.S. immigrants are sometimes ashamed to let their school friends see that their parents speak another language.

Which sentence is **not** relevant support for the argument that people at times turn their backs on their own cultural tradition?

A. Sentence 2
B. Sentence 3
C. Sentence 4
D. Sentence 5

Adequate Support

A valid argument must include not only relevant support but also an **adequate** amount of support—enough to prove the point. For example, it would not be valid to argue "Abortion is wrong" if one's only support was "My sister had an abortion and has regretted it ever since." Such an important issue would require more support than the attitude and experience of a single relative. Arguing a point that doesn't have adequate support is called "jumping to a conclusion."

✓ Check Your Understanding

In the argument below, three supporting items are given, followed by four possible points. The evidence adequately supports only one of the points; it is insufficient to support the other three. Choose the **one** point you think is adequately supported, and put a check mark (✓) beside it.

Support

- The first time I went to that beach, I got a bad case of sunburn.
- The second time I went to that beach, I couldn't go in the water because of the pollution.
- The third time I went to that beach, I stepped on a starfish and had to go to the emergency room to have the spikes removed from my foot.

Which **point** is adequately supported by the evidence on the preceding page?

_____ A. That beach is unsafe and should be closed.

_____ B. I've had a string of bad experiences at that beach.

_____ C. Beaches are not safe places.

_____ D. We're never going to get this planet cleaned up.

Explanation

The correct answer is B. Answer A is not adequately supported by three isolated instances; we'd need many more reports of dangerous conditions before considering having the beach closed. Answer C is even more poorly supported. We'd need many, many reports of dangerous conditions at beaches worldwide to come to the conclusion stated in C. Answer D is supported in part by the reference to pollution in the second statement of support, but the other two statements (about sunburn and the starfish) are not examples of pollution.

PRACTICE 4

For each group, read the three items of support (the evidence). Then check (✓) the **one** point that is adequately supported by that evidence.

Group 1

Support

● Many credit cards do not carry an annual fee.

● Some cards give you cash back, frequent-flier miles, or other benefits.

● Some credit cards charge a lower rate of interest than others.

Which **point** is adequately supported by all the evidence above?

_____ A. When used wisely, credit cards can be helpful.

_____ B. Credit cards charge high interest rates on unpaid balances.

_____ C. You need to shop around for the right credit card.

_____ D. Many people get into trouble by overusing credit cards.

Group 2

Support

- Some people put off writing or calling a friend because they feel they do not have time to do it right, but a quick note or call is often better than nothing.

- Sometimes it makes sense to do a routine chore quickly rather than perfectly in order to save time for something more important.

- Even a desk and office need not be perfectly neat; sometimes cleaning them up is just an excuse for putting off more important work.

Which **point** is adequately supported by all the evidence above?

____ A. Perfection is not always a worthwhile goal.

____ B. Striving for perfection always pays off in the end.

____ C. You can be better organized if you plan each day more carefully.

____ D. Getting things done haphazardly is always better than not getting them done at all.

Group 3

Support

- Some thieves who are sent to jail steal again as soon as they are released.

- A dog that has been hit for eating food off the table will often continue to gobble what it can find when the owner is not around.

- A teenage girl who is "grounded" because she sneaked out of the house may try to come up with a more creative plan to get out without being caught.

Which **point** is adequately supported by all the evidence above?

____ A. Many studies have found advantages and problems with punishment.

____ B. Punishment does not always have the intended effects.

____ C. Punishment is rarely effective.

____ D. Punishment can be effective in some cases.

Group 4

Support

- Elderly nursing-home patients who have little control over their activities tend to decline faster and die sooner than do those given more control over their activities.

- If two rats receive simultaneous shocks, but only one of them can turn a wheel to stop the shocks, the helpless rat becomes more vulnerable to ulcers and has lower immunity to disease.

- When allowed to adjust office furnishings and control interruptions and distractions, workers experience less stress and illness.

Which **point** is adequately supported by all the evidence above?

_____ A. It is possible to gain full control over our lives.

_____ B. Many negative life events are uncontrollable.

_____ C. Loss of control is a major problem in our society.

_____ D. A loss of control is stressful and makes one more vulnerable to ill health.

Argument in Textbook Writing

In most textbook writing, argument takes the form of well-developed ideas or theories (in other words, points) that are supported with experiments, surveys, studies, expert testimony, reasons, examples, or other evidence. Textbook arguments generally have solid support, but recognizing the author's points and asking yourself whether the support is relevant and adequate will help you be an involved and critical reader.

A Final Note

This chapter has dealt with the basics of argument, including the need for relevant and adequate support. In the next chapter, "Critical Reading," you will learn about some common errors in reasoning—also known as **logical fallacies**—that people may make when advancing an argument.

CHAPTER REVIEW

In this chapter, you learned the following:

- A good argument is made up of a point, or a conclusion, and logical evidence to back it up.

- To critically read an argument, you must recognize the **point** the author is making.

- To think through an argument, you need to decide if each piece of evidence is **relevant**.

- To think through an argument, you also need to decide if the author's support is **adequate**.

- Textbook arguments generally have solid support, but recognizing the author's point and looking for for relevant and adequate support will help you become a more involved and critical reader.

The final chapter in Part One—Chapter 10—will explain other aspects of being a critical reader: separating fact from opinion, detecting propaganda, and recognizing errors in reasoning.

 On the Web: If you are using this book in class, you can visit our website for additional practice in evaluating arguments. Go to **www.townsendpress.com** and click on "Learning Center."

REVIEW TEST 1

To review what you've learned in this chapter, complete each sentence or write the letter of the correct answer in the space provided.

_____ 1. The point of an argument can also be called its
     A. relevance.
     B. evidence.
     C. conclusion.

_____ 2. The support for an argument can be referred to as the (A. evidence; B. conclusion) that backs up the point.

_____ 3. Relevant support for an argument is information that (A. enthusiastically; B. partially; C. logically) supports the point.

_____ 4. If there is too little information to support a point, we say the support is
     A. dull.
     B. inadequate.
     C. irrelevant.

_____ 5. Textbook authors may support their arguments with
     A. experiments.   C. studies.
     B. surveys.   D. all of the above and more.

REVIEW TEST 2

A. In each group, one statement is the point, and the other statements are support for that point. Write the letter of the point in the space provided.

> *Hint:* If it sounds right to insert the word *because* in front of a sentence, you probably have a statement of support.

_____ 1. A. Chemicals in dark chocolate help protect arteries from heart disease.
     B. Dark chocolate can be good for the human body.
     C. Dark chocolate contains ingredients that fight depression.

_____ 2. A. A healthy adult tree can produce 5 pounds of pure oxygen a day.
     B. People should plant more trees around their homes.
     C. Mature trees can increase property value by 10 percent.
     D. Trees planted properly around buildings provide shade that cuts air-conditioning costs by 20 percent.

_____ 3. A. Teaching is a great way to learn because one needs to know the material well enough to explain it.
   B. By teaching a class, students will better appreciate their teachers' efforts.
   C. Some students may pay more attention when another student teaches, out of curiosity if nothing else.
   D. All students should be required to teach a class for a day.

_____ 4. A. In the 1700s, doctors in the American colonies were not required to attend college.
   B. In the mid-1800s, most doctors completed just two years of medical school.
   C. The training for doctors has changed dramatically over the past few centuries.
   D. Today, doctors receive about 10 years of education after high school.

B. Each point is followed by three statements that provide relevant support and three that do not. In the spaces, write the letters of the **three** relevant statements of support.

5–7. **Point: Drinking coffee can have unpleasant effects.**
   A. Some people don't like the taste of decaffeinated coffee.
   B. Coffee in the evening can interfere with sleep at night.
   C. As addictions go, coffee is less dangerous than tobacco.
   D. Too much coffee can cause the hands to shake.
   E. Drinking too much coffee can lead to a faster heartbeat and light-headedness.
   F. Most coffees cost under ten dollars a pound.

   Items that logically support the point: _____   _____   _____

8–10. **Point: Some people have very poor telephone manners.**
   A. They never identify themselves, but just begin the conversation.
   B. They often make their calls on cell phones.
   C. They have an unlisted telephone number.
   D. They conduct conversations with people around them at the same time they're talking on the phone.
   E. Some people don't like to talk on the phone.
   F. They often call around 6 p.m., which is most people's dinner hour.

   Items that logically support the point: _____   _____   _____

REVIEW TEST 3

A. In the space provided, write the letter of the irrelevant sentence in each paragraph—the sentence that changes the subject.

_____ 1. ¹Most people who have trouble with schoolwork don't lack intelligence—instead, they are tripped up by their own attitudes toward the work. ²For example, the "I can't do it" state of mind gets in many students' way. ³Instead of making an honest effort to do the work, the "I can't do it" type gives up before he or she begins. ⁴This type often also has trouble on the job. ⁵Then there's the "I'm too tired" attitude. ⁶Students with this problem give in to the temptation to nap whenever there is work to be done. ⁷Another view that leads to low achievement is "The instructor is boring." ⁸Students with that attitude expect every course to be highly entertaining and claim they can't be expected to learn anything otherwise.

Which sentence does **not** support the argument that people who have trouble with school work are tripped up by their own attitudes rather than a lack of intelligence?

A. Sentence 2   c. Sentence 4
B. Sentence 3   d. Sentence 7

_____ 2. ¹Sigmund Freud was one of the most important scientists of the twentieth century. ²A loving father, he had three sons and three daughters. ³He was among the first to study mental disorders, such as hysteria and neurosis, in a systematic way. ⁴He developed the theory of the unconscious and showed how people's behavior is greatly affected by forgotten childhood events. ⁵His discoveries are the basis of psychoanalysis, a method of treating mental illness that is still important today.

Which sentence is **not** relevant support for the argument that Freud is one of the most important scientists of the twentieth century?

A. Sentence 2   c. Sentence 4
B. Sentence 3   d. Sentence 5

_____ 3. ¹People's ability to remember what they see is less dependable than they think. ²In a famous experiment performed at Harvard, researchers showed people a videotape of a basketball game and asked them to count how many times players passed the ball. ³After about 45 seconds, a man dressed in a gorilla suit walked slowly across the scene, passing between the players. ⁴Although he was visible for five seconds, 40 percent of the viewers did not notice him at all. ⁵When the tape was played again, and they were asked simply to watch it, they saw him easily. ⁶Not surprisingly, some insisted that it could not be the same tape. ⁷They simply could not believe they had "tuned out" something as bizarre as a gorilla on the basketball floor. [8]At least they had a good story to tell when they got home.

Which of the following statements does **not** support the author's argument that people's ability to remember what they see is less dependable than they think?

A. Sentence 5   C. Sentence 7
B. Sentence 6   D. Sentence 8

B. For each group, read the three items of support (the evidence). Then, in the space provided, write the letter of the **one** point that is adequately supported by that evidence.

Remember that the point, or conclusion, should follow logically from the evidence. Do not jump to a conclusion that is not well supported.

Group 1

Support

- Many daycare facilities have health and safety standards that are barely satisfactory.
- Long waiting lists exist at most good daycare centers.
- Daycare centers can't get enough qualified help.

_____ 4. Which **point** is adequately supported by all the evidence above?
   A. Daycare is unreasonably expensive.
   B. Mothers with young children should not work.
   C. Our present birthrate must be drastically reduced.
   D. Our present daycare system is inadequate.

Group 2

Support

- Nearly all of those accused during the Salem, Massachusetts witch trials of 1692 had little political power or legal protection.
- On the basis of rumor and hearsay, innocent people in Salem were accused, tried, convicted and executed for the crime of witchcraft.
- The trial and execution of alleged witches in the Salem area ended suddenly when the wife of a "witch judge" found herself accused of practicing witchcraft.

_____ 5. Which **point** is adequately supported by all the evidence above?
   A. Many innocent people have been persecuted with charges of witchcraft over the centuries.

B. People in positions of power were less likely to be charged with witchcraft.

C. The Salem witch trials of 1692 were a shameful episode in American colonial history.

D. Some of the people executed during the Salem witch trials were guilty of serious crimes.

REVIEW TEST 4

Can failing a course be good for students? Here is a chance to apply your understanding of argument to an essay that addresses that question.

To help you continue to strengthen your skills, the reading is followed by questions not only on what you've learned in this chapter but also on what you've learned in previous chapters.

Words to Watch

Below are some words in the reading that do not have strong context support. Each word is followed by the number of the paragraph in which it appears and its meaning there. These words are indicated in the article by a small circle (°).

> *validity* (1): soundness or worth
> *trump card* (4): a tactic that gives one an advantage (like a trump suit in card games)
> *flustered* (6): nervously confused
> *composure* (6): calmness and self-control
> *radical* (6): extreme
> *conspiracy* (11): plot

IN PRAISE OF THE F WORD

Mary Sherry

1   Tens of thousands of eighteen-year-olds will graduate this year and be handed meaningless diplomas. These diplomas won't look any different from those awarded their luckier classmates. Their validity° will be questioned only when their employers discover that these graduates are semiliterate.

2   Eventually a fortunate few will find their way into educational-repair

shops—adult-literacy programs, such as the one where I teach basic grammar and writing. There, high-school graduates and high-school dropouts pursuing graduate-equivalency certificates will learn the skills they should have learned in school. They will also discover they have been cheated by our educational system.

3   As I teach, I learn a lot about our schools. Early in each session I ask my students to write about an unpleasant experience they had in school. No writers' block here! "I wish someone had made me stop doing drugs and made me study." "I liked to party and no one seemed to care." "I was a good kid and didn't cause any trouble, so they just passed me along even though I didn't read well and couldn't write." And so on.

4   I am your basic do-gooder, and prior to teaching this class I blamed the poor academic skills our kids have today on drugs, divorce, and other impediments to concentration necessary for doing well in school. But, as I rediscover each time I walk into the classroom, before a teacher can expect students to concentrate, he has to get their attention, no matter what distractions may be at hand. There are many ways to do this, and they have much to do with teaching style. However, if style alone won't do it, there is another way to show who holds the winning hand in the classroom. That is to reveal the trump card° of failure.

5   I will never forget a teacher who played that card to get the attention of one of my children. Our youngest, a world-class charmer, did little to develop his intellectual talents but always got by. Until Mrs. Stifter.

6   Our son was a high-school senior when he had her for English. "He sits in the back of the room talking to his friends," she told me. "Why don't you move him to the front row?" I urged, believing the embarrassment would get him to settle down. Mrs. Stifter looked at me steely-eyed over her glasses. "I don't move seniors," she said. "I flunk them." I was flustered°. Our son's academic life flashed before my eyes. No teacher had ever threatened him with that before. I regained my composure° and managed to say that I thought she was right. By the time I got home I was feeling pretty good about this. It was a radical° approach for these times, but, well, why not? "She's going to flunk you," I told my son. I did not discuss it any further. Suddenly English became a priority in his life. He finished out the semester with an A.

7   I know one example doesn't make a case, but at night I see a parade of students who are angry and resentful for having been passed along until they could no longer even pretend to keep up. Of average intelligence or better, they eventually quit school, concluding they were too dumb to finish. "I should have been held back," is a comment I hear frequently. Even sadder are those students who are high-school graduates who say to me after a few weeks of class, "I don't know how I ever got a high-school diploma."

8   Passing students who have not mastered the work cheats them and the employers who expect graduates to have

basic skills. We excuse this dishonest behavior by saying kids can't learn if they come from terrible environments. No one seems to stop to think that—no matter what environments they come from—most kids don't put school first on their list unless they perceive something is at stake. They'd rather be sailing.

9   Many students I see at night could give expert testimony on unemployment, chemical dependency, abusive relationships. In spite of these difficulties, they have decided to make education a priority. They are motivated by the desire for a better job or the need to hang on to the one they've got. They have a healthy fear of failure.

10   People of all ages can rise above their problems, but they need to have a reason to do so. Young people generally don't have the maturity to value education in the same way my adult students value it. But fear of failure, whether economic or academic, can motivate both.

11   Flunking as a regular policy has just as much merit today as it did two generations ago. We must review the threat of flunking and see it as it really is—a positive teaching tool. It is an expression of confidence by both teachers and parents that the students

have the ability to learn the material presented to them. However, making it work again would take a dedicated, caring conspiracy° between teachers and parents. It would mean facing the tough reality that passing kids who haven't learned the material—while it might save them grief for the short term—dooms them to long-term illiteracy. It would mean that teachers would have to follow through on their threats, and parents would have to stand behind them, knowing their children's best interests are indeed at stake. This means no more doing Scott's assignments for him because he might fail. No more passing Jodi because she's such a nice kid.

This is a policy that worked in   12 the past and can work today. A wise teacher, with my husband's and my support, gave our son the opportunity to succeed—or fail. It's time we return this choice to all students.

Reading Comprehension Questions

Vocabulary in Context

_____ 1. In the excerpt below, the word *impediments* (ĭm-pĕd′ə-mənts) means
A. questions.
B. skills.
C. obstacles.
D. paths.

> " . . . I blamed the poor academic skills our kids have today on drugs,
> divorce, and other impediments to concentration . . . " (Paragraph 4)

Central Point and Main Ideas

_____ 2. Which sentence best expresses the central point of the selection?
A. Before students will concentrate, the teacher must get their attention.
B. Many adults cannot read or write well.
C. English skills can be learned through adult literacy programs.
D. The threat of failure should be returned to our classrooms.

_____ 3. Which sentence best expresses the main idea of paragraph 6?
A. According to his teacher, Sherry's son sat at the back of the room,
talking to his friends.
B. Mrs. Stifter said that she didn't move seniors; she flunked them.
C. The fear of failure motivated Sherry's son to do well in English.
D. Sherry was at first nervous and confused to learn that her son might
fail English.

Supporting Details

_____ 4. According to the author, many students who get "passed along"
A. are lucky.
B. don't get into trouble.
C. eventually feel angry and resentful.
D. will never learn basic grammar and writing skills.

_____ 5. According to the author, a fear of failure
A. is healthy.
B. does not motivate people.
C. hurts more than it helps.
D. affects young students, but not her adult students.

Transitions

_____ 6. Read the two sentences below and then answer the question that follows.

> "Many students I see at night could give expert testimony on unemployment, chemical dependency, abusive relationships. In spite of these difficulties, they have decided to make education a priority." (Paragraph 9)

What does the second sentence do?
A. It defines a problem and presents a solution.
B. It shows a time order relationship.
C. It compares the attitudes of day students to the attitudes of night students.
D. It contrasts the students' difficulties with their willingness to make education a priority.

Patterns of Organization

_____ 7. The main pattern of organization of paragraph 6 is
A. time order.
B. list of items.
C. definition and example.
D. comparison.

Inferences

_____ 8. The author implies that our present educational system is
A. doing the best that it can.
B. the best in the world.
C. not demanding enough of students.
D. very short of teachers.

Purpose

_____ 9. The author's primary purpose in this article is
A. to inform readers about the advantages and disadvantages of giving failing grades to students.
B. to persuade readers that failure (or the threat of failure) can be good for students.
C. to entertain readers with the true story of one teacher's experiences.

Argument

10. Label the point of the following argument from the reading with a **P**; label the two statements of support for the point with an **S**. Label with an **X** the one statement that is neither the point nor the support of the argument.

___ A. Fear of failure motivated the author's son to do well in English.

___ B. Fear of failure is a good motivator.

___ C. Some people learn skills after high school in adult literacy programs.

___ D. Some kids won't put school first unless they know they might fail.

Discussion Questions

1. Do you know anyone who has failed or almost failed a course? What effect did the experience have on that person?

2. Most people think of failing a course as a negative experience. Why, then, does Sherry consider the threat of failure to be a positive teaching tool? Do you agree?

3. People often look back on their education and realize that some of the teachers they learned the most from were their strictest teachers. Who do you think you learned more from, strict teachers or lenient ones? Give examples to support your point.

4. Besides the threat of failure, what are some other ways that teachers can motivate students? What have teachers done to make you want to work harder for a class?

Note: Writing assignments for this selection appear on page 627.

Check Your Performance   ARGUMENT

Activity		Number Right	Points		Score
Review Test 1	(5 items)	_____	× 2	=	_____
Review Test 2	(10 items)	_____	× 3	=	_____
Review Test 3	(5 items)	_____	× 6	=	_____
Review Test 4	(10 items)	_____	× 3	=	_____
			TOTAL SCORE	=	_____%

Enter your total score into the **Reading Performance Chart: Review Tests** on the inside back cover.

ARGUMENT: Mastery Test 1

A. In each group, one statement is the point of an argument, and the other statements are support for that point. Write the letter of the point of each group.

_____ 1. A. Chimpanzees, who cannot swim, have drowned in zoo moats trying to save others.

     B. Some chimpanzees and monkeys are surprisingly sensitive to the plight of others.

     C. Given the chance to get food by pulling a chain that would also deliver an electric shock to a companion, rhesus monkeys will starve themselves for several days.

     D. Female chimps will sometimes head off a fight by taking stones out of the males' hands.

_____ 2. A. Colonial Boston had three well-used whipping posts in its public square.

     B. In some Italian cities, thieves and prostitutes were forced to run naked through the streets while being beaten with birch rods.

     C. In France, the hangman's scaffold was a permanent fixture in every city and town, and after the hanging, the corpse was allowed to remain until it crumbled.

     D. Far from being carried out "behind closed doors," hundreds of years ago punishments and executions were public events.

_____ 3. A. Pepsi's slogan "Come Alive, You're in the Pepsi Generation" read to Chinese customers as "Pepsi Brings Your Ancestors Back from the Dead."

     B. Perdue Chicken's slogan "It Takes a Tough Man to Make a Tender Chicken" was interpreted in Spanish as "It Takes an Aroused Man to Make a Chicken Affectionate."

     C. Some American companies have found that their product slogans don't translate well into other languages.

     D. KFC's patented slogan "finger-lickin' good" was understood in Japanese as "Bite Your Fingers Off."

_____ 4. A. The pessimistic view of human nature holds that people are basically lazy and have to be forced to work.

     B. Political and business leaders often base their policies on one of several assumptions about people.

     C. The optimistic view presumes people are interested in doing a job well and are capable of directing themselves.

     D. A middle-of-the-road theory is that while people do not dislike work, they do not work efficiently without appropriate direction.

(Continues on next page)

387

B. Each point is followed by three statements that provide relevant support and three that do not. In the spaces, write the letters of the **three** relevant statements of support.

5–7. **Point: My boss is a very unpleasant man to work for.**

    A. He barks orders and never asks for an employee's opinion.

    B. His fashion-plate wife is said to be even nastier than he is.

    C. His office is decorated in dull browns and grays.

    D. Even when he invites employees out to lunch, he expects them to pick up their own checks.

    E. He changes his mind so often that an employee who pleased him on Friday can be in the doghouse by Monday.

    F. He once accumulated so many parking tickets that the police actually came to his home to arrest him.

Items that logically support the point: _____   _____   _____

8–10. **Point: Stress has a negative effect on health.**

    A. Stress triggers a person's "flight or fight" response, which can save him or her from danger.

    B. Stress can cause an irregular heartbeat, which can lead to a heart attack.

    C. Stress can be caused by scary events or by pleasant ones, such as a romantic encounter.

    D. Stress depresses the immune system, making people more vulnerable to illness.

    E. Stress raises blood pressure, increasing the chance of stroke.

    F. Yoga, meditation, and breathing exercises can all be used to reduce stress.

Items that logically support the point: _____   _____   _____

ARGUMENT: Mastery Test 2

A. In each group, one statement is the point of an argument, and the other statements are support for that point. In the space provided, write the letter of the point of each group.

_____ 1. A. Poaching (illegal hunting) is threatening the survival of animal species throughout the world.

B. In Asia, poaching has driven Bengal tigers, snow leopards, and musk deer to the brink of extinction.

C. In Africa, poaching has claimed thousands of leopards, cheetahs, rhinos, and elephants.

D. In North America, illegal hunting has greatly reduced the number of bald eagles, grizzly bears, timber wolves, and giant otters.

_____ 2. A. During the Spanish-American War, U.S. soldiers were supplied with tin cans containing decayed meat.

B. Due to a lack of food safety standards, vendors in the 1800s often sold food that would not today be considered fit for people to eat.

C. Store-bought butter was often stale and mixed with gelatin, fat, or even mashed potatoes.

D. To improve the color of milk from diseased cattle, dairymen sometimes added molasses, chalk, or plaster of Paris.

_____ 3. A. Most fur products are made from animals bred for that purpose, so few endangered species are threatened by the fur industry.

B. Animal-rights activists should not attack others for using animals for fur and medical experiments.

C. Many treatments that save human lives were developed through animal testing programs.

D. Animals bred for fur coats are generally well cared for because breeders want a healthy coat.

(Continues on next page)

B. Each point is followed by three statements that provide relevant support and three that do not. In the spaces, write the letters of the **three** relevant statements of support.

4–6. **Point:** Convenience stores live up to their name.

A. Convenience stores are close to home.

B. Small local businesses should be supported by the community.

C. Some convenience store chains sell products under their own brand name.

D. Convenience stores are open until late or all night.

E. Parking is right outside the convenience store's door.

F. The produce at most of our supermarkets is usually terrible.

Items that logically support the point: _____   _____   _____

7–9. **Point:** Eating yogurt is healthful.

A. Yogurt contains natural antibiotics that can prevent certain kinds of infection.

B. Yogurt is available in nearly all food stores.

C. Yogurt kills the bacteria that can cause diarrhea.

D. You can substitute yogurt in many recipes calling for milk or sour cream.

E. Yogurt is a staple of the diet in many Middle Eastern countries.

F. Eating yogurt has been shown to lower cholesterol levels.

Items that logically support the point: _____   _____   _____

C. Read the following paragraph, and then answer the question that follows.

[1]Sexual harassment in the workplace must be recognized for the serious problem it is. [2]Too many people make light of the problem, believing sexual harassment to be nothing more than pleasant flirtation between coworkers. [3]However, many women, and even some men, have been driven to quit their jobs because of unwanted sexual attention from their supervisors. [4]An employer can more or less subtly pressure employees to grant sexual favors in order to keep their jobs. [5]Even employers who do not demand sex can make their employees miserable through unwelcome remarks about their bodies or dress. [6]Supervisors who sexually harass their employees must have a need to feel important or powerful. [7]All degrees of sexual harassment have the effect of creating a hostile and degrading atmosphere in the workplace. [8]To protect people from having to work in such an environment should be the aim of laws against sexual harassment.

_____ 10. Which sentence is **not** relevant to the argument that laws should protect people from unwanted sexual attention?

A. Sentence 3   C. Sentence 5

B. Sentence 4   D. Sentence 6

ARGUMENT: Mastery Test 3

A. In the following groups, one statement is the point of an argument, and the other statements are support for that point. In the space provided, write the letter of the point of each group.

_____ 1. A. Franklin Roosevelt's masterful use of radio in his "fireside chats" gave many Americans the feeling that they knew him personally.

B. Some American presidents have been highly successful at using mass communication to get their message across.

C. John F. Kennedy's wit and self-assurance came across during his televised press conferences and contributed significantly to his popularity.

D. Ronald Reagan was known as "the great communicator" for his seemingly effortless ability to convey strength and sincerity to the American people.

_____ 2. A. In the 6th century B.C., ships that came into port sent criers around town with signboards to announce their arrival.

B. The ancient Phoenicians painted advertisements on stones near the paths where people often walked.

C. The first printed advertisement was prepared by printer William Caxton in England in 1478 to sell one of his books.

D. Far from being a recent invention, advertising has been used to drum up business for thousands of years.

B. In the space provided, write the letter of the sentence that is **not** logical support for the argument in each paragraph.

_____ 3. ¹Proms are one traditional part of the high-school experience that should be discontinued. ²For one thing, proms are just too expensive. ³Between the girl's dress, the guy's tuxedo, flowers, tickets, and probably dinner in a restaurant, it's way too much money for an average high-school couple to spend. ⁴Rich parents, however, are glad to show off their wealth by supporting such expensive occasions. ⁵Secondly, proms encourage destructive forms of social competition. ⁶Teenagers get caught up in worrying about who has the best-looking date, who spends most on a dress, or who arrives in a rented limousine. ⁷And finally, proms often turn into excuses for underage drinking-and-driving excursions.

Which sentence is **not** relevant to the argument that high-school proms should be discontinued?

A. Sentence 2   C. Sentence 4
B. Sentence 3   D. Sentence 5

(Continues on next page)

_____ 4. ¹Statistics show that people travel more safely in airplanes than in cars. ²For that reason, it seems foolish to be afraid of flying and not be concerned about safety in a car. ³The figures are clear—planes, per passenger mile, are safer than cars. ⁴But statistics do not tell the whole story. ⁵Automobile accidents usually involve only a few people per occurrence and kill or injure only some of the victims. ⁶They involve situations which drivers believe they can avoid through skill or caution. ⁷On the other hand, airplane accidents usually involve large numbers of people and high death rates. ⁸One hundred percent is not uncommon. ⁹Surviving an airplane accident requires luck, not skill or caution, and passengers are totally dependent upon their crew. ¹⁰And to add insult to injury, passengers have paid unreasonably high amounts for tickets for this unsafe type of transportation. ¹¹There's no question about it: when driven by a safe and sober driver, a car is a safer bet than an airplane.

Which sentence is **not** relevant support for the argument that when a car is driven by a safe and sober driver, it is a safer bet than an airplane?

A. Sentence 5   C. Sentence 9
B. Sentence 8   D. Sentence 10

_____ 5. ¹Non-human animals, even highly intelligent ones, are not capable of using language. ²In the 1930s, a husband and wife research team raised a young chimpanzee along with their human baby, treating the two youngsters exactly alike. ³The chimp didn't learn any language at all. ⁴It wasn't reported how the human baby was affected. ⁵In the 1950s, another team of married researchers gave a young chimp extensive language lessons. ⁶She finally learned to make sounds resembling "papa," "mama," and "cup," but nothing more. ⁷More recently, several chimps and gorillas have been taught to use some American Sign Language. ⁸But they use ASL only to request food or social rewards, not to communicate complex ideas or feelings.

Which sentence is **not** relevant support for the argument that that non-human animals cannot use language?

A. Sentence 3   C. Sentence 5
B. Sentence 4   D. Sentence 6

ARGUMENT: Mastery Test 4

A. Each point is followed by three statements that provide relevant support and three that do not. In the spaces, write the letters of the **three** relevant statements of support.

1–3. **Point: We should spend more of our tax dollars on mass transit systems such as subways, commuter rail lines, and buses.**

    A. Our streets and roadways are becoming choked with traffic.

    B. Hybrid cars, which get great gas mileage, are becoming increasingly popular.

    C. Mass transit systems don't pollute nearly as much as automobiles.

    D. The New York City Subway's first underground line opened in 1904.

    E. There are currently over 200 million cars in the United States.

    F. If more people took mass transit to work, we would reduce our dependence on foreign oil.

Items that logically support the point: __C__ __D__ __F__

4–6. **Point: College students are particularly vulnerable to alcohol-related problems.**

    A. People who have an alcoholic parent are at greater risk of becoming alcoholics themselves.

    B. In America, most states limit the sale of alcohol to people who are 21 and older.

    C. Many university customs and traditions encourage dangerous practices of alcohol use.

    D. Alcohol use increases college students' already high risk for suicide, automobile crashes, and falls.

    E. In recent years, some colleges and universities have attempted to crack down on campus drinking.

    F. University campuses are heavily targeted by advertising and promotions from the alcohol beverage industry.

Items that logically support the point: __C__ __D__ __E__

(Continues on next page)

7–9. **Point:** Americans should cut down on their consumption of bottled water.

    A. Studies indicate that the tap water in most communities is perfectly fit to drink.

    B. Bottled water is very convenient when a person is participating in outdoor activities.

    C. Discarded water bottles are contributing to our growing trash problem.

    D. These days, there are many varieties of bottled water.

    E. Bottled water must be transported by truck to stores and vending machines, thus contributing to air pollution.

    F. Many people believe that drinking bottled water is healthier than drinking tap water.

Items that logically support the point: ___C___   ___E___   ___F___

B. For the group below, read the three items of support (the evidence). Then, in the space provided, write the letter of the point that is adequately supported by that evidence.

Support

● Music is often quite effective in helping emotionally disturbed children communicate.

● Music can help relieve anxiety in patients about to undergo surgery.

● Music can help relieve persistent arthritis pain.

___D___ 10. Which point is adequately supported by all the evidence above?

    A. Everyone should listen to music each day.

    B. Music is one of our most effective medical tools.

    C. More people should enter the field of music therapy.

    D. Music is a useful treatment for physical and emotional ailments.

ARGUMENT: Mastery Test 5

A. Each point is followed by three statements that provide relevant support and three that do not. In the spaces, write the letters of the **three** relevant statements of support.

1–3. **Point: Professional boxing should be banned.**

    A. Too many boxers have been critically injured and even killed in the ring.

    B. Most important boxing matches are broadcast on a pay-per-view basis.

    C. Women's boxing is becoming increasingly popular.

    D. Boxing encourages people's cruelest, most savage instincts.

    E. Boxing has given many young at-risk men a source of self-discipline and pride.

    F. Boxers who survive their careers are often left with permanent brain damage.

Items that logically support the point: _____ _____ _____

4–6. **Point: Feeling guilty is not all bad.**

    A. Some people feel guilty because they can't do everything others ask of them.

    B. Feelings of guilt can encourage a person to think about his or her behavior and act differently the next time.

    C. People who feel guilt are less likely to commit a crime than those who feel no guilt for their wrongdoings.

    D. People often feel guilty even when they have done nothing wrong.

    E. Parents often feel guilty when their children, even their adult children, do something wrong.

    F. People who feel guilt have more understanding of and compassion for other people's imperfections.

Items that logically support the point: _____ _____ _____

B. Read the paragraph below, and then answer the questions that follow.

    [1]The death penalty is popular with voters, who are frightened of violent crime, but it is not very effective in reducing the murder rate. [2]In the 1960s and 1970s, when murder rates were lower than today, the death penalty was hardly ever used. [3]Even today, the states that use the death penalty most also often have the highest murder rates. [4]In addition, every death sentence

(Continues on next page)

costs taxpayers hundreds of thousands of dollars in appeals and lawyers' fees. ⁵The number of executions that take place in a state doesn't seem to matter either. ⁶There have actually been some years in which states that had many executions experienced higher homicide rates than states with fewer executions.

_____ 7. Which statement is the point of the argument?
   A. The death penalty is popular with voters, who are frightened of violent crime.
   B. The death penalty is not very effective in reducing the murder rate.
   C. The murder rate has gone up in this country since the 1960s and 1970s.
   D. Executions cost more than they are worth.

_____ 8. Which sentence is **not** relevant support for the point of the argument?
   A. Sentence 3   C. Sentence 5
   B. Sentence 4   D. Sentence 6

C. Read the paragraph below, and then answer the questions that follow.

¹"I feel sorry for poor people, but it's not really my concern. ²I can't do anything about it. ³Right?" ⁴Wrong. ⁵Poverty is a problem that should concern every American of every economic class. ⁶When one American in eight—in *eight*—is living below the poverty line, that should worry every one of us. ⁷You and I may be comfortable today, but many of those millions of our fellow countrymen and women were once comfortable as well. ⁸The loss of jobs, the changing economy, and the slashing of social programs have meant that much of the American middle class is now hanging on by its fingertips, living from paycheck to paycheck, and feeling the ground give way beneath its feet. ⁹Other important social issues, such as the continued existence of racism, also demand attention in our country. ¹⁰In addition, we should care about poverty whether we ever personally experience it or not. ¹¹It is not merely an economic issue; it is a moral one. ¹²As a former vice president, Hubert Humphrey, once said, "A society is judged by how it treats its most vulnerable citizens."

_____ 9. Which statement is the point of the argument?
   A. Poverty should be the economic and moral concern of every American.
   B. The middle class is hanging on by its fingertips.
   C. Poverty is a moral issue.
   D. Poverty has never been so widespread.

_____10. Which sentence is **not** relevant support for the point of the argument?
   A. Sentence 5   C. Sentence 9
   B. Sentence 8   D. Sentence 12

ARGUMENT: Mastery Test 6

A. Each point is followed by three statements that provide relevant support and three that do not. In the spaces, write the letters of the **three** relevant statements of support.

1–3. **Point:** It makes sense to give alternative sentences, not jail, to some nonviolent offenders.

    A. Everyone is entitled to legal representation.

    B. Alternative sentences cost less than jail.

    C. The crime rate goes up every year.

    D. Prisons are overcrowded.

    E. The courts always have a backlog of cases.

    F. Evidence suggests that alternative sentences offer a better chance of rehabilitating the offender.

Items that logically support the point: _____   _____   _____

4–6. **Point:** Religion is a powerful force in modern American life.

    A. The main religion in America is Christianity.

    B. Television evangelists can collect millions of dollars from contributors.

    C. Religious leaders are often influential voices on public issues in America.

    D. In America, there is no state religion.

    E. The Pilgrims came to America seeking religious freedom.

    F. Public opinion polls show that a majority of Americans consider religion personally important to them.

Items that logically support the point: _____   _____   _____

B. In the following groups, one statement is the point of an argument, and the other statements are support for that point. In the space provided, write the letter of the point of each group.

_____ 7. A. Harsh drug laws have not ended illegal drug use.

    B. Legalizing drugs would put illegal street dealers out of business, thereby also putting an end to violent "turf battles" between dealers.

    C. Much of America's drug problem could actually be eliminated by legalizing narcotics.

    D. Profits from drug sales could be taxed to support drug treatment and education programs.

(Continues on next page)

_____ 8. A. Death Valley, California, at 282 feet below sea level, is the lowest spot in America.

B. Temperatures in Death Valley can range from a high of 132° F to a low of 37° F.

C. The valley receives less than two inches of rain per year.

D. Death Valley is a place of extremes.

C. For each group below, read the three items of support (the evidence). Then, in the space provided, write the letter of the point that is adequately supported by that evidence.

Group 1

Support

● A growing number of Japanese women are choosing to stay single, viewing their traditional marriage role as a "raw deal."

● The cost of living and raising a child in Japan is very high.

● Long work days and lengthy commutes leave many Japanese working people too exhausted to deal with children.

_____ 9. Which point is adequately supported by all the evidence above?

A. Japanese women are demanding changes in their society.

B. Japanese people work longer hours than workers in any other country.

C. Japanese families have traditionally been large.

D. There are a number of reasons why the birthrate in Japan is falling.

Group 2

Support

● Dolphins appear to be able to talk to one another through a language of squeals and grunts.

● There have been reports of dolphins helping people who were lost at sea.

● Dolphins in captivity have learned to perform sophisticated tasks, such as fetching objects in a particular order.

_____ 10. Which point is adequately supported by the evidence above?

A. There are no other animals as intelligent as dolphins.

B. Dolphins appear to be highly intelligent animals.

C. Dolphins are better off in captivity.

D. Dolphins are good parents.

10 Critical Reading

Skilled readers are those who can *recognize* an author's point and the support for that point. **Critical readers** are those who can *evaluate* an author's support for a point and determine whether that support is solid or not. In this book, you have already had practice in evaluating support—deciding when inferences are valid and when they are not (pages 273–293) and determining whether supporting evidence is relevant (pages 367–372) and adequate (pages 372–375).

This chapter will extend your ability to read critically in three ways. It will explain and offer practice in each of the following:

● Separating fact from opinion

● Detecting propaganda

● Recognizing errors in reasoning

Separating Fact from Opinion

As the illustration suggests, facts are solidly grounded and can be checked for accuracy; opinions are afloat and open to question.

Look at the photograph below of my great-grandmother's gravestone and the information that it provides. In the spaces provided, do the following:

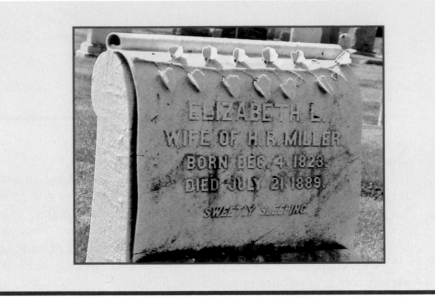

1. Write what you think are the **facts** on the gravestone.
2. Write what you think is the **opinion** it contains.

Facts: _____

_____

Opinion: _____

Fact

A **fact** is information that can be proved true through objective evidence. This evidence may be physical proof or the spoken or written testimony of witnesses. The photograph above presents mostly facts: Elizabeth L. Miller was born on December 4, 1823, and died on July 21, 1889. She was the wife of H.R. Miller.

Following are some more facts—they can be checked for accuracy and thus proved true.

Fact: The Quad Tower is the tallest building in this city.

(A researcher could go out and, through inspection, confirm that the building is the tallest.)

Fact: Albert Einstein willed his violin to his grandson.

(This statement can be checked in historical publications or with Einstein's estate.)

Fact: On September 11, 2001, terrorists destroyed the New York World Trade Center, killing thousands.

(This event was witnessed in person or on television by millions, and it is in records worldwide.)

Opinion

An **opinion** is a belief, judgment, or conclusion that cannot be objectively proved true. As a result, it is open to question. For instance, on my great-grandmother's gravestone, we are told that she is "sweetly sleeping." Of course I certainly *hope* that she is sleeping sweetly, but I have no way of knowing for sure. The statement is an opinion.

Or consider this example: After watching a movie, someone might state that the film was too sentimental. The statement is an opinion because it cannot be objectively proved. Another person might see the same movie and find it realistic. Neither statement can be proved; both are opinions.

Here are some more opinions:

Opinion: The Quad Tower is the ugliest building in the city.

(There's no way to prove this statement because two people can look at the same building and come to different conclusions about its beauty. *Ugly* is a **value word**, a word we use to express a value judgment. Value or judgment words are signals that an opinion is being expressed. By their very nature, these words represent opinions, not facts.)

Opinion: Einstein should have willed his violin to a museum.

(Who says? Not his grandson. This is an opinion.)

Opinion: The attack on the World Trade Center was the worst act of terrorism in the history of humankind.

(Whether something is "worst" is always debatable. *Worst* is another value word.)

Writing Facts and Opinions

To get a better sense of fact and opinion, take a few minutes to write three facts about yourself and then to write three of your opinions. Here, for example, are three facts about me and three of my opinions.

Three facts about me:

- I am six feet tall.
- I do my writing on a Macintosh computer.
- I have two sisters and one wife.

Three of my opinions:

- Schools should encourage students to do a great deal of reading.
- Macintosh computers are much easier to use than PC's.
- People should not get special treatment just because they are rich.

Now write your facts and opinions in the space below.

Three facts about you:

- _____
  _____
- _____
  _____
- _____
  _____

Three of your opinions:

> *Hint:* To make sure that these are opinions, do not begin them with "I." For example, do not write "I think handguns should be banned." Simply write, "Handguns should be banned."

- _____
  _____
- _____
  _____
- _____
  _____

Points about Fact and Opinion

There are several points to keep in mind when considering fact and opinion.

1 Statements of fact may be found to be untrue.

Suppose you discovered that the Quad Tower is only the second-tallest building in the city. The statement would then be an error, not a fact. It is not unusual for evidence to show that a "fact" is not really true. It was once considered to be a fact that the world was flat, for example, but that "fact" turned out to be an error.

2 **Value words** (ones that contain a judgment) often represent opinions. Here are examples of these words:

Value Words

best	great	beautiful
worst	terrible	bad
better	lovely	good
worse	disgusting	wonderful

Value words often express judgments—they are generally subjective, not objective. While factual statements *report on* observed reality, subjective statements *interpret* reality. For example, the observation that it is raining outside is an objective one. The statement that the weather is bad, however, is subjective, an evaluation of reality. (Some people—for example, farmers whose crops need water—consider rain to be good weather.)

3 The words *should* and *ought to* often signal opinions. Those words introduce what people think should, or ought to, be done. Other people will disagree.

Couples should definitely not live together before marriage.

Couples ought to live together before getting married to be sure they are compatible.

4 Don't mistake widely held opinions for facts. Much information that sounds factual is really opinion. A real estate agent, for example, might say, "At the price listed, this rancher is a great buy." Buyers would be wise to wonder what the value word *great* means to the agent. Or an ad may claim that a particular automobile is "the most economical car on the road today," a statement that at first seems factual. But what is meant by *economical*? If the car offers the most miles per gallon but the worst record for expensive repairs, you might not agree that it's economical.

As we will see in later parts of this chapter, advertisers and politicians often try to manipulate us by presenting opinions as if they were facts. For instance, one politician may claim that another will be soft on terrorism or will waste our tax dollars. But accusations are often not facts. Clear-thinking citizens must aim to get below the surface of claims and charges and determine as much factual truth as possible.

5   Finally, remember that much of what we read and hear is a mixture of fact and opinion. Our job, then, is to draw upon existing fact and opinion and to arrive at an informed opinion. On our Supreme Court, for example, nine justices deliberate in order to deliver informed opinions about important issues of our time. But even these justices often disagree and deliver split decisions. The reality is that most of what matters in life is very complex and cannot be separated into simple fact and opinion. Our challenge always is to arrive at the best possible informed opinion, and even then there will be people who disagree with us.

Fact and Opinion in Reading

In general, textbook authors try to be as factual as possible. Most textbook material is based on scientific observation and study, and textbook authors do their best to present us with all the facts and objective informed opinion. On the other hand, many essays, editorials, political speeches, and advertisements may contain facts, but those facts are often carefully selected to back up the authors' opinions.

✔ Check Your Understanding

To sharpen your understanding of fact and opinion, read the following statements and decide whether each is fact or opinion. Put an **F** (for "fact") or an **O** (for "opinion") beside each statement. Put **F+O** beside the **two** statements that are a mixture of fact *and* opinion. Then read the explanation that follows.

> *Hint:* Remember that opinions are signaled by value words—words such as *great* or *hard* or *beautiful* or *terrible* that express a value judgment. Take care to note such words in your reading.

_____ 1. Last night, a tree outside our house was struck by lightning.

_____ 2. The waiters at that restaurant are rude, and the food costs twice as much as it's worth.

_____ 3. Ostriches do not hide their heads in the sand.

_____ 4. Brad Pitt and Halle Berry are the most gorgeous movie stars in Hollywood today.

_____ 5. Low-flow showerheads save water, so all homeowners should be required to buy and install them in their showers.

_____ 6. *Watchers*, by Dean R. Koontz, is a terrifying novel that is bound to keep you awake at night.

_____ 7. The Grimm brothers collected their fairy tales from other storytellers.

_____ 8. There is nothing like a bottle of Coca-Cola to satisfy thirst.

_____ 9. In the late 1890s, when Coke was first sold, it included a small amount of cocaine, which was then legal.

_____10. One of the most delicious of soft drinks, Coca-Cola was first intended to cure various ills, including headaches.

Explanation

1. This is a statement of fact. You and your family might have seen or heard the lightning strike, or you could go outside later and see the type of damage done to the tree.

2. This is an opinion. Not every customer is likely to agree that all the waiters are rude and that the food is overpriced. The word *rude* is a value word.

3. This is a fact (contrary to popular belief) which can be checked through observation and scientific reports.

4. This is an opinion. Not everyone would regard Brad Pitt and Halle Berry in this way. Here the value word *gorgeous* shows us that a judgment is being expressed.

5. The first part of this statement is a fact; tests confirm that low-flow showerheads save water. The second part of the statement—that such showerheads should be *required*—is an opinion.

6. This is an opinion. The book may or may not be so scary that it would keep you awake at night.

7. This is a fact. It can be confirmed through the Grimms' writings and through research on the background of their stories.

8. This is an opinion. Many people might prefer cold water or some other drink as a thirst-quencher.

9. All the details here are facts that can be looked up and confirmed in historical records.

10. The first part of the statement is an opinion—not everyone would consider Coke to be one of the most delicious of soft drinks. (*Delicious* is another value word.) The second part of the statement is a fact that could be confirmed by researching historical records of the time.

PRACTICE 1

Some of the statements below are facts, and some are opinions; in addition, **two** include fact and opinion. Label facts with an **F**, opinions with an **O**, and statements of fact *and* opinion with an **F+O**.

_____ 1. German shepherds are the scariest dogs alive.

_____ 2. The dog that bites people the most often, according to one twenty-seven-year study, is the German shepherd.

_____ 3. German shepherds, which always make poor pets, are used in police work and as guide dogs for the blind.

_____ 4. Smoking has been found to be one cause of lung cancer.

_____ 5. Executives of corporations that pollute the environment should be jailed.

_____ 6. According to scientists, all the water on Earth has been recycled for millions of years, and we drink the same water as the dinosaurs did.

_____ 7. Because many studies have concluded that smoking is a health hazard, cigarettes should be banned.

_____ 8. Scientists predict that one-third of the people who begin smoking under the age of 18 will die prematurely because of their habit.

_____ 9. There's no illness harder to cope with than depression.

_____ 10. Depression is most common among persons between the ages of 25 and 44.

Detecting Propaganda

Advertisers, salespeople, and politicians are constantly promoting their points: "Buy our product," "Believe what I say," and "Vote for me." Often they lack adequate factual support for their points, so they appeal to our emotions by using propaganda techniques.

Part of being a critical reader is having the ability to recognize these propaganda techniques for the emotional fluff that they are. The critical reader strips away the fluff to determine whether there is solid support for the point in question. None of us wants to accept someone else's point as a result of emotional manipulation.

This section will introduce you to six common propaganda techniques:

- Bandwagon
- Plain Folks
- Testimonial
- Name Calling
- Transfer
- Glittering Generalities

While there are other propaganda techniques, the ones described below are among the most common. They all use emotional appeals to distract from the fact they are not providing solid evidence to support their points.

1   Bandwagon

Old-fashioned parades usually began with a large wagon carrying a brass band. Therefore, to "jump on the bandwagon" means to join a parade, or to do what many others are doing. The **bandwagon** technique tells us to buy a product or support a certain issue because, in effect, "everybody else is doing it."

A TV commercial may claim that more and more people are watching the evening news with anchorperson Kerrie Berger. Or a cell phone ad may show people in many different kinds of occupations using a certain cell phone. Or a political ad may feature people from all walks of life speaking out in support of a certain candidate. The ads imply that if you don't jump on the bandwagon, the parade will pass you by.

Here are two examples of real TV ads that have used the bandwagon appeal:

> With appealing music in the background, flashing scenes show many people wearing the sponsor's jeans.

> On a beautiful day, almost everyone on the beach leaves in a hurry in order to attend the sponsor's sale.

● Check (✓) the ad below that uses the bandwagon appeal.

_____ 1. A famous actress explains that she loves to use a certain hair coloring.

_____ 2. A cable company claims that more and more people are switching to it to access the Internet.

2 Testimonial

Famous athletes often appear on television as spokespersons for all sorts of products, from soft drinks to automobiles. Movie and TV stars make commercials endorsing products and political issues. The idea behind the **testimonial** approach is that the testimony of famous people influences the viewers that admire these people.

What consumers must remember is that famous people get paid to endorse products. In addition, these people are not necessarily experts about the products, or the political issues, they promote.

Here are two examples of real ads that have used the appeal of testimonials:

> An actor promotes a product intended to help a man's sexual performance.

> Popular country singers speak out on behalf of certain political candidates.

● Check (✓) the ad below that uses a testimonial.

_____ 1. An ad for a new movie shows people waiting to buy tickets in a line that extends halfway around the block.

_____ 2. A sports star praises the brand of sneakers he is putting on.

3 Transfer

The most common type of propaganda technique is **transfer**, in which products or candidates try to associate themselves with something that people admire or love. In the illustration on page 407, we see a political candidate holding a sign saying "Vote for Me" and standing next to a beauty queen wrapped in a U.S.A. banner.

There are countless variations on this ad, in which a beautiful and sexy woman (or an American flag or some other symbol of the U.S.A.) is used to promote a product or candidate or cause. The hope is that we will *transfer* the positive feelings we have toward a beautiful or sexy-looking person to the product being advertised, or that we will *transfer* the patriotism that we feel to a product or candidate. Over the years, advertisers have found that beauty and sex "sell" and that appeals to patriotism often succeed. In short, transfer usually works.

Here are two examples of real ads that have used the appeal of transfer:

> A beautiful woman in a slinky red dress is shown driving the sponsor's car.

> A hospital chain uses a portrait of Benjamin Franklin in its ads and claims that it, like Franklin, stands for new ideas.

● Check (✓) the ad below that uses transfer.

_____ 1. With the tune of "God Bless America" in the background, an announcer asks viewers to support the home baseball team by coming out to games.

_____ 2. A world-famous bike rider and cancer survivor appears in an ad for a company that sells anti-cancer medications.

4 Plain Folks

Some people distrust political candidates who are rich or well-educated. They feel that these candidates, if elected, will not be able to understand the problems of the average working person. Therefore, candidates often use the **plain folks** technique, presenting themselves as ordinary, average citizens. They try to show they are just "plain folks" by referring in their speeches to hard times in their lives or by posing for photographs while wearing a hard hat or mingling with everyday people.

Similarly, the presidents of some companies appear in their own ads, trying to show that their giant corporations are just family businesses run by ordinary folks.

Here are two examples of real ads that have used the appeal of plain folks:

> Average-looking American kids are shown at home trying and enjoying a cereal.

> A president of an insurance company is shown with his family, talking about his concern for their safety and well-being if he should not be there some day.

● Check (✓) the ad below that uses plain-folks approach.

_____ 1. A very attractive young woman wraps herself in a robe that has been washed in a particular brand of laundry detergent.

_____ 2. A grandmother, serving a canned vegetable soup to her grandson, says, "This has all the simple, healthy, and delicious ingredients I use in my own vegetable soup."

5   Name Calling

Name calling is the use of emotionally loaded language or negative comments to turn people against a rival product, candidate, or movement. An example of name calling would be a political candidate's labeling an opponent "soft," "radical," or "wimpy."

Here are two examples of name calling taken from real life:

> The fast-food industry labels critics of their industry as "food police," "cookie cops," and "the grease Gestapo."

> During a taste test, consumers describe the other leading brand of spaghetti sauce as "too salty" and "thin and tasteless."

- Check (✓) the ad below that uses name calling.

    _____ 1. An ad for hard liquor shows a beautiful woman in a strapless gown having a drink and being admired by several handsome men.

    _____ 2. "My opponent has lived in our state for only two years," says a candidate for state senator. "Let's not put an outsider into state office."

6   Glittering Generalities

A **glittering generality** is an important-sounding but unspecific claim about some product, candidate, or cause. It cannot be proved true or false because no evidence is offered to support the claim. Such claims use general words such as "great," "magical," or "ultimate." "Simply the best," an ad might say about a certain television set. But no specific evidence of any kind is offered to support such a generality. "The right candidate for our city," a campaign slogan might claim. But what does "right" really mean? It and similar phrases sound good but say nothing definite.

Here are two examples from real ads that use glittering generalities:

> A store ad claims, "Fashions that will bring out the rainbow in you."
> A canned-food ad boasts of "nutrition for today."

- Check (✓) the ad below that uses a glittering generality.

    _____ 1. "Ed Dalton—a candidate that really cares," says the announcer.

    _____ 2. A well-known athlete says he uses a certain kind of aspirin.

PRACTICE 2

In each pair of sentences below, the first sentence does not illustrate a propaganda technique, but the second one does. On the line, write the letter of the propaganda technique used in the second sentence.

A. bandwagon	B. testimonial	C. transfer
D. plain folks	E. name calling	F. glittering generalities

_____ 1. ● Kiddy Kare is the largest daycare center in town.

● Our competitor's daycare center is more concerned about profits than about children.

_____ 2. ● Sureguard sunglasses filter out harmful ultraviolet rays.

● "I'm proud to wear Sureguard sunglasses," says actress Jennifer Barnes. "You'll love them, too."

_____ 3. ● In a recent election poll, Margo Levy was ahead of the other candidate.

● Add your vote to the landslide victory Margo Levy will win in next week's election.

_____ 4. ● Twin Oaks is a residential development near Des Moines, Iowa.

● There's nothing else quite like Twin Oaks, a great residential community where you will be proud to live.

_____ 5. ● As a young man, candidate Alan Wilson had a variety of jobs working in a department store and in his family's TV station.

● As a young man, candidate Alan Wilson learned what it means to work hard by spending long hours lifting boxes and sweeping floors.

_____ 6. ● A college degree opens up job doors.

● Comedian Jerry Klein says, "A college degree opens up job doors."

_____ 7. ● I'm voting for Jones because he has had ten years of experience on the Senate's Committee on International Affairs.

● I'll bet my French poodle and German shepherd know more about foreign affairs than Smith does. My vote goes to Jones.

_____ 8. ● Markey's Used Cars will be open on the Fourth of July.

● A patriotic march plays, and a giant American flag waves over a used-car lot. "Celebrate your freedom of choice on the Fourth of July!" says the announcer. "At Markey's, we'll honor the holiday by making some star-spangled deals."

_____ 9. ● The presidential candidate supports our country's farmers.

● The presidential candidate has her own small farm, so she knows the farmers' concerns.

_____10. ● At Triple-A Technical School, you can learn the skills needed to become a plumber, mechanic, or electrician.

● Set the world on fire with skills you learn at Triple-A Technical School!

Recognizing Errors in Reasoning

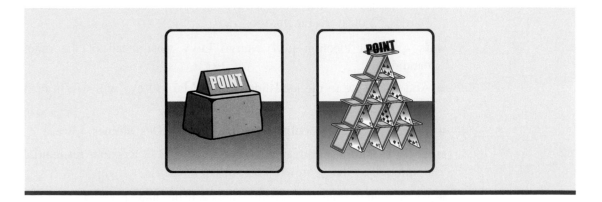

So far in this chapter, you have gotten practice in separating fact from opinion and in spotting propaganda. In this section you will learn about some common errors in reasoning—also known as **fallacies**—that take the place of the real support needed in an argument. As shown in the illustration, a valid point is based on a rock-like foundation of solid support; a fallacious point is based on a house of cards that offers no real support at all. Regrettably, these fallacies appear all too often in political arguments, often as the result of deliberate manipulation, other times as the result of careless thinking.

You've already learned about two common fallacies in Chapter 9, "Argument." One of those fallacies is sometimes called **changing the subject**. Attention is diverted from the issue at hand by presenting irrelevant support—evidence that actually has nothing to do with the argument. The second fallacy covered in Chapter 9 is sometimes called **hasty generalization**—in which a point is based on inadequate support. To be valid, a point must be based on an adequate amount of evidence. To draw a conclusion on the basis of insufficient evidence is to make a hasty generalization.

Below are six other common fallacies that will be explained in this section.

Three Fallacies That Ignore the Issue
- Circular Reasoning
- Personal Attack
- Straw Man

Three Fallacies That Oversimplify the Issue
- False Cause
- False Comparison
- Either-Or

In all of these fallacies, a point is argued, but no true support is offered for that point.

Fallacies That Ignore the Issue

Circular Reasoning

Part of a point cannot reasonably be used as evidence to support it. The fallacy of including such illogical evidence is called **circular reasoning**; it is also known as **begging the question**.

Here is a simple and obvious example of such reasoning:

Mr. Green is a great teacher because he is so wonderful at teaching.

The supporting reason ("he is so wonderful at teaching") is really the same as the conclusion ("Mr. Green is a great teacher"). We still do not know *why* he is a great teacher. No real reasons have been given—the statement has merely been repeated.

Can you spot the circular reasoning in the following arguments?

1. Vitamins are healthful, for they improve your well-being.
2. Since people under 21 are too young to vote, the voting age shouldn't be lowered below age 21.
3. Abortion is an evil practice because it is so wrong.

Let's look more closely at these arguments:

1. The word *healthful*, which is used in the conclusion, conveys the same idea as *well-being*. We still don't know why vitamins are good for us.
2. The idea that people under 21 are too young to vote is both the conclusion and the reason of the argument. No real reason is given for why people under 21 are too young to vote.
3. The claim that abortion "is so wrong" simply restates the idea that it is an evil practice. No explanation is given for why abortion is evil or wrong.

In all these cases, the reasons merely repeat an important part of the conclusion. The careful reader wants to say, "Tell me something new. You are reasoning in circles. Give me supporting evidence, not a repetition."

- Check (✓) the item that contains an example of the circular reasoning fallacy.

　　_____ 1. The government should lower our taxes because taxes are entirely too high.

　　_____ 2. I'm not going to be paid what I'm worth until I get a boss who cares about being fair.

Personal Attack

This fallacy often occurs in political debate. Here's an example:

> Senator Brill's opinions on public housing are worthless. He can't even manage to hold his own household together—he's been married and divorced three times already.

Senator Brill's family life may or may not reflect a weakness in his character, but it has nothing to do with the value of his opinions on public housing. **Personal attack** ignores the issue under discussion and concentrates instead on the character of the opponent.

Sometimes personal attacks take the form of accusing people of taking a stand only because it will benefit them personally. For instance, here's a personal attack on a congressman who is an outspoken member of the National Organization for Women (NOW): "He doesn't care about NOW. He supports it only in order to get more women to vote for him." This argument ignores the congressman's detailed defense of NOW as an organization that promotes equal rights for both men and women. The key to recognizing personal attack is that it always involves an opponent's personal life or character, rather than simply his or her public ideas.

- Check (✓) the item that contains an example of personal attack.

　　_____ 1. Why support Ray O'Donnell's highway safety proposal? He's got the biggest collection of speeding tickets in the district.

　　_____ 2. I feel my salary should be higher because it is so low.

Straw Man

An opponent made of straw can be defeated very easily. Sometimes, if one's real opponent is putting up too good a fight, it can be tempting to build a scarecrow and battle it instead. For example, look at the following excerpt from a debate on the death penalty.

> Ms. Collins opposes capital punishment. But letting murderers out on the street to kill again is a crazy idea. If we did that, no one would be safe.

Ms. Collins, however, never advocated "letting murderers out on the street to kill again." In fact, she wants to keep them in jail for life rather than execute them. The **straw man** fallacy suggests that the opponent favors an obviously unpopular cause—when the opponent really doesn't support anything of the kind. Then that made-up position is opposed.

● Check (✓) the item that contains an example of straw man.

_____ 1. The people who are in favor of gun control are obviously not concerned about criminals taking control of this fine country.

_____ 2. Rose Curtis is a declared lesbian and should not be allowed to run for public office.

Fallacies That Oversimplify the Issue

False Cause

You have probably heard someone say as a joke, "I know it's going to rain today because I just washed the car." The idea that someone can make it rain by washing a car is funny because the two events obviously have nothing to do with each other. However, with more complicated issues, it is easy to make the mistake known as the fallacy of **false cause**. The mistake is to assume that because event B *follows* event A, event B *was caused by* event A.

Cause-and-effect situations can be difficult to analyze, and people are often tempted to oversimplify them by focusing on one "cause" and ignoring other possible causes. To identify an argument using a false cause, look for alternative causes.

Consider this argument:

The Macklin Company was more prosperous before Ms. Williams became president. Clearly, she is the cause of the decline.

(*Event A:* Ms. Williams became president.
Event B: The Macklin Company's earnings declined.)

However, Ms. Williams has been president for only a few months. What other possible causes could have been responsible for the decline? Perhaps the policies of the previous president are just now affecting the company. Perhaps the market for the company's product has changed. In any case, it's easy but dangerous to assume that just because A *came before* B, A *caused* B.

● Check (✓) the item that contains an example of false cause.

_____ 1. I knew I shouldn't have taken the baby to the park today. Now he's got a cold.

_____ 2. Of course the legalization of prostitution will work in America. It has worked in European countries, hasn't it?

False Comparison

When the poet Robert Burns wrote, "My love is like a red, red rose," he meant that both the woman he loved and a rose are beautiful. In other ways—such as having green leaves and thorns, for example—his love did not resemble a rose at all.

Comparisons are often a good way to clarify a point. But because two things are not alike in all respects, comparisons (sometimes called analogies) often make poor evidence for arguments. In the error in reasoning known as **false comparison**, the assumption is that two things are more alike than they really are. For example, read the following argument:

> It didn't hurt your grandfather to get to work without a car, and it won't hurt you either.

To judge whether or not this is a false comparison, consider how the two situations are alike and how they differ. They are similar in that both involve a young person's need to get to work. But the situations are different in that the grandfather didn't have to be at work an hour after his last class. In fact, he didn't go to school at all. In addition, his family didn't own a car he could use. The differences in this case are more important than the similarities, making it a false comparison.

- Check (✓) the item that contains an example of the false comparison.

  _____ 1. After visiting Hal today, I came home with a headache. I must be allergic to his dog.

  _____ 2. I don't know why you're so worried about my grades. Albert Einstein had lousy grades in high school, and he did all right.

Either-Or

It is often wrong to assume that there are only two sides to a question. Offering only two choices when more actually exist is an **either-or** fallacy. For example, the statement "You are either with us or against us" assumes that there is no middle ground. Or consider the following:

> People opposed to unrestricted free speech are really in favor of censorship.

This argument ignores the fact that a person could believe in free speech as well as in laws that prohibit slander or that punish someone for falsely yelling "Fire!" in a crowded theater. Some issues have only two sides (Will you pass the course, or won't you?), but most have several.

- Check (✓) the item that contains an example of the either-or fallacy.

  _____ 1. School prayer is a positive force in parochial schools, so why not try it in our public schools?

  _____ 2. If you don't study at least three hours a night, you're not really serious about being in college.

PRACTICE 3

A. In the space provided, write the letter of the fallacy contained in each argument. Choose from the three fallacies shown in the box below.

> A **Circular reasoning** (*a statement repeats itself rather than providing a real supporting reason to back up an argument*)
>
> B **Personal attack** (*ignores the issue under discussion and concentrates instead on the character of the opponent*)
>
> C **Straw man** (*an argument is made by claiming an opponent holds an extreme position and then opposing that extreme position*)

_____ 1. Supporters of state lotteries apparently don't think people should work hard for what they get. They believe it's better to get something for nothing.

_____ 2. Earl will make a lousy class treasurer because he's just a conceited jerk.

_____ 3. Pollution is wrong because it dirties the environment.

_____ 4. Mr. Vincent supports sex education in junior high school. Maybe he thinks it's okay for 13-year-olds to be having babies, but I don't agree.

_____ 5. Watering new grass is important, since new lawns need a lot of water.

B. In the space provided, write the letter of the fallacy contained in each argument. Choose from the three fallacies shown in the box below.

> A **False cause** (*the argument assumes that the order of events alone shows cause and effect*)
>
> B **False comparison** (*the argument assumes that two things being compared are more alike than they really are*)
>
> C **Either-or** (*the argument assumes that there are only two sides to a question*)

_____ 6. Stay away from Gary's filthy dorm room. After the last time I went there to study, I actually got a rash.

_____ 7. Did you tell the boss off, or did you act like a wimp again?

_____ 8. There's a sign in the dorm lounge saying that excessive alcohol is dangerous. Well, so what? Too much pizza can be dangerous, too.

_____ 9. Do you always tell the truth, or are you a liar?

_____10. Last time there was an eclipse, the stock market went down. I'm going to sell all my stock before next week's eclipse takes place.

CHAPTER REVIEW

In this chapter, you learned that critical readers evaluate an author's support for a point and determine whether that support is solid or not. Critical reading includes the following three abilities:

● **Separating fact from opinion.** A **fact** is information that can be proved true through objective evidence. An **opinion** is a belief, judgment, or conclusion that cannot be proved objectively true. Much of what we read is a mixture of fact and opinion, and our job as readers is to arrive at the best possible informed opinion. Textbooks and other effective writing provide informed opinion—opinion based upon factual information.

● **Detecting propaganda.** Advertisers, salespeople, and politicians often try to promote their points by appealing to our emotions rather than our powers of reason. To do so, they practice six common propaganda techniques: bandwagon, testimonial, transfer, plain folks, name calling, and glittering generalities.

● **Recognizing errors in reasoning.** Politicians and others are at times guilty of errors in reasoning—fallacies—that take the place of the real support needed in an argument. Such fallacies include circular reasoning, personal attack, straw man, false cause, false comparison, and either-or.

 On the Web: If you are using this book in class, you can visit our website for additional practice in critical reading. Go to **www.townsendpress.com** and click on "Learning Center."

REVIEW TEST 1

To review what you've learned in this chapter, answer the following questions.

Fact and Opinion

1. *(A fact, An opinion)* _____ can be proved true through objective evidence.

2. *(An editorial, A political speech, A news report)* _____ is likely to be totally factual.

3. Most of what we read is *(fact, opinion, a mixture of fact and opinion)*

   _____.

4. *(Facts, Opinions)* _____ often include words that express judgments.

Propaganda Techniques

_____ 5. Propaganda is intended to (A. inform; B. persuade).

_____ 6. An important difference between a testimonial and a plain-folks appeal is that testimonials feature (A. famous; B. ordinary) people.

_____ 7. The (A. transfer; B. plain-folks) technique associates a product with symbols and images that people respect.

Fallacies

_____ 8. TRUE OR FALSE? The fallacy of personal attack ignores the true issue.

_____ 9. TRUE OR FALSE? The fallacy of straw man got its name because an opponent made of straw would be easily defeated.

_____ 10. In the either-or fallacy, the argument ignores the possibility of an additional
   A. cause for something happening.
   B. side to a question.
   C. comparison.

REVIEW TEST 2

Read the following statements and decide whether each is fact or opinion. Put an **F** (for "fact") or an **O** (for "opinion") beside each statement. Put **F+O** beside the **one** statement that is a mixture of fact and opinion.

_____ 1. The best exercise for a healthy heart is walking.

_____ 2. The heart pumps slightly more than a gallon of blood per minute through approximately 60,000 miles of blood vessels in the body.

_____ 3. More Bibles have been printed than any other book in history.

_____ 4. The Roman Catholic concept of God is more correct than the Protestant or the Jewish view.

_____ 5. Butterflies are the most beautiful of all insects.

_____ 6. The most amazing thing about butterflies is that their taste sensors are located in their feet, so that by standing on food, they can taste it.

_____ 7. Falling coconuts kill about 150 people worldwide each year, and sharks kill about 10 people.

_____ 8. The greatest danger in swimming in the ocean is of being attacked by a shark.

_____ 9. At the beginning of the twentieth century, only one of ten married women held a paying job.

_____10. For self-fulfillment, mothers in today's world should hold down an outside job as well as care for their children.

REVIEW TEST 3

A. Each of the passages below illustrates a particular propaganda technique. On the line next to the passage, write the letter of the technique being used.

_____ 1. Leslie Kendall, the television actress whose lovely hair is her trademark, reveals that her secret is Flirt shampoo. "Flirt softens my hair and gives it great body," Leslie says. "Thanks to Flirt, my hair has never looked better."

    A. Plain folks   C. Name calling

    B. Testimonial   D. Bandwagon

_____ 2. Monroe Archer is a millionaire and the president of a large corporation, yet he has never lost touch with his small-town roots. Despite his power and fame, he still likes returning to his hometown to enjoy a summer band concert and a simple supper at Charley's Diner.

    A. Name calling   C. Plain folks

    B. Bandwagon   D. Testimonial

_____ 3. "I wear Form Fit jeans—if I wear anything at all," whispers a shapely model in tight jeans and low-cut T-shirt.

    A. Bandwagon   C. Transfer

    B. Name calling   D. Glittering generalities

_____ 4. Come one! Come all! Everybody's going to Linwood Furniture for the big eighth annual sale, a sale so big we rented a tent to hold the crowds.

    A. Name calling   C. Transfer

    B. Bandwagon   D. Testimonial

_____ 5. Cast your vote next Tuesday for Greg Lewis. This fine man has much to offer his community and his nation. As your representative, he pledges to do his best to improve conditions and to bring you closer to the fulfillment of your highest dreams.

    A. Glittering generalities   C. Bandwagon

    B. Transfer   D. Name calling

B. In the space provided, write the letter of the fallacy contained in each argument. Choose from the three fallacies shown in the box below.

> **A   Circular reasoning** (*a statement repeats itself rather than providing a real supporting reason to back up an argument*)
>
> **B   Personal attack** (*ignores the issue under discussion and concentrates instead on the character of the opponent*)
>
> **C   Straw man** (*an argument is made by claiming an opponent holds an extreme position and then opposing that extreme position*)

_____ 6. Congressman Nagel's policy on welfare is nonsense. What do you expect from a man known to have cheated on his wife?

_____ 7. You can always trust an animal lover because people who like animals are more trustworthy than other people.

_____ 8. The mayor wants to allow liquor stores in town. He may not mind having all those drug pushers around, but I certainly do.

Now choose from the two fallacies shown in the box below.

> **A   False cause** (*the argument assumes that the order of events alone shows cause and effect*)
>
> **B   Either-or** (*the argument assumes that there are only two sides to a question*)

_____ 9. I ate in the company cafeteria yesterday, and today I have the flu. That's the last time I'll eat there.

_____ 10. There are only two types of citizens in this town: those who support building a new stadium and those who don't care about our town's future.

REVIEW TEST 4

A humble over-the-counter drug, a fixture in most family's medicine cabinets, has been shown over and over again to be no less than a hero of preventive medicine. Should it be a matter of public policy to encourage Americans to take a daily dose?

Words to Watch

inexorable (1): unavoidable
infuriating (1): maddening
mandate (2): require
substantially (3): largely
rationale (5): a reason
analgesic (6): painkiller
bolstering (9): supporting
caveats (14): warnings, cautions
unequivocally (16): definitely

THE 2,000-YEAR-OLD WONDER DRUG

David B. Agus

1   The inexorable° rise in health care spending, as all of us know, is a problem. But what's truly infuriating°, as we watch America's medical bill soar, is that our conversation has focused almost exclusively on how to pay for that care, not on reducing our need for it. In the endless debate about "health care reform," few have zeroed in on the practical actions we should be taking now to make Americans healthier.

2   An exception is Mayor Michael R. Bloomberg of New York, who is setting new standards that we would do well to adopt as a nation. In the last several years, he's changed the city's health code to mandate° restrictions on sodas and trans fats—products that, when consumed over the long term, harm people. These new rules will undoubtedly improve New Yorkers' health in years to come.

3   Such bold moves prompt a provocative question: when does regulating a person's habits in the name of good health become our moral and social duty? The answer, I suggest, is a two-parter: first, when the scientific data clearly and overwhelmingly demonstrate that one behavior or another can substantially° reduce—or, conversely, raise—a person's risk of disease; and second, when all of us are stuck paying for one another's medical

bills (which is what we do now, by way of Medicare, Medicaid and other taxpayer-financed health care programs).

4   In such cases, encouraging a healthy behavior, or discouraging an unhealthy one, ought to be a matter of public policy—which is why, for instance, we insist on vaccinating children for the measles, mumps, rubella and polio; we know these preventive strategies save lives.

5   Under that rationale°, then, why not make it public policy to encourage middle-aged people to use aspirin?

6   Developed in 1897 by the German chemist Felix Hoffmann, aspirin, or acetylsalicylic acid, has long proved its value as an analgesic°. Two millenniums before that, Hippocrates, the father of modern medicine, used its active ingredient—which he extracted from the bark and leaves of the willow tree—to help alleviate pain and fevers.

7   Since then, we've gained insight into both the biological mechanism and the effects of this chemical compound. Many high-quality research studies have confirmed that the use of aspirin substantially reduces the risk of cardiovascular disease. Indeed, the evidence for this is so abundant and clear that, in 2009, the United States Preventive Services Task Force strongly recommended that men ages 45 to 79, and women ages 55 to 79, take a low-dose aspirin pill daily, with the exception for those who are already at higher risk for gastrointestinal bleeding or who have certain other health issues. (As an anticoagulant, aspirin can increase the risk of bleeding—a serious

and potentially deadly issue for some people.)

8   New reports about aspirin's benefits in cancer prevention are just as convincing. In 2011, British researchers, analyzing data from some 25,000 patients in eight long-term studies, found that a small, 75-milligram dose of aspirin taken daily for at least five years reduced the risk of dying from common cancers by 21 percent.

9   In March, *The Lancet* published two more papers bolstering° the case for this ancient drug. The first, reviewing five long-term studies involving more than 17,000 patients, found that a daily low-dose aspirin lowered the risk of getting adenocarcinomas—common malignant cancers that develop in the lungs, colon and prostate—by an average of 46 percent.

10   In the second, researchers at Oxford and other centers compared patients who took aspirin with those who didn't in 51 different studies. Investigators found that the risk of dying from cancer was 37 percent lower among those taking aspirin for at least five years. In a subsection of the study group, three years of daily aspirin use reduced the risk of developing cancer by almost

25 percent when compared with the aspirin-free control group.

11   The data are screaming out to us. Aspirin, one of the oldest remedies on the planet, helps prevent heart disease through what is likely to be a variety of mechanisms, including keeping blood clots from forming. And experts believe it helps prevent cancer, in part, by dampening an immune response called inflammation.

12   So the question remains: given the evidence we have, why is it merely voluntary for physicians to inform their patients about a health care intervention that could not only help them, but also save untold billions in taxpayer dollars each year?

13   For some men over the age of 45 and women over 55, the risks of taking aspirin outweigh any benefits—and patients should talk with their doctors before taking any medication, including something as familiar as aspirin.

14   But with such caveats° in place, it still ought to be possible to encourage aspirin's use in those for whom the potential benefits would be obvious and the risks minimal. Just as we discourage smoking through advertising campaigns, for example, shouldn't we suggest that middle-aged Americans speak to their doctors about aspirin? Perhaps pharmacists or even health insurance companies should be enlisted to help spread the word about this disease-prevention drug?

15   The right policy will have to be hammered out, of course. But if we're going to address the country's sky-high medical bill, we're going to have to address the need for Americans to be active in protecting their own health.

16   Everyone may want the right to use tobacco products and engage in other behaviors that are unequivocally° linked with disease—or have the right not to wear a seat belt and refrain from other actions that may protect their well-being. But, if so, should society have the obligation to cover the costs of the consequences?

17   As the former Supreme Court Justice Potter Stewart once said, "There is a big difference between what we have the right to do and what is right to do." Health care reform should, at long last, focus on the latter.

Reading Comprehension Questions

Vocabulary in Context

_____ 1. In the excerpt below, the word *alleviate* (ə-lē′vē-āt′) means
   A. locate.
   B. reduce.
   C. increase.
   D. define.

> "Two millenniums before that, Hippocrates, the father of modern medicine, used [aspirin's] active ingredient—which he extracted from the bark and leaves of the willow tree—to help alleviate pain and fevers." (Paragraph 6)

Central Point and Main Ideas

_____ 2. Which sentence best expresses the central point of the selection?
   A. The government should be able to regulate a person's eating and drinking habits in order to lower health care costs for everyone.
   B. Many studies have confirmed that a small dose of aspirin taken daily decreases the risks of developing cancer and helps prevent heart disease.
   C. Because aspirin has been found to lower the risk of heart disease and cancer, we should encourage older adults to take a low-dose aspirin pill daily.
   D. Mayor Michael Bloomberg of New York is setting new public-health standards that we would do well to adopt as a nation.

_____ 3. The implied main idea of paragraphs 12–14 is that
   A. if more people took aspirin on a daily basis, we could save billions in taxpayer dollars each year.
   B. advertising campaigns are the best way to encourage aspirin's use.
   C. pharmacists and health insurance companies should be enlisted to help spread the word about aspirin.
   D. we should be doing much more than we are now to promote the benefits of taking aspirin.

Supporting Details

_____ 4. According to the selection, one way that aspirin helps prevent heart disease is by
   A. lowering blood pressure in overweight people.
   B. lowering plaque build-up in arteries.
   C. keeping blood clots from forming.
   D. dampening an immune response called inflammation.

Transitions

_____ 5. The sentence below expresses a relationship of
A. contrast.   C. comparison.
B. addition.   D. cause and effect.

> "Just as we discourage smoking through advertising campaigns, for example, shouldn't we suggest that middle-aged Americans speak to their doctors about aspirin?" (Paragraph 14)

Patterns of Organization

_____ 6. Paragraphs 8–10 mainly
A. define a problem and present a solution.
B. list the results of studies showing that aspirin lowers the risk of developing cancer.
C. contrast the health benefits of aspirin with possible risks involved in taking it every day.
D. provide a brief history of the use of aspirin in medicine.

Inferences

_____ 7. We can infer that the author of this selection believes that
A. physicians should be required to prescribe low-dose aspirin for all their older patients.
B. more studies need to be done before we can safely say that aspirin lowers the risk of developing cancer and heart disease.
C. people should be free to do whatever they want, as long as they don't harm others.
D. when it comes to health care, it's not fair to make everyone pay for the unhealthy behavior of some.

Purpose and Tone

_____ 8. On the whole, the author's tone in this selection is
A. angry.   C. detached.
B. concerned.   D. sarcastic.

Critical Reading

_____ 9. A TV commercial featuring a middle-aged doctor who tells us that he takes a small dose of aspirin every day to guard against cancer and heart disease is illustrating the propaganda technique of
A. glittering generalities.   C. testimonial.
B. transfer.   D. bandwagon.

_____ 10. The statement "If you don't take aspirin every day, you're not serious about protecting your health" is an example of the logical fallacy of

   A. personal attack.
   B. straw man.
   C. false cause.
   D. either-or.

Discussion Questions

1. If aspirin truly is the wonder drug that the author claims it is, would you support *requiring* all those for whom it is not dangerous to take it? Why or why not?

2. The author clearly approves of Mayor Bloomberg's restrictions on sodas and trans fats. However, others feel that Bloomberg has gone too far in restricting these items. Where do you stand on this issue? Explain.

3. Referring to our right to smoke and to not wear a seat belt, the author quotes Supreme Court justice Potter Stewart: "There is a big difference between what we have the right to do and what is right to do." What are some other behaviors that we may "have the right to do," but that aren't "right to do?" Make a list of them and then compare your list with your classmates' lists. What conclusions can you draw from these lists?

4. The author suggests that it is our moral and social duty to regulate a person's habits in the name of good health. Do you agree? Explain. If you agree that certain behaviors should be legally controlled for the good of society, what limits, if any, would you place on government's ability to regulate personal behavior?

Note: Writing assignments for this selection appear on pages 627–628.

Check Your Performance   CRITICAL READING

Activity		Number Right	Points	Score
Review Test 1	(10 items)	_____	× 2.5 =	_____
Review Test 2	(10 items)	_____	× 2.5 =	_____
Review Test 3	(10 items)	_____	× 2.5 =	_____
Review Test 4	(10 items)	_____	× 2.5 =	_____
			TOTAL SCORE =	_____%

Enter your total score into the **Reading Performance Chart: Review Tests** on the inside back cover.

CRITICAL READING: Mastery Test 1 (Fact and Opinion)

A. Identify facts with an **F**, opinions with an **O**, and the **one** combination of fact *and* opinion with an **F+O**.

_____ 1. Local TV news shows devote too much coverage to violent crimes, accidents, and fires.

_____ 2. The percentage of people who get their news from the Internet is rising, while the percentage of broadcast-news viewers is declining.

_____ 3. High-school students should be required to study a foreign language.

_____ 4. Although it is now considered a "dead" language, Latin was the language of the Roman Empire and later, the Roman Catholic Church.

_____ 5. Some American presidents were large men: Grover Cleveland's nieces and nephews called him "Uncle Jumbo," and William Howard Taft tipped the scales at 330 pounds.

_____ 6. Both Grover Cleveland and William Howard Taft rank as above-average presidents.

_____ 7. The core of a pencil is made out of graphite and clay, not lead.

_____ 8. It is always better to use a ball-point pen rather than a pencil when taking notes in class.

_____ 9. In the late 1800s, it was common for American children under fifteen to work in mines, in factories, and in the homes of the wealthy.

_____ 10. In the 20th century, child labor laws put a stop to such outrageous practices as having five-year-olds working sixteen-hour days.

(Continues on next page)

B. Identify facts with an **F**, opinions with an **O**, and the **one** combination of fact *and* opinion with an **F+O**.

_____ 11. Cats are much easier to care for than dogs.

_____ 12. A cat once fell from a building's twentieth floor and suffered only a pelvic fracture.

_____ 13. The Model T Ford was the most significant invention of the twentieth century.

_____ 14. In 1924, the Model T Ford could be purchased for $290.

_____ 15. Bessie Smith, known as the "empress of the blues," was killed in a car accident in 1937.

_____ 16. No singer alive today can sing the blues better than Bessie Smith did.

_____ 17. The first bathing suits for women were created in the mid-1800s.

_____ 18. Invented by a man, they were ridiculous-looking, high-necked costumes that included knee-length skirts, elbow-length sleeves, black stockings, and shoes.

_____ 19. Once such suits became wet, they could weigh as much as the bather, and there is evidence they may have caused drowning on more than one occasion.

_____ 20. Only a man could have invented something quite so impractical for women.

CRITICAL READING: Mastery Test 2 (Fact and Opinion)

A. Identify facts with an **F**, opinions with an **O**, and the **one** combination of fact *and* opinion with an **F+O**.

_____ 1. The globefish keeps from being eaten by gulping so much water that it becomes too large to be swallowed by its enemies.

_____ 2. The globefish is nature's strangest creature.

_____ 3. Comic strips are never suitable reading for young children.

_____ 4. In 1907, the *San Francisco Chronicle* began publishing the first daily comic strip—"Mr. Mutt," later named "Mutt and Jeff."

_____ 5. Sushi, a Japanese dish, usually consists of rice and uncooked fish.

_____ 6. People who refuse to eat sushi are missing a delicious taste experience.

_____ 7. Americans have become much too concerned about material success and owning things.

_____ 8. Studies show that Americans use as much as 50 percent of their paychecks to pay back consumer loans.

_____ 9. For their clothing alone, consumers each year pay out millions of dollars, dollars that should go instead to such worthy projects as health care research and housing for the homeless.

_____ 10. It is time for Americans to become less selfish and contribute more to the community.

(Continues on next page)

B. Identify facts with an **F**, opinions with an **O**, and the **one** combination of fact *and* opinion with an **F+O**.

_____ 11. Organ transplantation is the most important medical achievement of the twentieth century.

_____ 12. Through transplants, more than two thousand people each year receive a heart that once belonged to someone else.

_____ 13. In the Middle Ages, it was commonly believed that the seat of human intelligence was the heart.

_____ 14. The Middle Ages was the worst time to be alive; for example, in the mid-fourteenth century, bubonic plague killed millions of people.

_____ 15. During the Middle Ages, it was mainly the clergy that could read and write; most other people—including royalty—did not have these skills.

_____ 16. Because of its location on the San Andreas Fault, San Francisco experienced several major earthquakes in the 1800s.

_____ 17. Due to its stunning location and magnificent architecture, San Francisco is the most beautiful city in America.

_____ 18. Bram Stoker's *Dracula* begins with the story of Jonathan Harker, a young English lawyer hired by Count Dracula.

_____ 19. After he arrives at Dracula's castle in Transylvania, Jonathan finds himself the prisoner of the Count, who he slowly realizes is a bloodthirsty vampire.

_____ 20. From that point on, the reader will find it impossible to stop reading what is clearly the most enjoyably scary horror story of all time.

CRITICAL READING: Mastery Test 3 (Propaganda Techniques)

A. Each pair of items below illustrates a particular propaganda technique. On the line next to each pair, write the letter of the main technique being used.

_____ 1. ● The inventor of an artificial heart encourages people at risk of heart disease to try a drug which lowers cholesterol.

● "I get each day off to a roaring start with Zip breakfast cereal," says champion stock car racer Miles Leonard.

    A. Testimonial   C. Bandwagon
    B. Plain folks   D. Name calling

_____ 2. ● A man in painter's overalls is dipping his brush into a can of Olsen Paint. "Most of the week I'm president of Olsen Paint," he says. "On Saturdays, I'm a housepainter myself. So I know what people look for in a quality house paint."

● "I shop for my family's wardrobe at Wilson's Department Store. I want good values, not necessarily designer labels," says Anna Hendricks, bank clerk and homemaker.

    A. Transfer   C. Bandwagon
    B. Name calling   D. Plain folks

_____ 3. ● After six terms, the incumbent, Representative Lou Snark, is part of the pampered Washington crowd, out of touch with the people who elected him. Vote for Loretta Reese!

● Unlike some other brands of dog food which contain artificial "fillers," Hearty Dog contains wholesome, all-natural ingredients.

    A. Transfer   C. Bandwagon
    B. Name calling   D. Plain folks

_____ 4. ● The U.S. Heritage Committee has selected Bubble-O as the official soft drink of the Heritage Celebration to be held in the nation's capital this summer. Bubble-O: an important part of your heritage.

● A beautiful, nearly nude model lies on blue satin sheets in an ad for a skin care product containing cocoa butter.

    A. Plain folks   C. Bandwagon
    B. Glittering generalities   D. Transfer

(Continues on next page)

_____ 5. ● A Pacekeeper pickup truck is climbing a dirt road in the desert. "Pacekeeper," says the announcer. "The perfect vehicle to drive you into a new century."

   ● Buy your next suit at West's Tall Men's Store, and you'll be walking tall.

   A. Plain folks   C. Bandwagon
   B. Glittering generalities   D. Transfer

_____ 6. ● Don't miss out on the vacation cruise enjoyed by thousands of travelers. Ask your agent for details about Sea Fair's very popular tour of the Caribbean.

   ● You can be part of the growing number of people who are saying "No" to drugs and "Yes" to achievement. Be part of the crowd that makes a difference.

   A. Testimonial   C. Bandwagon
   B. Plain folks   D. Glittering generalities

B. Below are descriptions of four actual ads. On each line, write the letter of the main propaganda technique that applies to the ad.

A Bandwagon	D Plain folks
B Testimonial	E Name calling
C Transfer	F Glittering generalities

_____ 7. An ad for Tide laundry detergent features a cute little girl wearing a star-spangled red, white, and blue dress. "Stay true to her reds, whites, blues, and everything in between," reads the ad.

_____ 8. An ad for Bermuda tourism proclaims: "Bermuda: Feel the love."

_____ 9. A TV commercial for the Showboat casino shows crowds of people enjoying themselves around various gaming tables and asks the question, "Showboat . . . who _doesn't_ want to play?"

_____ 10. Actress Sally Field urges post-menopausal women to take Boniva to build strong, healthy bones.

CRITICAL READING: Mastery Test 4 (Propaganda Techniques)

A. Each pair of items below illustrates a particular propaganda technique. On the line next to each pair, write the letter of the main technique being used.

_____ 1. ● An ad for NyQuil Cough Syrup says, "Unlike those cough medicines you take every four hours, NyQuil Cough Syrup is made to last through the night."

● Sal's Pizza is like the thick cardboard we use to wrap take-home orders of Cheesy Pizza. Eat Cheesy Pizza if you're a pizza lover; eat Sal's if you love cardboard.

    A. Glittering generalities   C. Testimonial
    B. Name calling   D. Plain folks

_____ 2. ● A cable company advertises that more and more people are making the switch to its cable service.

● A small group comes onto a crowded beach carrying buckets of Deep Southern brand fried chicken. Other people nearby notice the group, leave, and come back with buckets of Deep Southern fried chicken. Soon everyone on the beach is either eating Deep Southern or going to get some.

    A. Glittering generalities   C. Transfer
    B. Name calling   D. Bandwagon

_____ 3. ● Try Choco-Chip Cookies—the cookies with goodness that doesn't quit.

● An Arnold Autofocus camera is the camera of your dreams. This delightful camera will make all your photography a pleasure. You'll love your new Arnold Autofocus.

    A. Glittering generalities   C. Transfer
    B. Name calling   D. Bandwagon

_____ 4. ● We cannot tell a lie—we honor America's presidents with beauty and savings. Come to Cherry Tree Carpets to see the amazing quality and discounts at our Presidents' Day Sale.

● An ad for a brand of cigarettes shows a hip young couple performing a graceful dance move.

    A. Glittering generalities   C. Transfer
    B. Name calling   D. Bandwagon

(Continues on next page)

_____ 5. ● "Out here in farm country, I work hard and live simply," says a farmer. "I don't look for fancy, but I do require quality. That's why, for everyday down-home toughness, I drive a Wellbilt truck."

● A big-city mayoral candidate is shown dropping off his daughter at the public school she attends in that city.

   A. Glittering generalities   C. Testimonial
   B. Name calling   D. Plain folks

_____ 6. ● Movie star Brad Clooney says, "I think this is the most entertaining movie I've ever been part of."

● Television actress Tamara Archer encourages overweight women to try the diet system that helped her shed seventy-five pounds.

   A. Glittering generalities   C. Testimonial
   B. Name calling   D. Plain folks

B. Below are descriptions of four actual ads. On each line, write the letter of the main propaganda technique that applies to the ad.

A	Bandwagon	D	Plain folks
B	Testimonial	E	Name calling
C	Transfer	F	Glittering generalities

_____ 7. What is it about owning a Weber grill that can make you wear your heart on your sleeve? Everything. From the thoughtful design to the careful construction to the way it treats your $40 filets, it all adds up to an ownership experience as beautiful as the grill itself. That's why millions of people around the world love their Weber grills.

_____ 8. A picture of a new-model Jeep simply states, "Jeep: There's only one."

_____ 9. In an ad for Samsung televisions, a beautiful young woman in a slinky black dress looks at a television which features Samsung's new black-screen technology.

_____ 10. Actor James Brolin is shown with a bottle of Flex-a-min dietary supplement. He says, "I have a pretty active lifestyle, and I can't let sore, stiff joints slow me down. So I take Flex-a-min every day. It works for me."

CRITICAL READING: Mastery Test 5 (Errors in Reasoning)

A. Each pair of items below illustrates a particular error in reasoning. On the line next to each pair, write the letter of the logical fallacy contained in both items. Choose from the three fallacies shown in the box below.

> A **Circular reasoning** (*a statement repeats itself rather than providing a real supporting reason to back up an argument*)
>
> B **Personal attack** (*ignores the issue under discussion and concentrates instead on the character of the opponent*)
>
> C **Straw man** (*an argument is made by claiming an opponent holds an extreme position and then opposing that extreme position*)

_____ 1. ● Governor Donovan's views on higher education are worthless. His own son dropped out of college.

  ● Ms. Jones is an atheist and should not be hired as a math teacher.

_____ 2. ● My neighbor Fred didn't support our invasion of Iraq. He obviously doesn't care if the terrorists attack us again.

  ● A local association wants to establish a halfway house for former mental patients in our neighborhood. But the neighbors oppose the idea; they say they don't want dangerous psychopaths roaming our streets.

_____ 3. ● Ronald Reagan was a great president because he was so effective in office.

  ● The government should raise the minimum wage because the minimum wage today is entirely too low.

_____ 4. ● Our congressman supports gay rights. How can he dare consider himself a Christian?

  ● I would never vote for Sarah Ratcliffe for mayor. Her own daughter was convicted of drinking and driving.

_____ 5. ● People should not wear fur coats because it's the wrong thing to do.

  ● Football is fun to watch because it's such an enjoyable game.

(Continues on next page)

B. In the space provided, write the letter of the fallacy contained in each pair of arguments. Choose from the three fallacies shown in the box below.

> A   **False cause** *(the argument assumes that the order of events alone shows cause and effect)*
>
> B   **False comparison** *(the argument assumes that two things being compared are more alike than they really are)*
>
> C   **Either-or** *(the argument assumes that there are only two sides to a question)*

_____ 6. ● Is he a good doctor, or did he get his medical degree overseas?

   ● Young people must choose between a career that will help their fellow human beings and one that will earn them a decent living.

_____ 7. ● Back in my day, private-school teachers were allowed to give pupils who misbehaved a good whack with a ruler, so I don't see why teachers today can't do the same.

   ● Children are like flowers—you only have to feed them and let them have plenty of sunshine, and they'll grow up hardy and beautiful.

_____ 8. ● My son is failing algebra. Evidently his teacher, Mr. Williamson, isn't doing a good job.

   ● A month after the president took office, the stock market went into a tailspin. I don't think he knows the first thing about managing the economy.

_____ 9. ● Are you going bar-hopping with us, or are you going to chicken out?

   ● You'll either have to get a good job soon or face the fact that you'll never be successful.

_____ 10. ● Ever since the new mayor took office, our town has had a string of burglaries. He must be soft on crime.

   ● The day Rosa wore her pink crystal bracelet, she finished first in the 100-meter run. Now she plans to wear that bracelet every time she races.

CRITICAL READING: Mastery Test 6 (Errors in Reasoning)

A. Each pair of items below illustrates a particular error in reasoning. On the line next to each pair, write the letter of the logical fallacy contained in both items. Choose from the three fallacies shown in the box below.

> **A** **Circular reasoning** (*a statement repeats itself rather than providing a real supporting reason to back up an argument*)
>
> **B** **Personal attack** (*ignores the issue under discussion and concentrates instead on the character of the opponent*)
>
> **C** **Straw man** (*an argument is made by claiming an opponent holds an extreme position and then opposing that extreme position*)

_____ 1. ● George wants the firm to hire more women and minorities. He doesn't seem to care how qualified our workers are.

   ● Anthony is in favor of building the new sports arena just a few blocks from here. He must not care if gangs of roughnecks trash our neighborhood.

_____ 2. ● I would never vote for Gary Blakely for Congress. At one time, he was being treated for depression.

   ● Councilman Hawkins is wholly unqualified to be elected mayor. Everyone knows he's been cheating on his wife.

_____ 3. ● Hank Aaron was one of the greatest baseball players of all time because he had great athletic ability.

   ● Todd is so cheap because he absolutely refuses to spend money on anything.

_____ 4. ● Senator Meyer's position on health care is nonsense. I understand his own wife suffered a nervous breakdown.

   ● Who can take Jake Green's argument for raising the sales tax seriously? Judging by the age of his wardrobe and car, the man hasn't paid a sales tax himself in decades.

_____ 5. ● Governor Rudolph favors tightening fuel efficiency standards on new vehicles. What does he want to do, bankrupt the whole American auto industry?

   ● My brother-in-law is opposed to the building of a new Wal-Mart outside of town. Evidently he wants to make it even harder for our young people to get jobs.

(Continues on next page)

B. In the space provided, write the letter of the fallacy contained in each pair of arguments. Choose from the three fallacies shown in the box below.

> **A** **False cause** *(the argument assumes that the order of events alone shows cause and effect)*
>
> **B** **False comparison** *(the argument assumes that two things being compared are more alike than they really are)*
>
> **C** **Either-or** *(the argument assumes that there are only two sides to a question)*

_____ 6. ● I did well on the finals last semester after having Oreos for breakfast. I must remember to buy a bag of Oreos before this semester's finals begin.

● I got a rash a couple of days after swimming in Jeremy's pool. That's the last time I swim there.

_____ 7. ● Mrs. Newhart didn't buy any Girl Scout cookies from my daughter. She must not believe in supporting a good cause.

● Do you support stricter gun control laws, or are you in favor of more tragedies like the mass shootings at the Aurora movie theater and Sandy Hook Elementary School?

_____ 8. ● When I was a kid, we never took our dogs and cats to the vet, so I don't see why my children shell out a lot of money to take their pets there.

● Back in my day, our teachers never went out on strike, so I don't know why teachers today feel they need to do so.

_____ 9. ● The houseplant I bought at Eden's Garden Center died a month after I bought it. They must be selling sickly plants.

● James is always reading, and now he needs glasses. That's what too much reading will do to you.

_____ 10. ● Unless you work out daily and carefully monitor your intake of fats, you're not really serious about staying in shape.

● Are you going to tell your girlfriend who's boss, or are you going to let her keep walking all over you?

Part Two

Ten Reading Selections

1 The Yellow Ribbon
Pete Hamill

Preview

When is a yellow handkerchief like a pair of open arms? For the answer, read this selection, which first appeared in a *New York Post* newspaper column by Pete Hamill. The story became the inspiration for the popular song "Tie a Yellow Ribbon 'Round the Old Oak Tree." This moving article probably also suggests the origin of using yellow ribbons as a symbol of America's wish to see her troops return home safely.

Words to Watch

cocoon (2): protective covering
bluntness (13): abruptness
exaltation (22): joy

1   They were going to Fort Lauderdale, the girl remembered later. There were six of them, three boys and three girls, and they picked up the bus at the old terminal on 34th Street, carrying sandwiches and wine in paper bags, dreaming of golden beaches and the tides of the sea as the gray cold spring of New York vanished behind them. Vingo was on board from the beginning.

2   As the bus passed through Jersey and into Philly, they began to notice that Vingo never moved. He sat in front of the young people, his dusty face masking his age, dressed in a plain brown ill-fitting suit. His fingers were stained from cigarettes and he chewed the inside of his lip a lot, frozen into some personal cocoon° of silence.

3   Somewhere outside of Washington, deep into the night, the bus pulled into a Howard Johnson's, and everybody got off except Vingo. He sat rooted in his seat, and the young people began to wonder about him, trying to imagine his life: Perhaps he was a sea captain, maybe he had run away from his wife, he could be an old soldier going home. When they went back to the bus, the girl sat beside him and introduced herself.

4   "We're going to Florida," the girl said brightly. "You going that far?"

5   "I don't know." Vingo said.

6   "I've never been there," she said. "I hear it's beautiful."

7   "It is," he said quietly, as if remembering something he had tried to forget.

8   "You live there?"

9   "I did some time there in the Navy. Jacksonville."

10   "Want some wine?" she said. He smiled and took the bottle of Chianti and took a swig. He thanked her and retreated again into his silence. After a while, she went back to the others, as Vingo nodded in sleep.

11   In the morning they awoke outside another Howard Johnson's, and this time Vingo went in. The girl insisted that he join them. He seemed very shy and ordered black coffee and smoked nervously, as the young people chattered about sleeping on the beaches. When they went back on the bus, the girl sat with Vingo again, and after a while, slowly and painfully and with great hesitation, he began to tell his story. He had been in jail in New York for the last four years, and now he was going home.

12   "Four years!" the girl said. "What did you do?"

13   "It doesn't matter," he said with quiet bluntness°. "I did it and I went to jail. If you can't do the time, don't do the crime. That's what they say and they're right."

14   "Are you married?"

15   "I don't know."

16   "You don't know?" she said.

17   "Well, when I was in the can I wrote to my wife," he said. "I told her, I said, Martha, I understand if you can't stay married to me. I told her that. I said I was gonna be away a long time, and that if she couldn't stand it, if the kids kept askin' questions, if it hurt her too much, well, she could just forget me. Get a new guy—she's a wonderful woman, really something—and forget about me. I told her she didn't have to write me or nothing. And she didn't. Not for three and a half years."

18   "And you're going home now, not knowing?"

19   "Yeah," he said shyly. "Well, last week, when I was sure the parole was coming through I wrote her. I told her that if she had a new guy, I understood. But if she didn't, if she would take me back, she should let me know. We used to live in this town, Brunswick, just before Jacksonville, and there's a great big oak tree just as you come into town, a very famous tree, huge. I told her if she would take me back, she should put a yellow handkerchief on the tree, and I would get off and come home. If she didn't want me, forget it, no handkerchief, and I'd keep going on through."

20   "Wow," the girl said. "Wow."

21   She told the others, and soon all of them were in it, caught up in the approach of Brunswick, looking at the pictures Vingo showed them of his wife and three children, the woman handsome in a plain way, the children still unformed in a cracked, much-handled

snapshot. Now they were twenty miles from Brunswick and the young people took over window seats on the right side, waiting for the approach of the great oak tree. Vingo stopped looking, tightening his face into the ex-con's mask, as if fortifying himself against still another disappointment. Then it was ten miles, and then five, and the bus acquired a dark hushed mood, full of silence, of absence, of lost years, of the woman's plain face, of the sudden letter on the breakfast table, of the wonder of children, of the iron bars of solitude.

22   Then suddenly all of the young people were up out of their seats, screaming and shouting and crying, doing small dances, shaking clenched fists in triumph and exaltation°. All except Vingo.

23   Vingo sat there stunned, looking at the oak tree. It was covered with yellow handkerchiefs, twenty of them, thirty of them, maybe hundreds, a tree that stood like a banner of welcome blowing and billowing in the wind, turned into a gorgeous yellow blur by the passing bus. As the young people shouted, the old con slowly rose from his seat, holding himself tightly, and made his way to the front of the bus to go home.

Basic Skill Questions

Vocabulary in Context

_____ 1. In the sentence below, the word *fortifying* (fôr′tə-fī′ĭng) means
A. strengthening.
B. watching.
C. hurrying.
D. losing.

"Vingo stopped looking, tightening his face into the ex-con's mask, as if fortifying himself against still another disappointment." (Paragraph 21)

_____ 2. In the excerpt below, the word *acquired* (ə-kwīrd′) means
- A. needed.
- B. took on.
- C. stopped.
- D. lost.

> "Then it was ten miles, and then five, and the bus acquired a dark hushed mood. . . ." (Paragraph 21)

Central Point and Main Ideas

_____ 3. Which sentence best expresses the main idea of this selection?
- A. Prison sentences can ruin marriages.
- B. If you commit a crime, you must pay for it.
- C. Vingo did not know what to expect.
- D. Vingo returned from prison to find that his wife still loved him.

_____ 4. Which sentence best expresses the main idea of paragraph 3?
- A. The bus stopped at a Howard Johnson's.
- B. The young people began to be curious about Vingo.
- C. Vingo might have been a sea captain.
- D. Everyone got off the bus except Vingo.

Supporting Details

_____ 5. TRUE OR FALSE? Vingo felt he should not have been put in prison.

Transitions

_____ 6. The relationship between the two sentences below is one of
- A. time.
- B. contrast.
- C. comparison.
- D. illustration.

> ". . . I told her that if she had a new guy, I understood. But if she didn't, if she would take me back, she should let me know." (Paragraph 19)

_____ 7. The transition words *as*, *when*, *after*, *now*, and *then*, which Hamill uses throughout this selection, all signal
- A. cause and effect.
- B. examples.
- C. contrast.
- D. time.

_____ 8. The relationship expressed in the phrase "a tree that stood like a banner of welcome" (paragraph 23) is one of
   A. contrast.
   B. comparison.
   C. cause and effect.
   D. time.

Patterns of Organization

_____ 9. The main pattern of organization of paragraph 2 is
   A. cause and effect.
   B. comparison and/or contrast.
   C. list of items.
   D. time order.

_____10. The main pattern of organization of the entire selection is
   A. cause and effect.
   B. comparison and/or contrast.
   C. list of items.
   D. time order.

Advanced Skill Questions

Inferences

_____11. We can infer that the young people were going to Florida
   A. on business.
   B. to visit relatives.
   C. on vacation.
   D. to get married.

_____12. The author implies that Vingo thought
   A. he would someday be in prison again.
   B. there might be no yellow handkerchief on the tree.
   C. his wife was wrong for not writing to him in prison.
   D. his wife was sure to want him back.

_____13. TRUE OR FALSE? The statement that Vingo "rose from his seat, holding himself tightly" (paragraph 23) implies that Vingo was trying to contain his emotions.

_____14. By telling us that the picture of Vingo's family was a "cracked, much-handled snapshot," the author implies that
   A. Vingo didn't know how to take good care of photos.
   B. the pictures were not really of Vingo's family.
   C. Vingo had looked at the snapshot a great deal while in jail.
   D. the photo was relatively new.

Purpose and Tone

_____15. The main purpose of "The Yellow Ribbon" is to
   A. inform readers that a convict's life can be rebuilt after prison.
   B. persuade readers to avoid a life of crime.
   C. entertain readers with a heartwarming story.

_____16. In paragraphs 17 through 21, the author's tone becomes increasingly
   A. bitter.
   B. amused.
   C. suspenseful.
   D. disbelieving.

Argument

_____17. Which of the following points is well supported by the evidence below?
   A. Vingo was nervous about something.
   B. Vingo was on the verge of a nervous breakdown.
   C. Vingo had a hostile personality.
   D. Vingo disliked young people.

> "[Vingo's] fingers were stained from cigarettes and he chewed the inside of his lip a lot, frozen into some personal cocoon of silence." (Paragraph 2)

_____18. Which statement does **not** support the following point?

Point: Vingo deserved the yellow handkerchiefs.

   A. He admitted his mistake.
   B. He paid for his crime by serving four years in jail.
   C. He probably caused his wife and children a lot of pain and embarrassment.
   D. He seemed to regret causing his wife pain.

Critical Reading

_____19. In telling this narrative, Hamill
  A. stresses his own opinions.
  B. leaves out any of Vingo's opinions.
  C. reveals the bus driver's opinions.
  D. reveals through the young people's actions how they feel about Vingo.

_____20. Judging by the first sentence of the selection, Hamill got some facts for this narrative by
  A. observing everything as a passenger on the bus ride.
  B. only imagining what might have happened on such a ride.
  C. interviewing at least one passenger.
  D. using a tape recording of the bus ride.

Summarizing

Following is an incomplete summary of "The Yellow Ribbon." In the space provided, write the letter (A, B, or C) of the item below that best completes the summary.

_____   A man named Vingo had just been released from prison and was on a bus headed home. Some young people were also on the bus, and they got Vingo to tell his story. He said he had written to his wife when he went to prison to explain he would understand if she found another man. He hadn't heard from her since but still loved her very much. So he recently wrote to her, telling her to put a yellow handkerchief on a well-known oak tree in town if she wanted him to come home. If the handkerchief wasn't on the tree, he wouldn't get off the bus there. . . .

  A. Vingo showed pictures of his wife and children to the young people, who got caught up in waiting to see the oak tree. As the bus got closer to Vingo's hometown, the bus became quiet and filled with suspense.
  B. The young people got caught up in Vingo's situation. After a tense ride to his hometown, he and his fellow travelers finally got his wife's answer: not one, but scores of handkerchiefs fluttering on the tree.
  C. Vingo would just continue on the bus to Florida, which is where the young people were going. He understood that while he was in prison, his wife might have started a new life for herself and their children.

Discussion Questions

1. According to the information in the selection, what is Vingo's attitude toward his wife?

2. Has Vingo assumed responsibility for his crime, in your opinion?

3. While there is much we don't learn about Vingo in this very short narrative, Hamill does provide us with clues to some important aspects of his personality. What evidence is there that he is a decent man, a person who we could feel deserves a second chance?

4. Many people are thrilled, some even to tears, by this story. Why do you think "The Yellow Ribbon" has such a powerful effect on readers?

Note: Writing assignments for this selection appear on page 629.

Check Your Performance		THE YELLOW RIBBON	
Activity	Number Right	Points	Score
Basic Skill Questions			
Vocabulary in Context (2 items)	_____	× 4 =	_____
Central Point and Main Ideas (2 items)	_____	× 4 =	_____
Supporting Details (1 item)	_____	× 4 =	_____
Transitions (3 items)	_____	× 4 =	_____
Patterns of Organization (2 items)	_____	× 4 =	_____
Advanced Skill Questions			
Inferences (4 items)	_____	× 4 =	_____
Purpose and Tone (2 items)	_____	× 4 =	_____
Argument (2 items)	_____	× 4 =	_____
Critical Reading (2 items)	_____	× 4 =	_____
Summarizing (1 item)	_____	× 20 =	_____
		TOTAL SCORE =	_____ %

Enter your total score into the **Reading Performance Chart: Ten Reading Selections** on the inside back cover.

2 College Athletes Should Be Paid

Ann Kaufmann

Preview

College athletics are hugely profitable—for the schools and the coaches. Is it right that the student-athletes remain unpaid? In this essay, Ann Kaufmann looks at the history of the college sports system, the justification for and against paying players, and some proposals for sharing the profits with the athletes who generate them.

Words to Watch

replicas (8): copies
compensation (9): money given to pay for loss, damage, or work done
contention (10): claim
chronic (14): long-lasting
royalties (15): percentages of income from the sale of something

1   Every fall hundreds of thousands of college football fans jam into stadiums throughout the United States, while millions more watch on TV. And every March, nearly 80 million people tune in to "March Madness," the National Collegiate Athletic Association's (NCAA's) men's college basketball championship tournament. Together, college football and men's basketball generate more than $6 billion in annual revenue—mostly through the sale of TV rights. Of this sum, the NCAA takes in nearly $800 million a year.

2   Because college football and men's basketball are so amazingly profitable, head football coaches at public universities earn on average more than $2 million a year. And top college basketball coaches routinely earn $4 million a year. Salaries for *assistant* coaches now commonly exceed $200,000, with some earning as much as $700,000.

3   Given these handsome salaries, how much do the players themselves earn? Well, if you follow college sports, you probably already know that these athletes aren't paid anything. In fact, they can be suspended for accepting so much as a free lunch from a fan. To do so would violate their status as amateurs, which the NCAA views as lying at the heart of college sports. According

to NCAA officials, the NCAA exists to protect college athletes from "excess commercialism."

4   However, in the past few years, critics have begun arguing that the NCAA doesn't protect college players. Rather, it cheats them out of the profits they help generate. The NCAA responds to this argument by pointing out that student athletes get something very valuable—athletic scholarships. But critics wonder just how much of a "gift" athletic scholarships actually are. Recent studies estimate that these scholarships fall on average about $3,500 short of the full cost of attending college annually. In addition, until very recently athletic scholarships had to be renewed every year. If an athlete "underperformed," was seriously injured, or even if he didn't fit into the offensive/defensive strategy of a new coach, there was a good chance his scholarship would be terminated. In October 2011, the NCAA began permitting colleges and universities to offer multiyear scholarships, but does not require them to do so. Some powerhouse schools, such as LSU, Alabama, and Texas, were opposed to this measure. Without the benefit of a four-year scholarship, college players can be "cut," just as if they were professional players.

5   Those opposed to the current system also challenge the notion that "student athletes" are getting a quality education. They point out that college football and basketball players often spend upwards of 50 hours a week during the season at their sport. Such an intense schedule makes it almost

impossible for them to take any but the easiest courses.

6   Of course, the "carrot" held out to these athletes is the dream of making it to the NFL or NBA. But for the vast majority of college athletes, the dream of a pro career is just a dream. Today, the NBA drafts only one percent of men's college basketball players, while two percent of football players make it to the NFL. And by the time most college athletes figure out that they're not going to make the pros, they're hopelessly behind academically. Rather than a "win/win" situation, what they face is a "lose/lose" situation: if they quit football or basketball to spend more time on their studies, they lose their athletic scholarships.

7   Desmond Howard, who won the 1991 Heisman Trophy while playing for the Michigan Wolverines, questions the current system. "You see everybody getting richer and richer," he says. "And you walk around and you can't put gas in your car? You can't even fly home to see your parents?"

8   Not surprisingly, college players

are sometimes tempted to take money "under the table." At the start of the 2010 football season, A. J. Green, a wide receiver at Georgia, confessed that he'd sold his own team jersey from a bowl game the year before, to raise cash for a spring-break vacation. While Green served a four-game suspension for violating his amateur status, the Georgia Bulldogs store profited by selling replicas° of his jersey for $39.95 and up. The NCAA banned the University of Southern California (USC) from taking part in bowl games in 2010 and 2011 because star running back Reggie Bush had accepted gifts from agents several years earlier. And in 2011, a University of Miami booster was found to have provided dozens of University of Miami football players with money, cars, and even prostitutes. Every year brings similar scandals.

9   Although the NCAA punishes players for accepting cash and gifts, civil rights historian Taylor Branch views the NCAA itself as the true villain of college sports. According to Branch, "The tragedy at the heart of college sports is not that some college athletes are getting paid, but that more of them are not." In fact, Branch challenges the whole concept of "student athletes." He sees this term as a thinly disguised way to keep athletes from being able to sue for workers' compensation° if they are injured playing for their college or university. Because they are "student athletes," they are denied the basic rights of other university employees.

10   Joe Nocera, a columnist for the *New York Times*, also makes a strong case for why men's college football and basketball players should be paid. As he puts it, "The NCAA's . . . contention° that it is protecting the players from 'excessive commercialism' is ludicrous; the only thing it's protecting is everyone else's revenue stream." To Nocera it's a simple matter of justice that college athletes should share in the wealth. To accomplish that goal, he lays out a plan for paying them a fair portion of the enormous profits they help generate.

11   Nocera's plan consists of five elements. The first element would require college coaches to offer athletes real contracts, just as professional teams do. One college or university might think a star halfback is worth $40,000 a year; another might think he's worth $60,000. When a player chooses a school, he and his recruiters would automatically discuss money.

12   The second element in the plan is a salary cap for every team, along with a minimum annual salary for every scholarship athlete. A salary cap would equalize the amount every team could pay its players. Thus, it would prevent super-rich athletic departments, such as those at the University of Texas and Oklahoma State, from recruiting all the top players. Nocera proposes a $3 million salary cap for the football team and $650,000 for the basketball team. The minimum salary would be $25,000 per athlete. Critics of Nocera's plan point out that smaller schools may not be able to pay their athletes these sums. That's probably true. According to Nocera, schools that truly couldn't afford to pay their players would be forced to

cut back on their football and men's basketball programs. Who knows? They might even return to their basic mission of educating students.

13   The third element would be that every player who stays in school for four years would also get an additional two-year scholarship. He could use this scholarship to either complete his bachelor's degree or get a master's degree. A six-year scholarship would allow players to take fewer courses during their years of athletic eligibility. As a result, they would stand a better chance of succeeding at the courses they do take. It would also enable those players who do graduate within four years to pursue a graduate degree. This focus on academics would better prepare athletes for a future without football or basketball. The days of *having* to major in physical education just because it's easy would be gone.

14   The fourth element of the plan is that each player would have lifetime health insurance. As things now stand, if a college football player or basketball player is injured while playing sports, the college has no legal responsibility to pay his medical bills. And many former college football players suffer chronic° pain by the time they are in their thirties—due to the punishment their bodies took while playing college ball.

15   The fifth element is that an organization would be created to represent both current and former college athletes. This organization might take the form of a players' union, which would manage the health insurance, bargain with the NCAA to set the salary caps and salary minimums, pay out royalties°, and serve as an all-around counterweight to the NCAA.

16   Will Nocera's plan ever become a reality? Some doubt it. However, a lawsuit called the O'Bannon case now threatens the NCAA's longstanding refusal to pay its players. The case is named after the lead plaintiff, Ed O'Bannon, who led UCLA to a national basketball title in 1995. The other plaintiffs include basketball greats Oscar Robertson and Bill Russell. Together they are suing the NCAA for licensing their images without compensating them. If the NCAA loses, the decision could lead to a "restructuring" of the relationship between college athletes and the NCAA. Who knows? It might eventually lead to paying the players.

17   Some protest that doing away with amateurism would ruin the college "brand." But amateurism isn't the reason fans love college sports. What they love is cheering on the teams that represent their schools. That would be just as true if the athletes were being paid. It's a similar situation to what happened with the Olympics. Years ago, only amateur athletes could take part in the Olympics. And what happened when pro athletes finally could take part? The Olympics only got better.

18   Others argue that if colleges began to pay football and men's basketball players, then they would have to pay athletes who play other sports, such as wrestling, lacrosse, and tennis. But college football and men's basketball aren't like other college sports. Because of the huge profits they generate, college

football and men's basketball players should be considered employees as well as students. As James Duderstadt, the former president of the University of Michigan, put it, "Most sports can be justified as part of what a university does. But big-time football and men's basketball are clearly commercial entertainment and have been pulled away from the fundamental purpose of a university."

Paying college football and men's 19 basketball players would cause the vast majority of the "under the table" payment scandals to go away. Rather than being the only ones *not* to profit from the enormous revenues they generate, these athletes would at long last receive a slice of the pie. Let's do the right thing and give it to them.

Basic Skill Questions

Vocabulary in Context

_____ 1. In the excerpt below, the word *violate* (vī′ə-lāt′) means
   A. support.
   B. go against.
   C. increase.
   D. determine.

> "In fact, they can be suspended for accepting so much as a free lunch from a fan. To do so would violate their status as amateurs, which the NCAA views as lying at the heart of college sports." (Paragraph 3)

_____ 2. In the excerpt below, the word *ludicrous* (lōō′dĭ-krəs) means
   A. sensible.
   B. ridiculous.
   C. common.
   D. worthy of thoughtful discussion.

> "As he puts it, 'The NCAA's . . . contention that it is protecting the players from "excessive commercialism" is ludicrous; the only thing it's protecting is everyone else's revenue stream.'" (Paragraph 10)

Central Point and Main Ideas

_____ 3. Which sentence best expresses the central point of the selection?
- A. Just as the Olympics improved when its athletes were paid, college football and men's basketball would improve if its athletes were paid.
- B. Because college football and men's basketball are so demanding and so profitable, the athletes who play them should be paid.
- C. It's wrong that college football and men's basketball coaches get paid huge salaries while their players receive only scholarships that don't even cover the full cost of attending college.
- D. *New York Times* columnist Joe Nocera has offered a plan for making college football and men's basketball more fair to the players.

_____ 4. Which sentence best expresses the main idea of paragraph 4?
- A. Colleges and universities have recently started to offer athletes multiyear scholarships.
- B. The NCAA harms college athletes more than it helps them.
- C. Athletic scholarships aren't as great a gift as the NCAA claims they are.
- D. Without the benefit of a four-year scholarship, college players can be "cut," just as if they were professional players.

_____ 5. Which sentence best expresses the main idea of paragraphs 5–6?
- A. It's wrong to hold out to college athletes the dream of making it to the NFL or NBA.
- B. The great majority of college football and men's basketball players never make it to the professional level and also don't get a quality education.
- C. Because college football and basketball players practice so much, they don't have time to take any but the easiest courses.
- D. By the time college athletes figure out they're not going to make the pros, they're far behind academically.

Supporting Details

_____ 6. TRUE OR FALSE? The NCAA currently requires colleges and universities to offer athletes four-year scholarships.

_____ 7. One part of Joe Nocera's plan is to
   A. provide money to small schools that otherwise couldn't afford to pay their athletes.
   B. make it easier for super-rich athletic departments to pay athletes more money than other schools.
   C. require colleges to pay small salaries to wrestling, lacrosse, and tennis players as well as larger salaries to football and basketball players.
   D. offer six-year scholarships to athletes who stay in school for four years.

_____ 8. The plaintiffs in the O'Bannon case are suing the NCAA for
   A. not providing workmen's compensation to them when they were injured.
   B. refusing to pay their health insurance.
   C. licensing their images without paying them.
   D. selling replicas of their college uniforms without paying them royalties.

Transitions

_____ 9. The sentences below express a relationship of
   A. comparison.
   B. cause and effect.
   C. contrast.
   D. time.

   "However, in the past few years critics have begun arguing that the NCAA doesn't protect college players. Rather, it cheats them out of the profits they help generate." (Paragraph 4)

Patterns of Organization

_____10. Paragraphs 11–15
   A. list the major points in a plan to pay college football and men's basketball players.
   B. compare and contrast how college football and basketball players will be paid at large schools with how they will be paid at small schools.
   C. give reasons why college football and basketball players should be paid.
   D. provide step-by-step directions for setting up a system for paying college athletes.

Advanced Skill Questions

Inferences

_____11. Paragraphs 1–3 suggest that
   A. college football and basketball coaches are overpaid.
   B. excess commercialism is harming college sports.
   C. college football and men's basketball are already extremely commercial.
   D. college football and men's basketball have not always been as profitable as they are today.

_____12. On the basis of paragraph 6, we can infer that
   A. making it to the pros is a realistic goal for many college football and basketball players.
   B. those people who encourage college athletes to dream of making it to the NFL or NBA are guilty of manipulating the athletes.
   C. most college football and men's basketball players should quit their sport so that they can spend time on their studies.
   D. most college athletes spend more time dreaming of making it to the NFL or NBA than working hard to get there.

_____13. We can conclude from paragraphs 7–8 that
   A. most college football players have enough spending money.
   B. most college football players take money "under the table."
   C. the NCAA tends to "look the other way" rather than punish players for accepting cash and gifts.
   D. because they aren't paid, some college athletes feel there is nothing wrong with taking "under the table" payments.

_____14. Paragraph 9 suggests that Taylor Branch
   A. believes that only college football and men's basketball players have the right to be called "student athletes."
   B. believes that the NCAA should be disbanded.
   C. used to play college football himself.
   D. views the situation of student athletes as a civil rights issue.

Purpose and Tone

_____15. The main purpose of this article is to
   A. inform readers that college football and men's basketball players are being unfairly treated.
   B. persuade readers to support a plan to pay college football and men's basketball players.
   C. entertain readers with stories about the difficulties facing student athletes.

_____16. Desmond Howard's tone in paragraph 7 can be described as
      A. indignant.
      B. straightforward.
      C. humorous.
      D. revengeful.

_____17. The overall tone of the selection can be described as
      A. matter-of-fact.
      B. concerned.
      C. detached.
      D. pleading.

Argument

_____18. Write the letter of the statement that is the point of the following argument. The other statements are support for that point.
      A. Because college football and men's basketball players have to spend so much time practicing, they are not prepared for a future without football or basketball.
      B. Today, only one percent of men's college basketball players make it to the NBA, while only two percent of college football players make it to the NFL.
      C. Receiving a scholarship to play college football or basketball is not necessarily a ticket to a bright future.
      D. One-year scholarships can be terminated if an athlete underperforms, is seriously injured, or doesn't fit in with the offensive/defensive strategy of a new coach.

_____19. Write the letter of the statement that is the point of the following argument. The other statements are support for that point.
      A. The NCAA does not really care about the well-being of college football and men's basketball players.
      B. Although the NCAA takes in nearly $800 million a year, it suspends college athletes who accept "under the table" payments.
      C. Because they are termed "student athletes," college football and basketball players cannot sue their colleges and universities for worker's compensation.
      D. The NCAA routinely licenses images of college athletes without compensating them.

Critical Reading

_____20. Someone who argues that college football and men's basketball players should not be paid because they are amateurs is illustrating the logical fallacy of
  A. straw man.
  B. circular reasoning.
  C. either-or.
  D. false cause.

Outlining

The following outline of paragraphs 11–15 of "College Athletes Should Be Paid" is missing two major supporting details and three minor supporting details. Complete the outline by filling in the missing details, which are listed after the outline.

Central point: *New York Times* columnist Joe Nocera has laid out a plan for paying college athletes a fair share of the enormous profits they help generate.

A. College football and men's basketball players would be offered real contracts.
  1. Salaries for a halfback might range from $40,000 to $60,000.
  2. Recruiters would discuss money with prospective student-athletes.

B. _____
  1. _____
  2. Salaries would be capped at $3 million for the football team and $650,000 for the basketball team.
  3. _____
  _____
  4. Schools that couldn't afford to pay their players would be forced to cut back on football and men's basketball.

C. Every player who stays in school for four years would receive an additional two-year scholarship.
  1. A player could either complete his bachelor's degree or use this scholarship to get a master's degree.
  2. _____
  _____
  _____

D. _____

E. An organization would be created to represent both current and former athletes.
  1. It would take the form of a players' union.
  2. Organization would manage health insurance, bargain with the NCAA to set salary caps and minimums, pay out royalties, and serve as all-around counterweight to the NCAA.

Items Missing from the Outline

- Every player would receive lifetime health insurance.
- The salary cap would prevent super-rich athletic departments from recruiting all the top players.
- Every team would have a salary cap.
- The minimum salary would be $25,000 per athlete.
- Players could take fewer courses during their years of athletic eligibility and have a better chance to succeed at the courses they do take.

Discussion Questions

1. Do you know of anyone who received a scholarship to play college football or men's basketball? If so, was this person's college career successful? Why or why not?

2. Historian Taylor Branch states that it is tragic that college football and men's basketball players are not paid. Do you agree or disagree? Explain.

3. According to Joe Nocera, schools that truly couldn't afford to pay their players would be forced to cut back on their football and men's basketball programs. Do you agree or disagree that some colleges should de-emphasize college football and men's basketball? Who might benefit if they did so? Who might lose out?

4. As the selection indicates, college football and men's basketball are enormously popular—and profitable. Overall, do you think our country's "love affair" with these sports is a good thing, a bad thing, or maybe a little of both? Explain.

Note: Writing assignments for this selection appear on page 630.

Check Your Performance   COLLEGE ATHLETES SHOULD BE PAID

Activity	Number Right	Points	Score
Basic Skill Questions			
Vocabulary in Context (2 items)	_____	× 4 =	_____
Central Point and Main Ideas (3 items)	_____	× 4 =	_____
Supporting Details (3 items)	_____	× 4 =	_____
Transitions (1 item)	_____	× 4 =	_____
Patterns of Organization (1 item)	_____	× 4 =	_____
Advanced Skill Questions			
Inferences (4 items)	_____	× 4 =	_____
Purpose and Tone (3 items)	_____	× 4 =	_____
Argument (2 items)	_____	× 4 =	_____
Critical Reading (1 item)	_____	× 4 =	_____
Outlining (5 items)	_____	× 4 =	_____
		TOTAL SCORE =	_____%

Enter your total score into the **Reading Performance Chart: Ten Reading Selections** on the inside back cover.

3 Shame

Dick Gregory

Preview

When we receive help, most of us feel grateful. But what if the help is given in an inconsiderate way? In this autobiographical piece, the comedian and social activist Dick Gregory shows that the good intentions of a giver are not enough if they don't take the recipient's pride into account.

Words to Watch

light-complected (1): light-skinned
stoop (2): an outside stairway, porch, or platform at the entrance to a house
mackinaw (28): a short, plaid coat or jacket
googobs (29): Gregory's slang for *gobs*, a large amount

1   I never learned hate at home, or shame. I had to go to school for that. I was about seven years old when I got my first big lesson. I was in love with a little girl named Helene Tucker, a light-complected° little girl with pigtails and nice manners. She was always clean and she was smart in school. I think I went to school then mostly to look at her. I brushed my hair and even got me a little old handkerchief. It was a lady's handkerchief, but I didn't want Helene to see me wipe my nose on my hand. The pipes were frozen again, there was no water in the house, but I washed my socks and shirt every night. I'd get a pot, and go over to Mister Ben's grocery store, and stick my pot down into his soda machine. Scoop out some chopped ice. By evening the ice melted to water for washing. I got sick a lot that winter because the fire would go out at night before the clothes were dry. In the morning I'd put them on, wet or dry, because they were the only clothes I had.

2   Everybody's got a Helene Tucker, a symbol of everything you want. I loved her for her goodness, her cleanness, her popularity. She'd walk down my street and my brothers and sisters would yell, "Here comes Helene," and I'd rub my tennis sneakers* on the back of my pants and wish my hair wasn't so nappy and the white folks' shirt fit me better. I'd run out on the street. If I knew my place and didn't come too close, she'd wink at me and say hello. That was a good feeling. Sometimes I'd follow her

_____

* All sneakers used to be called "tennis sneakers."

463

all the way home, and shovel the snow off her walk and try to make friends with her Momma and her aunts. I'd drop money on her stoop° late at night on my way back from shining shoes in the taverns. And she had a Daddy, and he had a good job. He was a paper hanger.

3   I guess I would have gotten over Helene by summertime, but something happened in that classroom that made her face hang in front of me for the next twenty-two years. When I played the drums in high school it was for Helene and when I broke track records in college it was for Helene and when I started standing behind microphones and heard applause I wished Helene could hear it, too. It wasn't until I was twenty-nine years old and married and making money that I finally got her out of my system. Helene was sitting in that classroom when I learned to be ashamed of myself.

4   It was on a Thursday. I was sitting in the back of the room, in a seat with a chalk circle drawn around it. The idiot's seat, the troublemaker's seat.

5   The teacher thought I was stupid. Couldn't spell, couldn't read, couldn't do arithmetic. Just stupid. Teachers were never interested in finding out that you couldn't concentrate because you were so hungry, because you hadn't had any breakfast. All you could think about was noontime, would it ever come? Maybe you could sneak into the cloakroom and steal a bite of some kid's lunch out of a coat pocket. A bite of something. Paste. You can't really make a meal of paste, or put it on bread for a sandwich, but sometimes I'd scoop a few spoonfuls out of the big paste jar in the back of the room. Pregnant people get strange tastes. I was pregnant with poverty. Pregnant with dirt and pregnant with smells that made people turn away, pregnant with cold and pregnant with shoes that were never bought for me, pregnant with five other people in my bed and no Daddy in the next room, and pregnant with hunger. Paste doesn't taste too bad when you're hungry.

6   The teacher thought I was a troublemaker. All she saw from the front of the room was a little black boy who squirmed in his idiot's seat and made noises and poked the kids around him. I guess she couldn't see a kid who made noises because he wanted someone to know he was there.

7   It was on a Thursday, the day before the Negro payday. The eagle always flew on Friday.* The teacher was asking each student how much his father would give

---

* In Gregory's day, ten-dollar bills were known as "eagles." On payday, people would have some ten-dollar bills to spend.

to the Community Chest*. On Friday night, each kid would get the money from his father, and on Monday he would bring it to the school. I decided I was going to buy a Daddy right then. I had money in my pocket from shining shoes and selling papers, and whatever Helene Tucker pledged for her Daddy, I was going to top it. And I'd hand the money right in. I wasn't going to wait until Monday to buy me a Daddy.

8 I was shaking, scared to death. The teacher opened her book and started calling out names alphabetically.

9 "Helene Tucker?"

10 "My Daddy said he'd give two dollars and fifty cents."

11 "That's very nice, Helene. Very, very nice indeed."

12 That made me feel pretty good. It wouldn't take too much to top that. I had almost three dollars in dimes and quarters in my pocket. I stuck my hand in my pocket and held onto the money, waiting for her to call my name. But the teacher closed her book after she called on everybody else in the class.

13 I stood up and raised my hand.

14 "What is it now?"

15 "You forgot me."

16 She turned toward the blackboard. "I don't have time to be playing with you, Richard."

17 "My Daddy said he'd . . . ."

18 "Sit down, Richard, you're disturbing the class."

19 "My Daddy said he'd give . . . fifteen dollars."

20 She turned around and looked mad. "We are collecting this money for you and your kind, Richard Gregory. If your Daddy can give fifteen dollars, you have no business being on relief*."

21 "I got it right now, I got it right now, my Daddy gave it to me to turn in today, my Daddy said . . . ."

22 "And furthermore," she said, looking right at me, her nostrils getting big and her lips getting thin and her eyes opening wide, "we know you don't have a Daddy."

23 Helene Tucker turned around, her eyes full of tears. She felt sorry for me. Then I couldn't see her too well because I was crying, too.

24 "Sit down, Richard."

25 And I always thought the teacher kind of liked me. She always picked me to wash the blackboard on Friday, after school. That was a big thrill, it made me feel important. If I didn't wash it, come Monday the school might not function right.

26 "Where are you going, Richard?"

27 I walked out of school that day, and for a long time I didn't go back very often. There was shame there.

28 Now there was shame everywhere. It seemed like the whole world had been inside that classroom, everyone had heard what the teacher had said, everyone had turned around and felt sorry for me. There was shame in going to the Worthy Boys Annual Christmas Dinner for you and your kind, because everybody knew what a worthy boy

---

* In Gregory's day, the charitable organization we call the United Way was known as the Community Chest.

* welfare

was. Why couldn't they just call it the Boys Annual Dinner, why'd they have to give it a name? There was shame in wearing the brown and orange and white plaid mackinaw° the welfare gave to three thousand boys. Why'd it have to be the same for everybody so when you walked down the street, the people could see you were on relief? It was a nice warm mackinaw and it had a hood, and my Momma beat me and called me a little rat when she found out I stuffed it in the bottom of a pail full of garbage way over on Cottage Street. There was shame in running over to Mister Ben's at the end of the day and asking for his rotten peaches, there was shame in asking Mrs. Simmons for a spoonful of sugar, there was shame in running out to meet the relief truck. I hated that truck, full of food for you and your kind. I ran into the house and hid when it came. And then I started to sneak through alleys, to take the long way home so the people going into White's Eat Shop wouldn't see me. Yeah, the whole world heard the teacher that day, we all know you don't have a Daddy.

29   It lasted for a while, this kind of numbness. I spent a lot of time feeling sorry for myself. And then one day I met this wino in a restaurant. I'd been out hustling all day, shining shoes, selling newspapers, and I had googobs° of money in my pocket. Bought me a bowl of chili for fifteen cents, and a cheeseburger for fifteen cents, and a Pepsi for five cents, and a piece of chocolate cake for ten cents. That was

a good meal. I was eating when this old wino came in. I love winos because they never hurt anyone but themselves.

The old wino sat down at the counter and ordered twenty-six cents' worth of food. He ate it like he really enjoyed it. When the owner, Mister Williams, asked him to pay the check, the old wino didn't lie or go through his pocket like he suddenly found a hole.   30

He just said: "Don't have no money."   31

The owner yelled: "Why in hell you come in here and eat my food if you don't have no money? That food cost me money."   32

Mister Williams jumped over the counter and knocked the wino off his stool and beat him over the head with a pop bottle. Then he stepped back and watched the wino bleed. Then he kicked him. And he kicked him again.   33

I looked at the wino with blood all over his face and I went over. "Leave him alone, Mister Williams. I'll pay the twenty-six cents."   34

The wino got up, slowly, pulling himself up to the stool, then up to the counter, holding on for a minute until his legs stopped shaking so bad. He looked at me with pure hate. "Keep your twenty-six cents. You don't have to pay, not now. I just finished paying for it."   35

He started to walk out, and as he passed me, he reached down and touched my shoulder. "Thanks, sonny, but it's too late now. Why didn't you pay it before?"   36

I was pretty sick about that. I waited too long to help another man.   37

Basic Skill Questions

Vocabulary in Context

_____ 1. In the excerpt below, the word *pledged* (plĕjd) means
   A. repeated.
   B. studied.
   C. promised to give.
   D. brought home.

> "I had money in my pocket . . . and whatever Helene Tucker pledged for her Daddy, I was going to top it." (Paragraph 7)

_____ 2. In the sentence below, the word *hustling* (hŭs′lĭng) means
   A. complaining.
   B. relaxing.
   C. studying hard.
   D. working energetically.

> "I'd been out hustling all day, shining shoes, selling newspapers, and I had googobs of money in my pocket." (Paragraph 29)

Central Point and Main Ideas

_____ 3. Which sentence best expresses the central point of this selection?
   A. Dick Gregory had a long-standing crush on a girl named Helene Tucker.
   B. The charity Gregory received was given in a way that labeled him as poor, which made him ashamed.
   C. As both a receiver and a giver, young Gregory learned that how something is given is as important as what is given.
   D. Gregory grew up in a poor and fatherless family.

_____ 4. Which sentence best expresses the main idea of paragraph 2?
   A. The author adored Helene Tucker, a symbol of everything he wanted.
   B. Everybody has a symbol of everything he or she wants.
   C. Helene Tucker made the author feel ashamed of his looks.
   D. Unlike the author, Helene Tucker had a father.

_____ 5. Which sentence best expresses the main idea of paragraph 5?
   A. Gregory liked to eat paste.
   B. The teacher assumed that Gregory was stupid.
   C. The teacher never realized that Gregory was hungry all the time.
   D. The teacher assumed that Gregory was stupid and never realized that his poor work was the result of hunger.

Supporting Details

_____ 6. After the teacher told the class that Gregory was the type of person the Community Chest helped and that he was fatherless, Gregory
   A. never went back to school.
   B. felt sorry for himself for a while.
   C. stopped working.
   D. felt that Helene Tucker did not feel sorry for him.

_____ 7. As support for his central point, the author uses several
   A. statistics.   C. personal experiences.
   B. expert opinions.   D. famous quotations.

Transitions

_____ 8. The sentence below contains a(n)
   A. contrast signal.   C. illustration signal.
   B. comparison signal.   D. cause-effect signal.

   "I got sick a lot that winter because the fire would go out at night before the clothes were dry." (Paragraph 1)

_____ 9. The relationship of the second sentence below to the first is one of
   A. addition.   C. contrast.
   B. comparison.   D. illustration.

   "I stuck my hand in my pocket and held onto the money, waiting for her to call my name. But the teacher closed her book after she called on everybody else in the class." (Paragraph 12)

Patterns of Organization

_____10. The main pattern of organization of paragraph 28 is
   A. time order.   C. definition and example.
   B. list of items.   D. contrast.

_____11. The pattern of organization used in paragraphs 30–36 is
   A. list of items.   C. cause and effect.
   B. time order.   D. comparison.

Advanced Skill Questions

Inferences

_____12. TRUE OR FALSE? The author implies that the wino taught him a valuable lesson.

_____13. In paragraph 5, the author implies that
    A. he is stupid.
    B. teachers understood him well.
    C. it was difficult for him to concentrate in school.
    D. the only way he ever got food was to steal it.

Purpose and Tone

_____14. TRUE OR FALSE? One of the author's purposes is to inform readers of how he learned the meaning of shame.

_____15. The word that best describes the tone of the last paragraph of the selection is
    A. angry.   C. sentimental.
    B. objective.   D. ashamed.

Argument

_____16. TRUE OR FALSE? The teacher's conclusion that Gregory was stupid did not take into account all the relevant evidence.

_____17. Which evidence from the selection supports Gregory's statement that, after the school incident, he felt shame everywhere?
    A. Gregory stuffed the plaid mackinaw into a garbage can.
    B. Gregory was always chosen to wash the blackboards on Fridays.
    C. Helene Tucker's eyes were full of tears.
    D. Gregory wanted to pay for the wino's dinner.

Critical Reading

_____18. Which of the following is a statement of opinion?
    A. "I was sitting in the back of the room, in a seat with a chalk circle drawn around it."
    B. "Paste doesn't taste too bad when you're hungry."
    C. "She turned toward the blackboard."
    D. "Helene Tucker turned around, her eyes full of tears."

_____19. In a TV commercial for a public university, a famous comedian states that he benefited from attending that university and so can others. The commercial is employing the propaganda technique of
    A. glittering generalities.   C. testimonial.
    B. plain folks.   D. bandwagon.

_____20. The following statement illustrates the logical fallacy of
A. either-or.
B. false cause.
C. false comparison.
D. personal attack.

"Students today have it far easier than we had it. They get free lunches in school."

Outlining

The following outline of "Shame" is missing two major supporting details and three minor supporting details. Complete the outline by filling in the missing details, which are listed after the outline.

Central point: Young Gregory learned both the shame of being let down by those who were supposed to help him and the shame of letting down another person.

A. _____

    1. Intends to impress Helene Tucker by pledging to Community Chest

    2. _____

    3. _____

B. _____

    1. Earns a lot of money one day and goes to a restaurant for a good meal

    2. Sees wino being beaten for not being able to pay for his meal

    3. _____

Items Missing from the Outline

- Offers to pay for meal, but too late
- Becomes ashamed of his own failure to help another
- Is humiliated by teacher
- Becomes ashamed of his poverty
- Leaves school and avoids it in the future

Discussion Questions

1. Why did Gregory include both the classroom and the restaurant anecdotes in one selection? What is the difference between the shame he felt in the first incident and the shame he felt in the second? What are the similarities between the two incidents?

2. The Community Chest incident could have had very different results if Gregory's teacher had handled the situation in another way. What do you think she should have done when Gregory said, "You forgot me"?

3. One type of irony is an event or an effect that is the opposite of what might be expected. In what ways are the following parts of "Shame" ironic?

   ● I never learned hate at home, or shame. I had to go to school for that.
   ● If I knew my place and didn't come too close, she'd wink at me and say hello. That was a good feeling.
   ● I looked at the wino with blood all over his face and I went over. "Leave him alone, Mister Williams. I'll pay the twenty-six cents." The wino got up. . . . He looked at me with pure hate.

4. Has anyone ever tried to help you in a way that didn't take all your needs into account? If so, how did you feel toward that person? In what ways might activities that are meant to help people also hurt them?

Note: Writing assignments for this selection appear on pages 630–631.

Check Your Performance   SHAME

Activity	Number Right	Points	Score
Basic Skill Questions			
Vocabulary in Context (2 items)	_____	× 4 =	_____
Central Point and Main Ideas (3 items)	_____	× 4 =	_____
Supporting Details (2 items)	_____	× 4 =	_____
Transitions (2 items)	_____	× 4 =	_____
Patterns of Organization (2 items)	_____	× 4 =	_____
Advanced Skill Questions			
Inferences (2 items)	_____	× 4 =	_____
Purpose and Tone (2 items)	_____	× 4 =	_____
Argument (2 items)	_____	× 4 =	_____
Critical Reading (3 items)	_____	× 4 =	_____
Outlining (5 items)	_____	× 4 =	_____
		TOTAL SCORE =	_____ %

Enter your total score into the **Reading Performance Chart: Ten Reading Selections** on the inside back cover.

4 The Bystander Effect
Dorothy Barkin

Preview

On a chilly March night, thirty-eight people witnessed a brutal attack—and hardly raised a finger to stop it. That kind of unwillingness to get involved is the topic of this article by Dorothy Barkin, who analyzes the confusion and lack of responsibility bystanders often feel when witnessing a crime or medical emergency. She begins by describing four crisis situations—and placing you right there at the scene. How would you react?

Words to Watch

intervene (2): interfere
phenomena (4): facts
apathy (23): indifference
diffusion (32): spreading thin
paralysis (32): inability to act

1   It is a pleasant fall afternoon. The sun is shining. You are heading toward the parking lot after your last class of the day. All of a sudden, you come across the following situations. What do you think you'd do in each case?

> **Situation One:** A man in his early twenties dressed in jeans and a T-shirt is using a coat hanger to pry open a door of a late-model Ford sedan. An overcoat and a camera are visible on the back seat of the car. You're the only one who sees this.

> **Situation Two:** A man and woman are wrestling with each other. The woman is in tears. Attempting to fight the man off, she screams, "Who are you? Get away from me!" You're the only one who witnesses this.

> **Situation Three:** Imagine the same scenario as in Situation Two except that this time the woman screams, "Get away from me! I don't know why I ever married you!"

Situation Four: Again imagine Situation Three. This time, however, there are a few other people (strangers to you and each other) who also observe the incident.

2   Many people would choose not to get involved in situations like these. Bystanders are often reluctant to intervene° in criminal or medical emergencies for reasons they are well aware of. They fear possible danger to themselves or getting caught up in a situation that could lead to complicated and time-consuming legal proceedings.

3   There are, however, other, less obvious factors which influence the decision to get involved in emergency situations. Complex psychological factors, which many people are unaware of, play an important part in the behavior of bystanders; knowing about these factors can help people to act more responsibly when faced with emergencies.

4   To understand these psychological phenomena°, it is helpful to look at what researchers have learned about behavior in the situations mentioned at the beginning of this article.

Situation One: Research reveals a remarkably low rate of bystander intervention to protect property. In one study, more than 3,000 people walked past 214 staged car break-ins like the one described in this situation. The vast majority of passers-by completely ignored what appeared to be a crime in progress. Not one of the 3,000 bothered to report the incident to the police.

Situation Two: Another experiment involved staging scenarios like this and the next situation. In Situation Two, bystanders offered some sort of assistance to the young woman 65 percent of the time.

Situation Three: Here the rate of bystander assistance dropped down to 19 percent. This demonstrates that bystanders are more reluctant to help a woman when they believe she's fighting with her husband. Not only do they consider a wife in less need of help; they think interfering with a married couple may be more dangerous. The husband, unlike a stranger, will not flee the situation.

Situation Four: The important idea in this situation is being a member of a group of bystanders. In more than fifty studies involving many different conditions, one outcome has been consistent: bystanders are much less likely to get involved when other witnesses are present than when they are alone.

5   Thus, membership in a group of bystanders lowers the likelihood that each member of the group will become involved. This finding may seem surprising. You might think there would be safety in numbers and that being a member of a group would increase the likelihood of intervention. How can we explain this aspect of group behavior?

6   A flood of research has tried to answer this and other questions about bystanders in emergencies ever since the infamous case of the murder of Kitty Genovese.

7   In 1964 in the borough of Queens in New York City, Catherine "Kitty" Genovese, twenty-eight, was brutally murdered in a shocking crime that outraged the nation.

8   The crime began at 3 a.m. Kitty Genovese was coming home from her job as manager of a bar. After parking her car in a parking lot, she began the hundred-foot walk to the entrance of her apartment. But she soon noticed a man in the lot and decided instead to walk toward a police call box. As she walked by a bookstore on her way there, the man grabbed her. She screamed.

9   Lights went on and windows opened in the ten-story apartment building.

10   Next, the attacker stabbed Genovese. She shrieked, "Oh, my God, he stabbed me! Please help me! Please help me!"

11   From an upper window in the apartment house, a man shouted, "Let that girl alone!"

12   The assailant, alarmed by the man's shout, started toward his car, which was parked nearby. However, the lights in the building soon went out, and the man returned. He found Genovese struggling to reach her apartment—and stabbed her again.

13   She screamed, "I'm dying! I'm dying!"

14   Once more, lights went on and windows opened in the apartment building. The attacker then went to his car and drove off. Struggling, Genovese made her way inside the building.

15   But the assailant returned to attack Genovese yet a third time. He found her

slumped on the floor at the foot of the stairs and stabbed her again, this time fatally.

16   The murder took over a half hour, and Kitty Genovese's desperate cries for help were heard by at least thirty-eight people. Not a single one of the thirty-eight who later admitted to having witnessed the murder bothered to pick up the phone during the attack and call the police. One man called after Genovese was dead.

17   Comments made by bystanders after this murder provide important insight into what group members think when they consider intervening in an emergency.

18   These are some of the comments:

19   "I didn't want my husband to get involved."

20   "Frankly, we were afraid."

21   "We thought it was a lovers' quarrel."

22   "I was tired."

23   The Genovese murder sparked a national debate on the questions of public apathy° and fear and became the basis for thousands of sermons, editorials, classroom discussions, and even a made-for-television movie. The same question was on everybody's

mind—how could thirty-eight people have done so little?

24   Nine years later, another well-publicized incident provided additional information about the psychology of a group witnessing a crime.

25   On a summer afternoon in Trenton, New Jersey, a twenty-year-old woman was brutally raped in a parking lot in full view of twenty-five employees of a nearby roofing company. Though the workers witnessed the entire incident and the woman repeatedly screamed for help, no one came to her assistance.

26   Comments made by witnesses to the rape were remarkably similar to those made by the bystanders to the Genovese murder. For example, one witness said, "We thought, well, it might turn out to be her boyfriend or something like that."

27   It's not surprising to find similar excuses for not helping in cases involving a group of bystanders. The same psychological principles apply to each. Research conducted since the Genovese murder indicates that the failure of bystanders to get involved can't be simply dismissed as a symptom of an uncaring society. Rather, the **bystander effect,** as it is called by social scientists, is the product of a complex set of psychological factors.

28   Two factors appear to be most important in understanding the reactions of bystanders to emergencies.

29   First is the level of ambiguity involved in the situation. Bystanders are afraid to endanger themselves or look foolish if they take the wrong action in a situation they're not sure how to interpret. A person lying face down on the floor of a subway train may have just suffered a heart attack and be in need of immediate medical assistance—or he may be a dangerous drunk.

30   Determining what is happening is especially difficult when a man is attacking a woman. Many times lovers do quarrel, sometimes violently. But they may strongly resent an outsider, no matter how well-meaning, intruding into their affairs.

31   When a group of bystanders is around, interpreting an event can be even more difficult than when one is alone. Bystanders look to others for cues as to what is happening. Frequently other witnesses, just as confused, try to look calm. Thus bystanders can mislead each other about the seriousness of an incident.

32   The second factor in determining the reactions of bystanders to emergencies is what psychologists call the principle of moral diffusion°. Moral diffusion is the lessening of a sense of individual responsibility when someone is a member of a group. Responsibility to act diffuses throughout the crowd. When a member of the group is able to escape the collective paralysis° and take action, others in the group tend to act as well. But the larger the crowd, the greater the diffusion of responsibility, and the less likely someone is to intervene.

33   The more social scientists are able to teach us about how bystanders react to an emergency, the better the chances that we will take appropriate action when faced with one. Knowing about moral

diffusion, for example, makes it easier for us to escape it. If you find yourself witnessing an emergency with a group, remember that everybody is waiting for someone else to do something first. If you take action, others may also help.

Also realize that any one of us 34 could at some time be in desperate need of help. Imagine what it feels like to need help and have a crowd watch you suffer—and do nothing. Remember Kitty Genovese.

Basic Skill Questions

Vocabulary in Context

_____ 1. In the sentence below, the word *scenario* (sĭ-nâr′ē-ō′) means
   A. fight.
   B. relationship.
   C. suggested scene.
   D. quotation.

> "Imagine the same scenario as in Situation Two except that this time the woman screams, 'Get away from me! I don't know why I ever married you!'" (Paragraph 1)

_____ 2. In the excerpt below, the word *assailant* (ə-sā′lənt) means
   A. observer.
   B. bystander.
   C. victim.
   D. attacker.

> "Next, the attacker stabbed Genovese. . . . From an upper window in the apartment house, a man shouted, 'Let that girl alone!'
>
> "The assailant, alarmed by the man's shout, started toward his car . . ." (Paragraphs 10–12)

_____ 3. In the excerpt below, the word *ambiguity* (ăm′bĭ-gyōō′ĭ-tē) means
   A. argument.
   B. uncertainty.
   C. lack of interest.
   D. crowding.

> "First is the level of ambiguity involved . . . Bystanders are afraid to endanger themselves or look foolish . . . in a situation they're not sure how to interpret." (Paragraph 29)

Central Point and Main Ideas

_____ 4. Which sentence best expresses the central point of this selection?
   A. People don't want to get involved in emergencies.
   B. Kitty Genovese was murdered because no one helped enough.
   C. People don't care what happens to others.
   D. Understanding why bystanders react as they do in a crisis can help people act more responsibly.

_____ 5. Which sentence best expresses the main idea of paragraph 27?
   A. Bystanders always have the same excuses for not helping.
   B. There has been research on bystanders since the Genovese murder.
   C. The "bystander effect" is a symptom of an uncaring society.
   D. Research shows that a number of psychological factors, not a simple lack of caring, keeps bystanders from getting involved.

_____ 6. The sentence that makes up paragraph 28 states the main idea of
   A. paragraph 29.
   B. paragraphs 29–30.
   C. paragraphs 29–31.
   D. paragraphs 29–32.

Supporting Details

_____ 7. Bystanders are most likely to help
   A. a woman being attacked by her husband.
   B. in any emergency when others are around.
   C. a woman being attacked by a stranger.
   D. when property is being stolen.

_____ 8. According to the author, when there is a group of bystanders,
      A. everyone is more likely to help.
      B. it is easier to understand what is happening.
      C. they are not influenced at all by each other.
      D. each is more likely to act after someone else takes action.

_____ 9. The author supports her statement that "bystanders are much less likely to get involved when other witnesses are present" with
      A. opinions.
      B. quotations from experts.
      C. research and examples.
      D. no evidence.

Transitions

_____10. In the excerpt below, what does the second sentence do?
      A. It compares the behavior of some bystanders with the behavior of others.
      B. It contrasts the behavior of confused bystanders with that of calm bystanders.
      C. It adds more detail to the first sentence.
      D. It establishes a cause and effect relationship.

      "Frequently other witnesses, just as confused, try to look calm. Thus bystanders can mislead each other about the seriousness of an incident." (Paragraph 31)

_____11. In the excerpt below, what does the second sentence do?
      A. It contrasts the comments made by witnesses to the rape with comments made by witnesses to the Genovese murder.
      B. It illustrates a point made in the first sentence.
      C. It compares two serious crimes.
      D. It establishes a cause and effect relationship.

      "Comments made by witnesses to the rape were remarkably similar to those made by the bystanders to the Genovese murder. For example, one witness said, 'We thought, well, it might turn out to be her boyfriend or something like that.'" (Paragraph 26)

Patterns of Organization

_____12. The pattern of organization of paragraphs 7–16 is
   A. comparison and/or contrast.
   B. list of items.
   C. definition and example.
   D. time order.

Advanced Skill Questions

Inferences

_____13. The reading suggests that people tend to believe
   A. theft is okay.
   B. loss of property is worse than bodily harm.
   C. bodily harm is worse than loss of property.
   D. rape is worse than murder.

_____14. From the article, we can conclude that Kitty Genovese's killer
   A. knew his victim.
   B. was unaware of the witnesses.
   C. stabbed her too quickly for her to get help.
   D. kept attacking when he realized no one was coming to help her.

_____15. From the article, we can conclude that of the following situations, the bystander is most likely to get involved when
   A. a man passes a clothing store from which people are carrying away clothes.
   B. a college student sees a man collapsing on a street where no one else is present.
   C. a neighbor sees a father and son fighting in their yard.
   D. a softball team sees the coach angrily chasing his wife.

Purpose and Tone

_____16. The main purpose of this article is to
   A. inform readers about the bystander effect and the factors that contribute to it.
   B. persuade people to be more helpful in emergency situations.
   C. both of the above.

_____17. The tone of the last paragraph of this article can be described as
    A. surprised.
    B. confused.
    C. pleading.
    D. lighthearted.

Argument

_____18. Write the letter of the statement that is the point of the following argument. The other statements are support for that point.
    A. "When a member of the group is able to escape the collective paralysis and take action, others in the group tend to act as well."
    B. "If you take action [in an emergency], others may also help."
    C. "Bystanders are afraid to endanger themselves or look foolish if they take the wrong action in a situation they're not sure how to interpret."

Critical Reading

_____19. The following sentence is a statement of
    A. fact.
    B. opinion.
    C. fact and opinion.

    "In more than fifty studies involving many different conditions, one outcome has been consistent: bystanders are much less likely to get involved when other witnesses are present than when they are alone." (Paragraph 4)

_____20. A man who explains that a woman was raped because she wore sexy clothing is illustrating the logical fallacy of
    A. false cause.
    B. straw man.
    C. personal attack.
    D. circular reasoning.

Summarizing

Add the ideas needed to complete the following summary of "The Bystander Effect."

Witnesses to crisis situations are less likely to help when only property is at risk and when a woman is being attacked by a man who may be her husband. Numerous studies have shown that witnesses' resistance to helping is also increased when there are other _____ _____. A famous example is the case of Kitty Genovese, who was stabbed to death at 3 a.m. while returning to her apartment. The attack went on for over half an hour. Thirty-eight people listened to her cries for help, but _____ _____. In another example, employees of a roofing company ignored a rape taking place on a nearby parking lot. Two psychological factors seem to explain _____ _____. One is the level of uncertainty in the situation. If the bystanders don't know how to _____ _____ a situation, they don't want to take action. The other factor is the principle of moral diffusion. The larger the crowd that is watching, the less responsibility _____ _____. Understanding these factors can help people be more useful in emergency situations.

Discussion Questions

1. Have you ever been in a situation in which the bystander effect played a part? Would your behavior be any different in light of what you have learned from this article?

2. The author states in paragraph 31, "Bystanders look to others for cues as to what is happening. Frequently other witnesses, just as confused, try to look calm." Why do you think witnesses would try to look calm during an emergency?

3. In paragraph 33, the author suggests that if you understand what causes "the bystander effect," you can act appropriately in an emergency: "If you take action, others may also help." If, say, you were in a group of onlookers while a fight was in progress, what could you do that would encourage others to intervene?

4. How does the conclusion of this article clarify the author's purpose for the reader? How does the article's beginning fit in with that purpose?

Note: Writing assignments for this selection appear on pages 631–632.

Check Your Performance   THE BYSTANDER EFFECT

Activity	Number Right	Points		Score
Basic Skill Questions				
Vocabulary in Context (3 items)	_____	× 4	=	_____
Central Point and Main Ideas (3 items)	_____	× 4	=	_____
Supporting Details (3 items)	_____	× 4	=	_____
Transitions (2 items)	_____	× 4	=	_____
Patterns of Organization (1 item)	_____	× 4	=	_____
Advanced Skill Questions				
Inferences (3 items)	_____	× 4	=	_____
Purpose and Tone (2 items)	_____	× 4	=	_____
Argument (1 item)	_____	× 4	=	_____
Critical Reading (2 items)	_____	× 4	=	_____
Summarizing (5 items)	_____	× 4	=	_____
		TOTAL SCORE	=	_____%

Enter your total score into the **Reading Performance Chart: Ten Reading Selections** on the inside back cover.

5 Growing Less Dumb
Eileen Brenoff

Preview

There are a lot of not-great things about growing older, including achy knees, thinning hair, and sagging skin. But growing older has its compensations, too. In this essay, the author reflects on the ways she has grown better and wiser with age.

Words to Watch

perspective (10): viewpoint
rigid (11): unbending
petrified (11): terrified
spontaneous (11): unplanned
infuriates (16): makes extremely angry

1   In the area of Indiana where I grew up, shops cater to the tourists who come to see the local Amish people, with their 19th century lifestyle and horse-drawn buggies. One popular local souvenir sold in those shops is kitchen plaques printed with what are supposedly Amish sayings—folksy things like "Kissing don't last; cooking do," or "Throw the horse over the fence some hay."

2   I was never tempted to buy one of those corny plaques. But I'll admit, one of the sayings on them has come into my mind recently. It's not about cooking or kissing or farm life. It's this: "We grow too soon old and too late smart."

3   I think whoever came up with that line was on to something. At 54, I don't consider myself old (no wisecracks from you 18-year-olds in the back row, please), and there are plenty of times I could be smarter. But if I'm not always smart, at least I believe I'm becoming a little less dumb as the years go on.

4   What am I less dumb about today than when I was younger? I think of a number of things. For starters, I believe that I am less dumb about worrying; I am less dumb about decisions; I am less dumb about other people's opinions, and in general I am less dumb when judging other people.

5   First of all, let's talk about worrying. What were you worried about a week ago? How about two weeks ago? Can you remember? No? Well, neither can

I, and that's my point. When I was younger, I worried a lot. I was really good at it. I could take one minor worry—say, a tickle at the back of my throat—and spin it into a long, complicated worry that could ruin an entire day. "My throat feels scratchy. Maybe I'm getting a cold. In fact, maybe it's not just a cold. Maybe it's strep. Strep is really nasty. And oh, shoot, I'm supposed to go to the movies with Keith on Saturday. That's only three days away. Lemme see . . . if it is strep, and I get antibiotics tomorrow, will I still be contagious on Saturday? But I still won't feel good and the date will be a disaster and Keith will never ask me out again and you KNOW who he'll ask out next, that cute Suzanne from biology class, and . . . " By the time I had worked that worry over thoroughly, my imagination had Keith and Suzanne married and living in a half-million dollar house at the shore with their 2.5 adorable children, while I was friendless and miserable and living in a cold rented room with a goldfish as my only companion.

6   Let me just point out that this was a dumb way for me to spend my time.

7   The fact is, I've slowly come to realize, that the things I worry about hardly ever happen. A few days after I've worked myself into a lather over some issue, the problem has generally either disappeared or been resolved in some perfectly satisfactory way. All my worrying had absolutely no impact, except to make me anxious and depressed. So one way that I am now less dumb is this: When I find myself starting to obsess about a possible problem—when those "What ifs?" start running through my head—I have learned to say a firm "STOP THAT!" to myself. I remind myself that the things I was worried about last week or last month have, in general, not actually happened; and if they *did* happen, well, then I dealt with them.

8   The second thing I am less dumb about now is making decisions. When I was younger, decisions scared me, so I wanted the people around me to do the deciding. I am talking about things as minor as choosing what to order in a restaurant ("Are you going to have the clam chowder? I'll get the clam chowder if you do") to as major as deciding where to go to college ("A girl in my home room's brother goes to State U and he likes it, so maybe I'll go there.") Never mind that I really wanted the taco salad; never mind that I didn't know a thing about State U or the girl's brother. I felt safer having someone else take the responsibility for my decision. The outcome? I ended up doing everything from eating food I didn't enjoy to attending a college that was ill suited to my needs.

9 Really, really dumb.

10 Slowly I've learned that making my own decisions is not only smarter, but it's very empowering. In order to make good decisions, I've had to start giving *myself* the same consideration that I used to reserve for other people. I've learned to respect *my* preferences and opinions and instincts, instead of hoping that someone else might magically know what's best for me. Sure, when I have an important decision to make, I still consult the people close to me; but it's to get their perspective° on my own thinking, not to ask them to tell me what to do. For better or worse, the decision is mine—I own it. And that's a lot more satisfying than my dumb old way.

11 In addition, I am less dumb about this: I worry MUCH less than I used to about what other people think. When I reflect upon my younger self, especially when I was in my teens and twenties, I imagine myself moving through life in a rigid° shell of self-consciousness. I was petrified° that I might draw attention to myself by doing something weird. And to me, "something weird" meant something fun, creative, joyous, outrageous, spontaneous° . . . you get the idea. If it was outside the tight little mold of what "normal" people were doing, I didn't have the courage to do it anyway. I was too afraid of what people would think. Would they stare? Would they laugh?

12 But you know something funny? When I think back to the people I knew during those years, I have only the dimmest memories of the ones I thought of as "normal." They all blend together in my mind—the girls with the stylish outfits and perfect hair; the boys with the varsity letters and pricey cars. For the most part, I can't even remember their names. The people who I do remember are the ones like Mike, who threw himself into every school play with passion and great good humor; Caroline, who dyed her hair pink long before it was fashionable; Serena, who would sing at the top of her lungs in the hallways, and Carl, who sat in the courtyard at lunchtime playing his bongo drums. I liked those people; I admired them; I wish I'd had the courage to be more like them.

13 I'm glad to say I'm not that dumb anymore. I can't remember the last time I hesitated to do or say something because I was worried, "What will people think?" I have taken to heart the wise words of former first lady Eleanor Roosevelt, who said, "You wouldn't worry so much about what others think of you if you realized how seldom they do." Now, I sing in public; I speak up in meetings; I ask for extra napkins in restaurants; I change my hair color on a whim. I talk to strangers, I play patty-cake with other people's babies, and I pet strangers' dogs. In short, I have a blast. I wish I'd had as much fun when I was 15.

14 Finally, I am less dumb in my judgments of other people. When I was younger, I tended to think in very black and white terms. People were good or they were bad; an action was either right or it was wrong. To take an extreme example, if I heard of a person accused of abusing children, my response would

be, "Just kill him—don't even bother with a trial. Get rid of him like you would a mad dog." And the thought of anyone hurting a child still makes me sick deep in my soul. But as the years have gone by, I have learned some sad truths. One of them is that people who hurt children were often themselves harmed in the same awful way. They were not born monsters; at one point, they were the innocent victims. So my attitude now is different. I think, "Keep him away from children, forever. But look at him as another human being. If he was terribly wounded in life, try to help him."

15   For another example, my earlier black-and-white thinking made me assume that our political leaders in Washington were doing what they should do, and that I didn't really need to pay very much attention to their actions. They knew more than I did about what needed to be done, right?

16   I think I'm less dumb about that now, too. I pay a lot closer attention to what our elected officials are doing. Now my attitude is, "Hey, I want my representatives to stand up for everyday folks, for people who are just trying to stay above water in today's hard times." I've come to harshly judge the politicians who seem concerned mainly about tax breaks for the wealthy and the best interests of banks and big corporations. I want to call them out when they disregard the poor and the middle class and everyday people in this country. It infuriates° me when I see them ignore the economic realities most of us live with and hear them say, "If you're not doing well in life, it's because you're lazy and don't want to work." I want to say to them, "Hey, you probably started on third base, and you want to condemn people who never had a chance to get to first?" I want to ask them, "How in your endless pursuit of wealth did you let your heart grow so hard?" I don't wish them ill, but I definitely judge them as people who have lost their humanity.

17   Yes, I've changed with the years, and in general I'm happy about those changes. I'm more tolerant in some ways, less in others, and a lot more ready to speak my mind and live my life without apology. Let me just conclude by saying that, all in all, I am not the dumb kid I was once upon a time. But, you know what they say, at least in Indiana: We grow too soon old and too late smart. Maybe you can grow smart at a younger age than I did.

Basic Skill Questions

Vocabulary in Context

_____ 1. In the excerpt below, the term *obsess about* (əb-sĕs′ ə-bout′)means
    A. laugh at.
    B. complain about.
    C. try to ignore.
    D. think about constantly.

> "So one way that I am now less dumb is this: When I find myself starting to obsess about a possible problem—when those "What ifs?" start running through my head—I have learned to say a firm "STOP THAT!" to myself. I remind myself that the things I worried about last week or last month have, in general, not actually happened." (Paragraph 7)

Central Point and Main Ideas

_____ 2. Which sentence best expresses the central point of the selection?
    A. Brenoff believes that she, like most people, has spent too much time worrying.
    B. As she's grown older, Brenoff has become more tolerant in some ways, less tolerant in others, and a lot more ready to speak her mind.
    C. Although Brenoff was never tempted to buy a corny Amish plaque, she believes that the Amish were right about what's important in life.
    D. Brenoff has become less dumb in several important ways and hopes that her readers will become less dumb, too.

_____ 3. The main idea of paragraphs 5–6 is that
    A. most people can't remember what they worried about two weeks ago.
    B. Brenoff now realizes that it was dumb of her to spend so much time worrying.
    C. Brenoff used to worry that she would become friendless and miserable because of a disastrous date.
    D. Brenoff now realizes that she was dumb to worry about so much about whether a cold would develop into strep.

_____ 4. Which sentence best expresses the implied main idea of paragraph 12?
  A. Although she once admired "normal" people, Brenoff now barely remembers them.
  B. Brenoff used to enjoy being around lively people, such as Mike, Caroline, Serena, and Carl.
  C. The definition of "normal" has changed greatly since Brenoff was young.
  D. Brenoff remembers and admires those classmates who stood out from the crowd and wishes that she had had the courage to be more like them.

Supporting Details

_____ 5. When Brenoff was young, she often worried about
  A. being thought of as "corny."
  B. doing something "weird."
  C. not having enough money to fit in with the "normal" people.
  D. not going to the right college.

_____ 6. One mistake that Brenoff made as a result of failing to take responsibility for her decisions was
  A. going to the prom with someone she didn't really like.
  B. attending a college that didn't meet her needs.
  C. marrying the brother of one of her friends.
  D. voting for a politician who supported the death penalty for child abusers.

_____ 7. These days Brenoff harshly judges
  A. people who stand out from the crowd by doing what they want.
  B. people who defend child abusers.
  C. people who are lazy and refuse to work.
  D. politicians who are mainly concerned about tax breaks for the wealthy.

Transitions

_____ 8. The relationship of the second sentence below to the first sentence is one of
  A. cause and effect.
  B. contrast.
  C. illustration.
  D. comparison.

  "But as the years have gone by, I have learned some sad truths. One of them is that people who hurt children were often themselves harmed in the same awful way." (Paragraph 14)

Patterns of Organization

_____ 9. Paragraph 14 mainly
  A. presents a series of steps involved in forming judgments of people.
  B. lists reasons why the author no longer thinks in very black and white terms.
  C. contrasts how the author judged child abusers when she was young with how she judges them now.
  D. compares child abusers to other types of criminals.

_____10. The main pattern of organization of the entire selection is
  A. cause and effect.
  B. list of items.
  C. comparison.
  D. illustration.

Inferences

_____11. From paragraph 5, we can infer that
  A. Brenoff was sickly as a teen.
  B. Brenoff never did marry and have children.
  C. Brenoff did not have a lot of self-confidence when she was a teen.
  D. Brenoff's one true love was a boy named Keith.

_____12. Paragraph 14 suggests that Brenoff
  A. has met people who have abused children.
  B. no longer believes in the death penalty for people who abuse children.
  C. believes that some people are born evil.
  D. believes that people who abuse children should not be imprisoned.

_____13. We can conclude from the selection that
  A. today's young people are smarter than when Brenoff was young.
  B. Brenoff feels that as people grow older, they have fewer worries.
  C. Brenoff enjoys life more today than she did when she was a teenager.
  D. all of the above.

Purpose and Tone

_____14. The author's purpose in writing this selection is to
  A. entertain readers with stories about how dumb she was when she was a teenager.
  B. inform readers of how she learned to stop worrying, make good decisions, stop being afraid of what other people think, and judge people fairly.
  C. persuade readers that they should try to "grow smart" at a younger age than she did.
  D. all of the above.

_____15. The word that best describes the tone of paragraphs 5–6 is
  A. compassionate.
  B. self-mocking.
  C. nostalgic.
  D. angry.

Argument

_____16. Which of the statements below does _not_ support the point of the argument?

  Point: Brenoff has become "less dumb" as she has grown older.

  A. She no longer asks people to tell her what to do.
  B. She no longer worries much about what other people will think of her.
  C. She pays a lot closer attention to what our elected officials are doing.
  D. She hopes that her readers can grow smart at a younger age than she did.

_____17. Which evidence from the selection supports Brenoff's statement that she has more fun now than when she was 15?
  A. For the most part, she can't remember the names of the "normal" people she knew in school.
  B. She pays more attention to what our elected officials are doing.
  C. She sings in public, speaks out at meetings, and asks for extra napkins at restaurants.
  D. She harshly judges politicians who seem concerned mainly about tax breaks for the wealthy and the best interests of banks and big corporations.

Critical Reading

_____18. Because Brenoff often let the people around her do the deciding when she was young, she would probably have been strongly influenced by which propaganda technique?
A. Glittering generalities
B. Plain folks
C. Bandwagon
D. Name calling

_____19. People who say, "If you're not doing well in life, it's because you're lazy and don't want to work" are committing the logical fallacy of
A. circular reasoning.
B. false comparison.
C. false cause.
D. either-or.

_____20. People who believe that elected officials are doing what they should because they were elected to do the right thing are committing the logical fallacy of
A. circular reasoning.
B. false comparison.
C. false cause.
D. either-or.

Outlining

The following outline of "Growing Less Dumb" is missing two major supporting details and three minor supporting details. Complete the outline by filling in the missing details, which are listed after the outline.

Central point: Eileen Brenoff believes that she is "less dumb" now than when she was younger.

    A. She is less dumb about worrying.
        1. She used to spin minor worries into long, complicated worries (example: she once worried that a tickle at the back of her throat would ruin a date and lead her to become friendless and miserable).
        2. Now she has come to realize that the things she worries about hardly ever happen, so she stops herself from worrying.

B. _____

    1. She used to let others make decisions for her (example: I'll get the clam chowder if you do).

    2. _____

    _____

C. _____

    1. She used to be afraid of drawing attention to herself by doing "something weird."

    2. She now realizes that people seldom think about what she does, so she does what she likes (example: singing in public).

D. She is less dumb in her judgment of other people.

    1. She used to think in very black and white terms (example: child abusers should be killed).

    2. _____

    _____

    3. _____

    _____

    4. She pays a lot closer attention to elected officials now and harshly judges those who seem mainly concerned about tax breaks for the wealthy and interests of banks and big corporations.

Items Missing from the Outline

- She worries much less than she used to about what other people think.
- Now she realizes that even child abusers were once innocent victims and wants them to be given help.
- She is less dumb about making decisions.
- She once thought that political leaders knew what they were doing, so she didn't need to pay attention to them.
- Now she has learned to respect her own preferences and instincts, and she makes her own decisions.

Discussion Questions

1. Brenoff ends her essay by saying that she hopes her readers grow smart at a younger age than she did. In what ways have you, like Brenoff, become "less dumb" than when you were younger? Do you think it's possible to become "smart" at a young age? Why or why not?

2. Brenoff says she now realizes that "the things I worry about hardly ever happen." Her worrying solved nothing; it only made her anxious and depressed. Do you agree with Brenoff that worrying is a "dumb" way to spend one's time? Or is worrying sometimes justified? Explain.

3. In Brenoff's opinion, people who condemn others for not doing well in life have "lost their humanity." Do you agree? Do you think that people don't do well in life because they're lazy and don't want to work? Or are there other reasons that some people don't succeed?

4. Brenoff thinks that whoever came up with the slogan "We grow too soon old and too late smart" had realized something important. Are there any slogans or sayings that you think are particularly meaningful—maybe even meaningful enough to live by? If so, explain what they are and why they hold special meaning for you.

Note: Writing assignments for this selection appear on page 632.

Check Your Performance

GROWING LESS DUMB

Activity	Number Right	Points	Score
Basic Skill Questions			
Vocabulary in Context (1 item)	_____	× 4 =	_____
Central Point and Main Ideas (3 items)	_____	× 4 =	_____
Supporting Details (3 items)	_____	× 4 =	_____
Transitions (1 item)	_____	× 4 =	_____
Patterns of Organization (2 items)	_____	× 4 =	_____
Advanced Skill Questions			
Inferences (3 items)	_____	× 4 =	_____
Purpose and Tone (2 items)	_____	× 4 =	_____
Argument (2 items)	_____	× 4 =	_____
Critical Reading (3 items)	_____	× 4 =	_____
Outlining (5 items)	_____	× 4 =	_____
		TOTAL SCORE =	_____%

Enter your total score into the **Reading Performance Chart: Ten Reading Selections** on the inside back cover.

6 Coping with Nervousness
Rudolph F. Verderber

Preview

Do you have trouble relaxing when you speak in front of a group? Do your legs tremble, does your heart pound, is your mouth dry? For many people, public speaking can be a nerve-racking experience. However, there are ways to deal with the nervousness. In this selection from his widely used college textbook *Communicate!* Seventh Edition, Rudolph F. Verderber provides information that may make your future speaking assignments less painful.

Words to Watch

virtually (2): almost
channel (3): direct
adrenaline (4): a hormone that stimulates and strengthens parts of the body
flabbergasted (5): amazed
eliciting (5): drawing out
psyching . . . up (9): preparing (oneself) psychologically
initial (10): first

1   Most people confess to extreme nervousness at even the thought of giving a speech. Yet you must learn to cope with nervousness because speaking is important. Through speaking, we gain the power to share what we are thinking with others. Each of us has vital information to share: we may have the data needed to solve a problem; we may have an idea for a procedure that will save money for our company or group; we may have insights that will influence the way people see an issue. We can only imagine the tremendous loss to business, governmental, educational, professional, and fraternal groups because anxiety prevents people from speaking up.

2   Let's start with the assumption that you are indeed nervous—you may in fact be scared to death. Now what? Experience has proved that virtually° anyone can learn to cope with the fear of public speaking. Consider the following points:

3   **1. You are in good company.** Not only do most beginning speakers

suffer anxiety at the thought of speaking in public, but many experienced speakers confess to nervousness when they speak as well. Now, you may think, "Don't give me that line—you can't tell me that [fill in the name of a good speaker you know] is nervous when speaking in public!" Ask the person. He or she will tell you. Even powerful speakers like Abraham Lincoln and Franklin D. Roosevelt were nervous before speaking. The difference in nervousness among people is a matter of degree. Some people tremble, perspire, and experience shortness of breath and increased heartbeat. As they go through their speech, they may be so preoccupied with themselves that they lose contact with the audience, jump back and forth from point to point, and on occasion forget what they had planned to say. Others, however, may get butterflies in their stomachs and feel weak in the knees—and still go on to deliver a strong speech. The secret is not to get rid of all of your feelings but to learn to channel° and control your nervousness.

4   **2. Despite nervousness, you can make it through a speech.** Very few people are so bothered by anxiety that they are unable to proceed with the speech. You may not enjoy the experience— especially the first time—but you can do it. In fact, it would be detrimental if you were not nervous. Why? Because you must be a little more aroused than usual to do your best. A bit of nervousness gets the adrenaline° flowing—and that brings you to speaking readiness.

**3. Your listeners aren't nearly as   5
likely to recognize your fear as you might think.** "The only thing we have to fear," Franklin Roosevelt said, "is fear itself." Many speakers worry that others will notice how nervous they are— and that makes them even more self-conscious and nervous. The fact is that people, even speech instructors, will greatly underrate the amount of stage fright they believe a person has. Recently, a young woman reported that she broke out in hives before each speech. She was flabbergasted° when other students said to her, "You seem so calm when you speak." Try eliciting° feedback from your listeners after a speech. Once you realize that your audience does not perceive your nervousness to the degree that

you imagine, you will remove one unnecessary source of anxiety.

6   **4. The more experience you get in speaking, the better you become at coping with nervousness.** As you gain experience, you learn to think more about the audience and the message and less about yourself. Moreover, you come to realize that audiences, your classmates especially, are very supportive, especially in informative speech situations. After all, most people are in the audience because they want to hear you. As time goes on, you will come to find that having a group of people listening to you alone is a very satisfying experience.

7   Now let's consider what you can do about your nervousness. Coping with nervousness begins during the preparation process and extends to the time you actually begin the speech.

8   The best way to control nervousness is to pick a topic you know something about and are interested in. Public speakers cannot allow themselves to be saddled with a topic they don't care about. An unsatisfactory topic lays the groundwork for a psychological mindset that almost guarantees nervousness at the time of the speech. By the same token, selecting a topic you are truly interested in will help you focus on what you want to communicate and so lay the groundwork for a satisfying speech experience.

9   A second key to controlling nervousness is to prepare adequately for your speech. If you feel in command of your material and delivery, you'll be far more confident. During the preparation period, you can also be "psyching yourself up°" for the speech. Even in your classroom speeches, if you have a suitable topic, and if you are well prepared, your audience will feel they profited from listening to you. Before you say, "Come on, who are you trying to kid!" think of lectures, talks, and speeches you have heard. When the speaker seemed knowledgeable and conveyed enthusiasm, weren't you impressed? The fact is that some of the speeches you hear in class are likely to be among the best and most informative or moving speeches you are ever going to hear. Public speaking students learn to put time and effort into their speeches, and many classroom speeches turn out to be surprisingly interesting and valuable. If you work at your speech, you will probably sense that your class looks forward to listening to you.

10   Perhaps the most important time for coping with nervousness is shortly before you give your speech. Research indicates that it is during the period right before you walk up to give your speech and the time when you have your initial° contact with the audience that your fear is most likely to be at its greatest.

11   When speeches are being scheduled, you may be able to control when you speak. Are you better off "getting it over with," that is, being the first person to speak that day? If so, you may be able to volunteer to go first. But regardless of when you are scheduled to speak, try

not to spend your time thinking about yourself or your speech. At the moment the class begins, you have done all you can to be prepared. This is the time to focus your mind on something else. Try to listen to each of the speeches that come before yours. Get involved with what each speaker is saying. When your turn comes, you will be far more relaxed than if you had spent the time worrying about your own speech.

12   As you walk to the speaker's stand, remind yourself that you have ideas you want to convey, that you are well prepared, and that your audience is going to want to hear what you have to say. Even if you make mistakes, the audience will be focusing on your ideas and will profit from your speech.

When you reach the stand, pause   13 a few seconds before you start and establish eye contact with the audience. Take a deep breath to help get your breathing in order. Try to move about a little during the first few sentences—sometimes, a few gestures or a step one way or another is enough to break some of the tension. Above all, concentrate on communicating with your audience—your goal is to share your ideas, not to give a performance.

Basic Skill Questions

Vocabulary in Context

_____ 1. In the excerpt below, the word *detrimental* (dĕt′rə-mĕn′tl) means
   A. helpful.
   B. expensive.
   C. harmful.
   D. funny.

   "Despite nervousness, you can make it through a speech. . . . In fact, it would be detrimental if you were not nervous. Why? Because you must be a little more aroused than usual to do your best." (Paragraph 4)

_____ 2. In the sentence below, the word *conveyed* (kən-vād′) means
   A. prevented.
   B. communicated.
   C. forgot.
   D. delayed.

   "When the speaker seemed knowledgeable and conveyed enthusiasm, weren't you impressed?" (Paragraph 9)

Central Point and Main Ideas

_____ 3. Which sentence best expresses the central point of the selection?
  A. Nearly everyone feels nervous about speaking in public.
  B. It is possible to control the fear of public speaking.
  C. You can control your nervousness about speaking by picking a topic that interests you.
  D. Even famous speakers report feeling nervous before giving speeches.

_____ 4. Which sentence best expresses the main idea of paragraph 3?
  A. Nearly everyone gets nervous before giving a speech, but good speakers are able to channel and control their nervousness.
  B. Franklin D. Roosevelt and Abraham Lincoln were nervous before speaking.
  C. Giving a speech can be a stressful experience.
  D. Speakers who tremble, perspire, and experience shortness of breath and increased heartbeat may lose contact with the audience.

_____ 5. Which sentence best expresses the main idea of paragraphs 7–13?
  A. When preparing a speech, choose a topic you know something about and are interested in.
  B. You will feel far more confident about a speech if you prepare adequately for it.
  C. There are various things you can do to cope with nervousness during the preparation for and beginning of a speech.
  D. According to research, it is just before you walk up to give your speech and the time of your first contact with the audience that your fear is likely to be at its greatest.

Supporting Details

_____ 6. The supporting details in paragraphs 3–6 are
  A. reasons public speaking is important.
  B. suggestions for avoiding the fear of public speaking.
  C. evidence that people learn to deal with the fear of public speaking.
  D. steps in the process of public speaking.

_____ 7. Nervousness
  A. is rarely experienced by people who give speeches on a regular basis.
  B. can actually help a speaker to do his or her best.
  C. cannot be effectively controlled.
  D. always interferes with the effectiveness of a speech.

_____ 8. One way to control being nervous about a speech is to
      A. speak loudly.
      B. prepare adequately.
      C. avoid eye contact.
      D. all of the above.

Transitions

_____ 9. The sentence below expresses a relationship of
      A. addition.
      B. time.
      C. cause and effect.
      D. contrast.

       "Despite nervousness, you can make it through a speech." (Paragraph 4)

_____ 10. The relationship of the second sentence below to the first is one of
      A. addition.
      B. illustration.
      C. contrast.
      D. cause and effect.

       "As you gain experience, you learn to think more about the audience and the message and less about yourself. Moreover, you come to realize that audiences, your classmates especially, are very supportive, especially in informative speech situations." (Paragraph 6)

Patterns of Organization

_____ 11. The main pattern of organization of paragraphs 3–6 is
      A. list of items.
      B. time order.
      C. contrast.
      D. definition and example.

_____ 12. The main pattern of organization of paragraphs 7–13 is
      A. time order.
      B. contrast.
      C. comparison.
      D. definition and example.

Advanced Skill Questions

Inferences

_____13. The author suggests that
   A. thinking about your speech shortly before giving it is likely to make you more nervous.
   B. you should revise your speech up until the last possible moment.
   C. it is always best to try to be the first speaker of the day.
   D. with proper preparation, you will certainly not be nervous once your speech begins.

_____14. The author suggests that with practice, you
   A. can completely get over all fear of speaking in public.
   B. will find it is no longer so necessary to be in command of your speech material.
   C. will choose better and better topics for your speeches.
   D. will experience less fear when speaking.

_____15. The author implies that
   A. it is possible to think about your speech too much.
   B. everyone has worthwhile ideas to share in a speech.
   C. making mistakes in a speech doesn't ruin it.
   D. all of the above.

Purpose and Tone

_____16. The purpose of this reading is
   A. to inform.
   B. to persuade.
   C. both of the above.

_____17. The tone of this reading is
   A. optimistic and helpful.
   B. outspoken and critical.
   C. sympathetic and forgiving.
   D. excited and joyous.

Argument

_____18. One of the following statements is the point of the author's argument in paragraph 1. The other statements are support for that point. Write the letter of the point of the argument.
A. Speaking is important.
B. Speaking gives us the power to share our thoughts with others.
C. Through speaking, we can provide the data needed to solve a problem.
D. We may be able to share a money-saving idea for our company.

Critical Reading

_____19. The sentence below is
A. a fact.
B. an opinion.
C. both fact and opinion.

"Research indicates that it is during the period right before you walk up to give your speech and the time when you have your initial contact with the audience that your fear is most likely to be at its greatest." (Paragraph 10)

_____20. The following statement illustrates the logical fallacy of
A. circular reasoning.   C. false comparison.
B. false cause.   D. either-or.

"Either you get rid of your nervousness or you'll never become an effective public speaker."

Outlining

Complete the outline by filling in the missing major and minor details. The missing items are listed in random order below the outline.

Central point: You can cope with the nervousness of public speaking.

A. Introduction: Since speaking is important, it's important to learn to cope with nervousness.

B. _____

   _____

   1. Even good speakers get nervous; they just learn to channel and control their nervousness.

   2. Nervousness won't stop you from completing a speech, and it will even help you.

3. Your nervousness during a speech won't show nearly as much as you might think it will.

4. The more experience you get in speaking, the better you become at coping with nervousness.

C. _____

_____

1. Pick a topic you know something about and are interested in.

2. _____

_____

3. Try to control your nervousness just before you walk up to give your speech.

a. Try to schedule your speech at a comfortable time.

b. Focus your mind on something other than your speech.

4. _____

_____

a. As you walk to the speaker's stand, focus on your ideas and the fact that you're well prepared.

b. When you reach the stand, do a few things to break some of the tension.

1) Pause a few seconds and establish eye contact with the audience.

2) Take a deep breath.

3) Move about a little during your first few sentences.

4) Concentrate on communicating with your audience.

Items Missing from the Outline

● There are various ways to cope with your nervousness about public speaking.

● Prepare adequately for your speech.

● Use certain techniques as you walk to the speaker's stand and just after.

● People can learn to cope with the fear of public speaking.

Discussion Questions

1. What have your public speaking experiences been like? Have some speeches gone better than others? If so, what were the differences, and what do you think were the reasons for those differences? What did you find helpful in preparing and giving speeches?

2. Why might it be a good idea to speak on a topic you know a great deal about and are interested in? Can you think of any examples from the speeches you've given or heard?

3. You may need to give speeches in your classes, but do you think you will have to speak in public after you graduate from school? In what situations might you have to give a speech or even a presentation to a small group?

4. Obviously, Verderber feels that nervousness is no reason to avoid speaking in public. What other activities have you willingly done despite the fact that they made you nervous in some way? Was being nervous in these situations helpful in some ways? If so, how?

Note: Writing assignments for this selection appear on page 633.

Check Your Performance   COPING WITH NERVOUSNESS

Activity	Number Right	Points	Score
Basic Skill Questions			
Vocabulary in Context (2 items)	_____	× 4 =	_____
Central Point and Main Ideas (3 items)	_____	× 4 =	_____
Supporting Details (3 items)	_____	× 4 =	_____
Transitions (2 items)	_____	× 4 =	_____
Patterns of Organization (2 items)	_____	× 4 =	_____
Advanced Skill Questions			
Inferences (3 items)	_____	× 4 =	_____
Purpose and Tone (2 items)	_____	× 4 =	_____
Argument (1 item)	_____	× 4 =	_____
Critical Reading (2 items)	_____	× 4 =	_____
Outlining (4 items)	_____	× 5 =	_____
		TOTAL SCORE =	_____%

Enter your total score into the **Reading Performance Chart: Ten Reading Selections** on the inside back cover.

7 Compliance Techniques: Getting People to Say Yes

Shelley E. Taylor, Letitia Anne Peplau, and David O. Sears

Preview

People who make a living selling products or ideas do not rely on mere chance as they make their pitch. They use time-proven techniques to convince buyers that they are getting a good deal. This selection from *Social Psychology*, Eighth Edition, reveals some widely used compliance techniques. See if you recognize any of them.

Words to Watch

compliance (1): going along with someone else's wishes
induce (2): persuade
explicitly (2): in a clear way
implicitly (2): in a way that is not obvious
replicated (4): duplicated
self-perception (5): how one views oneself
proposition (10): suggested plan
unscrupulous (10): without moral standards

1   Research has investigated the specific techniques that people use to gain compliance°. Robert Cialdini has studied car salesmen, con artists, and other professionals who earn a living by getting people to buy their products or go along with their schemes. He and other social psychology researchers have identified several important compliance techniques.

The Foot-in-the-Door Technique

2   One way of increasing compliance is to induce° a person to agree first to a small request. Once someone has agreed to the small action, he or she is more likely to agree to a larger request. This is the so-called foot-in-the-door technique. It is used explicitly° or implicitly° in many advertising campaigns. Advertisers often concentrate on getting consumers to do something connected with the product—even sending back a card saying that they do not want it. The advertisers apparently think that any act connected with the product increases the likelihood that the consumer will buy it in the future.

3   A classic study by Freedman and Fraser demonstrated this effect. Experimenters went from door to door and told homemakers they were working for the Committee for Safe Driving. They said they wanted the women's support for this campaign and asked them to sign a petition that was to be sent to the state's senators. The petition requested the senators to work for legislation to encourage safe driving. Almost all the women agreed to sign. Several weeks later, different experimenters contacted the same women and also other women who had not been approached before. At this time, all the women were asked to put in their front yards a large, unattractive sign that read "Drive Carefully."

4   The results were striking. Over 55 percent of the women who had previously endorsed the petition (a small request) also agreed to post the sign (a relatively large request). In contrast, less than 17 percent of the other women agreed to post the sign. Getting the women to agree to the initial small request tripled the amount of compliance to the large request. This effect has been replicated° in several studies.

5   Why this technique works is not entirely clear. One explanation is that people who agree to a small request get involved and committed to the issue itself, to the behavior they perform, or perhaps simply to the idea of taking some kind of action. Another explanation is based on self-perception° theory. The idea here is that in some ways the individual's self-image changes as a result of the initial act of compliance. In the safe-driving experiment, for example, a woman may have thought of herself as the kind of person who does not take social action, who does not sign petitions, who does not post signs, or, perhaps, who does not agree to things that are asked of her by someone at the door. Once she has agreed to the small request, which was actually difficult to refuse, she may have changed her perception of herself slightly. Once she has agreed to sign a petition, she may come to think of herself as the kind of person who does this sort of thing. Then, when the second request was made, she was more likely to comply than she would have been otherwise.

The Door-in-the-Face Technique

Sometimes a technique opposite to   6

the foot-in-the-door also works. First asking for a very large request and then making a smaller request can increase compliance to the small request. This is sometimes called the door-in-the-face technique, since the first request is typically so outrageously large that people might be tempted to slam the door in the requester's face. In one study, subjects were asked to volunteer time for a good cause. Some were asked first to give a huge amount of time. When they refused, as almost all did, the experimenter immediately said then perhaps they might agree to a much smaller commitment of time. Other subjects were asked only the smaller request, while a third group was given a choice between the two. The results were striking. In the small-request-only condition, 17 percent of subjects agreed. In the choice condition, 25 percent of subjects complied with the smaller request. But in the condition where subjects had first turned down a big request, 50 percent agreed to the smaller request.

7   This effect is familiar to anyone who has ever bargained about the price of a used car or been involved in negotiations between a labor union and management. The tactic is to ask for the moon and then settle for less. The more you ask for at first, the more you expect to end up with eventually. The idea is that when you reduce your demands, the other person thinks you are compromising and the amount seems smaller. In a compliance situation, such as asking for money for charity, the same might apply. Five dollars doesn't seem

like so much when the organization initially asked for a hundred dollars.

8   Clearly, both the foot-in-the-door and the reverse tactic work at times, but we do not yet know when each will be more effective. Both seem to work best when the behavior involved is prosocial, that is, when the request is to give money or help a worthwhile cause. One difference seems to be that the door-in-the-face technique works when the smaller request follows the larger request immediately and is obviously connected. The foot-in-the-door technique works even when the two requests are seemingly unconnected.

The Low-Ball Technique

9   Consider how likely you would be to agree to the following requests. In one case, a researcher calls you on the phone and asks you to participate in an experiment scheduled for 7:00 in the morning. In a second case, a researcher calls and asks you to participate in a study. Only after you initially agree to participate does the researcher inform you that the study will be scheduled at 7:00 a.m. When Robert Cialdini and his associates compared these two procedures, they found that the second approach was much more effective. When students were told from the outset that an experiment would be conducted early in the morning, only 25 percent agreed to participate and showed up on time. In contrast, using the second approach of initially concealing the time of the study, 55 percent of students agreed to the request and almost all of them actually showed up for the early

morning appointment. Once having agreed to participate, few people backed out of their agreement when they were informed about the time of day.

10   This tactic, in which a person is asked to agree to something on the basis of incomplete information and is later told the full story, is called the low-ball technique. Essentially, the person is tricked into agreeing to a relatively attractive proposition°, only to discover later that the terms are actually different from those expected. This technique appears to work because once an individual has made an initial commitment to a course of action, he or she is reluctant to withdraw, even when the ground rules are changed. Although this technique can be effective (Burger & Petty, 1981), it is clearly deceptive. To protect consumers from unscrupulous° salespersons, laws have been enacted to make low-balling illegal for several industries, such as automobile dealerships.

11   Our discussion of the foot-in-the-door, door-in-the-face, and low-ball techniques by no means exhausts the possible tactics people use to gain compliance. Research by Jerry Burger has begun to explore another strategy that he calls the **that's-not-all technique**. Consider this situation: A salesperson describes a new microwave oven to a potential customer and quotes a price. Then, while the customer is mulling over

the decision, the salesperson adds, "But that's not all. Today only, we're having a special deal. If you buy the microwave now, we'll give you a five-piece set of microwave dishes at no additional cost." In actuality, the dishes always come with the oven, but by presenting the dishes as a "special deal" or something "just for you," the salesperson hopes to make the purchase even more attractive. The essence of this technique is to present a product at a high price, allow the customer to think about the price, and then improve the deal either by adding an additional product or by lowering the price.

12   In a series of seven experiments, Burger has demonstrated the potential effectiveness of the "that's-not-all" approach. In one illustrative study, experimenters held a psychology club bake sale on campus. At random, half the people who stopped at the table and asked about the cupcakes were told that they could buy a prepackaged set including one cupcake and two cookies for 75 cents. In this control condition, 40 percent of those who inquired actually purchased a cupcake. In the "that's-not-all condition," people who inquired were first told that the cupcakes were 75 cents each. A moment later, they were told that actually, they would get not only the cupcake but also 2 cookies for the 75-cent price. In this "that's-not-all" condition, 73 percent of people bought a cupcake, a substantially higher proportion than in the control condition.

Basic Skill Questions

Vocabulary in Context

_____ 1. In the sentence below, the word *endorsed* (ĕn-dôrst′ *or* ĭn-dôrst′) means
A. rejected.
B. asked for.
C. supported.
D. ignored.

> "Over 55 percent of the women who had previously endorsed the petition (a small request) also agreed to post the sign (a relatively large request)." (Paragraph 4)

_____ 2. In the excerpt below, the words *mulling over* (mŭl′ ĭng ō′vər) mean
A. regretting.
B. paying for.
C. agreeing to.
D. thinking about.

> "A salesperson describes a new microwave oven to a potential customer and quotes a price. Then, while the customer is mulling over the decision, the salesperson adds, 'But that's not all. Today only, we're having a special deal.'" (Paragraph 11)

Central Point and Main Ideas

_____ 3. Which sentence best expresses the central point of the selection?
A. Certain techniques are widely used to persuade consumers to buy a product or go along with a plan.
B. The "foot-in-the-door" technique relies on people's tendency to agree to a larger request after they have agreed to a small one.
C. Anyone who has bargained to buy a car will recognize the "door-in-the-face" technique.
D. Social psychologists study why people are influenced by certain kinds of sales techniques.

_____ 4. Which sentence best expresses the main idea of paragraph 5?
A. While it is not certain why the "foot-in-the-door" technique works, there are some likely explanations.
B. People adjust their actions based on changes in their self-perception.
C. It is difficult to refuse a small, reasonable request.
D. A woman may not have considered herself to be the sort of person who takes social action.

_____ 5. Which sentence best expresses the main idea of paragraph 7?
   A. The "door-in-the-face" technique is commonly used when one bargains for a used car.
   B. When someone starts out making a large request and then replaces it with a smaller one, the second request seems reasonable by contrast.
   C. Compared with one hundred dollars, five dollars does not seem like much.
   D. People often begin negotiations by asking for more than they expect.

Supporting Details

_____ 6. The major supporting details of the reading are a series of
   A. questions.
   B. events.
   C. techniques.
   D. steps.

_____ 7. One explanation given for why the foot-in-the-door technique works is that agreeing to a small task
   A. makes the person feel he or she has done enough.
   B. angers the person.
   C. improves a person's opinion of the requester.
   D. changes the person's self-image.

Transitions

_____ 8. The relationship of the second sentence below to the first one is one of
   A. cause and effect.
   B. comparison.
   C. illustration.
   D. time.

   "Almost all the women agreed to sign. Several weeks later, different experimenters contacted the same women and also other women who had not been approached before." (Paragraph 3)

_____ 9. In the excerpt below, what does the second sentence do?
   A. It establishes a cause and effect relationship.
   B. It presents a solution to a problem.
   C. It contrasts the responses of two groups of people to a smaller request.
   D. It adds more detail to the first sentence.

   "In the choice condition, 25 percent of subjects complied with the smaller request. But in the condition where subjects had first turned down a big request, 50 percent agreed to the smaller request." (Paragraph 6)

Patterns of Organization

_____10. The main pattern of organization of paragraph 6 is
   A. list of items.
   B. time order.
   C. definition and example.
   D. comparison.

_____11. The main pattern of organization of paragraph 8 is
   A. list of items.
   B. time order.
   C. definition and example.
   D. comparison and/or contrast.

Advanced Skill Questions

Inferences

_____12. We can infer from paragraph 3 that
   A. women are more likely to be concerned about safe driving than men.
   B. the experimenters were aggressive and pushy in their dealings with the homemakers.
   C. the "Safe Driving" signs were deliberately made unattractive.
   D. the researchers were truly employees of the Committee for Safe Driving.

_____13. We can conclude from paragraph 5 that
   A. experiments often reveal very little.
   B. even though an experiment proves something, that doesn't mean it is fully understood.
   C. human behavior is generally easy to explain.
   D. we will never know why the foot-in-the-door technique works.

_____14. We can conclude that the "that's-not-all" technique works because
   A. people like to buy things.
   B. microwave ovens are especially popular these days.
   C. people buy what they need or want.
   D. people like to feel that they are getting more for their money.

Purpose and Tone

_____15. The tone of the reading can be identified as
   A. upbeat and positive.
   B. scholarly and matter-of-fact.
   C. concerned and angry.
   D. forgiving and understanding.

Argument

_____16. Which of the statements does **not** support the point of the argument?

   **Point: There are ways to make it more likely that people will do what you
   want them to do.**

   A. Experiments have shown that some compliance techniques work.
   B. Salespeople find that certain techniques work better than others.
   C. There is nothing wrong with trying to influence people.
   D. People are more likely to buy something if they are made to feel it's
      a great bargain.

Critical Reading

_____17. The sentence below is
   A. all factual.
   B. all opinion.
   C. a mix of fact and opinion.

   "To protect consumers from unscrupulous salespersons, laws have
   been enacted to make low-balling illegal for several industries, such as
   automobile dealerships." (Paragraph 10)

_____18. A fund-raising group which displays a large sign illustrating how many
   people have already donated to their cause is using the propaganda
   technique of
   A. plain folks.
   B. bandwagon.
   C. testimonial.
   D. glittering generalities.

_____19. A TV commercial which encourages us to purchase "The amazing Miracle Knives—guaranteed to make meal preparation a breeze" is using the propaganda technique of
A. plain folks.
B. bandwagon.
C. testimonial.
D. glittering generalities.

_____20. The following statement illustrates the logical fallacy of
A. false comparison.
B. either-or.
C. false cause.
D. circular reasoning.

"This product is a great buy because it's a real bargain."

Summarizing

Study notes on this reading might be made up of a summary of each compliance technique, including 1) a definition, 2) an example, and 3) an explanation of why the technique works. Complete the summary below by filling in the incomplete or missing items.

Compliance Techniques

1. Foot-in-the-door technique—getting a person to agree first to a small request so that he or she is more likely to agree to a larger one. This technique may work either because people become more committed or because they change their self-image. It works even when the requests appear unconnected.

Example: Women were more likely to agree to put a large, unattractive "Drive Carefully" sign in their front yards if they had first signed a petition asking senators to work for legislation encouraging safe driving.

2. Door-in-the-face technique—first asking for a very large request and then

_____

_____

This works when the smaller request follows the larger one immediately and is obviously connected to it.

Example: Study subjects were more likely to volunteer a small amount of time for a good cause if they were first asked _____

_____

3. Low-ball technique—_____

_____

This may work because people are reluctant to withdraw after making a commitment.

> Example: Students were more likely to take part in an experiment at 7 a.m. if they weren't told about the time until after agreeing to participate.

4. That's-not-all technique—presenting a product at a high price, allowing the customer to think about the price, and then improving the deal either by adding an additional product or by lowering the price.

> Example: _____

_____

_____

Discussion Questions

1. While reading this selection, did you recognize techniques that have been used to influence you to make a purchase or support someone's plan? How were the techniques used?

2. Which of the compliance techniques do you feel is most clearly deceptive? Why?

3. The authors state that no one is really sure why the foot-in-the-door technique is effective, but they offer two possible explanations. Does either of these theories seem to you to adequately explain why the technique works? Can you think of an alternative explanation?

4. Imagine that you are in the business of selling home computers. Describe how you would use the foot-in-the-door technique, the door-in-the-face technique, and the low-ball technique to try to make a sale.

Note: Writing assignments for this selection appear on pages 633–634.

Check Your Performance   COMPLIANCE TECHNIQUES

Activity	Number Right	Points		Score
Basic Skill Questions				
Vocabulary in Context (2 items)	_____	× 4	=	_____
Central Point and Main Ideas (3 items)	_____	× 4	=	_____
Supporting Details (2 items)	_____	× 4	=	_____
Transitions (2 items)	_____	× 4	=	_____
Patterns of Organization (2 items)	_____	× 4	=	_____
Advanced Skill Questions				
Inferences (3 items)	_____	× 4	=	_____
Purpose and Tone (1 item)	_____	× 4	=	_____
Argument (1 item)	_____	× 4	=	_____
Critical Reading (4 items)	_____	× 4	=	_____
Summarizing (4 items)	_____	× 5	=	_____
		TOTAL SCORE	=	_____%

Enter your total score into the **Reading Performance Chart: Ten Reading Selections** on the inside back cover.

8 Lizzie Borden
James Kirby Martin and others

Preview

A prosperous businessman and his wife lay dead, murdered with an ax. Their unhappy daughter had the motive and opportunity to kill. Modern experts strongly believe that Lizzie Borden was guilty of her parents' murder. Yet she was swiftly found innocent. In this selection taken from the history textbook *America and Its People*, Second Edition, Lizzie's acquittal is examined in light of the social views of the late nineteenth century.

Words to Watch

maintained (1): claimed
alienated (3): set apart from
grisly (5): causing horror
preponderance (7): great amount
unanimous (7): agreed upon by everyone
affirmed (7): stated
preconceived (9): decided before knowing all the facts
docile (9): obedient
frivolous (9): silly

1   Andrew Borden had, as the old Scottish saying goes, short arms and long pockets. He was cheap, not because he had to be frugal but because he hated to spend money. He had dedicated his entire life to making and saving money, and tales of his unethical and parsimonious business behavior were legendary in his hometown of Fall River, Massachusetts. Local gossips maintained° that as an undertaker, he cut off the feet of corpses so that he could fit them into undersized coffins that he had purchased at a very good price. Andrew, however, was not interested in rumors or the opinions of other people; he was concerned with his own rising fortunes. By 1892 he had amassed over half a million dollars, and he controlled the Fall River Union Savings Bank as well as serving as the director of the Globe Yard Mill Company, the First National Bank, the Troy Cotton and Manufacturing Company, and the Merchants Manufacturing Company.

2   Andrew was rich, but he did not live like a wealthy man. Instead of living alongside the other prosperous Fall River citizens in the elite neighborhood known as "the Hill," Andrew resided in an area near the business district called "the Flats." He liked to save time as well as money, and from the Flats he could conveniently walk to work. For his daughters Lizzie and Emma, whose eyes and dreams focused on the Hill, life in the Flats was an intolerable embarrassment. Their house was a grim, boxlike structure that lacked comfort and privacy. Since Andrew believed that running water on each floor was a wasteful luxury, the only washing facilities were a cold-water faucet in the kitchen and a laundry-room water tap in the cellar. Also in the cellar was the only toilet in the house. To make matters worse, the house was not connected to the Fall River gas main. Andrew preferred to use kerosene to light his house. Although it did not provide as good light or burn as cleanly as gas, it was less expensive. To save even more money, he and his family frequently sat in the dark.

3   The Borden home was far from happy. Lizzie and Emma, ages 32 and 42 in 1892, strongly disliked their stepmother, Abby, and resented Andrew's penny-pinching ways. Lizzie especially felt alienated° from the world around her. Although Fall River was the largest cotton-manufacturing town in America, it offered few opportunities for the unmarried daughter of a prosperous man. Society expected a woman of social position to marry, and while she waited for a proper suitor, her only respectable social outlets were church and community service. So Lizzie taught a Sunday school class and was active in the Women's Christian Temperance Union, the Ladies' Fruit and Flower Mission, and other organizations. She kept herself busy, but she was not happy.

4   In August, 1892, strange things started to happen in the Borden home. They began after Lizzie and Emma learned that Andrew had secretly changed his will. Abby became violently ill. In time so did the Bordens' maid Bridget Sullivan and Andrew himself. Abby told a neighborhood doctor that she had been poisoned, but Andrew refused to listen to her wild ideas. Shortly thereafter, Lizzie went shopping for prussic acid, a deadly poison she said she needed to clean her sealskin cape. When a Fall River druggist refused her

request, she left the store in an agitated state. Later in the day, she told a friend that she feared an unknown enemy of her father's was after him. "I'm afraid somebody will do something," she said.

5   On August 4, 1892, Bridget awoke early and ill, but she still managed to prepare a large breakfast of johnnycakes, fresh-baked bread, ginger and oatmeal cookies and raisins, and some three-day-old mutton and hot mutton soup. After eating a hearty meal, Andrew left for work. Bridget also left to do some work outside. This left Abby and Lizzie in the house alone. Then somebody did something very specific and very grisly°. As Abby was bent over making the bed in the guest room, someone moved into the room unobserved and killed her with an ax.

6   Andrew came home for lunch earlier than usual. He asked Lizzie where Abby was, and she said she did not know. Unconcerned, Andrew, who was not feeling well, lay down on the parlor sofa for a nap. He never awoke. Like Abby, he was slaughtered by someone with an ax. Lizzie "discovered" his body still lying on the sofa. She called Bridget, who had taken the back stairs to her attic room. "Come down quick; Father's dead; somebody came in and killed him."

7   Experts have examined and reexamined the crime, and most have reached the same conclusion: Lizzie killed her father and stepmother. In fact, Lizzie was tried for the gruesome murders. Despite a preponderance° of evidence, however, an all-male jury found her not guilty. Their verdict was unanimous° and was arrived at without debate or disagreement. A woman of Lizzie's social position, they affirmed°, simply could not have committed such a terrible crime.

8   Even before the trial began, newspaper and magazine writers had judged Lizzie innocent for the same reasons. As historian Kathryn Allamong Jacob, an expert on the case, noted, "Americans were certain that well-brought up daughters could not commit murder with a hatchet on sunny summer mornings." Criminal women, they believed, originated in the lower classes and even looked evil. They did not look like round-faced Lizzie, and did not belong to the Ladies' Fruit and Flower Mission.

9   Jurors and editorialists alike judged Lizzie according to their preconceived° notions of Victorian womanhood. They believed that such a woman was gentle, docile°, and physically frail, short on analytical ability but long on nurturing instincts. "Women," wrote an editorialist for *Scribner's*, "are merely large babies. They are shortsighted, frivolous°, and occupy an intermediate stage between children and men." Too uncoordinated and weak to accurately swing an ax and too gentle and unintelligent to coldly plan a double murder, women of Lizzie's background simply had to be innocent because of their basic innocence.

Basic Skill Questions

Vocabulary in Context

_____ 1. In the excerpt below, the word *parsimonious* (pär′sə-mō′nē-əs) means
   A. generous.
   B. lazy.
   C. stingy.
   D. deadly.

> ". . . tales of his unethical and parsimonious business behavior were legendary in his hometown . . . Local gossips maintained that as an undertaker, he cut off the feet of corpses so that he could fit them into undersized coffins that he had purchased at a very good price."
> (Paragraph 1)

_____ 2. In the excerpt below, the word *amassed* (ə-măst′) means
   A. spent.
   B. found.
   C. accumulated.
   D. donated.

> "By 1892 [Andrew Borden] had amassed over half a million dollars . . . "
> (Paragraph 1)

Central Point and Main Ideas

_____ 3. Which sentence best expresses the central point of the selection?
   A. Andrew Borden's unpleasant personality and cheap ways probably led to his murder.
   B. The case of Lizzie Borden should be reopened and reexamined to determine if she was truly guilty.
   C. Despite much evidence of her guilt, Lizzie Borden was found innocent of murder because of society's beliefs about women of her social class.
   D. In the late 1800s, Americans assumed that middle-class women who were well brought up were weak and gentle people who could not possibly commit a murder.

_____ 4. The main idea of paragraph 2 is expressed in its
   A. first sentence.
   B. second sentence.
   C. third sentence.
   D. last sentence.

_____ 5. Which sentence best expresses the main idea of paragraph 8?

    A. Lizzie had a round face and belonged to the Ladies' Fruit and Flower Mission.

    B. Americans couldn't believe a pleasant-looking, respectable woman like Lizzie could be a killer.

    C. Trials in the late 1800s were widely covered in newspapers and magazines.

    D. Americans of Lizzie's day believed that killers looked evil.

Supporting Details

_____ 6. The supporting details of paragraph 2 are mainly about

    A. the ways in which Andrew Borden saved money.

    B. Lizzie's and Emma's embarrassment with their home.

    C. the reason the Bordens often sat in the dark.

    D. the fact that the Bordens used kerosene rather than gas for light.

_____ 7. The odd occurrences in the Borden home began after

    A. Bridget Sullivan was hired to be the maid.

    B. Andrew Borden brought Abby home to be Lizzie and Emma's stepmother.

    C. Andrew Borden changed his will.

    D. Lizzie joined the church's Fruit and Flower Mission.

Transitions

_____ 8. The relationship between the two parts of the sentence below is one of

    A. cause and effect.

    B. contrast.

    C. time order.

    D. addition.

> "Instead of living alongside the other prosperous Fall River citizens in the elite neighborhood known as 'the Hill,' Andrew resided in an area near the business district called 'the Flats.'" (Paragraph 2)

_____ 9. In the following excerpt, what does the second sentence do?

    A. It establishes a cause and effect relationship.

    B. It contrasts Lizzie Borden's behavior with that of other women.

    C. It defines a term in the first sentence.

    D. It compares Lizzie Borden to other women of social position.

> "Society expected a woman of social position to marry, and while she waited for a proper suitor, her only respectable social outlets were church and community service. So Lizzie taught a Sunday school class and was active in the the Women's Christian Temperance Union, the Ladies' Fruit and Flower Mission, and other organizations." (Paragraph 3)

Patterns of Organization

_____10. Paragraph 2 is organized as a
   A. series of events in the Borden household.
   B. list of ways in which the Bordens lived very thriftily.
   C. comparison and contrast between the members of the Borden household.
   D. definition of *wealthy* followed by examples.

_____11. The pattern of organization of paragraphs 4–6 is
   A. time order.
   B. list of items.
   C. comparison and contrast.
   D. definition and example.

Advanced Skill Questions

Inferences

_____12. We can infer from the mention of Andrew Borden's changing his will that
   A. he had decided to leave all of his money to his daughters.
   B. he was a lawyer.
   C. his new will was unfavorable to Lizzie.
   D. his new wife was not going to inherit any of his money.

_____13. The authors imply that Bridget, Andrew, and Abby all became ill at about the same time because
   A. they became sick from living in the cold, dark house.
   B. they suffered from food poisoning as a result of eating three-day-old mutton.
   C. Lizzie poisoned them.
   D. Bridget poisoned them, but pretended to be ill herself to hide her actions.

_____14. Which of the following statements is a valid conclusion based on the information in paragraph 9?
   A. The editorialist for *Scribner's* expressed opinions that were unusual for the day.
   B. Lizzie Borden was an exceptionally unintelligent, gentle person.
   C. Men were thought to be more competent, mature, and intelligent than women.
   D. The ax used in the Borden murders was very heavy.

Purpose and Tone

_____15. The main purpose of this selection is to
   A. persuade the reader that society's views about women led to Lizzie Borden's being found innocent of two murders that she probably committed.
   B. inform the reader about the everyday life of a well-known nineteenth-century family and about a famous trial of the time.
   C. entertain the reader with a crime story.

_____16. In general, the authors' tone is
   A. sad and hopeless.
   B. objective and analytical.
   C. light and amusing.
   D. bitterly critical.

Argument

_____17. Which statement does **not** support the following point?

   Point: Lizzie Borden was probably guilty.

   A. She had attempted to buy poison shortly before the killings.
   B. She was miserable living with her stingy father and disliked her stepmother.
   C. She was alone in the house with her parents when the killings occurred.
   D. She was active in church and community organizations.

_____18. One of the following statements is the point of an argument. The other statements support that point. Write the letter of the point.
   A. The common belief that upper-class women were unable to swing an ax well was false.
   B. The jurors' reasoning in finding Lizzie Borden innocent was faulty.
   C. The jurors' idea that criminals looked a certain way was mistaken.
   D. The jurors' belief that women were too gentle and unintelligent to plan a murder was false.

Critical Reading

_____19. The sentence below contains
   A. only facts.
   B. only opinions.
   C. a mixture of both fact and opinion.

   "By 1892 he had amassed over half a million dollars, and he controlled the Fall River Union Savings Bank as well as serving as the director of the Globe Yard Mill Company, the First National Bank, the Troy Cotton and Manufacturing Company, and the Merchants Manufacturing Company." (Paragraph 1)

_____20. The following excerpt is an example of which logical fallacy?
   A. False comparison
   B. Either-or
   C. False cause
   D. Circular reasoning

   "Too uncoordinated and weak to accurately swing an ax and too gentle and unintelligent to coldly plan a double murder, women of Lizzie's background simply had to be innocent because of their basic innocence." (Paragraph 9)

Summarizing

In the space provided, write the letter of the paragraph (A, B, or C) that best summarizes the reading "Lizzie Borden."

As you read the three choices, keep in mind that a good summary will include general statements that sum up the selection. It will cover the key elements of the reading. Some specific details may be included as well.

_____ is the best summary of the reading.

   A. Lizzie Borden lived the respectable life expected of a woman of social position. One day she and her sister discovered that their father, Andrew, had secretly changed his will. Strange things then began to happen in the Borden household. First of all, their stepmother, Abby, became violently ill. After that, the Bordens' maid, Bridget Sullivan, and Andrew himself became ill too. Then Lizzie went shopping for a deadly poison, prussic acid. She said she needed it to clean her sealskin cape. However, the local druggist refused to sell the poison to her. Lizzie later told a friend that she feared an enemy would do something to her father. On August 4, Lizzie was alone in the house with her stepmother. As Abby was making a bed in the guest room, someone came into the room unobserved and killed her with an ax. Later that day, Andrew came home for lunch and, feeling unwell, lay down on the parlor sofa and napped. He never woke up. Like Abby, he was axed to death. Although there is strong evidence that Lizzie was the murderer, she was found innocent in a trial.

B. Lizzie Borden lived the respectable life expected of unmarried women of her social class, but she wasn't happy. Although her father, Andrew, was rich, he was miserly, and the Borden home was grim. In addition, Lizzie disliked her stepmother, Abby. In 1892, she and her sister learned their father had changed his will. Soon after, Abby and then the maid and Andrew became very ill. After that, Lizzie tried unsuccessfully to buy a deadly poison. Then, on August 4, both Abby and Andrew were found axed to death. Lizzie was tried for the crimes. Although experts today conclude she was guilty, the jury found her innocent. Like others of their day, they believed that upper-class women were too gentle, weak, and stupid to plan and carry out a murder. Also, they believed that criminal women came from the lower classes and looked evil.

C. Andrew Borden was rich but miserly. The Borden home, therefore, lacked comforts. It had no running water on each floor, and the only toilet in the house was in the cellar. To save money, since kerosene was cheaper than gas, the house was not connected to the town gas main. And to save yet more money, the Bordens often sat in the dark. Furthermore, the house was in a neighborhood near the business district, not the elite neighborhood that his daughters, Lizzie and Emma, felt was equal to their social class. The sisters also disliked their stepmother, Abby. Women of the time were expected to marry and, while waiting for the proper man, to do volunteer work for the church and community. So Lizzie taught a Sunday school class and was active in such organizations as the Women's Christian Temperance Union and the Ladies' Fruit and Flower Mission. One day she discovered her father had changed his will; not long after that, he and Abby were found axed to death.

Discussion Questions

1. On the basis of the information in the reading, do you agree or disagree with the experts who say Lizzie was guilty? Explain your answer.

2. As you read this selection, what impression did you form of life in the Borden household? What particular details helped you form that opinion?

3. The authors imply that the story about Andrew Borden's cutting off the feet of corpses to make them fit undersized coffins was a rumor, not a proved fact. Why, then, do you think they include the story in this piece?

4. Do you believe that any of the notions about women that existed in Lizzie Borden's day are still at work in some ways today? Explain your answer.

Note: Writing assignments for this selection appear on page 634.

Check Your Performance   **LIZZIE BORDEN**

Activity	Number Right	Points		Score
Basic Skill Questions				
Vocabulary in Context (2 items)	_____	× 4	=	_____
Central Point and Main Ideas (3 items)	_____	× 4	=	_____
Supporting Details (2 items)	_____	× 4	=	_____
Transitions (2 items)	_____	× 4	=	_____
Patterns of Organization (2 items)	_____	× 4	=	_____
Advanced Skill Questions				
Inferences (3 items)	_____	× 4	=	_____
Purpose and Tone (2 items)	_____	× 4	=	_____
Argument (2 items)	_____	× 4	=	_____
Critical Reading (2 items)	_____	× 4	=	_____
Summarizing (1 item)	_____	× 20	=	_____
		TOTAL SCORE	=	_____ %

Enter your total score into the **Reading Performance Chart: Ten Reading Selections** on the inside back cover.

9 Nonverbal Communication
Anthony F. Grasha

Preview

When we think of communication, we usually think of language. But a great deal of human communication takes place without speaking. When we are angry, we may make a fist. When we are happy, our faces give us away. The extent to which we reveal our feelings without words, however, goes much further than we are often aware of. In this excerpt from a college textbook titled *Practical Applications of Psychology,* Third Edition, Anthony F. Grasha provides an overview of just how much we really say without words.

Words to Watch

norms (2): normal standards
culprit (6): guilty one
manipulate (7): use
utterances (7): expressions
quivering (8): trembling

1   The way we dress, our mannerisms, how close we stand to people, eye contact, touching, and the ways we mark our personal spaces convey certain messages. *Such nonverbal behaviors communicate certain messages by themselves and also enhance the meaning of our verbal communications.* Pounding your fist on a table, for example, suggests anger without anything being spoken. Holding someone close to you conveys the message that you care. To say "I don't like you" with a loud voice or waving fists increases the intensity of the verbal message. Let us examine the concepts of *personal space* and *body language* to gain additional insights into the nonverbal side of interpersonal communication.

NONVERBAL MESSAGES: The Use of Personal Space

2   Edward Hall notes that we have personal spatial territories or zones that allow certain types of behaviors and communications. We allow only certain people to enter or events to occur within a zone. Let us look at how some nonverbal messages can be triggered by behaviors that violate the norms° of each zone. The four personal zones identified by Hall are as follows:

3   **1. Intimate distance.** This personal zone covers a range of distance from body contact to one foot. Relationships between a parent and child, lovers, and close friends occur within this zone. As a general rule, we allow only people we know and have some affection for to enter this zone. When people try to enter without our permission, they are strongly repelled by our telling them to stay away from us or by our pushing them away. Why do you think we allow a doctor to easily violate our intimate distance zone?

4   **2. Personal distance.** The spatial range covered by this zone extends from one to four feet. Activities like eating in a restaurant with two or three other people, sitting on chairs or on the floor in small groups at parties, or playing cards occur within this zone. Violations of the zone make people feel uneasy and act nervously. When you are eating at a restaurant, the amount of table space that is considered yours is usually divided equally by the number of people present. I can remember becoming angry and generally irritated when a friend of mine placed a plate and glass in my space. As we talked I was visibly irritated, but my anger had nothing to do with the topic we discussed. Has this ever happened to you?

5   **3. Social distance.** Four to twelve feet is the social distance zone. Business meetings, large formal dinners, and small classroom seminars occur within the boundaries of the social distance zone. Discussions concerning everyday topics like the weather, politics, or a best

seller are considered acceptable. For a husband and wife to launch into a heated argument during a party in front of ten other people would violate the accepted norms for behavior in the social zone. This once happened at a formal party I attended. The nonverbal behaviors that resulted consisted of several people leaving the room, others looking angry or uncomfortable, and a few standing and watching quietly with an occasional upward glance and a rolling of their eyeballs. What would violate the social distance norms in a classroom?

6   **4. Public distance.** This zone includes the area beyond twelve feet. Addressing a crowd, watching a sports event, and sitting in a large lecture section are behaviors we engage in within this zone. As is true for the other zones, behaviors unacceptable for this zone can trigger nonverbal messages. At a recent World Series game a young male took his clothes off and ran around the outfield. Some watched with amusement on their faces, others looked away, and a few waved their fists at the culprit°. The respective messages were "That's funny," "I'm afraid or ashamed to look," and "How dare you interrupt the game." What would your reaction be in this situation?

NONVERBAL MESSAGES:
The Use of Body Language

7   *Body language* refers to the various arm and hand gestures, facial expressions, tones of voice, postures, and body movements we use to convey certain messages. According to Erving Goffman, they are the things we "give off" when talking to other people. Goffman notes that our body language is generally difficult to manipulate° at will. Unlike our verbal utterances°, we have less conscious control over the specific body gestures or expressions we might make while talking. Unless we are acting on a stage or purposely trying to create a certain effect, they occur automatically without much thought on our part.

8   Michael Argyle notes that body language serves several functions for us. *It helps us to communicate certain emotions, attitudes, and preferences.* A hug by someone close to us lets us know we are appreciated. A friendly wave and smile as someone we know passes us lets us know we are recognized. A quivering° lip tells us that someone is upset. Each of us has become quite sensitive to the meaning of various body gestures and expressions. Robert Rosenthal has demonstrated that this sensitivity is rather remarkable. When shown films of people expressing various emotions, individuals were able to identify the emotion correctly 66 percent of the time even when each frame was exposed for one twenty-fourth of a second. *Body language also supports our verbal communications.* Vocal signals of timing, pitch, voice stress, and various gestures add meaning to our verbal utterances. Argyle suggests that we may speak with our vocal organs, but we converse with our whole body. *Body language helps to control our conversations.* It helps us to decide when it is time to stop talking, to interrupt the other person, and to know when to shift topics or elaborate on something because our listeners are bored, do not understand us, or are not paying attention.

Basic Skill Questions

Vocabulary in Context

_____ 1. In the excerpt below, the word *enhance* (ĕn-hăns′) means

    A. replace.   C. contradict.

    B. reinforce.   D. delay.

"The way we dress, our mannerisms . . . convey certain messages. *Such nonverbal behaviors communicate certain messages by themselves and also enhance the meaning of our verbal communications.*" (Paragraph 1)

_____ 2. In the excerpt below, the word *repelled* (rĭ-pĕld′) means
    A. greeted.   C. encouraged.
    B. turned away.   D. ignored.

> "When people try to enter without our permission, they are strongly repelled by our telling them to stay away from us . . ." (Paragraph 3)

Central Point and Main Ideas

_____ 3. Which sentence best expresses the central point of the selection?
    A. It is possible to express anger without words.
    B. People communicate with each other in various ways.
    C. We can convey nonverbal messages and emphasize verbal messages through the use of personal space and body language.
    D. According to Michael Argyle, body language has several functions.

_____ 4. Which sentence best expresses the main idea of paragraph 7?
    A. We must plan our body language.
    B. It is hard to control body language.
    C. Actors use body language to create an effect.
    D. *Body language* refers to the nonverbal ways we communicate, usually without conscious control.

_____ 5. The main idea of paragraph 8 is expressed in its
    A. first sentence.
    B. second sentence.
    C. next-to-last sentence.
    D. last sentence.

Supporting Details

_____ 6. According to Rosenthal's work, we
    A. frequently understand body language.
    B. rarely understand body language.
    C. always understand body language.
    D. never understand body language.

_____ 7. To support his central point, the author uses
    A. examples.   C. opinions of other experts.
    B. research.   D. all of the above.

_____ 8. The major supporting details of the reading are
    A. nonverbal messages and verbal messages.
    B. communicating well and communicating poorly.
    C. intimate distance and body language.
    D. communicating through personal space and through body language.

Transitions

_____ 9. In the following excerpt, what does the second sentence do?
  A. It illustrates and adds detail to the first sentence.
  B. It establishes a cause and effect relationship.
  C. It shows a time order relationship.
  D. It contrasts verbal and nonverbal forms of communication.

  > *"Such nonverbal behaviors communicate certain messages by themselves
  > and also enhance the meaning of our verbal communications.* Pounding
  > your fist on a table, for example, suggests anger without anything being
  > spoken." (Paragraph 1)

Patterns of Organization

_____10. The pattern of organization of paragraph 3 (as well as 4, 5, and 6) is
  A. time order.
  B. cause and effect.
  C. definition and example.
  D. list of items.

_____11. On the whole, paragraph 8
  A. compares and contrasts body language and verbal expression.
  B. lists the functions of body language.
  C. defines body language and gives examples of it.
  D. uses time order to narrate an incident about body language.

Advanced Skill Questions

Inferences

_____12. TRUE OR FALSE? Just as body language generally occurs automatically,
  so do our reactions to the use or misuse of our personal space.

_____13. Goffman's ideas on body language (paragraph 7) imply that
  A. we usually are aware of our own body language.
  B. our body language might reveal emotions we wish to hide.
  C. we can never manipulate our body language.
  D. we should learn to manipulate our body language.

_____14. We can conclude from the reading and our own experience that body
  language
  A. communicates positive and negative messages of all sorts.
  B. is best at communicating friendly messages.
  C. communicates poorly.
  D. communicates rarely.

_____15. Two students reviewing together for a test would be working within
     A. an intimate distance.
     B. a personal distance.
     C. a social distance.
     D. a public distance.

Purpose and Tone

_____16. The author's primary purpose in this selection is to
     A. inform us about nonverbal communication and how it works.
     B. persuade us that nonverbal communication is as important as conversation.
     C. entertain us with anecdotes involving funny or embarassing public behavior.

_____17. On the whole, the author's tone is
     A. humorous.
     B. objective.
     C. scornful.
     D. enthusiastic.

Argument

_____18. Write the letter of the statement that is the point of the following argument. Note that two other statements support the point, and that one statement expresses another point.
     A. I became angry and generally irritated when a friend of mine placed a plate and glass in my space.
     B. As we talked I was visibly irritated, but my anger had nothing to do with the topic we discussed.
     C. Business meetings take place within the boundaries of the social distance zone.
     D. Violations of the personal zone make people feel uneasy and act nervously.

Critical Reading

_____19. The sentence below is
     A. totally factual.
     B. only opinion.
     C. both fact and opinion.

     "When shown films of people expressing various emotions, individuals were able to identify the emotion correctly 66 percent of the time even when each frame was exposed for one twenty-fourth of a second." (Paragraph 8)

_____20. An ad featuring a beautiful young woman draped over a luxury convertible is using the propaganda technique of

A. bandwagon.   C. testimonial.

B. transfer.   D. plain folks.

Outlining

Complete the following outline of "Nonverbal Communication" by using the information in the boldfaced headings, italics, and numbers in the selection. (Five items need to be added to the outline.)

Central point: Our use of personal space and body language communicates meaning and emphasizes verbal communication.

A.   _____

    1. Intimate distance

    2. Personal distance

    3. _____

    4. _____

B.   Nonverbal messages: the use of body language

    1. Definition and explanation of body language

    2. Functions of body language

        a.   _____

            _____

        b.   _____

        c.   Helps control our conversations

Discussion Questions

1.   What are your answers to the following questions from the selection? Why do you think the author included these questions?

    ● Why do you think we allow a doctor to easily violate our intimate distance zone?

    ● I can remember becoming angry and generally irritated when a friend of mine placed a plate and glass in my space. . . . Has this ever happened to you?

    ● What would violate the social distance norms in a classroom?

2. This selection includes headings, italics, labels, and numbered items. How are these related to the author's purpose?

3. What are some examples of a dating or business situation in which someone's body language might contradict his or her verbal communication?

4. Give examples from your own experience of all four types of personal space.

Note: Writing assignments for this selection appear on page 635.

Check Your Performance   NONVERBAL COMMUNICATION

Activity	Number Right	Points	Score
Basic Skill Questions			
Vocabulary in Context (2 items)	_____	× 4 =	_____
Central Point and Main Ideas (3 items)	_____	× 4 =	_____
Supporting Details (3 items)	_____	× 4 =	_____
Transitions (1 item)	_____	× 4 =	_____
Patterns of Organization (2 items)	_____	× 4 =	_____
Advanced Skill Questions			
Inferences (4 items)	_____	× 4 =	_____
Purpose and Tone (2 items)	_____	× 4 =	_____
Argument (1 item)	_____	× 4 =	_____
Critical Reading (2 items)	_____	× 4 =	_____
Outlining (5 items)	_____	× 4 =	_____
		TOTAL SCORE =	_____ %

Enter your total score into the **Reading Performance Chart: Ten Reading Selections** on the inside back cover.

10 The Power Within
John Langan

Preview

Year after year, teachers watch the latest group of college students arrive in their classrooms. After a while, an observant teacher can begin to predict, with pretty good accuracy, which students will succeed and which will not. Here a veteran teacher explains that the most important factor is not a student's IQ. Read on to discover the real secrets behind college (and life!) success.

Words to Watch

slouching (10): hunched over
resignation (11): acceptance of defeat
peers (17): buddies
succumb (19): surrender
passive (29): inactive
clique (42): gang

1   In the first college writing class that I taught, I had a student who was drowning.

2   Gerald was a quiet young man who wore sunglasses, did not speak in class, and sat in the back of the room. I didn't know he was drowning until I collected a mid-semester assignment which asked students to write about what they had done—or not done—to take charge of their lives.

3   I still remember reading Gerald's essay, listening to the voice of a young person flooded with pain and regret. It was so moving I asked him if I could copy and share it with other students. He agreed, and then, several weeks later, he stopped coming to class and I never saw him again. All that remains are his words:

MY LIFE

4   Somewhere, a little piece of me is lost and crying. Someplace, deep in the shadows of my subconscious, a piece of my soul has sat down and anchored itself in defeat and is trying to pull me down into the darkness with it. This might sound strange to someone who is not familiar with the inner conflicts that can tear and pull at a person's soul until he begins to stop and sink in his own deep-hollow depths. But sinking doesn't take much. It takes only one little flaw which left unattended will grow and grow . . .

until, like cancer, it consumes the soul.

5   I know now, and I have always known, that help comes first from within. I know that if one doesn't come to one's own rescue, then all is lost. I know it is time for me to look at myself, which I would rather avoid. But in order to break free of my own chains, I must look at myself.

6   I could relate the incidents of youth. I could tell of many past failures and what I think caused them. But I won't, for one example will show where I'm at. At the beginning of this summer I set my goals. These goals consisted of the college courses I wanted to complete and where I wanted to be physically and mentally when the summer was over. Listed among the goals to be accomplished were courses I needed in writing and accounting. But now I am so far behind in both courses it looks as if I will fail them both. I ask myself, "Why?" I know that if I work enough, I can handle the courses. So why am I so lazy? Why is it that the things I seem to want most, I either give up or in some way do not strive for? These are the questions I must try to answer.

7   I think I've spent too much of my life just waiting for good things to come. I've waited for a magic rainbow to appear in the sky and to drop a pot of gold in my lap. I've been hurt so much in life and I just wanted it handed to me.

8   But it's time for me to stop chasing rainbows. It's time to stop looking into the sky waiting for help to arrive. It's time for me to start bailing the rot out of my mind, to stop dreaming and not acting, before I have nothing left to hope for. I can see now that I've never given it the total effort, that I've always been afraid I would fail or not measure up. So I've quit early. Instead of acting on my dreams, I've laid back and just drifted along. I've lived too much time in this world unfulfilled. I've got to make my dreams work. I must do this now, and what it takes is the doing. Somehow I must learn to succeed at success rather than at failure, and the time to start is now.

9   I have known other students over the years who, like Gerald, were involved in an inner battle. It's often clear they regard themselves as unlikely to succeed in school. They walk into the classroom carrying defeat on their shoulders the way other students carry textbooks under their arms.

10   I'd look at them slouching° in their seats and staring into space and think, "What terrible things have gone on in their lives that they've quit already? They have so little faith in their ability to learn that they're not even trying." Such students often suddenly disappear one day, just as Gerald did, and no one pays much notice because they had already disappeared in spirit long before.

11   When I have seen such students with resignation° in their eyes, I have wanted to shake them by the shoulders and say, "You are not dead. Be proud and pleased that you have brought yourself this far. Yes, life has probably been very hard, but you can still be someone. Get off the bench. Come onto

the playing field. Give it a shot. You'll never learn to succeed if you don't try."

Running from the Power Within

12   For years I have watched what happens when a school year unfolds. As the crunch of work begins, students are put up against the wall. Like it or not, they must define their role in school. There are only two roads to take. One road is to do the work: to click off the stereo or television, reject the invitation to go out, shut off the cell phone, stop everything and anything else, and go do the essentially lonely work that studying is. The other road is to escape the work.

13   Below I describe escape routes I've seen students take. If you see yourself in any of these situations, you need to know it. Self-knowledge is power. Once you are aware of what you are doing, you can begin to deal with it.

"I Can't Do It."

14   Some people will let themselves be discouraged by bad grades. They'll think, "There's no use trying. I'm just not any good at this." But the only way people will really know that they cannot do something is by first trying—giving it their best shot. They must not let a defeatist attitude keep them from making a real effort. If you think you "can't do it," the reason may be that you have given up far too soon.

"I'm Too Busy."

15   Some people make themselves too busy, perhaps working more hours on a part-time job than they need to. Others get overly involved in social activities. Others allow personal or family problems to become so distracting that they cannot concentrate on their work. There are situations in which people are so busy or troubled that they cannot do their work. But there are also situations where people exaggerate conflicts or stress. They create an excuse for not doing what they know they should do.

"I'm Too Tired."

16   People with this excuse usually become tired as soon as it's time to write a paper or study a book or go to class. Their weariness clears up when the work period ends. The "sleepiness syndrome" also expresses itself in the imagined need for naps during the day and then ten hours or more of sleep at night. Such students are, often literally, closing their eyes to the hard work that school demands.

"I'll Do It Later."

17   Everyone tends at times to procrastinate—to put things off. Some students, however, constantly postpone

assignments and study. Time and time again they put off what needs to be done so they can watch TV, talk to a friend, hang out with their peers,° or do any one of a hundred other things. They typically wind up cramming for tests and writing last-minute papers, and they often seem surprised and angry at their low grades.

"I'm Bored with the Subject."

18 Students sometimes explain that they are doing poorly in a course because the instructor or the subject matter is boring. These students want education to be entertainment—an unrealistic expectation. On the whole, courses and instructors balance out: Some are boring, some are exciting, many are in between. If a course is not interesting, students should be all the more motivated to do the work so that they can leave the course behind once and for all.

"I'm Here, and That's What Counts."

19 Some students spend their time at school lost in a dangerous kind of fantasy. They feel, "All will be well, for here I am in school. I have a student ID in my pocket, a sweatshirt with the school name on it, and textbooks on my desk. All this proves I am a student." Such students have given in to a fantasy we all at times succumb° to: the belief that we will get something for nothing. But we find out soon enough that such a hope is a false one. Life seldom gives us something for nothing—and school won't either.

20 We have probably all known students who escape. They make excuses. They never really determine to try their best. They know what they should do but don't do it. They fool themselves, time and time again. They try to have as much fun as they can, and they keep saying, "Tomorrow. Tomorrow I will get serious. Tomorrow I will start working hard." There is often a terrible hurt deep inside them. And for some reason a switch within never turns on, a spark of determination never ignites. They are individuals who are unable to take charge of their own lives and to work hard, as Gerald puts it, "to succeed at success."

Turning On the Power Within

21 Wouldn't be great if we could go to a drugstore and buy motivational pills? These personal power pills would energize our attitude. We would turn on to success and take charge of our lives and pursue worthy goals. We would be determined and self-disciplined, and nothing would stop us. Of course, there are no such pills. What I am going to offer you instead are some thoughts. Read and think about them and see if you can get them into your soul.

Thought #1
Having a Dream

22 Several years ago, my wife and I were vacationing in New Mexico. As we drove into one small town, we suddenly came upon a huge billboard. I was so struck by

what it said that I stopped our car and wrote down the words.

> **If you never have a dream, you'll never have a dream come *true*.**

23   You need to have a dream within you—a belief and resolve in your heart that you will take charge of your life and make yourself proud.

24   Consider this basic truth about human nature: We all want to respect ourselves. We all want to live our lives in such a way that we think well of our behavior and others think well of us. We do not want to be disrespected or seen as bad people. An equally basic truth is that the only way we can get respect is to earn it. At a certain point in growing up, we realize that life doesn't give us something for nothing. What is important and meaningful is what we earn through trying hard and working hard.

25   Take a minute to think about the following question: Imagine two people. The first person has drifted unhappily through life, putting in a minimal effort at a series of jobs and maybe even at times living off others. One morning the telephone rings and someone says to this person, "Congratulations. You have just won a million dollars in the state lottery." The second person works hard and eventually earns a million

dollars; that person is well-regarded by others and has a strong sense of accomplishment and self-worth. Which person would you rather be—the one who *won* a million dollars or the one who *earned* a million dollars?

26   Of course, we'd all like to wake up one morning and learn that we've just won a million dollars. But let's face it: this isn't very likely. In fact, it's close to impossible. So if you're realistic, chances are you would choose to be the person who worked hard, overcame obstacles, and achieved success. If you relate to that person, your attitude may be something like this: "I want to respect myself and have others respect me. To get this respect, I'm going to work hard to succeed. At this stage in my life, that means doing well in school because education is clearly a key to success." And if you've made mistakes in the past (and many of us have), your attitude should be: "I can change my behavior. I'm going to learn to work hard so I can get somewhere and be someone."

Thought #2
Your Attitude about Learning

27   Think about your own attitude toward learning. Put a check by the item or items that apply to you. (If you agree with some sentences in an item but not others, cross out the ones you do not agree with.)

28   _____ School has never really turned me on. I feel I can start to study if I need to, but I don't want to. What's wrong with being a bit lazy? Life is supposed to be about enjoying yourself and having

some fun. I want to take it easy and have as much good time as I can for now.

29   _____ I suppose I am passive° about studying, but it's not all my fault. I'm tired of being told what to do. I'm tired of being force-fed what other people think I need to learn. A lot of the stuff is not going to be of any value to me as far as I can see. I can't wait to get out of school and be on my own so I can start living my life.

30   _____ If I study too much, I'll miss out on the good times that school has to offer. I won't have time to go to games or parties. And I don't want to be alone. If I start studying, some of my friends are going to think twice about hanging out with me.

31   _____ I want to do more in school, but I'm afraid of really giving it a good effort. What if I try my best and I still get lousy grades? People will just laugh at me. I don't want to look foolish, so I'm probably just going to drift along and not call any attention to myself.

32   _____ I guess I've just been out of it for a long time. There are probably lots of reasons why. I never got any encouragement along the way. I pretty much just let things happen to me. I feel like a piece of driftwood that's been tossed about on a stormy sea. I do want to do something and to become someone. I've felt like this for a while, and at times I really want to get serious. But so far I just haven't done so.

33   _____ I'm not an active student who tries my best all the time. But I'm not a zombie either. I do some studying, just not as much as other people would like me to. I should probably do more, and I'm going to work on that and try to do a better job of taking charge of my studies.

34   _____ I feel something stirring within me. For a long time I was dead to learning, but I want to get somewhere. I'm ready to be a serious student. It's true that some of the stuff I have to study is boring, and some teachers do not care. But I feel now that these are just hurdles that will not stop me. I'm going to start doing more to get where I want to go.

35   _____ I'm on the move, and I have taken charge of my life. There is something inside me that is strong and determined to succeed. I feel in my heart of hearts that nothing is going to stop me. It's my life, and I'm going to work hard and respect myself and gain success and happiness.

36   So where do you fit? The items above will help you think about what your attitude is and how you can improve it.

Thought #3
Doing the Work

37   The heart of the matter is not the speed at which a person learns; the heart of the matter is his or her determination—"I *will* learn." I have seen people who had this quality of determination or persistence do poorly in a course (often because of out-of-class problems or events), come back and repeat it, and finally succeed.

38   Through knowing such determined people, I've come to feel that the single most important factor for school survival and success is an inner commitment to doing the work. When the crunch comes—and the crunch is the plain hard work that school requires—the person with the commitment meets it head-on; the person without the commitment avoids it in a hundred different ways.

39   On the following scale of *Passive* to *Determined*, where would you rate yourself?

Passive   Determined
1 2 3 4 5 6 7 8 9 10

40   Why have you rated yourself at that point on the scale? What strengths can you build upon? What are the personal challenges you must overcome?

Thought # 4
An Unequal Playing Field

41   There is a popular idea in America that has always made me uneasy. It is the idea that success is within us—that we can all "pull ourselves up by our bootstraps" and triumph over tough odds.

42   Now there is truth to this idea, but it is not the whole truth. Life is like a race, and there are different lanes on the racetrack. Some of us are in lanes where there are no obstacles on the track. Some of us are in lanes where there are all kinds of obstacles—for example, personal health challenges, family neglect or abuse, poverty,

racism, a neighborhood environment with violence and drugs, a school where one's peers are not into studies but into "respecting themselves" by being in the right clique,° wearing the right kind of footwear, having the right hair style, or whatever.

43   If you're in a track that is full of obstacles, you can get worn down. You can start losing hope. And then it is harder to ignite the spark of determination within. In such circumstances, you must try your best to be a hero. You must battle the odds. You must keep alive a belief deep inside yourself that you can make your world a better one. And the first step in doing that is to know your life has been hard but that you will not give up. If you have read this essay so far, chances are that you can do it. You can be a fighter. You can be a hero.

Thought # 5
A Quotation to Live By

44   If I could pass along one quotation, it would be this line from the great religious and political leader Mahatma Gandhi: **"Be the change you want to see in the world."** These ten words are all simple ones, but put together they express an idea with unlimited power. The key to changing your world is to take personal responsibility for your actions and behavior. No one else can do this for you; it must be you alone.

45   To put Gandhi's idea another way, each one of us has his or her own ship to sail. Some people don't sail their own ships; they just kind of drift with the

tides. That's not a very satisfying way to live one's life, just drifting along with others who are also drifting, and yet a lot of people do it. If their friends and peers are into enjoying the moment and taking the easy way out and not into setting larger goals in life, that's what they do.

46   I urge you to actively sail your own ship. That ship of yours is unique and precious, and no one else should sail it for you. That ship is the journey of your life. You get to go on that journey only once, with a one-way ticket, so make the most of it. Dream dreams, set meaningful goals, make something happen. Don't just drift along with the tides. Become someone.

47   In the opening story, my student Gerald realized he was not sailing his own ship, and you could almost hear him crying out in disillusionment and regret. Do not let that happen to you. You do not want to wake up some day with a taste of dust and ashes in your mouth and a terrible pain in your soul.

Thought # 6
The Fear of Loneliness

48   Perhaps the biggest reason it is so hard to take responsibility for one's life and sail one's own ship is the fear of being alone.

49   To grow, we must sometimes set sail in new directions and leave acquaintances and friends behind. At such times, we must have the courage and strength to depend on ourselves. We must be ready to handle the loneliness that may be part of marching to the beat of our own drummer. We must not cling to the crowd when it prevents our personal growth. When the adventurer Columbus set sail for America, it was a terrifying thing to do. But he discovered a new world, and if we have the courage to sail our own ship, so might we.

Thought #7
The Opportunity to Help Others

50   There are many self-help books on the market that present the following idea: If you take charge of your life, you can achieve financial success. That may (or may not) be true, but it is not the full story of what happiness is about. As you seek to grow, the larger goal to keep in mind is that by gaining power for yourself, you will gain the power to be of help to others.

51   Robert Kennedy said, "The purpose of life is to contribute in some way to making things better." Dr. Martin Luther King wrote, "Life's most persistent and urgent question is, 'What are you doing for others?'" If we take control of our lives and achieve a measure of success, we will have the opportunity to work on behalf of others. At that stage, many religious leaders believe, we become fully blessed.

Thought #8
The Power of Regular Reading

52   If you have read this essay so far, you may be saying, "OK, I'm ready to do what it takes. I'll stick to my studies because I know they're a means to an end. I'll have some fun and games but remember they're a side show and

not the main event. I'm OK with being alone a bit along the way. But what else can I do to keep myself inspired? What practical strategy do you have for me?"

53   I do have one strategy: Read. No one expresses the power of reading better than Oprah Winfrey: "I can't imagine," she said, "how I could have become the person I am now without books. How would I know there was another world beyond my small, isolated, feeling-abandoned world? Books became synonymous with freedom. They showed that you can open doors and walk through."

54   Many people (and I am one of them) believe that regular reading is the very heart of education. Here is what the experts say:

55   **1. Reading provides language power.** Research has shown *beyond any question* that frequent reading improves vocabulary, spelling, and reading speed and comprehension, as well as grammar and writing style. If you become a regular reader, all of these language and thinking abilities develop almost automatically.

56   **2. Reading increases job power.** In today's world more than ever before, jobs involve the processing of information, with words being the tools of the trade. Studies have found that the better your command of words, the more success you are likely to have. Nothing will give you a command of words like regular reading.

3. Reading creates human power. 57 Reading enlarges the mind and the heart. It frees us from the narrow confines of our own experience. Knowing how other people view important matters helps us decide what we ourselves think and feel. Reading also helps us connect with others and realize our shared humanity. The novelist C.S. Lewis wrote, "We read in order to know that we are not alone." We become less isolated as we share the common experiences, emotions, and thoughts that make us human. We grow more sympathetic and understanding because we realize that others are like us.

Regular reading can, in short, 58 change your life. It can open the door to a lifetime of pleasure, learning, and personal growth. But you must be the one to decide whether to walk through that door.

Finally . . .

There are no fireworks to set off here, 59 just some final words.

Understand that your ship is yours 60 alone to sail, and no one else can sail it for you. The power within you is enormous, but you must turn it on. Work on your studies. Reread this essay. Order some books. I wish you a strong and courageous heart as you set sail on the adventure of your life.

Basic Skill Questions

Vocabulary in Context

_____ 1. In the sentence below, the word *syndrome* (sĭn′drōm′) means
     A. complaint.
     B. reaction.
     C. pattern.
     D. idea.

       "The 'sleepiness syndrome' also expresses itself in the imagined need for naps during the day and then ten hours or more of sleep at night." (Paragraph 16)

_____ 2. In the excerpt below, the words *synonymous* (sĭ-nŏn′ə-məs) *with* mean
     A. related to.
     B. the same as.
     C. unlike.
     D. more important than.

       "How would I know there was another world beyond my small, isolated, feeling-abandoned world? Books became synonymous with freedom. They showed that you can open doors and walk through." (Paragraph 53)

Central Point and Main Ideas

_____ 3. Which sentence best expresses the central point of the selection?
     A. Some students fail to realize that they have the ability to become heroes.
     B. There are a number of escape routes that students take to avoid studying.
     C. To succeed in school, students must first honestly examine their attitude about learning.
     D. Students can succeed in school by turning on the power within themselves.

_____ 4. The main idea of paragraphs 37–38 is that
     A. some people must repeat courses before they succeed at them.
     B. Langan has known some very determined people.
     C. school is hard work.
     D. determination is the key to success in school.

_____ 5. The main idea of paragraphs 41–43 is that
     A. Langan is uncomfortable with the idea that we can all "pull ourselves up by our own bootstraps."
     B. if you're on a track that is full of obstacles, it's easy to get worn down.
     C. people who face more obstacles than others must try their best to be heroes.
     D. in some schools, being in the right clique is more important than studying.

Supporting Details

_____ 6. According to Langan, happiness is best achieved by
  A. achieving financial success.
  B. gaining the opportunity to work on behalf of others.
  C. gaining power for yourself.
  D. overcoming obstacles such as personal health challenges, family neglect or abuse, and bad neighborhoods.

_____ 7. The major supporting details of paragraphs 14–19 are
  A. excuses students use to avoid studying.
  B. obstacles that make it impossible for some students to succeed.
  C. ways that students deal with failure.
  D. typical attitudes toward learning.

Transitions

_____ 8. The sentence below expresses a relationship of
  A. addition.
  B. cause and effect.
  C. comparison.
  D. time.

  "When I have seen such students with resignation in their eyes, I have wanted to shake them by the shoulders and say, "You are not dead." (Paragraph 11)

_____ 9. The relationship of the second sentence below to the first sentence is one of
  A. comparison.
  B. cause and effect.
  C. illustration.
  D. contrast.

  "If you're in a track that is full of obstacles, you can get worn down. . . . And then it is harder to ignite the spark of determination within." (Paragraph 43)

Patterns of Organization

_____ 10. Paragraph 25
  A. narrates in time order a day in the life of a lottery winner.
  B. illustrates what it feels like to win a million dollars.
  C. contrasts a lottery winner with a person who worked hard and earned a million dollars.
  D. gives reasons why it's better to earn a million dollars than to win a million dollars.

_____11. The main pattern of organization of this selection is
   A. time order.
   B. contrast.
   C. list of items.
   D. definition and example.

Advanced Skill Questions

Inferences

_____12. On the basis of paragraphs 41–43, we can infer that
   A. some students use real obstacles as an excuse for giving up.
   B. many students exaggerate the obstacles they face.
   C. it is nearly impossible to become a hero.
   D. most students face similar obstacles in life.

_____13. On the basis of Gerald's essay, we can conclude that he
   A. lacked the intelligence to succeed in school.
   B. eventually became a success.
   C. was not a good writer.
   D. was his own worst enemy when it came to school.

Purpose and Tone

_____14. In general, the author's tone is
   A. tolerant.
   B. solemn.
   C. encouraging.
   D. matter-of-fact.

_____15. The author's main purpose is to
   A. inform readers of strategies to succeed in school and in life.
   B. persuade readers that they can succeed in school and in life.
   C. entertain readers with the silly excuses some students use to get out of studying.

Argument

16. Complete the following argument by adding a statement of support.

   Point: Leaders agree that helping others is life's larger goal.

   Support: Robert Kennedy said, "The purpose of life is to contribute in some way to making things better."

   Support: _____

   _____

_____ 17. Write the letter of the statement that is the point of the following argument. The other statements are support for that point.
  A. Research has shown beyond any question that frequent reading improves vocabulary, spelling, and reading speed and comprehension, as well as grammar and writing style.
  B. Reading is the heart of education.
  C. Reading increases the chance for job success.
  D. Reading frees us from the narrow confines of our own experience.

Critical Reading

_____ 18. The sentence below contains
  A. facts.
  B. opinions.
  C. both facts and opinions.

   There are many self-help books on the market that present the following idea: If you take charge of your life, you can achieve financial success.

_____ 19. Students who like to do what their friends are doing would probably be strongly influenced by the propaganda technique of
  A. name-calling.
  B. bandwagon.
  C. glittering generalities.
  D. testimonial.

_____ 20. Students who believe that if they study too much, they will miss out on the good times that school has to offer are committing the logical fallacy of
  A. false cause (*the argument assumes that the order of events alone shows cause and effect*).
  B. circular reasoning (*a statement repeats itself rather than providing a real supporting reason to back up an argument*).
  C. either-or (*the argument assumes that there are only two sides to a question*).
  D. false comparison (*the argument assumes that two things being compared are more alike than they really are*).

Outlining

Complete the following outline of the selection. Some items and parts of items are already filled in for you.

Central point: **Students can become successful if they take charge of their lives by activating the power within themselves.**

A. Gerald—an example of a student with a self-defeating attitude.

B. Running from the Power Within—escape routes students take to avoid studying.
   1. "I can't do it."
   2. _____
   3. "I'm too tired."
   4. "I'll do it later."
   5. _____
   6. "I'm here and that's what counts."

C. Turning On the Power Within—some motivational thoughts.
   1. _____
   2. Know your attitude about learning.
   3. _____
   4. Battle the odds of an unequal playing field.
   5. Live by the quotation: "Be the change you want to see in the world."
   6. Be ready to handle loneliness.
   7. Seek to help others.
   8. Read a lot because reading:
      a. Provides language power.
      b. _____
      c. Creates human power.

Discussion Questions

1. In the course of your education, have you met any students like Gerald—or have you ever had a bit of Gerald in yourself? What do you think people like Gerald have to do to take charge of their lives?

2. What escape routes are you most likely to use to avoid studying? What can you do to avoid them?

3. Describe someone you know (it could be you) who has a dream—and who is the better off for it. Also describe someone you know who does *not* have a dream. Do you agree or disagree that it's important to have a dream?

4. In "The Power Within," the author quotes such inspirational figures as Mahatma Gandhi, Robert Kennedy, Dr. Martin Luther King, and Oprah Winfrey. Who inspires you? Why?

Note: Writing assignments for this selection appear on page 636.

Check Your Performance   **THE POWER WITHIN**

Activity	Number Right	Points	Score
Basic Skill Questions			
Vocabulary in Context (2 items)	_____	× 4 =	_____
Central Point and Main Ideas (3 items)	_____	× 4 =	_____
Supporting Details (2 items)	_____	× 4 =	_____
Transitions (2 items)	_____	× 4 =	_____
Patterns of Organization (2 items)	_____	× 4 =	_____
Advanced Skill Questions			
Inferences (2 items)	_____	× 4 =	_____
Purpose and Tone (2 items)	_____	× 4 =	_____
Argument (2 items)	_____	× 4 =	_____
Critical Reading (3 items)	_____	× 4 =	_____
Outlining (5 items)	_____	× 4 =	_____
	TOTAL SCORE =		_____%

Enter your total score into the **Reading Performance Chart: Ten Reading Selections** on the inside back cover.

Part Three

Relationships and Combined-Skills Tests

1 Relationships Tests

Understanding relationships between ideas is a key part of good comprehension. The tests that follow will give you practice at mastering the common types of relationships that have been explained in Chapters 5 and 6 of this book.

RELATIONSHIPS: Test 1

For each pair of sentences below, answer the question about the relationship between the sentences.

_____ 1. ● Witnesses and victims are sometimes better able to recall the details of a crime when hypnotized.
● A witness to the kidnapping of a group of California school children was hypnotized and was able to recall all but one digit of the kidnapper's license number.

What does the second sentence do?

A. It establishes a cause and effect relationship.
B. It presents an event that happened later in time than the event in the first sentence.
C. It gives an example to support what is stated in the first sentence.
D. It contrasts with the first sentence.

_____ 2. ● Going at high speed, the luxury liner *Titanic* collided with an iceberg and rapidly sank to the bottom of the North Atlantic before rescue ships could arrive to pick up passengers.
● Scientists believe that the reason the *Titanic* sank so rapidly is that the rivets used to hold together plates forming the ship's metal hull were of poor quality and broke during the collision.

How are the two sentences related?

A. They repeat the same idea.
B. They provide a cause and an effect.
C. They contradict each other.
D. They present two events in the order in which they happened.

_____ 3. ● One public service slogan that really caught on with the American public was "Friends Don't Let Friends Drive Drunk."
● "A mind is a terrible thing to waste," is another memorable public service slogan.

What is the relationship between the two sentences?

A. Statement and example   C. Comparison
B. Cause and effect   D. Addition

_____ 4. ● After New York City's Times Square had become dirty and run-down, public officials led a successful effort to "clean up" the area and turn it into a tourist attraction.
● California politicians and developers worked to renovate Hollywood Boulevard, turning it from a crime-ridden strip into a major tourist draw.

How are the two sentences related?

A. They contradict each other.
B. They present two events in the order in which they happened.
C. They repeat the same idea.
D. They compare similar situations.

_____ 5. ● In Shakespeare's time, boys and men played both male and female roles on the English stage.
● It wasn't until 1662, 46 years after Shakespeare's death, that King Charles II declared that all female roles should be played only by actresses.

What is the relationship between the two sentences?

A. Addition   C. Contrast
B. Comparison   D. Time order

_____ 6. ● A recent survey suggests that women seem to grieve through talking and crying.
● Most men choose to grieve through action, such as spending more time on hobbies.

What does the second sentence do?

A. It contrasts with the first sentence.
B. It explains the meaning of the first sentence.
C. It provides an example of the first sentence.
D. It presents an effect of the cause stated in the first sentence.

_____ 7. ● Stress inoculation is a strategy that helps people prepare for stressful events ahead of time.
● If you're petrified about speaking in front of a class, practicing in front of friends may prevent your freezing up on the day of the presentation.

What is the relationship between the two sentences?

A. Time order   C. Addition
B. Contrast   D. Statement and example

_____ 8. ● Most scientists now believe that birds evolved from small, predatory dinosaurs called theropods.
● Like birds, theropods had light, hollow bones and stood erect on two feet, with their ankles held above the ground.

What does the second sentence do?

A. It establishes a cause and effect relationship.
B. It presents an event that happened later in time than the event in the first sentence.
C. It draws a comparison between birds and theropods.
D. It presents additional information about birds.

_____ 9. ● As TV gained in popularity during the 1950s, the movie industry increased the size of movie screens to make going out to the movies more attractive.
● Movie producers began spending huge amounts of money on elaborate productions that TV shows couldn't hope to match.

How are the two sentences related?

A. They state a cause and an effect.
B. They contradict each other.
C. The second sentence presents additional information on the same topic.
D. The second sentence repeats the information given in the first sentence.

_____ 10. ● Famed home run hitter Babe Ruth was well known, during his career, for partying and ignoring team rules.
● Although Ruth wanted to manage a team after he retired as a player, no major league owner would give him the chance to be a manager.

What is the relationship between the two sentences?

A. Cause and effect   C. Addition
B. Comparison   D. Illustration

_____ 11. ● The United States entered World War II after the Japanese attacked Pearl Harbor on December 7, 1941.
● During the war, military production became a priority, and Americans learned to use less of such things as sugar, coffee, and gasoline, which had become scarce.

How are the two sentences related?

A. They repeat the same idea.
B. They contradict each other.
C. They compare similar situations.
D. They describe two situations in the order in which they occurred.

_____ 12. ● Genuine paper money has tiny red and blue fibers embedded throughout.
● Counterfeit bills display lines that are printed on the surface, not embedded in the paper.

What does the second sentence do?

A. It provides an example of the statement in the first sentence.
B. It contrasts with the first sentence.
C. It presents an effect of the cause stated in the first sentence.
D. It presents additional information about genuine paper money.

_____ 13. ● Often people are stigmatized for harmful behaviors they may no longer engage in.
● Labels such as "compulsive gambler," "ex-convict," "recovering alcoholic," and "former mental patient" can stick to a person for life.

What is the relationship between the two sentences?

A. Comparison   C. Contrast
B. Time order   D. Statement and example

_____ 14. ● The most common biological cause of mental retardation is fetal alcohol syndrome, caused by a mother's use of alcohol while pregnant.
● Down syndrome, which results from the presence of an extra chromosome, represents a second major cause of mental retardation.

What does the second sentence do?

A. It contrasts with the first sentence.
B. It presents additional information about the causes of mental retardation.
C. It presents an effect of the cause stated in the first sentence.
D. It repeats the information given in the first sentence.

_____ 15. ● Throughout the centuries, wearing high heels has immobilized women and resulted in bunions, corns, twisted ankles, spinal deformities, and shortened calf muscles.
● Extremely tight corsets were equally bad for women, causing shortness of breath, fainting, and miscarriages.

What is the relationship between the two sentences?

A. Comparison   C. Contrast
B. Cause and effect   D. Statement and example

_____ 16. ● At the end of World War II, Nazi war criminal Adolf Eichmann escaped to Argentina, where he lived under an assumed identity for roughly fifteen years.
● Israeli agents eventually captured Eichmann, flew him to Israel, where he was then tried and convicted of crimes against humanity and crimes against the Jewish people, and finally hanged.

How are the two sentences related?

A. They state a cause and an effect.
B. They present two events in the order in which they occurred.
C. They compare similar situations.
D. They contradict each other.

_____ 17. ● Binge drinking on campus violates the standards of conduct expected of those in an academic setting.
● The other side of binge drinking is that it represents conformity to peer culture, especially in fraternities and sororities.

What does the second sentence do?

A. It contrasts with the first sentence.
B. It establishes a cause and effect relationship.
C. It presents an event that happened later in time than the event in the first sentence.
D. It gives an example to support what is stated in the first sentence.

_____ 18. ● Emotion contagion occurs when an individual responds to the emotions of another, without fully understanding what that individual is feeling.
● In a nursery, when one infant starts to cry, all the other infants nearby begin crying as well.

What is the relationship between the two sentences?

A. Comparison   C. Contrast
B. Cause and effect   D. Statement and example

_____ 19. ● In colonial America, 10 to 30 percent of children did not survive their first year of life.
● Many parents waited until it seemed likely that the infant would survive to name their child.

How are the two sentences related?

A. They compare similar situations.
B. They state a cause and an effect.
C. They contradict each other.
D. They contain a statement and an example.

_____ 20. ● According to the National Association of Convenience Stores, 5.5 million hours and 22 million dollars are wasted by businesses on the extra time and effort needed to handle pennies.
● It costs much more to manufacture, store, and distribute pennies than the coins are actually worth.

What is the relationship between the two sentences?

A. Statement and example   C. Addition
B. Cause and effect   D. Time order

_____ 21. ● Whale oil was heavily used in the 1700s and first half of the 1800s in lamps and as candle wax.
● When kerosene was developed from coal in the 1850s, the use of whale oil to light homes and businesses was virtually eliminated.

What does the second sentence do?

A. It contrasts with the first sentence.
B. It provides an example of the statement in the first sentence.
C. It repeats the information given in the first sentence.
D. It compares whale oil and kerosene.

_____ 22. ● In the 1920s, women encouraged each other to smoke cigarettes in public, since they deserved to enjoy the same pleasures as men.
● Magazine ads urged women who were trying to lose weight to "reach for a Lucky cigarette instead of a sweet."

How are the two sentences related?

A. They contradict each other.
B. They provide a cause and an effect.
C. They present two examples of the growing acceptance of women's right to smoke.
D. They compare similar situations.

_____ 23. ● Unlike women, many men believe that "being strong" is often more important than having close friendships.

● Research shows that owing to this belief, only one male in ten has a close male friend to whom he reveals his innermost thoughts.

What is the relationship between the two sentences?

A. Addition   C. Time order
B. Contrast   D. Cause and effect

_____ 24. ● The ancient Greeks and Romans considered suicide acceptable if it was committed as a refusal to submit to tyrannical authorities or if one's honor was already lost.

● Suicide was frowned upon as a cowardly and disgraceful act if it was done in response to minor misfortunes.

What is the relationship between the two sentences?

A. Cause and effect   C. Statement and example
B. Time order   D. Contrast

_____ 25. ● Hall of Famer Jackie Robinson, who broke major league baseball's color barrier during the 1947 season, paved the way for black superstars such as Willie Mays, Hank Aaron, Bob Gibson, and Ken Griffey, Jr.

● Major league baseball's first Latino superstar, Roberto Clemente, made it easier for the Latino stars who came after him, including Orlando Cepeda, David Ortiz, Pedro Martinez, and Alex Rodriguez.

How are the two sentences related?

A. They contain a statement and an example.
B. They state a cause and an effect.
C. They compare similar situations.
D. They contradict each other.

RELATIONSHIPS: Test 2

For each pair of sentences below, answer the question about the relationship between the sentences.

_____ 1. ● In zombie movies, zombies almost always have a slow, shuffling way of walking and a craving for human flesh.
● Moreover, they exist in a decaying state, with discolored skin and eyes.

What is the relationship between the two sentences?

A. Cause and effect   C. Addition
B. Contrast   D. Time order

_____ 2. ● In the Middle Ages, Europeans believed that bathing opened the pores and encouraged deadly gases to invade the body.
● Consequently, most Europeans didn't wash, or even get wet, if they could avoid it.

What is the relationship between the two sentences?

A. Addition   C. Time
B. Contrast   D. Cause and effect

_____ 3. ● Although Thomas Edison was a great inventor, not all of his ideas were good ones.
● For instance, he developed a plan to build giant electromagnets that would catch enemy bullets in flight and send them back the way they had come.

What is the relationship between the two sentences?

A. Comparison   C. Statement and example
B. Contrast   D. Time order

_____ 4. ● E-readers such as Amazon's Kindle and Barnes & Noble's Nook have reduced the number of books that people buy, causing many bookstores to go out of business.
● Likewise, now that people are able to download songs from iTunes and other servers, brick and mortar music stores such as Tower Records are a thing of the past.

What is the relationship between the two sentences?

A. Addition   C. Contrast
B. Comparison   D. Statement and example

_____ 5. ● Three-quarters of the deadliest mass murders in U.S. history have occurred since 1980.
● Some of this slaughter is due to the availability of assault weapons.

What is the relationship between the two sentences?

A. Time order   C. Comparison
B. Addition   D. Cause and effect

_____ 6. ● The Black Death, an outbreak of bubonic plague that killed millions, first affected western European populations in 1347 in the port city of Messina, Sicily.
   ● Ships carrying the plague then left Messina and sailed northward, spreading the disease to the northern Italian cities of Genoa and Venice.

What is the relationship between the two sentences?

A. Time order   C. Contrast
B. Addition   D. Statement and example

_____ 7. ● Keeping your back straight and your shoulders from lurching forward adds to the impression that you're confident and in control of your feelings.
   ● On the other hand, if you want to appeal to someone's sympathetic side, you can sag a little all around, because you will look more in need of help.

What is the relationship between the two sentences?

A. Cause and effect   C. Contrast
B. Time order   D. Addition

_____ 8. ● One thing young women in abusive relationships should do is confide in someone trustworthy, such as a teacher, guidance counselor, doctor, friend, or parent.
   ● A second thing they should do is contact the National Domestic Violence Hotline: 1-800-799-7233.

What is the relationship between the two sentences?

A. Addition   C. Statement and example
B. Cause and effect   D. Comparison

_____ 9. ● When President Garfield was shot by a madman in 1881, a metal detector that had been brought in to locate the bullet in Garfield's body gave confused results.
   ● The reason was that the device had been reading the president's bedsprings.

What is the relationship between the two sentences?

A. Statement and example   C. Comparison
B. Cause and effect   D. Contrast

_____ 10. ● A chemical found in copperhead venom is being used to attack breast cancer cells and to prevent cancer from spreading.
   ● In a similar manner, a new drug derived from deadly cone shell venom has been used to target chronic pain.

What is the relationship between the two sentences?

A. Time order   C. Contrast
B. Statement and example   D. Comparison

_____ 11. ● King Henry VIII of England had his second wife, Anne Boleyn, beheaded after she gave birth to a daughter, Elizabeth, rather than the son he wanted.
● Years later, Elizabeth took the throne after the death of her father and older sister Mary and became one of England's greatest rulers.

What is the relationship between the two sentences?

A. Cause and effect   C. Time order
B. Contrast   D. Addition

_____ 12. ● Some patients who are trying to quit smoking use a chewing gum containing nicotine to reduce nicotine consumption over time.
● Another method of reducing a craving for cigarettes is using the nicotine patch, which delivers a continuous flow of nicotine through the skin.

What is the relationship between the two sentences?

A. Comparison   C. Statement and example
B. Addition   D. Cause and effect

_____ 13. ● Volcanic eruptions such as those caused by Mt. St. Helens in Washington State and Mt. Pinatubo in the Philippines have resulted in destruction and death.
● Yet the lava spewed out by volcanoes makes very fertile soil, which is good for growing crops.

What is the relationship between the two sentences?

A. Addition   C. Cause and effect
B. Contrast   D. Time order

_____ 14. ● Some very popular books have been challenged or banned by school districts and public libraries across America.
● For example, some parents have objected to the Harry Potter books because the books were said to promote witchcraft, while others objected to *The Color Purple* because it contained gay characters.

What is the relationship between the two sentences?

A. Contrast   C. Addition
B. Statement and example   D. Cause and effect

_____ 15. ● One of the first motion pictures ever filmed showed a giant locomotive train heading straight for the audience.
● Because they weren't used to seeing pictures that moved, people in the audience screamed and ducked under their seats.

What is the relationship between the two sentences?

A. Contrast   C. Addition
B. Statement and example   D. Cause and effect

_____ 16. ● Ida B. Wells (1862–1931) was a civil rights leader who became famous for leading a campaign against lynching.

● Wells also worked tirelessly to gain women the right to vote.

What is the relationship between the two sentences?

A. Contrast   C. Time order
B. Comparison   D. Addition

_____ 17. ● The plot of Herman Melville's classic novel _Moby Dick_ revolves around men on board a ship trying to kill a great white whale.

● In like fashion, the plot of the popular book and movie _Jaws_ tells the story of men in a boat pursuing and killing a great white shark.

What is the relationship between the two sentences?

A. Addition   C. Comparison
B. Cause and effect   D. Statement and example

_____ 18. ● If you were in a U.S. store and wanted to buy something to help you see in the dark, you'd ask the clerk where the flashlights are.

● However, if you were in England and needed the item, you would have to ask for an "electric torch."

What is the relationship between the two sentences?

A. Contrast   C. Statement and example
B. Addition   D. Comparison

_____ 19. ● To turn a corpse into a mummy, ancient Egyptians first washed the body with water from the Nile River.

● Next, they removed all organs except the heart, which was thought to house a person's spirit.

What is the relationship between the two sentences?

A. Contrast   C. Time order
B. Addition   D. Comparison

_____ 20. ● A loss leader is a product or service that sells at a loss but encourages people to shop at a specific store, where they will buy other products.

● A classic example of a loss leader is milk or sugar—two things people usually need—being sold at less than cost to draw customers into that supermarket.

What is the relationship between the two sentences?

A. Cause and effect   C. Contrast
B. Statement and example   D. Comparison

_____ 21. ● The ancient Chinese thought that it was distasteful to serve meat in large pieces that resembled the original animal.
● Therefore, they preferred to cut the meat into bite-size pieces in the kitchen.

What is the relationship between the two sentences?

A. Time order   C. Comparison
B. Statement and example   D. Cause and effect

_____ 22. ● In the classic monster movie *Godzilla,* the mutant reptile Godzilla incinerates much of Tokyo with his fiery breath.
● Just as Godzilla appears in a number of movies, fire-breathing dragons appear and reappear in many legends and tales.

What is the relationship between the two sentences?

A. Addition   C. Comparison
B. Statement and example   D. Contrast

_____ 23. ● Famed author Mark Twain paid for a promising African American student named Warner T. McGuinn to attend Yale Law School.
● McGuinn eventually became a mentor to a young lawyer named Thurgood Marshall, who would later become the first African-American to serve on the United States Supreme Court.

What is the relationship between the two sentences?

A. Cause and effect   C. Statement and example
B. Contrast   D. Time order

_____ 24. ● Like the attention given to serial killers, the attention given to road rage may be overdone.
● One research study estimates that the odds of dying because of road rage are only 1 in 9.5 million; the odds of being killed in an auto accident are 1 in 16,000.

What is the relationship between the two sentences?

A. Comparison   C. Statement and example
B. Cause and effect   D. Addition

_____ 25. ● General George A. Custer believed that defeating hostile Native Americans in eastern Montana would enable him to command higher fees as a public speaker after he retired from the U.S. Army.
● Instead, a combined force of Lakota Sioux, Cheyenne, and Arapaho warriors killed Custer and 267 of his men at the Little Bighorn River on June 25, 1876.

What is the relationship between the two sentences?

A. Cause and effect   C. Addition
B. Contrast   D. Time order

2 Combined-Skills Tests

Following are twenty-five tests that cover many of the skills taught in Part One and reinforced in Part Two of this book. Each test consists of a short reading passage followed by questions on any of the following: vocabulary in context, central points and main ideas, supporting details, relationships, inferences, purpose and tone, argument, and critical reading.

COMBINED SKILLS: Test 1

Read the passage below. Then write the letter of the best answer to each question that follows.

[1]I remember the day we were driving to a friend's house. [2]We were trying to turn left into a residential neighborhood, but there was a car stopped, blocking the lane ahead. [3]I could see a man in the car holding a woman around the neck with his right arm and slugging her in the face with his left fist. [4]I jumped out of the car and pulled open her door. [5]As I pulled her out of the car, he swung open his door and headed for us both. [6]It occurred to me then that I had always inserted myself into these situations on the premise that a man wouldn't hit a woman, and that premise clearly didn't apply here. [7]But as he stepped toward us, my husband was standing there. [8]"Calm down, man," my husband said. [9]He walked the man back along the road, talking to him, almost whispering to him, as I took the woman across the street, into someone's yard under a tree, and went to the house to get help. [10]Her face was covered in blood. [11]The police came, but the woman wouldn't press charges. [12]The police would not arrest him based on what I saw without her complaint, and so we all got back in our cars and drove away.

[13]I saw them both about a year later at the grocery store, an old yellow bruise on her cheek. [14]I suppose I had always thought that even strangers could intervene and make things right, if only they would, and this was a hard lesson that it wasn't that easy. [15]You couldn't always fix everything.

_____ 1. In sentence 6, the word *premise* means
    A. belief.
    B. misunderstanding.
    C. report.
    D. invitation.

_____ 2. In sentence 14, the word *intervene* means
    A. seek revenge.
    B. come between.
    C. explain.
    D. decide.

_____ 3. When the writer pulls the injured woman out of the car, her husband
    A. fights with the abusive man.
    B. shouts at the abusive man that he has called the police.
    C. walks the abusive man back along the road, talking to him.
    D. remains in the car in order to call the police on his cell phone.

_____ 4. The passage
   A. contrasts abusive men with men who aren't abusive.
   B. compares the writer's attitude toward abuse to her husband's attitude.
   C. presents a sequence of events in time order.
   D. lists reasons why some women accept being abused.

_____ 5. On the basis of sentence 6, we can infer that the writer
   A. knows that the man who slugged and choked the woman won't hit her.
   B. regrets that she ever got involved with the couple.
   C. wants to attack the man herself.
   D. fears that the man will attack her.

_____ 6. The author's tone is mainly
   A. tolerant.
   B. apologetic.
   C. concerned.
   D. frightened.

_____ 7. You could conclude from the passage that the writer
   A. will be unwilling to intervene in another case of domestic abuse.
   B. will try once more to get the woman to press charges against the abusive man.
   C. regrets becoming involved in the couple's business.
   D. now sees that there is little anyone can do if a woman who is being abused refuses to press charges against her abuser.

_____ 8. Which of the following statements best expresses the main idea of the passage?
   A. Sometimes there is no "quick fix" for abusive relationships.
   B. Some women love their men so much that they are willing to endure being abused by them.
   C. Violent behavior can be observed even in seemingly "nice" neighborhoods.
   D. Domestic violence is the most serious social problem facing Americans today.

COMBINED SKILLS: Test 2

Read the passage below. Then write the letter of the best answer to each question that follows.

[1]In his book *About Alice*, in which he remembers his late wife, the writer Calvin Trillin writes about Alice and her beliefs about parenting. [2]He describes a time that Alice volunteered at a camp for children with disabilities. [3]Alice was especially good friends with a little girl she called by her initial, L. [4]L. had genetic diseases that kept her from growing normally and from digesting food. [5]She had difficulty walking. [6]She had to be fed through a tube at night. [7]Still, the little girl was, in Alice's words, "the most optimistic, most enthusiastic, most hopeful human being I had ever encountered." [8]As Alice became closer to the little girl, she became more curious about L. [9]What had given her such strength, such joy and optimism? [10]What was her secret? [11]Then one day at camp, while the children were playing a game, L. asked Alice to hold her mail. [12]On top of the pile was a note from L.'s mother. [13]Alice glanced at it and saw the words that L.'s mother had written to her daughter. [14]"If God had given us all the children in the world to choose from, L., we would only have chosen you."

_____ 1. Alice learned the secret of L.'s optimism when she
   A. met the girl's charming mother.
   B. read a note that L. had written to her mother.
   C. glanced at a note that L.'s mother had written to her daughter.
   D. helped feed her through a tube at night.

_____ 2. The relationship between sentence 7 and sentences 4–6 is one of
   A. cause and effect.
   B. addition.
   C. comparison.
   D. contrast.

_____ 3. The author implies that
   A. some parents are willing to overlook their children's disabilities.
   B. the secret of L.'s optimism was that she knew her parents loved her dearly.
   C. Alice had never met a child who had as many disabilities as L.
   D. Alice envied L.'s joyful nature.

_____ 4. We can infer that Calvin Trillin
  A. was shocked when he learned that his wife had secretly read the note that L.'s mother had written her.
  B. could not understand his wife's curiosity about L.
  C. admired his wife for volunteering at a camp for children with disabilities.
  D. was annoyed that his wife spent time volunteering at a summer camp rather than staying at home with him.

_____ 5. We can infer that L.'s mother
  A. was frustrated that her disabled daughter required so much assistance.
  B. was more than equal to the challenge of being the parent of a disabled child.
  C. felt guilty about sending her disabled daughter off to summer camp.
  D. also suffered from serious disabilities.

_____ 6. The author's main purpose is to
  A. inform us about some of the needs of a particular disabled child.
  B. persuade us that disabled children deserve better treatment.
  C. entertain us with a heartwarming story of the power of love.

_____ 7. The tone of the passage can be described as mainly
  A. admiring.
  B. concerned.
  C. humorous.
  D. detached.

_____ 8. Which is an appropriate title for this selection?
  A. Little Girl Lost
  B. Doing More for Disabled Children
  C. An Uncomplaining Child
  D. The Power of Love

COMBINED SKILLS: Test 3

Read the passage below. Then write the letter of the best answer to each question that follows.

¹I think of myself as a "good" person. ²I obey the law. ³I don't intentionally mistreat my family or friends. ⁴I do volunteer work and generally try to be a decent human being. ⁵And yet there are moments when I realize that there is darkness in my soul. ⁶By that I mean there is a place in me that is fully capable of hatred and violence.

⁷I feel that dark place overwhelm me as I follow the story of Malala Yousafzai, the 14-year-old Pakistani schoolgirl who was shot in the head by Taliban militants. ⁸These men boarded her school bus and shot her at point-blank range for the "crime" of speaking out for the right of girls to be educated, a right the Taliban denies. ⁹The assassination attempt left Malala barely clinging to life. ¹⁰After more than two months in a British hospital, she had recovered enough to be released for weeks more of outpatient treatment. ¹¹Even from her hospital bed, Malala continued to demonstrate her indomitable courage. ¹²She telephoned other threatened young women in Pakistan to encourage them to keep struggling for their right to go to school. ¹³In response to her survival, the Taliban says that they will find a way to murder her later.

¹⁴As I think of the men who shot Malala, I feel that dark place in my soul swallow me up. ¹⁵I imagine myself with a gun, face to face with those monsters. ¹⁶I imagine myself making them experience the same terror that she experienced. ¹⁷I imagine giving myself over to that darkness in my soul. ¹⁸I imagine myself, yes, killing them and being glad to do so. ¹⁹So am I a "good" person after all? ²⁰Am I any different than those men, whose own darkness led to their attempted murder of a child? ²¹Wouldn't they justify their crime as easily as I could justify killing them? ²²If they are monsters—and I believe they are—would killing them make me a monster, too? ²³These questions trouble me, and I cannot answer them to my full satisfaction. ²⁴I suspect that this dark place exists deep within all of us.

_____ 1. In sentence 11, the word *indomitable* means
   A. recovering.
   B. foolish.
   C. unstoppable.
   D. unsteady.

_____ 2. The Taliban shot Malala Yousafzai because she
   A. spoke out in favor of religious freedom.
   B. had dishonored her family by leaving her house without permission.
   C. tried to get an education.
   D. spoke out in favor of the right of girls to be educated.

_____ 3. The pattern of organization in sentences 8–13 is one of
     A. cause and effect.
     B. time order.
     C. contrast.
     D. illustration.

_____ 4. Sentence 13 is a statement of
     A. fact.
     B. opinion.

_____ 5. The passage suggests that
     A. under certain circumstances, we are all capable of doing terrible things.
     B. Malala Yousafzai is a hero.
     C. The Taliban militants who shot Malala Yousafzai are evil people.
     D. all of the above.

_____ 6. The tone of sentences 14–24 can be described as
     A. concerned and sympathetic.
     B. angry but ambivalent.
     C. sorrowful but optimistic.
     D. revengeful and determined.

_____ 7. Which of the following sentences best expresses the main idea of the passage?
     A. All over the world, girls have a right to be educated.
     B. The men who shot a 14-year-old Pakistani schoolgirl should not be judged harshly because we all have evil within ourselves.
     C. When thinking about what he would like to do to the men who nearly murdered Malala Yousafzai, the author suggests that we all have dark places within us.
     D. Malala Yousafzai, a schoolgirl who spoke out for the right of girls to get an education, is a hero.

_____ 8. What is the most appropriate title for this selection?
     A. Taliban Militants
     B. A Heroic Schoolgirl
     C. My Own Dark Places
     D. A Shooting on a School Bus

COMBINED SKILLS: Test 4

Read the passage below. Then write the letter of the best answer to each question that follows.

¹Most people dislike bats, and surely the most feared of all the species is the dreaded vampire bat. ²Vampire bats live up to their horror-story reputation as greedy and efficient stealers of blood.

³Depending upon its type, the vampire bat may prefer to dine on the blood of mammals (including humans) or birds. ⁴The bat begins its meal by circling above its usually sleeping target for several minutes, probably to allow heat-sensitive patches on its face to determine where best to bite. ⁵It then inflicts a small wound with its teeth, which are so razor-sharp that they make the incision virtually painless. ⁶The wound bleeds freely as long as the bat continues feeding, thanks to a substance in the bat's saliva that prevents clotting. ⁷As many as a half dozen of the bat's fellows may join it to feed from one wound.

⁸Vampire bats have such great appetites for blood that they may drink more than their own weight at one feeding, thus making it briefly impossible for them to fly. ⁹A single vampire drinks about twenty-five gallons of blood in its lifetime. ¹⁰Although vampire bats are sometimes responsible for the death of humans or animals, those deaths are not due to loss of blood. ¹¹Rather, the deaths are the result of rabies or other diseases spread by the bats.

_____ 1. In sentence 5, *incision* means
   A. heat-sensitive patch.
   B. cut.
   C. blood.
   D. saliva.

_____ 2. Sentences 10 and 11
   A. narrate events.
   B. define a term.
   C. compare two things.
   D. discuss a cause and effect relationship.

_____ 3. The main patterns of organization of the second paragraph are cause-effect and
   A. contrast.
   B. comparison.
   C. time order.
   D. definition and example.

_____ 4. We can conclude that vampire bats use their heat-sensitive patches
    A. for personal temperature control.
    B. to find where blood is close to their victims' skin.
    C. to find sleeping victims.
    D. to find out which potential victims have the best blood.

_____ 5. The passage suggests that
    A. bats are usually solitary feeders.
    B. all vampire bats have rabies.
    C. vampire bats intend to kill their victims.
    D. vampire bats prefer victims that lie still.

_____ 6. The author's main purpose is to
    A. inform readers about how vampire bats are able to locate and drink blood.
    B. persuade readers that vampire bats deserve to be feared.
    C. entertain readers with scary details about vampire bats.
    D. predict that vampire bats will soon become extinct.

_____ 7. On the whole, the tone of the passage is
    A. fearful.
    B. objective.
    C. disbelieving.
    D. playful.

_____ 8. Which is the most appropriate title for this passage?
    A. Vampire Bats' Feeding Habits
    B. Bats and Disease
    C. Bats in Social Groups
    D. How Bats Live

COMBINED SKILLS: Test 5

Read the passage below. Then write the letter of the best answer to each question that follows.

[1]Have you ever seen someone walk across a bed of hot coals and wondered how in the world he or she did it? [2]"Firewalkers" seem to trot right across the fire without a hint of a grimace and without any damage done to the soles of their feet. [3]And while firewalkers would like their performances to appear to be the result of some secret and mystical power, the "secrets" behind firewalking are really pretty simple. [4]To begin with, you may have noticed that firewalking always happens at night. [5]The reason for this is that if the walks happened during daylight, the fiery coals would appear to be no more than a pile of gray ashes. [6]In reality, the coals that you see the firewalkers move across have been burning for a very long time, so they are covered with a thick layer of ash. [7]However, in darkness, the red glow of the coals is visible. [8]And *after* the firewalker steps onto the coals, sparks and flames often shoot up, giving the impression of walking through fire. [9]But the fact is, if the walker moves quickly enough, his or her feet are protected by ash, which is a remarkably poor conductor of heat. [10]A walker would have to stand still on the coals for a few seconds in order for them to actually cause a burn. [11]Therefore, the real skill of a firewalker lies in his or her ability to move calmly and slowly enough to amaze an audience, yet quickly enough to avoid roasted feet.

_____ 1. As used in sentence 2, the word *grimace* means
   A. bored expression.
   B. smile.
   C. doubt.
   D. pained expression.

_____ 2. In order for their feet to get burned, firewalkers would have to stand on hot coals for
   A. about 15 seconds.
   B. a fraction of a second.
   C. a few seconds.
   D. a minute or more.

_____ 3. Sentence 6 expresses a relationship of
   A. cause and effect.
   B. time.
   C. comparison.
   D. contrast.

_____ 4. The passage discusses
   A. stages in the training of a professional firewalker.
   B. reasons why firewalking isn't as risky as it seems.
   C. a definition and example of the term _firewalker_.
   D. differences between professional and amateur firewalkers.

_____ 5. We can infer that if firewalkers performed during the day,
   A. many of them would get seriously burned.
   B. their audiences would not be as impressed with them.
   C. the coals they walk across would be hotter.
   D. both A and C.

_____ 6. The author of this passage would probably agree with which of the following statements?
   A. Firewalkers are fakes who should be arrested for tricking people.
   B. Firewalking should be outlawed since it can lead to serious burns.
   C. It is easy to learn to be a firewalker.
   D. Firewalking involves skill rather than magic.

_____ 7. The author's tone can be described as
   A. mocking.
   B. amazed.
   C. critical.
   D. straightforward.

_____ 8. Which statement best states the main idea of the passage?
   A. To many people, firewalking seems amazing.
   B. Firewalkers do not possess mystical powers, but instead they have an awareness of some simple secrets.
   C. Coals which have been burning for a long time produce lots of ash, which is a poor conductor of heat.
   D. Firewalkers must not walk too slow or too fast.

COMBINED SKILLS: Test 6

Read the passage below. Then write the letter of the best answer to each question that follows.

¹*When I fall in love, it will be forever*, goes the old song by Nat King Cole. ²But will it be? ³Is the state of being in love something that can really last forever? ⁴As it turns out, the answer is a resounding *no*. ⁵A recent study of nearly 2,000 married couples found that newlywed bliss wears off after about two years. ⁶At that point, the huge surge of happiness that was felt at the beginning of the relationship has dwindled back down to the level of happiness prior to falling in love.

⁷The bad news is that many couples interpret this shift away from constant passion and excitement as a sign they should split up. ⁸After all, they want to be in love; and, according to all the songs on the radio and the romantic movies in the theaters, it should be forever. ⁹The good news, however, is that this switch from passionate love to what's known as companionate love—deeply affectionate, but less sexual—is entirely natural. ¹⁰It happens to all couples.

¹¹It may seem unfair, but there are evolutionary and practical reasons for this gradual disappearing of passion. ¹²If we remained forever in the throes of obsession, we'd never get anything done. ¹³We'd neglect our health, children, jobs, and the world around us. ¹⁴Humans are hardwired, in fact, to eventually lose *obsessive* interest in everything. ¹⁵The new car, a hobby, a new flavor of cheesecake—in time the excitement always dims. ¹⁶If it doesn't (take, for example, too much cheesecake), life is thrown out of balance.

¹⁷Natural as it may be, however, the cooling of romantic love still bothers us. ¹⁸We may look at it logically and accept that it is an expected transition, but we still feel pretty let down. ¹⁹Why? ²⁰Because humans are also hardwired to want surprise and change in their lives. ²¹When a relationship is new, every little thing (the way one sneezes, dessert preferences, eye color) is a surprise. ²²In time, however, everything becomes pretty darned predictable.

²³Luckily, with a little imagination and commitment, couples can continue to surprise each other in small ways long after the initial thrill is gone. ²⁴A bouquet of flowers, an unexpected trip, or just a few heartfelt words can go a long way to keeping a relationship strong. ²⁵And for those who have children, there's even more good news. ²⁶The sudden newness of an empty nest is such a big change that many couples rediscover one another and find themselves enjoying a second honeymoon.

²⁷So while it may be true that the obsessive brand-new love we fall into doesn't last forever, real love quite often does.

_____ 1. In sentence 12, the term *in the throes of* means
   A. struggling with.   C. excited by.
   B. in expectation of.   D. unaware of.

_____ 2. According to the selection, humans are hard-wired to
  A. fall passionately in love.
  B. desire commitment.
  C. want surprise and change.
  D. want love to last forever.

_____ 3. The relationship between sentence 9 and the two sentences that come before it is one of
  A. addition.   C. cause and effect.
  B. illustration.   D. contrast.

_____ 4. The organizational pattern of the third paragraph is
  A. a series of steps in a process.
  B. a comparison of two or more items.
  C. an explanation for why something occurs.
  D. a contrast between two emotions.

_____ 5. The passage suggests that
  A. modern views of love are influenced by popular music.
  B. people like being passionately in love.
  C. obsessive love is impractical.
  D. all of the above.

_____ 6. The author's tone can be described as
  A. amused and playful.   C. nostalgic and sentimental.
  B. straightforward and optimistic. D. detached and analytical.

_____ 7. The author's main purpose in writing this selection is to
  A. predict how many American marriages will fail because of unrealistic ideas about love.
  B. persuade people to stay together even though they are no longer passionate about each other.
  C. explain why passionate love always turns into companionate love.
  D. inform couples of ways to keep passionate love alive.

_____ 8. Which of the following sentences best expresses the main idea of the selection?
  A. Contrary to popular belief, it's impossible to stay in love forever.
  B. There are a number of ways in which couples can keep their relationship strong.
  C. It's natural for passionate love to change into companionate love, which is deeply affectionate but less sexual.
  D. Although most of us would like to remain in passionate love, we'd neglect the world around us if we did.

COMBINED SKILLS: Test 7

Read the passage below. Then write the letter of the best answer to each question that follows.

¹Little League baseball in its present form should be abolished. ²For one thing, the pressure that children are put under to succeed may harm them more than help them. ³One mother discovered her son taking Maalox tablets from the medicine chest whenever a game approached. ⁴He explained that they helped relieve the stomach burn he would feel during the game. ⁵Other children have been found taking tranquilizers. ⁶Another drawback to today's Little League baseball is that some parents take the game too seriously and set a bad example for their children. ⁷Recently, a disillusioned coach said, "At our field, we put the bleachers way back from the dugout where the players are. ⁸That way, parents can't be hissing down advice to their children all the time and getting them upset." ⁹A final reason Little League should be abolished is that it doesn't offer enough success to most players. ¹⁰Instead, the game revolves around the more developed kids who are able to hit and throw the ball harder than the smaller children. ¹¹In one recent game, most of the batters were clearly afraid of the speed of the hardball, which was pitched by a boy bigger than many of the other players.

¹²A workable alternative to Little League hardball would be slow-pitch softball. ¹³The ball is pitched slowly and underhand, which offers a high level of success to kids without a high level of ability. ¹⁴Slow-pitch softball would get more children involved in the game, and help people remember that it *is* a game—not an adult arena where one is branded with success or failure.

_____ 1. In sentences 1 and 9, the word *abolished* means
    A. supported.
    B. done away with.
    C. expanded.
    D. imitated.

_____ 2. According to the author, one advantage of slow-pitch softball is the
    A. weight of the ball.
    B. age of the players.
    C. size of the field.
    D. lesser degree of skill required.

_____ 3. The relationship of sentence 6 to the sentences that come before it is one of
    A. time.
    B. addition.
    C. contrast.
    D. comparison.

_____ 4. Sentence 1 is a statement of
   A. fact.
   B. opinion.
   C. fact and opinion.

_____ 5. From the passage, you can conclude the author would agree with the idea that
   A. it's not whether you win or lose; it's how you play the game.
   B. competition in baseball helps prepare people for competition in life.
   C. children's games should imitate adults' games.
   D. sports should help children learn that there are winners and losers in life.

_____ 6. The author's main purpose is to
   A. inform readers how Little League baseball works.
   B. persuade readers that Little League baseball is harmful to children.
   C. entertain readers with true stories involving Little League games.
   D. predict that Little League baseball will soon be abolished.

_____ 7. The main idea of paragraph 1 is best stated in
   A. sentence 1.
   B. sentence 2.
   C. sentence 9.
   D. sentence 11.

_____ 8. What is the most appropriate title for this selection?
   A. The Pressures on Today's Children
   B. Slow-Pitch Softball
   C. Let's Reform Little League
   D. Sportsmanship in Baseball

COMBINED SKILLS: Test 8

Read the passage below. Then write the letter of the best answer to each question that follows.

> [1]The social psychologist Philip Zimbardo set out to test a theory that the anonymity of city life encourages crime. [2]He arranged to have automobiles abandoned in two different locations: New York City and Palo Alto, California, a medium-sized suburban community. [3]The cars' license plates were removed and their hoods were raised to signal that the autos were abandoned. [4]Then each car was secretly watched for sixty-four hours.
>
> [5]The person assigned to watch the New York car did not have long to wait. [6]Within ten minutes the car received its first auto strippers—a father, mother, and eight-year-old son. [7]The mother appeared to be a lookout, while the son aided the father's search of the trunk, glove compartment, and motor. [8]He then handed his father the tools necessary to remove the battery and radiator. [9]Total time of destructive contact: seven minutes.
>
> [10]This, however, was only the first "contact." [11]By the end of the sixty-four hours, the car had been vandalized twenty-four times, often by well-dressed, seemingly middle-class adults. [12]What remained when the experiment was over was a useless hunk of metal. [13]In contrast, the Palo Alto car was approached only once: when it started to rain, a passerby stopped to lower the hood.
>
> [14]According to Zimbardo, the crucial factor in the different fates of the two cars was anonymity. [15]In a large city, where the chances of being recognized outside one's own neighborhood are extremely slim, even "upstanding citizens" can afford a temporary turn at thievery. [16]In a smaller community, on the other hand, the higher probability of being recognized and caught keeps people honest.

_____ 1. In sentence 14, the word *crucial* means
- A. least interesting.
- B. most important.
- C. most unlikely.
- D. most helpful.

_____ 2. According to the passage, Zimbardo's main purpose in doing the experiment was to
- A. illustrate a point.
- B. test a theory.
- C. catch thieves.
- D. teach honesty.

_____ 3. The pattern of organization in sentences 5 through 9 is one of
    A. time order.
    B. list of items.
    C. comparison.
    D. contrast.

_____ 4. The relationship between sentences 15 and 16 is one of
    A. time.
    B. comparison.
    C. contrast.
    D. cause and effect.

_____ 5. Sentence 13 is a statement of
    A. fact.
    B. opinion.
    C. both fact and opinion.

_____ 6. The passage suggests that
    A. people who vandalize cars always travel in groups.
    B. New Yorkers are more dishonest than people in most other big cities.
    C. social pressure promotes honesty.
    D. the car used in Palo Alto was probably in better condition than the car in New York City.

_____ 7. The tone of the passage can be described as mainly
    A. objective.
    B. doubtful.
    C. alarmed.
    D. scornful.

_____ 8. Which statement best states the main idea of the passage?
    A. Philip Zimbardo is a creative social psychologist.
    B. People are now more dishonest than ever.
    C. In big cities, ordinary people's chances of being recognized outside of their neighborhood are quite slim.
    D. Zimbardo's experiment suggests that the impersonal nature of city life encourages crime.

COMBINED SKILLS: Test 9

Read the passage below. Then write the letter of the best answer to each question that follows.

[1]Perception is strongly influenced by attention. [2]Unfortunately, if you daydream during a lecture, little or nothing will reach your brain. [3]Attending is not always easy, so so you take notes and make conscious efforts to remain alert. [4]Did you notice an error in the previous sentence? [5]You probably were concentrating on the content, and although your eyes saw the word *so* repeated, you ignored it. [6]Similarly, you were probably not focusing any attention on your thumb until you read this sentence. [7]You simply cannot attend to every stimulus around you, so only certain things are selected. [8]Have you ever driven down a highway with your gas needle nearing "empty"? [9]Chances are you became preoccupied with the location of gas stations. [10]Another day when your tank was full but your stomach was empty, the gas stations might have been overlooked, but every diner and restaurant would have caught your eye. [11]Attention is usually focused on needed things. [12]If you are hungry or thirsty right now, you might have a problem keeping your attention focused on the reading rather than on the refrigerator.

_____ 1. As used in sentence 3, the word *attending* means
   A. showing up.
   B. paying attention.
   C. taking care.
   D. waiting.

_____ 2. In sentence 9, the words *preoccupied with* mean
   A. fully interested in.
   B. forgetful about.
   C. expert in.
   D. confident about.

_____ 3. According to the author, we usually concentrate on
   A. what we are expected to pay attention to.
   B. random things.
   C. daydreaming.
   D. needed things.

_____ 4. The relationship between sentences 5 and 6 is one of
   A. time.
   B. contrast.
   C. comparison.
   D. illustration.

_____ 5. Sentence 12 discusses a
    A. series of events.
    B. contrast.
    C. comparison.
    D. cause and effect.

_____ 6. You might conclude from the paragraph that it would be a good idea to
    A. forget about taking notes in classes.
    B. avoid being hungry when you go to your classes.
    C. take a difficult class just before lunchtime.
    D. eat less.

_____ 7. What is the best title for this selection?
    A. Daydreaming
    B. Perception
    C. The Relationship between Perception and Attention
    D. How Hunger Influences Attention

_____ 8. Which statement best expresses the main idea of the paragraph?
    A. You are unlikely to notice an error in writing if you are concentrating on its content.
    B. If you are hungry, you will focus on eating.
    C. Unfortunately, when students daydream during lectures, nothing will reach their brains.
    D. Perception is strongly influenced by attention, which is usually focused on needed things.

COMBINED SKILLS: Test 10

Read the passage below. Then write the letter of the best answer to each question that follows.

[1]If you're a member of the millennial generation—ages 18 to 34—who never got beyond 12th grade, expect hard times, say people who study the transition from youth to adulthood.

[2]"There's nothing for these kids," said Maria Kefalas, a St. Joseph's University sociologist. [3]"Absolutely nothing."

[4]It's not simply the recession and its robust half-life that stymie high-school-only young people.

[5]Thirty years of jobs moving from Main Street to Mumbai and elsewhere; of the American workplace being wired with robots and computers that perform the jobs that factory workers and office clerks once did; of neutered unions, shrunken wages, and diminished benefits—all of this has changed the nature of work and has made people who use their hands, backs, and working-class smarts nearly as obsolete as VCRs.

[6]"I don't see a future or an ability to retire," said Brian Haney, 31, an unemployed Northeast Philadelphia resident with only a high-school degree. [7]"There'll be one low-wage job after another ahead of me. [8]It's just a nightmare."

[9]The national unemployment rate for people ages 18 to 19 with only high-school degrees is 22.7 percent, according to new, non-seasonally adjusted calculations by the U.S. Bureau of Labor Statistics.

[10]Although the economy is improving, high-school-only graduates still find themselves pressured on all sides. [11]They compete with immigrants for unskilled construction work. [12]They're aced out of traditional service jobs by young people with college degrees who can't find work on their own level. [13]And they're applying for the same underpaying jobs at the mall that their friends are, all of them members of a star-crossed generation that's huge in number but short on options.

[14]Of course, high-school graduates understand that a postsecondary education—a certificate, an associate's degree, or a bachelor's—is the best way up and out. [15]But scholarly rigor isn't for everyone. [16]And postsecondary prices are out of reach for many blue-collar people.

[17]A generation ago, that would have been fine; there was plenty of decent-paying blue-collar work.

[18]But that America is gone.

[19]What exists now is a country that can no longer be called the land of opportunity for all.

[20]"These kids are part of a generation that was still being told they can do anything," Kefalas said. [21]"Well, no, you can't. [22]There are huge barriers now. [23]Kids say they're going to be lawyers, veterinarians. [24]It makes me crazy, because it'll never happen."

_____ 1. In sentence 4, the word *stymie* means
     A. affect.   C. help to motivate.
     B. hold back.   D. frustrate.

_____ 2. In sentences 6–8, Brian Haney's tone can be described as
    A. defensive and self-pitying.   C. distressed and indignant.
    B. pessimistic and fearful.   D. angry and scornful.

_____ 3. The writer's main purpose in writing this selection is to
    A. persuade young people to continue their education.
    B. predict what must happen to make the American economy able to provide enough good-paying jobs for the millennial generation.
    C. inform readers of the economic challenges high-school graduates face.
    D. entertain readers with stories of young people who have succeeded in the face of long odds.

_____ 4. The relationship between sentences 14 and 15 is one of
    A. cause and effect.   C. illustration.
    B. contrast.   D. comparison.

_____ 5. Which of the following *doesn't* the author present as a reason why it's difficult for people with only high-school degrees to get a job?
    A. Jobs have moved from Main Street to Mumbai.
    B. Robots and computers now perform much factory and office work.
    C. Many recent high-school graduates have poor verbal and math skills.
    D. High-school graduates are competing with college graduates who can't find work in their own field.

_____ 6. The selection suggests that
    A. it's a waste of time to get a high-school diploma.
    B. as the economy continues to improve, most high-school graduates will be able to find decent-paying blue-collar work.
    C. there will always be a demand for people who are willing to work hard.
    D. we shouldn't tell kids that they can do anything, because it isn't true.

_____ 7. This selection mainly
    A. contrasts job opportunities for high-school-only young people with job opportunities for college graduates.
    B. lists reasons why young people who have only a high-school diploma are not finding good-paying jobs.
    C. provides a short history of trends in the American labor market.
    D. defines the term *millennial generation* and compares it to past generations.

_____ 8. Which of the following sentences best states the main idea of the passage?
    A. The U.S. job market looks bleak for young people with only a high-school diploma.
    B. Unfortunately, many high-school graduates can't afford post-secondary education.
    C. Kids who think they're going to be lawyers and veterinarians are in for a rude awakening.
    D. Most members of the millennial generation will never be able to retire.

COMBINED SKILLS: Test 11

Read the passage below. Then write the letter of the best answer to each question that follows.

¹The Internet has often been referred to as "the information highway." ²We can zip along this highway at top speed and learn infinite details about everything from anteaters to zombies. ³It has been argued that the computer is one of the most remarkable learning tools ever invented. ⁴But is information the same thing as education? ⁵Some experts argue that computers are actually detrimental to learning.

⁶One recent study has shown that the spread of home computers and high-speed Internet access is associated with significant declines in math and reading scores. ⁷The primary reason for this, it is believed, is that the Internet is creating a culture of short attention spans. ⁸The hyperlink world has made it increasingly difficult for us to engage in deep thought and to take our time when confronted with, say, a difficult math equation or a complex concept. ⁹After all, we're on a highway—who wants to slow down?

¹⁰The antidote to this growing problem of instant information gratification could well be an activity that the Internet seems to have replaced for many: reading books. ¹¹It's a fact that reading leads to educational gains. ¹²Research has revealed that kids who grow up in a home with 500 books end up staying in school longer and making better grades. ¹³A book, unlike the Internet, requires readers to immerse themselves in different worlds. ¹⁴It involves contemplation and reflection and, perhaps most importantly, slowing down in order to consider what an author is saying.

¹⁵However, it is often difficult to get people—young people in particular—to see the benefits of reading books. ¹⁶They argue that the Internet helps them learn about what's going on *now*. ¹⁷Books are old-fashioned and full of old ideas, while the Internet keeps them informed of current trends, culture, and controversy. ¹⁸Basically, computers are cooler.

¹⁹To be sure, the Internet promotes a kind of learning that is quite different from what is learned by reading books. ²⁰But it is still the literary world that helps one become cultivated and open-minded. ²¹To read a book and journey into the author's mind and artistry is to gain an experience that may very well last forever. ²²It is an experience, then, that is the very opposite of rushing along a highway and snatching up bits of information for the moment—it is education for a lifetime.

_____ 1. As used in sentence 5, the word *detrimental* means
   A. favorable.
   B. harmful.
   C. relevant.
   D. comparable.

_____ 2. Which of the following sentences best states the main idea of the passage?
   A. The Internet is creating a culture of short attention spans.
   B. Because young people think computers are cool, it is difficult to get them to read books.
   C. Unlike the Internet, a book requires readers to immerse themselves in different worlds.
   D. We become truly educated by reading books, not by using the Internet.

_____ 3. According to the passage, kids who grow up in a home with 500 books
   A. don't know as much as kids who spend lots of time on the Internet.
   B. are considered old-fashioned by their peers.
   C. stay in school longer and make better grades.
   D. are unable to keep up on current trends, culture, and controversy.

_____ 4. The relationship of sentence 7 to sentence 6 is one of
   A. contrast.   C. illustration.
   B. cause and effect.   D. addition.

_____ 5. On the basis of sentences 15–18, we can infer that
   A. many of today's young people have little or no interest in the past.
   B. computers are cooler than books.
   C. today's young people are less trend-conscious than past generations.
   D. all of the above.

_____ 6. Sentence 21 is a statement of
   A. fact.
   B. opinion.

_____ 7. The author's main purpose is to
   A. inform readers about the harmful effects of "the information highway."
   B. entertain readers by making fun of people with very short attention spans.
   C. persuade readers that books offer a more valuable experience than being on the Internet.
   D. predict that in a few years books will again become popular.

_____ 8. The author's tone can be described as
   A. scornful.
   B. pessimistic.
   C. serious.
   D. pleading.

COMBINED SKILLS: Test 12

Read the passage below. Then write the letter of the best answer to each question that follows.

¹We live in an era in which more women are entering formerly male-dominated professions, demanding equal pay for equal work, and generally rejecting the societal double standard which has held them back from reaching their full potential. ²Yet many women are still bound by old-fashioned and harmful ideas about sexuality. ³An epidemic of "date rapes" on college campuses is evidence that warped beliefs about sexuality are barriers that women—as well as men—need to break in order to achieve a full human partnership. ⁴As many as 25 percent of all college women may become victims of rape or attempted rape. ⁵Women at the beginning of their college careers are especially vulnerable to date rape. ⁶They may be living in coed dorms with men whom they assume they can trust. ⁷They are eager to appear cool and sophisticated, not paranoid or uptight. ⁸Most destructively of all, many women still subscribe, at least subconsciously, to the belief that they "owe" sexual favors to a man they date. ⁹After a sexual attack by a date, many women are racked with guilt rather than anger. ¹⁰Were they to blame, they ask themselves, because they drank too much? ¹¹Because they wore a short skirt? ¹²Similarly, men have grown up in a culture which suggests that once they have spent "good money" entertaining a date, they are owed sex in return.

_____ 1. In sentence 8, the words *subscribe . . . to* mean
   A. describe.
   B. agree with.
   C. ignore.
   D. argue with.

_____ 2. The relationship of sentence 2 to sentence 1 is one of
   A. addition.
   B. illustration.
   C. contrast.
   D. comparison.

_____ 3. The relationship of sentence 12 to sentences 9–11 is one of
   A. time.
   B. contrast.
   C. comparison.
   D. cause and effect.

_____ 4. You can conclude that the author believes
   A. many men and women should change their attitudes about sexuality.
   B. attitudes about rights in the workplace have changed more than attitudes about sexuality.
   C. victims of date rape often feel responsible for having been attacked.
   D. all of the above.

_____ 5. The main purpose of this passage is to
   A. inform readers about interesting sexual attitudes.
   B. use facts to argue that sexual attitudes need improving.
   C. entertain readers with dramatic sexual images.
   D. predict the future of the American sex scene.

_____ 6. The author's tone can be described as
   A. sarcastic.
   B. optimistic.
   C. arrogant.
   D. concerned.

_____ 7. The point made in sentence 2 is best supported by
   A. sentence 1.
   B. sentence 4.
   C. sentence 8.
   D. sentence 12.

_____ 8. The main idea of the passage is that
   A. women are now close to reaching their full potential.
   B. societal attitudes toward sexuality are old-fashioned and harmful.
   C. colleges should provide better security in coed dorms.
   D. men's sexual attitudes are strongly in need of change.

COMBINED SKILLS: Test 13

Read the passage below. Then write the letter of the best answer to each question that follows.

¹Mary was watching a mystery on television. ²The end of the movie was near, and she was totally engrossed. ³Then her baby started crying. ⁴She shouted at him to shut up. ⁵His response was intensified crying. ⁶Mary got angry and shook him. ⁷The baby cried even louder. ⁸Meanwhile, the mystery's conclusion took place, and Mary missed it. ⁹Angrily, she slapped her son's face. ¹⁰In this situation, someone was pursuing a goal— seeing the end of a suspenseful television show. ¹¹But something happened to block the achievement of that goal. ¹²The person thus became frustrated, anger built up, and direct aggression occurred.

¹³Aggression is not always aimed at the original frustrater. ¹⁴For example, consider a businessman who had a hard day at the office. ¹⁵He was about to close a deal with a client when his boss clumsily interfered and lost the sale. ¹⁶On the way home in his car, the frustrated businessman blew his horn angrily at a car ahead when it didn't immediately pull away from a stoplight. ¹⁷As he entered his home, his dog jumped up on him, only to receive a quick kick. ¹⁸He then shouted at his wife during supper. ¹⁹All these aggressive behaviors are examples of displaced aggression. ²⁰Aggression against the person who caused the original frustration can often be harmful. ²¹In this case, assaulting or swearing at the boss could cost the businessman his job. ²²When the original frustrater has status and power over the frustrated person, aggression may be displaced onto a less threatening target, who may have nothing at all to do with the original frustration.

_____ 1. In sentence 2, the word *engrossed* means
  A. involved.
  B. disgusted.
  C. disappointed.
  D. bored.

_____ 2. The topic of the first paragraph is
  A. parent-child relationships.
  B. direct aggression.
  C. displaced aggression.
  D. suspense.

_____ 3. Aggression is more likely to be displaced if the original frustrater
  A. is a family member.
  B. has power over the frustrated person.
  C. is angry at the frustrated person.
  D. is unfair to the frustrated person.

_____ 4. The relationship between sentences 11 and 12 is one of
    A. definition and example.
    B. comparison.
    C. contrast.
    D. cause and effect.

_____ 5. The organizational pattern of the second paragraph is
    A. a series of steps in a process.
    B. a contrast of events.
    C. illustration and explanation of a general concept.
    D. a comparison of two or more events.

_____ 6. The writer's main purpose in writing this selection is to
    A. predict how aggression influences relationships.
    B. inform readers about two types of aggression.
    C. persuade readers to be careful not to take out their aggression on the wrong people.
    D. entertain readers with dramatic anecdotes about aggressive behavior.

_____ 7. What is the best title for the selection?
    A. Family Relationships
    B. The Causes of Aggression
    C. Direct and Displaced Aggression
    D. Displaced Aggression

_____ 8. Which sentence best states the main idea of the selection?
    A. A great deal of frustration is aimed against family members.
    B. When frustration and anger build up, direct or displaced aggression may occur.
    C. Sometimes a frustrater may have a great deal more power or status than the person who is frustrated.
    D. Direct aggression is more satisfying than indirect aggression.

COMBINED SKILLS: Test 14

Read the passage below. Then write the letter of the best answer to each question that follows.

¹Thousands of years ago, ancient Greeks firmly believed that many illnesses, from colds to migraines, were caused by too much blood in the body. ²Because they didn't realize that blood constantly circulated through the body, they felt that blood could become stagnant and rot inside people. ³As a result, Greek physicians regularly prescribed "bloodletting," a procedure that involved cutting patients and draining blood from them—sometimes more than a quart! ⁴Often, patients who had been only slightly ill with a little head cold became deathly ill from blood loss. ⁵Meanwhile, as recently as 120 years ago, many doctors prescribed what was known as the "Rest Cure" for female patients who complained of sadness or lack of energy. ⁶This "cure" involved confining the patient to bed for months at a time and strictly forbidding any creative activity. ⁷Doctors believed that pastimes of painting or writing or playing music were much too intense for even a healthy woman. ⁸Therefore, tired or disturbed women should certainly avoid creative activities. ⁹Additionally, little to no social interaction was allowed since it was felt that the distraction of friends and loved ones would further exhaust a patient. ¹⁰The result of this "cure" was that moderately depressed women often became terribly depressed at best, and suicidal at worst. ¹¹From ancient Greek medicine to near-modern medicine, sometimes the treatment has been more dangerous than the illness!

_____ 1. In sentence 2, the word *stagnant* means
   A. powerful.
   B. inactive.
   C. overheated.
   D. cold.

_____ 2. The ancient Greeks didn't realize
   A. that bodies sometimes contain too much blood.
   B. that colds and migraines differ from other illnesses.
   C. that blood circulates throughout the body.
   D. all of the above.

_____ 3. As recently as 120 years ago, doctors believed that
   A. creative activity could benefit only healthy women.
   B. depression could be cured through intense activity.
   C. creative activities such as painting or writing were too intense for even healthy women.
   D. most women were emotionally disturbed.

_____ 4. The relationship of sentence 3 to sentence 2 is one of
   A. contrast.
   B. cause and effect.
   C. comparison.
   D. time.

_____ 5. We can infer that doctors who prescribed the "Rest Cure" for women
   A. did not realize that their "cure" was driving some women to suicide.
   B. believed that, in general, women were "the weaker sex."
   C. had no knowledge of how to effectively treat depression.
   D. all of the above.

_____ 6. The passage suggests that bloodletting
   A. led to the deaths of a number of patients.
   B. often drove patients to suicide.
   C. was sometimes an effective method of treating blood disorders.
   D. all of the above.

_____ 7. The author's tone seems to be
   A. nostalgic.
   B. detached.
   C. ashamed.
   D. critical.

_____ 8. The main idea of the passage is expressed in
   A. sentence 1.
   B. sentence 2.
   C. sentence 5.
   D. sentence 11.

COMBINED SKILLS: Test 15

Read the passage below. Then write the letter of the best answer to each question that follows.

[1]It would be a mistake to assume that primitive societies are mentally backward—unable to benefit from their environment or understand how to cope effectively with it. [2]Given the general level of technology available, they do adapt to and manipulate their environment in a sophisticated and understanding manner. [3]Countless examples can be cited to illustrate this point. [4]Among some Eskimo groups, wolves are a menace—a dangerous environmental feature that must be dealt with. [5]They could perhaps be hunted down and killed, but this involves danger as well as considerable expenditure in time and energy. [6]So a simple yet clever device is employed. [7]A sharp sliver of bone is curled into a springlike shape, and seal blubber is molded around it and permitted to freeze. [8]This is then placed where it can be discovered by a hungry wolf, which, living up to its reputation, "wolfs it down." [9]Later, as this "time bomb" is digested and the blubber disappears, the bone uncurls and its sharp ends pierce the stomach of the wolf, causing internal bleeding and death. [10]This method, though harsh, is undeniably practical. [11]It is a simple yet fairly safe technique that involves an understanding of the environment as well as wolf psychology and habits.

_____ 1. As used in sentence 6, the word *employed* means
   A. hired.
   B. recognized.
   C. used.
   D. known.

_____ 2. The relationship between the two parts of sentence 5 is one of
   A. time.
   B. comparison.
   C. contrast.
   D. addition.

_____ 3. The author implies that among primitive societies, the Eskimos' cleverness is
   A. superior.
   B. typical.
   C. rare.
   D. inferior.

_____ 4. The author implies that certain societies are considered "primitive" because of their
    A. attitude toward animals.
    B. level of technology.
    C. creative ability.
    D. understanding of their environment.

_____ 5. The author's attitude toward the Eskimos who created the device appears to be
    A. accusing.
    B. disgusted.
    C. objective.
    D. puzzled.

_____ 6. Which is an appropriate title for this selection?
    A. Mentally Backward Societies
    B. Dangerous Environmental Features
    C. Intelligence in Primitive Societies
    D. Land of the Eskimos

_____ 7. Which sentence best expresses the main idea of the passage?
    A. The greatest challenge to a society is controlling its environment.
    B. Eskimos are able to control wolves.
    C. With increased technology, primitive societies should be able to cope even more effectively with their environment.
    D. Primitive societies can deal shrewdly and effectively with the demands of their environment.

_____ 8. The author supports the main idea with a
    A. list of several reasons.
    B. comparison of two things.
    C. contrast between two things.
    D. detailed example.

COMBINED SKILLS: Test 16

Read the passage below. Then write the letter of the best answer to each question that follows.

[1]It's not easy to tell when someone's lying to you. [2]But most liars feel a little bad about their deception, whether it's complimenting Grandma on her tasteless cake or covering up a major scandal. [3]And often that twinge of guilt, anxiety, or fear is strong enough to give lies away. [4]The tone of a person's voice, for example, is one of the best cues. [5]Research indicates that people's voices often get noticeably higher in pitch when they lie. [6]Also, they're more likely to stammer or stumble over words. [7]Liars also often sound distant when they're making something up, using few descriptive phrases or hand motions. [8]In one study, students pretending to like a person they in fact disliked said such things as, "Yeah, I really like her because she's a good person." [9]In addition, liars tend to lace their speech with denials and hedging, such as, "I didn't really read the book very carefully, so I'm not sure," or "I don't remember for sure who I played against in that tournament." [10]And they're prone to frequent blinking and fidgeting, such as head-scratching or nail-biting. [11]On the other hand, many behaviors we think are signs of deception are not. [12]Shifty eyes, for example, are not a good sign that someone is lying. [13]When people speak slowly, take a long time to answer questions, shift their gaze or their posture, or don't smile much, they're *perceived* to be deceptive. [14]According to researchers, however, these behaviors are as likely to show up during lie-telling as during truth-telling.

_____ 1. As used in sentence 10, the words *prone to* mean
   A. responsive to.
   B. afraid to show.
   C. likely to hide.
   D. likely to show.

_____ 2. According to the selection, one behavior that does *not* indicate that someone is lying is
   A. a higher-sounding voice.
   B. stammering and stumbling over words.
   C. shifty eyes.
   D. head-scratching and nail-biting.

_____ 3. Sentences 4–10
   A. provide examples of types of behavior which indicate that a person is lying.
   B. list reasons why some people feel the need to lie.
   C. compare liars to honest people.
   D. define the term *deceptive behavior*.

_____ 4. The relationship of sentence 11 to sentence 10 is one of
   A. cause and effect.
   B. contrast.
   C. addition.
   D. comparison.

_____ 5. On the basis of this passage, we can infer that
   A. there are certain cues which tend to indicate whether or not a person is lying, but they're not foolproof.
   B. most liars are eventually found out.
   C. liars have no feelings of guilt over their behavior.
   D. fidgeting and frequent blinking are sure signs that a person is lying.

_____ 6. The author would probably agree with which of the following statements?
   A. Lying is no big deal since everyone does it.
   B. Most politicians are liars.
   C. People should never lie.
   D. Liars tend to exhibit certain behaviors.

_____ 7. The author's tone is mainly
   A. sympathetic and tolerant.
   B. scornful and superior.
   C. solemn and objective.
   D. informal but instructive.

_____ 8. What is the best title for the selection?
   A. We All Lie
   B. Foolproof Methods of Lie Detection
   C. Lie Detection: An Inexact Science
   D. How Detectives Obtain the Truth

COMBINED SKILLS: Test 17

Read the passage below. Then write the letter of the best answer to each question that follows.

¹According to a recent survey by the travel company Expedia.com, a third of employed U.S. adults don't use all of their allotted vacation time; they feel too much job pressure. ²And their allotted time isn't much to begin with: on average, fourteen days. ³Contrast that with the average number of paid vacation days allotted to employees in some other industrialized nations: seventeen in Australia, nineteen in Canada, twenty-four in the United Kingdom, twenty-seven in Germany, and thirty-nine in France. ⁴In fact, about a fourth of U.S. employees don't receive *any* paid vacation time. ⁵In addition, many Americans who do take vacation days continue to work via cell phones and computers. ⁶Approximately a fourth of U.S. vacationers check their business voicemail or e-mail while on "vacation." ⁷Also, it's standard for U.S. employers to require a year on the job before granting two weeks of vacation. ⁸Finally, the United States is the only leading industrialized nation that doesn't legally require any minimum vacation time. ⁹Canada and Japan require at least two weeks of paid vacation, China at least three, and all the other leading industrialized countries at least four. ¹⁰Going without vacations leads to stress, resentment, depression, and burnout, which reduce job performance and impair health. ¹¹U.S. companies that have implemented mandatory vacations of at least three weeks have seen increased productivity and profits. ¹²For these reasons, U.S. law should mandate minimum vacation times.

_____ 1. In the first sentence, the word *allotted* means
   A. required.
   B. surrendered.
   C. permitted.
   D. demanded.

_____ 2. In contrast to many other industrialized nations, the United States
   A. requires that employers grant their employees two weeks of paid vacation.
   B. doesn't legally require any minimum vacation time.
   C. recommends but doesn't require that employees receive paid vacation time.
   D. requires that employers grant their employees three weeks of paid vacation.

_____ 3. Many Americans don't use all their allotted vacation time because
   A. they fear that their employers will penalize them if they do.
   B. they enjoy working.
   C. it's now so easy to work from home via cell phones and computers.
   D. they feel too much job pressure.

_____ 4. This selection mainly
    A. lists reasons why Americans receive little paid vacation.
    B. defines the term *paid vacation* and provides examples of paid vacations in other countries.
    C. contrasts how much paid vacation workers in other industrialized countries receive with how little American workers receive.
    D. compares attitudes toward work of Europeans and Americans.

_____ 5. The author suggests that
    A. even while many American workers are on vacation, they're still working.
    B. workers in other nations receive too much paid vacation.
    C. productivity would suffer if American workers received more paid vacation time.
    D. Americans work long hours, but the quality of the work they perform is poor.

_____ 6. The writer's main purpose in writing this selection is to
    A. predict whether American workers would take time out for longer paid vacations if these were offered to them.
    B. persuade readers that the United States should require employers to provide minimum vacation time.
    C. entertain readers with amusing stories about how Americans continue to work when they're supposed to be vacationing.
    D. inform readers about differences in the amount of vacation time workers in industrialized countries receive.

_____ 7. Sentence 12 expresses
    A. a fact.
    B. an opinion.

_____ 8. The main idea of the selection is expressed in
    A. sentence 1.
    B. sentence 2.
    C. sentence 8.
    D. sentence 12.

COMBINED SKILLS: Test 18

Read the passage below. Then write the letter of the best answer to each question that follows.

[1]We all know deserts are dry places, but just what is meant by the term *dry*? [2]That is, how much rain defines the boundary between humid and dry regions? [3]Sometimes it is defined by a single rainfall figure, for example, twenty-five centimeters (ten inches) of precipitation per year. [4]*(Rainfall* refers to the quantity of water that falls in the form of rain, snow, etc. in an area in a given amount of time.) [5]However, the concept of dryness is a relative one that refers to any situation in which a water deficiency exists. [6]Thus, climatologists define *dry climate* as one in which yearly precipitation is less than the potential loss of water by evaporation. [7]Dryness, then, is related not only to total annual rainfall but also to evaporation. [8]Evaporation, in turn, greatly depends upon temperature. [9]As temperatures climb, potential evaporation also increases. [10]Fifteen to twenty-five centimeters of precipitation can support forests in northern Scandinavia, where evaporation into the cool, humid air is slight and a surplus of water remains in the soil. [11]However, the same amount of rain falling on New Mexico supports only a sparse vegetative cover because evaporation into the hot, dry air is great. [12]So clearly no specific amount of precipitation can serve as a universal boundary for dry climates.

_____ 1. In sentence 3, the word *precipitation* means
  A. weather conditions.
  B. humidity in the air.
  C. water that falls to the earth in any form.
  D. dry places.

_____ 2. Scientists who study weather consider a dry climate to be one in which
  A. ten inches of water fall each year.
  B. potential evaporation is greater than the rainfall.
  C. there is no rainfall at all.
  D. it gets very hot.

_____ 3. The higher the temperature is,
  A. the greater the rainfall.
  B. the smaller the rainfall.
  C. the greater the potential evaporation.
  D. the smaller the potential evaporation.

_____ 4. In the discussion in the passage, temperature is
   A. a cause.
   B. an effect.

_____ 5. The relationship between sentences 10 and 11 is one of
   A. time.
   B. comparison.
   C. contrast.
   D. cause and effect.

_____ 6. The main purpose of the passage is to
   A. explain the relationships between dryness, evaporation, and temperature.
   B. persuade us that a hot, dry climate is better for people than a cool, humid one.
   C. entertain us with vivid descriptions of life in a dry climate.
   D. predict that in the future, more of the Earth will become a desert.

_____ 7. The author implies that one reason evaporation in northern Scandinavian forests is slight is that
   A. the rainfall is low there.
   B. there is no rainfall there.
   C. the air there is cool.
   D. a heavy ground cover prevents the moisture from evaporating.

_____ 8. Which sentence best expresses the main idea of the selection?
   A. When temperatures are lower, there is less evaporation.
   B. A dry climate is one in which the rainfall is less than the potential evaporation, which depends on temperature.
   C. Evaporation in a northern forest is slight in comparison with the evaporation in a desert region like that of New Mexico.
   D. Rainfall is the amount of water that falls to earth as rain, snow, sleet, and hail.

COMBINED SKILLS: Test 19

Read the passage below. Then write the letter of the best answer to each question that follows.

¹It's Friday afternoon, and you have almost survived another week of classes. ²You are just looking forward dreamily to the weekend when the English instructor says: "For Monday you will turn in a five-hundred-word composition on college football."

³Well, that puts a good big hole in the weekend. ⁴You don't have any strong views on college football one way or the other. ⁵You get rather excited during the season and go to all the home games and find it rather more fun than not. ⁶On the other hand, the class has been reading Robert Hutchins in the anthology and perhaps Shaw's "Eighty-Yard Run," and from the class discussion you have got the idea that the instructor thinks college football is for the birds. ⁷You are no fool, you. ⁸You can figure out what side to take.

⁹After dinner you sit down at the computer that you got for high-school graduation. ¹⁰You might as well get it over with and enjoy Saturday and Sunday. ¹¹Five hundred words is about two double-spaced pages with normal margins. ¹²You open a new document, think up a title, and you're off:

Why College Football Should Be Abolished

¹³College football should be abolished because it's bad for the school and also bad for the players. ¹⁴The players are so busy practicing that they don't have any time for their studies.

¹⁵This, you feel, is a mighty good start. ¹⁶The only trouble is that it's only thirty-two words. ¹⁷You still have four hundred and sixty-eight to go, and you've pretty well exhausted the subject. ¹⁸It comes to you that you do your best thinking in the morning, so you shut down the computer and go to the movies. ¹⁹But the next morning you have to do your washing and some math problems, and in the afternoon you go to the game. ²⁰The English instructor turns up too, and you wonder if you've taken the right side after all. ²¹Saturday night you have a date, and Sunday morning you have to go to church. ²²(You shouldn't let English assignments interfere with your religion.) ²³What with one thing and another, it's ten o'clock Sunday night before you sit down at the computer again.

_____ 1. In sentence 17, the word *exhausted* means
  A. created.
  B. researched.
  C. completely covered.
  D. forgotten.

_____ 2. The relationship between the first part of sentence 18 (before the comma) to sentence 19 is one of
   A. cause and effect.
   B. contrast.
   C. comparison.
   D. addition.

_____ 3. The overall pattern of organization is
   A. time order.
   B. list of items.
   C. definition and example.
   D. comparison.

_____ 4. The author's tone can be described as
   A. angry and worried.
   B. encouraging and respectful.
   C. humorous and sarcastic.
   D. ambivalent and bewildered.

_____ 5. To make his points, the author has chosen to use a
   A. factual anecdote.
   B. fictional anecdote.

_____ 6. The author suggests that the student
   A. is more skilled at putting things off than at writing compositions.
   B. would miss a party in order to attend church on Sunday.
   C. actually enjoys writing compositions.
   D. should have found out his instructor's view on football before writing the composition.

_____ 7. The author implies in the second paragraph that the student
   A. agrees with Robert Hutchins's views on football.
   B. has no interest in football at all.
   C. has paid no attention to class discussions.
   D. feels his composition should defend the instructor's point of view.

_____ 8. Which sentence best expresses the main idea of the passage?
   A. College football should not be abolished.
   B. A college composition assignment requires time and thought to complete.
   C. English instructors should not assign homework for the weekends, when students have little available time.
   D. Composition assignments should be based on class reading assignments and discussion.

COMBINED SKILLS: Test 20

Read the passage below. Then write the letter of the best answer to each question that follows.

¹Why do American schools fail to create lifetime readers? ²There are two basic and related "facts of life" that parents and educators seem to ignore. ³The first fact is that human beings are pleasure-centered. ⁴We will voluntarily do over and over that which brings us pleasure. ⁵For example, we go to the restaurants we like, order the foods we like, listen to the radio stations that play the music we like, and visit the relatives we like. ⁶Conversely, we avoid the restaurants, foods, music, and relatives we dislike.

⁷What does this pleasure principle have to do with reading? ⁸Children love stories, so every time we read to a child at home or at school, we send a "pleasure" message to the child's brain. ⁹You could even call it a commercial, conditioning the child to associate books and print with pleasure. ¹⁰However, all too often, parents don't read to their children; and, to make matters worse, schools send "unpleasure" messages about reading. ¹¹Endless hours of worksheets, intensive phonics instruction, and seemingly unconnected test questions can be—to a child—tedious or boring, threatening, and meaningless. ¹²If a child seldom experiences the "pleasures" of reading at home and meets only the "unpleasures" at school, then the natural reaction will be avoidance.

¹³The second basic fact is that reading is an accrued skill. ¹⁴In other words, reading is like riding a bicycle, driving a car, or sewing: in order to get better at it, you must do it. ¹⁵And the more you do it, the better you get at it. ¹⁶The last twenty-five years of reading research confirms this simple formula. ¹⁷Regardless of sex, race, nationality, or socioeconomic background, the students who read the most are the ones who read the best, achieve the most, and stay in school the longest. ¹⁸In contrast, those who don't read much cannot get better at it. ¹⁹And most Americans (children and adults) don't read much, and therefore aren't very good at it.

²⁰Why don't Americans read much? ²¹The reason is that a lack of "pleasure" messages in the home, coupled with the large number of "unpleasure" messages about reading they received throughout their school years, nullify any attraction a book might offer. ²²They avoid books and print the same way a cat avoids a rocking chair.

_____ 1. In sentence 6, the word *conversely* means

    A. in addition.

    B. in contrast.

    C. as a result.

    D. next.

_____ 2. The author feels that children are encouraged to read by
A. doing worksheets.
B. riding a bicycle.
C. having phonics instruction.
D. being read to.

_____ 3. Sentence 12 expresses a relationship of
A. cause and effect.
B. comparison.
C. contrast.
D. addition.

_____ 4. The passage discusses
A. stages of reading education.
B. a list of methods for teaching reading to children.
C. the reasons Americans do not become skillful, lifetime readers.
D. a definition of the phrase *lifetime readers* with examples.

_____ 5. Sentences 16 and 17 state
A. a fact.
B. an opinion.

_____ 6. The author's tone can be described as
A. critical and analytical.
B. joyful and optimistic.
C. tolerant and amused.
D. pleading and hopeful.

_____ 7. Sentence 22 implies that most Americans
A. carelessly seek out books and print.
B. purposely stay away from books and print.
C. have no opinion about books and print.
D. are often harmed by books and print.

_____ 8. Which sentence best states the main idea of the passage?
A. Most Americans don't read much or well because parents and educators often fail to make reading a pleasant experience.
B. Reading to children sends a message to them to associate books and print with pleasure.
C. People, being pleasure-centered, will voluntarily avoid activities they dislike and repeatedly do activities that bring them pleasure.
D. Twenty-five years of reading research has shown that the students who read the most are those that read the best.

COMBINED SKILLS: Test 21

Read the passage below. Then write the letter of the best answer to each question that follows.

¹In general, when a philosophy can fit onto a bumper sticker, it is not much of a philosophy. ²It is a simple-minded catch phrase. ³Rarely has that truth been so evident as with the smug slogan: "Government is not the answer to the problem. ⁴Government *is* the problem."

⁵What a bunch of malarkey. ⁶What a simplistic, short-sighted, load of garbage. ⁷"Government is the problem," huh? ⁸Fine. ⁹Then certainly the people who hold this view will be more than happy to relinquish the benefits provided to them by the government. ¹⁰Let these stalwart, independent-minded, the-government-doesn't-do-squat-for-me individuals try existing without the "problem" of government.

¹¹Let them live without the protection provided by the government-funded police and firefighters, and without the safety provided by an army, navy, air force, and national guard. ¹²Let them live without clean air and water, insured by governmental regulations and their city water department. ¹³Let them give up their municipal waste disposal system, which they use every time they flush their toilets. ¹⁴Take away the government-maintained roads they use to drive to work every day. ¹⁵Don't let them check the weather reports before heading out, either—those forecasts are based on data collected by the National Weather Service, a government agency. ¹⁶Oh, and once they're on the road, should they have the misfortune to have an accident—well, too bad. ¹⁷Yes, the rest of us are aided by the government requirement that all motorists be insured, but they'll surely prefer to pay for all the damages themselves.

¹⁸They'll gladly give up using the government-run post office and its mail delivery system, right? ¹⁹And at work, they'll be satisfied to know that no pesky government agencies are overseeing the health and safety of their workplace. ²⁰They'll feel great about using elevators that are never inspected, running power tools made without safety regulations, and working in facilities constructed without government-imposed building and electrical codes. ²¹As they age, they'll happily do without their Social Security benefit, and they'll allow an illness or injury to financially ruin them, rather than participate in Medicare.

²²Sounds great, huh? ²³Ah, the joys of living in a society where government minds its own darn business instead of intruding in the lives of private citizens. ²⁴Government is the problem. ²⁵Right.

_____ 1. In sentence 9, the word *relinquish* means
      A. expand.
      B. explain.
      C. replace.
      D. give up.

_____ 2. According to the passage, those who oppose government should be willing to live without all of the following *except*
 A. municipal waste disposal systems.
 B. car insurance.
 C. mail delivery.
 D. air conditioning.

_____ 3. The relationship of sentence 20 to sentence 19 is one of
 A. illustration.   C. comparison.
 B. addition.   D. contrast.

_____ 4. The overall pattern of organization of the selection is
 A. cause and effect.   C. definition and example.
 B. list of items.   D. compare and contrast.

_____ 5. The author implies that
 A. our taxes are too high for the government services we get.
 B. there are too many government regulations.
 C. few people would actually want to live without government services.
 D. we should cut government spending on wasteful programs such as Medicare and Social Security.

_____ 6. The author's tone can be described as
 A. doubtful and defensive.
 B. sarcastic and mocking.
 C. objective and straightforward.
 D. worried and concerned.

_____ 7. Which of the following sentences best states the main idea of the passage?
 A. A philosophy that can fit onto a bumper sticker is not much of a philosophy.
 B. Rather than being "the problem," government is vitally important to our daily lives.
 C. The people who think that government is the problem will be happy to live without the "problem" of government.
 D. The government's most important function is to oversee the health and safety of our workplaces.

_____ 8. Which is the most appropriate title for this selection?
 A. Our Out-of-Control Government
 B. Silly Bumper Stickers
 C. People Who Do Without Government
 D. Government Is *Not* the Problem

COMBINED SKILLS: Test 22

Read the passage below. Then write the letter of the best answer to each question that follows.

[1]The power of advertising to influence public attitudes and behaviors is well-illustrated by how diamonds have been "sold" to the public. [2]In 1938, some three-quarters of all diamonds mined in South Africa, the world's leading producer, were sold for engagement rings in the United States. [3]Most of these stones, however, were smaller and of poorer quality than those bought in Europe, where diamonds were purchased mostly by the aristocracy. [4]In addition, the diamonds that Americans purchased had an average price of only $80. [5]It was at this time that a South African diamond executive from the De Beers company engaged a New York advertising agency, N.W. Ayer, to prepare a plan for creating a new image for diamonds among Americans. [6]After researching the declining market for diamonds in the United States, the ad agency came up with a plan that stressed the need to strengthen the association in the public's mind of diamonds with romance. [7]Since young men bought over 90% of engagement rings, it would be crucial to impress on them the idea that diamonds were a gift of love: the larger and finer the diamond, the greater the expression of love. [8]Similarly, young women had to be encouraged to view diamonds as an integral part of any romantic courtship. [9]To accomplish this, movie stars, those shining examples of romance for the mass audience, were given diamonds to use as their symbols of indestructible love. [10]Magazine stories were written which stressed the size of diamonds that celebrities presented to their loved ones, and photographs conspicuously showed the glittering stone on the hand of a well-known woman. [11]Even the British royal family was enlisted to wear diamonds rather than other jewels. [12]Finally, the advertising agency came up with the slogan "A Diamond Is Forever," now considered to be the most recognized advertising slogan ever. [13]The advertising campaign succeeded in spectacular fashion. [14]By the end of the 1950s, the retail sales of diamonds had increased by over 50%, and a diamond ring was considered, by virtually everyone, a necessity to engagements.

_____ 1. In sentence 8, the word *integral* means
   A. minor.
   B. necessary.
   C. inexpensive.
   D. extra.

_____ 2. In the late 1930s,
   A. diamond sales in the United States increased by 50%.
   B. most diamonds were purchased by American movie stars and European aristocrats.
   C. few young men bought their fiancées diamond engagement rings.
   D. the diamonds Americans purchased had an average price of only $80.

_____ 3. The De Beers Company wanted to
  A. become the world's sole exporter of diamonds.
  B. encourage Americans to purchase many inexpensive diamonds.
  C. encourage Americans to purchase larger and finer diamonds.
  D. limit the amount of diamonds that could be exported by South Africa.

_____ 4. Sentence 3 expresses a relationship of
  A. cause and effect.
  B. comparison.
  C. illustration.
  D. contrast.

_____ 5. Sentences 9–12
  A. list ways that diamonds were "sold" to the public.
  B. contrast European attitudes toward diamonds with American attitudes.
  C. compare men's attitudes toward diamonds to women's attitudes.
  D. present a series of steps in time order.

_____ 6. The passage suggests that
  A. it was entirely natural for Americans to think of diamonds as a necessity to engagements.
  B. the American public has been cleverly manipulated into spending money on expensive diamonds.
  C. Americans would be better off if they spent their money on luxury goods other than diamonds.
  D. only movie stars and other wealthy people really believe that "A Diamond Is Forever."

_____ 7. Sentence 14 is a statement of
  A. fact.
  B. opinion.

_____ 8. Which is the most appropriate title for the passage?
  A. Diamonds Aren't Forever
  B. How Diamonds Have Been Sold to the Public
  C. A Brief History of De Beers Diamonds
  D. Advertising in Action

COMBINED SKILLS: Test 23

Read the passage below. Then write the letter of the best answer to each question that follows.

[1]The Hawthorne experiment was conducted in the late 1920s and early 1930s. [2]The management of Western Electric's Hawthorne plant, located near Chicago, wanted to find out if environmental factors, such as lighting, could affect workers' productivity and morale. [3]A team of social scientists experimented with a small group of employees who were set apart from their coworkers. [4]The environmental conditions of this group's work area were controlled, and the subjects themselves were closely observed. [5]To the great surprise of the researchers, the productivity of these workers increased in response to any change in their environmental conditions. [6]The rate of work increased even when the changes (such as a sharp decrease in the level of light in the workplace) seemed unlikely to have such an effect.

[7]It was concluded that the presence of the observers had caused the workers in the experimental group to feel special. [8]As a result, the employees came to know and trust one another, and they developed a strong belief in the importance of their job. [9]The researchers believed that this, not the changes in the work environment, accounted for the increased productivity.

[10]A later reanalysis of the study data challenged the Hawthorne conclusions on the grounds that the changes in patterns of human relations, considered so important by the original researchers, were never measured. [11]However, even if the original conclusions must be revised, they nonetheless raise a problem for social scientists: Research subjects who know they are being studied can change their behavior. [12]Throughout the social sciences, this phenomenon has come to be called the Hawthorne effect.

_____ 1. In sentences 2 and 5, the word *productivity* means
      A. attendance.   C. rate of work.
      B. human relations.   D. health.

_____ 2. The pattern of organization of the second paragraph is
      A. list of items.   C. definition and example.
      B. time order.   D. cause and effect.

_____ 3. The author implies that a sharp decrease in light did not affect workers' output because the workers
      A. experienced less eyestrain.
      B. had to pay more attention to what they were doing.
      C. knew they were being observed, and this motivated them.
      D. in the experiment were paid more than other workers.

_____ 4. Employers might conclude from the Hawthorne experiment that they
should
   A. keep plant lighting low.
   B. constantly change environmental conditions.
   C. consistently let workers know that their work is important.
   D. keep social scientists away from their workers.

_____ 5. The Hawthorne experiment suggests that
   A. workers' attitudes are more important than their environment.
   B. social scientists are good workers.
   C. productivity in electric plants tends to be low.
   D. even those Hawthorne workers who were not in the experiment
improved their productivity.

_____ 6. The Hawthorne effect is a problem for social scientists because
   A. researchers usually do not measure the changes in human relations
among workers.
   B. the results of a study will be questionable if the subjects are aware
that they are being observed.
   C. the Hawthorne research was done too long ago, when working
conditions were quite different.
   D. the group of employees who were studied was small.

_____ 7. The author's main purpose is to
   A. explain the Hawthorne effect.
   B. prove the importance of research.
   C. amuse with a surprising experiment.
   D. suggest ideas for future research.

_____ 8. Which sentence best expresses the main idea of the passage?
   A. The famous Hawthorne experiment took place in the late 1920s and
early 1930s.
   B. The Hawthorne experiment took place because the management
of an electric plant wanted to find out the impact of environmental
factors on workers.
   C. An experiment revealed the fact, known as the Hawthorne effect,
that research subjects may behave differently if they know they are
being studied.
   D. A reanalysis of data from an experiment at an electrical plant
showed that the researchers were careless about how they conducted
their study.

COMBINED SKILLS: Test 24

Read the passage below. Then write the letter of the best answer to each question that follows.

[1]Although teenage pregnancy and birthrates in the United States dropped dramatically during the 1990s, they remain many times higher than in other industrialized countries, where adolescents begin sexual activity just as early or earlier. [2]Teenage birthrates in recent years have been nearly five times as high in the United States as in Denmark, Finland, France, Germany, Italy, and Spain and twelve times as high as in Japan. [3]Experts disagree about why the U.S. rates are so high. [4]Some observers point to such factors as the reduced stigma on unwed motherhood, media glorification of sex, the lack of a clear message that sex and parenthood are for adults, the influence of childhood sexual abuse, and the failure of parents to communicate with children. [5]Contrasts with the European experience suggest the importance of other factors as well. [6]First of all, Europe's industrialized countries have provided universal, comprehensive sex education for a much longer time than the United States. [7]Comprehensive programs encourage young teenagers to delay intercourse but also aim to improve contraceptive use among sexually active adolescents. [8]Such programs include education about sexuality and acquisition of skills for making responsible sexual decisions and communicating with partners. [9]They provide information about risks and consequences of teenage pregnancy, about birth control methods, and about where to get medical and contraceptive help. [10]Secondly, European countries also provide access to reproductive services. [11]Contraceptives are provided free to adolescents in Britain, France, and Sweden. [12]Sweden showed a fivefold reduction in the teenage birth rate following the introduction of birth control education, free access to contraceptives, and free abortion on demand. [13]Indeed, U.S. teens who use contraception in their first sexual experience are much less likely to bear a child by age 20. [14]In the United States, the provision and content of sex education programs is a political issue. [15]Some critics claim that community- and school-based sex education leads to more or earlier sexual activity, even though evidence shows otherwise.

_____ 1. In sentence 7, the word *comprehensive* means
        A. limited.   C. costly.
        B. complete.   D. immoral.

_____ 2. Other industrialized countries have teenage pregnancy and birth rates that are
        A. about the same as those of the United States.
        B. much higher than those of the United States.
        C. slightly lower than those of the United States.
        D. much lower than those of the United States.

_____ 3. Some critics of sex education programs believe that sex education
    A. leads to more or earlier sexual activity.
    B. is ineffective in reducing teen pregnancy.
    C. effectively reduces teen pregnancy but leads to increased rates of sexually transmitted diseases.
    D. has no effect on teens' sexual behavior.

_____ 4. All of the following have been given as reasons for America's high rate of teenage pregnancy *except*
    A. media glorification of sex.
    B. the influence of childhood sexual abuse.
    C. widespread availability of condoms.
    D. the failure of parents to communicate with their children.

_____ 5. This selection mainly
    A. lists possible reasons why European countries have lower teenage pregnancy and birth rates than the United States.
    B. compares sex education programs in the U.S. to those in Europe.
    C. presents a series of measures, in the order in which they were adopted, that some European countries have employed to reduce their rates of teen pregnancy.
    D. defines the term *comprehensive sex education* and provides examples of it.

_____ 6. The author's main purpose is to
    A. inform.   C. entertain.
    B. persuade.   D. predict.

_____ 7. On the whole, the tone of this passage is
    A. defensive.   C. uncertain.
    B. outraged.   D. straightforward.

_____ 8. The passage suggests that
    A. sexual activity among American teenagers would rise dramatically if more teens were provided with community- and school-based sex education.
    B. teenage pregnancy and birth rates will continue to drop dramatically even if American teens are not provided with comprehensive sex education and free access to contraceptives.
    C. teenage pregnancy rates in the United States could be reduced if the United States provided universal sex education, free access to contraceptives, and abortion on demand.
    D. it is immoral to provide teenagers with free access to contraceptives and abortion on demand.

COMBINED SKILLS: Test 25

Read the passage below. Then write the letter of the best answer to each question that follows.

[1]Imagine being on a treadmill, wearing a face mask connected to oxygen-measuring equipment. [2]You are walking at a leisurely pace, at the slowest setting, so your oxygen consumption is fairly low. [3]As the speed of the treadmill increases, your metabolism increases, and as a result, your oxygen consumption goes up as well. [4]Your muscle cells are using the extra oxygen to break down carbohydrates, which they use for fuel, and turn them into energy, so their metabolism is said to be aerobic (with air). [5]You are now jogging along at a comfortable speed, still supplying ample oxygen to your muscle cells, so your exercise is still aerobic. [6]As you increase your speed, your oxygen consumption will continue to rise, but at some point, it will stop rising. [7]That is because your heart and lungs have reached their maximum capacity for supplying oxygen to the muscles via the bloodstream. [8]But you can still run a lot faster. [9]Your speed keeps increasing and eventually you are running as fast as you can, but your oxygen consumption has not changed. [10]Your muscle cells can keep on firing without getting the extra oxygen they need because they are able to break down carbohydrates without using oxygen. [11]This is called anaerobic (without air) metabolism. [12]Sprinters, who run at top speed, perform most of their hundred-meter race anaerobically; in contrast, long-distance runners, who have time to vary their speed, perform most of their event aerobically.

[13]Anaerobic metabolism is far less efficient than aerobic metabolism but is capable of generating very high quantities of energy for short periods of time. [14]It also generates lactic acid as a byproduct. [15]This accumulates in the muscles and is associated with muscle fatigue and general exhaustion. [16]That is why sprinting cannot be kept up for very long. [17]After sprinting, the lactic acid that has accumulated in the muscles has to be broken down, and this requires oxygen, which explains why we puff and pant after a hard run.

_____ 1. The body's energy is usually obtained through the breakdown of
   A. carbohydrates.
   B. lactic acid.
   C. the bloodstream.
   D. oxygen.

_____ 2. When you run, your body begins anaerobic metabolism
   A. as you begin to pick up speed.
   B. after sprinting is completed.
   C. when your heart and lungs cannot supply sufficient oxygen.
   D. when the lactic acid in your muscles must be broken down.

_____ 3. Aerobic metabolism
   A. is more efficient than anaerobic metabolism.
   B. breaks down carbohydrates without oxygen.
   C. generates lactic acid.
   D. happens for only brief periods.

_____ 4. The main overall patterns of organization of the passage are cause and effect and
   A. list of items.
   B. comparison.
   C. contrast.

_____ 5. The purpose of this passage is to
   A. inform us about what happens to our bodies during walking, running, and sprinting.
   B. persuade us that we need to exercise regularly to keep our metabolisms going.
   C. entertain us with a vivid and detailed account of how our bodies work.

_____ 6. We can infer that when we feel we are out of breath, we are low on
   A. lactic acid.
   B. carbohydrates.
   C. muscle cells.
   D. oxygen.

_____ 7. The passage implies that during sprinting,
   A. there is a dangerous strain on the heart.
   B. the body's reserve of carbohydrates increases.
   C. the body breaks down carbohydrates both with and without oxygen.
   D. the body needs less energy than usual.

_____ 8. Which statement best expresses the main idea of the passage?
   A. Walking, jogging, and sprinting create different energy demands on the human body and also consume different amounts of oxygen.
   B. Running at top speed cannot be kept up nearly as long as jogging because of the different ways that energy is supplied to the muscles.
   C. Muscle cells can keep on firing in the absence of oxygen because they are able to break down carbohydrates for short periods.
   D. When lactic acid accumulates in someone's muscles, the person experiences muscle fatigue and general exhaustion.

Sample Answer Sheet

Use the form below as a model answer sheet for the twenty-five combined-skills tests.

Name _____ Date _____

Section _____ SCORE: (Number correct) _____ x 12.5 = _____ %

COMBINED SKILLS: Mastery Test ____

1. _____

2. _____

3. _____

4. _____

5. _____

6. _____

7. _____

8. _____

Appendixes

Pronunciation Guide

Each word in Chapter 1, "Vocabulary in Context," is followed by information in parentheses that shows you how to pronounce the word. (There are also pronunciations for the vocabulary items that follow the readings in Parts One and Two.) The guide below and on the next page explains how to use that information.

Long Vowel Sounds

ā	pay
ē	she
ī	hi
ō	go
ōō	cool
yōō	use

Short Vowel Sounds

ă	hat
ĕ	ten
ĭ	sit
ŏ	lot
ŏŏ	look
ŭ	up
yŏŏ	cure

Other Vowel Sounds

â	care
ä	card
îr	here
ô	all
oi	oil
ou	out
ûr	fur
ə	ago, item, easily, gallop, circus

Consonant Sounds

b	big
d	do
f	fall
g	dog
h	he

Consonant Sounds

j	jump
k	kiss
l	let
m	meet
n	no
p	put
r	red
s	sell
t	top
v	have
w	way
y	yes
z	zero
ch	church
sh	dish
th	then
th	thick
zh	usual

Note that each pronunciation symbol above is paired with a common word that shows the sound of the symbol. For example, the symbol ā has the sound of the *a* in the common word *pay*. The symbol ă has the sound of the *a* in the common word *hat*. The symbol ə, which looks like an upside-down *e* and is known as the schwa, has the unaccented sound in the common word *ago*. It sounds like the "uh" a speaker often says when hesitating.

Accent marks are small black marks that tell you which syllable to emphasize as you say a word. A bold accent mark (ʹ) shows which syllable should be stressed. A lighter accent mark (ʹ) in some words indicates a secondary stress. Syllables without an accent mark are unstressed.

Writing Assignments

A Brief Guide to Effective Writing

Here in a nutshell is what you need to do to write effectively.

Step 1: Explore Your Topic through Informal Writing

To begin with, explore the topic that you want to write about or that you have been assigned to write about. You can examine your topic through **informal writing**, which usually means one of three things.

First, you can **freewrite** about your topic for at least ten minutes. In other words, write, for ten minutes, whatever comes into your head about your subject. Write without stopping and without worrying at all about spelling or grammar or the like. Simply get down on paper all the information about the topic that occurs to you.

A second thing you can do is to **make a list of ideas and details** that could go into your paper. Simply pile these items up, one after another, like a shopping list, without worrying about putting them in any special order. Try to accumulate as many details as you can think of.

A third way to explore your topic is to **write down a series of questions and answers** about it. Your questions can start with words like *what, why, how, when,* and *where.*

Getting your thoughts and ideas down on paper will help you think more about your topic. With some raw material to look at, you are now in a better position to decide on just how to proceed.

Step 2: Plan Your Paper with an Informal Outline

After exploring your topic, plan your paper, using an informal outline. Do two things:

- **Decide on and write out the main point of your paper.** It is often a good idea to begin your paragraph with this point, which is known as the *topic sentence*. If you are writing an essay of several paragraphs, you will probably want to include your main point somewhere in your first paragraph. In a paper of several paragraphs, the main point is called the *central point*, or *thesis*.

- **List the supporting reasons, examples, or other details that back up your point.** In many cases, you should have at least two or three items of support.

Step 3: Use Transitions

Once your outline is worked out, you will have a clear "road map" for writing your paper. As you write the early drafts of your paper, use **transitions** to introduce each of the separate supporting items (reasons, examples, or other details) you present to back up your point. For instance, you might introduce your first supporting item with the transitional words *first of all*. You might begin your second supporting item with words such as *another reason* or *another example*. And you might indicate your final supporting detail with such words as *last of all* or *a final reason*.

Step 4: Edit and Proofread Your Paper

After you have a solid draft, edit and proofread the paper. To evaluate your paper, ask yourself these questions:

1 Is the paper **unified**? Does all the material in the paper truly support the opening point?

2 Is the paper **well supported**? Is there plenty of specific evidence to back up the opening point?

3 Is the paper **clearly organized**? Does the material proceed in a way that makes sense? Do transitions help connect ideas?

4 Is the paper **well written**? When the paper is read aloud, do the sentences flow smoothly and clearly? Has the paper been checked carefully for grammar, punctuation, and spelling mistakes?

Writing Assignments for the Twenty Readings

Note: The discussion questions accompanying the twenty readings can also make good topics for writing. Some of the writing assignments here are based on these questions.

Part One Readings

Night Watch

1. Imagine that you are the son of the old man in the story. The day after your father died, you arrived and heard the story of the other Marine who had been with him in his last hours. How do you think you would feel about the situation? Would you feel primarily grateful, sad, angry, regretful, confused, or something else? Write a paragraph that describes what you think your reaction might be. If your response would be a mix of several emotions, say so. Along with stating your feelings, tell why you feel as you do.

2. The young Marine stayed by the old man's bedside, he said, because "I figured he really needed me." Tell in a paragraph about a time you felt needed. Who was it who needed you, and in what way? How did you respond to that person? Did you feel able to give the person what he or she wanted from you? Was feeling needed a pleasant experience, or did it seem like a burden? Here's a sample topic sentence for this paragraph: "Once my older brother really needed my help, and it felt very good to be able to help him."

3. It's not uncommon to see people reach out to help their loved ones. But the final paragraph of this article states that "in a uniquely human way . . . there are people who care what happens to their fellow human beings"—in other words, they care about people to whom they have no particular obligation. Think of experiences you have had, or heard about, in which people went out of their way to assist someone they do not know well, if at all. Write an essay that tells the stories of two or three such incidents. You might conclude your essay by talking about what, if anything, the "givers" in such situations gain by their actions.

Here's to Your Health

1. Few people go through life without being exposed to the negative effects of alcohol. In a paragraph, describe an unpleasant or dangerous incident you have been aware of, or experienced yourself, in which alcohol played a part. Who was involved? What happened? In what way did alcohol contribute to the situation? How did the incident end?

2. The advertising and sale of cigarettes are topics of much debate. There are already some legal restrictions in place: cigarettes are no longer advertised on television, they are not to be sold to minors, and warning labels on cigarettes inform consumers of health risks associated with smoking. In your opinion, are such restrictions needed or helpful? Should more restrictions be imposed on the tobacco industry, or should cigarettes be advertised and sold like any other product? Write a paragraph that explains your opinions about how or if cigarettes should be regulated and why.

3. As this article shows, alcohol is advertised as something that makes people more successful, sexier, healthier, and happier. The abuse of alcohol, however, often has quite the opposite effect. Write an essay in which you describe what alcohol advertisements would look like if they showed the negative side of drinking. What images would you choose to include in such advertisements? You might organize your essay by addressing several of the positive "myths" about alcohol mentioned in the article and describing an ad that would contradict each myth.

Child-Rearing Styles

1. Near the end of the article, the author lists six recommendations to parents who want to raise "competent, socially responsible, independent children." Choose one of those six recommendations and write a paragraph that demonstrates how it was (or was not) practiced in your own home. Illustrate the paragraph with examples from your childhood. Conclude by stating how you were positively or negatively affected by those examples.

2. Reread the author's descriptions of the three parenting styles: authoritative, authoritarian, and permissive. Think of a parent you know who is a good example of one of those three styles. Then write a paragraph that describes how that person interacts with his or her child. Provide one or more examples that demonstrate the adult's approach to parenting. You might try using some dialogue to emphasize a point or two. In conclusion, comment on how you think the parent's style is affecting the child.

3. It is not uncommon to hear parents say of their children, "I don't understand— we raised them all just the same, and yet they've turned out so differently." On the basis of your own experience growing up and your observations of other families, write an essay that comments on several possible explanations for why siblings develop different—sometimes dramatically different— personalities. Provide vivid real-life examples to illustrate your points. A possible central point for this essay might be: "Inherited personality, different parental treatment, and birth order account for many of the differences between siblings."

Rowing the Bus

1. Logan writes, "In each school, in each classroom, there is a George with a stricken face." Think of a person who filled the role of George in one of your classes. In a paragraph, describe why he or she was the target of teasing, and what form that teasing took. Include a description of your own thoughts and actions regarding the student who was teased.

2. Fearing that his life would be made miserable, the author decided to stop being friends with George. How do you feel about that decision? Do you think it was cruel? Understandable? Were there other options Logan might have tried? Write a paragraph in which you explain what you think of Logan's decision and why. Suggest at least one other way he could have acted, and tell what you think the consequences might have been.

3. In this essay, Logan provides many vivid descriptions of incidents in which bullies attack other students. Reread those descriptions and consider what they teach you about the nature of bullies and bullying. Then write an essay that supports the following main idea: "Evidence in 'Rowing the Bus' suggests that most bullies share certain characteristics." Mention two or three such characteristics, and provide evidence from the essay that illustrates how they are present in acts of bullying. In your concluding paragraph, you might write about what these characteristics tell us about bullies.

Wonder in the Air

1. In explaining why he refused at first to encourage his daughter's belief in Santa Claus, Gammage states that he wanted to be able to answer his daughter's questions about China "from an established position of truth-telling." Do you think Jin Yu will later doubt her father because he "lied" to her about Santa Claus? Or won't it make a difference? Write a paragraph which explains your thinking.

2. Write a paragraph that supports one of the following main ideas: "I believe that parents should encourage their children to believe in Santa Claus, the Easter Bunny, and the tooth fairy" or "I believe that it is important for parents to discourage their children's belief in Santa Claus, the Easter Bunny, and the tooth fairy." Explain your thinking, giving specific examples from your life experiences as well as from Gammage's observations in the article.

3. Although Gammage and his wife originally decided that "no lies" would be their one firm parental rule, they eventually come to realize that this rule is not realistic. What do you think are two or three good (and realistic) parental rules? Write an essay in which you state and then discuss each rule. Be sure to explain why you think each rule would benefit both parents and children.

Students in Shock

1. Students face a good deal of pressure in their new environment, as this essay shows. But they are not the only ones susceptible to "shock." Anyone in a demanding new situation can experience depression, frustration, and hopelessness. For example, someone who is new to a job, to a neighborhood, to marriage, or to parenthood might experience his or her own brand of shock. Write a paragraph that explores the possible causes of shock in a person facing a specific situation. You may choose one of the situations listed here, or another that occurs to you. Suggest ways the person might reduce the pressure he or she feels.

2. When you experience stress, what helps you to relax? Write a paragraph that describes your own favorite stress-reduction technique. Is it exercising, talking with a friend, taking a bath, playing golf, punching a pillow? You might begin with a vivid description of how stress affects you, then contrast that with a description of how your favorite technique changes your mood. Explain in detail how you go about using the technique.

3. Stress, anxiety, depression, burnout—these words are common parts of our modern vocabulary. What do you think are some of the main sources of this widespread stress? Write an essay that describes several common causes of stress. You could use as your central point a sentence similar to this: "There are three common reasons why people today are so stressed out." For each cause of stress you mention, provide specific ways in which it affects people. Add interest to your essay by using examples from the lives of people you know or have observed.

Relationships in the 21st Century

1. Not so long ago, living together as an unmarried couple was considered scandalous. Now, as this article makes clear, it is part of the mainstream. Do you consider this development a positive, negative, or neutral one? Write a paragraph explaining your answer.

2. According to Verderber, U.S. couples are now postponing marriage until their mid-20s and even beyond, and today's first-time bride and groom are older than ever before. What do you think is the "right" age to marry? Why? Write a paragraph responding to this question.

3. Verderber concludes his selection by stating that "cohabitation neither weakens nor strengthens marriage." Drawing from your observations, what are elements that **do** either strengthen or weaken marriage? Write an essay in which you isolate three factors that you think are important in making a marriage (or other committed relationship) either succeed or fail. You may choose three "success" factors, three "failure" factors, or two of one and one of the other. Provide specific examples that demonstrate how the factor you are discussing leads to a relationship's success or failure.

The Scholarship Jacket

1. Marta remembers herself at 14 as, "Pencil thin, not a curve anywhere, I was called 'Beanpole' and 'String Bean,' and I knew that's what I looked like." Write a paragraph in which you describe yourself at a particular age. You may choose to focus on your appearance or on internal qualities. Here are a couple of sample topic sentences: "The summer I was 12, I was in a bad mood nearly all of the time." "I went through a growth spurt when I was 15 that left me feeling as gangly and awkward as a baby giraffe."

2. Marta stresses again and again how important the scholarship jacket was to her and how hard she worked to win it. Write a paragraph about something you worked hard to achieve when you were younger. How long did you work toward that goal? How did you feel when you finally succeeded? Or, as an alternative, write about not achieving the goal. How did you cope with the disappointment? What lesson, if any, did you learn from the experience?

3. One reason Marta wanted the scholarship jacket so much is that she did not have the chance to participate in school sports. She wanted to make a name for herself somehow, and being a fine scholar was the way that she chose. In your high school, what were (or are) a few ways that people could become well-known? Those ways might be positive, such as being a top scholar or musician, or less so, such as being a class troublemaker. Write an essay in which you identify three categories of well-known students in your school, and describe the kind of people who belong in each category.

In Praise of the F Word

1. Has someone you know (or have you) received an F for a course? Write a paragraph describing what happened. What led to the poor performance? What effect did that experience have? Was failing a motivation to work harder? What were the effects, positive and negative, of receiving the failing grade?

2. This article concerns one way of motivating students—the threat of failure. Thinking back on your own classroom experience, what would you say are some other effective ways of motivating students to do their best? Write a paragraph that describes one other method teachers and instructors can use to motivate their students. Provide examples of times you have seen this method put into practice and how effective it seems to be.

3. Sherry believes that giving students F's when they deserve to fail would encourage them to take more responsibility for their performance. Most people agree that individuals truly overcome a problem only when they take responsibility for it, rather than expecting it to magically disappear or to be solved by someone else. In an essay, describe two or three people you know (you might be one) who have accepted responsibility for dealing with a difficult problem. The problems could be an unhappy marriage, an issue at work or school, or a crisis like substance abuse. How did the people demonstrate their willingness to take responsibility for their problems? What action did each take? How was the situation changed by what they did?

The 2,000-Year-Old Wonder Drug

1. After reading the case for promoting the use of aspirin, write a paragraph in defense of one of these statements:

   ● It should be public policy to require the use of aspirin.

   ● It should be public policy to recommend the use of aspirin.

   ● The government should not be involved in telling people what medicines to take.

   Provide specific evidence to support your opinion.

2. Mayor Bloomberg of New York has generated a great deal of controversy in his attempts to ban super-sized sodas from being sold in his city. He reasons that the ban may at least force people to think about the link between sugary soft drinks and diseases such as diabetes. Would you support such a ban in your town? Why or why not? Write a paragraph explaining your position.

3. As this article mentions, certain preventive strategies have already become matters of public policy. Children are required to be vaccinated; motorists are required to wear seat belts; tobacco products are not sold to minors. What are some other strategies to prevent disease or injury you can think of? Would you support making them a matter of public policy? Write an essay in which you describe three such strategies and explain why you would favor making them the law of the land.

Part Two Readings

The Yellow Ribbon

1. Vingo's wife had to decide whether to forgive Vingo and welcome him back into her life. Think of a time when you had to decide whether or not to forgive someone. Write a paragraph that describes that situation. Begin by explaining who the other person was and what your relationship had been like. Then describe what he or she did to hurt or offend you and how you felt about what happened. Continue by explaining how you made the decision whether or not to forgive the person. End your paragraph by saying how you feel about your decision now.

2. In "The Yellow Ribbon," Hamill provides various clues to Vingo's character. His body language, his conversation with his fellow passengers, what he has to say about his past and his family, and his attitude as the bus nears his hometown all contribute to the reader's opinion of what kind of man he is. Write a paragraph that supports the following topic sentence: "Details in the story suggest that Vingo is a decent man who deserves the yellow ribbons." Find specific evidence in the story to back up that statement.

3. Vingo had to wait in suspense to discover something important about his future. Most people have had the experience of waiting a long time (or what seemed like a long time) to find out something important. Such situations might have involved a job, pregnancy, romance, health, or school. Write an essay about a situation in which you (or someone you know) had to wait for something. Tell the story a little at a time, as Hamill does, in order to keep the reader in suspense until the end. Begin by explaining what was being waited for and why it was important. Continue by describing the wait and the emotions experienced as time went by. Use time transitions (see page 184) to help the reader follow your story. Finish by telling how the wait finally ended and how you (or the person you are writing about) felt once it was over.

College Athletes Should Be Paid

1. Many college football and basketball players are encouraged to dream of eventually moving on to the NFL and NBA. However, as Kaufmann explains, this is a dream that will most likely lead to a rude awakening, since the reality is that only 1 to 2 percent of these players will succeed in becoming professional athletes. Have you ever had a dream that was shattered when you learned the truth about how things really work? Write a paragraph describing your experience. Your "shattered illusion" experience can be anything from learning the truth about Santa Claus to learning the truth about an extremely competitive or difficult career path.

2. Kaufmann writes, "Not surprisingly, college players are sometimes tempted to take money 'under the table.'" Do you sympathize with players who accept cash or gifts? Or do you think such players should be seriously punished? Write a paragraph in which you explain and defend your point of view.

3. As Kaufmann points out, both athletes and non-athletes have criticized the NCAA rules prohibiting college athletes from receiving money and gifts. Some athletes are now accepting these gifts, evidently believing that certain rules deserve to be broken. Although the statement "rules are made to be broken" is not always the best advice, we've all broken rules. Write an essay in which you discuss a time when you broke a rule that you thought was either unfair or unnecessary. In the body of your essay, first present the rule and explain why you thought it was wrong. In the next paragraph, discuss breaking the rule—how you broke it and how that made you feel. In the third paragraph, discuss what happened. Did you get caught, or did you get away with it? Did your behavior help make a change in the rules?

Shame

1. When have you, like Gregory, regretted the way you acted in a particular situation? Perhaps you didn't speak up when someone was being teased, or perhaps you spoke harshly to someone because you were in a bad mood. Write a paragraph that describes the situation and how you acted. Conclude by explaining why you feel you acted wrongly and what you wish you had done instead.

2. Teachers are powerful figures in the lives of children. At times, because of impatience, poor judgment, a misunderstanding, anger, or some other reason, a teacher may hurt a student's feelings. Write a paragraph about a situation you experienced (or observed) in which you believe a teacher acted inappropriately and made a student feel bad. Be sure to explain not only what the teacher did but also how the student was affected.

3. A dictionary defines a word by briefly explaining its meaning. In this article, Dick Gregory defines the word *shame* in a different manner. He describes two incidents in his life in which shame played a central part. Write an essay in which you define a powerful word by narrating one or more events. Some words to consider include *gratitude, fear, jealousy, pride, joy, anger, kindness,* and *disappointment.* Your central point might be stated something like this: "Two incidents that happened ten years apart taught me the real meaning of _____." Focus on those parts of the incidents that illustrate the meaning of the word. Your essay will be more powerful if you, like Gregory, include significant bits of description and dialogue.

The Bystander Effect

1. This article suggests that people act quite differently when they are alone and when they're in a group, or in public. Write a paragraph that contrasts your own behavior when you're alone and when you're in a specific public setting. Examples of public settings might be a party, football game, dance, family gathering, or workplace. The tone of your paragraph could be serious or humorous. Provide lively examples of your behavior to illustrate your points.

2. "The Bystander Effect" is filled with anecdotes of people who stood back when help was needed, preferring to wait for someone else to act. Think of an individual who has acted in the opposite way, someone who perceived a need and quickly offered assistance. The situation might have involved an emergency like the ones mentioned in the article, or it might have concerned a more long-term need, such as an illness or a financial problem. Be specific in describing what the need was and how the individual reacted. Conclude by stating how the situation might have turned out if the individual had not helped.

3. Barkin defines *moral diffusion* as "the lessening of a sense of individual responsibility when someone is a member of a group." Drawing upon your own experience and knowledge of the world, write an essay that gives two examples of moral diffusion at work. For each example, describe what group is involved, how group members decline to take individual responsibility, and what happens as a result. Examples you might use include soldiers who commit war crimes and then say they were "just following orders," students who allow a classmate to be harassed because they don't want to get involved, or neighborhood people who let a park become overrun with trash because it's not their job to pick it up.

Growing Less Dumb

1. In the selection, Brenoff states that she's come to the realization that the things she worries about hardly ever happen. Write about a time in your life when you "worried yourself into a lather" about something, only to have the problem disappear or get resolved. In writing your paper, be sure to describe what the situation was that you found yourself worrying about as well as how it got resolved.

     Alternatively, write a paragraph describing something you worried about that actually *did* happen, and how you dealt with it.

2. Many people have trouble making decisions, so they tend to let other people make choices for them. Why do you think decision-making is difficult for some people? Write a paragraph in which you explain reasons why making decisions can be difficult.

3. In "Growing Less Dumb," Brenoff describes four different ways of thinking when she was younger that, now as an older adult, she believes were pretty dumb. She worried too much, she feared making her own decisions, she was overly concerned about what other people thought of her, and she judged people too quickly. Write an essay in which you describe three things you thought or did when you were younger that you think are pretty dumb now. Be sure to use vivid examples of these past three "dumb" behaviors and, as Brenoff does, explain how you think or act differently today.

Coping with Nervousness

1. What makes you nervous? What is something you occasionally—or often—need to do that makes your mouth go dry and your knees knock? Write a paragraph, in a serious or humorous vein, about a situation that makes you nervous and how you react to it. Some topics to consider include speaking in public, asking someone for a date, and applying for a job. Provide lots of vivid details so the reader can see and feel your nervousness.

2. Imagine that you were required to give a "how-to" speech on a process that you are very familiar with. What would you choose to talk about? Write a paragraph in which you state your topic and then give clear, step-by-step instructions on how to complete the process. Use time transitions (see page 184) to make your instructions easy to follow.

3. Verderber suggests that people who can master their nervousness, rather than allowing it to control them, will enjoy a sense of accomplishment. Think of a problem that you have faced and overcome. It might be a particular fear, like the one described in the article. Or you may have conquered a problem with a difficult person, overcome a bad habit, or figured out a solution to a problem in your life. Write an essay that explains, first, what problem existed and how it affected you; second, how you decided to deal with the problem; and finally, what happened as a result of your actions and how you felt about what you'd done.

Compliance Techniques: Getting People to Say Yes

1. Why do you think that compliance techniques are so often effective? What do they appeal to in the mind of the consumer that is lacking in the more straightforward approach of simply making a product available to those who want to buy it? Write a paragraph that explains a few reasons you think people are so easily influenced by compliance techniques.

2. Have you ever agreed to perform a service or to buy something and then later felt you had been persuaded by a clever, manipulative, or deceptive sales technique? Write a paragraph that describes the process that you and the seller engaged in. Use time transitions (page 184) to make the sequence of events clear to the reader. Explain how you believe you were manipulated into the agreement or purchase.

3. Think of a product you might want to sell or a service you might want people to agree to perform. Write an essay that tells how you could accomplish your goal by using three of these four compliance techniques: the foot-in-the-door, the door-in-the-face, the low-ball, and the that's-not-all techniques. Give a detailed explanation of the steps you would follow in each case. In conclusion, state which technique you believe would work best and why.

Lizzie Borden

1. On the basis of the information presented in the article, write a paragraph that supports one of the following main ideas: "I believe that Lizzie Borden was guilty of the murder of her parents" or "I think there is reason to doubt that Lizzie Borden killed her parents." Explain your thinking, backing up your opinions with evidence from the text.

2. Think of a time you were wrongly suspected of doing something bad. It might have involved anything from breaking a dish when you were a child to committing a crime. Write a paragraph describing that experience. Tell what you were suspected of and what (if any) evidence pointed to you. Were you able to prove you were innocent? How did you feel about being a target of suspicion?

3. The author suggests that a stereotype existing in Lizzie's day had a very specific effect—that she was found innocent of murder because of it. What are some stereotypes that exist today? How are people of certain ethnic groups, genders, sexual preferences, or economic groups stereotyped? Write an essay in which you explain how you believe certain groups are stereotyped. What effects might occur because people believe those stereotypes?

Nonverbal Communication

1. Write a paragraph that describes a time when you were made uncomfortable by another person's nonverbal communication. Tell where the incident occurred, who else was there, and what the relationship was between you and the person whose communication disturbed you. Then describe specifically what the other person did that made you uncomfortable and how you responded. You may also want to refer to the article and describe what kind of personal space was violated by this person's behavior.

2. As you may know, the "personal space zones" described in the article are not the same worldwide. For example, people from some Middle Eastern countries are accustomed to standing close together as they talk, even if they do not know one another well. On the basis of your reading of this article and your knowledge of human nature, how do you think a person from such a country might be perceived in America? How might an American visiting such a country be viewed? Write a paragraph that describes how people from the two cultures might judge one another based on their nonverbal communication.

3. Think of some people you see often but do not know well—perhaps people like store owners, your mail carrier, school secretaries, a bus driver, or a new neighbor. On the basis of their nonverbal communication, what do these people seem to be like? Write an essay in which you introduce each person and tell what impression you have formed of him or her. Be as specific and descriptive as possible as you tell about these people's nonverbal behavior and what it seems to say about them.

The Power Within

1. The author mentions Mahatma Gandhi, Robert Kennedy, and Dr. Martin Luther King—leaders whom many people find inspirational. Write a paragraph about a person (he or she need not be famous) who inspires you. In writing your paragraph, be sure to describe what this person does or has done that is inspiring, as well as what you would like to accomplish by following this person's example.

2. Write a paragraph about a person you know (it could be you) who has shown a determination to succeed despite an "unequal playing field" or other obstacles in life. Describe the challenges the person has had to face. Then explain what he or she has done to overcome the challenges.

3. In "The Power Within," the author details six "escape routes" that students take to avoid studying. Write an essay in which you describe several escape routes that you or your peers are most likely to take. After presenting examples and details of each escape route, explain what must be done in each case to *not* escape in that way.

Limited Answer Key

An important note: To strengthen your reading skills, you must do more than simply find out which of your answers are right and which are wrong. You also need to figure out (with the help of this book, the teacher, or other students) *why* you missed the questions you did. By using each of your wrong answers as a learning opportunity, you will strengthen your understanding of the skills. You will also prepare yourself for the review and mastery tests in Part One, the reading comprehension questions in Part Two, and the relationships and combined-skills tests in Part Three, for which answers are not given here.

Answers to the Practices in Part One

1 Vocabulary in Context

Practice 1: Examples

1. Examples: *I couldn't find my car keys, I dropped a bowl of soup, my computer crashed twice;* A
2. Examples: *the TV is talking to them, others can steal their thoughts;* C
3. Example: *the giant land tortoise can live several hundred years;* B
4. Examples: *going to town concerts and ball games, visiting neighborhood friends, playing board games;* A
5. Examples: *gardening, chat groups on the Internet;* A
6. Example: *picking up the language and customs of their new home;* A
7. Examples: *financial help, free medical care;* C
8. Examples: *learning, reasoning, thinking, language;* B
9. Examples: *the phones were constantly ringing, people were running back and forth, several offices were being painted;* B
10. Examples: *accepting a bribe from a customer, stealing from an employer;* C

Practice 2: Synonyms

1. embarrasses
2. examine
3. practical
4. confusing
5. overlook
6. necessary
7. opponents
8. arrival
9. charitable
10. customary

Practice 3: Antonyms

1. Antonym: *long;* A
2. Antonym: *financial loss;* B
3. Antonym: *openly;* B
4. Antonym: *plainly;* B
5. Antonym: *active;* A
6. Antonym: *clear;* C
7. Antonym: *benefit;* B
8. Antonym: *increase in value;* B
9. Antonym: *careless;* C
10. Antonym: *weak;* C

Practice 4: General Sense

1. B
2. C
3. A
4. B
5. C
6. A
7. C
8. B
9. C
10. B

2   Main Ideas

Practice 1

1. S
   S
   G
   S

2. S
   S
   S
   G

3. S
   G
   S
   S

4. S
   S
   S
   G

5. S
   S
   S
   G

6. S
   S
   G
   S

7. S
   G
   S
   S

8. S
   G
   S
   S

9. G
   S
   S
   S

10. S
    S
    G
    S

Practice 2

(Answers will vary.)

Practice 3

1. P   4. P
   S   S
   S   S
   S   S

2. S   5. S
   S   P
   P   S
   S   S

3. S
   S
   S
   P

Practice 4

1. S   4. S
   S   S
   P   S
   S   P

2. P   5. S
   S   P
   S   S
   S   S

3. S
   P
   S
   S

Practice 5

Group 1
A. SD
B. SD
C. MI
D. T

Group 2
A. MI
B. SD
C. SD
D. T

Group 3
A. T
B. SD
C. SD
D. MI

Group 4
A. MI
B. SD
C. SD
D. T

Group 5
A. MI
B. SD
C. T
D. SD

Practice 6 *(Wording of topics may vary.)*

Paragraph 1
Topic: Stories
Main idea: Sentence 1

Paragraph 2
Topic: ESP
Main idea: Sentence 2

Paragraph 3
Topic: Gay marriage
Main idea: Sentence 1

Paragraph 4
Topic: Driving (*or* Poor attitudes about driving)
Main idea: Sentence 10

Paragraph 5
Dark chocolate (*or* Health benefits of dark chocolate)
Main idea: Sentence 1

Practice 7
1. 1
2. 3
3. 2
4. 5
5. 1

3 Supporting Details

Practice 1 *(Wording of answers may vary.)*

A. **Main idea:** Parents can take several steps to discourage TV watching and encourage reading.

  1. Have only one TV set, and place it in the family room.
  2. Connect reading with eating.
  3. Don't put a TV set in a child's bedroom.

B. **Main idea:** Colleges of the early nineteenth century were distinctly different from today's schools.

  1. Students were mostly white males.
  Minor details: College was considered a final polishing for upper-class gentlemen.

  2. All students had to take the same courses.
  Minor details: They studied ancient languages, literature, natural science, mathematics, and political and moral philosophy.

  3. Colleges were small.
  Minor details: Most had only a few dozen students, three or four professors, and three or four tutors.

  4. Student life was more regulated.
  Minor details: Strict curfews determined when students had to turn off their lamps, and attendance at religious services was required.

Practice 2 *(Wording of answers may vary.)*

A. Introduce yourself
   Refer to physical setting
   Ask a complimentary question
   Seek direct information

B. *Major detail*: Smaller labor force
   Minor detail: Milking machines use only one operator.

   Major detail: Higher milk output
   Minor detail: American cows give 7.5 times more milk than Brazilian cows.

Practice 3

A. C
B. B

Practice 4 *(Wording of answers may vary.)*

A. Passive listening—trying to make sense out of a speaker's remarks without being able to interact with the speaker
   Ex.—Students listen to an instructor's lecture without having the chance to ask questions.

B. Self-serving bias—the practice of judging ourselves leniently
   Ex.—When *he* lashes out angrily, we say he's moody. When *we* lash out angrily, we say we're under pressure.

4   Implied Main Ideas

Practice 1

Paragraph 1	Paragraph 3
1. D	5. C
2. B	6. B

Paragraph 2
3. D
4. A

Practice 2

1. C
2. D
3. B

Practice 3 *(Wording of answers may vary.)*

1. *Topic:* Reasons for lying
   Implied main idea: People tell lies for several reasons.

2. *Topic:* Being an only child
   Implied main idea: Being an only child has its drawbacks.

3. *Topic:* Opposition to capital punishment
   Implied main idea: People oppose the death penalty for different reasons.

Practice 4

1. C
2. B

5   Relationships I

Practice 1 *(Answers may vary.)*

1. also	4. First
2. For one thing	5. Third
3. In addition	

Practice 2 *(Answers may vary.)*

1. After	4. before
2. Then	5. while
3. during	

Practice 3 *(Wording of answers may vary.)*

A. Main idea: For several reasons, pork was America's most popular meat a hundred years ago.
1. Pigs grew quickly.
2. Pigs required little attention.
3. Pigs could be preserved cheaply.

B. Main idea: . . . aging process.
1. Our bodies simply wear out.
3. Our body chemistry loses its delicate balance.
4. Our bodies, with age, reject some of their own tissues.

Practice 4 *(Wording of answers may vary.)*

Main idea: The 1960s were a time of profound events in America.
1. 1963—assassination of President Kennedy
2. 1965—urban riots in black ghettos
3. 1968—protests against increasing American presence in Vietnam

Practice 5 *(Wording of answers may vary.)*

Main idea: People pass through three stages in reacting to unemployment.
1. Shock, followed by relief
2. Strong effort to find a new job
3. Self-doubt and anxiety if no job is found

Practice 6 *(Wording of answers may vary.)*

Main idea: Taking certain steps will help you to remember your dreams.
2. Put a pen and notebook near your bed.
3. Turn off your alarm so you can wake up gradually.
4. Write down the dream immediately.

Practice 7

1. B	6. A
2. A	7. A
3. A	8. B
4. B	9. A
5. B	10. B

6 Relationships II

Practice 1 *(Answers may vary.)*

1. For instance	4. including
2. for example	5. illustration
3. such as	

Practice 2

A. Shaping; *definition*—1; *example 1*—2; *example 2*—10
B. Irony—saying one thing but meaning another
   Example—To end the famine in Ireland, Swift suggests the Irish should raise babies to be eaten.

Practice 3 *(Answers may vary.)*

1. Similarly	4. as
2. Just like	5. Just as
3. in the same way	

Practice 4 *(Answers may vary.)*

1. however	4. despite
2. Although	5. In contrast
3. but	

Practice 5

A. Contrast: Japanese employment practices and U.S. employment practices

B. Contrast: school and home

Public discipline in school	Private scolding at home
Much competition in school	Minimal competition at home

Practice 6 *(Answers may vary.)*

1. Because	4. Since
2. as a result	5. Therefore
3. so	

Practice 7

A. *Cause:* Chronic stress
Effect: Painful muscle tension
Effect: Weakening of body's immune system
Effect: Psychological disorders

B. *Main idea (effect):* There are several reasons people daydream.
Major supporting details (causes):
1. To tolerate boring jobs
2. To endure deprivation
3. To discharge hostile feelings
4. To plan for the future

Practice 8

1. A	6. B
2. C	7. C
3. B	8. A
4. C	9. C
5. A	10. B

7 Inferences

Practice 1

A. 1. C
2. B
3. C
4. B

B. 5. C
6. B
7. A
8. C

C. 9. B
10. A
11. B
12. B

Practice 2

A. 3, 4, 6
B. 1, 4, 6
C. 1, 4, 6

Practice 3

1. Simile, B
2. Simile, C
3. Metaphor, B
4. Metaphor, C
5. Metaphor, C

Practice 4

1. B	6. B
2. B	7. A
3. C	8. A
4. C	9. C
5. A	10. B

Steps in Reading a Graph or Table

- *Title of graph:* Changes in U.S. Work Force, 1900–2010
- *Source of graph: Statistical Abstract* 2012; James M. Henslin, 2013
- *Span of years covered:* 1900–2010
- *Types of work covered:* White-collar, blue-collar, and farming

Practice 5

2, 3, 4

8 Purpose and Tone

Practice 1

1. P	6. E
2. I	7. P
3. P	8. I
4. I	9. E
5. E	10. I

Practice 2

1. B
2. C
3. A

Practice 3

1. D
2. B
3. A
4. C
5. E

Practice 4

A. 1. admiring
   2. sympathetic
   3. critical
   4. objective
   5. ironic

B. 6. straightforward
   7. sarcastic
   8. threatening
   9. self-pitying
   10. sympathetic

Practice 5

1. J
2. C
3. A

4. D
5. F

Practice 6

1. B
2. A
3. B

4. A
5. B

Practice 2

1. A, C, F
2. C, E, F
3. A, C, F
4. B, D, E

Practice 3

1. B
2. B
3. B
4. C

Practice 4

1. C
2. A
3. B
4. D

9 Argument

Practice 1

1. A. S
   B. P

2. A. S
   B. P

3. A. S
   B. P
   C. S

4. A. P
   B. S
   C. S

5. A. S
   B. P
   C. S

6. A. S
   B. P
   C. S

7. A. S
   B. P
   C. S

8. A. S
   B. P
   C. S
   D. S

9. A. S
   B. S
   C. P
   D. S

10. A. S
    B. S
    C. S
    D. P

10 Critical Reading

Practice 1

1. O
2. F
3. F+O
4. F
5. O
6. F
7. F+O
8. F
9. O
10. F

Detecting Propaganda

- *Bandwagon:* 2
- *Testimonial:* 2
- *Transfer:* 1
- *Plain Folks:* 2
- *Name Calling:* 2
- *Glittering Generalities:* 1

Practice 2
1. E
2. B
3. A
4. F
5. D
6. B
7. E
8. C
9. D
10. F

Fallacies That Ignore the Issue
- *Circular Reasoning:* 1
- *Personal Attack:* 1
- *Straw Man:* 1

Fallacies That Oversimplify the Issue
- *False Cause:* 1
- *False Comparison:* 2
- *Either-Or:* 2

Practice 3

A.		B.	
1.	C	6.	A
2.	B	7.	C
3.	A	8.	B
4.	C	9.	C
5.	A	10.	A

Acknowledgments

Text Credits

Agus, David B. "The 2,000-Year-Old Wonder Drug." From *The New York Times*, December 12, 2012. Reprinted by permission of PARS International.

Barkin, Dorothy. "The Bystander Effect." Copyright © 1991 by Trend Publications. Reprinted by permission.

Barry, Dave. Selections on pp. 324 and 358. Reprinted by permission.

Brenoff, Eileen. "Growing Less Dumb." Reprinted by permission of the author.

Dunayer, Joan. "Here's to Your Health." Reprinted by permission.

Ellerbee, Linda. Excerpt from *Move On* on p. 312. Copyright © 1991 by Linda Ellerbee. Published by The Putnam Publishing Group.

Gammage, Jeff. "Wonder in the Air." Originally published as "Yes, Jin Yu, There Is Wonder in the Air." From the *Philadelphia Inquirer*, December 30, 2006. Used with permission of the *Philadelphia Inquirer*. Copyright © 2013. All rights reserved.

Grasha, Anthony F. "Nonverbal Communication," from *Practical Applications of Psychology*, 3rd ed., copyright © 1987. Printed and Electronically reproduced by permission of Pearson Education, Inc., Upper Saddle River, New Jersey.

Gregory, Dick. "Shame," from *Nigger: An Autobiography* by Dick Gregory. Copyright © 1964 by Dick Gregory Enterprises, Inc. Used by permission of Dutton, a division of Penguin Putnam Inc.

Hamill, Pete. "The Yellow Ribbon." Copyright © 1971 by Pete Hamill. Used by permission. All rights reserved.

Henslin, James M. "Relationships in the 21st Century" and chart on page 293 from *Essentials of Sociology: A Down-to-Earth Approach,* 10th ed., copyright © 2013. Printed and Electronically reproduced by permission of Pearson Education, Inc., Upper Saddle River, New Jersey.

Kellmayer, John, and Alina Wyden. "Students in Shock." Reprinted by permission.

Kaufmann, Ann. "College Athletes Should Be Paid." Reprinted by permission of the author.

Landers, Ann. "College Student Deplores the Drinking Around Her." Permission granted by Ann Landers/Creators Syndicate.

Lamott, Anne. Excerpt on p. 268. Copyright © 1994 by Anne Lamott. Published by Anchor Books.

Logan, Paul. "Rowing the Bus." Reprinted by permission.

Lubrano, Alfred. Excerpt on p. 582 adapted from "Diminished Diplomas." Posted December 31, 2012 on www.philly.com.

Martin, James Kirby; Roberts, Randy; Mintz, Steven; McMurry, Linda O.; and Jones, James H. "Lizzie Borden," from *America and Its Peoples*, 2nd ed., copyright © 1993. Reprinted by permission of Pearson Education, Inc., Upper Saddle River, New Jersey.

McGowan, Christopher. Excerpt on p. 612 from *The Raptor and the Lamb*. Copyright © 1977 by Christopher McGowan. Published by Henry Holt.

Orwell, George. Excerpt on pp. 287–288 from "A Hanging," in *Shooting an Elephant and Other Essays* by George Orwell. Copyright © 1950 by Sonia Brownell Orwell and renewed 1978 by Sonia Pitt-Rivers. Reprinted by permission of Houghton Mifflin Harcourt Publishing Company. All rights reserved.

Papalia, Diane E., and Sally Wendkos Olds. "How Parents' Child-Rearing Styles Affect Their Children," from *Psychology*, 2nd ed. Copyright © 1988 by McGraw-Hill, Inc. Reprinted by permission of The McGraw-Hill Companies.

Popkin, Roy. "Night Watch." Originally appeared in *The National Observer*. Reprinted by permission of Dow Jones & Company, Inc. Copyright © 1964 by Dow Jones & Company, Inc. All rights reserved worldwide. Also reprinted with permission from the September 1965 *Reader's Digest*.

Rhodes, Richard. Excerpt on p. 318 from *A Hole in the World*. Copyright © 1990 by Richard Rhodes. Published by Simon and Schuster.

Roberts, Paul. Excerpt on p. 600 adapted from "How to Say Nothing in 500 Words." From *Understanding English* by Paul Roberts. Copyright © 1958 by Paul Roberts.

Roker, Al. Excerpt #10 on p. 356 adapted from *Don't Make Me Stop This Car.* Copyright © 2000 by Al Roker. Published by Scribner.

Salinas, Marta. "The Scholarship Jacket," from *Nosotras: Latina Literature Today*, edited by Maria del Carmen Boza, Beverly Silva, and Carmen Valle. Copyright © 1986 by Bilingual Press/Editorial Bilingue, Arizona State University, Tempe, AZ. Reprinted by permission.

Sherry, Mary. "In Praise of the F Word." Used with the permission of Mary Sherry.

Taylor, Shelley E., Letitia Anne Peplau, and David O. Sears. "Compliance Techniques," from *Social Psychology*, 8th ed. Copyright © 1994 by Prentice-Hall. Reprinted by permission of the authors.

Trelease, Jim. Excerpts on pages 143, 169, and 602 adapted from *The Read-Aloud Handbook*. Copyright © 2001 by Jim Trelease. Published by Penguin Books.

Verderber, Rudolph E. "Presenting Your Speech," from *Communicate!* 7th ed. Copyright © 1993 Wadsworth, a part of Cengage Learning, Inc. Reproduced by permission. www.cengage.com/permissions

Photo Credits

Part One

Chapter 2, p. 86 © Corbis Bridge/Alamy; Chapter 3, p. 126 © Blend Images/Alamy; Chapter 4, p. 162 © Weston Colton/ Ruberball/ Corbis; Chapter 5, p. 204 courtesy Maria Breidenbach; Chapter 6, p. 248 © Wavebreak Media Ltd./Alamy; Chapter 9, p. 383 © Somos Images/Alamy; Chapter 10, p. 400 courtesy John Langan; p. 424 © Smartstock/iStockphoto.

Part Two

Chapter 1, p. 444 © Somos Images/Alamy; Chapter 2, p. 452 © PCN Photography/ Alamy; Chapter 3, p. 464 © Corbis Bridge/ Alamy; Chapter 4, p. 474 © Andrew Butterton/Alamy; Chapter 5, p. 484 Private Collection; Chapter 6, p. 496 © Blend Images/Alamy; Chapter 7, p. 506 © Craig Holmes/Alamy; Chapter 8, p. 517 © Everett Collection Inc./Alamy; Chapter 9, p. 527 © iStockphoto/Thinkstock RF.

Index

"2,000-Year-Old Wonder Drug, The," David B. Agus, 423–425

Addition, words that show, 72–73, 108, 148–150, 182–183, 266
Agus, David B., "The 2,000-Year-Old Wonder Drug," 423–425
Antonyms, as context clues, 28–30
Argument, 363–398
adequate support, 372–375
    chapter review, 376
    mastery tests for, 387–398
    point and support, 364–366
    relevant support, 367–372
    review tests for, 377–386
    in textbook writing, 375

Bandwagon propaganda technique, 407–408
Barkin, Dorothy, "The Bystander Effect," 472–476
Begging the question, 413
Brenoff, Eileen, "Growing Less Dumb," 483–486
"Bystander Effect, The," Dorothy Barkin, 472–476

Cause and effect
    pattern of organization, 233–238
    words that show, 233–235, 266
Central idea: see Central point
Central point, 79, 150
    definition of, 79, 150

Changing the subject fallacy, 367–372, 412
"Child-Rearing Styles," Diane E. Papalia and Sally Wendkos Olds, 125–126
Circular reasoning fallacy, 413–414
"College Athletes Should Be Paid," Ann Kaufmann, 451–455
Combined-skills tests, 563–614
Comparison, words that show, 227–228, 266
Comparison and/or contrast pattern of organization, 230–233
"Compliance Techniques: Getting People to Say Yes," Shelley E. Taylor, Letitia Anne Peplau, and David O. Sears, 505–508
Context clues
    antonyms, 28–30
    examples, 22–25
    general sense of the sentence or passage, 31–34
    synonyms, 26–27
Contrast, words that show, 229–230, 266
"Coping with Nervousness," Rudolph F. Verderber, 495–498
Critical reading, 399–440
    chapter review, 418
    detecting propaganda, 407–412
    fallacies that ignore the issue, 413–415
    fallacies that oversimplify the issue, 415–416
    mastery tests for, 429–440
    recognizing errors in reasoning, 412–418
    review tests for, 419–428
    separating facts from opinion, 399–406

Definitions, textbook, 34, 224–225
Definition and example pattern of
        organization, 223–226
Details, supporting (*see* Supporting Details)
Diagramming (maps), 111
Dunayer, Joan, "Here's to Your Health,"
        85–88

Either-or fallacy, 416
Errors in reasoning, 412–418
Examples
        as context clues, 22–25
        with definitions, 34, 223–225
        words that introduce, 222–226

Fact, definition of, 400
Fact and opinion, 399–406
        points about, 403–404
Fallacies, 412–416
        that ignore the issue, 413–415
                circular reasoning, 413–414
                personal attack, 414
                straw man, 414–415
        that oversimplify the issue, 415–416
                either-or, 416
                false cause, 415
                false comparison, 416
Fallacy, definition of, 412
False cause fallacy, 415
False comparison fallacy, 416
Figures of speech, 285–287

Gammage, Jeff, "Wonder in the Air,"
        203–205
General sense of the sentence or passage,
        as context clue, 31–34
General versus specific ideas, for finding
        main idea, 60–63
Glittering generalities, 410
Graphs, inferences in, 290–293
Grasha, Anthony F., "Nonverbal
        Communication," 526–528
Gregory, Dick, "Shame," 463–466
"Growing Less Dumb," Eileen Brenoff,
        483–486

Hamill, Pete, "The Yellow Ribbon," 443–445
Hasty generalization fallacy, 372–375, 412
Henslin, James M., "Relationships in the 21st
        Century," 299–302
"Here's to Your Health," Joan Dunayer, 85–88

Illustration, words that show, 222–223, 266
Implied main idea, 141–180
        central ideas, 150–155
        chapter review, 155
        definition of, 141
        figuring out in paragraphs, 143–148
        figuring out in longer passages, 150–155
        mastery tests for, 169–180
        putting into words, 148–150
        review tests for, 156–168
Inferences, 273–318
        chapter review, 294
        defined, 273
        in everyday life, 273–274
        in graphs and tables, 290–293
        guidelines for, 277
        in literature, 282–289
        mastery tests for, 307–318
        in reading, 274–282
        review tests for, 294–306
Informed opinion, 404
"In Praise of the F Word," Mary Sherry,
        381–383
Irony, a note on, 329–330

Kaufmann, Ann, "College Athletes Should Be
        Paid," 451–455
Kellmayer, John, and Alina Wyden, "Students
        in Shock," 247–250
Key words, for finding main ideas, 71–73
        addition words, 72–73
        list words, 71–72

Langan, John, "The Power Within," 533–542
Limited answer key, 637–644
List of items pattern of organization, 186–189
List words, 71–72, 107–108
"Lizzie Borden," James Kirby Martin and
        others, 516–518
Logan, Paul, "Rowing the Bus," 161–165

Main idea, 57–102
    chapter review, 80
    definition of, 57
    implied (*see* Implied main idea)
    locations, 73–78
    mastery tests for, 91–102
    and pattern of organization, 196–197
    recognizing, 59–73
        as general versus specific idea, 60–63
        using key words, 71–73
        using topic, 64–70
    review tests for, 81–90
    in sentence, 64–70
    and topic, 64–70
    in topic sentence, 64
Main idea sentence, 64
Major details, 105–106
Mapping, 111–114
Martin, James Kirby, and others, "Lizzie
    Borden," 516–518
Metaphor, 284–287
Minor details, 105–106

Name calling propaganda technique, 410
"Night Watch," Roy Popkin, 41–42
"Nonverbal Communication," Anthony F.
    Grasha, 526–528
Note-taking techniques, 106–119

Opinion
    definition, 401
    informed, 404
Outlining, 106–111
    tips for, 107–109

Papalia, Diane E., and Sally Wendkos Olds,
    "Child-Rearing Styles," 125–126
Patterns of organization, 186–198
    cause and effect, 235–238
    comparison and/or contrast, 230–233
    definition and example, 223–226
    list of items, 186–189
    time order, 186, 190–195
    main ideas and, 196–197, 238–240
Personal attack fallacy, 414

Plain-folks propaganda technique, 409
Point, author's, 57-59
    and specific ideas, 60–63
    central, of a selection, 79, 150
Point and support, in arguments, 364–366
Popkin, Roy, "Night Watch," 41–42
"Power Within, The," John Langan, 534–542
Pronunciation guide, 617–618
Propaganda, 407–412
    bandwagon, 407–408
    definition, 407
    glittering generalities, 410
    name calling, 410
    plain folks, 409
    techniques, 407
    testimonial, 408
    transfer, 408–409
Purpose, 319–324
Purpose and tone, 319–362
    chapter review, 336
    mastery tests for, 351–362
    review tests for, 337–350

"Reading for Pleasure and Power," 10–15
    rewards of regular reading, 10–11
    special offer of books, 15
    suggestions for regular reading, 13–14
Reading performance chart, inside back cover
"Relationships in the 21st Century," James M.
    Henslin, 299–302
Relationships I, 181–220
    chapter review, 198
    combined mastery tests, with
        Relationships II, 267–272
    mastery tests for, 209–220
    review tests for, 199–208
    (*See also* Patterns of Organization;
        Transitions)
Relationships Tests, 551–562
Relationships II, 221–272
    chapter review, 241
    combined mastery tests, with
        Relationships I, 267–272
    mastery tests for, 253–264
    review tests for, 242–252

Relationships II—*Cont.*
  (*See also* Patterns of Organization;
    Transitions)
"Rowing the Bus," Paul Logan, 161–165

Salinas, Marta, "The Scholarship Jacket,"
    343–346
"Scholarship Jacket, The," Marta Salinas,
    343–346
"Shame," Dick Gregory, 463–466
Sherry, Mary, "In Praise of the F Word,"
    381–383
Simile, 285–287
Straw man fallacy, 414–415
"Students in Shock," John Kellmayer and
    Alina Wyden, 247–250
Study note-taking techniques, 106–119
    mapping, 111–114
    outlining, 106–111
    summarizing, 114–119
Study tips/hints, 17–18, 224–225
Summarizing, 114–119
Supporting details, 103–140
    chapter review, 119
    definition of, 59, 103
    major and minor, 105–106
    mapping, 111–114
    mastery tests for, 129–140
    outlining, 106–111
    review tests for, 120–128
    summarizing, 114–119
Synonyms, as context clues, 26–27

Tables, inferences in, 290–293
Taylor, Shelley E., Letitia Anne Peplau,
    and David O. Sears, "Compliance
    Techniques: Getting People to Say Yes,"
    505–508
Testimonial propaganda technique, 408
Thesis, 79, 150
Time, words that show, 184, 266

Time order pattern of organization, 190–195
    series of events and stages, 191–193
    series of steps (directions), 194–195
Tone, 325–335
    list of words that describe, 326–327
Topic, 64–70
    definition of, 64
    finding the, 64–70
Topic sentence, 64
Transfer propaganda technique, 408–409
Transitions, 181–185, 221–223, 227–230,
    233–235
    defined, 182
    that show addition, 182–183, 266
    that show cause and effect, 233–235, 266
    that show comparison, 227–228, 266
    that show contrast, 229–230, 266
    that show illustration, 222–223, 266
    that show time, 184, 266
    tips about, 185

Value words, 401, 403
Verderber, Rudolph F., "Coping with
    Nervousness," 494–498
Vocabulary in context, 21–56
    antonyms, 28–30
    chapter review, 35
    examples, 22–25
    general sense of the sentence or passage,
        31–34
    mastery tests for, 45–56
    review tests for, 36–44
    synonyms, 26–27
    types of context clues, 22

"**W**onder in the Air," Jeff Gammage, 203–205
Writing assignments, 619–636
    Brief Guide to, 619–620

"**Y**ellow Ribbon, The," Pete Hamill, 445–445